THE BLACK HILLS:

OR,

THE LAST HUNTING GROUND OF THE DAKOTAHS.

A COMPLETE HISTORY

Of the Black Hills of Dakota from their First Invasion in 1874 to the Present Time, Comprising a Comprehensive Account of How They Lost Them; of Numerous Adventures of the Early Settlers; Their Heroic Struggles for Supremacy against the Hostile Dakotah Tribes, and their Final Victory; The Opening of the Country to White Settlement, and its Subsequent Development.

BY

ANNIE D. TALLENT

Published by Brevet Press
Copyright 1974 by BREVET PRESS,
a division of BREVET INTERNATIONAL, INC.,
Northwestern Bank Building, Sioux Falls,
South Dakota 57102

Library of Congress Catalog Card Number: 74-76330
ISBN: 0-88498-017-0

All rights reserved

No part of this work covered by the copyright hereon may be reproduced or used in any form or by any means—graphic, electronic or mechanical, including photocopying, recording, taping or information storage retrieval systems—without written permission of the publisher.

Second Edition

Manufactured in the United States of America
Pine Hill Press, Freeman, South Dakota 57029

PUBLISHER'S PREFACE

Annie D. Tallent was the first white woman to enter the Black Hills. She did so in 1874, with the Gordon Party. Almost 25 years later she chronicled her story and others in her book, "The Black Hills; or, Last Hunting Ground of the Dakotahs." Essentially her book is a history of the first quarter century of white occupation of the Black Hills.

Through the years, the book has become increasingly difficult to obtain. We, at Brevet Press, have felt for some time now that the book should be reprinted. At the same time, we are compelled to recognize that the perspective of Annie Tallent is not the same that many people have today. It seemed appropriate, therefore, to ask another woman, one of our times, to write an introduction to this reprinted work. Virginia Driving Hawk Sneve, a Brulé Sioux Indian and an editor of Brevet Press, agreed to do so.

No small part of the fascination of history lies in its fleeting, evanescent "truths." Even as in science, one era's dogma is the next's heresy, and both may be the object of the future's patronizing disdain. Annie Tallent's "The Black Hills; or, Last Hunting Ground of the Dakotahs" juxtaposed with Virginia Driving Hawk Sneve's Introduction that precedes it suggests something of this elusive quality of history, of the historian's inability to fix finally and forever an ultimate truth to the chronicle of human events.

Mrs. Tallent, was, of course, a product of her age. Her point of view is that of the nineteenth century pioneer who saw the Indian as more than merely an impediment to a self-serving notion of progress. Indeed, to ascribe purely malicious, greedy motives to settlers of the Annie Tallent stamp is to misunderstand or distort the attitudes of another time. For all their sanctimony, those settlers by and large believed implicitly in the justness of their endeavor. For them the Indian *was* a savage, an obstacle to civilizing forces whose righteousness and beknighted destiny was self-evident.

Now, some one hundred years later, the currents of history have undergone their inexorable and perhaps predictable shift. Mrs. Sneve represents the position of the twentieth century Indian—proud of her cultural heritage, impatient for reform, and deeply offended by the Annie Tallents of the past, whose misconceptions and prejudices contributed to the sorry lot of the Indian today. Small wonder, then, that her Introduction should reflect the bitterness of the generations of her people subjected to discrimination and degradation at the hands of their white conquerors.

This book and its Introduction are an effort to strike a balance between those contrary views of one segment of our common history. If the publisher is unwilling to take a position in the usual sense of that phrase, that is, to denigrate the opinions of either Mrs. Sneve or Mrs. Tallent at the expense of the other, the reason for this seeming reticence can be traced to that belief in the slippery nature of historical ''truths'' noted above. We have all of us, particularly in our time, heard the rant of proselyters who are firmly convinced of the moral rectitude of their ways. Sadly, history will not support such simplistic, keyhole visions. The reader is urged, then, to approach both Mrs. Sneve's Introduction and Mrs. Tallent's narrative with an open mind and to judge each by the forberant standards of history's longer view.

Donald P. Mackintosh
Publisher

*Yours truly
Annie D. Tallent*

INTRODUCTION TO SECOND EDITION

THE BLACK HILLS: OR, LAST HUNTING GROUND OF THE DAKOTAHS, Annie Tallent's malicious, bigoted treatment of the Dakota or Sioux Indians, would best serve mankind if it were burned rather than reprinted in this edition to continue to perpetuate a distorted, untrue portrait of the American Indian. However, Annie Tallent is a revered and sacred figure in South Dakota's history. Schools have been named after this woman, and an annual award to an outstanding female teacher is presented in her name. Destruction of Annie Tallent's book would be considered heresy by the non-Indians in South Dakota.

Fortunately, the publisher and editors of this edition recognized the innate prejudice present in Mrs. Tallent's book and wished to offset her biased presentation by prefacing the text with a review from the viewpoint of an American Indian. I have written this introduction from my viewpoint—that of a Brulé Sioux.

I recognize, of course, that Annie Tallent wrote her book from the viewpoint of the time in which she lived. Her treatment of the Sioux reflects that of the white settlers of the 1880's. When she wrote, " . . . there are no good Indians, but dead Indians," she was obviously in accord with the anti-Indian policy of the United States government. The reader of this edition is urged to understand that Mrs. Tallent's presentation was wholly one-sided. But, also understand that this cannot excuse the damage done to the image of the Indians by Annie Tallent and other "experts" of the period who were abysmally ignorant of the Indians they wrote about.

"The Dakotahs, or Nadowessious . . . ," Annie Tallent wrote on page one of her book, "were doubtless a valorous people considered from an Indian standpoint . . . ," but she clearly did not consider them such. She believed that the Sioux went to war, not in self-defense against extermination, but because they were natural killers. She said that the Sioux used the excuse of the government breaking treaties to go to war even though she weakly admitted that perhaps the treaties were at times disregarded. Yet Mrs. Tallent ignored the wrong doing of the whites and placed the blame for the hostilities directly on the Indians. In fact, she asked if such treaties should ever have been entered into for they tended to " . . . arrest the advance of civilization, and retard the development of the rich resources of our country . . . "

The truth was that the whites wanted the land and its gold. The Indians, who were in the way, were simply removed without regard for any dignity or pride they might have had as human beings.

It was true, as Annie Tallent wrote, that the Indians knew there was gold in the Black Hills. Indeed, the presence of the yellow rock was known long before the white men discovered it. But the Indians had no use for it and when they learned of the white men's coveteous desire for the gold the Indians fought—not to keep the white people away from the gold, but to prevent the invasion of sacred lands. Mrs. Tallent retold the unauthenticated story of early white men discovering gold in the Black Hills and being ambushed by Indians who killed the whites, confiscated the gold which they then traded for "glittering gewgaws so dear to the hearts of savages." Mrs. Tallent makes no mention of the Indian tales of how gold was taken from the whites by Indian bands who hid it in an inaccessible mountain of the Black Hills. Hidden, not because the Indians wanted the gold, but because they rightly recognized that if it were permitted out of the Hills more avaricious white men would come.

Annie Tallent fell in love with the Black Hills the minute the Gordon Party illegally entered the area. Yet, even after she lovingly and poetically described the majestic magnificence of the Dakota mountains, Mrs. Tallent did not understand the Sioux's similar feelings for the Hills. She made light of the Sioux's reverence for the Black Hills, which to them was the abode of *Wakantanka*. To Annie Tallent, the Sioux's mystic love was merely a superstitious myth that originated in the imagination of a simple-minded people who were not enlightened by civilization.

Mrs. Tallent believed, as did many white people of the period, that the Sioux never made proper use of the resources of the Black Hills. According to her, the Indians only visited the Hills to hunt, to fish, to secure the tall slim pines for their lodge poles (later in the book Mrs. Tallent bewails the fact that the white settlers were decimating the forests) and to worship. She reasoned, then, that the white men were justified in taking the Black Hills from the "savages" who should never have been given exclusive ownership of land they never really used. She wrote, "The gold-ribbed Black Hills were to be snatched from the grasp of savages, to whom they were no longer profitable even as a hunting ground, and given over to the thrift and enterprise of the hardy pioneer, who would develop their (the Black Hills) wonderful resources and thereby advance the interests and add to the wealth of our whole country." The interests of the Indians were ignored. Their wealth was stolen and they were doomed to a life of poverty and despair.

Still, a glimmer of pity for the Indians can be detected in Mrs. Tallent's writing. She admitted that the Gordon Party violated the 1868 Treaty and understood why the Sioux looked upon the whites as invaders. She ever bewailed the fact that the Gordon Expedition opened the way for other illegal entry into the Black Hills and how in one short year the area was transformed from a wilderness into a scene of busy life. She mourned the impressive silence, the profound solitude that once reigned and was lost forever. But she reasoned that all could be excused because the white people were more interested in the gold than in anything else.

The Gordon Party started for the Black Hills on October 6, 1874, and traveled surreptitiously westward in defiance of the law. They were not intimidated by the Sioux who had on "paint and feathers" to stop the tresspassers in their domain. Annie Tallent was proud that the Gordon Party were trespassers and outlaws. She regarded the furtive maneuvering which the expedition employed to avoid discovery as a "wonderfully brilliant conception." But she considered the Sioux, who engaged in defensive warfare, as "sneaking savages."

When the Gordon Party was apprehended and escorted out of the Black Hills by troopers of the Second United States Cavalry, Mrs. Tallent reported that they had been in greater danger than they had known of being massacred by "incensed savages." When the invaders and their military escort reached the Red Cloud Agency, they became fully aware of the displeasure of the Sioux. However, Mrs. Tallent felt that she was innocent of any crime. Apparently she considered the men of the party to be the ones guilty of trespassing and she could not understand why the Sioux made menacing gestures toward her. It did not occur to Annie Tallent that her presence indicated to the Indians that the white party was not a transient group. The Sioux knew that white men brought women and children with them only with the intention of staying and that more whites would follow.

Throughout her book Annie Tallent recounts many incidents of the suffering of white soldiers and settlers at the hands of the Indians. Those who died she thought of as martyrs in the righteous cause of progress and civilization. She had great admiration and respect for the pioneers who did not let the threat of death deter them from reaching the Black Hills and the gold. She had only disdain and scorn for the marauding Sioux eager to scalp any "poor pilgrim" found treading upon Indian land. Nowhere did she note that the Sioux were unafraid of death, nor did she mention that many of them died in defense of their way of life.

All attempts by the government to keep the gold seekers out of the Black Hills failed and it became necessary, as Mrs. Tallent wrote, "to make a new treaty with the Sioux so that the rich resourceful land could be economically developed by hard-working pioneers." In reporting the negotiations of the

Treaty Commissions with the Sioux, Mrs. Tallent declared that the Indians were insolent and defiantly made unreasonable demands. She admitted that under the terms of the new treaty of 1876 the Indians lost a great deal, but she rationalizes that loss by stating:

"They (the Indians) were assured of a continuance of their regular daily rations, and certain annuities in clothing each year, guaranteed by the treaty of 1868, and what more could they ask or desire, than that a living be provided for themselves, their wives, their children, and all their wild, careless, unrestrained life, exempt from all the burdens and responsibilities of civilized existence? In view of the fact that there are thousands who are obliged to earn their bread and butter by the sweat of their brows, and that have hard work to keep the wolf from the door, they should be satisfied."

Annie Tallent's opinion was, of course, the expression of the United States government, which but a few years before had been engaged in a Civil War to emancipate the Blacks. This same government in 1876 doomed thousands of Indians to the enslavement of a life of dependency on government hand-outs and confinement to economically unproductive reservations.

It follows naturally that Annie Tallent glorified General George A. Custer. She recorded the "tragedy" of the Little Big Horn in order to preserve the name and courage of that dead "hero" and the troops of his beloved Seventh whom Tallent described as "soldiers as valiant and brave as ever bestrode a horse or shouldered a carbine." According to Mrs. Tallent, the direct cause of the Little Big Horn engagement was the refusal of hostile Indians to voluntarily settle on the reservations and that it became necessary "to compel obedience and bring in these recalcitrant bands."

The Seventh and their leader, Mrs. Tallent reported, realized the hardships and dangers of such a campaign but proceeded "with resolute faces and courageous hearts, confident of success." Then she adds that the very name, Seventh Cavalry, had been the synonym of victory. To the Indians the Seventh was synonymous with death. They recalled the courageous action of these troopers and their glorious leader who, on November 27, 1868, slaughtered Black Kettle and more than a hundred of his Cheyenne band (only eleven were warriors) in a surprise dawn attack on the Washita River in Oklahoma.

Annie Tallent did not find it difficult to mentally depict the action at the Little Big Horn:

"We can plainly see in the picture a burly savage—malignant hate portrayed in every lineament of his ugly painted face, with glistening blade in hand, bending low over each prostrate (white) form—perchance, many not yet dead. We can see the reeking scalp of each separate victim waved exultantly in the air, and now we can see them stripped of their clothing and their pockets rifled.''

Perhaps Mrs. Tallent did not know that to the Indians these white soldiers at the Little Big Horn looked very much like the ones who butchered women and children at Washita.

Annie Tallent not only perpetrated horror stories of the Indians, but she was guilty of misstatement and actual falsehood when she wrote of individual Indians. She called Sitting Bull a whiley Brulé chieftain when in fact he was a Hunkpapa Holy Man. She described Gall as being vindictive and said nothing of his influence on his people to cooperate with the whites. She wrote that Crazy Horse was guilty of depredations, but still dismissed him as being merely reckless and ignored his genius as a strategic commander. She referred to Roman Nose as a Brulé Sioux and obviously knew nothing of this Cheyenne's heroic leadership of his people.

Annie Tallent goes on to reflect the prevalent opinion of her time when she expresses the belief that the Allotment Act of 1887 was a good thing for the Indians. The proponents of the Act were well-meaning white persons who believed that when the savages were peaceably settled on their own land and became productive farmers, they would make rapid strides towards self-support and eventually reach the ultimate goal and the eternal happiness of civilization. These humanitarians and Mrs. Tallent neglected to note that much of the reservation land was impossible to farm and their expectation of hunters turning into successful farmers has, of course, proven unrealistic. The Act itself became another means of robbing the Indian of more of his land.

Mrs. Tallent's deplorable ignorance of the Sioux is most apparent in her last chapter when she wrote of the Messiah Ghost Dance and ''The Fatal Battle of Wounded Knee.''

With great authority, but with no reference to her source of information, Mrs. Tallent wrote that the religion of the Sioux was polytheistic. ''They,'' she wrote, ''not only worshipped numerous objects, which they deified and invested with more or less potent attributes, according to their incomprehensibility, chief among whom were their two antagonistic deities— the good and the evil spirits—and believed in and practiced the shedding of atoning blood to propitiate their incensed divinities, through the mediation of their medicine-men, whom they regard as the personification of the great Wakan—.''

Unfortunately, Annie Tallent is not present to defend her statements, but if she could somehow appear, I would accuse her of abominable untruth. For truly, the Sioux believed in only one Great Spirit, *Wakantanka,* God. The numerous objects which Mrs. Tallent believed the Sioux worshipped were symbolic of *Wakantanka*. Neither was a medicine man the personification of that God, but only a man gifted with healing powers who was as well the spiritual leader of the people.

Mrs. Tallent erred further when she called medicine men "a class of lazy, but shrewd, impostors, who, claiming supernatural powers, have by their incantations and sorceries, imposed upon the credulity of these (the Sioux) benighted people, the most absurd superstitions, among which was the belief that some day a 'Messiah' would appear." Mrs. Tallent did not or could not understand that medicine men were at times possessors of psychic powers which led them to have great influence over their tribes. These men did not, as Mrs. Tallent believed, "go about compounding medicines" to convince the Sioux that a Messiah would save them.

Neither did a fanatical white evangelist named Hopkins, as Mrs. Tallent wrote, begin the Messiah belief. A Paiute, Woyoka, in the southwestern United States founded the religion of the Ghost Dance and it was brought to the Dakotas by Kicking Bear. Few whites, Mrs. Tallent not among them, recognized the Ghost Dance as being entirely Christian. The ceremony and ritual differed, but the belief was indentical to that of the Christian church. Nonviolence and brotherly love was the doctrine. The Indians were not to fight but only to dance and sing.

"Hideously painted and arrayed in their invulnerable 'ghost dance' shirts:" Mrs. Tallent described, "to the weird music of the tom-tom and other savage devices for making a great noise, the poor deluded creatures danced round and round . . ."

The "poor creatures" may have been deluded, but it was a delusion caused by the desperation of their reservation existence and by years of being deluded by the promises of the United States.

The Ghost Dance religion and the Sioux's belief that with its faithful practice dead relatives would return and the white men would leave forever was a comforting factor to a destitute people. Their anger and grief over Sitting Bull's death was assuaged by the nonviolent tenets of the new religion and a truly bloody uprising was prevented.

But Mrs. Tallent certainly did not understand why the Sioux danced and neither did the agent at Pine Ridge who panicked and sent for troops. Both should have heeded the Oglala leader, Red Cloud, who sorrowfully understood the desperation of his people which led them to believe in the Dance. Yet he knew the whites did not understand when he said, "The white men were frightened and called for soldiers. We hoped we could tell them our troubles and get help. The soldiers meant to kill us. We did not believe it, but some were frightened and ran away."

The culmination of all the fear and misunderstanding was what Mrs. Tallent called the "battle" at Wounded Knee where, she said, many women and children were unfortunately killed—almost 300 of them.

At last, Annie Tallent finished with the Dakotahs and tales of their last hunting ground. Her telling of the events of Wounded Knee was just as bigoted and untrue as the statements in the preceding pages of her book. Wounded Knee was a good place for her book to end, for that massacre stifled the dignity, pride, and spirit of the Sioux for generations just as thoroughly as did Annie Tallent's words.

Virginia Driving Hawk Sneve

To My

Fellow-Pioneers

This Work

Is Respectfully Inscribed.

INTRODUCTION

By some strange influence upon the processes of the human mind, trifling occurrences and incidents in the lives of nations, as well as individuals, frequently assume large proportions, and grow in interest year by year as they go by. "As distance lends enchantment to the view," so time throws the glamour of romance over receding events.

Belief in these bits of proverbial wisdom, and the hope that the mellowing influence of nearly a quarter of a century may have likewise invested the unwritten chapters of Black Hills pioneer history with added interest, together with the helpful encouragement of many friends throughout the Hills, first induced the author to undertake the task resulting in the production of this little work. It seemed proper, too, that the part enacted by those who stood in the front ranks, in the thick of the fray, in the sanguinary battle for the settlement of the Black Hills, should be placed upon record before they "shuffled off the mortal coil," or, ere passing years should leave but a shadowy memory of their courage and brave endurance, and future generations be thus compelled to accept the story of their struggles and heroism as a vague and unsatisfactory tradition.

The original plan and scope of the work did not contemplate a full and comprehensive history in all its broad significance, but a compilation of all information in relation to the Black Hills, obtainable without labored research, and a truthful record of such incidents and occurrences as stand out in bold relief in the memory of the author, who was amongst them and in a manner identified with their aims, and a sharer in their hardships. The scope, however, has been broadened, so as to embrace, as nearly as practicable, all the important events that have transpired in the Black Hills during their twenty-three years of history.

The work is far from being all that had been desired and hoped for, as in going back through the dimly-lighted corridors of the vanishing years in search of the footprints of history, it has been found that the imprints had become more or less illegible, and, in some instances, wholly obliterated. However, it may serve to aid some future skilled historian, whose penetrating vision will be able to read the much that lies unwritten between the lines of these pages.

An intimate acquaintance with the many vicissitudes and difficulties incident to the early settlement and subsequent development of the Black Hills has somewhat lessened the labor of the arduous undertaking, and really furnishes the only justification that can be offered for this feeble attempt to place upon historic annuals the struggles, the failures, and successes of our early pioneers.

The word pioneers is here used in a far broader sense than its common acceptation implies. It is applied not alone to those who blazed the way over the trackless plains in 1874, or dodged the "blue coats" in 1875, or traveled over the blood-stained trails to the Black Hills in 1876, but also to those who were pioneers of the chief great civilizing forces employed in achieving our present civilization.

Owing to the limitations of this volume, it was made necessary to choose from a long roster of few individual examples to illustrate the dangers, the hardships and privations, experienced alike by nearly all, which few must stand for the great rank and file of deserving pioneers.

In presenting this work to the people of the Black Hills, the author, let it be understood, disclaims for it any pretensions to literary merit, and pleads wholly guiltless of any incendiary designs on the world or any of its rivers, claiming only to be a simple relation of facts expressed in plain, homely diction, without the slightest attempt at rhetorical embellishment. And, moreover, if in relating the incidents woven into this story, the first person, singular number, is frequently used, it is not with any feelings of egoism nor in any spirit of boastfulness, but rather that as an actual participant in the occurrences described, it became a real necessity. However, with all its imperfections, it is herewith submitted, with many misgivings, to the reading public.

THE AUTHOR.

CONTENTS

Chapter I

The Dakotahs	1
First Invasion of Black Hills	3
First Movement Looking Toward Colonization of Black Hills in 1872	4
Adventures on the Border	6

Chapter II

The Custer Black Hills Expedition	10
Gold Found by Indians	12
Organization of First Expedition	13

Chapter III

Preparations for the Journey	15
Sioux City Gold Hunters	20
The First Defection	21

Chapter IV

Crossing the Niobrara	24
Bill of Fare on the Plains	27
Sickness in Camp	30
Almost a Tragedy Within the Fold	31

Chapter V

Crossing the Bad Lands	33
A Death in Camp	34
An Amusing Incident	36
First Sight of the Black Hills	38

CONTENTS

Chapter VI

Crossing the Cheyenne River 39
Indians Discovered.. 39
Strike Custer's Trail and Journey Through the Black Hills—
　A Revelation.. 42
Reach French Creek and Find Gold 44
Christmas Day in the Black Hills in 1874........................ 46

Chapter VII

Building Stockade.. 48
Life in Stockade During Winter of 1874-5 49
Messengers Carry out the Glad Tidings........................... 54
Two More Leave the Stockade 59
Stockade Party Taken out of the Hills by the Government 61

Chapter VIII

Riding out of the Hills on a Government Mule 63
Reach Fort Laramie... 68
Terrible Experience of Troops sent after our Expedition 69
A Street Interview With "Wild Bill" 72

Chapter IX

The Black Hills—Its Mountains, Forests, Climate,
　Productions, etc. 75
The Black Hills Never the Home of the Indians 81
Some Indian Traditions 82
Immigration to Black Hills in 1875-76 84

Chapter X

The First to Enter the Black Hills in 1875 86
The First Expedition in 1875.................................... 88
Scientific Expedition Sent to Black Hills 89

Chapter XI

The Cession of the Black Hills 95
Advent of Gen. Crook in Black Hills............................. 98
Miners Leave Hills by Order of Gen. Crook 99

CONTENTS

Miners Return to Hills 101
The Cavalry Force Withdrawn 101
Custer City in 1875 102
French Creek the Mecca of Pioneers in 1875 103

Chapter XII

Some of the Pioneers of 1875, and How They Got to
    the Black Hills....................................... 104
The Major Part of the Expedition 115

Chapter XIII

How Some of the Pioneers Fooled Uncle Sam 116

Chapter XIV

First Discovery of Placer Gold in Northern Hills 124
First Locations of Deadwood Gulch 127
First to Bring Merchandise to the Black Hills 131
First Gold Dust Taken out of the Black Hills 136

Chapter XV

Early Freight and Passenger Transportation to Black Hills 138
Early Postal Facilities in the Black Hills 141

Chapter XVI

The Yellowstone Expedition or the Indian Campaign of 1876 146
The Custer Column 149

Chapter XVII

News of the Terrible Disaster Reaches the Black Hills 164
The Summer Campaign—Gen. Geo. Crook 168

Chapter XVIII

The Year 1876 in Black Hills 175
Some of the Expeditions of 1876 175

Chapter XIX

Montana Expeditions 184
The Centennial Party 192
Outward-Bound Pilgrims 193

Chapter XX

Chapter of First Events 195
Second Suit in Equity in the Black Hills 196
First Person Killed 198

Chapter XXI

Custer in 1876 213
Massacre of Metz Family 218
Hostiles Returning From Little Big Horn 219
Raids on Custer 220
Scalped a Man Alive 221

Chapter XXII

Rapid City in 1876 226
Block House Built 234
Upper Rapid 234
Location of Ranches in Rapid Valley in 1876 234

Chapter XXIII

A Trip From Cheyenne to Deadwood in 1876 235
A Personal Reminiscence 241

Chapter XXIV

Placer Mining in Deadwood Gulch in 1876 245
Placer Mining Processes 248
Hydraulic Placer Mining 250
Early Quartz Mining in the Black Hills 252
Peculiarities of Miners 254

Chapter XXV

Deadwood in 1876 255
Sunday in Deadwood—Pioneer Days 261

CONTENTS xxiii

Deadwood by Lamplight 261
How We Celebrated Our Natal Day in 1876 263
Platting of South Deadwood 266
First Murder in Northern Hills 267
Murder of Wild Bill 270

Chapter XXVI

Indian Raid on Montana Herd 273
Wolf Mountain Stampede 275
Telegraph Line Reaches Deadwood 278
Failure of Bill for Territory of Lincoln 280

Chapter XXVII

Black Hills Opened to Settlement 283
Judges of the Black Hills District and Circuit Courts 284
Highway Robbers and Road Agents 285
How a Deadwood Lady Saved Her Watch 288
Deadwood Famous Treasure Coach 288

Chapter XXVIII

CUSTER COUNTY 292
The Mines of Custer County 294
The Mica Mines of Custer County 298
Custer City 300
Sylvan Lake 301
Custer in 1877 303
Hermosa 307

Chapter XXIX

PENNINGTON COUNTY—Its Organization 308
County Seat 312
Schools and Churches 312
Library Association 316
Secret Orders—Manufacturing 317
Chlorination Works—Water System of Rapid City 317
School of Mines 322
Rapid City—Incorporated 324
Rapid City Fire Department and Banking Institutions 327

CONTENTS

Chapter XXX

Horse Stealing Around Rapid City in 1877 331
Mining Stampedes in Rapid City 332

Chapter XXXI

Hill City 335
Queen Bee—Sheridan 340
Rochford 342
Pactola 346
Harney 347
Hayward 348
Rockerville 349
Castleton, Sitting Bull, Silver City, and Keystone 352

Chapter XXXII

LAWRENCE COUNTY 355
Deadwood 357
The Great Fire 362
Deadwood's Water System 364
The Great Flood 365

Chapter XXXIII

New Deadwood 370
Deadwood's Reduction Works 370
Deadwood's First Railroad 372
Banking Institutions 374

Chapter XXXIV

History of Homestake Mines 380
Lead City 387
Emergency Hospital 392
Hearst Free Library—Newspapers, etc. 393

Chapter XXXV

Central City 396
Churches 396

CONTENTS xxv

Terraville 401
Crook City 402

Chapter XXXVI

Spearfish 406

Chapter XXXVII

Horse Thieves and Cattle Rustling on the Northern Frontier 420
Fight With Exelbee Gang—Sequel to the Fight 423
How Spearfish Came to be Called "The Queen City" 424
Spearfish Normal School 425
Organization 429

Chapter XXXVIII

Galena Silver Camp 433
Terry 435
Bald Mountain Refractory Ore Deposit 437

Chapter XXXIX

Our Pioneers 445
Society of Black Hills Pioneers 446
Black Hills and Historical Society of 1877 456

Chapter XL

MEADE COUNTY 458
Sturgis 462
Schools, Churches 465
Banks Manufactures, and Water System 469
Electric Light System 471

Chapter XLI

Fort Meade 476
Tilford 480
Piedmont 481
Black Hawk 483

Chapter XLII

FALL RIVER COUNTY 484
Thermal Springs 486

Chapter XLIII

Hot Springs of Minnekahta................................. 495
Public Institutions—Fire Department and Electric Light Systems ... 498
Cascade, Wind Cave 506
Edgemont 508

Chapter XLIV

BUTTE COUNTY 510
Minnesela 512
Belle Fourche 513
Cattle Shipping Industry................................... 516
Building Wyoming and Missouri River R. R................. 517
Cattle Outfits of Black Hills 517

Chapter XLV

Organization of Dakota Territory and Subsequent Struggle
    for Statehood 519
Sioux Treaties 519
Assessed Valuation of South Dakota....................... 525
South Dakota Permanent School Fund 525

Chapter XLVI

The Treaty of 1889 for the Great Sioux Reservation
    in Dakota 527
The Messiah Craze, etc..................................... 529
The Arrival of a Military Force at Pine Ridge 531
The Advent of Gen. Miles and the Disarmament
    of the Hostiles 536

LIST OF ILLUSTRATIONS

Frontispiece	Front
Stone Showing Record of Early Black Hills History	8
H. N. Ross	12
The Pioneers of 1874	19
The Gordon Stockade, 1876	49
Eaf Witcher, March, 1875	56
The Needles Near Harney's Peak	76
Devil's Tower Showing Millions of Tons of Fallen Rocks	78
Prof. Walter P. Jenny	90
Red Cloud	100
Spotted Tail	101
Wm. Lardner	127
Fred. T. Evans	138
H. N. Witcher	139
Transportation From Pierre to Deadwood	143
Sitting Bull	147
Gen. Custer's Last Charge	156
Gen. Custer's Last Battle	162
Gen. Custer	163
Sioux Indians in War Costumes	176
Attack on Wagon Train en Route to Black Hills in 1876	182
Black Hills Treasure Coach	190
Dr. D. W. Flick	197
A. W. Merrick	199
Porter Warner	202
Col. James M. Wood	203
Jack Langrishe	205
Capt. C. V. Gardner	208
Milton E. Pinney	209
Judge Thomas Hooper	213
Custer in 1876	215
S. M. Booth	216
Scene at Red Canyon After the Murder of the Metz Party	218
Thomas E. Harvey	223

LIST OF ILLUSTRATIONS

Ellis T. Peirce, Black Hills Humorist 224
John R. Brennan 228
Block House at Rapid City—1876 233
Capt. Jack Crawford, the Poet Scout 242
No. 4, above Discovery, on Deadwood 246
Cabin on Claim No. 2, Deadwood Gulch 247
White Rocks Overlooking Deadwood 256
Deadwood in 1876 257
Witcher's Freight Train on the Streets of
    Deadwood in 1876 260
Gen. A. R. Z. Dawson 265
James Halley 278
Judge Granville G. Bennett 283
Hon. Gideon C. Moody 284
Custer City 299
Sylvan Lake 302
Joseph Kubler 305
The Start for Harney Peak 306
A Distant View of Harney's Peak 310
Rapid City in 1878 313
Richard B. Hughes 315
Rapid City Chlorination Plant and School of Mines 319
Beecher's Rocks, Near Custer 320
Rapid City, Looking North, in 1899 326
Judge John W. Nowlin 330
Hill City in 1876 336
Old U. S. Courthouse, Sheridan 341
Rochford at the Beginning of the Boom, 1878 344
Stage Coach, Main Street, Deadwood 359
Deadwood After the Great Flood of 1883 367
The Deadwood and Delaware Smelter, Deadwood,
    South Dakota 371
Frank J. Washabaugh 376
Deadwood From Forest Hill 378
The Great Homestake Works at Lead 383
The Homestake Hoisting Works, 2,000 Horse-power
    Used, Lead City 385
Lead City, Black Hills, South Dakota 391
Central City in 1878 397
Seth Bullock 401

LIST OF ILLUSTRATIONS xxix

Terraville Gold Mining Camp 402
Crook City in 1876 403
Spearfish in 1876, with Lookout Mountain
   in the Background 409
Spearfish Town in 1877 414
Picture Gallery in Spearfish in 1877 417
Spearfish in Lead 430
Terry, Mining Center of the Great Refractory Ore District
   of the Black Hills 435
Golden Reward Gold Mine, Deadwood 439
Kildonan Chlorination Mine at Pluma, Between
   Deadwood and Lead 442
Group of Presidents of Society of Black Hills Pioneers 451
Building Erected at Lead by P. A. Gushurst 453
Sturgis in 1899 459
Meade County Courthouse 461
Street Scene in Sturgis, 1898 472
Rough Riders Leaving Sturgis for Cuba, May, 1898 474
Fort Meade, Bear Butte in the Background 478
"Comanche" 480
Horseshoe Curve on the Fort Pierre R. R. Between
   Lead and Piedmont 481
Col. Wm. Thornby 488
Dr. R. D. Jennings 493
The First House on the Original Town-Site of Hot Springs,
   Built by Dr. R. A. Stewart 496
South Dakota Soldiers Home, Hot Springs 499
Interior of Plunge Bath, Hot Springs 502
Hot Springs 506
Cowboy Scene in the Black Hills 511
Cattle Shipping Pen at Belle Fourche 514
Grand Council Between Friendly and Hostile Chiefs 532
Buffalo Bill Holding a Conference With Sitting Bull 535

THE BLACK HILLS;

OR,

The Last Hunting Ground of the Dakotahs.

CHAPTER I

THE DAKOTAHS

As this book is designed to be only a history of the events and incidents connected with the white settlement of the Black Hills, as stated in the introduction, it seems unnecessary to go back to the races that had occupied this portion of the great American continent long centuries ago, and of which we have no knowledge save that which is based upon vague tradition, nor does it seem necessary to more than briefly refer to the mournful history of the tribes of the great Sioux Nation, or the Dakotahs, who have been driven from the East towards the setting sun until their last and most cherished hunting ground was lost to them forever.

The Dakotahs, or Nadowessioux—abbreviated by the French explorers and trappers to Sioux—were doubtless a valorous people considered from an Indian standpoint, and are credited with many deeds of wonderful prowess in their numerous conflicts with the hostile tribes to the eastward, against whom they maintained their broad possessions for at least 200 years undisturbed— and we know not how much longer.

About the middle of the seventeenth century the Dakotahs occupied a vast stretch of territory extending from the 48° of north latitude to the Missouri river, and stretching westward to the main range of the Rocky Mountains.

In 1837 they ceded to the United States all their land lying east of the Mississippi river, since which time they have been losing their once wide domain slice by slice until at the time of the invasion of the Black Hills in 1874, they were confined to the limit prescribed by the treaty of 1868, which will be referred to farther on.

My readers need not be told in detail how that once powerful people were reduced in number, by almost constant conflicts with other tribes to the eastward of the Great Lakes, nor of how, by the numerous French and Indian wars, and their consequent defeats, they were finally forced to abandon the country, so long occupied by them, around the small lakes and headwaters of the Mississippi, and driven down and westward onto the plains of the Missouri, preceded by the Cheyennes, not of the various cessions of their territory made by them to the general government, nor of how they fought the onward march of civilization, inch by inch, until all the Western frontiers were marked by a trail of the blood of innocent women and children; or, mayhap, by their capture and torture even worse than death; nor of the consequent wars with the United States, by which they were almost exterminated, and finally driven to the wall. All this is already a matter of common history, with which most school girls and boys are familiar at the present day.

It is well known that, up to the year 1877, there had been almost perpetual hostilities on the part of the Indians, on the excuse of broken treaties, etc., the suppression of which cost the government many millions of treasure, as well as the sacrifice of thousands of human lives, and which decimated the Indian tribes, till now there is but a pitiful remnant of them left. While it cannot be claimed that treaty obligations have not been sometimes violated on the part of the government—as in the cases of Colorado and Montana, when vast hordes of adventurers and gold-seekers crossed and recrossed the Indian domain, despite treaty stipulations, frightening and killing the game upon which they almost solely depended as means of sustenance.

The treaty of 1868, guaranteeing to the Indians as a permanent reservation, all the territory lying between the Missouri river on the east, and the western boundary of Dakota on the west, and from the north boundary of the State of Nebraska on the south, to the forty-sixth parallel of latitude on the north; also stipulated that the country north of the Platte river in Nebraska, and east of the summit of the Big Horn mountains in Wyoming, should be held and considered unceded Indian territory, and that no white person or persons should be permitted to settle upon, or occupy any portion of same, not to pass through without the consent of the Indians; and also conceded the right to the Indians to hunt south of the North Platte, as far as the Republican Fork of the Smoky Hill river, for a term of years, or, as long as the buffalo might range in sufficient numbers to justify the chase, and prohibited soldiers from entering the unceded territory, north of the Platte. The treaty of 1868 also stipulated that the government should remove all military posts and government roads within the limits of their reservation, the right to establish which was granted by the treaty of 1851. In the following year, 1869, notwithstanding the treaty of 1868, all Indians found off their permanent reservation, were considered hostile, and under the jurisdiction of military authority. That the provisions of the above treaty were sometimes violated by the Indians there can be no doubt, and that its provisions were disregarded by the invasion of their reservation in 1874-5-6 is indisputable, but, ignoring the ethical side of the question, should such treaties as tend to arrest the advance of civilization, and retard the development of the rich resources of our country, ever have been entered into? This is a question which demands much thoughtful consideration. Although having deep-seated convictions on this troublesome Indian problem, as it is not within the province of this book to give them expression, the question may as well be turned over to the moralist and political economist for discussion.

THE FIRST INVASION OF THE BLACK HILLS

Prior to the year 1874, that portion of the Indian Territory known as the Black Hills, was a part and parcel of the happy hunting ground of the red man, and had for long centuries lain in an isolation almost complete as "Darkest Africa." Up to that year none of the several expeditions sent to this Western country for the purpose of exploration or subduing the hostilities of the Indians, had succeeded individually or collectively in penetrating the mountain fastnesses of the Black Hills, with the sole exception of Gen. Harney, who, with members of his staff, climbed the rugged peak, which was honored with that brave officer's name, and on its lofty summit unfurled our national emblem for the first time to the mountain breeze, and under its sacred folds pledged to it their allegiance and undying loyalty in numerous bumpers of sparkling champagne, as evidenced by the many empty bottles discovered on the spot by the pioneers about two decades later. And thereby hangs a romantic tale.

The first military and scientific expedition sent out for the purpose of exploration, known as the Warren Expedition, failed to consummate the plan of penetrating the Black Hills, as will be seen by the following extract from the report of Lieutenant Warren to the government. He says: "Setting out from Fort Laramie on the 4th of September, 1856, we proceeded direct for the Black Hills, via Raw Hide Butte, Old Woman's Creek, the Southern Fork of the Cheyenne, and Beaver Creek; up a branch of this last stream we entered the Hills (the foot-hills). We continued north to the vicinity of Inyan Karce (or the peak which makes the mountain), a remarkably high basaltic peak, one of the highest of the moutains and so far to the north that we had a full view of the prairie beyond. Here we were met by a very large force of the Dakotahs who made such earnest remonstrance and threats against our proceeding into their country that I did not think it prudent for us as a scientific expedition to venture further in this direction. Some of them were for attacking us immediately, as their numbers would have insured success, but the lesson taught them by Gen. Harney, in 1855, made them fear they would meet with retribution, and this I endeavored to impress upon them. We were at this time almost in sight of the place where these Indians had plundered Sir George Gore, in 1856, for endeavoring to proceed through their country.''

The expedition of Capt. Reynolds, sent out in 1859 with the object of exploring to the north and west of the Black Hills, around the headwaters of the Yellowstone and Missouri river, its line of march being along the northern slope, and on its southward march the western slope of the Black Hills, made no attempt to enter the Hills; so I think the assertion is justified that no military or scientific expedition ever penetrated the interior recesses of the Black Hills until the year 1874.

FIRST MOVEMENT LOOKING TO THE COLONIZATION OF THE BLACK HILLS, IN 1872

It is a matter of unwritten history, however, that an unsuccessful attempt was made to organize a formidable expedition to colonize the Black Hills in 1872, the project having its origin in the exceedingly fertile brain of Charlie Collins, then editor of the Sioux City *Times,* Iowa. It may not be out of place here to refer back to an earlier scheme which, while not pertinent to this history, will reveal the peculiar mental bent of this adventurous man.

His first dream, beginning in 1869, was of a gigantic colonization scheme which contemplated the founding, somewhere on the banks of the Missouri river, a powerful Irish-American empire, whose guiding star would lead towards the British dominions on the north. The plan devised by himself and his co-operator, John P. Hodnett, then U.S. Assessor for Dakota Territory, was to organize, in different parts of the country, colonies of Irish-Americans to enter homesteads and settle upon that portion of the Sioux (Brule) reservation lying on the east adjacent to the river, opposite the mouth of White river, so that—as in substance stated by himself—when ''England's difficulty,'' and ''Ireland's opportunity'' should arise, a patriotic army of Irish-American colonists could conveniently, and without interference, invade the British domain and wipe out, root and branch, their long-time oppressors from the face of the American continent.

Thus it will be discerned that the scheme, while designed for the betterment of the condition of native and American born Irishmen in this country, had the earmarks of Fenianism plainly impressed upon its face. The plan was submitted to the Fenian Convention held in St. Louis in the fall of 1869, which resulted in the selection of a committee to visit the region referred to and examine its resources, and if satisfactory to inaugurate the work of colonization. Its projectors even succeeded in securing the passage of a bill through Congress, authorizing a colony corporation, for the management of affairs—the purchase of land, agricultural implements, etc., designating for officers such names as A. T. Stewart, Jim Fiske, Jr., Ben Butler, Wendell Philips, and others whose names were then household words.

So popular became the apparently philanthropic scheme that a famous millionaire dry goods merchant offered a half million dollars, to aid in furtherance of the project. In short, the committee selected to visit and report upon the resources of the region of prospective settlement, being, for the most part tenderfeet, unaccustomed to the terrible hardships of a journey over the untrodden wilds of Dakota, returned with a very poor opinion of the Indian domain, and submitted a majority report unfavorable to the scheme. A minority of the committee, who reported favorably, had selected the site where Brule City now stands, as the seat of empire and named it Limerick. The majority report however, dealt a vital blow to the project and it collapsed. Mr. Collins then turned his attention to the scheme for the settlement of the Black Hills as before stated.

To boom the enterprise and attract public attention, he during the spring and summer of 1872, published in the *Times* a series of highly sensational articles which were distributed broadcast over the land, announcing that an expedition was organizing in Sioux City with the object of exploring and revealing to the world the hidden mysteries of the Black Hills of Dakota.

En passant, it should be stated here that Charlie Collins, although erratic and visionary to a degree, was a writer of no mean ability—a man of generous impulses and liberal to a fault, thoroughly westernized in feeling and sentiment, and withal a born organizer. With facile pen he portrayed in glowing colors the golden treasure concealed within the rock-ribbed hills and the gulches of the land he pictured; drawing for the most part on his resourceful imagination for material, or rather for the immaterial, as the existence of gold in the Black Hills was then scarcely more than a vague conjecture, based on Indian tradition. Albeit these articles had the effect of drawing many to Sioux City, to which its enterprising people were, naturally, by no means averse. Among those who were thus attracted was T. H. Russell, a fronteirsman of considerable experience, having been a pioneer of Colorado, and familiar with mining life among the camps of the Rockies. Through the Indian wives of some of his mountaineer acquaintances he had gained an intimate knowledge of the traditions of the existence of gold in the Black Hills, in which traditions he was a firm believer.

On his arrival in Sioux City he was naturally greatly disappointed to find that the expedition so glowingly described in the columns of the *Times,* as yet existed only on paper; however, entering into the spirit of the enterprise, Collins and Russell, jointly with others, began at once the work of organization.

Prominent among the organizers were Charles S. Soule, manager of the Northwestern Transportation Company, Dan Scott, editor of the Sioux City *Journal*; Harnett & Howard, and many others. Gen. A. C. Dawes, general passenger agent of the Kansas City & St. Joe Railroad, also lent valuable assistance to the project.

Pamphlets were compiled and published at the *Times* office, setting forth the grand possibilities of the Black Hills, their distance from Sioux City, cost of transportation, etc. Plentifully supplied with these pamphlets, Capt. Russell made a tour of the towns along the Missouri river as far down as Kansas City, judiciously distributing his literature to such as, in his judgment, were liable to join. The success of the trip proved all that could be desired, hundreds from the Missouri river towns enrolling members of the expedition, which was dated to start on September 1, 1872. As, apparently, no care had been taken to keep the expedition secret, the movement finally attracted the attention of the military authorities of the government, when Gen. Hancock, then in command at Fort Snelling, issued the following peremptory order to the post commanders on the Missouri river: "That any expedition organized for the purpose of penetrating the Black Hills, be immediately dispersed, the leaders arrested and placed in the nearest military prison." This order inflicted the death blow to the projected expedition to the Black Hills in 1872. All preparation immediately ceased, and the expedition was abandoned, much to the disappointment and disgust of the organizers.

ADVENTURES ON THE BORDER

It is claimed upon authroity, which we have no good reason to dispute, that adventurous parties, at different dates, as far back as 1859, and perhaps before, had, despite the vigilance and extreme hostility of the Sioux, who guarded their domain against encroachment with a jealous eye, made some discoveries of the precious metal in the country west of the Black Hills in the Big Horn Mountains; and had also, according to Indian traditions— substantiated by tangible evidences discovered by prospectors in 1876-7— ventured around the western and northern bases and a short distance into the foothills or spurs of the Black Hills.

LAST HUNTING GROUND OF THE DAKOTAHS

There was a story published years ago, for the authenticity of which I am not able to vouch, and which, therefore, must be accepted at its face value, that a party of nineteen men detached themselves at Fort Laramie from a large party of gold hunters en route for California—influenced by current reports of rich gold discoveries in the Black Hills, made their way thither, found rich gold deposits, and worked claims, and were all massacred by the Indians, save one, who shortly after died.

Prospectors coming into the Hills during the great rush of 1876, claim to have found proofs corroborative of the above story in the shape of old sluice boxes, gradually crumbling into decay, corroded mining implements, and other evidences that gold hunters had mined in some of the gulches along the northern border of the Hills, even as far back as 1833.

Among the private collection of fossils and other curios in possession of John Cashner, of Spearfish, South Dakota, there is a simple flat stone, carefully preserved and framed, which furnishes material for an exceedingly interesting bit of early Black Hills history. It is an irregular sandstone tablet about twelve inches square and two and one half inches thick, bearing an inscription which, if genuine, reveals a truly pathetic story. This tablet was discovered in March, 1887, in the middle draw of Lookout Mountain, by Lewis Thoen, of Spearfish, while quarrying for building stone. It was found concealed under a large, flat rock, the crevice between which and the ground underneath was filled in by the drifting sands of years and overgrown with vegetation, giving the discovery every appearance of genuineness.

Learning of this cold, mute witness of an early Black Hills tragedy, the author, partly to gratify a natural curiosity and partly to be enabled to vouch for its existence, visited the cabinet of Mr. Cashner and found the stone as above described. On the table is inscribed, apparently by the blade of a pocket knife and in somewhat irregular lines, as will be seen by the accompanying cut, the following tragic story. On one side is recorded: "Came to these Hills in 1833, seven of us DeLacompt Ezra Kind G. W. Wood T Brown R Kent Wm King Indian Crow. all ded but me Ezra Kind. Killed by Inds beyond the high hill got our gold June 1834." On the reverse side: "Got all of the gold we could carry our pony all got by the Indians. I have lost my gun and nothing to eat and Indians hunting me."

This story, besides having in itself many of the elements of probability is, as related by old hunters who had spent years amongst them, also verified by Indian tradition, which tells that upon a time, a band of Sioux hunters in quest of game, came upon a stream, muddied, as they supposed, by beavers, and in following it up, found the small party of gold hunters, swooped down upon them, killing all but one, who escaped, and appropriated their gold, which was afterward sold to the Hudson Bay Company for $18,000 (or probably its equivalent in fire water, beads, and other glittering gewgaws so dear to the hearts of savages). The fact that this tradition tallies with the record on the stone tablet, certainly entitles the story to much credence.

The supposition is, that this gold was mined in the vicinity of Gold Run, about twelve miles from Lookout mountain, in a direct line. The theory appears to be that Ezra Kind, after making his escape from the Indians, went into hiding in the middle draw of Lookout mountain, where he inscribed his sad story on a piece of sandstone, which he concealed under a large rock, where he hoped it might some day be found; then either died from starvation or was finally killed by the Indians.

The spot where the tablet was accidentally discovered, which was also visited, seemed well adapted for the cache, being some ten or twelve feet below the level of the ground about it, two large scrub oaks marking the spot. Back towards the mountain about 100 yards, the draw deepens to eighteen or twenty feet and is overhung with large bushes, making an admirable place for concealment from Indians.

The publication of the story of the above discovery in some of the principal newspapers of the country brought letters from parties who claimed to be relatives of some of the unfortunate missing men, which tends to strengthen somewhat its credibility.

Father De Smet, the venerable Catholic missionary, often visited the Hills with his savage proteges, but how far into the interior of the Black Hills proper he ever penetrated, is uncertain.

Let it be borne in mind that what was named the Black Hills embraced a large scope of territory extending from the 103d meridian of longitude on the east to the Big Horn and Wind rivers on the west, and from the Laramie and Sweetwater rivers on the south to the Yellowstone on the north, so that it is quite easy to believe that portions of that territory had been visited and prospected for gold at a much earlier date than 1874.

In speaking of the Black Hills proper, reference is had to the main uplift, embraced between the two forks of the Cheyenne river.

It may safely be asserted then, that no adventurous spirits ever penetrated very far into the interior of the Black Hills previous to the year 1874, and, as we have no positive proof of any such exploration, it may be assumed that up to that time they had remained a vague mystery. However, they were destined to remain a mystery no longer. Thenceforth the beautiful pine-clad Black Hills were no longer to echo to the shrill war-whoop of the Sioux, nor the turf of the fair, smiling valleys lying between, respond to their stealthy tread. In 1874 the campfires of the red man were extinguished in the Black Hills, never again to be rekindled. The spirit of adventure and aggression was then abroad in the land; the handwriting was on the wall. The gold-ribbed Black Hills were to be snatched from the grasp of savages, to whom they were no longer profitable even as a hunting ground, and given over to the thrift and enterprise of the hardy pioneer, who would develop their wonderful resources and thereby advance the interests and add to the wealth of our whole country.

CHAPTER II

THE CUSTER BLACK HILLS EXPEDITION

On July 2d, 1874, an expedition under the command of Gen. Geo. A. Custer, left Fort Abraham Lincoln with ten companies of cavalry, two of infantry, a detachment of white and Indian scouts, interpreters, miners, teamsters, etc., in all about 1,000 men, under orders from the Governmental Department, to make a reconnoissance of the country from that point to Bear Butte on the north of the Hills, and explorations of the country adjacant thereto, on the southwest, south, and southeast, and into the interior eastward for the purpose presumably of learning something of the topography and geological formation of the Hills, and also of their general character and possible resources. The prime object of the expedition, however, would appear to be to ascertain their exact geographical position, relative to the military posts, Lincoln and Laramie, with a view to the establishment of other posts within or near the Black Hills, in case future complications with the Sioux rendered it necessary.

The following extract from the report of William Ludlow, chief of engineers, Department of Dakota, accompanying the expedition, will make clear its real object:—

"In case of any future complication with the Sioux, or the needs of bordering civilization should make it necessary to establish military posts on this reservation, indications all point to the Black Hills as the most suitable point, both on account of their geographical position, and on the abundance of wood, water, and grass to be found there. To explain the value of its position, it should be stated that the trails from the camp of the hostile Sioux on the Yellowstone to the agencies near the Missouri, where live the reservation Indians, and where the issues of annuities are made, lead by a southeasterly course through the Hills, the abundance of game, and ample security of which make them a ready refuge in time of war, and a noble hunting ground in time of peace. It was therefore desirable to gain positive information regarding them, and to connect them as well, by reconnoissance with the posts of Lincoln and Laramie. To accomplish these results was the object of this expedition."

In this connection the opinion is ventured that there might have been another object underlying the action of the government, and one of more vital interest to the people of the country, who were looking with covetous eyes, towards this rich domain, namely, their ultimate redemption from the hands of the Indians, and their consequent opening to white settlement, in case the vague rumors that had reached the world, of their fabulous richness, should be borne out by the facts.

Be that as it may, a hasty exploration was made—all that was possible in the limited time fixed for the work (sixty days time), sufficiently extensive, however, to answer the purpose for which the expedition was organized, and to gain a partial knowledge of the formation of the Hills, and their general topographical features.

The expedition entered the Hills on the west, at a point near Inyah-Kara, penetrated southeastward as far as Harney's Peak, thence southward across the southern limits of the Hills to the south fork of the Cheyenne river.

From this point, Charlie Reynolds, Custer's chief of scouts, was sent alone across the Indian infested country with dispatches to Fort Laramie, and it is alleged that the famous scout suffered exposure and privations on the journey, from the efforts of which he never fully recovered.

Returning to Harney's Peak the expedition spent a few days prospecting in the region of the Peak, then took up their march along the Box Elder, and finally after some difficulty found its way out of the Hills at a point nearly opposite Bear Butte, which embraced all the territory explored.

But very little prospecting was done, and that principally on the heads of the streams draining the area around Harney's Peak, where only five days were spent, the longest time at any one point, in proof of which I will quote from General Custer's Report to the War Department, in detailing the work of the expedition, the following:—

"It will be understood that within the limits of the Black Hills we were almost constantly marching, never halting at any one point for a longer time than one day—except one, and that was near Harney's peak, where we remained five days; most of the command, however, being employed in operations during the halt. From this it will be seen that no satisfactory or conclusive examination of the country could be made regarding its mineral deposits; enough, however, was determined to establish the fact that gold is distributed throughout an extensive area within the Black Hills. No discoveries, as far as I am aware, were made of gold deposits in quartz, although there is every reason to believe that a more thorough and extended search would have discovered it. Seeking for gold was not one of the objects of the expedition; consequently, we were but illy-prepared to institute or successfully prosecute a search for it, even after we became aware of its existence in the country."

H. N. ROSS
One of the Mining Experts of the Custer Expedition of 1874

It will be seen from the above that, although prospects of gold were found in the gulches of the streams flowing from the region of Harney's Peak, no deposits of gold in quartz were discovered. The fact was revealed to the pioneers of 1874 in their search for gold, very shortly after, that the prospecting done by the Custer expedition was a mere bagatelle; besides, there was such a wide discrepancy of statements in the reports of the experts accompanying the expedition, in regard to even the existence of gold in the Black Hills, that the public mind was thrown into a greater degree of uncertainty than before, for, while General Custer and the mining experts of the expedition claimed to have found gold, Prof. Winchell, geologist, was equally positive in his claim that he did not see a single one of the shining particles. The sequel has demonstrated, however, that the Professor probably did not see the gold because he wouldn't. There is an old adage which says: "There are none so blind as those who won't see."

Be that as it may, it was left to the pioneers of 1874 to relieve the public mind from the uncertainly into which it was thrown by these conflicting reports, and to prove to them beyond any doubt the existence of the precious metal in which the people of the country were, at the time, more deeply interested than in any other question. In this state of uncertainty they awaited, with no little anxiety, a report from the pioneers who were already on their perilous way before the final reports of the Custer expedition were made public.

GOLD FOUND BY THE INDIANS

Such of my readers as are familiar with the history of the early missionaries among the Indians, will doubtless remember the stories told of the wonderfully rich specimens of gold, platinum and other precious metals shown by the Indians at the mission, and who, when asked where they were found, would always point in the direction of the Black Hills, but would never consent to conduct any white person to the place, they having doubtless been warned against the cupidity of the whites by their friends, the missionaries. In view of the recent rich discoveries in the Hills it is quite safe to believe that right in or near the Black Hills, those wonderful specimens were found.

DE SMET EXPLAINS THE USE OF A GUN TO THE INDIANS

The subjoined story has been handed down from those missionary days, which the writer is sufficiently credulous to believe. In substance the story runs thus: "De Smet, in one of his trips among the Sioux Indians, before the discovery of gold in California, promised a Sioux chief a present of a pistol, the use of which he had been at some trouble to explain. Accordingly he procured a horse pistol at one of the fur companies' trading posts, some powder, and caps. On his return to the home of the chief he redeemed his promise, purposely neglecting to bring any bullets. The chief overcame the difficulty by going away and returning after a brief absence with a handful of yellow metal nuggets, which he requested be melted into bullets. The missionary, finding that the nuggets were gold, cautioned the Indians against making known the existence of gold in their country, as the 'pale faces' would undergo untold hardships to possess it."

So, it will be seen that the region of the Black Hills and westward of them was renowned, in the legends of the Indians, for their precious metals, and judging from the rich specimens obtained by the Jesuit Missionaries, this country will prove something more than a mere glittering generality.

ORGANIZATION OF FIRST EXPEDITION

Upon the return of the Custer exploring expedition in the summer of 1874, Collins and Russell, deeming the time auspicious for such a movement, renewed their efforts to organize a Black Hills Expedition. In furtherance of the scheme they proceeded at once to Chicago, opened an office on Clark street, and began the work of drawing in recruits. Their efforts were being rapidly crystallized by the enrollment of numerous members, but the publicity given the enterprise soon attracted the attention of Gen. Sheridan—then stationed at Chicago, who immediately issued orders to the commander of the frontier posts, similar to the one issued by Gen. Hancock two years before, which again dealt a vital blow to the project.

Apparently abandoning the enterprise, they gave up their office in Chicago and returned to Sioux City, where the following dispatch was sent to the Associated Press by Chas. S. Soule: "In view of the recent order of Gen. Sheridan, the Collins & Russell expedition has been abandoned for the present." This dispatch was merely a blind to put the military authorities off their guard, for right upon its heels, hundreds of letters marked "confidential" were mailed from the *Times* office, in reply to those asking for information in reference to the expedition—stating that the dispatch promulgated was a blind; that the expedition was a foregone conclusion, and also, cautioning all who contemplated going to keep their own counsel and make known their intentions only at the *Times* Office.

How many of those numerous correspondents reported at headquarters has not been ascertained, but it is a well-known fact that despite the gigantic efforts of those indefatigable workers, the expedition, in point of numbers, did not materialize to any great extent, as only twenty-six men, all told, had the hardihood to defy the authorities and undertake the perilous journey. These few got together, made their secret arrangements, purchased their supplies and equipments—paying for them in cold cash out of their individual pockets, as far as known—and launched secretly out for the Black Hills without exciting the slightest suspicion on the part of the Government officials or creating a single ripple on the surface of affairs in the pioneer outfitting city.

This first expedition to the Black Hills has been called by some the Gordon expedition, in honor of John Gordon, the leader of the expedition on its journey into the Hills.

This appellation, however, appears to be a misnomer, as it cannot be ascertained that the guide of the expedition was in any direct way sponsor for its organization.

It appears from reliable data obtained, that Collins and Russell, by virtue of their mutual efforts to effect an organization in conjunction with other prominent citizens of Sioux City, as before recorded, are rightfully entitled to that distinction. Therefore, by that token, the first expedition will be recorded on the pages of this history as the Collins-Russell Expedition.

CHAPTER III

PREPARATIONS FOR THE JOURNEY

The following account of the secret preparations for and the journey of the expedition over the plains to the Black Hills, with incidents of the trip, partakes somewhat of the nature of historical narration, rather than a bare record of facts, which it is hoped may render the reading thereof less tiresome.

Sioux City, the scene of the first movement for the invasion of the Sioux domain, was, at the time of the opening of this story, an enterprising and rapidly growing young city, not far back from the threshold of the then Western frontier—an admirable outfitting point for the unsettled regions to the Westward, and favorably located geographically for carrying out the enterprise of its bold projectors, who were then projecting the secret arrangements for the perilous journey.

Almost any day during the latter part of September, 1874, there might have been seen small groups of determined looking men standing on the street corners, or in the hotel lobbies—engaged in earnest discussion of some apparently absorbing topic—an occurrence common enough in any well regulated city; the only thing remarkable about these gatherings being that their personnel was always the same, and whenever closely approached they would immediately disperse, a circumstance which might have led a critical observer to suspect them of some dark conspiracy, and if any curiously inclined person had felt disposed to follow their movements, when the shadows began to fall, they might perhaps have been found at some pre-appointed place in secret conference behind closed doors. Strangers they were, for the most part, who had gathered there, from widely separated localities—extending from the northern lakes to the southern gulf—drawn thither by the current rumors that an expedition was about to leave that convenient point for the Black Hills.

Bright, crisp October comes, and if we board a ferry boat and cross over to the west bank of treacherous Missouri river with its numerous snags and shifting sands, we will find our little party of Black Hills adventurers rendezvoused in a grove near by a small village named Covington, making active but quiet preparations for breaking camp, and strangely enough, with them a woman and small boy—the former none other than the author of this story. Speculation was rife around the little community, and many questions were asked as to the destination of the outfit, but the men were absolutely noncommittal, and it was then demonstrated that a woman too, can sometimes keep a secret. The necessity for secrecy becomes obvious when it is known that the movement was in direct violation of the express orders of the United States government, whose vigilance the expedition hoped to escape.

Preparations for the journey were soon completed. Tents were hurriedly taken down, carefully folded, and with their poles strapped to the sides of the respective wagon boxes; bright, new cooking utensils, coffee pots and frying pans predominating, were fastened in artistic array along the outside wherever convenience and taste dictated. The inevitable water buckets were suspended from the wagon reaches underneath, and last but by no means least the "grub boxes," were lifted to their places at the rear, where they were held in place by an arrangement similar to that employed for the baggage of passengers on the early stage coaches, when everything was in readiness for moving.

In the afternoon of that memorable day of October 6th, 1874, the first expedition to the Black Hills cut loose its prairie craft from its moorings on the banks of the "Big Muddy," and followed the "Star of Empire," westward right through the heart of the Sioux reserve. As the train filed out of camp on that October day—the new wagons, whose white covers bore a "strange device," gleaming brightly in the afternoon sun, in the lead, the horsemen on the flanks, the pedestrians—among whom I tripped jauntly along in the rear—it must have presented an imposing pageant to the very few observers.

The expedition, in its entirety, was composed of twenty-six men, one woman, and a boy, six canvas-covered wagons, each drawn by two pairs of fat, sleek, and a few of them somewhat frisky cattle—by the way, they were neither so fat nor sleek, and not in the least frisky at the end of the journey. There were also five saddle horses, and two beautiful greyhounds, whose frequent frantic chases after the poor timid antelope and rabbit, proved the source of much diversion to the expedition on its long, monotonous march across the bleak, treeless plains. Those long-limbed, pointed-nosed, fleet hounds—named, respectively, Dan and Fan, were noble specimens of their kind, of indisputable lineage, and the pets of the entire party.

When a few miles out from the starting point, the train halted for the night, when the question, as to who should lead the expedition, and pilot the piratical craft safely to its destination, came up for consideration. After some lively canvassing, as to the best man to intrust with so important an undertaking, the choice finally fell upon John Gordon, who, claiming to have traveled over the country as far as the foot-hills, several years before, was deemed the best fitted, by virtue of such knowledge of the route, to be our guide and leader.

However, the expedition had not proceeded far on the journey beyond the line of public travel before it became apparent that our guide's knowledge of the geography of the country was, to say the least, somewhat vague and uncertain. He had, doubtless, penetrated the country over government roads, used for the transportation of supplies for the military posts to the west of the Black Hills, but not, it was thought, in the direction of the objective point of the expedition. Be that as it may the train was enabled by the aid of a small pocket campass, carried by Lyman Lamb, who took daily bearings, to keep the general direction, and, although the train may have traversed a good deal of unnecessary territory, our leader was indefatigable in his efforts to find the most practicable ground over which to travel, and finally landed the expedition safely—though somewhat the worse for wear, in the Black Hills. It was his daily custom to ride out every morning in advance of the train to mark out the line of march for the day, by virtue of which he was entitled to unbounded credit.

The expedition was splendidly equipped with munitions for its defense— each man having provided himself with the most approved Winchester rifle, besides small arms, and sufficient ammunition to last by economy for a period of eight months. Fidelity to history compels me to record, however, that at divers times, some of our men indulged in the careless pastime of firing their precious cartridges at targets, on which occasions I had grave misgivings as to whether there would be any left to kill Indians with in case it became necessary. At times I was strongly tempted to expostulate with them on their thoughtless waste of ammunition, but I quickly controlled that inclination, concluding that, perhaps, they knew their own business—at least they might think they did and take occasion to remind me of that fact. I did, however, venture to approach them timidly one day when I thought them uncommonly reckless, and say solemnly: "Boys, don't you think you will need all this ammunition that you are virtually throwing away when we get out among the Indians?" "Oh, shoot the Indians," answered one of the boys, irreverently. Now, deeming this a potent and convincing argument against the position I had assumed, and plainly significant, I meekly yielded the point and referred no more to the subject.

Our wagons were packed to the guards with sundry provisions, chiefly flour, bacon, beans, also sugar, coffee, a modicum of tea, a limited quantity of canned goods, butter, etc. It was estimated that our supply of the staple articles was sufficient to last, at least, eight months, and, as the owners of each outfit purchased their own supplies, the luxuries were more or less abundant, according to the purses of the purchasers.

Besides the supply of munitions and provisions, we were provided with all the necessary paraphernalia for camping, mechanics' tools, and, to complete the outfit, with picks, shovels, and gold pans.

Let it be understood that the members of the expedition, while arranging for the journey, had been divided into what is called, in army parlance, messes, a kind of copartnership being entered into, the respective partners pooling their resources for the purchase of supplies and other property necessary for transportation, with the understanding that, at dissolution, the assets be equally divided among the partners.

The grouping was as follows: No. 1 being composed of Capt. Tom Russell, Lyman Lamb, Eaf. Witcher and Angus McDonald. No. 2, B. B. Logan, Dan McDonald, or Red Dan, Dan McDonald, or Black Dan (the last two, bearing the same patronymic, were distinguished by the color of the shirts they invariably wore), James Dempster, James Powers, J. J. Williams, and Thomas Quiner. 3d, John Gordon, J. W. Brockett, Newton Warren, H. Bishop, Chas. Long, Chas. Cordeiro and Moses Aarons. 4th, R. R. Whitney, Harry Cooper, David Aken, and John Boyle. 5th, Chas. Blackwell, Thos. McLaren, Henry Thomas, D. G. Tallent, Annie D. Tallent, and Robt. E. Tallent, then a boy nine years of age, making twenty-eight in all.

Now that we had got safely away from Sioux City, the problem was how to escape suspicion. So on the canvas covers of the wagons was painted, in large, red letters, "O'Neill's Colony;" intended as a misleading device, which, however, turned out to be a rather transparent one, as very few seemed to be deceived thereby.

The people of the small towns through which we passed, along the route, regarded our train with a good deal of justifiable curiosity, and our ears were frequently greeted with such questions as: "Hullo, where are you going?" "Where are you bound for, strangers?"

For answer their attention was usually called to the painted words on the canvas.

"Oh, you can't fool me;" "What are you giving us?" and other localisms would be heard in reply.

If they had only been permitted to have taken a look into the hidden recesses of our wagons, and discovered the aforesaid picks, shovels, and gold pans, their evident suspicions would have been amply verified. No doubt vague rumors had reached those people in advance that an expedition was on its way to the Black Hills, in reference to which the subjoined extracts from Nebraska newspapers will show the trend of public opinion.

Group of Members of the First Expedition now Remaining in the Black Hills
1. JOHN J. WILLIAMS 2. THOS. H. RUSSELL 3. EAF. WITCHER
4. LYMAN LAMB 5. ANNIE D. TALLENT 6. ROBT. E. TALLENT

SIOUX CITY GOLD HUNTERS

The West Point *Republican* says the following extract from the Oakdale *Journal* refers to the Sioux City party under Capt. Russell, a well-known and reliable frontiersman, and adds: "Although attempting a dangerous task, we apprehend that every man fully realizes the situation and is prepared to face death at any moment."

Here is what the Oakdale paper says:—

"We were misinformed last week in regard to the destination of the supposed emigrant party which passed up the valley recently. Instead of being sturdy sons of toil destined, in the future, to delve in the rich soil of Holt County, their destination was the Eldorado of the Northwest—the coveted gold fields of the Black Hills. They were resolute, determined looking fellows, and one scarcely knows which to do first—admire their courage or condemn their judgment in thus venturing into an Indian country in the present temper of the red men. That they will have to fight their way inch by inch, across the Sioux territory, is a fact patent to every one conversant with the facts in the case.

"We fear they have counted without their host, for they go into a country where dwell Indians enough to surround their little party a hundred deep. If they are captured they have no reason to expect mercy at the hands of the relentless, bloody Sioux."

Until we had left the last vestige of civilization behind us, each day of our journey was very much like the preceding one, the same routine of camp duties to perform, such as pitching tents, gathering wood, building fires, over which our evening meals were cooked at night, and taking down and folding tents, preparing our hasty breakfast just as the autumn days began to dawn. Each member of the party was required to serve his turn in the performance of all camp duties, which was really no hardship at that stage of journey, as no night patrol to guard the camp was necessary.

Our train traveled rather slowly, each day covering an average distance of from fifteen to twenty miles, not a bad record, when it is considered that cattle are not noted for their speed.

Spots, well supplied with wood and water, and favorable for grazing, were selected for camping grounds, usually by some one sent out in advance for that purpose. At night, upon arriving at the ground selected, no time was lost, each man proceeded with alacrity in the performance of the duties falling to his share. Supper being disposed of and the remnants gathered up—not even one very small basketful—a couple of hours were then spent in telling stories and singing songs, and, by the way, there were some capital story-tellers in our party, and a few exceptionally fine singers—notably, young

Harry Cooper, whose rich tenor voice, as it floated out on the still night air, made one think of the New Jerusalem.

The only drawback to the enjoyment was, that by the rules adopted I was required to furnish my share of the entertainment by singing a song or telling a story. Story-telling being more in my line, I would sometimes rehearse a tale calculated to "harrow up the soul, freeze the young blood," etc.—usually one in which tomahawks and scalping-knives conspicuously figured. At the close of these outdoor musicals all would retire to their tents to sleep—perchance to dream of home or "the girls they left behind them."

I must confess here that I enjoyed those social hours spent around the smouldering camp-fire after our days' journeys were ended. Yes, it was truly glorious out under heaven's dark canopy, with its myriads of bright stars twinkling lovingly down upon us like a very benediction—more especially so in that we realized that we were soon to become trespassers and outlaws without the pale of civilization.

THE FIRST DEFECTION

Soon after we left the little village of Norfolk behind, and were slowly nearing the last settlement, one of the members of our expedition became suddenly very ill—so alarmingly sick that he felt it necessary to at once sever his connection with the enterprise, of which he had been one of the chief promoters, and speedily return to Sioux City. Now, I was uncharitable enough to think at the time, that the poor fellow just became "awfully" homesick, and my opinion has not materially changed since then. As it is not essential to this history, and for fear that I may have done him a mental injustice, his name shall be withheld. Yet, after all, there perhaps was not one of us who did not experience occasional twinges of homesickness as we approached the danger line, and visions of exposure, hardships, sickness, and even death rose up before us, and the fierce warwhoop of the Sioux was already ringing in our ears. The outlook was by no means alluring, and one could scarcely be blamed for turning his back upon such a prospect. Besides, it is certainly no discredit to be homesick, but rather a proof that in all the wide world there is no place like home.

This defection left the expedition with only twenty-five men to face the perils of the journey over the plains. However, we were in a measure compensated for our loss by a valuable addition to our number, soon after.

A little later, one of our members, whom for prudential reasons we shall designate as Mr. A., incidentally came across a man who was the owner of a very diminutive donkey, which he was anxious to sell—offering him at what he represented as a great bargain. Mr. A., being of a speculative turn of mind, and thinking that he knew a good thing when he saw it, after carefully diagnosing his small anatomy, purchased the little equine for a reasonable consideration. After a critical examination of the property I mentally decided, without prejudice, that the expedition had lost but little by the exchange, and, in behalf of the donkey, I will say that only on two or three occasions had we reason to be sorry that he joined the expedition.

However, when it was afterwards seen what prodigious burdens were loaded upon the docile little creature, and the way he was yanked about by the bits—emphasized by an occasional vigorous kick, I came to the conclusion that the poor little beast had indeed fallen into rather hard lines. Ah, me, many were the wordy combats I had with the purchaser on account of what I deemed cruelty to animals—in which, much to my discomforture, I always came out second best. I was on safe ground from a moral standpoint, but as he was the owner of the property he had a decided practical advantage. I was reminded one day during active hostilities, that the donkey was his and that he felt at liberty to kick him whenever he was in a kicking mood without asking leave of any one.

It is highly amusing now to recall these exciting passages on the journey over the plains—and all on account of a donkey.

It is quite remarkable now how a trip over the plains, with all its trying discomforts, brings to the surface the most unlovely elements of a man's character, or a woman's either for that matter.

Now don't let anyone be led into the belief that our comrade was a monster of cruelty—far from it. On the other hand, he was one of the kindest and best fellows in the outfit. He merely wanted to demonstrate to the sometimes headstrong little creature, that he was master, and felt compelled to resort to heroic methods to convince him of the fact.

We had now arrived at our ostensible destination, O'Neill settlement, on the western verge, while really, our journey had but just begun. All the exposure, the hardships, and dangers had yet to be encountered. As there no longer seemed to be any great necessity for secrecy, our plans and objects were pretty freely discussed with the few settlers at this point, with the understanding, however, that no information be given regarding our movements.

The people looked upon our undertaking as foolhardy in the extreme, and used all their native eloquence in trying to persuade me, at least, to change my mind and return before it was too late. But all their well-meant advice went for naught.

Did I ever feel tempted to turn back? No, not at this stage of our journey, but later on, when trouble and misfortune seemed to gather darkly over us, when the pitiless storms of winter overtook us, when sickness and death entered our midst, and bore away one of our little band—then, ah, yes, I would have hailed with glad thankfulness any opportunity to return to the comforts and safety of home, but no such opportunity was likely to occur.

Turning back, after we had penetrated the hostile country, was altogether out of the question, even if such a course had been permitted, as the exposure and danger of a backward journey would have been as great, if not even greater, than to advance, so the only way was to keep together and press resolutely on to the end.

After a day spent in the O'Neill settlement for rest, our journey westward was resumed, and I now recall, how utterly horrified those kind people looked as our train pulled out of camp.

They assured us that we were rushing headlong right into the jaws of death, and to be candid I was much of the same opinion, yet we were not disposed to profit by their well-meant advice.

When about two days out from the last settlement, we were met by a party of United States surveyors who had been sent out to establish the Nebraska State line, but who, on account of the Indians, were forced to return without fully completing the work. They urged us not to proceed on our journey, saying that the Sioux had on their war paint and feathers, and in no mood to permit white men to enter their domain. The expedition was not to be intimidated, but, despite all warnings to the contrary, and fully conscious of the perils ahead, proceeded along the valley of the Elkhorn river, about on the line now occupied by the N. W. & M. V. R. R. to a point about halfway between O'Neill and Long Pine, not far from old Fort Niobrara, where our train diverged to the right, then traveling in a northwesterly direction to the Niobrara river, which was reached on the 31st day of October.

Three weeks had now elapsed since leaving camp on the bank of the Mississippi river, yet only a very small part of our journey had been accomplished.

The novelty, as well as the poetry of the trip, had by this time entirely worn off, and had instead become painfully realistic and prosaic. A few of our number would have willingly turned their backs on the promised land and returned had it been possible. Our stock had already begun to show the effects of their long march.

CHAPTER IV

"CROSSING THE NIOBRARA"

At this point the expedition encountered the first real difficulty of the journey. It was found that ice had already formed on both sides of the river, while in the middle of the stream the current was very swift. The bed of the channel was covered with quicksand and very treacherous, hence any attempt to ford the river at that time seemed like a hazardous undertaking. After a brief consultation on the difficulties of the situation, it was decided to halt, and remain for a few days to give the stock time to feed and recuperate, or, until, by the melting of the ice on the edge of the stream, the crossing might be safely effected. We were astir at dawn on the following morning, and found, much to our satisfaction, that the ice, the result of a higher temperature, was fast losing its hold upon the banks, and, piece by piece floating swiftly down with the current.

During the halt several of our men started out to make a reconnoissance of the country ahead of us as far as the Fort Randall road, on the Keya Paha, to ascertain the most practicable route, and also to look for any signs of the proximity of Indians, returning late with the report that no Indians had been seen.

At 10 o'clock on the morning of the 2d of November, preparations were completed for crossing the treacherous stream, and by noon we were all landed safely on the opposite side, albeit not without a hard struggle, as the quicksands on the bed made it extremely difficult for the cattle to keep their feet, the shifting sands causing some of them to fall several times during the crossing.

Let it be understood that henceforth on our journey, all orders from headquarters were to be obeyed to the letter, "without asking the reason why or daring to make reply."

By the way, have my readers ever observed how prone some men are, when vested with a "little brief authority," to become arbitrary and domineering? I have, and it is enough to make the angels weep. Of course, now that we were no longer under the protection of the law, the necessity of having a leader became apparent. It also became vitally important that certain regulations and rules of discipline be laid down and rigidly enforced. All fully realized that if every man was permitted to be a law unto himself, it would result in confusion worse confounded.

From this point our march was continued north and west, following for some distance the line of the Nebraska State survey, thence in the same direction to the Keya Paha river and the Fort Randall Government road.

While in camp at this point a small detachment of United States cavalry, with an ambulance, was seen passing along the road to the westward only a short distance away, but notwithstanding the fact that our stock was scattered all around, feeding in plain view, we were not discovered, strangely enough. Their appearance naturally created no little excitement in our midst for a short time. I remember we were all in mortal fear lest the irrepressible donkey might betray us into the hands of the soldiers, it being his custom to indulge in the pastime of braying lustily from the time he was set free from his burden on reaching camp, and all along through the silent watches of the night, at short intervals until the dawn of the morning, and, although he was Lilliputian as to size, his braying was as loud, sonorous and prolonged, as the notes of a fog horn on the great lakes. However, as good luck would have it, he did not bray at that crisis, at least not until the soldiers were well out of hearing, and had disappeared from sight beyond an adjacent hill, when we again breathed freely.

Forsooth, that little midget of a donkey was the source of a great deal of trouble and inexpressible anxiety to us all along the line through the hostile country on account of that unfortunate habit of his. While we all felt it necessary to walk around on tip-toe, so to speak, talk in subdued whispers and extinguish our fires before dark, he would bray away at his own sweet will without let or hindrance. Finally we were forced, in sheer self-defense, to resort to the expedient of putting a muzzle on him for several nights during the most critical part of our journey; of course, that had to be discontinued as he must eat if he was expected to carry burdens, besides, we felt it was not quite democratic to suppress freedom of speech.

We now began to realize that we were treading on forbidden ground—that we were without the pale of the law and cut off from communication with the outside world—that henceforth danger would menace us from every quarter.

At any time we were liable to be met or overtaken by roving bands of Indians, who we felt sure would look with no favor upon our aggressive movements. On the other hand, we were still more afraid of the authorities we had secretly defied.

We were in constant expectation of seeing a troop of cavalry come upon us from the rear, seize our train, burn our wagons and supplies, march us back in disgrace, and possibly place us in durance vile.

To guard against such a contingency, a rather curious piece of strategy was resorted to. Every few miles our train would move several times in ever-increasing circles, then off in another direction, zigzagging over the ground in what I thought a very peculiar manner. At first I was greatly surprised and somewhat alarmed at these erratic movements, and really thought that the boys had suddenly taken leave of their senses, but when it was explained to me that it was done to lead possible pursuers off our track I was greatly relieved and felt assured and the heads of our men were still level. In fact, I regarded the maneuvering as a wonderfully brilliant conception.

It now became necessary that some precautionary measures against probable Indian depredation should be adopted; therefore, a code of such rules and regulations as were needed for our own personal safety and the protection of our stock, was agreed upon, which were in substance as follows:—

All camp duties must be completed, and fires extinguished before dusk. No loud talk or other unnecessary noise shall be allowed. All members of the expedition owning stock shall be required to perform guard duty at night—three to patrol the outskirts of the camp until midnight, then three others to take their places until morning, or daylight—no members shall be exempt from guard duty except in cases of sickness.

These requirements seemed comparatively light, at first, but, as the train advanced into the Indian country, and the storms came, and the weather grew colder and colder, the thermometer going sometimes to twenty-five or thirty degrees below zero, with no fires to warm by, they became a terrible hardship. Not a few murmurings were heard from the men who had this hard duty to perform, and as the days went by and no trouble came, a spirit of insubordination began to manifest itself—in truth, there was for a time some talk of a mutiny, which was, however, averted by the better judgment of the majority.

This standing night guard was especially a hardship on those who were compelled to leave their warm beds, and go out into the bitter cold at midnight to patrol their beats until the morning. Their boots became as hard and unmanageable as cast iron, with the extreme cold and frost, and it was with the greatest difficulty they succeeded in pulling them on. As they tugged, pulled, pounded, and struggled with their refractory footwear, I could hear from my comfortable quarters on the ground floor of my bedroom, frequent and rather forcible ejaculations, which sounded to me wonderfully like snatches of a prayer, or quotations from the "Litany," as they floated in to me through the folds of my tent. I suspected at the time,—not without good valid grounds, however, that they were not intended for either. I felt a great sympathy for the boys, and often advised them to go to bed with their boots on, but, although they received my suggestion with some degree of tolerance, my advice was never followed.

BILL OF FARE ON THE PLAINS

Perhaps some of my readers may like to know how we fared during our long journey over the plains. Well, until the settlements were left behind, we lived on the fat of the land through which we passed, being able to procure from the settlers along the route many articles which we were after compelled to do entirely without.

From that time to the end of our journey, or rather until we returned to civilization, the luxuries of milk, eggs, vegetables, etc., could not, of course, be had for love or money.

Our daily "bill of fare," which, in the absence of menu cards, was stereotyped on memory's tablets, consisted of the following articles, to wit: For breakfast, hot biscuit, fried bacon, and black coffee; for dinner, cold biscuit, cold baked beans, and black coffee; for supper, black coffee, hot biscuit, and baked beans warmed over. Occasionally, in lieu of hot biscuits, and for the sake of variety, we would have what is termed in camp parlance, flapjacks. The men did the cooking for the most part, I, the while, seated on a log or an inverted water bucket, watching the process through the smoke of the camp fire, which, for some unexplainable reason, never ceased for a moment to blow directly in my face, shift as I might from point to point of the compass. I now recall how greatly I was impressed with the dexterity and skill with which they flopped over the flapjacks in the frying-pan. By some trick of legerdemain, they would toss up the cake in the air, a short distance, where it would turn a partial somersault, then unfailingly return to the pan the other side up. After studying the modus operandi, for some time one day, I asked permission to try my skill, which was readily granted by the cook, who doubtless anticipated a failure. I tossed up the cake as I had seen them do, but much to my chagrin, the downcoming was wide of the mark. The cake started from the pan all right, but instead of keeping the perpendicular, as by the laws of gravitation it should have done, it flew off, at a tangent, in a most tantalizing manner, and fell to the ground several feet away from the pan, much to the amusement of the boys. I came to the conclusion that tossing pancakes was not my forte.

To relieve the monotony of our daily fare, our tables (?) were quite frequently provided with game of various kinds, such as elk, deer, antelope, grouse, etc., large bands of antelope being seen almost daily along the route over the plains. Each outfit had their own hunters, who supplied, for the most part, their respective messes, with game, but Capt. Tom. Russell, who was the real "Nimrod" of the party, and a crack shot, bagged much more game than he needed, which surplus was distributed among the camps. Besides being a good hunter and skillful marksman, Capt. Tom Russell ever proved himself a brave and chivalrous gentleman, during the long, trying journey, and somehow I always felt safer when he was near.

There were several others in the party, too, who won the reputation of being skilled hunters, and judging by the marvelous stories told of the great number of deer, elk, and other animals killed, which could not be brought into camp, they deserved to stand at the head of the profession. If there is anything in the wide world, more than another, of which the average man feels proud, it is of the quantity of game he captures.

Speaking of game brings to mind an experience, the very remembrance of which always causes an uprising and revolution in the region of the principal organ of digestion. Some of the boys, in their very commendable desire to provide the camp with game, one day captured an immense elk, bringing in the choicest parts for distribution among the different messes, and judging from the flavor and texture of the flesh of the animal it must have been a denizen of the Hills since the time of the great upheaval, and to make a bad matter worse, our chef for the day conceived the very reprehensible idea of cooking the meat by a process called "smothering."

Having a deap-seated, dyed-in-the-wool antipathy to smothered meats of all kinds, I employed all the force of my native eloquence in trying to persuade him to adopt some more civilized method of cooking, but no, he was determined to smother it or not cook it at all, as by that process, he said, all the flavor of the meat would be retained, and he continued: "If my way doesn't suit you, cook it yourself." Accordingly it was cooked his way and brought to the table—the word table is here used figuratively—and truth compels me to admit that it looked very tempting, so, as I was abnormally hungry that night, I conveyed to my mouth, with a zeal and alacrity worthy of a batter cause, an exceedingly generous morsel of the meat; but, oh, ye shades of my ancestors! it was speedily ejected and then and there I pronounced it the most villainous morsel I had ever tasted in all my checkered career, and the cook was compelled to concur in that opinion. "Ugh!" although more than two decades have passed since then, I can taste it yet. The trouble, however, was more in the elk than in the cooking.

All formality was thrown to the winds at meal time, each one helping himself or herself with a liberality and abandon, that was truly astonishing and, I might add, alarming, in view of the fact that our larders were becoming rapidly depleted, and that we were completely cut off from our base of supplies. Our coffee was drank from tin cups and our bacon and beans eaten from tin plates. Yes, we had knives and forks—not silver, nor even silver-plated, yet we enjoyed our meals, for with appetites whetted with much exercise and fresh air we were always ravenously hungry, and could eat bacon and beans with the keenest relish.

Strange as it now seems, while journeying over the plains I was for the most time blessed, or cursed, with a voracious, almost insatiable appetite—in fact, was always hungry during my waking hours, and what is most remarkable, none of the others were afflicted with the malady.

At the outset of the journey I had protested strongly against the kind of food on which we were being regaled, declaring that I never could be tempted to eat such abominable stuff, and prophesying my own demise from starvation within a month. Later, however, as I trudged along on foot in the rear of the wagon, I would often, between meals, stealthily approach the wagon, surreptitiously raise the lid of the ''grub'' box and abstract therefrom a great slice of cold bacon and a huge flapjack as large around as the periphery of a man's hat—and a sombrero hat, at that—and devour them without ever flinching or exhibiting the slightest disgust.

IN THE HEART OF THE INDIAN COUNTRY

As we advanced further into the Indian domain, Capt. Russell and our leader Mr. Gordon began to bring back to camp startling reports of fresh trails discovered, and moccasin tracks recently made, giving unmistakable evidence that the dreaded savages were not far away. ''Well, boys, we are almost sure to have a moccasin dance to-night, and we must be prepared to give the braves a fitting welcome,'' warned the captain. However, as we were not treated to an exhibition of their terpsichorean skill, nor molested at that time, the conclusion was reached, that these fresh trails were made by the Indians returning from their summer hunt, to winter quarters at their various agencies. All unconscious were they of the near proximity of the invaders, who, though brave, were not insensible to the perils which at the time surrounded them, and, figuratively speaking, slept nightly, on their arms, to be ready for an attack at the first warning cry from the faithful sentinels on guard. We were in great danger of being discovered at any moment, as we were crossing their trails every day at this stage of our journey—and frequently their camp fires were found yet burning.

SICKNESS IN CAMP

Soon after leaving the settlements, a number of our little party, including myself, were stricken with a malady which finally culminated in the death of one of our number, and in view of the exposure and hardships, and manner of living, it seemed a miracle that more did not succumb to their dreadful effects. Baked beans, hot biscuits, and alkali water, are not conducive to longevity.

About this time two or three other members of our expedition began to show acute symptoms of home-sickness, viz.: Charles Blackwell, the sickest on the list, Eaf. Witcher, and, to confess the truth, I had had by this time several spasms of the disease myself, although I had resolutely refused to acknowledge it. Eaf, however, having a good saddle horse, and therefore, in a sense, independent of the train, determined to return to cilivization at all hazards—which he felt that he was at perfect liberty to do.

His arrangements were speedily made. The contents of his grip, such as needles, thread, buttons, pins, etc., etc., were divided among his friends, the pins falling to my lot. He bade us all "God speed" on our dangerous journey that night, as he was to start on his homeward march before the dawn of the following day. But, alas, the "best laid plans o' mice and men aft gang aglee." A council was called that night (I was never admitted to their conferences), at which a preamble and resolutions, something like the following, were adopted:—

Whereas, we, in council assembled, have by sagacity and shrewd management, succeeded in eluding the vigilance of the powers that be, up to date; and whereas we believe that any direct or indirect communication with the outside world would be dangerous to the success, and prejudicial to the interests of our expedition; therefore, be it resolved, That no member of the expedition shall be permitted to return to civilization which we all voluntarily left; and, be it further resolved, That any attempt to return shall be deemed treasonable to the expedition, and that the offender shall be punished, by being disarmed and placed under guard, until the dangerous inclination subsides.

This seemed an arbitrary proceeding in a democratic country like the United States, where every man is guaranteed the liberty of going or coming, according to the bent of his own inclinations, provided in so doing he does not interfere with the rights of others, but, it must not be forgotten that we were at the time a law unto ourselves. Eaf. made a vigorous protest against this high-handed exercise of power. "Perhaps some of you think that I am afraid of the Indians; but I want you all to understand that I am no coward," said he, "I am just heartily sick of this whole disagreeable business," he added. That no braver fellow ever shouldered a Winchester is believed; that he possessed a wonderful amount of pluck, and was capable of great physical endurance is shown later. Impelled by a spirit of true democracy, I ventured a plea for individual personal liberty, and got snubbed for my pains. The powers were inexorable. Eaf. became afterward reconciled to the situation,—saying to me one day a little later: "Well, this is a rather unpleasant experience, but, if you are able to endure the fatigue, the exposure, and all the other disagreeable things of a journey like this, surely I ought not to complain." "I believe," he continued, "if you were not here we should become totally demoralized." Such an expression was, of course, very comforting to me, as I had always felt myself a great incumbrance to the expedition.

ALMOST A TRAGEDY WITHIN THE FOLD

Shortly after crossing the South Fork of the White river, an occurrence took place which came very near resulting in a terrible tragedy. According to the account given by one who was an eye-witness of the unfortunate affair, the trouble originated substantially as follows:—

John Gordon, the leader of our party, who, by some curious and illogical process of reasoning had evolved the strange idea that he owned the expedition in fee simple and in consequence of this foolish delusion, exercised the little brief authority conferred upon him with all the arrogance of an autocrat, on the one side, and Charles Cordeiro, in whose veins bounded the hot blood of a long line of Moorish ancestors, and who was stanch and true to the traditions of his race, on the other side, were the prime factors in the difficulty.

The country through which we were traveling at the time being broken and very rough, Mr. Gordon in his capacity of leader had ordered some work done along the line of march to render it more practicable for the passage of our train.

Mr. Cordeiro being a little slow in obeying the mandates of the august leader, was duly reprimanded for his want of alacrity, and a few bitter invectives—more forcible than euphonious—were hurled at the delinquent. Mr. Cordeiro then, I believe, returned the compliment by inviting his opponent to take a journey to the tropical domain presided over by Pluto and his fair queen Proserpine.

Mr. Gordon, not willing to be outdone in politeness, then applied to Mr. Cordeiro an epithet or cognomen not recognized in the nomenclature of our race, which naturally aroused the ire of the fiery Moor, who prided himself greatly on his ancestry, to such a white heat that he quickly raised his gun, leveled it directly at the heart of his traducer, and fired, missing his mark. Just before firing, however, he heard a cry of: "Hold, don't shoot!" and turning his head suddenly to see whence the cry proceeded, he looked right into the muzzle of a gun in the hands of Mr. Bishop, one of Mr. Gordon's backers; in so doing his aim became unsteady, his gun deflected a little, hence his failure. In endeavoring to extricate his revolver from his belt, after his gun had missed, he stumbled and fell, when Mr. Gordon rushed upon his fallen foe with drawn knife, and in his uncontrollable rage would probably have finished his victim then and there, had it not been for the prompt and brave interference of Lyman Lamb, who opportunely rushed upon the scene, seized the hand of the excited leader and wrested the knife therefrom. By this time others of our party had gathered around the scene or conflict and insisted that the disgraceful exhibition be brought to a speedy termination.

THE TWO VERSIONS

Mr. Cordeiro claimed that Mr. Gordon was advancing toward him with his hand upon his revolver, at the same time saying: "Now, Charley, let's settle this matter right here." Gordon, on the other hand, alleging that he did not have his hand on his revolver, but simply said: "Now, Charley, let's have an understanding." Which version is correct is not known.

Mr. Gordon and his sympathizers were clamorous in their demands that summary punishment be meted out to the offender, but the level-headed and unprejudiced members, who were largely in the majority, said no; and they would have prevented any violence at the risk of their lives. Finally after a good deal of argument pro and con, the belligerents consented to accept terms of peace, which were, that Mr. Cordeiro be dispossessed of his arms for a period of ten days, when they were to be restored in case of peaceable behavior. A resolution was also passed, making it a high crime for any member of the party to threaten the life of any other member, under a heavy penalty, the nature or extent of which is not now remembered, possibly, the death penalty. The opposing forces then stacked their arms, and sweet peace once more reigned in our midst.

Which was considered the more guilty party? Well, opinion among the members was pretty evenly divided. How many of us would be willing to tamely accept insult?

Human nature manifests itself the same out in the solitude of the inhospitable prairie, as in more settled communities, and even the most amiable of our race anywhere, will scarcely submit to be trampled upon beyond a certain point. And that point is where forbearance ceases to be a virtue.

CHAPTER V

CROSSING THE BAD LANDS

Long before reaching the White river, water became very scarce—long stretches of barren arid country were being traversed, without finding a drop, either for ourselves or stock—snow having to be melted at times for both purposes. Upon reaching the White river we were reduced to the necessity of loading one of our wagons with blocks of ice, cut from the almost solidly frozen stream, which was melted from time to time as it became necessary for our own use, or for watering our stock.

The water thus secured was in a high degree offensive and nauseating, wholly unfit for man or beast, and not until nearly famished with thirst could I be tempted to drink a drop of the vile compound. How often in those trying days did our minds wander back to an "old moss-covered bucket, as it rose dripping from fondly remembered wells." Oh, the boon of clear, sparkling, cold water—more precious by far than the nectar of the gods.

Thus laden with the unpalatable conglomeration of chalk and congealed water—and I know now what other ingredients, which was to serve us for drink for the two or three days following—we continued on our dreary march across the Mauvaises Terres, or Bad Lands, and language is inadequate to describe the utter desolation of the country through which we passed. Long ranges of hills, cut up by a perfect labyrinth of ravines or gorges into all sorts of fantastic shapes, into various architectural forms, resembling fortresses, castles, and even small villages, confronted us on every hand. There was but little vegetation, with here and there a solitary pine tree to relieve the barrenness in this noted paradise of the scientists. The only sign of animal life to be seen while crossing this "Inferno," was a single mountain sheep that stood on the extreme summit of one of the white chalky bluffs to our right, making a wonderfully attractive picture as with head erect he surveyed in apparent wonderment our slowly moving train, doubtless the first spectacle of the kind he had ever witnessed. Was he sole monarch of that entire God-forsaken domain? At any rate I felt convinced that no human being could long abide in such a place.

Numerous evidences that we were traveling over a region that had at some time in the dead past been the bed of an ocean were discovered; pieces of fossil bones, and petrified shells of various kinds and large size, lay scattered over the surface, some of which we gathered. Of course, those things called up interesting reflections, but as we were not at the time in search of the fossilized remains of animals, large or small, vetebrate or invertebrate, that had existed in prehistoric times, nor very scientifically inclined, we paid but little attention to those wonderful deposits. I would like to ask, who would be scientific, with feverished tongue and parched lips, and visions of the scalping knife flourishing over their heads? Besides we were nearly suffocated with the alkali dust that rose in clouds at every step and every revolution of the wheels of our train—notwithstanding it was almost winter. The whole aspect of this region of desolation suggested the thought, that a Heaven-directed curse had, at some time, swept over the land, withering and consuming everything in its path, both animate and inanimate. It must be borne in mind that this region was seen at its worst, being the time when all vegetation was cut down by the frost. It is asserted that, in many portions of the Bad Lands, the grasses grow quite luxuriantly, and frequently springs of good water are found. We, however, failed to find any such luxury as a spring of water(or water of any kind that was fit for drink), and oh, the intolerable thirst! I would have been willing to have given my kingdom (had I one), not like Richard III for a horse, but for a single draught of the water that comes bubbling up from the depths of some cold mountain spring.

A DEATH IN CAMP

On the morning before our train reached the valley of the Bad river (but I am at a loss to understand why it is called a river, as there was not a drop of water to be found within the radius of several miles of the valley), the condition of our sick patient became so serious, that it was suggested and urged by some of the more humane of the party that the train halt for a few days, or until the suffering man got better. I think none of us realized that he would die. It was decided,, however, that, as we were in the very heart of the hostile country, delay would be dangerous and unjustifiable, in that the lives of the whole party would be jeopardized—and, it was argued, that his bed could be so adjusted, that by traveling slowly he would suffer no great discomfort. Accordingly, one of the wagons was emptied of its contents and a comfortable bed prepared upon which the sick man was laid, nevermore to rise.

All that day I walked along on foot by the side of the wagon, with the long agonizing wails of the dying man ringing in my ears; every cry piercing my heart like a two-edged sword, he begging to be shot, and thus relieved from his terrible suffering. This thought no doubt was suggested to his mind by the sight of a gun strapped to the canvas above his head, which was very soon removed. About one hour before arriving at our camping ground his cries ceased, and we all fervently hoped he had fallen asleep. Upon reaching camp and looking into the wagon it was seen that he, indeed, was peacefully sleeping, the sleep that knows no wakening. "Ah, pity 'tis, 'tis true," that the poor pilgrim had fought the supreme battle alone, with no tender hand to wipe away death's gathering teardrops, or smooth his dying pillow—but—yes, did not the pitying angels hover above and around him, even 'neath that coarse canvas?

Gloom, like a dark pall, hung over our little camp on the dreary, lonely prairie that night. Death was in our midst and every gust of wind that blew adown the valley seemed laden with the wails and groans of our departed companion.

I must record here that everything kind hands could do, with the medicines available, was done for his relief and comfort.

Now, notwithstanding the extreme dangers of the situation, it became imperative that we camp for a day in order that the last sad rites be performed for our dead comrade, J. J. Williams, a skilled artisan, and a genius in many ways, taking charge of the preparations for the burial.

A coffin of small hewn timbers, strongly pinned together with wooden pins, was constructed, in which the body was decently laid, then a cover, also of hewn timbers was pinned down in like manner. Surely no prowling wolves or coyotes could ever reach him in his impregnable bed! A grave was then dug on a little grassy eminence overlooking the lonely valley, then sadly and tenderly his comrades lowered him into his final resting-place, there to await the call of the last trumpet on resurrection morn.

A cross, also of small, smooth, hewn timber was erected over his grave. On the pedestal of the cross was written the following inscription: "Died on the 27th of November, 1874, on his way to the Black Hills, Moses Aarons, aged 32 years. 'May he rest in peace.' "

No audible prayer was uttered; no funeral dirge was sung; each one stood reverently with bowed, uncovered head, around the grave until the first earth fell upon his rude coffin, then turned sadly away. I would give much to know whether that solitary grave has remained undisturbed, all the long years since then.

There is a tradition handed down to us, that Indians will never disturb a grave surmounted by a cross, as they have the greatest veneration for this symbol of Christ's death,—hence the erection of the cross.

At 3 o'clock p.m. November 28th, the simple ceremonies being over, our train moved on, leaving our late companion in the desolate spot, far from home and friends, where the summer's breeze and winter's blast would wail a perpetual requiem athwart his lone grave.

It all seemed to me peculiarly sad at the time, and I could but look back with wet eyes at the slowly receding cross, bathed in the pale light of a late November sun, until it was finally hidden from my view. Ah, how deeply I felt impressed with the inscrutable mysteries of Providence! But it was not for us to understand why a man, more or less accustomed to the hardships of life, should be cut down in all the glory and strength of his young manhood, while a delicate woman, wholly unused to exposure, or any of the privations and hardships incident to such a journey, should be given strength to endure and overcome all the difficulties of that terrible march.

Truly "God's ways are mysterious and past finding out."

AN AMUSING INCIDENT

It has been said that there is but a step from the sublime to the ridiculous; so likewise there is but a step from the pathetic to the ludicrous; for, right upon the heels of the sad and impressive scene we had just witnessed, followed an incident which caused a good deal of amusement in our midst, and illustrated how very near laughter and tears are together. Mr. Blackwell had the good fortune of capturing a beautiful silver gray fox, the skin of which is accounted of great value, and after divesting the beauty of its sheeny outer garment he left the carcass to be food for the hungry coyotes that were very numerous on the plains. However, the ravenous beasts came very near being cheated out of the feast intended for them, and by one of the hearty pioneers, too, who innocently supposing the flesh good for food lingered behind the train for the purpose of securing the coveted meat.

Shortly after reaching camp that night the donkey was seen approaching in the reflected rays of the sinking sun with the carcass of the fox standing bolt upright, stiff and stark on his back (frozen solid), and a more ludicrous spectacle could hardly be imagined. When the attention of the boys was called to the approaching donkey and his nude rider, with the owner marching gaily along beside them, the comical looking proposition created no end of merriment in the camp. It was perfectly irresistible.

When told that foxes were considered wholly unfit for human food, the poor fellow very reluctantly gave it back to the wolves. He did not see why foxes were not quite as wholesome and palatable as the opossum, the woodchuck, and the squirrel; neither did I.

In marching across the Bad Lands we found a great scarcity of both fuel and water, and had not the precaution been taken of loading wood onto the wagons before leaving the White river, the inevitable black coffee and hot bread would have been for awhile unknown quantities.

The difficulties of the march increased as the days went by. The cattle became completely worn out from their long journey over the rough, untraveled ground, without being allowed sufficient time to feed. Their hoofs became worn to the quick, and it looked as if some of them would have to be abandoned on the plains to die. To partially relieve them, they were provided with leather shoes, divided to fit the hoofs, which for a time remedied the difficulty, this, however, affording only temporary relief to the poor, emaciated creatures that were becoming day by day less able to carry their rapidly diminishing loads.

Slowly and toilfully we crept along over the hard frozen ground, with nothing to relieve the tiresome monotony of the march, save the amusement afforded us by the daily chases of the greyhounds after some kind of game. If the game happened to be a band of antelope, they, with a snort of defiance, would scamper away over the prairie with almost lightning speed, those not especially singled out by the hounds, turning now and then, with heads erect, and nostrils distended, to view the situation, and make sure that there was really sufficient cause for so much alarm on their part; and it was truly a beautiful sight. The hounds, selecting their victims from the band, would (Dan in the lead) scud away after them, in a perfect frenzy of excitement, usually running them to some point beyond our reach of vision, so that we rarely knew the real denouement of the exciting chase. If, on the other hand, the game chanced to be a rabbit, the chase proved to be a very disappointing and unsatisfactory affair to both Dan and Fan, on account of its shortness, as they were soon run to cover. The rabbit, bounding away in great leaps, covering a distance of twelve or fifteen feet at a jump, would suddenly disappear in its burrow, not far away, the dogs then returning, with a wofully crestfallen expression on their intelligent faces, and their tails dangling down, in a truly despondent manner. Nevertheless, we all felt exceedingly grateful to them for even this temporary diversion along the dreary road.

Let none of my readers be deluded into the belief that there was anything, either very romantic or pleasant connected with this part of our journey, unless shivering over the dying embers of a camp fire, silently watching the daylight gradually fade into darkness, until all the surrounding desolation was overspread with the sable wings of night, and then creeping, benumbed with cold, into bed, be romantic, or unless getting up at the early dawn, partaking of a hastily prepared breakfast, none too tempting to the appetite, and trudging off through the snow, day after day, be considered a pleasure. If any one labors under such a foolish delusion, let such individual take a journey under like conditions and circumstances, and be disenchanted.

FIRST SIGHT OF THE BLACK HILLS

We had our first glimpse of the Black Hills about ten o'clock a.m., December 31st. The Black Hills! The Black Hills! passed from lip to lip. A glad cry of relief went forth at the sight, and every heart sang paeans of joy and thankfulness, that our destination was so nearly reached. We could see plainly, away in the distance, to the left of us, the long line of dark shadowy hills, dimly outlined against the blue sky, and to the right, Bear Butte, standing alone like a huge sentinel guarding the entrance to that unknown land.

Of course, the Hills were yet a long distance away, but our goal was always after in sight to buoy up our spirits.

Several days before sighting the Hills some of our poor cattle had become so reduced and footsore, that it seemed impossible for them to proceed any farther with their loads. It appeared as if some would be compelled to abandon their wagons and stock of supplies, and make their way into the Hills as best they could with such provisions as they could carry, or adopt the alternative of going into winter quarters on the bleak prairie. This terrible alternative, however, was happily averted. The owners of the better conditioned stock acted the part of the good Samaritan, by relieving the disabled cattle of a part of their loads, thus increasing that of their own already overburdened stock. Two or three hundred pounds, more or less, was loaded on to the submissive donkey, and thus lightened we were all able to proceed together on our journey greatly to our relief.

CHAPTER VI

CROSSING THE CHEYENNE RIVER

On the morning of December 3d we found our train on the crest of a high precipitous bluff, near the point where the waters of Elk creek swell the current of the Cheyenne river, and in something of a dilemma.

To descend the almost perpendicular front of the bluff with the wagons looked impossible. Descend we must, however, or take the alternative of turning back, and traveling many miles in search of a more practicable point. Finally, they hit upon the expedient of letting the wagons down the steep incline by means of ropes, with which, fortunately, the party was well supplied. The cattle were unhitched, and driven across, and down the vertical bluff first, then the wagons, one by one, were lowered by means of ropes to the valley below.

INDIANS DISCOVERED

At this time occurred the most exciting episode of the entire journey. As the last wagon was being lowered, some one discovered moving objects a mile or so down the valley. Field glasses being brought to bear revealed that the animated objects were nothing more nor less than about two score of Indian ponies, feeding along the valley of the river,—a convincing evidence that their owners were near at hand. "Ah, then there was hurrying to and fro," but "no gathering tears, nor tremblings of distress." Oh, no, just a firm compression of the lips, a flashing of the eye, then a hurried examination of Winchesters, a buckling on of cartridges belts, and the boys were ready for action at the first sign of hostility on the part of the Indians. A fight seemed inevitable, and there were no cowards in our little band of men.

I was speedily and rather unceremoniously ushered into a covered wagon out of sight—under protest, however, for I am nothing if not curious, but there was some consolation in the thought that from my point of vantage, everything that transpired could be plainly seen. The reason assigned for such summary procedure was that the presence of a woman might lead the Indians to suspect that the party contemplated a longer stay within their domain than would be agreeable to them.

Very soon two mounted braves came dashing up the valley toward us, being very careful, however, not to come within gunshot of our train; then after a hasty survey of the situation, with a shrill warwhoop, they rode back at full speed to report the number of pale faces and their apparent strength.

Orders were then given to cross the river and halt for dinner, although an hour earlier than the usual time for our noonday meal. Soon after going into camp, five mounted Indians rode into our midst, and remained until the train was ready to pull out. The Indians improved the time by trying to barter away their ponies for ammunition and guns; and no doubt they would have given several of their ponies for one of the Winchesters, with which our party was equipped, and which they examined with a great deal of interest. Of course we had neither guns nor ammunition to barter away for ponies nor money.

These Indians seemed quite friendly, and to do them justice, they were really quite respectable looking Indians, as Indians go, but like all their race, the most inveterate of beggars. They were fitted out with a goodly supply of flour, bacon, sugar, and tobacco—yes, we had tobacco, and pipes too.

From my safe retreat 'neath the canvas, through a convenient aperture, I had a "bird's-eye" view of the whole procedure and to tell the truth, I felt much uneasiness on seeing the liberality with which the boys were doling out their precious stock of provisions to the graceless savages. In truth, I could scarcely refrain from uttering a warning cry from my hiding-place, from which I hoped soon to emerge, but I remembered the ammunition episode in the early part of the journey, and heroically closed my lips.

When the train received its marching orders the Indians, laden with the generous contribution, returned to their camp, a short distance below. These Indians, who proved to be a band of Cheyennes returning from a summer hunt to winter quarters—are reputed to be less warlike than many of the other tribes,—at all events, they gave us no farther trouble. Perhaps they stood in wholesome terror of the formidable equipments of our expedition and thought discretion the better part of valor. Had we encountered an equal number of the fierce and bloodthirsty Sioux, doubtless I should have a far different story to relate, or, perchance, there might not have been one left to tell the tale. I am of the opinion, however, that our plucky little band would have proved more than a match for the sneaking savages, as they were on the constant lookout, and always prepared for a surprise.

After this encounter, and, in view of a possible attempt to run off the stock of the train, a double guard was placed to patrol the outskirts of the camp, to watch the cattle, for several nights thereafter, when, as we were not molested, the force was reduced to its original number.

Two days after leaving the Cheyenne river, one of our cattle gave up the struggle, unable to proceed a step farther. The worn-out beast was unhitched from the wagon, the yoke removed from his galled shoulders, and he was turned out on the prairie to die, and the last we saw of the poor bovine he was lying exhausted on the ground, but, true to his instincts, chewing his "cud" vigorously.

As we approached the Hills, they began to assume a more definite shape. Instead of the great banks of vapory clouds as at first sight, there rose up, bold, rugged, abrupt mountains, all along their eastern limits, and the striking resemblance of Bear Butte to a huge bear, as outlined from our point of view, became easily discernible, growing more and more clearly outlined, as the train drew near.

Two days before reaching the point of entrance, it appeared that in a few hours, at most, we could reach the Hills, and I was greatly surprised when told that they were yet forty miles away. The next morning, they were so very near that I felt an impulse to reach out my hand and pluck a twig from the evergreens on the hillsides,—so deceptive is distance, in the rare atmosphere of the Black Hills,—especially to the unaccustomed eye. The delusion is not near so great when one becomes accustomed to the climate, the philosophy of which I do not understand.

At length on the 9th day of December our feet first pressed Black Hills' soil, at a point about four miles below Sturgis, where we took dinner in the midst of a howling snowstorm. Here we found a well-defined wagon road made by the heavy supply train, accompanying the Custer expedition on its exit from the Hills in the preceding August. On reaching the foothills at this point, to guard against an ambushed foe it was deemed advisable to press into service a day guard, an advance and rear guard, and also two flank guards, whose duty it was to patrol the ridges along each side of the moving train to apprise the party of any threatened danger, and it was no easy duty. We expected to find Indians galore in the Hills, skulking behind the bushes and trees, and I now recall how I magnified every bush and shrub along the top of the ridges, into the tufted heads of so many redskins, peering over the crests of the hills at our train. However, as no apparent danger seemed to threaten us, and as no evidence of the presence of Indians had been found, after two days the extra guard was released from duty.

Our first camp within the limits of the Hills was made in a canyon about two miles below where Piedmont now is, on the night of December 9th, wherefrom the train marched in a southerly direction up over the hill and down into the Box Elder Valley at a point not far from the mouth of Jim creek, then following up the Box Elder to the north fork of that stream and over the divide to Little Rapid creek, thence almost due south across Castle, Slate, and Spring creeks to our destination, two and one-half miles below Custer.

When we first struck the Custer wagon trail, we found along the way, horseshoes, kernels of corn, and other evidences that civilized people had but recently traveled over the ground, which so reminded me of home, or, I might as well confess the truth, I became for the first time so utterly homesick that—what did I do? Well, I sought the most convenient log, sat down upon it, and proceeded to shed a torrent of unavailing tears—and they were no crocodile tears, either. Would not some of my readers have been equally weak, I wonder?

Through the mystic influence of associations, very small things are, under circumstances, wonderfully potent in their appeal to the human heart. So in this case even a few grains of corn, scattered along the wild mountain trail, had the power to burst open the flood-gates and let the current of tears rush forth.

On the first night spent within the limits of the Hills, we all had a pretty bad Indian scare, which caused something of a panic in the camp. Long after the camp fires were extinguished and the guards posted on the outskirts, the inmates of the camp were suddenly aroused by the low warning cry of: "Boys, for God's sake, get up quick and get your guns, the camp is surrounded by Indians! We're in for it this time, sure." The boy's sprang up, pulled on their cast iron boots, grabbed their guns and rushed forth to meet the foe. I sat bolt upright in my lowly bed, and listened—my heart beating a rapid tattoo, meanwhile—but could hear nothing but the dismal howling of the hungry timber wolves, which, it finally turned out, two of the guards had magnified into the blood-curdling warwhoop of the Sioux. A few of the boys had never heard an Indian warwhoop; hence the mistake.

As our route was taken through some of the wildest portions of the Hills, the journey through them proved a delightful revelation—one continuous poem, replete with all that is grand, sublime and beautiful. We found the Black Hills a profound solitude, with peace, like a guardian angel, reigning over the whole wide expanse, and without a single vestige of civilization; and as we marched along under the shadows of the lofty hills, I remember how greatly I was impressed with their vastness, and our own comparative insignificance and littleness. Up and down over the rough divides our jaded cattle laboriously made their way. Down steep and dangerous declivities, into dark canyons, where the sun never shone save at midday, and where it seemed so awfully hushed, as to be almost oppressive, we pursued our course.

All along the route could be seen in places, on one hand, huge rocks piled high one upon the other, with almost mechanical regularity and precision, as if placed there by the hand of a master workmen—a great wall of natural masonry; on the other the everlasting hills, covered with majestic pines, that looked like stately sentinels guarding the valleys below, towering far, far up above our heads; then anon low lying ranges of hills, clothed with dense forests of pine, and away in the hazy distance, other ranges rising up like great banks of clouds against the horizon. For myself, I confess that I had then no knowledge of the geography of the country we were traversing, but as I remember the localities, it was on the divide between Rapid and Spring creeks that we first saw Harney's Peak, towering up in rocky grandeur, to the left of our line of march.

A noticeable feature of the country through which we passed, as we neared our objective point, was the many beautiful glades, with their scattered bunches of pines and hemlocks—a vivid picture of which I have in my mind as they appeared to me then, with the bright winter's sun shining down through their branches, flecking the brown earth beneath, with patches of burnished gold—spots where one might expect to see fairies dancing and skipping about on moonlight nights. A fit abode it seemed for our first parents,—in the days of their primeval innocency,—ere woman tempted (?) man to sin.

In passing through some of the deepest, darkest canyons of the Hills, my imagination would run riot at times, and I could not help glancing furtively from side to side of the ravines to see whether there were any gnomes or hobgoblins peering out at us from between the crevices of the great rocks, where these irrational creatures are supposed to hold high carnival, and I confess that I always felt a trifle relieved when we emerged from those uncanny places.

Altogether the journey through the Hills was a rare treat to one who had never before been among the mountains. The entire landscape was one well calculated to impress the beholder with awe, and incline him, if aught earthly could, to fall prostrate at the footstool of the Great Unseen behind all its wonderful majesty and beauty; and to make the scene still more impressive, an awful silence—a silence which only primeval forests know—hung over all. No sound was to be heard amid the solitude, save our own voices, which sounded strange and unnatural; the rumbling of the wagons over the rough trail, and the cracking of the drivers' whips, which reverberated from hill to hill and through the corridors of the woods in the most romantic manner. By the way, the drivers seemed to delight in cracking their whips and hallooing to the cattle, simply, I suspected, to hear the delightfully romantic effect.

Lyman Lamb was one of the Jehus of the party, and he showed himself quite as expert in that capacity as he has since in keeping county records. He did not, however, like the scriptural Jehu, ride in a chariot, drawn by fiery steeds, but on the contrary, drove his own cattle, walking by their side from the start to the finish, and the wonderful skill and dexterity with which he wielded his prodigious whip, and cracked its long lash, would have made a professional "whacker" green with envy, and excited my most profound and lasting admiration.

In all the vicissitudes of that long, trying journey Mr. Lamb proved himself one of Nature's noblemen—fearless and intrepid, and one upon whom it is always safe to rely.

Our march through the Hills was necessarily slow, owing to the weak condition of the cattle, it taking just two weeks from the time we entered the Hills to reach French creek. At last, after a hard journey full of bitter experiences, we arrived at our objective point, about two and one-half miles below Custer, on December 23d, 1874, having been seventy-eight days en route.

As soon as the train came to a halt, some of the boys rushed to the wagons for shovels and gold pans, and hastened to find the place where the miners of Custer's expedition claimed to have found the gold. Soon they were seen returning to camp waving their hats aloft in a very excited manner, myself joining them, by frantically waving my much traveled and weather-beaten hood in genuine sympathy. Eureka! They had found particles of gold in the bottom of each gold pan, and my readers may be assured that there was great rejoicing in our camp on French creek that winter's night.

Our poor emaciated cattle were unyoked for the last time, and turned out to subsist as best they could for the winter. Our tents were pitched, suppers prepared and eaten with the usual informality, and we then sat around our blazing campfires in the heart of the wilderness, not singing songs and rehearsing tales, as of yore, when we yet reposed under the folds of the American flag, but talking of and thinking out the difficult problem that confronted us; some, perchance, indulging in waking dreams of the piles of gold that were almost within their grasp.

Ah, if we could only have lifted the curtain, and taken a glance into the future, at the long years of weary waiting, our bright hopes would have given place to dark despair. In mercy, "Heaven from all creatures hides the Book of Fate." I often wonder if any of the little band of pioneers, who sat dreaming around that camp fire on French creek that night, have ever yet realized their hopes, or are they still chasing the illusive phantom, that somehow always manages to elude their grasp. I am quite clear on one point, and that is, that the author of this story has been reaching out for more than two decades after that delusive "will-o'-the-wisp," and is still employed in the same fruitless occupation.

Now that our journey was ended for a few months at least, our camp arrangements must be of a more permanent character, so we pitched our tents on the hill slope north of French creek near a copious spring and proceeded to make our surroundings as comfortable as was possible under the circumstances and limitations.

A wearied and worn, tattered and torn combination we were, to be sure, on reaching French creek on that 23d day of December, 1874. How could it be otherwise? I was painfully aware that I, at least, was in a very sorry plight. My shoes, especially, were in a sadly demoralized condition—a thin apology for shoes, although the second pair since leaving the haunts of man. What did I do for shoes? Why, I made a pair of moccasins of a deer skin that had been tanned and prepared by one of the boys for the purpose, and very comfortable moccasins they were, too. Did I walk much of the way on the journey? Oh, yes, all of the way after leaving the settlements, except during a week of sickness, and a few short rides on the back of the little burro.

Now some may regard such a feat as something quite wonderful, but there was really nothing remarkable about it, when it is remembered that the distance traveled was only from ten to fifteen miles a day, and the gait exceedingly slow—a mere pleasure walk. Anyhow, who would ride in a heavily loaded wagon drawn by worn-out, footsore cattle? Not I, indeed. Of course the ground traversed was very rough, and sometimes covered with snow, hence the deplorable state of my footwear.

Had it not been for certain precautions taken by us pedestrians on our way into the Hills, some would have been barefoot in all likelihood, long before reaching the end of the journey.

When there was snow on the ground we "packed" our feet to protect them against the loose snow, as well as the cold. Now I venture to assert that some of my readers do not even know what packing the feet means. I didn't know before I started to the Black Hills, and took a regular course in the art. Well, it means simply to bind a gunnysack—now don't pretend not to know what a gunnysack is—snugly around the feet and ankles, then bind it on with a stout cord to keep it in place. There is nothing equal to it as a protection to the feet, and I regard the man or woman who originated the idea, as a genius and a benefactor of the pioneers. Try it when you cross the plains on foot in the winter.

The next day, December 24th, was wash day, and day of general repairs in camp, and a formidable undertaking it was, as may be easily imagined. We had tubs, washboards, and plenty of soap in the outfit, but we were obliged to take turns in washing as there were not quite enough tubs to go round. When the garments were washed, they were spread on the bushes to dry, and when dry were ready to wear, as they were never ironed, everything being done after the most primitive fashion. It is needless to say that the boys did their own washing and mending. Lest some might think that we had ignored the laws of hygiene while en route, I want to state that frequent short halts had been made for washing and bathing purposes, notwithstanding the danger, for although branded as outlaws, we were not barbarians.

CHRISTMAS-TIDE IN BLACK HILLS IN 1874

Yule-tide had come, and it was hardly to be expected that the children's patron saint would think of running the gauntlet of the Indians to visit our obscure camp among the wilds, so, inspired by the spirit of "Peace on earth and good will towards men," and feeling that something should be done to keep the festive season green in our memories, I bethought me of a Christmas tree, without the genial saint. There were plenty of evergreens that could easily vie with the time-honored holly and mistletoe on every side, and beautiful Christmas tree near at hand in the valleys, but what was the good of a tree with nothing to put on it—no books, no toys, no confections, nothing but picks, shovels, gold pans, and an ox chain for ornamentation, and these would hardly be appropriate. The fondly remembered Christmas stocking was thought of, but here the same difficulty occurred. The whole category of supplies from baked beans down failed to furnish anything suitable for a Christmas gift, and so my great mental struggle to make the "eve" seem like Christmas went for naught.

Christmas morn dawned upon us, and at no time since our journey began did we realize so keenly how far removed, both by distance and environments, we were from home and all that it implies. Completely cut off from the whole Christian world with its precious privileges; no Merry Christmas greeting from the loved ones away back towards the rising sun; no sweet chimes of Christmas bells fell upon our ears; no grand organ notes, pealing forth the glad Hosannas, reached us among the mountain fastnesses; no church privileges—but, wait—was not the whole visible expanse a church, grander by far than any cathedral ever built by human hands? Was there not a powerful sermon in the beautiful quartz that lay scattered about on the hillsides, and a great moral lesson in every tree and bush that grew upon their lofty crests? Were not the mournful cadences of the wind, as it whispered through the pine branches above our tents, more touching than the sweetest song; and the awful silence that brooded over each hill, valley, and beautiful glade, more potent to lift the thoughts Heavenward, than the grandest choral music ever chanted by human voices? These were the thoughts that rose up in my mind, as I sat musing at the opening of my tent, on that Christmas day, nearly a quarter of a century ago.

What of our material comfort? Did we have a Christmas dinner? Alas, no. Roast turkey with cranberry sauce, plum puddings, and mince pies were not much in evidence on our tables that day—nothing but our coarse everyday fare, and no doubt the thoughts of every one of our little band went back over the dreary intervening waste, to the good cheer of the dear old homes.

The day after Christmas the storm clouds gathered, and soon snow began to fall,—coming down in great feathery flakes until the whole landscape was covered to a depth of two or more feet, on a dead level, and our tents were almost literally snowed under. Then the wind rose and blew a terrific gale—driving the loose snow before it, and piling it in great banks in the valley below, and the cold became intense.

Being on the southern slope of the hill we did not feel the cold much, but the cattle suffered terribly, both from cold and hunger, especially the latter, as they could not reach the cured grasses,—so abundant in the snow-covered valley. At night great fires were built of pitch pine logs, piled high, which threw out light and heat in every direction. The poor cattle, attracted by the grateful warmth, would come into camp and stand in a long line on each side of the fire, until somewhat thawed out, when they would wander back, one by one, into the darkness and fierce storm.

Was it reason or instinct that guided those dumb brutes in, systematically arranging themselves in rows, near the fire, and then leaving their comfortable positions without any compulsion, just as if they felt themselves intruders.

In less than a week the great storm was over and the weather became as warm and balmy as a June day.

CHAPTER VII

BUILDING THE STOCKADE

The time had now come when we must look this situation squarely in the face. We were in the Black Hills, but how long we would be permitted to remain was a problem which the future alone could solve. But whether our stay was to be long or short, the exigencies of the situation demanded that safer and more comfortable quarters be at once provided. The storms of midwinter were upon us, and danger, for aught we knew, might be even then lurking behind each bush and tree. Therefore, to guard against exposure and possible danger, the plan for building a place of defense was matured and speedily executed. Skillful and willing hands, were soon at work, and despite the fact that the work began in the midst of the worst snowstorm of the winter, in about two weeks the formidable structure, commonly known as the Gordon stockade, was completed and ready for occupancy.

For the benefit of those who have never seen that early stronghold, I will give a description of the structure, as I remember it after the lapse of nearly a quarter of a century, and, in view of the memorable winter spent within its gloomy walls, I am not likely to forget a single feature, from the top to the base, or from the great wooden gate to the opposite wall.

The walls of the stockade were built of heavy pine timber, thirteen feet in length, set close together in an upright position, three feet in the ground, forming an inclosure eighty feet square. Along the line of contact, between the timbers, other smaller timber were pinned with heavy wooden pins. At each of the four corners of this inclosure were bastions, standing out six feet from the main structure,—each provided with four embrasures, and along the two sides and one end, at intervals of about eight feet, were portholes. A large double gate twelve feet wide, built of hewn timber strongly riveted together with wooden pins, completed the structure, this gate being the only entrance to that impregnable fortress of the Hills. It has been pronounced by those who are good judges of defensive works the strongest fortification of the kind ever built in the West. Capt. Mix, in his description of our stronghold to Gen. Bradley, on his return with the prisoners to Fort Laramie said: "Why, if they had resisted I should have been obliged to return to the fort for artillery to dislodge them." At any rate, once within its strong walls we felt that we could defy the Indians as long as our ammunition lasted or until we were starved out. But would our ammunition last; would our provisions hold out until relief came? That was the problem.

Within the walls of the stockade were built seven log cabins, three on each side and one opposite the gate, with a space of about six feet intervening between them and the walls, designed for the sharpshooters at the portholes, and the bastions, leaving a large area in the center of the inclosure. In one of these log cabins the author spent the never to be forgotten winter of 1874-5. It is much to be regretted that ruthless hands were permitted to destroy that great early landmark of the Black Hills, which might have been preserved as a memorial to the pluck and perseverance of the men who built it. It is said that not a single stick is left to mark the spot where it stood.

LIFE IN THE STOCKADE

The seven cabins within the walls of the stockade, in which we were doomed to drag out the weary monotonous days of winter, were more or less pretentious, according to the taste and skill of the builders.

The first cabin on the right was conspicuous because of the peculiar construction of the roof, which consisted of small hewn timbers with a groove chiseled out in the center of each to carry off the water. As a substitute for shingles it was an ingenious contrivance. This same cabin had a floor of hewn

THE GORDON STOCKADE—PHOTOGRAPHED IN 1876

logs, a door of hand-sawed boards, a chimney, a fire-place, and an opening for a window, but no sash. This model cabin was built by what was known on our journey as the "Logan" outfit—each wagon with all its accessories and appurtenances, being called, while en route, an "outfit." Well, this Logan aggregation consisted of a half-dozen fine muscular fellows from the pineries of Wisconsin, who were not afraid of work, and not very much afraid of Indians. Some of them, as their names indicated, were brave Scotsmen, whose ancestors, at least, came frae the hills o' bonnie Scotland.

The second on the right belonged to the "Whitney" pro-position, the personnel of which was R. Whitney, D. Aken, John Boyle, and Harney Cooper, the young artist who charmed us all by his glorious voice while journeying over the plains.

The third on the same side, which compared favorably with the first, though of a somewhat different style of architecture, was constructed by Lyman Lamb, T. H. Russell, and Angus McDonald, who, poor fellow, was crushed to death by the falling of a tree, a few years ago, near Deadwood. This cabin was planned by Lyman Lamb, who also drew the plan for the great stockade.

The cabin opposite the gate, a well-built and substantial structure, was occupied by John Gordon, the leader of the expedition, H. Bishop, the owner of the aforementioned greyhounds, Chas. Long, and N. Warren, dubbed "Uncle Nute," and the best-natured man in the expedition. "Uncle Nute," by the way, was a master of the art of song. His voice could be heard blithely and joyously singing from early morn to dewy eve without cessation, in fact he sang always except when asleep, and his constant refrain was something about being "Down in the coal mines underneath the ground, and digging dusty diamonds all the season round."

The next cabin to the right in the circuit, and the most unpretentious of the seven, was our house, a low square structure without gables, consisting of one room which served the purposes of kitchen, dining room, bed room, and parlor. Like the others it was built of logs, not hewn but round as nature formed them, with not a single mark of ax or adz to mar their symmetry. The roof which slanted at an angle of about forty-two and a half degrees was constructed of poles covered over with alternate layers of hemlock boughs and mother earth. I think the poles were of the quaking asp variety, at least I thought so, when the wintry winds swept through the great open gate. It had a chimney, too, a sort of a nondescript affair, and a wide fireplace with a large flat stone in front of it, and several stones of lesser magnitude, arrayed with an eye to artistic effect, in a circle on the outside, otherwise our cabin was guiltless of floor or carpet. There was an opening fronting the area for a door, over which was hung a large coffee sack for a portiere, and a small square opening just opposite for a window, over which was tacked a piece of cloth bearing in large red letters the following legend, "XXX Extra Superfine," which completed the main part of the edifice.

Moreover, our house had a wing—a right wing, whose sole occupant was Chas. Cordeiro, the Moor. Now, although this annex was, architecturally speaking, a part and parcel of the main building, there was no communication between the two parts, save a small square opening cut through the log partition, for the mutual accommodation of the dwellers on each side, and through which reciprocal courtesies were daily interchanged. For instance, among our scanty supply of cooking utensils was a small iron kettle—perhaps the only one in the expedition, which our near neighbor took occasion to borrow, whenever he had a pot of beans, or a leg of venison to cook,—on the other hand, he had a sharp two-edged axe, which he always kept whetted to the keenness of a razor, to which we were ever made welcome, on demand. As these articles were being passed back and forth through this convenient aperture, our neighbor, when looking through from his little dingy room with his super-naturally intense black eyes, made a very suggestive picture, to me suggestive of a prisoner peering through the barred windows of a prison cell.

The next cabin on the left of the entrance was occupied by Eaf Witcher and Henry Thomas, and the last in the circuit belonged to Chas. Blackwell and Thos. McLaren, our former copartners,—the firm having dissolved by mutual consent, just before moving into the stockade. The inside furnishings of these cabins were of the crudest kind, all being cut or hewn from the pine trees hard by. Not a very attractive home, my readers may think. No, but the best that could be provided with the facilities at hand.

Now, all this may be very dry and uninteresting to the reader, and may not mean much, as viewed through the mist of over twenty intervening years, but it meant a great deal to those early pioneers—it meant untold hardships and deprivation of the comforts of life, and in giving these small details, it has been the desire of the author to present a true picture of the comfortless homes that afforded them shelter and place of refuge at that trying time, as by these glimpses into the past, something is shown of how, by brave endurance and self-sacrifice, the way was made clear for the civilization which followed.

A CONFLAGRATION IN CAMP

That life in camp on French creek, pending the building of the stockade, was not wholly barren of exciting incidents, will be shown by the following somewhat dramatic events, in which myself and the donkey enacted the leading parts.

Among our camping equipments was a gorgeous red, white and blue striped tent,—a thing of beauty and of pride, patterned after the stripes of our national flag, representing the thirteen original colonies now embraced in our

Union of States, and in which the various members of our firm were mutually interested.

Well, one day when alone in camp, while indulging in my usual post-prandial nap, with my head uneasily reclining on a huge roll of bedding within the tent, I felt a sort of dreamy sensation of abnormal warmth creeping over me, which grew hot, and still hotter, until the superlative of heat was reached, when I suddenly awoke to find myself almost completely enveloped in flame and smoke.

At a glance I saw that the entire front of the tent was in a blaze, which was spreading above and around me with lightning rapidity. Springing up, I hastily tore the opposite end of the tent free from its fastenings and scrambled out, dragging, by the strength of sheer desperation, the roll of bedding after me.

Just at this critical moment, when I had given up the tent as doomed to utter destruction, one of the men, opportunely, came into camp for some mechanical tool, and, seeing my dilemma, he quickly severed the guy ropes, thus letting the burning tent to the ground, when, by some vigorous tramping, the fire was soon smothered, but leaving only a few smoke-blackened fragments of the once beautiful canvas, that had protected us from the wind and rain, snow and sleet, for so many dreary nights in crossing the plains. Ah! I could have wept.

When the stockade builders returned from their work that night, I lost no time in revealing to those affected, the story of our irreparable loss—laying much stress upon the lamentable fact that we were then left without even a shelter over our devoted heads, and told them how it happened. No, I didn't tell them that I was asleep when the cause of the disaster originated. I explained to them how a small stream of flame had stolen out from the camp fire near by, and crept slowly and stealthily tentward, until it communicated with the canvas, and—

"Well, where were you all the time, while the fire was cr-e-e-ping up to the tent?" interrupted one of the boys, sarcastically.

"Where was I? Why, I was in the tent, of course." I answered, guiltily.

"And you didn't see the fire a-coming, eh?" he returned.

"Well, no, not until it was too late," I meekly replied.

"That's rather strange," he said, with just a hint of suspicion in his tone.

He then plainly intimated that, in his opinion, the catastrophe was altogether the result of criminal carelessnesss on my part. I silently stood accused, with not a word to offer in my own defense.

"Well, now, Tom, what's the use of crying over spilled milk?" chimed in another of the boys.

Now that the ordeal was over, impelled by a spirit of conciliation, I brought forth the charred remnants and laid them, as a peace offering, at their feet, with the suggestion that they apportion them, per capita, among them.

"Great Scott," said Tom, "what can we do with these rags? You might as well throw them in the fire and let them burn like the balance."

"Oh no, I won't do that," I said. "You may need them to patch your pants with when the flour sacks are all gone."

"That's what," said another.

So the gaudy pieces were put away and portions of them were finally used for the above mentioned purpose.

THE DONKEY GETS A GOOD SQUARE MEAL

While the stockade was in process of construction, I was, of necessity, left the sole guardian of the camp properties, supplies, etc., and therefore felt morally responsible for their safety.

I was not alone, however; my only companion was the donkey, who spent his time for the most part within the precincts of the camp, prowling around and gazing with pleading eyes and ears erect in at the opening of each tent—probably to spy out the lay of the land. That donkey of ours, since his advent into the Black Hills, had subsisted chiefly on mountain scenery and the choice tid-bits of bacon rinds and gunny sacks that had been thrown out by the campers.

Well, one day he took it into his long, wise head to treat himself for once to a good square meal, so, protruding his head and shoulders into one of the tents he seized about a half side of bacon, which was carefully wrapped in a piece of canvas, then, backing out with his ill-gotten booty, proceeded to masticate it at his leisure. I think he knew beforehand just where to find it.

Observing the whole daring procedure from a distance, and keenly realizing that I would be called upon to give an account of my stewardship, I immediately rushed to the rescue of the pillaged property. With that end in view, I approached the head of the little gourmand and was about to grasp the canvas that hung suspended from his mouth when he turned his heels upon me like a flash, and kicked as only that branch of the equine race can kick. But, skillfully dodging his vicious heels I escaped the contact. Several like attempts to rescue the property were made with similar results.

Having an unbounded regard for the heels of the mule race, and deeming "prudence the better part of valor," I then stood at a respectful distance and watched the bacon, canvas and all, disappearing down the burro's throat.

It was with feelings of no little trepidation that I approached the owners of the pillaged tent that night and informed them of what had happened during their absence, and of my heroic effort to save their property. After telling them how the donkey had eaten the entire proposition, one of them queried: "Did he fry the bacon, or eat it raw?" "No, I replied. "He didn't wait to cook it; he seemed to prefer it raw." To my great relief the boys regarded the whole affair as exceedingly comical, but for the life of me I couldn't see where the fun came in.

The 16th of January found us all settled in our respective quarters within the walls of the stockade. Every night at sundown the huge gate was closed and securely barred, after which there was no egress. Yet, even within those formidable walls, with the gate strongly barred, I did not feel that we were any too safe. Having no sentinels posted out, how easy for Indians to stealthily approach the stockade in the night or early morning, while its unguarded inmates were profoundly sleeping, scale its walls and massacre every one. Visions of such a possibility often came up before me, while I lay awake at night, listening to the midnight howlings of the wolves and the occasional scream of the wild cat, which sounded so like the human voice, that I sometimes felt absolutely sure that the savages must be right upon us. I could almost see the sheen of their brandishing scalping knives in the dark. However, such visions were soon banished—giving way to a more healthy condition of mind.

Now that we were safely entrenched and domiciled for the present, what of the future? Everything for which the expedition was undertaken had now been accomplished. The long hard journey with its varied vicissitudes had been made, and gold, the prime object, had been found. What next was to be done? Evidently it would not do to remain inactive in our safe retreat until our store of provisions was exhausted, or until our ammunition was all gone. Plainly, communication must be opened with the outside world at all hazards, and at once, before the Indians should start on the warpath, thirsting for vengeance on the trespassers on their rightful domain, and before the government should take extreme measures to prevent reinforcements from reaching us.

MESSENGERS CARRY OUT THE GLAD TIDINGS

We all felt satisfied that as soon as the people were assured of our success, immigration would at once begin, but to accomplish this some one must undertake the dangerous journey back to civilization. Who would have the hardihood to undertake such a ride over the bleak prairie in the depth of winter?

No difficulty was experienced on that score, as Gordon and Witcher were not only willing, but anxious to bear out the glad tidings, and both having good saddle horses, they were of course conceded the honor.

As the intelligence to be sent out must be accompanied by actual gold as an indisputable voucher, much had to be done in the way of making preparations for the journey. A rude rocker was constructed out of one of the wagon boxes, when several days were spent in rocking out gold from the bed of French creek, resulting in the production of a sufficient quantity of the glittering scales to prove its existence in paying quantities, beyond dispute.

Many letters, too, had to be written to our respective friends, for not since the day we left the settlements had a single word been communicated to those left behind. Besides, on the day we left camp on the banks of the "Big Muddy," the irrepressible Charlie Collins, who was present to bid the expedition Godspeed on its dangerous journey exacted a promise from several members of the party, myself among them, to send back, at the first opportunity, letters for publication in the Sioux City *Times,* of which he was then editor, and as fortunately we were supplied with material the promise was faithfully kept.

On the 6th day of February, 1875, a pack horse was loaded with the necessary supplies, blankets, ammunition, etc., when the two plucky men, John Gordon and Eaf Witcher, mounted their horses and started away from the stockade with the gold, and numerous messages to friends, on their winter's journey, across the untraveled, snow-covered plains; civilization, home, and friends before, and an uncertain fate behind for Sioux City. Many doubts were expressed as they rode away and disappeared in the timber as to the probability of their ever reaching their destination. For twenty-three days they braved the storms and keen cutting winds of the prairie, subsisting on poorly prepared food, frequently being unable to procure the necessary fuel to boil a cup of coffee. For twenty-three nights they wrapped their blankets about them and laid down on the frozen ground or in a hole excavated in a snow drift, and during much of that time their horses had to paw away the snow to reach the grass which afforded them but a bare sustenance. Poor brutes!

The route taken by them was in a southeasterly direction to the Niobrara river, thence along the valley of that stream to Yankton, thence down the Missouri river to Sioux City. Three days before reaching Yankton their supplies became so nearly exhausted that they were reduced to quarter rations, and the horses had almost reached the point of starvation. When about a day's journey distant from Yankton, Mr. Gordon's horse gave out and he was obliged to halt a day to let him recuperate. Meanwhile Eaf, who it is alleged gave Mr. Gordon the slip, was riding away on his more powerful

EAF WITCHER
Taken March 1, 1875, on his return from the Black Hills to Sioux City

American horse post-haste to Sioux City, reaching that point twenty-four hours in advance of his comrade. When Gordon arrived next day with the gold Eaf was having a gala time indeed. He was being feted and banqueted, and I don't know but that he was carried around the streets upon the shoulders of some of its citizens. As to that tradition is silent. Be that as it may, when poor Mr. Gordon arrived on the scene, the enthusiasm of the people had reached its zenith.

The people of Sioux City naturally felt much gratified and elated at the success of the first expedition, as it was at that post it had equipped only a few months before.

When the letters, with glaring headlines, appeared in the daily newspapers on the following morning, there was a perfect furore of the wildest excitement, which however was not long confined to Sioux City alone. The story soon spread to the remotest bounds of our country, and became the almost universal topic of conversation.

From that time government lines were drawn closer around the Sioux domain, and hundreds soon began to gather along the borders, seeking for some loophole to slip through; many succeeded, some failed, as we know.

When our messengers left the stockade the mutual understanding was, that they would immediately proceed to organize another expedition, steal a march on the government, and return to our relief with reinforcements and additional supplies.

Now some may come to the conclusion, from this scheme, that the pioneers of 1874 were regular fillibusters; but no they were neither fillibusters, freebooters, nor pirates, but peaceable, law-abiding citizens of the United States—however, "with keen eyes to the main chance."

Mr. Gordon, in accordance with the plan formulated, lost no time in organizing another expedition, which managed somehow to elude the vigilance of the government, and get pretty well on its way to the Hills, when it was intercepted by a military force, the wagons and supplies burned, and Gordon, the leader, placed under military surveillance.

The twenty-two men, now left in the stockade, spent the long, weary weeks of waiting, according to their various inclinations; some rocked gold on French creek, when the weather was favorable, others spent their time in prospecting and hunting during the day, and—well, I hardly know how they did spent the long winter evenings. It is thought, however, that some of them played whist and the old-fashioned game of euchre, or an occasional friendly game of draw poker for pastime, as such terms as "Honors are easy," "I pass," etc., could frequently be heard from the neighboring cabins. Why, what else could they do, in the absence of newspapers and books, to occupy the mind? By the way, I did manage to smuggle in "Milton's Paradise Lost," and a funny romance, entitled "The English Orphans," on leaving civilization, which were read, re-read and read again, until every word from Alpha to Omega was printed in ever-living characters upon the tablets of my memory. So imbued did I become with the spirit and sentiment of those works, that I felt at times, as if paradise was indeed lost to me,—never to be regained, while at other times I felt myself growing very much like "Sal. Furbish" in the English Orphans. Didn't I enjoy life in the stockade? Oh, that mine enemy might be condemned to spend a winter under like circumstances and conditions,—but no, I could not wish that even my deadliest foe be so cruelly punished.

Imagine yourself imprisoned within the gloomy walls of an inclosure, and more closely confined within the still gloomier walls of a cell-like cabin, with no work for mind or hand to do, and with an uncertain fate hanging over your head, and you may be able to form a faint conception of the misery of life in the old stockade during the memorable winter of 1874-5. The very remembrance causes ague chills to creep rapidly along the spinal column. Sooner by far would I take my chances with the Sioux Indians out on the open plain. This gloomy picture of life in the stockade, let it be understood, its but a reflex of my own individual experience, and not my companions, who perhaps took a more optimistic view of the situation. Yet, it is certain that time hung heavily on the hands of every one within the walls of the stockade.

When vigilance began to relax and the warm days of early spring came I frequently ventured out to wander about on the sunny slopes of the adjacent hills, incidentally looking for gold which I expected to find scattered about quite plentifully along the hillsides and in the gulches. No, I didn't find any worth speaking of. I was pre-eminently a tender-foot then, since, however, I have had numerous object lessons, which have made me a wiser if not better woman. In taking these long rambles I was very careful not to lose sight of the stockade, as despite its gloom it afforded a haven of safety in case of danger.

These pleasant excursions were brought, by an amusing incident, to an abrupt termination. One day while seated on a large boulder of quartz on the top of a low hill drinking the wonderful beauty of the surrounding landscape, my eyes chanced to glance down the valley below, when they became riveted by a sort of fascination on a clump of bushes, among which I detected a slight unnatural movement. While looking, lo, the bushes became violently agitated, swaying back and forth in a very suspicious manner as if an Indian was lurking among its branches.

I hesitated no longer. Over boulders and jagged rocks I went down the slope, but I have never been quite able to understand just how I reached the bottom of that hill. All I know is that I got there and didn't stand on the order of my going. Along up the valley I ran with the fleetness of a professional sprinter, through the bushes, over fallen trees, clearing every obstruction with a bound. I fairly flew, fear adding speed to my wings, until reaching within a short distance of the stockade, when I was forced to make a slight detour to avoid the bullets that were coming directly towards me on my line of flight. The boys were shooting at a mark blazed on a tree a little below the stockade, where I stopped to look back to see how many Indians were following on my trail, and I must confess to a feeling of no little disappointment that I was not being pursued by a band of Sioux, in war paint. Such a splendid chance to become the heroine of a thrilling adventure and a hairbreadth escape was lost.

I arrived at the stockade breathless and excited, and when questioned as to the cause of my perturbation, I answered, evasively, "Oh, nothing much. It was probably nothing more than a mountain lion, or wild cat, or perchance an innocent rabbit." It is needless to say that from that time I kept religiously behind the entrenchments.

TWO MORE LEAVE THE STOCKADE

Shortly after Messrs. Gordon and Witcher left for Sioux City with the gold, two more of our number began to devise ways and means for returning to civilization. To accomplish their purpose, they by their combined ingenuity, planned a small vehicle to transport their supplies, blankets, and other belongings to Fort Laramie. The affair was to be a kind of dual combination of part cart and part sled, and really showed a good deal of foresight on the part of the designers, who shrewdly reasoned that while there was deep snow in the hills there might be none outside. No, they were not intending to draw the very peculiar rig themselves, although if their going out had hinged upon that alternative, they would not for a moment have hesitated to hitch themselves to the car, but fortune smiled upon the two homesick tender feet for once, at least. Blackwell and McLaren were providentially the owners of a single ox—free from all incumbrance, that was to be used as the motor power, and for which a kind of harness was made of skins and such other material as was available. This one emaciated ox was all that was left to the poor fellows of their original investment in the expedition.

On the morning of the 14th day of February, their unique contrivance being complete, the vehicle was loaded with provisions, blankets, etc., the motive power attached, and the fragile-looking outfit was ready to pull out on its terribly perilous journey to Fort Laramie.

It would indeed be difficult to imagine anything more grotesquely ludicrous than the spectacle they presented, as they marched away from the stockade. Of course, we all felt sad to see them go, but we could not help laughing at the little outfit as it started away from the stockade. The poor, bony, half-starved ox trigged out in his motley harness, hitched to the Liliputian vehicle—not much larger than a good-sized hand sled, piled up high with its load of supplies, blankets, etc., and the wheels of the contrivance strapped on top, venturing out in the winter, on a journey of two hundred miles through a hostile country, was a sight—the very pathos of which made it irresistibly funny. It scarcely seemed possible that they would ever reach Fort Laramie alive.

As night approached, the wrecked craft returned. Something had given out or weakened, obliging them to put back to the stockade for repairs. The next morning they started away again, and the poor fellows were seen no more.

Blackwell and McLaren never returned to the Hills, for, according to their own declaration, they had had enough of them to last the balance of their lives, and would have turned back long before reaching the Hills, had it been possible. Mr. Blackwell especially was homesick from the day he left the last settlement. A brave fellow he was, nevertheless. "Well," he said one day, while en route, "this is the worst pill I was ever compelled to swallow," and as I have swallowed a good many doses of the same kind of pills, I am prepared to vouch for the probable correctness of his assertion.

The infection spread, for about three weeks later, or on the 6th of March, four others of our already small band marched away from the stockade for Fort Laramie, viz., Newton Warren (happy Uncle Nute), D. McDonald (Red Dan), J. J. Williams, and Henry Thomas,—but, ah, I forgot, there were five of them—the donkey left the Black Hills at the same time for good, and never after did his musical notes echo through the picturesque hills of the great Golconda. Two of the deserters, having saddle horses, rode away with blankets strapped onto their saddles behind, and guns across the pommels in front; another had the donkey, but tradition is silent as to whether he rode him out or packed him with his belongings and walked by his side,—that must be left to conjecture. J. J. Williams, with gun across his shoulder, and pack on his back, walked out, and through the deep snow of the trackless forest it was no easy task, methinks. Our force was now reduced to eighteen men.

Six weeks had elapsed since our messengers had left us, and grave doubts began to arise in our minds as to the probability of reinforcements ever reaching us. Perhaps by this time the strong arm of the government had intervened to prevent any farther trespass on the Sioux domain. Still we looked anxiously from day to day for some tidings from the men, who had carried the proof of our safety and success to the world.

Our situation, nothwithstanding the strength of our position, was neither an enviable, nor a pleasant one; realizing, as we did, that the Indians would soon be leaving (if they had not already left), the agencies on their mission of revenge. In view of this, well knowing the modes of the Indians, every precaution was taken to guard against their depredations, or an attack. All combustible substances, such as fragments of pine, brush, etc., were gathered into piles and burned; even the grass for some distance around the stockade was burned to the roots. Every one familiar with the methods of the

Indians knows, that burning the enemy out is their sure resort, when all other means fail.

During the month of March, 1875, the pioneers of 1874 surveyed and platted the first town site in the Black Hills, on French creek, in that little dimple in the hills where stood the stockade. By the aid of a picket, rope, and a small pocket compass, the site was laid out into blocks and streets and christened Harney City in honor of the great Indian fighter, Gen. Harney. Log foundations were laid on the corner lots of the principal streets by the fortunate ones who drew them. It is now amusing to recall how anxious I was to draw a desirable or central corner lot, in what was confidently prophesied was destined to become the metropolis of the coming golden empire.

April was finally ushered in with one of the blinding snow storms so common in Dakota during that month. The wind blew fierce and cold, piling up the snow in drifts all through the nooks and crannies of the Hills, and scattering our poor cattle in every direction—anywhere to find shelter from the driving storm.

THE STOCKADE PARTY TAKEN OUT OF THE HILLS BY THE MILITARY

One evening during this storm, just as the great gate was about to be closed and barred for the night, four men, unheralded and unbidden, rode boldly right into our stronghold, causing no little consternation and excitement in our usually quiet little community. At first sight they were thought to be the vanguard of our expected reinforcements, but upon a second look it was seen that two of our visitors were in military uniform, while, in the other two we recognized the familiar faces of our quondam comrades, J. J. Williams and Dan McDonald, who, as emissaries of Uncle Sam, had also donned soldier's clothes. The blue coats and brass buttons betrayed their mission. It developed then that the four men who had left the stockade on the 6th of March, had after a hard journey of eight days reached Fort Laramie in safety, though not without encountering Indians. As the little party were crossing the head of Red Canyon, they were confronted by two well-armed mounted braves riding directly towards them. Naturally the boys were slightly alarmed at the prospect of an encounter with the two burly savages, but they immediately leveled their guns at the approaching Indians, who by frantic gesticulations made it known that they were not hostile, but "good Injuns." They also encountered a large band of Indains and squaws with papooses, on the Cheyenne river, who made no hostile demonstrations.

After a few days for rest and recuperation two of the party proceeded on their journey homeward, while the other two were detained to guide the soldiers back to the quarters of the pioneers in the Hills. And that is how we were at last found.

The four mounted men who rode, unannounced, into our midst on the evening of the 4th of April, proved to be J. J. Williams, Dan McDonald, and two lieutenants in the Second United States Cavalry, detailed from their camp twelve miles below, bearing orders to our party to make immediate preparations for leaving the Black Hills. The entire force sent to remove the trespassers, consisted of a troop of cavalry, about twenty-five pack mules and a large train of wagons, to carry rations and forage, and an ambulance for the use of the female trespasser, all under the command of Capt. Mix, of the Second United States Cavalry.

We were proclaimed prisoners, although no formal arrests were made, and given just twenty-four hours to hunt our scattered stock and make other needful preparations for leaving the stockade. Instructions were given, that nothing but the necessary articles of clothing, blankets, etc., and enough provisions to serve until reaching Fort Laramie, could be transported.

The next day was a busy one—a day spent in preparing to give up all that we had risked our lives to attain. Some started out in search of the stock, that had been scattered to the four winds by the storm, while others were putting together such few articles as could be taken, and caching or hiding such property as must be left behind. All mining implements, mechanics' tools, chains, etc., had to be left.

The writer of this story cached a trunk containing all her worldly goods, and although she has been searching diligently for more than two decades, her eyes have never yet been gladdened by a sight of the trunk, or a single article of its contents.

The limited time allowed us for preparations had expired. The search for the stock had proved, in part, fruitless—only about half having been found; our goods and chattels had been cached and our little bundles tied up, and we were ready to be marched out of the land of promise, to that from which we came.

CHAPTER VIII

RIDING OUT OF THE BLACK HILLS ON A GOVERNMENT MULE

I wonder if any of my fair readers ever rode a government mule, or any kind of mule for that matter, for a mule is a mule the world over. If not, they, of course, know nothing of the exhilaration, the real keen enjoyment such a ride affords, and have lost much of earth's pleasures. I have had that delectable experience, and it furnished me more genuine amusement to the square inch than I ever had either before or since, and this is how it happened. The troops ordered in to take us out of the Black Hills, supposing it impracticable to reach the stockade through the rugged hills with their wagons, went into camp, about twelve miles below, thus making it necessary to send in pack mules to carry out our belongings.

About 9:30 o'clock on the morning of the sixth of April, a troop of cavalry with their high stepping, glossy steeds, and about twenty-five pack mules, put in their appearance at the stockade, and, as everything was in readiness, it took but a short time to load and strap our goods on to the pack saddles. That being accomplished, it developed that there was one more mule than was needed for packing purposes. Now, to this extra pack mule—whether by previous design or otherwise is a matter for conjecture—was assigned the honor (?) of carrying out the first white woman to enter the Black Hills.

The boys, or most of them, having no saddle horses, of course had to walk to the camp below, so started a little in advance driving the few cattle that were found before them; but—what was I to do?

Just as I was revolving this vital question in my mind, one of the men having charge of the mules—or a muleteer—appeared at the door of our cabin, where I stood in a somewhat uncertain state of mind, and inquired: "Well, mum, what are you a goin' to do? Ride or Walk?" Fully appreciating his generosity in thus allowing me the choice of two alternatives, I told him with some asperity, that I had walked into the Black Hills, and, if necessary, could easily walk out, but, I added, "as the snow is pretty deep, I would prefer to ride if there was a way provided."

"Did you ever ride much on horseback?" he asked. I very modestly informed him that I was a skilled horsewoman, and was perfectly at home on the saddle, as I had ridden more or less from childhood up.

"Oh, well, I think we can fix it all right. The command is ready to march, and we had better be a startin'," he said.

Thus urged I donned my hood and wraps and followed him out through the wide gate, with a throb in my heart, and a tear in each eye—I felt it was for the last time—and there, before my astonished vision, stood the prancing, dancing steed I had been expected to ride, transformed into an old, scarred mule, several hands higher than any mule I had ever seen before; with head bowed down with the weight of accumulated years, and a long apprenticeship in military service, and the full modicum of "cheek" of the traditional government mule, and, to cap the climax, a masculine saddle on his back. I stood aghast.

"Jupiter, Olympus," I cried, "you don't expect me to ride that beast to camp, a distance of twelve miles, do you?" "I guess you'll have to, or walk," he answered. After making a careful mental estimate of the distance from the saddle to the ground, I concluded it would be an extremely hazardous undertaking, so I pleaded: "No, I can't do it. If I should be thrown, it would be almost certain death." "All right, you're the doctor," he answered nonchalantly.

Now, if I had been modeled after the pattern of the "new woman," or if I had been a little less conservative, the difficulty, in part, might have been overcome. However, I finally concluded to accept the situation, so asked the muleteer to tighten up the saddle girth a little and I would try it. Did you ever know of a woman venturing on a saddle, without first making sure that the girth was safely tight?

My attendant signified his willingness to humor my whim, so unbuckling the strap, he gave it a vigorous pull, when the mule, in physical protest against the proceedings, began to increase, by inflation and expansion, his already abnormal circumference; and, in further protest, uttered a series of such alarming groans or grunts, at the same time looking back with appealing eyes, moist with unshed tears,—as much as to say, "Please, don't," that I was moved to relent, thinking that the poor brute was in the last throes of dissolution. So I told the man to leave the girth as it was, and I would take my chances.

At that moment, the inspiring bugle notes gave the signal "mount," when the whole command simultaneously vaulted into their saddles—that is, all but the muleteer and I. Another bugle signal of "Forward, march!" was sounded, and the column marched on in double file. I was struck at the time by the beauty and perfection of the discipline maintained in the regular army.

"Now, just put your foot in my hand, and I'll help you onto the mule," said my attendant. I did as directed, and with an agile spring that would have done credit to an acrobat, I was landed safely into the saddle.

"There you are," said he, and sure enough, there I was, perched on the back of a "government mule." He placed my foot in the stirrup, carefully arranged my somewhat abbreviated riding skirt, then after one long, lingering look at the old stockade and its environents, to get a last impression of the place where I had spent so many weary, anxious days and nights, we started off down the valley at a tolerably brisk pace, soon overtaking and joining the calvacade which was a little in advance. Just at this juncture we came to a point where French creek crossed the gulch, and do you suppose that mule could be induced by any peaceable measures to wade the stream? No, not a bit of it. I urged and coaxed and patted and thrust my heel vigorously into his side (I had no spurs), but without avail. Forced to resort to heroic methods, I threatened a while, (no, I didn't punctuate my threats with any very strong adjectives) and finally dealt him a sudden blow with my whip (a willow rod cut from the bushes bordering French creek), whereupon the mule suddenly reared, and made a flying leap across, landing on the opposite side on all fours. Of course I was greatly astonished at such an eccentric feat on the part of the mule—especially so, as I had considered him old enough to be more dignified, but was not in the least disconcerted. I managed somehow to maintain my equilibrium on the saddle, notwithstanding the fact that I was taken completely off my guard. "Be careful now and hold fast to the saddle or he will throw you in to the middle of next week," cried my escort in apparent alarm. So as I had no ambition to be precipitated into the future in such an unceremonious manner, I did afterward hold on to the saddle with such a grip that no natural forces—not even an earthquake, could have unseated me.

At each of the crossings of that crooked, meandering stream, the mule resolutely refused to go into the water, always leaping across after his own fashion. However, after several crossings were successfully made I had learned to adapt myself to the motions of the mule, and had gained so much confidence in my own skill that I soon loosened my vice-like grip on the saddle altogether.

At one of the crossings, while I was fiercely struggling to obtain the mastery over the stubborn proclivities of the mule, a dashing young lieutenant suddenly wheeled out of his position on the flank of the column, rode back, and politely offered to exchange mounts with me. What impelled him to such an act of gallantry was, and is, largely conjectural; however, as I had a pretty well-grounded suspicion that some of the troopers, both privates and officers, were having a good deal of amusement at our expense—that is, mine and the mule's—I positively but courteously declined the proffer. Did they select that mule for my use with "malice prepense?" or did they not? That was the question. With this suspicion uppermost in my mind I assured him that I was well satisfied with my mount and was getting along splendidly. I was determined to ride that mule to camp despite his eccentricities, or die in the attempt; besides, to be candid, I would not have dared to venture on the back of the splendid, high-mettled animal rode by the dashing, debonnair young lieutenant.

After about two hours' ride we came in sight of the military camp dotted over with numerous white tents, and the blue-coated soldiers, who had already reached camp, moving about under the scattered trees. A little removed from the others was noticed a smaller group of tents, the headquarters of Capt. Mix and his staff—a distinction always observable in military camps, I have learned since then.

Anxious to avoid making any further display of equestrienneship, I decided to dismount at this point and walk into camp, a distance of a quarter of a mile or such a matter, so I slid down from the saddle—as gracefully as could be expected from such a lofty position, but instead of standing on my feet as I naturally expected to do, I fell to the ground in a helpless heap, benumbed in every limb, utterly paralyzed. The muleteer, who had kept faithfully at my side since leaving the stockade, quickly dismounting, very compassionately offered to assist me to my feet, but I peremptorily ordered him away and told him to hasten with all possible speed into camp, with my mule, and tell the boys that a woman was lying helpless, perchance dying, back on the trail, desiring immediate spiritual consolation. The obedient muleteer had not proceded far towards camp, however, before a peculiar sensation, like the puncture of a million needles, began to creep over me, and when upon essaying to rise, I found that I could stand on my feet; the blood went coursing through my cramped members and soon I was briskly wending my way into camp, none the worse for my twelve miles' ride on a government mule.

On my arrival at camp I was escorted to a comfortable tent, that had been provided for my accommodation, where I was directly visited by Capt. Mix, whom I had not before seen. Very soon the captain's aid appeared at the entrance and handed in a sumptuous lunch—a lunch that would have tempted the appetite of the most dainty epicure—with the compliments of Capt. Mix, and to which my readers may be assured ample justice was done. Enjoy it? Well, rather; I had become very tired of bacon and beans straight.

Here we were told by Capt. Mix that we had been in far greater peril than we dreamed of, for, he said, on reaching a high point about fifty miles from the Hills, with his command, the signal fires kindled by the Indians who had already surrounded the Hills could plainly be seen, and also that forced marches had been ordered that our imperiled little party might be reached before being massacred by the incensed savages. It was found on reaching camp, that an ambulance had been provided to convey the female prisoner from the Black Hills, much to said prisoner's gratification.

The next day, April 7th, at the customary bugle signal, the march was resumed towards Fort Laramie, nothing of special importance occurring until nearing Red Cloud Agency. When a few miles distant from that point the train was met by a Frenchman, named Baptiste, bearing a message from the agent in charge at the post, warning Capt. Mix of the hostile attitude of the Indians, who were, he said, making threats of sanguinary vengeance on the invaders as soon as they showed their faces at the agency, and advising the captain to conceal all the Black Hillers under the canvas of the wagons of the train. Capt. Mix told the boys of the fate in store for them, and advised them all to get to cover as quickly as possible; the boys, however, resented the proposition with much scorn. They were not made of the kind of material implied in such a course. Not only did they not hide under the canvas covers, but on reaching the agency they circulated freely among the Indians who were gathered there in large number awaiting their arrival—of course their guns were well in hand, and no doubt their very boldness disarmed the savages—but instead of proceeding to wreak vengeance on the real culprits, they seemed to vent their entire displeasure on the only innocent member of the party. The ambulance in which I was seated was immediately surrounded by about a dozen of the most diabolical looking specimens of the human form it had ever been my misfortune to see. They surveyed me with such malignant curiosity from every possible point of view, expressing their entire disapproval of me by numerous suggestive gestures and grunts, that I really became greatly alarmed for my own personal safety, and ordered the curtains of the ambulance closed that I might be hidden from their vindictive gaze. Even then their hideous faces could be seen peering in at me through every aperture, causing a sensation to creep over me, as if pierced by a dozen sharp-pointed arrows.

I don't know why, but those mistaken and misguided savages seemed to regard me as the arch-trespasser of the party—the very head and front of the whole offending; and I feel sure that had it not been for the presence of the troops, I would have been speedily disposed of then and there, and my scalp would have graced the belt of one of those inhuman savages. We were afterward informed that the military force had some difficulty in preventing an outbreak, so wrought up were the Indians over such a wanton breach of their treaty rights.

Our stay at the agency was not a prolonged one, and greatly was I relieved when the welcome bugle notes sounded the signal to "march!"

Although prisoners, we were treated with the utmost consideration by both officers and men on our march to Fort Laramie. Every day a carefully prepared lunch was sent to our tent with the compliments of the gallant captain. Whether this was done as a mere act of common courtesy, or prompted by a feeling of commiseration for my truly forlorn appearance, and my "lean and hungry look" was, and is still, an open question. I am afraid the latter is the correct interpretation thereof.

REACH FORT LARAMIE

In about ten days from the time we left camp in the Hills, we came in sight of Fort Laramie, and the American flag floating proudly above the government buildings, the sight of which caused the fires of patriotism, that had been smouldering within us for the six months previous, to burn up with renewed intensity, for, be it understood, we were all patriotic Americans to the core, and, like the prodigal son, were returning to the paternal arms of Uncle Sam.

When about two miles from the fort, a gay cavalcade of ladies, on horseback, were seen approaching the train, presumably to meet their returning husbands and friends, and incidentally to get a glimpse of the prisoners, whom they regarded with excusable curiosity.

They brought the alarming information that the Platte River was swollen nearly out of its banks, and so rapidly rising, that in less than an hour it would be impossible to ford the stream. There was no bridge at that time. The train pushed on with all possible speed, soon reaching the banks of the turbulent Platte. On the surface of the stream, logs, roots of trees, and even some whole trees, roots and branches, and all manner of debris went rushing along with the dreadful swish of the current towards the Missouri. There was no time to be lost, so the horses and their heavy wagons plunged in, heading up stream and almost floating on the bosom of the powerful current, and reached the opposite shore in safety.

The ladies on horseback, the troop of cavalry, and the pack mules, including my friend, forged through the angry waters; the ladies with skirts sweeping the stream, accomplishing the daring undertaking first.

We were then marched to the fort where we were detained two days, enjoying its hospitality, when the party was released, without parole, and given full transportation to Cheyenne, Wyoming, where we arrived with neither flour in our sacks, nor scrip in our purses.

Here members of the first expedition to penetrate the Black Hills separated, the author and family remaining in Cheyenne during the summer of 1875 awaiting developments in the Sioux problem; the rest of the party, after a short delay, boarding a train for Sioux City, the point from which the expedition had embarked in early October of the preceding year, where they were received right royally by its citizens.

When our returning expedition had reached to a distance of about ten miles from Cheyenne, it was met by that stanch friend and abettor of the enterprise, Charlie Collins, who had traveled all the way from Sioux City to bid the pioneers welcome home.

Yes, we were back again within the pale of civilization and the law, after an absence of nearly seven months. Thus ended the memorable journey in and out of the Black Hills, with its dangers and hardships, of the first expedition, the members of which gained nothing save a very dearly-bought experience.

The way had been opened, however, for the mad rush which speedily followed—in fact, it had already begun ere we reached Fort Laramie, for, as was afterward learned, a party of men were hanging about Red Cloud Agency, waiting to slip into the Hills as soon as the troops having the prisoners in charge had fairly passed out of sight.

Some of the members of the first expedition returned to the Hills during the summer of 1875, others in the early spring of 1876—to whom reference will be made further on—while a few never returned, preferring not to face the perils and hardships of a second journey to the new Eldorado. Not all the gold of Ophir, nor the wealth of India, would have tempted some of those few to repeat their first experience.

TERRIBLE EXPERIENCE OF TROOPS SENT AFTER OUR EXPEDITION

It was then learned that as soon as it became known to the military authorities that an expedition had really been organized and was already on its way to the Black Hills, troops were immediately ordered out from Fort Robinson, and other military posts, to overtake or intercept the expedition and bring it back to suffer the penalty for disregard of government orders. The expedition was not to be found, however, by any of the parties sent out, as the sequel has shown, owing, in part, no doubt, to the skillful maneuvering and the bewildering gyrations of our train along the line.

The troops ordered out from Fort Robinson had a terrible experience in their fruitless search after our party, which was at the time safely encamped on French creek. The command consisting of Troop D., Third Cavalry, under the captaincy of Brevet Brig.-Gen. Guy V. Henry, and about fifteen men of the Ninth Infantry under Lieut. Carpenter, with wagons, rations, etc., for thirty days, started from Camp (now Fort) Robinson, the 26th of December on their winter's march toward the Black Hills. By the time the Cheyenne river was reached, the weather became so intensely cold—the thermometer going down to forty degrees below zero—that the hands of both officers and men were terribly frozen. They entered the Hills a short distance, but finding no trail started back on their homeward journey braving the keen cutting wind from the north and barely escaping being frozen to death. The story of their fearful suffering during their homeward ride, is best told in the language of the captain in command, in his graphic and interesting published account of his experience, a short time since. He says: "The cold was so intense that it was impossible to ride. Dismounting, we led our horses, as they, poor brutes, in their suffering, struggled to escape from their riders, who, in their frozen condition, had trouble to prevent. Our trail was lost or obliterated by the snow; our eyes were absolutely sightless from the constant pelting of the frozen particles, and thus we struggled on. A clump of trees or a hill for shelter from the killing, life-sapping wind, would have indeed been a sweet haven.

"With frozen hands and faces, men becoming weaker and weaker, many bleeding from the nose and ears, the weakest lying down, and refusing to move,—a precursor of death; with them the painful, stinging bite of frost, had been succeeded by the more solid freezing, which drives the blood rapidly to the center and produces that warm, delightful, dreamy sensation, the forerunner of danger and death. They had to be threatened and strapped to their saddles, for if left behind death would follow, and an officer's duty is to save his men. Ours now was a struggle for life; to halt was to freeze to death, to advance our only hope, as Red Cloud could not be far away, and some of us might be able to reach camp with life, though with frozen limbs.

"Weakened, till we could no longer walk, in desperation, the command, 'Mount,' was given. Stiffened and frozen, we clambered into our saddles. Forward, gallop, and we all knew this was a race for life. We were powerless. Brain nor eye could no longer help us. The instinct of our horses, would alone save those who could hold out. So, on we rushed, life and home in front, death behind. Suddenly, turning the curve of a hill, we came upon a ranch, inhabited by a white man and his squaw, and we were saved. Had the sun burst forth with the heat of summer, our surprise and joy could not have been greater than they were, to find this place of refuge and safety in the wilderness, and to be saved from the jaws of death by a 'squaw ranch!' I have since passed this ranch, and nothing has ever awakened stronger feelings of gratitude than the sight of that hovel. The horses were put in the corral. Those that were running wild with their powerless riders were caught. Men were put under shelter, and the process of thawing out frozen parts commenced, with its attendant pain and suffering.

"Every officer and man was frozen; some suffered more than others; and to this day many are suffering from the effects of this march by the loss of members. Even where there is no physical disability freezing leaves a nervous prostration, from which one never recovers. We found ourselves about fifteen miles from our post, and so great was the cold, that we could not persuade an Indian to carry a message to Red Cloud asking that wagons and ambulances to sent to our assistance.

"The next day we received medical attention, and the helpless were carried to the post.

"There could not have been a greater contrast between our departure and return. Entering my own quarters, I was not recognized, owing to my blackened swollen face. All my fingers were frozen to their second joints; the flesh sloughed off, exposing the bones. Other flesh gradually grew afterward, except on one finger, the first joint of which had to be amputated, while the joints of my left hand are so stiffened by freezing and extraneous deposits, that I am unable to bend or close my fingers."

The above narrative shows what many other officers and soldiers in the past have had to undergo on the plains in the performance of duty, and not a winter but has its maimed and suffering victims, who have borne their share in the battle of civilization, rendering victory possible through the protection of settlers, the building and extension of railroads, and the peopling of the Great West.

It is very easy indeed, for us, pioneers, to believe that the above tale of fearful suffering is not in the least exaggerated, when we recall that, at the very time our pursuers were struggling in the icy embrace of a veritable blizzard, right in the teeth of a genuine Norther, that cuts like a razor, we were piling up great log fires to ward off the intense cold, even though protected from the piercing wind by the surrounding hills. It is more difficult, however, to understand why they should turn on their homeward ride, in the face of such a storm, with the thermometer forty degrees below, instead of remaining in the shelter of the Hills until the cold abated, having plenty of rations, forage, etc., with them.

It appears that Gen. Henry, erroneously supposing that our expedition had entered the Hills at some point on their southern limits, expected to either overtake us or strike the trail that would lead directly to our camp in the Hills, when in fact we had entered at a point almost diametrically opposite. Manifestly we had a very narrow escape from capture, as it could not have exceeded thirty miles from the point reached by the troops to our camp on French creek.

It was learned, too, that a detachment of soldiers had also been dispatched on our trail from Fort Randall on the Missouri river. It transpired that as soon as the band of Cheyenne Indians, encountered by our expedition at the Cheyenne river crossing, had reached their agency, they gave information of having met a large party of white men traveling towards the Black Hills, when the military authorities at the above named post immediately sent a company of mounted infantry in hot pursuit. This company succeeded in finding our wagon trail which was followed into the Hills to some point on the Box Elder creek, when, their rations becoming exhausted, it was forced to give up the pursuit and return to the post. Soldiers attached to that company afterwards told that our train could not have been more than a day's journey in advance of them, as they had spent the night before turning back near our recently abandoned camp fires. From this, it appears that the company were not at all anxious to overtake and capture the expedition when so near its journey's end.

A STREET INTERVIEW WITH WILD BILL

One day during the summer of 1875, while walking along one of the principal streets of Cheyenne with a friend, there appeared sauntering leisurely towards us from the opposite direction a tall, straight, and rather heavily built individual in ordinary citizen's clothes, sans revolver and knives; sans buckskin leggins and spurs, and sans everything that would betoken the real character of the man, save that he wore a broad-brimmed sombrero hat, and a profusion of light brown hair hanging down over his broad shoulders. A nearer view betrayed the fact that he also wore a carefully cultivated mustache of a still lighter shade, which curled up saucily at each corner of his somewhat sinister looking mouth, while on his chin grew a small hirsute tuft of the same shade, and, barring the two latter appendages, he might easily have been taken for a Quaker minister. When within a few feet of us, he hesitated a moment as if undecided, then, stepping to one side, suddenly stopped, at the same time doffing his sombrero and addressed me in good respectable Anglo-Saxon vernacular substantially as follows:—

"Madam, I hope you will pardon my seeming boldness, but knowing that you have recently returned from the Black Hills, I take the liberty of asking a few questions in regard to the country, as I expect to go there myself soon. 'My name is Hickoc.' " I bowed low in acknowledgment of the supposed honor, but I must confess, that his next announcement somewhat startled me.

"I am called Wild Bill," he continued, "and you have, no doubt, heard of me,—although," he added, "I suppose you have heard nothing good of me."

"Yes," I candidly answered, "I have often heard of Wild Bill, and his reputation at least is not at all creditable to him." "But," I hastened to add, "perhaps he is not as black as he is painted."

"Well, as to that," he replied, "I suppose I am called a red-handed murderer, which I deny. That I have killed men I admit, but never unless in absolute self-defense, or in the performance of an official duty. I never, in my life, took any mean advantage of an enemy. Yet, understand," he added, with a dangerous gleam in his eye, "I never allowed a man to get the drop on me. But perhaps I may yet die with my boots on," he said, his face softening a little. Ah, was this a premonition of the tragic fate that awaited him?

After making a few queries relative to the Black Hills, which were politely answered, Wild Bill with a gracious bow, that would have done credit to a Chesterfield, passed on down the street out of sight, and I neither saw nor heard more of him until one day early in August, 1876, when the excited cry of "Wild Bill is shot," was carried along the main street of Deadwood.

During our brief conversation he incidentally remarked that he thought I possessed a good deal of "sand" to undertake so long and dangerous a journey into the Black Hills. Now, while Wild Bill, no doubt, intended that sentiment as a great compliment—it being his ideal of "pluck,"—would you believe I did not at first quite like the imputation. You see I was not as well versed in Western phraseology then, as I have since become.

It was a rather startling experience to be "held up" in the main thoroughfare of a large, busy town, in broad daylight, by a noted desperado, yet Wild Bill performed that daring exploit with a single wave of his swift unerring right hand. No reflection is meant on his memory when it is hinted that perhaps he was not well up in street etiquette. Be that as it may, I have been strongly impressed ever since with the thought that Wild Bill was by no means all bad. It is hard to tell what environments may have conspired to mould his life into the desperate character he is said to have been.

Before coming to Black Hills in 1876, Wild Bill was at one time sheriff somewhere in the State of Kansas—in which capacity he is reputed to have been a holy terror to law-breakers. He was also for many years notable as a government scout, having acted in that capacity during the Civil War. The greater part of his life had been spent on the plains, among the lawless element of the Western border, where, as an officer of the law, he was brought in frequent conflict with all such desperate characters as usually infest the frontier settlements; murderers, horse-thieves, road-agents, and other criminals, who seem to believe that the world owes them a living which they are bound to have at any cost. Wild Bill was in consequence mixed up in many a desperate encounter, in which the first to press the trigger came off victor, and he was usually the first.

Perhaps the most remarkable peculiarity in the make-up of Wild Bill, was his wonderful nerve, and marvelous swiftness as a shot—his aim being steady, and his shot like a flash of light, it is easy to believe that he never allowed a man to get the drop on him.

Whether he possessed any redeeming traits is a disputed question; that he had numerous ardent admirers is an admitted fact.

This bold dashing frontiersman, who met his fate in the Black Hills, upon a time, met a daring and accomplished equestrienne of the circus ring, called Madame Agnes Lake, and mutually admiring each other's dashing characteristics, they finally loved and were married in Cheyenne, Wyoming, in 1874. The widow survives her murdered husband and now lives somewhere in the State of Kansas.

CHAPTER IX

THE BLACK HILLS

The Black Hills, apparently an upheaval from the bed of a vast ocean, having its existence away back in the misty past, or, at some prehistoric period, comprising an area of about 6,000 square miles, are situated in Southwestern Dakota, and Eastern Wyoming, the greater part, or about two-thirds of the entire area, lying in South Dakota and embraced between the north and south forks of the Big Cheyenne river, which encircles them on three sides, north, east, and south. Along their entire eastern limits, rise up bold, rugged, and lofty ranges of hills, trending northeast and southwest, and extending several miles into the interior, giving them the appearance of almost complete inaccessibility, as seen at a distance by one approaching them from the east. A nearer approach and exploration, however, will discover the fact that such is by no means the case, as along any of the numerous streams that gather their waters in the hollows of the jagged granite peaks and flow eastward to the plains, will be found practicable avenues of entrance to the interior.

The highest point of this wonderful uplift is Harney's Peak, in the granite region of the southern Hills, which extends its giant naked crest above its surrounding sister peaks, to an elevation variously estimated at from 7,500 to 8,200 feet above the level of the sea. From the summit of this dominant peak, one may behold, spread out, a glorious panorama of pine-clad hills, luxuriant valleys, and far-reaching undulating plains,—which look, in the distance, like the billows of old ocean, and perhaps no more enchanting scene ever greeted the human vision.

This peak was named in honor of Gen. W. S. Harney, one of the first Peace Commissioners who were sent out by the Government and succeeded in effecting a treaty with the Sioux in 1865.

The second highest point is Crook's Tower,—to the northwest of Harney's Peak, which rises up to an altitude of 7,140 feet above the plane of the sea. Terry's Peak, in the northern Hills, claims a height of 7,076 feet above the ocean level, and Inyan Kara, west of the Hills, aspires to an altitude of 6,063 feet above the plane of the sea. This peculiar formation stands alone in the midst of a plain just west of the Hills proper, and bears the appearance, as its name signifies, of having been thrown up from the center of an earlier upheaval leaving the rim of the earlier uplift intact. The name Inyan Kara

THE NEEDLES NEAR HARNEY'S PEAK

interpreted from the Indian tongue, signifies, "A mountain within a mountain,"—as appropriate as the name is musical.

Bear Butte, north of the main uplift and distant therefrom about eight miles, rises up in solitary grandeur, 4,400 feet above the plane of the sea and 1,200 feet above the surrounding plains. The dim outlines of this lone mountain, about which cling many interesting Indian traditions, could be seen by the longing eyes of the travelworn pioneers for days before reaching their *ultima thule,* and perhaps never "since the morning stars sang together" was the sight of a mere inanimate object hailed with greater thankfulness. Bear Butte is entitled to become historic—to be remembered in song and story as in the past in Indian tradition, in that it served as a conspicuous landmark to the early explorers to the west and northward, and later to the pioneer, guiding him from afar to the golden gate, which it overlooks, and where it will forever keep its lonely vigil.

The most unique geological elevation in the region surrounding the Black Hills is the "Devil's Tower," which rises up from the valley of the Belle Fourche river like a huge fossil tree trunk, 800 feet high and a mile in circumference at its base. This structure, which is believed by those who have examined its formation to have once formed the pith of a volcanic cone, is gradually disintegrating and falling away, and will doubtless eventually crumble to a confused pile of broken rocks.

The mountainous region of the Black Hills includes the Harney range of granite peaks and ridges, which extends in an almost complete circle from the Buckhorn spurs north of Custer City, around to the castellated and massive pile known as Calamity Peak, about two miles east of that city; the limestone region in the west, and the volcanic uplifts, viz.: Terry's Peak, Crow's Peak, Bear Butte, Inyan Kara, Bear Lodge, and Devil's Tower, in the northwest.

The elevation of some of the principal points in and near the Black Hills, as ascertained by the observations and calculations of Samuel Scott, mining engineer of Custer City, is as follows:—(Above the ocean.)

Harney's Peak	7,403 ft.	Inyan Kara	6,063 ft.
Crook's Tower	7,140 ft.	Sundance Mt.	6,023 ft.
Terry's Peak	7,070 ft.	Crow's Peak	5,772 ft.
Bear Lodge	6,828 ft.	Black Buttes	5,650 ft.
Custer's Peak	6,812 ft.		

The most attractive features of the Black Hills region to the pioneers were the magnificent forests of pine covering the lower ranges and extending far up the lofty mountain slopes; and the beautiful groves of spruce and fir trees that grew along through the canyons of the Hills, stretching up their graceful heads, oftentimes 100 feet toward the top of the vertical walls on either side—always strongly suggestive of the thought that they were reaching up to greet the light of the sun's rays, whenever that orb deigned for a brief time to shed its beams down into their dark recesses; also the many charming natural parks afterwards found throughout the Hills, sometimes, strangely enough, right in the heart of the heavily timbered region, surrounded by lofty mountains and well watered by copious springs. Notably among the productive watered parks found hidden among the mountains in the depths of the forest is what is called Boulder Park, lying about six miles northeast of Deadwood, containing approximately a thousand acres of land.

Groves of ash, oak, elm and a few other varieties of deciduous trees were found to exist on the northern slopes of the Hills, and to a limited extent on their eastern and southern basis, while the many streams flowing therefrom,

78   THE BLACK HILLS; OR,

were found fringed with an abundant growth of cottonwood, box elder, birch, willow, etc.

The forests of the Black Hills are not to-day what they were twenty years ago. Those remorseless civilizers, the ax and the saw, have shorn them of much of their primitive luxuriance and beauty—denuding large areas of their

DEVIL'S TOWER, SHOWING MILLIONS OF TONS OF FALLEN ROCK

most valuable timber, leaving in their places nothing but unsightly stumps. Despite the stringent laws enacted for the protection of Black Hills forests a great deal of wanton destruction of valuable timber is carried on year by year.

Another active agent, that has made sad havoc in the forests of the Black Hills is the extensive timber fires that almost yearly sweep over the Hills, through the most heavily wooded territory, leaving in their pathway charred trees divested of all beauty. The timber of the Black Hills is, for the most part, pine of an excellent quality and of suitable dimensions for being sawed into lumber for building and various other purposes—in short the forests of the Hills are among the many of their valuable resources, and upon which, by reason of ever-increasing industries, there will be in the future extraordinary demand.

The area of the Black Hills covered by an excellent quality of pine timber is estimated at 3,000 square miles, which will produce an adequate supply for all local demands for generations yet to come.

PRODUCTIVENESS OF THE BLACK HILLS

Between the successive mountain ranges of the Black Hills are rich, fertile valleys covered with a luxuriant growth of grass and susceptible of a high condition of cultivation. Agriculture is carried on extensively in the numerous valleys interspersed throughout the Hills, immense crops of cereals, also potatoes and other tubers, in fact all kinds of vegetables being raised with wonderful success. Wild fruits, such as plums, grapes, cherries, currants, raspberries, gooseberries, strawberries, and juneberries are found in great abundance, and of large size and excellent quality, pronounced by experts to be equal if not superior in flavor to the cultivated fruits of the same kind.

Although no extensive attention has yet been given to fruit culture, experiment has proven that many varieties of apples and pears can be successfully cultivated. Systematic efforts have been made by nursery men near the eastern slopes of the Hills towards fruit culture, and several kinds of fruit, not indigenous to the Black Hills, have been grown with the most gratifying results. Perhaps the most extensive and successful fruit culturist in the Black Hills is C. Thompson, whose nursery is located a few miles out from Rapid City and upon whom was bestowed the award for the size and quality of fruit exhibited at the Dakota State Fair.

The soil of the valleys and plains surrounding the Black Hills is also exceedingly productive in the cereals, and all vegetables suitable to that latitude, the extensive beds of gypsum surrounding the Hills furnishing an inexhaustible source of fertilization to the lands lying adjacent thereto. The entire region outside of the timbered area is covered with an abundant growth of buffalo grass, which to-day furnishes grazing for thousands of cattle, horses and sheep, without other sustenance throughout the entire year. This "bunch grass," which principally grows in the valleys and on the bench lands, makes it's appearance early in the spring, reaches maturity in June, and cures where it stands, retaining all its nutritive qualities, thus constituting the best autumn and winter food for stock that nature has provided.

THE CLIMATE OF THE BLACK HILLS

The climate of the Black Hills though in many respects peculiar to itself, depends,—like all mountainous region, greatly upon locality. Through the dry season, extending from May to October, comparatively little rain falls on the surrounding plains, while through the mountainous region rainfalls are frequent and copious, and the more heavily timbered the region the more frequent the showers. The mountains serve as condensers, gathering and precipitating the moisture, with which the atmosphere is charged, by evaporation from remote localities, while the plains may be dry and parched by long continued drouth.

Dark thunder clouds, heavily charged with electricity, frequently hover over the mountain tops, and, after discharging their abundant moisture over the forest region, break and fade away before reaching the edge of the plains. Doubtless, the more extensive culture of timber areas on the treeless portions of the Hills region, will result in a corresponding increase of precipitation.

No great depth of snow falls save in the limestone ranges of the Hills where it remains the greater part of the season from December to May. Much more snow falls in the northern than in the southern Hills, or on the valleys outside, and it remains longer. The heaviest snow falls in the months of March and April, and sometimes even in May. The great flood of 1883, which wrought such destruction in the northern Hills, was occasioned by a heavy fall of snow in early May, followed by a warm rain.

The temperature of the Black Hills varies with elevation and topography. In exceptional cases in the history of the Hills, the thermometer has been known to indicate a range of 122 degrees, from twenty-five degrees below to ninety-seven above, seldom, however, reaching more than ninety-four degrees above to twenty degrees below zero, the main temperature varying according to location from eight to ten degrees. Owing to the dryness of the climate, in this favored region, the extremes of heat and cold are not felt as in the humid atmosphere of eastern localities in the same latitude.

DRAINAGE

In the drainage system of the Black Hills the principal streams are the Belle Fourche, or north fork, and the south fork of the Big Cheyenne river, Redwater, Sand, Spearfish, Whitewood, False Bottom, Alkali, Bear Butte, Elk, Box Elder, Rapid, Spring, Battle, French, Beaver, Red Canyon, and Fall River. Of these, Sand, Spearfish and False Bottom creeks, empty their waters into the Redwater, a tributary of the Belle Fourche, while all the other above named streams discharge into the South Fork of the Big Cheyenne river. A notable feature of the drainage system is that a number of the streams flowing eastward from the Hills, sink and find a subterranean channel as they approach the foothills, the water rising again to the surface, a short distance below, but sometimes carrying no surface water to the streams of which they are tributaries. As a matter of fact, the only streams of the system which unfailingly discharge their waters into the main rivers, throughout the year, are the Redwater, Spearfish, Rapid and Fall River creeks, the first three of which, furnish ample power for manufacturing and milling, besides a large surplus for irrigation purposes. Numerous springs producing an abundant supply of pure, soft water, are found in every part of the Black Hills.

MINERALS OF THE BLACK HILLS

The most notable characteristic of the Black Hills region is the abundance and wonderful variety of its mineral productions. Although young in point of development, they have already in operation some of the most productive gold mines in the world, and they are known to contain silver, iron, copper, galena, tin, nickel, plumbago, cobalt, mica, asbestes, antimony, salt, arsenic, and almost every other known metal. The oft repeated assertion that the Black Hills are the richest mineral region of equal area in the world is no doubt true.

THE BLACK HILLS NEVER THE HOME OF INDIANS

No evidence that Indians had at anytime made the Black Hills their home was found by the first pioneers, which, to them, was a matter of no little surprise, because contrary to all preconceived ideas on that point. The romantic mental picture drawn of the Black Hills, as the Indians' elysium, whither they hied them from the heat and fatigue of the summer hunt, to rest under the grateful shades of their beautiful groves, and smoke the pipe of peace or war, according to their mood, while the squaws gathered the wood, built the fires, and cooked the meals, the dusky maidens and boys meanwhile disporting themselves, according to their savage fancies, such as target practice with the bow and arrow, running, jumping, etc., sports of which the young braves are excessively fond; and the war dances, the ghost, and other dances, in the deep ravines, where the warwhoop would be sure to ring out with the most telling effect, was completely dissolved. It seems plain enough that the tastes and proclivities of savages cannot be gauged from a civilized standpoint, for, as it appeared, the Black Hills with all their varied attractiveness possessed no charms for the red men, while to white men they would have been a veritable paradise.

Ample evidences were afterwards found that they frequently visited the foothills, for the purpose of supplying themselves with lodge poles, rarely, however, venturing very far into the interior. The reason for this avoidance of the Hills is believed by many to be their superstitious fear of the terrible thunder storms, which frequently occur in the Hills, when the lightning, doubtless attracted by the mineral, sometimes plays fantastic freaks, that would make even the most philosophical pale-face quail. It has been asserted by those familiar with the habits of the Indian, that, when caught in the Hills by a threatened thunder-storm they would fly with a piercing shriek and in the wildest terror, out towards the plains, at the first flash of lightning, and the first low rumblings of thunder.

SOME INDIAN TRADITIONS

Of the many curious Indian traditions and legends handed down from the dead centuries, none, perhaps, are more interesting to us than the superstitions of the Dakotahs in regard to the Black Hills—superstitions having their origin in the fertile imaginations of these simple-minded people, living so close to the heart of nature, which they are wholly unable to comprehend. Owing to their complete ignorance of the infallible laws governing the great forces of nature, they are led to invest everything that is awe-inspiring and grand, all the magnificent, and, to them, incomprehensible objects in nature, with human or superhuman powers. Everything that moves, such as the sun, moon, wind, clouds, etc., they clothe with attributes of a god or man, in proportion to the power with which they are impressed.

According to Indian folk-lore, they believe that the Great Spirit sits enthroned, under some one of the lofty peaks of the Black Hills who, in his angry moods, shoots forth tongues of forked lightning, and hurls out forged thunderbolts from his abiding place, sometimes accompanied by violent wind, which, they claim, is kept stored in great tanks for such occasions, all of which they regard as direct manifestations of his dire displeasure,—and the terrible electrical storms that occasionally sweep over the Hills, twisting, splintering, and tearing up by the roots the great giants of the woods, leaving them lying in bewildering confusion along the mountain slopes, they regard as an exhibition of his still more wrathy paroxysms. It is not surprising, then, in view of this belief, that the Indians should have given the Black Hills an extremely wide berth. They, evidently, had no desire to approach or spend much time around the throne of an incensed deity.

Another superstition of theirs was, that the evil spirit had his realm in the dark ravines and gorges of the Hills, whose malign influence caused the sun to refuse to shine down into their dark recesses, while others of their numerous deities had their abodes somewhere among the mountain ranges. Still another story,—one of much significance current among the Sioux, was that a white man was kept confined, under one of the lofty mountains of the Hills, doomed to perpetual imprisonment, as a warning to trespassers upon their happy hunting ground. As the story goes, this prisoner, who, inconsistent as it may seem, is allowed to sally forth occasionally for a constitutional, is a person of colossal proportions, and is reputed to leave, in his perambulations, footprints twenty feet long. Which one of the Indian deities is his custodian, or to what nationality the prisoner belongs, tradition saith not. Moreover, there are other strange legends, which are told and accepted by them, with the same blind, unreasoning credulity, that has characterized, to a more or less extent, all the primitive and uncivilized nations of the world.

The year of 1874, beginning the first epoch in the pioneer history of the Black Hills, and the two subsequent years of 1875-6, forming as they do, the era comprehended between their invasion by the first expedition, and their legitimate occupancy in the early part of 1877, were truly momentous ones, a period pregnant with exciting and tragic events, not unmixed with incidents both pathetic and ludicrous, many of which occurred under the author's own observation, and in a few of which she participated.

Although those early pages, as a result of the then crude conditions, have to record a few cases of high crimes, and some of lesser magnitude, it may safely be asserted, that far less lawlessness prevailed during their chaotic period, than in any other mining region of which we have information. The stains upon the white pages of our history are comparatively few though not far between.

All through the summer of 1875, the United States troops were kept exceedingly busy in an unsuccessful attempt to keep back the hordes of gold seekers, who were continually making their way into the Hills, from every point of the compass, and in driving out those who had succeeded in eluding their vigilance. Vain effort! Experience has shown that adventurers or hunters after the yellow metal will not and cannot be stayed;—as well attempt to stop the swollen current of the Father of Waters at its flood tide, in its resistless rush to the Gulf,—throw obstacles across its course, and it will remorselessly sweep them out of its path, or overflow, and cut a new channel for its mighty volume of waters to speed on its way to the sea. Miners, methinks, when determined to reach a region where gold is reputed to exist, are quite as slippery as the proverbial eel, that slips through the hand, despite the firmness of the grasp. The case of the Black Hills furnishes an exemplification of the aptness of the above comparison, for even had a cordon of soldiers with extended bayonets, in close contact, have placed around the Hills, doubtless some loophole would have been found to slip through.

IMMIGRATION TO BLACK HILLS IN 1875-6

Immediately upon the removal of the first expedition from the stockade in 1875, adventurers began to make their way into the Hills, but not until late in the fall of 1875 and the spring of 1876 did the great rush of immigration take place, when, over every practicable route to the Hills, representatives of every trade and profession under the sun came rushing along, figuratively, tumbling over each other in their headlong haste to be the first to reach the New Eldorado, each individual sanguine of realizing fabulous wealth on reaching the end of his journey.

Some were in companies, varying in size, with wagons well loaded with supplies, and munitions of war; others on horseback, with blankets and guns strapped on their saddles, their waists encircled with cartridge belts and bristling with revolvers, knives, etc.,—veritable moving arsenals—while many were on foot, with all their equipments swung on a stick over their shoulders, sometimes traveling by day and hiding by night, resorting to various devices to cover up their trials, thus hoping to escape the vengeance of the marauding Sioux, who were, in the spring of 1876, on the warpath, fierce for the scalps of any poor pilgrim who might be found trading with sacrilegious feet on their cherished hunting ground. Yet, alas! many of them met their death at the hands of the ambushed foe,—how many can never be known. However, the numerous new-made graves, seen along the various highways into the Hills, marking the scenes of the dark tragedies enacted near by, revealed in mute but eloquent language, the sad fate of not a few,—graves of the poor victims, whose mutilated bodies were oftentimes found and hastily buried by other pilgrims following in their wake—graves with only a small piece of pine board to serve as a monument to mark the spot, and with no other epitaph than the one simple work—"Unknown," inscribed thereon. Yes, unknown, yet who had mother, wife, or sister, perhaps, who long waited and watched till the heart ached and the eyes grew weary, for some message from the absent ones who would never return.

We have all seen advertisements in some of the newspapers, of the Black Hills, reading thus: "Information wanted of, so and so (giving name, age, description, etc.), who left his home for the Black Hills in 1875 or 1876, as the case might be, since which time he has not been heard from. Any information regarding him will be thankfully received, etc." Many of those missing ones, perchance, lie buried in some of the unknown graves scattered along the lines of early travel into the Black Hills.

A journey into the Black Hills in 1875-6 from any point, was one fraught with danger, involving in 1875 the great probability of capture by the United States soldiers, and in 1876 that of meeting the deadly Sioux, who were then in open and active hostility. Thus they were literally facing possible death at every step of their journey over the plains. Notwithstanding the danger, the steady influx continued, some being forced to turn back before reaching their destination, the majority, however, managing to slip through into the Hills.

In one short year the whole aspect of the Black Hills was transformed from a wilderness into a scene of busy life, furnishing to those who had seen them in all their primitiveness a striking contrast indeed.

The impressive silence, the profound solitude, that had therefore reigned supreme over the hills and valleys, was rudely broken.

All along the banks of various streams and in numerous gulches of the Hills, never before trodden by civilized feet, might be seen the tents of hundreds of busy prospectors diligently delving for the shining particles with pick and shovel, whose noise awoke the slumbering echoes of the surrounding hills; and scores of others might be seen sitting prone, along the edges of the streams, with goldpans filled with gravel, scooping up the water, whose flow and ebb washed off the lighter substance, leaving that of the greater specific gravity in the bottom of their pans; then with magnifying glasses eagerly peering into the little arcs of black sand left in the bottom of their pans to discover the traces of gold. Did they find gold? Oh, yes, they always found colors, each one claiming an average of from fifteen to forty cents to the pan from grass roots down to bed-rock.

CHAPTER X

THE FIRST TO ENTER THE HILLS IN 1875

According to the most reliable information obtainable, the first to reach the Black Hills in the spring of 1875, was a small party, of which Wade Porter, Thos. Monahan, Rob't Kenyon, Wm. Coslett, Alfred Gay, and others, were members; with a sprinkling of squaw men and half-breed Indians. This party had rendezvoused near Red Cloud Agency in April, 1875, awaiting the return and passage of the troops having the prisoners in charge, ready to follow back their trail to the stockade. It is to be presumed that no time was lost, and that ere the troops had reached Fort Laramie with their prisoners, this party had entered the wide open gates of our once boasted stronghold in the Hills, and taken possession of the recently vacated cabins within the walls,—even before their rude hearthstones had hardly time to grow cold,—and it is further reasonable to suppose that no time was lost by them in ferreting out, and bringing forth to the light of day the various pieces of property that had been so carefully cached only a few days before, and, perchance, the cattle that had been driven to the recesses of the Hills by the furious snowstorm, at the time of the exodus of their owners, were soon found and appropriated by them,—all of which, no doubt, should be regarded as the legitimate booty of those having the good fortune of finding them. But I draw the line at the trunk. What became of the cached trunk? That is the problematic question. Alas! did it too fall into the hands of the half-breeds and squaw men? To a moral certainty some man found that trunk and appropriated its contents, but what use a man could possibly put some of the garments and other articles to, is somewhat puzzling. It certainly needed no wonderful detective skill to have found its hiding-place, as the attention of anyone entering the third cabin on the left of the entrance to the stockade, would at once be attracted to a rather suspicious looking spot in one of the corners of the cabin floor,—which would betray the secret. When I say floor, I mean ground floor, literally. According to a plausible theory, they first raked off the debris from the surface, then shoveled away a few inches of Mother Earth, removed the poles that spanned the small opening, and there about three feet below the surface it stood fully revealed; the trunk being lifted out, and the lid pried open, the work of desecration began. Garment after garment of the owner's personal wardrobe was taken out and curiously scrutinized,—

they no doubt wondering what, or how each article was to be utilized,—nothing extremely elaborate, it must be confessed, yet all she possessed. But the half has not yet been told. On reaching the bottom of the trunk, a small mahogany box was found in which was deposited, among other trinkets, a little golden locket, enwrapped in a small piece of tissue paper, grown yellow with the passage of years, which enclosed the shadow of a face,—a very dear face. A romance? Oh, no, there was no romance whatever connected with that long-treasured memento,—only the pictured face of a much beloved classmate, who had, years before, left her work unfinished and crossed over the border into the spirit land. The loss of this picture cut deep. The owner of that wardrobe was for many years after diligently searching for a dusky maiden, trigged out in the garments abstracted from that ill-starred trunk, and with a little golden locket suspended from her bronzed throat, or, perchance, from one of her dusky ears,—but without reward. The loser has long since ceased to regret the loss of her wardrobe of twenty years ago, but the picture never; and woe betide the luckless maid, or fully-matured dame, red or white, who is ever found wearing that cherished locket.

This same little party of golden hunters, who had followed up so quickly the exit trail of the first pioneers, after being comfortably domiciled in the deserted cabins, and possessing themselves of such cached property as could be found in and around the stockade, which included picks, shovels, gold pans, etc., proceeded without unnecessary delay to the work of prospecting,—some mining in the abandoned works on French creek, others scattering out through the Hills in search of richer fields. However, they were not long left uninterrupted in their labors. The military authorities soon learning of their bold escapade through the lines into the Hills, at once sent a detachment of mounted soldiers, lead by Raymond, a scout in the government service, to remove them, or any others who might be found in the Hills, to the agency. In the early part of May those of the party who remained on French creek were one day surprised and captured, with their provisions, and escorted back to Red Cloud agency, where, after a short duress, they were set at liberty and their property restored to them. It is to be presumed that their outward march was not characterized by the headlong haste with which they entered the Hills, not many days before. However, they soon returned to the Hills by a circuitous route. The other members of the party who escaped capture—among whom was Wade Porter, remained in the Hills, until the arrival of the Jenny Expedition, in June, with which they prospected to some extent under the protection of Col. Dodge's command, and were not afterwards disturbed, until they, with hundreds of others, who, in the meantime, had entered the Hills, were ordered out by Gen. Crook on August 10th, 1875.

THE FIRST EXPEDITION IN 1875

The first well-equipped expedition to embark for the Black Hills in the spring of 1875 was organized and outfitted at Sioux City, through the efforts of John Gordon, who, it will be remembered, left the stockade with Eaf Witcher, in the depth of winter, February 6th and rode back over the bleak plains to Sioux City, bearing the shining particles that were to set the whole country in a wild delirium. Obviously, no time had been lost by Gordon, in carrying out the plan agreed upon, before leaving the stockade, of fitting out an expedition as speedily as possible, and returning with reinforcements and supplies to the imperiled little band, left entrenched among the mountains.

The state of the public mind was highly auspicious at the time for the organization of a Black Hills expedition evidently, for in a little more than sixty days from the time the two hardy messengers left the Hills, the organization was complete; outfits were purchased and every one ready for marching orders. The members numbered 174 men, and two women, one of whom was the wife of Major Brockett—a member of the Collins and Russell expedition of 1874; the other a German women, whose name is not positively known. It is believed, however, that she was Mrs. Schlawig, whose husband kept a brewery in Deadwood in 1876. The train consisted of twenty-nine wagons, heavily freighted with provisions, saddle horses and all the other adjuncts of a well-equipped expedition.

The train was scheduled to leave Sioux City on the 20th of April, 1875, but owing to the mass of ice floating in the river the ferryboat was unable to cross, causing a delay of several days. On the morning of the 25th the whistle of the steam ferry blew the signal that the channel was clear, when the impatient gold adventurers hurried to the landing and were all soon landed on the opposite side of the river. On the following morning, April 26th, the train, under the captaincy of John Gordon, marched away from the west bank of the Missouri—strangely enough, without attracting the notice of Uncle Sam's watchful agents—and proceeded on its way westward across the State of Nebraska unmolested until, reaching a point on the Niobrara river between Snake and Antelope creeks, near the present site of Gordon, Neb., where, at 6 o'clock in the morning on the 25th of May, a company of infantry under Capt. Walker, and two troops of cavalry, and a battery of two Gatling guns, from Fort Robinson, in command of Capt. Mills, surrounded the expedition, seized and burned nearly the entire train, with its valuable cargo of merchandise, besides the blankets and personal belongings of many of the party.

One of the wagons, however, was saved from the general holocaust by the bravery and pertinacity of a woman—Mrs. Brockett. Mrs. Brockett occupied a seat on this wagon on the top of a load of merchandise belonging to her husband, and do you suppose she could be induced to yield up her point of vantage on that load of goods? No, indeed; not she! Most women would have meekly yielded, but Mrs. Brockett didn't. She could neither be persuaded, cajoled, nor frightened into giving up her "dead cinch" on that load of merchandise, but sat as immovable as a rock and as imperturbable as the famed Egyptian sphinx. The officer in command was completely nonplussed. He was too gallant a gentleman to order violent hands laid upon a lady; neither did he feel quite justified in turning a Gatling gun upon her, and of course it wouldn't do to cremate her alive; so, after exhausting every kind of strategy known to military tactics, he was finally compelled to face the wagon about with its load of merchandise—including the plucky Mrs. Brockett, who, with the rest of the party, were marched back under military escort to Yankton, where they were set across the river and admonished not to return with trespassing intent.

John Gordon, the leader of the expedition, was taken into custody and conducted to the nearest military prison (Fort Robinson), where he was held until August, 1875, when he was taken to Omaha, Neb., for trial, and released by Judge Dundy, of that city.

The train of this expedition belonged to the Sioux City and Black Hills Transportation Co., that being the initial trip of the line.

Despite the discouraging failure of his second adventure Gordon, after his release, with admirable pluck and perseverance returned to the Hills, but hard luck seemed to follow him. The fickle goddess refused to smile upon his efforts and would not be propitiated.

Meeting our former leader on the streets of Deadwood, one day, late in the 70's, I ventured to inquire how things were "panning out" for him in the Black Hills. He frankly confided to me that he had not as yet succeeded in striking "pay gravel." "Every venture has so far proved a disastrous failure; and what is worse, I am several hundred dollars out of pocket," he answered. By way of encouragement, I told him, in reciprocal confidence, that we, too, had gotten clear down to bed-rock, with not a dollar in sight, and as a further solace, took occasion to remind him that the brave were not always rewarded with success. Since that day I have never seen the leader and guide of the first expedition to the Black Hills.

SCIENTIFIC EXPEDITION SENT TO THE BLACK HILLS

In the spring of 1875, after the discovery of gold in the Black Hills, and even before the first expedition was removed from the stockade, the government, foreseeing the inevitable consequences of such discovery, and anticipating the difficulty of preventing trespassers from entering upon the Sioux reserve, and, at the same time, unwilling that the then existing treaty stipulation should be violated, deemed it expedient that immediate steps be taken, in the interest of miners as well as for the protection of the Indians, towards securing the right, by new treaty, or otherwise, to enter the Black Hills portion of the Sioux reservation for the purposes of prospecting and mining.

Preliminary to this, however, inasmuch as there were many conflicting rumors in regard to the existence of gold in paying quantities, the government decided to send reliable parties into the reputed gold-bearing region, to ascertain the true value and extent of its mineral deposits, or other possible resources. A report of the result of such investigation would furnish substantial information upon which to base an intelligent judgment, in the event of any subsequent negotiations for the acquisition of the Black Hills, and their abandonment by the Indians.

Accordingly, an expedition for that purpose was organized under the direction and control of the Interior Department and Walter P. Jenny, was appointed to take charge of the work,— receiving his commission, March 26th, 1875. On April 25th the expedition, fully manned and equipped, was gathered at Cheyenne, Wyoming, ready to embark for the Black Hills, to enter upon the important work intrusted to it. Owing to some misunderstanding, however, the necessary transportation facilities had not been furnished, which necessitated a delay of nearly a month.

At length, on the 20th day of May, everything being in readiness, the expedition started for Fort Laramie, where it was joined by a military escort, under the command of Lieut.-Col. R. T. Dodge, 23d Infantry, when the whole party moved on Black Hills-ward.

PROF. WALTER P. JENNY
Photographed about March, 1878, and a good representation of the youthful Geologist, at the time of the Black Hills Scientific Expedition in 1875

As the extent and scope of the work to be accomplished, was designed to be of far-reaching importance, both from a material and scientific standpoint, it was deemed advisable to change the original plan by adding to the corps an astronomer and topographer, Capt. P. H. Tuttle, of Cambridge University, and Dr. V. T. McGillicuddy, at present of Rapid City, South Dakota, being commissioned to the respective positions.

As much of the history of the Black Hills during the year 1875, is embodied in the reports of officers in charge of the scientific and military expeditions ordered into the Hills, and is therefore a matter of public record, I feel justified in copying such reports, either as a whole, or in part, as the only available source from which to obtain absolutely correct information in regard to the work and movements of said expeditions.

From Prof. Jenny's published account of the movements of the expedition under his charge, after leaving Cheyenne, I copy the following:—

"Arriving at Fort Laramie on May 20th, all arrangements were consummated, and crossing the Platte on the afternoon of the 24th of May, we joined the military escort, furnished by the War Department, consisting of Lieut.-Col. R. T. Dodge, Twenty-third Infantry, commanding; Lieut. M. F. Trout, Ninth Infantry, adjutant; Lieut. J. F. Trout, Twenty-third Infantry, quartermaster; Lieut. J. G. Bourke, Third Cavalry, topographer; and Surgeons Jaquette and Kane, with two companies of the Ninth Infantry under Capts. A. H. Bowan, Munson and Lieut. DeLaney; two companies of the Second Cavalry under Capt. Spaulding and Lieuts. C. F. Hall, J. H. Cole and F. W. Kingbury; four companies of the Third Cavalry under Capts. W. Hawley, G. Russell, and W. H. Wessels, and Lieuts. A. D. King, R. G. Whitman, James Lawson, J. G. Foster, and C. Norton, with a train of seventy-five wagons.

"This large command, numbering full 400 men, would seem at first unnecessarily strong for the mere purpose of protecting from Indians those who were pursuing the investigation in the Hills, but the attitude of the Indians on the penetration of this, the most cherished spot of their reservation, could not be foretold, and it was known that they had been not a little agitated by the invasions of Gen. Custer in the previous year, and by the subsequent visits and operations of miners. Though no bands of Indians were met during the work, our safety and freedom from their visits were probably due to the well-known magnitude and strength of the expedition.

"A great measure of the success of the exploration is due to the hearty co-operation of the officers of the command, but particularly to the commander, Col. Dodge, whose unwavering interest and determination to make the work successful, and whose constant assistance and courtesy were especially valuable and grateful during the entire course of the work. To Lieuts. Norton and Foster, who were detailed for topographical work, Dr. McGillicuddy is indebted for assistance in the prosecution of his mapping.

"Reaching the Black Hills on the east fork of the Beaver on the 3d day of June, the work of the survey was soon begun, and a permanent camp was established on French creek near the stockade erected by the miners during the previous winter. In order to pursue the work more rapidly and thoroughly a division of the party was made, as follows:—

"Mr. Jenny, with a corps of assistants, assumed more particularly the investigation of the mineral resources of the country, prospecting the gold deposits, etc., while the remainder of the party, Mr. Newton, Dr. McGillicuddy, and Capt. Tuttle continued the topgraphical and more complete geological study of the Hills. As the work of the survey progressed northward the main body of the escort of troops was transferred from one base of supplies to another, so as to keep up with the course of the expedition. In this manner, with scarcely a day's remission from work, the survey continued until the entire area of the Black Hills between the forks of the Cheyenne had been mapped, and its geology and mineral resources determined, as fully as the rapid progress would permit.

"Having passed over the entire country, and accomplished the object of the expedition, the various parties assembled on the Cheyenne, at the mouth of Rapid creek, and began the march homeward, reaching Fort Laramie via White River and the agencies of Spotted Tail and Red Cloud, on the fourteenth day of October, after an absence of four months and twenty days."

Having disbanded the expedition at Cheyenne, the officers of the survey returned east, and assembled in Washington early in November to complete their reports. While in the field, the various discoveries of the presence of gold in the different districts were announced to the Commissioner of Indian Affairs at Washington, and a preliminary report by Mr. Jenny on the mineral resources of the Hills, accompanied by a small preliminary map by Dr. McGillicuddy, was published in the annual report of the Commissioner of Indian Affairs for 1875. The completed observations of the mineral resources, climate, etc., possessing immediate and particular interest, were, by resolution of the Senate, called for in advance of the final report, and with a preliminary map were published in 1876.

The subjoined account, given by Professor Jenny, of his meeting with the miners on French creek, may be read with interest:—

"When I reached French creek, June 16th, 1875, about fifteen men were found camped four miles above the stockade, where they had been at work for several weeks, and had staked off claims, built small dams and were digging ditches, preparatory to commencing sluicing on the bars along the banks of the streams. These miners were very enthusiastic in regard to the mineral wealth of the gulch; they were reporting from five to twenty-five cents to the pan from the gravel, and made the most extravagant statements as to the yield which would be obtained as soon as they commenced working with sluices. But they were working under unfavorable circumstances, the water supply was very small—not exceeding fifty miner's inches, with every indication that it would soon fail entirely, and the grade of the valley was so small that it was difficult to get a good head of water for sluicing.

"On testing, by washing the pay gravel from the different prospect holes already opened, with a pan, and weighing the gold obtained, it was found that the usual yield along the streams was from four to eight colors to the pan (about one-tenth to one-fifth of a cent), and in favorable and somewhat limited localities, from a half cent to as high as one and a half cents were obtained from the gravel from off bed-rock.

"The gravel bars were rich enough in gold to pay if extensively worked under more favorable circumstances, but too poor to yield a remunerative return for the labor employed, except in a few limited deposits of gravel near the extreme head of the stream."

The following is a copy of Professor Jenny's dispatch to the Department at Washington from camp on French creek:—

"CAMP ON FRENCH CREEK, June 17th, 1875.
To Hon. E. P. Smith, Commissioner of Indian Affairs, Washington, D.C.:
I have discovered gold in small quantities on the north bend of Castle creek, in terraces of bars and quartz gravel. Arrived here yesterday. About fifteen men have located claims on the creek above here and have commenced working. Gold is found southward to French creek at this point. The region has not been fully explored, but the yield of gold is small and the richness of the gravel has been greatly exaggerated. The prospect, at present, is not such as to warrant extensive operations in mining.

WALTER P. JENNY, E. M.,
Geologist of Exploration of the Black Hills."

The thought may here occur to the mind of the reader, as it has to mine, that the results of the work of exploration of the Black Hills for mineral deposits, as shown by the reports of Professor Jenny to the Commissioner of Indian Affairs, was by no means of an encouraging nature. The infinitesimal prospects obtained were not calculated to inspire the belief that the placer mining in the territory examined could, by even the most approved processes, be made very remunerative. Of course, the existence of gold was demonstrated and much other valuable information obtained, in reference to their geology, topography, etc., yet the result certainly furnished but small evidence that the Black Hills would ever become the great mineral producing country into which it has since developed. But, when it is remembered that the marvelous placer deposits of the northern Hills had not yet been discovered, and when it is considered that no systematic mining was practicable and the prospects obtained were merely pan tests, from the surface down to bed-rock, at more or less widely separated points, the homeopathic character of the prospects obtained ceases to be a matter of surprise. However, by years of persistent work, with an ever-abiding faith in the final outcome, it has since been demonstrated that the Black Hills is pre-eminently a gold-producing country. Discoveries have been made, and are being made, almost daily, in both the northern and southern Hills, that have proved a wonderful revelation to the mining world.

CHAPTER XI

THE CESSION OF THE BLACK HILLS

All attempts of the government to keep the people out of the Black Hills, proved from the first unsuccessful. From the time the first expedition succeeded in secretly launching its "prairie craft" and eluding subsequent pursuit, and in finally planting its banners amid the natural battlements of the Hills, right within the "holy of holies" of the hunting ground of the Sioux, it became evident that the government would soon be compelled to yield to the popular demand, that some arrangement be made with the Indians, looking to the relinquishment of their claim to the Black Hills portion of their reservation. As a matter of fact, it was no part of the governmental policy, that this resourceful land should any longer be reserved for the sole use of savages, but to make favorable terms for its relinquishment possible it was necessary that an effort be made to maintain inviolate the provisions of the then existing treaty; therefore to accomplish the desired end, two things had to be done: first, to appoint a commission to treat with the Indians for the cession of the Black Hills, or for their occupancy for mining; second, to remove by military force, as far as practicable, all trespassers from the Indian reserve.

In pursuance of that policy, on the 18th day of June, 1875, a commission was appointed by the Secretary of the Interior, for the purpose of treating with the Indians; and on the 20th of September of the same year, the combined council of commissioners and Indians rendezvoused on the White river, about eight miles from Red Cloud Agency. The representatives of the government present were as follows: Hon. Wm. B. Allison, of Iowa; Brig.-Gen. A. H. Terry, U. S. A.; S. D. Hinman, Santee agency; W. H. Ashley, Beatrice, Nebraska; Hon. A. Comings, Missouri; G. P. Beauvais, St. Louis, Missouri; A. G. Lawrence, Rhode Island.

The following tribes of Indians were represented: The Ogalallas, Mineconjons, Brules, Uncapapas, Blackfeet, Sans Arcs, Yanktons, Santees, Cheyennes, and Arapahoes.

As might have been expected, their deliberations proved barren of good results. Owing to the dictation of a few degenerate, renegade white men, and the Indians half-breeds, their demands were so exorbitant as to render negotiations at that time out of the question. From $30,000 they raised their price finally to $70,000, in addition to which they wanted large herds of cattle, and horses, agricultural implements, the most approved guns, plenty of ammunition, and palatial residences that would compare favorably with those occupied by the wealthy pale-faces, with tapestry hangings, upholstered furniture, etc., for their chiefs; and it is hard to tell what their limit might have been if the conference had continued longer. The commissioners, of course, refused to consider these unreasonable demands, and the council broke up, without accomplishing their object.

It is stated by a gentleman who was present on that occasion, that before the pow-wow closed the Indians had become insolent and defiant, and when negotiations came to an end, some of the chiefs assumed an attitude of decided hostility,—hostility indicating that they would much like to bear away the scalps of the commissioners as trophies, in lieu of the $70,000 and other property demanded for their land. For a time an outbreak seemed imminent, which, however, was happily averted by the wiser counsels of the few.

It goes without saying that the failure of the commission to treat with the Indians was a source of keen disappointment to the hundreds of miners in the Hills, who were being so persistently harassed by the soldiers as to render any extensive or successful prospecting impracticable; and also to many who were standing outside the golden gate waiting for the permission and consent of the government to enter the forbidden country. Miners became clamorous for what they regarded as their rights, which they were determined to have at all hazards—if not with, then without, the consent of the government.

President Grant was quick to see that some further effort must be made to relieve the embarrassment of the situation, as the following extract from his message to Congress in reference to the matter, will show:—

"The discovery of gold in the Black Hills, a portion of the Sioux reservation, has had the effect to induce a large emigration to that point. Thus far the effort to preserve the treaty rights of the Indians of that section has been successful, but the next year will witness a large increase of such emigration. The negotiations for the relinquishment of the gold lands having failed, it will be necessary for Congress to adopt some measure to relieve the embarrassment growing out of the causes named.

"The Secretary of the Interior suggests that the supplies now appropriated for that people, being no longer obligatory under the treaty of 1868, but simply a gratuity, may be issued or withheld at his discretion."

Congress then took the matter under consideration, which resulted in the appointment of a second commission by the Secretary of the Interior. In August, 1876, this commission met again in council with the representatives of the various tribes, under instructions from the Interior Department to treat with the Indians on the following specific terms:—

1st. The Indians to relinquish all right and claim to any country outside the boundaries of the permanent reservation, as established by the treaty of 1868.

2d. To relinquish all right and claim to so much of that said reservation as lies west of the 103d meridian of longitude.

3d. To grant right of way over the permanent reservation to that point thereof which lies west of the 103d meridian of longitude, for wagon and other roads, from convenient and accessible points on the Missouri river, not exceeding three in number.

4th. To receive all such supplies as are provided for by said act and said treaty of 1868, at such points and places on their said reservation and in the vicinity of the Missouri river, as the President may designate.

5th. To enter into such agreement or arrangement with the President of the United States as shall be calculated and designed to enable said Indians to become self-supporting.

Negotiations this time proved successful, and on September 26th, 1876, at Red Cloud Agency, the following euphonious and suggestive signatures (in Indian chirography, I suppose), were attached to the treaty, namely: Red Cloud, American Horse, Young-Man-Afraid-of-His-Horse, Little Wound, Red Dog, Afraid-of-the-Bear, Three Bears, Fire Hunter, Quick Bear, Red Leaf, Five Eyes, White Bow, Good Bull, Lone Horse, Two Lance, Bad Wound, Veasel Bear, High Bear, He-Takes-the-Indian-Soldier, High Wolf, Big Thunder, and Slow Bull.

The above treaty was ratified by Congress, and approved by the President, on February 28th, 1877.

The territory ceded by this treaty is embraced between the two forks of the Cheyenne river, and is bounded on the west by the 104 degree meridian of longitude.

It will be seen by studying the provisions of this treaty, that by its terms the Indians from a material standpoint lost much, and gained but little. By the first article they lose all rights to the unceded Indian territory in Wyoming from which white settlers had then before been altogether excluded; by the second they relinquish all right to the Black Hills, and the fertile valley of the Belle Fourche in Dakota, without additional material compensation; by the third conceding the right of way over the unceded portions of their reservation; by the fourth they receive such supplies only, as were provided by the treaty of 1868, restricted as to the points for receiving them. The only real gain to the Indians seems to be embodied in the fifth article of the treaty. The Indians, doubtless, realized that the Black Hills was destined soon to slip out of their grasp, regardless of their claims, and therefore thought it best to yield to the inevitable, and accept whatever was offered them.

They were assured of a continuance of their regular daily rations, and certain annuities in clothing each year, guaranteed by the treaty of 1868, and what more could they ask or desire, than that a living be provided for themselves, their wives, their children, and all their relations, including squaw men, indirectly, thus leaving them free to live their wild, careless, unrestrained life, exempt from all the burdens and responsibilities of civilized existence? In view of the fact that there are thousands who are obliged to earn their bread and butter by the sweat of their brows, and that have hard work to keep the wolf from the door, they should be satisfied.

THE ADVENT OF GEN. CROOK IN THE BLACK HILLS

In the early part of July almost simultaneously with the appointment of the first commission to treat with the Sioux for their occupancy Gen. Crook arrived in the Hills with a military force, for the purpose of expelling all persons to be found in the Hills without the consent and sanction of the government.

This, it is believed, was undertaken more from considerations of policy in order to conciliate the Indians, who, it was thought, would refuse to negotiate, until trespassers were removed from their territory, than with any expectation, or even hope, that the effort would prove successful.

As a matter of fact Gen. Crook was plainly inclined to give the miners a wide latitude, and fulfilled his mission, it seemed, in a sort of perfunctory way. Major Pollock, however, who was in command of the military forces, was disposed to execute his orders to the very letter, and is credited with a great deal of "pernicious activity," in harassing the miners,—forcing them to dodge about from point to point to escape arrest and expulsion, and sometimes, in extreme cases, in placing them in "durance vile," and feeding them on hard tack and water. In short, Major Pollock kept the miners in perpetual hot water, during his nearly four months stay in the Black Hills.

One day, about the middle of October, a squad of cavalry, while scouring the Hills in search of trespassers, surprised a small party of some half-dozen miners, who were prospecting on Castle creek, took them into custody, relieved them of their property, and escorted them to military headquarters at Custer, where they were put in the "guardhouse," or some kind of an inclosure prepared for recalcitrant miners. After being kept prisoners for several days, they were sent to Cheyenne to be tried before the United States commissioner, who, concluding, doubtless, that he had no valid right to hold them, soon released them, and restored their property.

Among these prisoners were Wade Porter and T. H. Mallory, prominent miners in the Hills in 1875, both of whom had returned to the Hills, after having voluntarily left about the middle of August, in compliance with the order of Gen. Crook. This, it appears, was their second offense, in consequence of which they were made an example of. Soon after their discharge, nothing daunted, they with others again returned to the Hills, late in the fall of 1875, and remained during the winter following.

The history of these few is also the history in part of hundreds of other prospectors who were driven out at the point of the bayonet, only to return at the first favorable opportunity by some circuitous route, and re-enter at some other point, then scatter out through the gulches of the Hills. These offensive and defensive movements were kept up during the entire summer of 1875, the solution of the problem being no nearer at its close than at the beginning.

MINERS LEAVE THE HILLS BY ORDER OF GEN. CROOK

Pursuant to instructions from the government, Gen. Crook, on the 10th day of August, issued a call to the miners to meet at the stockade near Custer, for the purpose of entering into preliminary arrangements for leaving the Hills, until some terms for opening the country to settlement could be agreed upon with the Indians, and also, incidentally, to make rules and regulations for the protection of their claims, pending negotiations. As one of the conditions of their voluntary exodus the miners presented a petition to the commanding general, asking that six or more men of their own choosing be permitted to remain in the Hills to guard their claims during the absence of their owners. Gen. Crook, who was in full sympathy with the miners, was disposed to allow them every reasonable opportunity for throwing any kind of a safeguard around the property they were so reluctantly leaving, expressed a willingness to grant their petition, and further, would allow them five days in which to make preparations for leaving, provided they would then go out of the Hills, without compelling him to resort to force. Believing that their own interests would be best served by complying, the miners unanimously agreed to the proposed terms.

On the following morning, August 11th, a town-site company was organized, a site of a mile square was laid out and platted and named Custer. The blocks were divided into lots which were numbered from one up to twelve hundred. Tickets bearing these numbers were deposited in a box, from which on that day several hundred miners drew slips and became the owners of the lots corresponding in number with those drawn from the receptacle. A list of the names of lot owners was given into the custody of the men chosen as guardians of the miners' property interests, during their temporary absence. The men chosen to remain in the Hills were: Saml. Shankland, Thos. Hooper, A. D. Trask, Robt. Kenyon, W. H. Wood, Alex. Thompson, Alfred Gay, and H. F. Hull.

August 15th, 1875, hundreds of miners of their own volition turned their backs upon the new found Eldorado. Other miners, not within the reach

RED CLOUD

of Gen. Crook's proclamation, upon hearing of the action taken at the stockade, also left the Hills a few days later. Let it be understood, however, that a considerable number of miners and prospectors, scattered about at remote points, were never reached. A few others also, who were prospecting with the Jenny Expedition, among whom were John W. Allen, Brown, Carlin, Flarida, and Warren (our "Uncle Newt"), were not molested. There were a great many miners yet left in the Hills, and others constantly coming to take the places of those who had left.

SPOTTED TAIL IN THE BLACK HILLS

During the month of August, 1875, one of the head chiefs of the Sioux Nation, and twelve braves of his tribe, with their ponies, trappings, and dogs, accompanied by an Indian agent, arrived in the Black Hills, the object of the visit being to investigate and judge for themselves of the true value of the territory to be relinquished,—such knowledge to be used to the advantage of their people in the approaching council. That their estimate of the value of the Black Hills and their resources was great evidenced by the extravagant consideration demanded therefor a month later.

SPOTTED TAIL

MINERS RETURN TO THE HILLS

After the failure of the commission to agree upon any terms with the representatives of the Sioux, for the opening of the country to settlement, the miners, who had voluntarily left the Hills at the request of Gen. Crook, with renewed determination returned and repossessed themselves of their abandoned claims, also with them hundreds of others who entered the Hills for the first time.

The cavalry, meanwhile, were kept exceedingly active in their attempts to keep back the invaders, which efforts proved fruitless, as, if driven out at one point they were sure to re-enter at another.

THE JENNY EXPLORING EXPEDITION COMPLETES ITS WORK

The Jenny Exploring Expedition, having finished the important work that had been intrusted to it, left the Hills with its military escort, about the first of October, 1875. On the outward march Col. Dodge reported having met California Joe with about forty or fifty men, on the south fork of the Cheyenne river, en route for the Hills.

THE CAVALRY FORCE WITHDRAWN

About the 1st of December, 1875, Capt. Pollock and his cavalry force were withdrawn from the Hills, at which time all military opposition to immigration ceased. About the same time, the Indians doffed their feathers, rubbed off their war paint, and suspended active hostilities for the winter, to be renewed with increased violence and added horrors in the early spring of 1876. All opposition being removed, the rush began. Not only miners who could now prosecute their search for gold without molestation, but men of all professions; business men with their stock in trade; groceries, dry goods, restaurant furnishings, sawmills, saloon fixtures, billiard tables, etc., came for a time without let or hindrance. It is estimated that at least 11,000 people came to the Black Hills during the winter of 1875-6—from November 15, 1875, to March 1, 1876—the great majority of whom came first to Custer.

CUSTER IN 1875

Custer is beyond question entitled to the proud distinction of being the pioneer town of the Black Hills. Being the objective point of a large percentage of those coming to the Hills during the winter of 1875-6, it suddenly grew from a small mining camp of a few unfinished cabins to a town of very formidable proportions.

During the first three months of the year 1876, 1,400 buildings were erected on the site where, at the close of 1875, there had stood but one solitary finished building.

It is somewhat difficult to realize that on the spot where, less than two years before, civilized feet had never trod, but which meanwhile had become historic ground, a town of such magnitude should exist. Fact, however, is sometimes stranger than fiction.

During that period, structures of both lumber and logs sprung up on every hand as if by magic. The clear air of the beautiful park was resonant from morning till night, seven days in the week, with sound of ax, hammer, and saw; the surrounding hillsides swarmed with men, busy in felling trees and cutting them into logs to be used in the construction of cabins or hauled to the mill to be sawed into lumber. Ah, pity 'tis, that the beauty of our magnificent forests and groves should have to be so marred! This pioneer town of the Black Hills was built of structures both large and small (some of them quite pretentious) to be used for various purposes, all kinds of business being represented.

There were hotels, restaurants, dry goods and grocery stores; also meat shops, shoe shops, sawmills, and saloons galore.

Before the great stampede to Deadwood Gulch in the spring of 1876 Custer could boast a population variously estimated at from 6,000 to 10,000 people, in which numerous families were included.

FRENCH CREEK THE MECCA OF THE PIONEERS OF 1875

French creek was the "Mecca" towards which the hundreds of gold-seekers, who came to the Black Hills during the year 1875, first turned their eager faces. It had already become historic. It was on the borders of French creek, that Ross and McKay, the staunch miners who accompanied the Custer Expedition, found their most encouraging prospects. On French creek, also, on December 23d, just as the winter's sun was sinking behind the western Hills the boys of 1874 panned out the first shining particles, that gladdened their eyes and realized their hopes; and, too, on one of its banks, mid winter's snows and storms they built, in an incredibly short space of time, the strongest fortification of the kind ever constructed on the Western frontier, as well as the cabins within its walls, cabins that afforded temporary shelter and protection to hundreds of the miners and tenderfeet who subsequently came to the Hills. On the banks of French creek was washed out, with the aid of a rudely constructed rocker, the bright, coarse gold that was conveyed by two plucky men, in dead of winter, hundreds of miles over a bleak prairie, to Sioux City, to convince the world that gold in the Black Hills was not a myth, but a glittering reality. This French creek gold then, was the lodestone that attracted so many to that locality in 1875. I think it may be safely stated that nine-tenths of the miners coming into the Hills during that year, did their first prospecting on French creek, whence they scattered out to explore other localities, principally along the streams, having their headwaters in the Harney Peak area, viz.: Spring, Rapid, Box Elder, and Castle creeks, some going north into the Bear Lodge region, where it is claimed numerous large-sized nuggets were found. Along the above named streams placer gold was discovered, in perhaps paying quantities, but the glowing reports that were, during the summer, scattered broadcast over the land were doubtless greatly exaggerated, or perhaps in some instances the product of an exuberant fancy. However, the visible evidences of the real metal in the hands of many honest and legitimate miners, were sufficient to establish the fact that the Black Hills was destined to become pre-eminently a gold-bearing country and sufficiently encouraging to induce all classes, reckless of consequences, to join in the race towards the many gates opening into the Hills.

CHAPTER XII

SOME OF THE PIONEERS OF 1875, AND HOW THEY GOT TO THE BLACK HILLS

Among the many who were attracted to the Black Hills during the first year of their civilized, or it would better be said, half-civilized, existence, and who were intimately identified with their early history and subsequent development, are the following, naming them in the order of their arrival as to date as far as known: Dr. D. W. Flick, Sam'l Shankland, A. D. Trask, Joseph Reynolds, Thos. Hooper, Frank Bryant, Wm. Lardner, H. B. Young, Emil Faust, V. P. Shenn, and John R. Brennan.

Besides those above named there are hundreds of others who were more or less conspicuous figures in the fleeting drama of 1875, some of whom have long since left the Hills, others still residents, but of whom the writer could gain no direct or even indirect information. However, the experiences of these few, whose adventures have come to her knowledge, will illustrate those of the majority, perhaps, of the pioneers of 1875.

Dr. Flick and Mr. Shankland were both members of the second expedition to embark for the Black Hills in 1875, and among the few of a large party, who, after great hardships and exposures, and by a good deal of strategy to avoid falling into the clutches of the military, which was then the great bugbear, finally succeeded in reaching their goal, in the early summer of that year.

Dr. Flick has the distinction of having built the first log cabin erected in the Black Hills in 1875, and Mr. Shankland was one of the seven men left to guard the property of the expelled miners during that year, and both have been residents of the Black Hills since then.

In this connection it seems apropos that a brief account be here given of the trying experiences of that second expedition, which it is believed may prove interesting.

Early in the spring of 1875, a few days after the Gordon party had slipped quietly away from the banks of the Big Muddy, a large party of other gold-seeking adventurers, numbering 150, were gathered at Sioux City, awaiting transportation to the Black Hills.

They soon entered into contract with the H. N. Witcher Transportation Company to carry their goods and equipments to the Black Hills for eight cents per pound avoirdupois, then with a few saddle horses and a small pack train the expedition started on its journey westward, under the pilotage of Eaf Witcher, along the Niobrara river, south of the Nebraska State line, and thus quite outside of the Indian reservation.

When about 300 miles from Sioux City, near the point where Gordon's train had been captured and burned a short time before, the expedition was overtaken and joined by another party of something more than 100 men, under the guidance of Capt. Ely, of which Judge Rhinehart, now of Lead City, was a member, making altogether a formidable aggregation.

The journey westward proved an uneventful one until reaching Snake river, a small tributary of the Niobrara, where an event occurred which somewhat dampened the ardor of the gold-seekers, and threatened the success and even the very existence of the expedition itself. Up to that time, although the party had been constantly on the alert, through fear of governmental interference, no serious apprehension had been felt of an attack by the Indians. However, at this point they were made unpleasantly aware that Indians in plenty were near at hand.

One day a half dozen of the party, who had been detailed to serve as scouts along the line of march, came rushing headlong and excited into line, bringing the startling information that a large band of from 1,500 to 2,000 Indians had been encountered, who had relieved them of their blankets. As a matter of fact there were only 250 of the savages—quite enough, however, to strike terror to the heart of a tenderfoot. Naturally almost the entire party was thrown into a state of intense excitement and alarm; some wrung their hands and wept, while the majority at once proceeded to put the expedition substantial war footing. Selecting a favorable position the wagons of the train were quickly formed into a kind of corral for the protection of the stock; the tents were pitched outside, their guns got in readiness, and thus fortified and equipped they awaited in fear and trembling the expected enemy.

At this juncture Dr. Flick, who did not believe in the hostility of the Indians, electrified the expedition by announcing his readiness to go in search of the savage robbers, and try to recover the lost blankets, provided one of the men who had been relieved of their property would go with him to locate the Indians. One of the scouts reluctantly consented to risk his life in an attempt to regain possession of his almost indispensable bedding. So the two started bravely out in the probable direction of the Indians, but had not proceeded far, when, upon reaching the summit of a hill, they discovered coming up on the opposite side, a legion of Indians making directly towards them. Waiting until they had nearly reached the brow of the hill, the two men faced about, and returned to camp, followed closely by the Indians, who, when within a short distance of the camp, halted, presumably to hold a council of either war or peace. After a brief deliberation, twelve of the band, headed by their chief, Lame Lance, advanced a safe distance directly towards the camp of the pale-faces (and some of them were abnormally pale at the time), when they laid their guns on the ground, in token of their peaceable intentions, and went through a sort of pantomime, very expressive to those who understood its significance, and which, being interpreted, meant "We good Injuns." Upon being beckoned to approach, they came into camp, leaving their guns on the ground, where they had laid them. The chief, in the manner characteristic of his race, stated that the band were merely on a hunting expedition, and in proof of the honesty of his statement presented a document signed by the Secretary of the Interior permitting them to hunt off their reservation. After the usual amount of begging—they are born beggars, these red men of the plains—the twelve braves returned peaceably to their own camp, carrying with them a generous supply of crackers, sugar, tobacco, etc. Emboldened by this success, numerous others of the band came into the camp of the expedition asking for more, and when refused, they became insolent and defiant, making themselves exceedingly troublesome, by peering into the wagons of the train, as if determined to help themselves to whatever they wanted.

Finally, however, they were driven away and a strong guard of armed men placed around the camp and corral. As the members of the expedition, for the most part, had but small confidence in the good faith of their savage neighbors, believing the old saying that there are "no good Indians but dead Indians," their camp in plain view seemed a constant menace to their security, and thus no sleep came to their eyes nor slumber to their eyelids that night, with the exception of a few who were made of sterner stuff. Anxious to put miles of distance between the two camps, bright and early the next morning the train resumed its march directly westward, but not towards the Black Hills. From this time the Black Hills fever began rapidly to wane. Apparently the train and members of the expedition, the majority of whom were tenderfeet, had no intention of directing their course towards the Hills, seeming determined to keep outside of the Indian reservation. A few who were really anxious to go to the Black Hills insisted that the train cross the Nebraska line into the reservation and make directly for the Hills, and thus, perhaps, avoid collision with the military. It was becoming plainly evident that the expedition was doomed to go to pieces. At this juncture, Dr. Flick, hoping to ward off such a disaster, mounted a wagon—I suspect there were no stumps thereabouts—and made a vigorous speech, urging the duty of loyalty on the part of every member to the original purpose of the expedition, insisting that fear of Indian hostilities was utterly groundless, etc., and, as a matter of fact, there was but little danger from that quarter, at that early date in 1875, as by the summary removal of the pioneers of 1874 from the stockade, a short time before, the government had shown a determination to respect the treaty rights of the Indians, and they were satisfied.

On reaching the mouth of Antelope creek, about 400 miles from Sioux City and eighteen miles south of the Nebraska State line, the climax came. The roll of members being called, out of the entire expedition only fourteen men signified a willingness to undertake the rest of the journey to the Black Hills. Early the next morning, June 23d, 1875, during the "wee sma'" hours, a small party with the following personnel: Messrs. Dunlap, Shankland, Flick, Berry, Wright, Timmish, Burns, Mitchell, Bushnell, Atchinson, Webster, Nelson, and Forbes, with eight pack animals, left the expedition to its fate, and pulled out for their original destination,—Valentine Dunlap being constituted as guide. At 12 o'clock the next night, after traveling over a bluffy country, with short intervals of rest, the little party camped on the head of White Earth creek, where they partook of a midnight supper of cold beans, bread and coffee. At daylight they started out towards the White Earth river—camping at 9 o'clock a.m. for breakfast. They had hardly commenced their meal, before two Indians were discovered on a bluff above their camp, and supposing them to be government scouts, they deemed it advisable to pack up without finishing their breakfast and hurry on towards the Hills, before being overhauled by the military. Hungry and tired as they were—having been in camp only about forty minutes, they quickly packed their belongings and traveled on with their jaded animals, as rapidly as possible over the rough untraveled country towards the Black Hills, until they had put about twenty-five miles between them and the point where they had seen the supposed government scouts,—when, having been fortunate in finding a small slough or depression on the prairie, affording sufficient water for the purpose, they camped, prepared and drank a cup of coffee, then threw themselves down on the broad prairie for a few hours' sleep. After a short rest, they started out again, traveling with all the speed of which their worn-out pack animals were capable, reaching Wounded Knee at 11 o'clock at night, where they went into camp. Their sole anxiety and desire was to escape discovery and arrest by the soldiers, who they feared were then warm on their trail. We must not lose sight of the fact, that this adventurous little band were traveling on foot, and leading their pack mules, which, of course, greatly increased the danger of discovery;—for whoever heard of a mule that would not, without the slightest compunction betray even his very best friend?

On the evening of the third day after leaving the expedition the party arrived at the White Earth river, completely exhausted from almost constant travel and loss of sleep. Crossing that stream the next morning and going on in the direction of the Hills about twelve miles, they suddenly found themselves confronted on every hand by a bewildering maze of seemingly insurmountable bluffs. The very worst portion of the Bad Lands, in all their confusing grotesqueness, stared them in the face. The guide (Dunlap), after having climbed to the summit of one of the high chalky bluffs to survey the prospect, declared that it would be impossible to scale their precipitous sides with the pack mules, and if they attempted to go round them, they would become irremediably lost amid the intricate labyrinths of the cuts, gulches, gorges, etc. "We must go back on our trail, and try to find a more practicable route," said the guide. The majority of the party, relying upon the judgment of their leader, in whom they reposed the utmost confidence, as he claimed to be an experienced frontiersman and to have spent several years among the Indians, seemed willing to follow his advice. Dr. Flick alone strenuously opposed any retrograde movement, preferring to take the chance of being lost among the gloomy defiles of the Bad Lands rather than invite the extreme probability of running head-long right into the arms of a body of United States troopers. "I, for one, shall no longer follow the leadership of a man who would guide us blindly back into the very danger we have been most anxious to avoid," said the doctor. "I propose going to the Black Hills right along this line, and those of you who turn back will have good reason to regret it," he continued.

After spending some time in discussing the situation pro and con, the doctor, who had resolved to push his way in a direct line to the Hills at all hazards, began making preparation for his lone journey amid many protests. After putting together his outfit for the trip, the problem of transportation came up for solution. To carry his blankets and other equipments with sufficient provisions for an indefinite time, seemed an impossibility. Finally, after a great deal of persuasion, Chas. Webster, who held an undivided half interest in a diminutive, half-starved pack pony, with a saddle-worn abrasion on his back as large as the crown of a man's hat, in which the doctor also held a proprietary interest, was induced to risk the undertaking. "There's no danger of our getting lost. When we come to a hill we can't climb, we'll just go around it. We'll get to the Hills all right, and it won't take us many days, either," urged the doctor; "and," he continued, "when we get there, I believe we shall find someone from whom we can get supplies enough to keep us from starving, at least."

After packing the little undivided pony with such articles only as might be most needed, thus reducing the load to the least possible minimum of weight, the two plucky men started, straight as the swallows fly, for the Black Hills, uncertain as to what their fate might be. Upon going a little distance, they turned and waved their hands (I suspect they had no handkerchiefs) in token of farewell to their comrades, whom they expected never to see again.

Let us now leave the twelve who are about to double on their trail, and follow the two lone adventurers into the Hills. After a hard day's march over and around the barren precipitous bluff, through the ashes of that desolate region,—which has aptly been compared to Hades with its fires extinguished—they had the unexpected good fortune of camping that first night on the opposite bank of the Cheyenne river. Early the next morning, after a frugal breakfast of bread alone, they resumed their march Hills-ward, reaching the mouth of a clear, sparkling stream, teeming with fish, at 8 p.m. June 27th, where they camped for the night. The next morning they proceeded with much difficulty up the stream, which the doctor named "Tanglefoot"—Squaw creek, a branch of Battle creek—because of the almost impenetrable growth of underbrush along its banks. "I thought it the most beautiful stream I ever laid eyes upon," related the doctor. The sight of the fish was certainly one which might have filled the heart of Isaac Walton's least ardent disciple with great gladness,—and how much more, then, that of the two half-famished pilgrims who had not tasted meat for many days.

Did you find no game on your journey into the Hills, Doctor?" I inquired. "Oh, yes, plenty of it; elk, deer, grouse, and other game, but I did not dare to shoot for fear of discovery," replied the doctor. What a shining example of self-denial, to be sure, for a crack sportsman, who could at that time, in nine cases out of ten, bring down a bird on the wing at the first shot.

It was with extreme difficulty that our two travelers pushed their way up through the heavy undergrowth, along the beautiful "Tanglefoot," with their frail pony, handicapped as he was with his load of blankets, beans, and camp paraphernalia.

"Why," said the doctor, "our poor little pack-horse became so weak that we actually had to push him up hill." They were at last forced to lighten his load, by throwing off their supply of beans of forty pounds avoirdupois, which they thought could safely be dispensed with, as they had not indulged in the luxury of beans since leaving the Cheyenne river, the hazard involved in cooking them being considered too great; besides, everything was wet and sodden, as it rained continuously during the entire trip.

Any gold hunters, prospecting along Tanglefoot Gulch, during the few succeeding weeks, might have found the flotsam and jetsam of a small cargo of Black Hills, "grub," if not gold, to reward them for their search. Going north after leaving Tanglefoot, they soon found themselves at or near the base of Harney's Peak, and on the fifth day after leaving their companions in the Bad Lands, they climbed the dizzy heights to the summit of one of the jagged peaks of that ridge of the Harney Peak range called the "Needles," and looked down and abroad upon the glorious panorama of wooded hill, green valley, and smiling glade—a scene more beautiful, perchance, than had ever before dawned upon their visions. No sign, however, of human life and activity was visible in all the wide expanse. Can we be the only human beings in the Black Hills? was the mental query that occurred to them. Not a very cheering possibility truly to the two solitary men amid the fastnesses without supplies.

Descending from their lofty outlook into the valley below they traveled on and soon dropped into the valley of a little bubbling stream (Willow creek) dancing gaily southward into French creek. Cautiously descending the stream, and watching closely for some trace of human occupancy,—either soldiers, miners, or Indians, they were soon rewarded by discovering, clearly silhouetted against the southern sky, what appeared to be the figure of a man, moving along the crest of a distant hill, in advance of them. Keeping the object ever in view, they hurried on at a rapid pace, until within hailing distance, when the doctor, making a kind of trumpet of both hands, called out through it in his most most sonorous and penetrating tones: "Hullo there, white man or Indian?"

"Indian," came back in the unmistakable but welcome accents of a white man.

In double quick, the two tired and hungry men climbed the hill and were at his side.

"My name is Flick," said the doctor, at the same time extending his hand, "and my companion's name is Webster," he added, introducing his fellow-traveler.

"My name is Van Horn, and there is my camp," returned the man pointing to a group of tents, and a number of canvas-covered wagons, just at the foot of the hill.

"Well," ventured the doctor, "we are tired and ravenously hungry, and nearly barefoot, as you can see, and would like some breakfast. We have eaten nothing for the past five days but bread straight,—and bread made of flour and water alone, at that."

They were at once conducted to the camp below, and treated with the miner's proverbial hospitality, to a good square miner's meal, the first in many days. Thus, after a hard journey over hills, across yawning ravines, through valley and glade, sleeping on the ground at night without tents to protect them from the rain that had drizzled down almost unceasingly both day and night, and living on bread alone, our two heroic pioneers had at length found a temporary haven of rest.

After spending a few days, enjoying the prodigal hospitality of Van Horn's camp, meanwhile prospecting a little on their own account, they made their way to the military headquarters of Col. Dodge's command, then stationed at the stockade near Custer. Here the doctor found and introduced himself to Capt. G. Russell of the Third United States Cavalry, and a brother mason, to whom he made known their most urgent needs. It will be remembered that they had been forced to throw overboard their cargo of supplies, on the Tanglefoot, and, in consequence, were almost, if not entirely, out of the staple articles of diet.

"After an interchange of fraternal grips, Captain Russell asked, "Now, Doctor, what can I do for you?"

"Well, first I need a pair of boots, as you can plainly see," answered the doctor, at the same time, holding up for the captain's inspection what, by a liberal stretch of the imagination, might once have been considered a very respectable boot, but which, by virtue of mile after mile of travel on foot, through bush and bracken, and over jagged rocks, had well-nigh lost all resemblance to the "thing of beauty" and of pride, it once had been. "Number nine will do." "Next, I want about twenty-five pounds of bacon and a sack of flour," and—"Oh, yes, I would like a can of baking powder and a modicum of salt," concluded the doctor.

The articles were promptly ordered brought from the commissary stores, and delivered without price or conditions.

Some days after, Doctor Flick, no longer afraid to shoot, captured an immense mountain grizzly, whose shaggy cuticle he presented to Capt. Russell, with his compliments,—not Bruin's compliments but the doctor's.

We will now go back and ascertain the fate of Dunlap and his trusty followers. As soon as the two deserters from their ranks had disappeared behind an intervening bluff in the Bad Lands, they, with some misgivings doubtless, as to the consequences, commenced their backward march towards the White Earth river, upon reaching which they turned up the stream in search of "Sawyer's trail," which the guide assured them was not far distant. The party had not proceeded more than a half mile when a bunch of horses was seen grazing on the river bottoms not more than a mile away. Bringing them into nearer view by the aid of a magnifying glass, they were discovered to be United States cavalry horses. Instantly realizing their peril, they quickly led their horses behind a convenient bluff, where a hurried consultation was held as to the best plan of escape from the soldiers, whose mission they felt convinced was expressly to capture them. "Now we are in for it," said the guide in a low voice. They really were in pretty close quarters, as the general topography of the country made it impossible for them to fall back or advance any distance from their position behind the bluff without coming directly into view. Hoping to discover some way out of their dilemma, the guide crept stealthily up to the edge of the bluff on his hands and feet, when he saw the troopers already mounted and about to march out on their trail of the day before, which they had just left in search of ''Sawyer's trail.''

It seemed certain that in half an hour the soldiers would trace them to their hiding-place, in view of which certainty they became intensely excited. ''Some of us will probably be captured, in any event, and all of us if we remain together,'' said the guide. ''We had better separate, take different directions, and hide ourselves as best we can until dark, when possibly some of us, under cover of the night, may effect our escape,'' he urged. Acting upon this advice, without loss of time the members of the ''hemmed in'' little party, with their respective belongings, scattered out, panic-stricken, in every direction—every man for himself.

Shankland, Berry Wright, and Timmish started off in the direction of the river, which they hoped to reach in time to hide themselves and animals among the timber and brush along its banks. Traveling on with their utmost speed through the friendly protection of the brush, not daring to take time to look back, thinking the soldiers might be right upon them, they fortunately soon found a hiding-place among the rocks of a deep canyon making out from the river, and admirably fitted by nature for such a purpose, where they remained until night safe from immediate capture at least. Before entering their ''rocky retreat'' they were joined by Porter and Forbes, who had followed almost directly upon their heels in their precipitous flight. When darkness at last spread over them its protecting wings they breathed more freely, and ventured out from their confined quarters among the rocks, in search of a more roomy spot, where they could spread their blankets for a much-needed rest and sleep, and thus forget for a time their dangerous environments. Thinking themselves quite safe from discovery, as their feet had left no prints on the hard rock leading to their position in the canyon, they decided to remain for a few days for recuperation, during which time they subsisted entirely upon uncooked food, not deeming it safe to build fires.

Becoming tired of the general monotony of life in the canyon, on the second morning, ere the dawn of the day, they led their horses out of their retreat and again took up their line of march towards the Black Hills, haunted by an ever-present fear of arrest by the military. The details of the march into the Hills need not be narrated at length. A brief outline, marked by a few of the principal incidents of the journey, being deemed sufficient.

The party soon came to an inviting little grove convenient to water, where they camped and remained for two days and three nights, taking frequent observations, meanwhile, from an adjacent hill, looking for government scouts. Upon one occasion they were rewarded by seeing two mounted men about a half-mile distant, which again threw them into a panic; fortunately, however, they were not discovered. "We talked in whispers, and took every precaution against discovery, and just waited for fate to decide our destiny," related my informant.

On the third day they resumed their march, and after traveling about twelve miles over a level prairie country, they came to the ever-dreaded Mauvaises Terres, where in one of the deep gorges they camped for the night, feeling, for once, secure from arrest—as they though neither man nor beast could often be tempted to enter such a desolate region. The next day they made their way through a long winding canyon, too narrow in places, to admit of passage, often being compelled to widen the same by the use of picks, and sometimes being obliged to unpack and carry their freight on their backs through the more difficult places, and finally, after ten mortal hours of toiling through its devious windings they emerged into a flat country where, finding a little water of very inferior quality, they camped for the night.

The next day they reached and crossed the Cheyenne river, then traveling on with light hearts, but very tired feet, keeping all the time a sharp lookout for scouts, they reached what they called Trout creek, near the foothills, July 4th, where they spent the night without shelter of any kind from the furious rain-storm which occurred during the night. They started from camp the next morning, drenched to the skin, but joyous in the bright anticipation that, before the setting of the sun, they would be safely in the Black Hills, and beyond all danger of pursuit from the rear. However, in consequence of a heavy storm, which prevailed throughout the day, they were compelled to take refuge in a deep gorge in the foot-hills near which they found their first gold, panning out as high as ten cents to the pan. Notwithstanding these encouraging prospects, owing to a scarcity of water and danger of capture, they decided not to drive their stakes at that point, but proceed further into the mountains.

The following day, July 6th, after traveling about fifteen or twenty miles, they found themselves among the mountain ranges. Apprehending now but little danger of capture, they deemed it safe to halt for a couple of days and prospect a little as they went. Accordingly on July 7th, Shankland, Berry, and Porter, went about six miles further into the mountains, looking for gold, returning to camp at night, with nothing but a mountain grouse to reward them for their day's labor—their first game in the Hills, which, being dressed, was impaled on the end of a pointed stick, cooked before a pitch pine fire, and eaten without salt for supper. The next day, July 5th, the same party mounted their horses and rode back to the gulch where the gold had been discovered, for the purpose of ascertaining whether water could be found which might be conducted by means of a ditch to the point prospected, in which they were wholly unsuccessful.

The trip, however, proved not altogether without compensation, as they had the satisfaction of killing a huge mountain grizzly, whose choice cuts furnished their camp with the luxury of bear's meat for a few days.

On July 9th, after partaking of a breakfast of "bear on slapjack," they moved on some eight or ten miles and halted at the junction of two small streams, where the day was spent in supplying their sadly depleted larders with the fish in which the stream abounded. Following up the southwestern branch of the stream, some nine miles over a rough, unbroken country, they came upon the deserted camp of their former guide (Dunlap), which seemed to have been vacated not more than three hours before. The names Valentine Dunlap and Oaks Texas were discovered written in pencil on a birch tree near the camp.

Following up Dunlap's trail until all trace of it was lost, then keeping on in a southerly direction for several miles, they again came into the trail of their quandom guide, whom they were exceedingly anxious to overtake, that they might learn something of the fate of the other members of the party. With this object in view, they hurried along on the fresh trail of their guide over several miles of heavily wooded country into an extensive park, with a stream of water running through its center (Custer's Park). Ever watchful were they for some evidence of the presence of the military, who, if in the country, they suspected might be encamped not many miles from the base of Harney's Peak. For the purpose of reconnoitering the vicinity, Shankland and Porter mounted their horses and rode out to an elevated point, about two miles from camp, from where they discovered a large number of horses and mules and four men herding them. "We could hear the men chopping wood in their camp and also hear the dogs barking. We did not know what party it was, but thought it might be Jenny's military escort. Our plan was to steal quietly into the vicinity of the camp, and wait for an opportunity to interview some one happening to be out alone," related my informant, Mr. Shankland. Early the following morning, before the sun had tipped the lofty peaks, Shankland and Berry started out on foot to locate the military camp which they felt assured was not far away, soon coming to a point where the whole camp stood out in bold relief, before they were aware of its immediate vicinity. Falling back out of sight, they counseled together as to the best method of procedure, finally agreeing to climb up behind a large cliff of rocks, that loomed up not more than two hundred yards from the center of the camp, from where much that was said could be distinctly heard and understood, "We might have been taken for a couple of representatives of the Lo family, contemplating a raid upon the camp," said Mr. Shankland.

We will now leave the vigilant men behind the cliffs overlooking the camp of Col. Dodge's command on French creek, and go back along the line to the mouth of Antelope creek, where, nearly three weeks since we left

THE MAJOR PART OF THE EXPEDITION

After the small party of fourteen men left the expedition for the Black Hills on the morning of June 23d, the train at once pulled out westward until reaching what is called the "Sidney Cut-off," where another separation took place. From this point some of the party turned their faces towards the Black Hills, while the majority took up their line of march to Sidney, Nebraska, whence they scattered where they listed.

Among those who went towards the Hills from the Sidney Cut-off was Judge Rinehart, now of Lead City. No doubt many of the expeditions embarking for the Black Hills in 1875 may have had an equally trying if not altogether similar experience.

CHAPTER XIII

HOW SOME OF THE PIONEERS
FOOLED UNCLE SAM

The following account of how Joe Reynolds and his two companions bribed the government employees at old Fort Laramie to smuggle them across the swollen Platte on the government ferry boat, will illustrate some of the cunningly devised artifices practiced by gold-seeking adventurers to elude the watchfulness of Uncle Sam's soldiers at that frontier post in 1875, and will also show what imperfect knowledge some of them had of the geography of the Black Hills.

It was early in May, 1875, very soon after the removal of the Collins and Russell party from the stockade that Joseph Reynolds, Jas. Corneille, and Billy Jacobs, of Georgetown, Colorado, moved by an inspiration, suddenly made up their minds to go to the Black Hills. It did not take them long to put themselves in light marching order, for within forty-eight hours after their hasty decision they were equipped with good saddle horses, pack animals, guns, and provisions for sixty days, and on their way to the New Eldorado. Included in their outfit was a bottle of "antidote" for sudden colds, snake bites, and kindred maladies, which was to be used solely for medicinal purposes.

On reaching Fort Laramie, they found the Platte river swollen away out of its banks, and more than two hundred other Black Hills adventurers encamped near by, waiting for the river to get down to low water-mark, so that they might steal across under cover of night, away from the military reservation into the Sioux territory. Finding further progress barred for the time being, the trio decided after studying the situation, to leave their stock of supplies at the fort in charge of one of their number, while the other two made a flying trip to the Hills, with rations for ten days, to examine their resources, the result of which was to determine their future course. But how to get across the turbulent river was yet an unsolved problem.

In the belief that every man has his price, they decided finally to offer a bribe to the wagonmaster of a government train, with whom they had fallen in on their way from Cheyenne to Fort Laramie, who was about to board the ferry with a load of Indian supplies for Red Cloud Agency, to take them across the river as a part of his outfit. So Joe, as spokesman of the party, approached the wagon-master, and after a short preliminary talk leading up to the delicate proposition he purposed making, laid bare his plans. He told him he would give him ten round dollars to slip his little party across the river with his load of Indian freight, and explained how it could be done without detection.

As the plan outlined by Joe seemed both feasible and safe, the wagon-master, after a little apparent hesitancy, said: "All right, I'll do it; make your arrangements and we'll drive onto the boat."

Following closely along the lines dictated by Joe, they were soon taken across the river without exciting any suspicion. While *in transit*, Corneile (sic), the custodian of the flask, bethought him that, inasmuch as they would want to recross the ferry in the near future, it would be the part of wisdom to cultivate the freindship of the ferryman. So, pulling the flask from his pocket, and holding it temptingly towards him, said, blandly, "Won't you take something?" "Well, yes, I don't care if I do," responded the ferryman with alacrity,—and he did.

After traveling about twenty miles with the train, they diverged to the north—the trainmaster having told them that by keeping due north he thought they would strike French creek. So north they went, striking the Hills somewhere on their western limits on May 30th, 1875. Continuing in the same direction, they made a complete "arc of a circle" around the western and northern limits of the Hills, climbing to the summit of each prominent point to take their bearings, and, if possible, locate French creek.

It is needless to delay the narrative, by giving the details of their erratic wanderings. Let it suffice to state that they climbed successively, Inyan Kara, Devil's Tower, Bear Lodge Peak—where, while waiting for a dense fog to clear away, they did some prospecting with fairly encouraging results—then through Spearfish valley and south to Custer's Peak, and finally, on the 15th day of June, they climbed to the bald summit of Harney's Peak, where for the first time they located French creek which they reached on the same day in a sorry condition.

They had been on the march for twenty days, without having seen a white man, ten of which they had subsisted solely on venison straight, without salt. The next day, while prospecting in a shallow tunnel which had been dug by the stockade boys, they heard the sound of human voices, which they feared might belong to Indians; but soon distinguishing the accents of their own beloved vernacular, they hastily emerged from the tunnel to meet and greet their white brothers, one of whom proved to be A. D. Trask, now of Pactola, Pennington County. No sooner was the hearty interchange of greetings over than Reynolds asked Trask how much "grub" he had in his party. "Grub!" answered Trask, "well, we have a small jar of salt that I found cached under one of the cabins in the stockade which has been our main diet for the past twenty-four hours." Now, we all know that salt as a condiment is all right, but very unsatisfactory as a steady diet. "Have you more supplies than you really need?" inquired Trask of Reynolds. "More than we really need! Why, man alive, we haven't had a morsel to eat for ten days but venison, and venison without salt at that," answered Reynolds. "We have plenty of that and to spare," added Reynolds, cheerfully; "and as you have the salt, we shall fare pretty well." By the way, that little jar of salt is the only single article cached by the stockade party that has come to the writer's knowledge.

Within the next two days quite a number put in an appearance at the stockade, when a miners' meeting was called, for the purpose of organizing a mining district on French creek. The meeting, at which sixteen men were present, was held in the open, a short distance above where Custer City now stands. Officers were chosen, a district organized, rules and regulations to govern the same were passed and a recorder duly elected, but, as the minutes of the meeting have been lost, it is impossible to give details of its proceedings. It is related, however, that an exceedingly warm discussion was had, relative to the rule establishing the size of placer claims, the minority insisting upon twenty acres, the majority favoring 300 feet in length along the gulch, from rim to rim, which was the rule established. This is believed to be the first mining district ever organized in the Black Hills, and A. D. Trask, of Pactola, the first recorder chosen.

The morning after the meeting, the two men, having become convinced that the Black Hills was a pretty good country, and also that a more varied diet would prove conducive to health, mounted their horses and hied them away to their base of supplies at Fort Laramie. On their appearance at the ferry landing, the ferryman, recognizing them, seemed much surprised at the puzzling situation, which they soon made clear by confessing that they had been to the Black Hills, and that their joining the train was merely a bit of strategy. They then and there entered into a conspiracy with the ferryman, by which he was to take them across the river in three days for a consideration of ten dollars. According to the plan they were to come to the landing at 11 o'clock p.m. of the third day and scratch on the canvas at the back of his tent, when he was to slip quietly out and shove them with their outfits across. The Platte river was not yet fordable and the 200 or more gold-hunters were still awaiting near its banks.

As it neared the eleventh watch of the night of the third day, Reynolds, Corneile (sic), and Jacobs, led their horses away from camp and made a circuit around the outer limits of the post, to avoid the sentinels who were placed at intervals to guard the garrison against external savage attack, or internal conspiracy. Stealthily and noiselessly they were picking their way towards the ferry landing without the clatter of a hoof,—the horses seeming to appreciate the necessity for caution, when like a thunderbolt from a cloudless sky, they were startled nearly out of their boots, by the prolonged cry of "Eleven o'clock and all is well," but a few yards away from them. They came to a dead halt, paralyzed, scarcely daring to breathe. The darkness favored them, for the watchman passed around on his beat, so near that with an outstretched arm they could have almost touched him, but he did not discover them. As soon as the sound of his footsteps died away they hurried to the landing, led their horses over the approach, whose shifting sands gave back no sound, onto the ferry.

The signal was given but not a word was spoken. The ferryman came quietly out, unlocked the ferry, shoved them across and received his price.

They went again north to Bear Lodge Peak, where they prospected for a short time, thence to French creek, where they remained prospecting for placer and quartz until ordered out by Gen. Crook, in August of that year. Mr. Reynolds, with commendable enterprise, resolved not to leave the Hills, without taking with him something upon which to base an estimate of their mineral richness, so during the five days grace allowed the miners in which to make necessary arrangements to leave the Hills, he had 2,250 pounds of quartz mined from a ledge, situated about three and one-half miles above Custer City, then employed the Cast Brothers, who had a wagon and team, to transport the same to Cheyenne, paying them therefor two cents per pound, or $45 for the load. On reaching Cheyenne he sampled the ore and sent it to Georgetown, Colorado, to be tested. According to certificates of assay, the highest grade samples yielded seventeen dollars of gold per ton of quartz. That was the first ton of quartz of any kind, transported out of the Black Hills for treatment.

Robert Florman, who had prior to his coming to the Black Hills spent many years of his active life in a number of the most prominent mining regions of the United States, notably Colorado, Montana and New Mexico, in which he succeeded by shrewdness and unflagging energy in realizing several handsome fortunes, only to be lost in other less fortunate mining speculations, made his advent on French creek on July 14th, 1875. After a short stay on that stream, he went north to Spring creek, near the present site of Hill City, where he prospected quite extensively for placer gold, and also for gold in quartz during the summer of 1875, leaving the Hills late in the fall of that year. Returning to the northern Hills with his family in the early spring of 1876, he was fortunate in securing by purchase a claim on the famous "Deadwood Gulch," where he remained as long as the working of his claim proved profitable.

Mr. Florman afterwards became engaged in several other mining enterprises throughout the Hills, becoming in 1885 or 1886 a resident of Rapid City, to which he has unreservedly pinned his faith to the present time. He erected a number of the finest, most substantial, as well as the most expensive business blocks in Rapid City, and in doing this he staked his all upon the "hazard of a die," and lost. Mr. Florman by his thorough and extended knowledge of mines and mining and sagacity will doubtless yet wrest a fortune from the wonderful mineral resources of our country. What Mr. Florman does not know about ores of various kinds is hardly worth knowing.

As apropos to the above, I will here relate a brief story, in which is interwoven a sad episode, of the journey of Mr. and Mrs. Florman with their three little children from Cheyenne to the Black Hills in the spring of 1876, which forcibly illustrates the pluck, the nerve, the real heroism of one of the women pioneers of the Black Hills. As all early pioneers traveling over that route have good reason to remember, every step of the journey after leaving the protection of Fort Laramie was then menaced by the most deadly peril, yet in the face of this, almost alone most of the way, every breeze wafting back to them reports of the terrible Indian atrocities being perpetrated farther on towards the Hills, they with their helpless little children pushed resolutely onward to their destination.

Women of less courage and determination could scarcely have borne the intense mental and physical strain of such a journey under like circumstances.

Mr. Florman and family, with six men, arrived at the stage station, on the Cheyenne river, on or about April 24th, 1876, where they found encamped a party of about forty emigrants, including a number of women, in the most intense excitement and alarm. Here they also found ample evidence that the red demons had been putting in their murderous work. The four horses belonging to the Cheyenne and Custer Stage Company had just arrived at the station, bringing in the four men of Col. Brown's party, who had been attacked and dangerously wounded,—one fatally,—only a few miles up Red Canyon.

On that same evening, the report of the massacre of the Metz party was brought into the station, which, of course, greatly increased the alarm of the already panic-striken emigrants. Many,—especially those with families, urged that the party return at once to Fort Laramie, nearly 200 miles away.

Mr. Florman, however, opposed such a movement, insisting that the danger of returning to the post would be greater than that of the short march on to Custer, and proposed organizing a party for their mutual safety, that would be bound to stand by each other through evil as well as good report, until reaching Custer City. An organization, consisting of thirty-nine men, was soon effected, the members of which were Jules Coffee of Laramie, with fifteen cowboys who had just arrived at the station; the incoming stage with its ten male passengers; one Henry Feuerstein, with six men, and Mr. Florman's party of eleven, which included Mrs. Florman and their three children. This party started at 7 o'clock on the following morning, with their armor buckled on for Custer,—keeping their guns well in hand and their eyes on the alert for an ambushed foe. All along the trail through the Red Canyon, at intervals, they discovered shocking evidences of bloody deeds. They first came to the point where Brown's party had been attacked, the scene indicating that there had been a fierce conflict.

The stage was found lying in a ravine, riddled with bullets, and besmeared with the blood of the victims; their belongings, torn and hacked to pieces, lay scattered along and about the trail. Traveling about two miles further up the Canyon, they came upon the body of Mrs. Metz,—shot through the heart—who seemed to have been the last one of the party killed, as she had, apparently, run away from the scene of the first attack. Half a mile further on was found the body of the driver, and about a half mile still further on lay Mr. Metz, close to the wagon—shot through the head, and several times through the body. The colored woman was not found by the Florman party.

What was to be done? The bodies could not longer be left there as food for the vultures and coyotes.

Here Mrs. Florman exhibited the nerve, the spirit of self-sacrifice, that stamps her as a true heroine. Despite the probability that the deadly savages might be hiding in ambush, not far away; despite the fact that the poor mutilated bodies had lain for many hours uncared for, Mrs. Florman, with the courage of the Spartan women of old, proceeded at once to aid in preparing the dead—as far as the limitations would permit, for decent Christian burial. With gentle, tender hands, she helped to straighten out and compose the distorted members of the murdered woman; arrayed the body in the best garments that could be found among the scattered contents of the rifled trunks; then, after washing the face and brushing back the disheveled hair with caressing touch, her noble, self-imposed task was finished.

Brave woman! May thy crown be set with precious jewels, whose brilliancy time can never mar!

The remains were then placed in a wagon, that had been brought for the purpose, and sent back, under escort, to the Cheyenne stage station for temporary burial.

This grewsome duty being performed, the stage passengers, apparently forgetting their compact, mounted the stage and started off a rapid pace towards Custer, but were speedily brought to a dead halt by the loud peremptory cry of, "Halt! or you are dead men." Looking back they saw Mr. Florman, with gun in hand, pointed directly at them, and believing from the dangerous gleam in his eye that he meant business, they prudently halted. One of the passengers said afterwards: "I tell you, boys, Mr. Florman looked as though he really meant to shoot." They excused their course by saying that they considered the real danger of the journey past. Mr. Florman, however, thought otherwise,—as any one familiar with the habits of the Indians would have thought. He knew that the party was liable, at any moment, to be pounced upon, from behind some projecting headland or point of rocks, by the skulking savages. On that same evening they arrived at Pleasant Valley, where they found a large freight outfit, which gave them a feeling of comparative security for the night. The next morning they pulled out for Custer, where they arrived at noon, safely within the lines of the city guards—"the Custer minute men."

John W. Allen, another representative miner, came to the Black Hills in the early part of July, 1875. After prospecting at different points on French and Spring creeks—working for a time, it is stated, with good results on what is known as "Stand Off Bar," on the last named stream, he joined the Jenny Exploring Expedition, with which he remained during his stay in the Hills, greatly aiding it, by his extensive mining knowledge, in ascertaining their mineral resources. He was a member of the board of trustees of the first township organization of Custer; also in the early spring of 1876 aided in the township organization of Rapid City, in which he had the most unbounded faith. So great was his confidence in the future of the "Gate City," the "Denver" of the Black Hills, that he induced his less sanguine brother, Jas. W. Allen, to leave a lucrative business in Cheyenne and come and get possession of as many town lots in the future Denver as was possible. Jas. W. Allen, however, took but little stock in the prospective Denver, declaring, much to the disgust of his far-sighted brother, that he would not accept as a gift the whole town-site proposition.

John W. Allen later went to Deadwood, where in company with other parties, he engaged in extensive placer mining. He, jointly with Col. Daniel Thompson, became the owner of 42,000 feet of the deepest gravel beds on that gulch, to operate which they constructed several hundred feet of bed-rock flume with all the necessary protective appliances against floods. Notwithstanding those expensive appliances, however, the terribly destructive flood of 1883 either washed away or buried under heaps of debris their almost entire work. Later Mr. Allen went to the Alaskan gold fields, and somewhere among the icy glaciers he to-day lies buried.

A familiar figure to the early settlers of the Hills, especially of Custer, was Tom Hooper. He was one of the seven men who were permitted to remain in the Black Hills when the hundreds of miners were ordered out by Gen. Crook in August, 1875. Aided by a detachment of United States soldiers, Mr. Hooper made the first survey of the Custer town-site, in August of that year, using a small pocket compass and a couple of picket ropes for the purpose, making the plat of the site on a twelve-inch square piece of birch bark stripped from a tree on French creek, which plat has unfortunately been lost. In March, 1876, when the town was organized into a city, the people of the Black Hills, in convention assembled, established a Black Hills Superior Court, of which Tom Hooper was elected judge—a court whose jurisdiction was to be co-extensive with the entire Black Hills. In short Tom Hooper was closely identified with all the early movements, looking to the welfare and advancement of the pioneer town of the Black Hills, in which he was the first to practice the profession of law. He is now a prominent attorney at law in Sundance, Wyoming.

CHAPTER XIV

FIRST DISCOVERY OF PLACER GOLD IN THE BLACK HILLS

It appears from trustworthy information, that the first exploration of that portion of the northern Hills, bordering on Whitewood creek, was made by Frank Bryant and party in August, 1875. It is quite generally known that the government expedition, under Professor Jenny, although penetrating and prospecting the country as far to the northward as Bear Butte creek and other portions of the Hills to the northwest, made no explorations along Deadwood and Whitewood creeks, and the rich placer deposits, later found in the gulches of those streams, were to that expedition an entirely unknown quantity.

It seems beyond reasonable doubt, therefore, that Bryant and his little party of gold hunters, uncovered with pick and shovel, and washed out the first gold taken from Whitewood and lower Deadwood gulches.

Perhaps there are not many of our early pioneers who have had a more checkered experience, in all that goes to make up a miner's life with its vicissitudes, than Frank Bryant, and an account of some of his early adventures may prove of interest to those who care for pioneer history.

Frank Bryant, with a party of six others, viz.: John Pearson, Thos. Moon, Richard Lowe, James Peierman, Samuel Blodgett, and George Hauser, seven in all, arrived in the Hills, from some Missouri river point, in August, 1875, making their first camp at Spring Valley. On their way to the northern Hills,—their objective point, the party did its first prospecting on a small tributary of Elk creek, with unpromising results.

Frank Bryant was the possessor of a small map, furnished him before starting by Tom Labarge, Charley De Gray and Lephiere Narcouter, old employees of the American Fur Company, which served the party as a guide to their objective point.

The second place prospected by the Bryant party was at the mouth of Spruce gulch, on what was called on their map the Chaw-Skaw-Skaw-Walkapalla (afterwards named Whitewood creek), a beautiful stream of clear water, running then about 200 miners' inches, where was found good prospect on the surface gravel. Fortunately, having a saw in their outfit, they whipped out enough lumber to construct eight boxes, twelve feet long each, and commenced sluicing, but not being wholly satisfied with the results of the experiment, they soon began to look around for richer "diggings." This party built at the mouth of Spruce gulch, the first cabin in the northern Hills.

One of the party, Sam Blodgett, who had, while hunting, come upon a gulch, which to him looked favorable, after reporting the same to the other members of the party, returned to the gulch with John Pearson, to see what could be found, and the first dirt panned by them was taken from the point of the bar, on which now stands the Deadwood High School building. Other bars, for a distance of 300 or 400 yards up the creek, were also prospected, but as nothing encouraging was found, no locations were made. The places last prospected were on what was later called "Deadwood Gulch." This, as far as known, was the first prospecting done on Deadwood gulch.

About the middle of September the party left their works on the Whitewood, on a fruitless search for richer diggings. Turning their faces towards Terry Peak, they prospected on the way, Nevada and White Tail gulches (then unnamed), without finding pay gravel; then crossing to the opposite side of the peak, they prospected the Spearfish and its tributaries with similar results; they then proceeded down the Spearfish valley to the vicinity of Spearfish Buttes where they went into camp. On climbing the Butte 500 or 600 feet one of the party discovered, about three miles farther down the valley, a large cluster of tents which proved to be Col. Dodge's camp. Not wishing to be captured by the soldiers, of which there was not the slightest danger from that source, as Col. Dodge's command was not looking for miners, they secreted their camp until night when they pulled out under the cover of darkness for Sand creek, where they arrived on the morning of the next day. Here they hunted and jerked venison for a couple of days, when the little party divided up and went their respective ways.

Moon and Lowe followed Col. Dodge around to Bear Butte, whence they made their way back to the Missouri river for home, thoroughly disgusted with the Black Hills. Blodgett and Hauser joined the soldiers at Custer, and shortly after left for Fort Laramie. Bryant and Pearson went to Black Buttes, thence southeasterly to the head of Spring and Slate creeks, but finding no satisfying prospects they concluded to return to their abandoned works on the romantic Chaw-Skaw-Skaw-Walkapalla. On their way back they almost ran into the arms of a detachment of United States troops, only escaping arrest by hurriedly leading their sure-footed animals up among the shelving rocks of a precipitous ledge. When the shadows began to fall they ventured out of their hiding-place and slipped into the edge of the soldiers' camp, and had a confidential talk with a teamster, named Robinson—afterwards, one of the locators of the Big Missouri mine at Lead—who advised them to go to Fort Laramie and join Gen. Crook's command about to start for the Big Horn. The

Black Hills having been stripped of their charms, the two weary gold-hunters accepted Robinson's advice, and bright and early the next morning were on their way out to join Gen. Crook for the Big Horn. It is needless to state that Pearson was as glad as though he had found a gold nugget to get away from the Black Hills, and it is surmised that Bryant shed no copious tears at leaving.

On their way out they had an exciting and somewhat amusing adventure which came near getting them into serious trouble, and illustrates "how great a matter a little fire kindleth." On the second day of their journey outward, they came upon a water-hole, about ten feet in diameter and two feet deep, the rim of which was cut up with the tracks of wild animals, as if large herds of sheep and cattle had watered there, and at the time of their arrival there were thousands of wild bees on the spot, some drinking on the edge of the pool, others whirling and buzzing around overhead. It is reasonable to presume that there were some lively jigs danced around that water-hole among the angry bees for a while. Well, anyone who has ever been in a hornets' nest can appreciate the situation.

At a critical juncture, Pearson conceived the unhappy thought of setting fire to the grass, as a means of putting an end to the vicious onslaught of the bees. He started the fire, and as the wind was blowing a small gale at the time, and the grass was as dry as powder, it burned like a flash and spread over the prairie with the speed of a race horse, and the two men had to fight like Trojans to save their animals and packs from destruction. Finding it impossible to put out the fire they had so thoughtlessly kindled, and also fearing that the smoke, which could be seen for a long distance, might attract the notice of the Indians, they hurried away from the scene of conflagration as rapidly as their limitation would permit.

On the fourth day outward they camped at the old Government Farm, where they met Frank Norton, Ed. Davis, and Frank Smith on their way to the Black Hills, with whom they exchanged jerked venison for the staff of life (bread),—a glad exchange, as they had been subsisting for several weeks on "jerk" straight. On the Platte river they met Ed. Murphy, who afterwards made a stake on "Deadwood" gulch and later out of the Yellow creek mines. Ed. was hospitably entertained by the "boys," who treated him to some venison of their own "jerking," which he pronounced very fine. The next day they visited the Fort, and found much to their disappointment that Gen. Crook was not going to the Big Horn.

To make a long story short, they were soon on their way back to the Black Hills, Pearson going by wagon to the southern Hills, and Bryant, with W. H. Coder, William Cudney and two other men with whom he had become acquainted at Laramie, going directly to the northern Hills, and on the 8th day of November, 1875, Bryant was again camped on Whitewood creek, occupying the cabin built in August of the same year. On the same evening, November 8th, 1875, a notice was posted on a tree, about fifty feet east of the cabin, claiming—"by virtue of discovery—300 feet below the notice, and 600 feet below Discovery Claim and 300 feet above Discovery Claim for mining purposes.

    (Signed)   FRANK BRYANT,
                HENRY CODER,
          WILLIAM CUDNEY."

 J. B. Pearson later went to the northern Hills with the Lardner party, and was among the first locaters on Deadwood gulch, where he continued placer mining until some time in 1876, when, it is alleged, he commenced the erection of the second stamp mill in that vicinity, which was put in operation in April, 1877, operating for the most part on ore from the Black Tail mine, which he had located. He operated his twenty stamp mill for about three years, when he disposed of his property and prospected for a time in the southern Hills. In 1883 he became engineer of the De Smet mill at Central City. Mr. Pearson located what was known as the Giant and Old Abe mines, now the property of the Homestake Company, on December 11th, 1875. These are believed to be the earliest quartz mines located in the Hills.

THE FIRST LOCATORS ON DEADWOOD GULCH

 During the summer of 1875, William Lardner, who has the distinction of being among the first locators and one of the organizers of the first mining district, established on the great "bonanza gulch," with a small party of gold-seekers and a well-equipped little pack train, arrived in the Black Hills from Cheyenne, Wyoming. Soon after their arrival in the Hills they made their way to the north, in quest of the shining metal,—exploring as they went some of the streams and their tributaries, having their source in the Harney Peak region, and finally in early October pitched their tents on Little Rapid creek, a short distance above its mouth, near the point known as "Ross' Bar."

WM. LARDNER
One of the party making first locations on the famous "Deadwood Gulch" in November, 1875

One day, during their stay on that stream, two men, short of provisions,—a very common occurrence in those days,—arrived at their camp and reported that favorable indications of placer deposits had been encountered on a stream in the northern Hills. Those two men were J. B. Pearson and Dan Muskle, the latter of whom, it is inferred, had penetrated the Hills to Deadwood gulch and discovered good indications of the existence of placer gold, but becoming short of supplies, was forced to leave without making any location. How, when, and where Muskle fell in with J. B. Pearson is not understood, as the latter not many days before had parted with Frank Bryant at Fort Laramie. At any rate they came to the camp of the Lardner party together, and were supplied with provisions, when the whole party pulled up stakes and started for the northern Hills.

The entire party was composed of Wm. Lardner, Ed. McKay, Joe Englesby, Jas. Hicks, Wm. Gay, Alfred Gay, J. B. Pearson, Dan Muskle, and—Haggard,—nine in all. They lost no time in loading their pack-horses with blankets, picks, shovels, gold pans, and the necessary supplies, of which they had an abundance, caching the balance, for which they afterwards returned, when the party went northward across the north fork of Little Rapid; the headwaters of Whitewood, White Tail, and Little Spearfish creeks, through snow knee-deep, then over the rough mountains, through the Bald Mountain region to the new diggings on Deadwood gulch, where, a little below the mouth of Blacktail, "Discovery" claim was located in November, 1875. This was doubtless the first location made on the great bonanza gulch.

All of the original locations made by this party were, it appears, made above "Discovery"—No. 9 falling to the lot of Wm. Lardner and No. 4 above to Wm. Gay. As if by the irony of fate none of the fabulously rich claims, located a few weeks later below "Discovery" were secured by those first locators on Deadwood gulch. Seemingly with pernicious intent, those industrious little animals, the beavers, had constructed a dam across the stream, on what proved to be one of the richest claims on the gulch, thus backing up the waters of the creek, forming a veritable little lagoon across the narrow valley from hill to hill.

Owing to this circumstance, and the further fact that the gulch below was covered with a dense growth of underbrush, and strewn with a bewildering confusion of dead timbers, lying across each other at every known or conceivable angle, the outlook for prospecting was not considered inviting.

At a miners' meeting held in December, a mining district was organized, and appropriately named the "Lost Mining District"—the first organization of the kind in the northern Hills. Wm. Lardner was chosen recorder of the district, and by the rules established to govern the same, was vested with the right to charge a fee of $1.50 per claim for recording locations.

Of that little group of pioneers, who so eagerly and hopefully pushed their way through the deep snow to Deadwood gulch twenty-three years ago, Wm. Lardner alone remains in the Black Hills. All the other members of the party, excepting McKay, are reported dead. The tragic fate of one of the number, Wm. Gay, is doubtless well known to most of those who knew him in the early days. Wm. Gay was sentenced and hung in 1896 for shooting and killing an officer of the law in Montana.

Poor fellow, he did not meet his fate with the fearlessness and daring characteristic of him. When brought face to face with his awful doom, he who had braved the innumerable dangers of years of frontier life, and had, perchance, many a time in his checkered career looked into the muzzle of a gun aimed at his heart without flinching, cowered and cringed at the foot of the gallows in the most pitiable and abject terror.

About three weeks later, or towards the last of December, 1875, Mr. Lardner returned with pack horses to Little Rapid creek for the cached property, and reported the new rich discovery to a small party of prospectors on Castle creek, who the following day packed their tools and other belongings, and followed on his trail to Deadwood gulch.

This second party, composed of J. J. Williams, W. H. Babcock, Eugene Smith, and Jackson, arrived on Deadwood gulch about the 1st of January, 1876, all of whom located claims below "Discovery." It is asserted that Jackson located No. 1 below and afterward sold his claim to Hildebrand and Harding, experienced miners from Montana. J. J. Williams located No. 22 below Discovery, from which in a period of three months he washed out $27,000 in gold dust. He afterward sold his claim on Deadwood, and located No. 14 above Discovery on Whitewood creek from which he realized $35,000 of the precious metal, the reward of his indomitable perseverance. Mr. Williams helped lay out and found the city of Deadwood, of which for more than two decades he has been a resident, and where he is now engaged in the honorable avocation of a worker in wood.

The next to find their way to Deadwood gulch, were Wade Porter and Oscar Cline, about the middle of January, 1876. Porter had altogether a remarkable experience, as will be shown by the following brief recapitulation of his early career in the Black Hills. It will, perhaps, be remembered that he was one of the first party to reach French creek in 1875, and one of those of the party who escaped capture by the military squad dispatched to summarily remove them from the Hills. Hearing of the exodus of the miners in August, he soon after voluntarily left the Hills for Fort Laramie, where after a few days stay he joined a party of about thirty men fitted out with a large pack train, led by one Mallory, and started for Iron creek in the northern Hills, where Mallory reported having found rich diggings. Owing to a scarcity of water for sluicing purposes in that region, Porter with several others left Iron creek and went to Castle creek where he had formerly prospected. He had not been there long before the whole party was rounded up by a squad of Capt. Pollock's troopers, taken to Custer and placed in the "guard pen," where they were kept for several days, when they were taken to Cheyenne, tried before a United States commissioner, and released. Soon after their release a number of the party, including Porter, equipped themselves and again started for the northwestern Hills, by a circuitous route to avoid the soldiers. After prospecting a few weeks on Sand and Bear creeks, Porter and Cline decided to return to the gold diggings on Castle creek, and it was on this trip that they struck the trail of the Lardner party, on the Little Spearfish, which led them to Deadwood gulch, where they located claims in January, 1876.

One of the first of the Black Hills pioneers to catch the gold infection that began to spread over the land in the spring of 1876 was V. P. Shoun, whose imposing presence and distinctive personality is, doubtless, well-remembered by the early settlers of the Hills. Mr. Shoun was one of the 176 members of Gordon's unfortunate expedition, whose goods and chattels were seized and burned by military authority, while en route to the Black Hills in the spring of 1875. Soon after the release of the captured party, on the east bank of the Big Muddy, opposite Yankton, Mr. Shoun re-equipped and was again making his solitary way across the black prairies—ever on the alert for the "blue coats,"—for the Black Hills. At Spotted Tail Agency, where he tarried for a while to recuperate, he organized a small party of seven men, equipped with as many Sharp's rifles, 2,000 rounds of ammunition, twelve pack ponies, and four saddle horses, and thus reinforced, resumed his journey to the Hills about October 1st, 1875.

To guard against surprise by the soldiers, who were then vigilantly watching the approaches to the Hills, two of the party were kept on duty both day and night as scouts. When near Buffalo Gap, two troops of soldiers were seen by the scouts, who soon communicated the alarming intelligence to the other members who, by hiding behind a protecting hill, escaped discovery. Mr. Shoun had pretty good reason for wanting to give the United States soldiers a wide berth, for had he not seen them only a few months before apply the match that caused all his belongings, as well as those of his fellow-travelers, including clothing, supplies and much of their bedding, go up in smoke?

On reaching Custer, the party was taken in charge by D. T. Snively, and by him conducted to the protecting shelter of the stockade, then occupied by Sam Shankland and Robert Kenyon, who had been permitted to remain in the Hills by Gen. Crook, to look after the interests of the miners, a man named Murphy and two other men. In order to avoid a collision with Major Pollock's soldiers, Mr. Shoun secured the services and connivance of Bob Kenyon, who had become familiar with the topography of the Hills, to pilot them around the dreaded "blue coats," and put them on the trail for the north. By the courtesy of Bob, they were soon on their way towards Harney's Peak, where they hoped to find a safe asylum among the fastnesses, for a time at least.

On the 25th of October, the party selected a camping ground amid the dark, deep defiles of the Harney Peak range, where they unloaded their pack ponies, and stored their supplies among the shelving granite rocks, then led the ponies, relieved of their burdens, to an open park about ten miles distant, to graze. The spot selected for a camping ground must have been an ideal hiding-place, judging from Mr. Shoun's own standpoint, of which he says, using his exact diction: "We camped in such a place at the foot of Harney's Peak, that the devil himself could not have found us." Later Mr. Shoun went north to Deadwood gulch, and was one of the early claim owners and workers on that historic gulch.

Owing to the strict military espionage maintained along the lines to the Hills, in the spring of 1875, it had been found a losing venture to attempt the transportation of provisions in any considerable quantities, hence those coming to the Hills later were outfitted for the most part with pack animals carrying supplies for only a limited period, some for sixty, some for thirty days, and strangely enough a few, trusting to kind Providence for the future, with a little more than enough to last them to the gold fields, consequently having no base of supplies, miners and prospectors were frequently reduced to uncomfortable straits for something to eat.

THE FIRST TO BRING MERCHANDISE TO THE BLACK HILLS

Among the first to bring merchandise to the Black Hills to supply this demand of the miners and prospectors, was H. B. Young, then of the firm of Cuthbertson & Young, of Cheyenne, Wyoming. In early November, 1875, Mr. Young arrived in the Hills from Cheyenne, in charge of several loads of goods for the firm of which he was a member, making Hill City, then a mining camp of considerable importance, his base of commerical operations during the winter of 1875-6. Early in May, 1876, taking the current at its flood, he transferred his headquarters from Hill City to Deadwood, where he carried on an extensive jobbing trade with the retail dealers of Deadwood and other mining camps for the firm of Cuthbertson & Young, which was among the first to engage in wholesale commerical transactions in the Black Hills.

Later Mr. Young turned his attention to mining operations, his first venture being the purchase of 100 feet of the Homestake mine from Alex. Engh and Henry Harney, who together owned a one-half interest in the mine, the purchase price being three hundred dollars.

In the fall of 1877, Mr. Young sold his fractional interest in the mine to a representative of the Homestake Company for the handsome sum of $10,000, or at the rate of $150,000 for the whole mine. During the time between the purchase and sale, Mr. Young had made extensive developments of his fraction, taking out large quantities of ore for treatment, thereby greatly enhancing the selling value of his property.

Late in the fall of 1877, the firm of Cuthbertson & Young secured from the Homestake Company the contract for the transportation of the Homestake eighty stamp mill; the hoisting machinery and other appurtenances of the plant, from Cheyenne, Wyoming, to the Homestake mine, at the rate of six cents per pound, realizing therefrom the sum of $33,000, which may appear to those not considering the time, distance, and difficulties involved, a large sum. The tranportation of 275 tons of unwieldy machinery 250 miles in the depth of winter, over a comparatively untraveled country, handicapped with the frequent necessity of repairing roads, building bridges, etc., was no small undertaking.

A part of the Homestake machinery was carried to the Hills by an ox freight train, owned by A. J. Parshall of Cheyenne, via Red Cloud and Crook City. When the outfit reached the vicinity of the latter point on the route, it was caught and locked for many days in the fatal embrace of the memorable snowfall of March, 1878, when every bovine—save nine, of the 100 head of cattle, perished from exposure and starvation.

Who of the early residents of the Hills will not remember the great snowstorm beginning March 6th, 1878? I said snowstorm, but, as a matter of fact, there was no storm about it. There was no wind, no, not even a gentle zephyr to fan the feathery flakes into uneven billows as they fell. Thick and fast, however, they dropped fluttering down, straight from the clouds to earth, until its whole face was covered with a foot,—two feet,—three feet,—four feet, on a deed level, of the "beautiful." The unprecedented snowfall finally came to an end,—as all things will, but not before grave fears were entertained that the Black Hills was doomed to be irrecoverably snowed under. It has been said that every misfortune has its compensating features. Be that as it may, the deep snow of 1878 proved a veritable Klondike to the idle men and boys about Deadwood, as its business men were freely paying one dollar per hour to men for shoveling the snow from the roofs of their buildings, that were giving way under immense pressure.

Conspicuous among the pioneers of 1875 was John R. Brennan, who, by unyielding perseverance and indomitable pluck during his years of residence in the Black Hills, has succeeded in reaching the topmost rung of the ladder of success. He was prominent among the few brave men, who, in face of great danger, located and founded Rapid City, and whose experiences during those perilous times were more thrilling, perhaps, than ordinarily fall to the lot of pioneers. Mr. Brennan may be accounted one of the representative citizens of the Black Hills, by virtue of which numerous positions of honor and trust were from time to time conferred upon him during his long and continuous residence therein.

In March, 1876, Mr. Brennan was made a member of the first Board of Trustees of Rapid City. He opened and kept the first hostelry in Rapid City in a twelve by fourteen feet log cabin, situated on Rapid street between Fifth and Sixth streets. In 1878 he built and opened the American House, on the corner of Sixth and Main streets, which was consumed by fire in 1888. He was made president of the Hotel Harney Company, the building being constructed under his direction, and opened by him in 1886, the ownership passing from the company to Mr. Brennan in 1888.

In 1877 Mr. Brennan was appointed Superintendent of Public Instruction for Pennington County by Gov. Pennington, was also appointed first Postmaster of Rapid City during the same year; was at one and the same time Express, Stage, and Union Pacific Agent, for a period of ten years. In 1888 he was appointed President of the Board of Trustees of the School of Mines of Rapid City, by Governor Church, holding the office for four years. In 1892 he was appointed State Railroad Commissioner by Governor Sheldon, for two years, and was elected to the same position, in 1894, for two years.

It is thus a pleasure to record that one of the early pioneers of the Black Hills has occupied important niches in their history. The subjoined account of the journey of the party of which Mr. Brennan was a member, and some of their experiences after reaching the Hills, may prove of interest to residents thereof.

John R. Brennan, in company with Geo. W. Stokes, N. H. Hawley, and George Ashton, left Denver, Colorado, for the Black Hills, about the middle of October, 1875, with teams and wagons loaded with all the requisite equipment for such a journey, including provisions adequate for six months. On reaching Cheyenne, an inventory of the cash on hand was taken, where it was found that the combined wealth of the party was just twenty dollars. However, with this meager cash capital, but with a large surplus of determination and pluck, they pulled out from Cheyenne for the Hills. On the seventh day out from Denver, they reached the Platte river, near Fort Laramie, where they went into camp for seven days—this delay being made to avoid meeting with a squad of soldiers who were reported on their way out from the Hills to the Fort with a number of prospectors under arrest for trespassing on the Indian Reserve, and for the still further purpose of receiving recruits.

While in camp on the Platte, they were joined by a party of forty-five men, also bound for the Black Hills, among whom were California Joe (the noted scout), Dido King, afterwards commissioner of Lawrence County, and popularly known as "Honest Dick," Geo. Palmer, John Argue, Robert Ralston (who was captain of the party), and James Hepburn and wife—the only woman in the party.

This Mrs. Hepburn, who died a few years ago in Central, near Deadwood, was probably the first woman to enter the Hills in 1875,—barring Calamity Jane, who it is asserted, came in with Professor Jenny's military escort at an earlier date.

As soon as the military escort arrived with their prisoners at Fort Laramie, the party immediately broke camp and departed precipitately for the Hills via the Government Farm, Raw Hide Buttes, and Cottonwood, crossing the Cheyenne river at the point where Edgemont now stands; then up Red Canyon through Pleasant Valley to Custer Park, arriving there on November 12th, 1875. Here the party found and took possession of three log barracks built by the soldiers, occupying them for one night only. The next day they went down French creek to the stockade, two and a half miles below, where they remained and prospected five or six days, when, dividing into small parties, they scattered out to different points in the middle and southern Hills.

Brennan, Stokes, Palmer, Hawley, Byron, and Argue, located on what is known as Palmer's gulch, built three substantial log cabins and established themselves in their winter-quarters.

On December 20th, 1875, a miners' meeting was held at the cabin of Brennan, Stokes, and Palmer, which was as far as known the first regular miners' meeting ever held in the Black Hills, the minutes of whose proceedings have been preserved.

Below are the full proceedings:—

Meeting called to order by J. R. Brennan. Present: Geo. W. Stokes, Geo. Palmer, N. H. Hawley, G. Byron, Dick King, John Argue, T. C. Brady, Gus. Williams, and California Joe.

After objects of meeting were stated; on motion, T. C. Brady was elected chairman, and Geo. W. Stokes, secretary.

The following business was then transacted:—

Moved and seconded that the gulch be named "Palmer Gulch," and that a mining district be formed to be known as Palmer Gulch Mining District. Motion carried.

Moved and seconded that a committee of two be appointed to draft laws to regulate the district. Adopted.

Geo. Stokes and T. C. Brady were chosen to draft laws to govern the district.

On motion the Montana Company located on Stand-off Bar on Spring creek were invited to attend the meeting on the 25th inst. to assist in making laws to govern the district.

Nominations for recorder for the district were called for.

John R. Brennan, being the only name presented, was chosen recorder of the Palmer Gulch Mining District.

Reading report of committee on laws, price for recording claims was fixed at one dollar per claim; size of claim was fixed (temporarily), 300 feet up and down the gulch, and from rim to rim.

California Joe was then called upon to tell the meeting what he knew, in a general way, about the Hills, he having spent the summer with Professor Jenny in their explorations.

Joe was very enthusiastic on the subject, saying that, in his opinion, the Black Hills was the richest country in the United States, that he had prospected as far north as Elk creek, and south to French creek, and had found splendid prospects in every place between those two points. He called the attention of the meeting to the fact, that he had located and staked the first quartz claim in the Black Hills, said claim being situated one mile below his cabin on the gulch.

On motion, meeting adjourned to meet again on December 25th, to hear the report of the committee on laws.

GEO. W. STOKES,
Secretary.

This party prospected and worked nearly the entire winter on Palmer gulch and Spring creek, running a drain ditch 1,800 feet and sinking forty or fifty prospect holes, without realizing enough to pay for sharpening and repairing tools.

In the latter part of February, 1876, John R. Brennan in company with W. P. Martin, A. Brown, Mart. Pensinger, Wm. Marsten, Thos. Ferguson, and Dick King, left the party, went to Rapid valley and then located Rapid City on February 25th, 1876.

THE FIRST GOLD DUST TO BE TAKEN OUT OF BLACK HILLS

Emil Faust, also a pioneer of 1875, left Cheyenne, Wyoming, in October, 1875; with two four-horse teams, and wagons loaded with provisions for the Black Hills. By considerable stratagem, and making some tedious detours, to avoid meeting the soldiers under Capt. Pollock, who were leaving the Hills for Fort Laramie about that time, he succeeded in reaching Custer on the 24th of December, 1875, where he remained during the winter. Provisions becoming very scarce in the Hills, Mr. Faust in company with D. G. Tallent, who was returning from his second trip to the Black Hills, left Custer for Cheyenne, in the early part of March, 1876, taking with him $1,000 in gold dust for the purchase of supplies. This gold dust was mined from the placer deposits of French, Spring, and Castle creeks, and was the first gold of any considerable quantity carried out of the Black Hills.

Their journey was by no means over a bed of roses, as will be seen. On reaching the vicinity of Hat creek, they were overtaken by a terrific snowstorm—a veritable Dakota blizzard, and having no forage for their horses, and not much provisions for themselves, both came very near perishing with cold and hunger. As the snow was too deep for the horses to reach the grass, they were forced to dole out to them their scanty supplies to keep the poor beasts from starvation. Even the contents of their "grub-box,"—including a lot of nice ham sandwiches—had to be fed to them, while they themselves went "awfully" hungry. However, half-starved as they were, when the storm abated somewhat, they pushed their way through the snow and slush, towards Fort Laramie. At the "Government" farm they providentially met Judge Kuykendall with a small party on his way to the Hills with merchandise for the Deadwood market, of whom they procured in exchange for Black Hills gold dust enough supplies to last until reaching Cheyenne.

This is but an instance of the terrible hardships and privations endured by many of the early pioneers while traveling over the dreary wastes to the Black Hills.

After investing the $1,000 of gold in provisions for the miners Mr. Faust returned to the Hills, where he has ever since remained, and is now one of the prosperous, business men of the great mining metropolis of the Hills, Lead City.

CHAPTER XV

EARLY FREIGHT AND PASSENGER TRANSPORTATION TO THE BLACK HILLS

When the tide of emigration began to flow towards the Black Hills, in the early spring of 1875, the necessity for means of transportation for passengers and freight over the plains became apparent, and a few shrewd men of capital, seeing in this necessity an opportunity for profitable investment, lost no time in organizing companies and establishing lines from different points to the Black Hills for that purpose. Nor was their judgment and penetration at fault, for, during the years prior to the advent of the first railroad, the immense freight and passenger traffic between outfitting points and the Hills, not only yielded large results to the operators, but was an important factor in the business economy of the Black Hills; and from those standpoints may be regarded as the most prosperous years in their entire history.

FRED. T. EVANS
Who started the first passenger and freight transportation train from Sioux City to the Black Hills in April, 1875

The pioneer organization for the transportation of freight, was called the Sioux City & Black Hills Transportation Company,—the company being Fred. T. Evans, Judge Hubbard, John H. Clark, John Hornick,—Sioux City capitalists—of which Fred T. Evans was president. The first train of the line left Sioux City on April 26th, 1875, with the goods and equipments of Gordon's ill-fated expedition, which was almost totally destroyed by the military—wagons, goods and all,—at the point on the Niobrara route near where Gordon, Nebraska, now stands, as before related.

During the years 1876-7, this company shipped their merchandise from Sioux City up the Missouri river by steamer, first to Yankton, afterwards to Pierre, then from those respective points by wagon to the Hills. In 1878, their shipping point was changed from Sioux City to Chamberlain to connect with the Chicago, Milwaukee and St. Paul R.R., whence their goods were shipped by steamer to Pierre, and from there by wagon to all points in the Black Hills until 1888. This Evans' Transportation Company employed varying from 1,000 to 1,500 men and wagons, from 2,000 to 3,000 oxen, and from 1,000 to 1,500 mules, and the freight traffic of the line was something immense. Although the men employed on the line had frequent encounters with the Indians, the only loss sustained by the company during the period of its existence was 200 oxen stolen, and one man killed by the Indians at Crook City, in March, 1876, and two men killed and ten mules stolen in 1877 on the Cheyenne river.

Following closely upon the heels of the organization of the Sioux City and Black Hills Transportation Company came that of the Witcher Company, which carried on a very extensive freight business with the Hills during the first four or five years of its history. This company commenced operations along that line in the spring of 1875, the first train of the line starting on its initial trip a few days after the departure of the Gordon party with the Evans' transportation train.

It may be remembered that this unfortunate expedition, destitute of the quality of cohesion, broke up into fragments, while en route on the old Niobrara trail to the Hills. Subsequently the Witcher Company shipped their freight from Sioux City by boat to Yankton and Pierre successively, thence overland by wagon to different points in the Black Hills.

H. N. WITCHER
Who established the second passenger and freight transportation line from Sioux City to the Black Hills in April, 1875

Several other freight lines, doing a more or less extensive business with the Hills, were established prior to the opening of the country to settlement in 1877, notably Dick Dunn & Newbanks' transportation lines, running from Pierre, and J. M. Woods, Bramble and Miner, Jewett & Dickinson from Sidney.

The first regular express and passenger line to the Black Hills, called the Cheyenne and Black Hills Stage Line, running first from Cheyenne, afterwards from Sidney to Deadwood, was established during the year 1876.

The company Messrs. Gilman, Salisbury and Patrick, commenced operations along the line laid out, and made an earnest and determined effort to push the work to a speedy completion, and put the line in full operation in the early spring of that year, but owing to the persistent hostility of the Indians and their consequent depredations, it was found utterly impracticable. Their relay stations were burned, their stock run off, and their general agent killed by the Indians. Thus handicapped, they were compelled to partially suspend operations temporarily. However, despite the difficulties in the way, work was soon resumed, and some time in July a splendid four-horse coach, loaded with passengers, succeeded in safely reaching Custer. On its return trip, however, when a few miles out from Custer, the coach was attacked by a band of Indians, who after a chase of several miles, killed the driver, cut the horses from the coach and drove them away, harness and all, leaving the passengers stranded on the trail, who were in consequence compelled to walk back twelve miles to Custer for a new start. The difficulties of establishing a line of coaches 300 miles over an intensely hostile country are not easily surmounted, yet by an unyielding perseverance, the obstacles were at last overcome, and on September 25th, 1876, the first through coach of the line reached Deadwood.

In addition to its passenger traffic, this line carried large consignments of fast freight and express matter, amounting, it is estimated by some, to about 40,000,000 pounds annually. All Western and Southern, and a considerable portion of Eastern mail for the Hills was carried over this line. All of the Homestake bullion up to 1881, and nearly all of the early gold product of the Black Hills, was transported by the Cheyenne and Black Hills Stage Company during the perilous years, when "road agents," under the guise of honest men, surreptitiously watched the shipments, and "hold-ups" were a common occurrence, and when the golden treasure had to be guarded by intrepid nervy men armed with shot-guns.

The old historic Deadwood Treasure Coach that has since been "held up" and robbed, in regular Black Hills style, in numerous of the large cities of the United States and in many parts of the old world, to the intense delight, amid the wild plaudits of tens of thousands, among whom were some crowned heads, was planned and built by Superintendent Voorhees, of the Cheyenne and Black Hills Stage Company, for the safer transportation of Black Hills gold.

The Northwestern Express, Stage, and Transportation Company, organized under the laws of Minnesota, with R. Blakely as president, and C. W. Carpenter as secretary and treasurer, commenced running a daily line of stages in connection with the Northern Pacific Railroad from Bismarck to Deadwood on May 1st, 1877. In October, 1880, the line was transferred to

Pierre, to connect with the Chicago and Northwestern Railway, and in 1886 was transferred from Pierre to Chadron, Nebraska, to connect with the Fremont, Elkhorn and Missouri Valley Railroad on its completion to that point. In 1880, the company established a line of splendid Concord four-horse coaches, between Pierre and Deadwood, which it is estimated carried an average of 5,000 passengers yearly for a period of five years, during which time the line carried all the Northern and a large percentage of the Eastern mail for the Black Hills. The Homestake bullion was transported by this company, from Deadwood to Pierre, during the years 1881 and 1882. The heavy weight transportation alone on this line amounted to 11,000,000 pounds annually, employing 250 men, 600 horses and mules, and 2,000 oxen.

On the completion of the F. E. & M. V. R. R. to the Hills, all that kind of passenger and freight traffic with the Black Hills soon ceased and the lines discontinued. Stage coaches, ox and mule trains are now relegated to the dead past. The rumbling of the dashing tally-ho; the long strings of tired cattle, toiling slowly along with the trains of heavily freighted wagons; the ear-piercing crack of the long lashes of the picturesque bull-whackers, and the prolonged braying of the mules, are no more seen nor heard on the business throughfares of our cities.

EARLY POSTAL FACILITIES IN THE BLACK HILLS

Prior to the opening of the country for settlement in February, 1877, and the subsequent establishment of regular United States mail service for the Black Hills, the people, having been thrown upon their own resources for means of communication with the outer world, were compelled to avail themselves of chance opportunities for sending out letters—business or otherwise,—and had also to depend upon the same uncertain means for return messages. The large accumulation of mail for the Black Hills, at the various outfitting points, was usually intrusted to the care of trains leaving these points for the Hills, and as these trains were frequently held in siege by the hostile Indians for many days at a time, the mail did not always arrive when expected. However, after weeks of anxious waiting on the part of the long suffering people, it would, in most cases, reach its destination. On its arrival in Deadwood, the principal distributing point of the Hills, it would be taken in charge by a self-constituted postmaster, and laboriously arranged in alphabetical piles, ready for delivery—the *modus operandi* being as follows: The addresses were read aloud; each person upon the call of his name would elbow his way through the immense crowd of eager letter-seekers, to the delivery window, where, by the payment of fifty cents in "coin of the realm" or its equivalent in gold dust, he would receive his long looked for letter or letters. Fifty cents may seem a large price to pay for a single letter, but when it is considered that several clerks had to be employed in arranging and handing out the mail, and several others in weighing up the gold dust received in payment therefore, besides the percentage to the carriers, it was not, perhaps, unreasonable.

In the summer of 1876, about the last of July or perhaps the first of August, followed the Seymour and Utter Pony Express Mail Service with its corps of daring intrepid riders, conspicuous among whom were Charlie Utter (Colorado Charlie), H. G. Rockfellow, and Herbert Godard. Mounted on the fleetest of bronchos, with mail sacks strapped onto their saddles, and their guns and cartridges thrown across the pommels; silently and swiftly they flew over the Indian infested trail, first between Fort Laramie and Deadwood, and afterwards between Sydney and Deadwood, with the thousands of white-winged messages, never, as far as known, losing a single paper, or failing to arrive on schedule time. Although the service called for only a weekly mail, the riders by a frequent relay of fresh ponies, sometimes made the trip in the incredibly short space of forty-eight hours, much of the distance being traveled under cover of the night to avoid contact with the Indians. For this dangerous service the company received twenty-five cents for each letter delivered, but as the number of letters varied from 2,000 to 3,000 each trip the compensation was not insignificant.

That the riders had many thrilling experiences with the redskins on their trips, goes without saying; that they sometimes, too, had very narrow escapes, is illustrated by the following story from the pen of a young pioneer of 1876, (R. B. Hughes):—

"Among the riders employed by Seymour and Utter, to carry the mail from Deadwood to Fort Laramie, was Brant Street, now living the life of a quiet farmer in Dodge County, Nebraska. Street was engaged to ride pony express, and for a month or so went through the experiences common in those days to all men in that dangerous occupation. He carried, besides the mail sack tied to his saddle, nothing save a Remington rifle and a bag of cartridges slung across the pommel of the saddle. One afternoon, he was riding along on his down trip, about eight miles north of Hat Creek Station, not expecting trouble, for the Indians had been unusually quiet for a week or more, when a volley was fired upon him from the bush, and, in an instant, as he afterwards told the story, the world seemed to be full of redskins. His horse fell dead at the first fire. One ball struck the pommel of the saddle and another knocked heel from his boot. Extricating himself from the saddle as quickly as possible,

TRANSPORTATION FROM PIERRE TO DEADWOOD

and pulling off the gun and cartridges, he ran as fast as he could to a little arroyo close by, into which he threw himself at full length.

"As he ran the bullets sang and whistled about his ears and kicked up the dust at his feet. The Indians were rapidly closing in on him when he emptied his cartridges on the ground, and, as he expressed it, commenced pumping lead back at them. So warm did he make it for the Indians, that they soon began to look for cover and long range, from which they kept up an intermittent fusillade until night fell, when they withdrew. Street said afterward that the three or four hours he spent hugging the ground seemed longer than so many days at any other time of his life. The nerve of the man is shown in the fact that after darkness had settled down he crawled out to his dead horse, disengaged the pouches of mail, and carried them on his back to Hat Creek Station."

Brave and swift though these riders were, one of them at least is known to have fallen a victim to the deadly bullets of the redskins, as about the middle of August, a Sidney express rider was found scalped beside his mail bag, between Castleton and Deadwood.

In connection with this private mail service, a post office was established in Deadwood, nor for the distribution of mail as in regular United States service, but for a safe depository, where the people could go and get their mail under certain restrictions. Upon the arrival of the express, the pouches were emptied of their contents and the letters arranged alphabetically as before, when the letters would be handed out as called for—only one person's mail could be called for at a time. By right of priority, first come first served, each new one claiming mail, regardless of sex, being required by an unwritten law to take his position in the line in the rear, so that if one desired to get the mail of a friend, he would be compelled to take his place in the rear of the column and wait his turn. Of course it took a long time to call out two or three thousand letters from the voluminous piles and weigh up the gold-dust postage, and for that reason the line was usually long drawn out, a quarter of a mile, more or less, and those having to repeat the operation grew proportionately tired. There are many doubtless in the Black Hills to-day, who after the lapse of twenty-one years, grow tired at the recollection of having stood in line for three or four hours awaiting their turns to get a letter from the old home.

After two months of pony express mail service, the line was sold out to Mr. Clippenger of Fort Laramie, whose service proved so unsatisfactory to the people, that finally all mail matter for the Hills was ordered to be given into the care of the Cheyenne and Black Hills Stage Company for transportation, such service being at first rendered free of charge.

Occasionally, before the establishment of the Pony Express Service, letters for the Hills were intrusted to the care of parties of gold-seeking adventurers to be delivered directly into the hands of the parties addressed when found. Sometimes such persons were not readily found, in which case, letters frequently passed through several hands before reaching their addresses, and I now recall two occasions, on which I received very badly soiled, tattered and torn missives, bearing the unmistakable ear-marks of having been persued by other eyes than those for whom they were intended. However, we could not afford to be too fastidious in those days, and were glad to get even second-hand news. Such were the postal limitations in the Black Hills in 1876.

CHAPTER XVI

THE YELLOWSTONE EXPEDITION; OR,
THE INDIAN CAMPAIGN OF 1876

The Yellowstone Expedition of 1876 furnishes the theme for a tragic chapter in the history of the Black Hills. While the campaign may be considered by some more a matter of general history, inasmuch as the expedition had its inception in the necessity for throwing protection around the people of the Black Hills and the outlying settlements against the depredations of hostile Sioux, and also in that the Black Hills would more directly lose by its failure or profit by its success, than any other portion of our common country, it may be regarded as essentially a part of Black Hills history. Howbeit, believing it to be such, it seems fitting that a brief account of that memorable campaign, the causes leading thereto, its object and results, be recorded on these pages, that the name of the dead hero, whose trail the first pioneers followed into the wilderness, may be ever kept green in their memories.

Primarily, the invasion of the Black Hills in 1874, and the subsequent failure of the Sioux to obtain redress for such violation of treaty obligations in their council with the United States Commissioners in 1875, followed by the unrestricted influx of gold-seekers into their domain,—aggravated, doubtless, by a long list of fancied wrongs, treasured up for years,—yet unavenged, engendered the bitter hostilities, which resulted in the crowning tragedy of 1876—the tragedy of the Little Big Horn.

The more direct and immediate cause, however, precipitating the conflict, was the refusal of certain bands of hostile Indians to comply with the request of the Indian Department, that they be compelled to settle down on their reservation, subject to the control of the Indian agents. It was to compel obedience and bring in these recalcitrant bands, who were roaming at will over a very large scope of the Western public domain,—but rarely visiting their agencies (only when rations were drawn), that the campaign known as the Yellowstone Expedition, was authorized by the War Department and placed under the direction of Gen. Sheridan, in the winter of 1875-6.

About this time, Sitting Bull, the "medicine man" of these hostile bands, learning of the contemplated aggressive movements, began to concentrate his savage forces, and away out westward among the mountains of Southern Montana, he planted the hostile standard—at a point he thought

SITTING BULL

admirably located for his purpose—not too far away to preclude the possibility of making dashing raids on the distant settlements, yet near enough to the impregnable ramparts of the Big Horn mountains, to which, if closely pursued, he could make his escape, and at the same time accessible to foreign territory, where needed recruits could be obtained.

Pending the military warlike movements, the wily Brule chieftain—the most uncompromising and relentless of the foes of the pale-faces, and his savage coadjutors, the vindictive Uncapapas, Chief Gall, and Crow-king, and the reckless Crazy Horse, the ruling spirits of the hostile forces, were rapidly gathering in recruits from nearly all the tribes of the Sioux nation. Couriers and runners were sent out with the "war pipe" to the various reservations to stir up the spirit of war among the agency Indians; hundreds of them from both the upper and lower agencies, including all the renegade outlaws of the various tribes, hastened to swell the hosts of Sitting Bull on the Yellowstone.

The plan of the campaign for subduing these savage forces, which finally numbered in the aggregate from 6,000 to 8,000 Indians and squaws, including nearly 3,000 of the most warlike braves of the Sioux nation, was briefly as follows: A column from the Department of the Platte under Gen. Crook and one from Fort Abraham Lincoln, under Gen. Terry to be joined by Gen. Gibbons' command from Fort Ellis, on the Upper Yellowstone, were to co-operate, and in conjunction, surround and capture the hostile bands, or drive them onto their respective reservations.

In the execution of the above plan, about the 1st of March, 1876, Gen. Crook, in command of the first column consisting of ten companies of Third Cavalry and two of the Fifth Infantry, comprising altogether less than 900 men, moved out westward from Fort Laramie in quest of the savage foe, going into camp on the Powder river near old Fort Reno, where he remained on account of severe storms for several weeks, meanwhile reorganizing his army.

Soon after their arrival in camp, Gen. Reynolds, with the force of cavalry and pack-train, proceeded down the river and when about fifty miles below, on the 17th of March, he was met and repulsed by Crazy Horse and his band of 100 lodges, which obliged him to return to camp, and it was at the time of this delay and repulse that the Indians left their agencies by hundreds to join the hostiles.

As soon as the weather made it practicable, Gen. Crook resumed his march with a little more than 1,000 fighting men (a force wholly inadequate, as it turned out, to cope successful with the enemy in an almost totally unknown country), and about 200 more as scouts, teamsters, and packers, reaching Goose creek—a branch of the Tongue river—about the first of June, where he made a permanent camp.

The "hostiles," on the approach of Gen. Crook, of whose movements they kept themselves thoroughly well-informed through the medium of scouts and spies who were ever diligently scouring the country on the watch for any threatened danger, sent out a large party of their best fighting braves to discover the real strength of the approaching army, and, if expedient and practicable, precipitate a conflict.

On the 17th of June, Gen. Crook encountered these Indians somewhere near the headwaters of the Rosebud, where a battle ensued, in which the expedition was defeated and compelled to retreat—without, it is believed, any serious loss—placing it, however, for the time being, practically out of the campaign.

The victorious Indians after repeated fruitless attempts to decoy Gen. Crook into ambush in the canyons of the Rosebud, faced about and returned on their trail to the village near the Little Big Horn—the very trail, doubtless, struck and followed up by Custer and his brave troopers to their death eight days later.

The Sagacious Sitting Bull and his allies, upon being warned of the advance of Gen. Custer's column from the east, and easily discerning in the general movement the net that was being woven around them, determined not to be caught in its meshes unprepared, so with admirable foresight, they had located their village along the west bank of the Little Horn—thus commanding its waters—the key to the situation, and in near proximity to the Big Horn mountains, whither they could send their squaws if need be, and make their own escape perfectly safe from pursuit amid their frowning battlements.

It was near their chosen vantage ground, insolent and defiant in their conscious strength, that the yelling savage hosts of Sitting Bull, in all their gaudy panoply, and fairly bristling with the most approved arms, closed around and blotted out of existence, by sheer force of numbers, Custer and five troops of his beloved Seventh—soldiers as valiant and brave as ever bestrode a horse or shouldered a carbine.

THE CUSTER COLUMN

On the morning of May 15th, the second column of the Yellowstone Expedition, with Brig.-Gen. Terry in command of all the forces, numbering in the aggregate about 1,200 men, and 1,400 animals, left Fort Abraham Lincoln to join in the campaign against the hostile Sioux.

As the long line of cavalry, infantry, artillery, mounted scouts, pack mules, ponies, with the long train of supply wagons, marched out from the garrison, conspicuous at the head of the column might be seen Gen. Custer—every inch a soldier—and the gallant Seventh Cavalry with the twelve companies of splendidly disciplined troopers, mounted on their glossy, prancing, well-trained horses, the sheen of their carefully polished accoutrements gleaming brightly in the morning sun, making, methinks, to any lover of military display, a pageant worth going a long distance to see.

These brave soldiers and their heroic leader, while fully realizing the hardships and dangers which lay before them, and being inured to the hardships of Indian campaigns, with resolute faces and courageous hearts, confident of success—for had not the very name, Seventh Cavalry, been ever a synonym of victory,—pressed forward to defeat and death. Ah! did no thought or premonition, no vision of the awful calamity that awaited them on the bluffs, overlooking the picturesque valley of the Little Big Horn, come to them meanwhile? We cannot know. But let us follow their movements along their line of march thither, till the curtain drops, behind which the closing scene of the drama was enacted.

On the 20th of May, after four days' march, the expedition reached the Little Missouri river, about forty-six miles distant from Fort Lincoln, where a halt of one day was made for the purpose of ascertaining the truth or falsity of rumors current at the fort, that hostiles were gathered in large force on that stream and prepared to give battle.

Gen. Custer, with four companies of cavalry, a number of scouts, himself acting as guide, rode up the valley of the Little Muddy about twenty miles and back, without finding Indians or even any recent trace of them, which settled the question of Indians thereabouts beyond doubt. However, as the savages were liable to be encountered at any time, scouts were kept constantly employed scouring the country in advance, and on the flanks of the column all along its line of march.

Traveling directly westward, over a country then before untraveled by white men, the command reached the Powder river, about twenty miles above its mouth, June 9th, from which point the expedition marched northward down the river, through the almost impassable Bad Lands,—at first regarded as altogehter impracticable for wagons,—to its mouth, where the nearly exhausted supply of rations and forage was replenished from the loaded boats, which had steamed up the Yellowstone for that purpose. From this point, a large scouting party and several troops of cavalry under Major Reno, were sent out in advance to discover, if possible, some trace or trail leading to the rendezvous of the hostiles, who were supposed to be not very far away.

After three days for rest and recuperation, on the 15th of June, Gen. Custer, with six companies of cavalry, the Gatling battery, scouts and pack mules, moved west from the mouth of Powder river,—leaving all unnecessary incumbrances, such as wagons, tents, etc., behind—to the mouth of Tongue river, about forty miles distant, reaching that point on the evening of the 16th, Gen. Terry and staff following up the Yellowstone by steamer. From the mouth of Tongue river the column then continued its course westward to the mouth of the Rosebud, about midway between the Tongue and Big Horn rivers, which was reached on June 20th.

While in camp, at the mouth of the Rosebud, the scouting party returned and reported that the trail and deserted camp of a village of 380 lodges, indicating a force not less than 1,200 in all, had been discovered; also reporting that the Indians could have been overtaken in thirty-six hours, as the trail appeared to be not more than a week old.

Had this scouting party of perhaps more than 500 well-equipped soldiers and scouts, at once pressed forward on this fresh trail, instead of returning to the main division of the column, thereby losing much valuable time, the entire village, it is believed, would have been overtaken, surprised and captured, and thus, perchance, the terrible fate of Custer and his gallant command might have been averted. Evidently this failure to follow up the Indians placed Custer in great jeopardy, by giving the hostiles an intimation of his near approach, and giving them time to reach and join the forces on the Little Horn, and also opportunity to mature plans for effective offensive or defensive operations.

All plans being arranged, and preparations made, at noon of June 22d,—only three short days before the fatal battle,—our Gen. Custer with his gallant Seventh, his force of Ree and Crow scouts, and pack mules for carrying the necessary rations, moved bravely on up the valley of the Rosebud, hopeful of accomplishing great results; confident of achieving an easy and speedy victory over a small village of only 1,200 Indians. Fatal mistake!

Gen. Terry with the regiment of infantry and Gen. Gibbons' command, was to proceed up the river as far as the steamer could go, and then march to the point where he could co-operate with Gen. Custer.

Taking up the trail where the scouting party had turned back, Custer cautiously followed it up over the divide between the Rosebud and Big Horn rivers, preceded by his faithful and trusty scouts, who kept up a line of communication with the advancing column. The Crows soon became aware that they were nearing the dreaded Sioux—they could scent their natural enemies from afar.

At about 11 o'clock on the night of the 24th, in response to "officers' call," all troop commanders assembled at the headquarters of the commanding general and received marching orders—important information had been brought in, making it necessary to move forward at once—the hostile village had been precisely located by the scouts. The bugle call of "boots and saddles" was sounded and the sleepy troopers were soon in their saddles, and on their tortuous march through the brakes of the Wolf mountains, never halting until the morning.

The 25th, the fatal day of the battle, dawned delightfully; the sun rose in brightness resplendent—the sun whose last slanting rays were to cast their mellow beams athwart a scene, such as the world has rarely, if ever, witnessed. As the day advanced and the command were nearing the enemy, Custer ordered that no trumpet call be sounded except in an emergency; and instructed his officers to keep their respective troops within supporting distance of each other—not to get ahead of the scouts, nor linger too far in the rear. He told them in impressive words how much he relied upon their discretion and judgment, and above all upon their loyalty whatever might come. His tone and manner was gentle and subdued, with none of the usual brusqueness that characterized Gen. Custer. Was not the dark shadow of their coming doom brooding over him?

The 3,000 fighting warriors were by this time fully aware of the proximity of the long-haired chief and his handful of soldiers, and their spies were, even then, lying prostrate on the opposite slopes of the bluffs watching the advancing column over their crests. Before noon of that day, the command had crossed the divide, when Custer divided his regiment into three battalions, which before 1 o'clock were ready to advance along the lines indicated in their orders, against the enemy.

Capt. Benteen's battalion of three troops, consisting of troop "H," Capt. Benteen; troop "D," Capt. Wier; troop "K," Lieut. Godfrey; were ordered to a line of high bluffs on the left of the trail, three or four miles distant, to reconnoiter the field and prevent the escape of the Indians in that direction, and report the situation to the commanding general, and fight if necessary.

Major Reno in command of the advance battalion, composed of troop "M," Capt. French; troop "A," Capt. Moylan; troop "G," Lieuts. McIntosh and Wallace, under orders to charge the village, followed the trail, crossed the river at the ford, and marched his troops down towards the enemy, massed along the left bank of the Little Horn.

Gen. Custer with his battalion of five troops, viz.: troop "I," Capt. Keogh and Lieut. Porter; troop "F," Capt. Yates and Lieut. Riley; troop "C," Capt. Tom Custer and Lieut. Harrington; troop "E," Lieuts. Smith and Sturgis; troop "L," Lieuts. Calhoun and Crittenden; with scouts, numbering all told not more than 300 men, prepared to take his position on the bluffs to the right, at the lower end of the village.

For the last time those brave boys in blue cheerfully responded to the inspiring trumpet call of "mount." Once more in obedience to the bugle call, sweet and clear, of "Forward, March!" they rode bravely along the trail of the savages until near the ford, then up onto the bluffs to the right, overlooking the Little Horn. "Boldly they rode and well, into the jaws of—" but, the curtain drops. Well, what then? The sequel and scene of conflict tell us that, in a brief space, there was a short, fierce, terrible battle—the true details of which can never be known. We only know that not one of that gallant three hundred ever rode back to rehearse the story of Custer's last battle. The annihilation was complete. Ah! that was not all. What did the fiends incarnate then do? It is not at all difficult to conceive and draw a mental picture of their work. We can plainly see in the picture of a burly savage—malignant hate portrayed in every lineament of his ugly painted face, with glistening blade in hand, bending low over each prostrate form—perchance, many not yet dead. We can see the reeking scalp of each separate victim waved exultantly in the air, and now we can see them stripped of their clothing and their pockets rifled. We can see the murderous bandits flitting about all over the battle-ground among the dead, in a general scramble after the arms and accoutrements of the dead soldiers, which, with such few horses as had escaped the awful carnage, are handed over to the squaws and other non-combants; and lastly, we can see them mount their ponies and ride in hot haste, and red-handed, to attack the beleaguered battalions on the bluffs above. It did not take them long to accomplish all this, as there were legions of them, and, moreover, the picture is not overdrawn, but literally true.

The following particulars of the movements of Major Reno and Capt. Benteen in their two days' fight on the Little Big Horn, are gleaned partly from official reports, and partly from an article on the subject by Lieut.

Godfrey, one of Custer's troop commanders in Capt. Benteen's battalion. As Lieut. Godfrey was a participant in the battles, he is entitled to be regarded as unquestionable authority on the subject.

The story, shorn of all unnecessary details, is substantially as follows:—

Major Reno, after crossing the ford, moved his column down the valley of the Little Horn, in a line skirting the timber for perhaps two miles, then formed his battalion into a skirmish line, extending out from the timber across the valley—with the Ree scouts on the left, and advanced down toward the Indian village. The Indians who had rode up the valley to meet the soldiers, made a pretext of retreating—developing strength meanwhile, and firing occasional shots. Suddenly, at the opportune time, they made a bold dash on Reno's left flank, forcing his command back into the timber on the river bank, and putting the Ree scouts to an ignominious flight. It is told that the cowardly Rees fled precipitately—never stopping until they reached the supply camp, at the mouth of the Powder river.

Reno, not seeing Custer within supporting distance, did not obey the order to charge the village, but, being forced back on the defensive in the timber, ordered his troops to dismount and fight the enemy on foot. His position—sheltered by the timber, and protected to an extent by the river bank, was a good one, and it is thought could have been maintained for a long time without serious loss. Howbeit the Indians surrounded the command on every side, and sent their death-dealing missiles fast and furious into their ranks. Major Reno—on finding himself bespattered with the blood of his faithful scout (Bloody Knife), who fell riddled at his side, and hemmed in by overpowering numbers, at least five to one—gave the order to "mount and get to the bluffs," but owing to the noise of battle and the confusion, the order was not heard or not understood. It would appear that the troops were becoming sadly demoralized. The order of "mount and get to the bluffs" was repeated, and again not understood, and not until one of the troop commanders standing near Reno, communicated the order to the other troops, was it understood.

The command then, for the most part, mounted and made a hasty retreat across the river at a lower ford, and without the least semblance of military order, scrambled up the bluffs on the right. While crossing the river a number were shot—among them was the brave Capt. Hodgson, who, when he fell from his horse into the river, cried out in despairing tones, "For God's sake don't leave me here." At that moment a soldier held out the stirrup of his saddle and told him to take hold of it. Grasping the stirrup, he was dragged through the water to the opposite side, but when climbing the bank of the stream, he was struck by another ball and fell back into the water. An attempt was afterwards made to recover his body, but without success.

When scaling the bluff, it became apparent that but few of the Indians had followed up Reno's retreat, for reasons which soon became manifest. How long Reno's fight in the timber lasted is uncertain, as estimates of the time vary; probably, however, not more than twenty or thirty minutes. Reno's casualties, nearly all of which occurred during the retreat, were three officers, thirteen enlisted men and scouts killed; one officer, one interpreter and fourteen soldiers and scouts missing.

Soon after Reno's disorderly retreat to the bluffs, he was joined by Benteen's battalion, followed by the pack train on their way to join Custer. At that time Capt. Benteen, the hero of the Little Big Horn, first learned of Reno's fight and defeat in the valley. Just about the time of this junction of Reno and Benteen, it was discovered that the Indians for the greater part had abandoned the pursuit of Reno's retreating troops, but upon looking down the river it was seen that the bottom was swarming with mounted warriors, riding excitedly to and fro, evidently in great consternation; soon they were seen to ride swiftly down the valley out of sight.

It was at this very time that the Indians, having been warned of the appearance of more soldiers farther down the bluffs, surrounded and utterly annihilated Custer and his men.

It seems inexplicable, and only upon the hypothesis that they feared the movement of the Indians might be a ruse to decoy them from their point of vantage, that no concerted movement of the two battalions was made, at the time of this diversion, to reach Custer. In view of the facts, however, such a theory becomes baseless, as they obviously knew that a battle was in progress on the bluffs below; they knew that Custer was having a fight with the Indians, for, says Major Reno in his official report: "Almost at the same time I reached the top (of the bluff), mounted men were seen to be coming towards us, and it proved to be Capt. Benteen's battalion H, D, and K. We joined forces and in a short time the pack train came up. Still hearing nothing of Custer, and with this reinforcement I moved down the river in the direction of the village keeping on the bluffs. We heard firing in that direction and knew it could be only Custer. I moved to the summit of the highest bluff, and seeing and hearing nothing, sent Capt. Wier with his company to open communication with the command. He soon sent back word by Lieut. Hare that he could go no farther. I at once turned everything back to the first position, and which seemed to me best."

Capt. Benteen on learning that Capt. Wier and his battalion had, without orders, gone down the river with his troops, moved the other two troops of his command down the river in the direction Capt. Wier had gone, and from the top of the high bluff got his first view of the Indian village, and discovered Wier's troops in full retreat followed closely by the Sioux. What could a single company of calvary do against hundreds of armed savages?

It is plain then that it was after the junction of Reno's and Benteen's battalions, that the Custer battle was in progress, and not simultaneously with Reno's fight in the valley, as it supposed by some. Yes, they knew that Custer was having a fight with the Indians; shot after shot was heard from the direction of Custer's battle-ground, perhaps a little more than two miles below. What did those shots mean? They meant that Custer was having a fierce conflict with the red hosts that drove Reno in disorder to the bluffs a half hour before. Then again they heard two distinct volleys in rapid succession. What did those volleys mean? They meant that Custer was in deadly peril—a signal to the soldiers he had so often led to victory to hasten without delay to his support.

Custer's last desperate appeal reached the ears of the five or six hundred soldiers above, but no response came. Alas, the opportune time soon passed, for in less than one hour the Indians, flushed with their bloody victory, were hastening to drive them from their position on the bluffs.

Had the officer superior in command rallied the entire forces to his support, at the sound of the first shot from Custer's field, he would have won and deserved immortal honors. Strange as it appears, they seemed to feel no apprehension that Custer was in any real danger, believing that he was perfectly able to take care of himself, but how they could think so in view of Reno's disaster a short time before is somewhat puzzling.

It is believed, upon the very unsatisfactory information drawn from Indians who took part in the battle, that the ammunition of some of Custer's troops became exhausted, that two of his troops had dismounted to do battle on foot, and that their horses, made frantic by the waving of blankets and the yelling of the Indians, had been stampeded, bearing away with them the reserve ammunition in the saddle-bags.

It will be understood that when Benteen joined Reno on the bluffs, he was on his way with the pack train to join Custer in obedience to an urgent order—Custer's last order—which read as follows: "Benteen, come quick! Big Village; Bring packs. Cook, Adjutant. P.S. Bring packs." This order would indicate, that from some favorable point he had discovered the full strength of the Indian village, and realizing that the situation was desperate, had sent for reinforcements; and more ammunition.

About the time that Reno was moving in line down the valley toward the Indian village, some of his men saw Custer and a few of his battalion, standing

GENERAL CUSTER'S LAST CHARGE

dismounted on a bluff, cheering and waving their hats as if giving encouragement to Reno's men; and that was the last seen of him or any of his men, until found dead on the battlefield.

It is said, that the bluff where Custer was last seen was the one to which Reno escaped with his demoralized troops about an hour later.

The Indians, after the Custer battle, returned red-handed to the siege of the bluff, with a determination to wipe out, if possible, by virtue of numbers, the residue of the regiment. In brief, the Indians in a very short time gained possession of the surrounding points of vantage, and began to pour deadly shot, thick and fast, into the ranks of the soldiers, who, being on the defensive, could do little more than to maintain their positions; making occasional bold sorties to drive back the besiegers whenever they became too aggressive. When night came, the Indians, by that time in possession of all the surrounding hills, had the two commands completely environed, and had not darkness intervened to put a stop to further hostilities that night, they would, in all probability, have shared the fate of Custer.

That night, after the battle was over, the united tribes of Indians held high carnival in the village below, in savage celebration of their bloody victory—nor did they in the least try to conceal their unbounded joy.

Hundreds of huge bonfires were built through the village, and what with the continuous discharge of firearms (they had plenty of ammunition), the beating of tomtoms; wild exultant whooping and yelling, scalp-dancing, etc., pandemonium reigned supreme. All the night through they kept up their savage orgies in which, it is thought, human heads were paraded,—as several were found afterwards severed from the bodies. They were working themselves up to a pitch of frenzy that boded no quarter on the morrow to the weary men on the bluffs, who could from their position hear and see nearly the whole fantastic proceeding,—not a very inspiring spectacle under the circumstances, one would think.

When the fighting had ceased for the night, and the Indians had for the greater part withdrawn to the village, scouts were dispatched to find some trace of Custer's command, but they soon returned, reporting that the country was full of "Sioux." By this time, when they could breathe more freely, and think more rationally, everybody began to wonder what had become of Custer. "What's the matter with Custer?" "Why don't he send us word what he wants us to do?" All sorts of speculations were indulged in, and all kinds of theories advanced but the true one. The general opinion expressed was that he had had a battle, was repulsed, and had gone down the river to meet Terry, and would soon return to their relief.

The most intense excitement prevailed among the troops on the bluffs. A curious hallucination, in which there is something inexpressibly pathetic, took possession of the men—arising doubtless from the excessive mental and physical strain of the day past. Some imagined they could see, in the refracted light of the numerous Indian bonfires on the opposite bluffs, columns of troops advancing over the ridges; they fancied they could hear, amid the din and confusion of their savage orgies, the tramping of horses, the command of officers, and even the trumpeter's call. So confident were some that either Gen. Crook or Gen. Terry's command was approaching, that guns were fired, and "stable call" sounded to let them know their exact position, and that they were friends.

One man mounted a horse and galloped along the line, crying, "Don't be discouraged, boys, Crook is coming!" Poor fellows, it was but a phantasy; no reinforcements came to their support for the morrow's battle.

Realizing that with the dawn of day the Indians would return to the siege, the whole of that terrible night was spent in making preparations for their defense. The soldiers were put to work digging trenches, and as there were but few shovels and spades in the command, all kinds of implements, axes, hatchets, halves of canteens, tin cups, and even table knives and forks were brought into service.

Long before the sun had tipped the distant mountain peaks, and while the tired soldiers were yet digging in the trenches, the Indians opened fire upon them,—a few straggling shots at first, but as the day advanced they were heavily reinforced, and the firing became more general, fierce and furious, but not as effective as the savages could wish for, as many of the troops were then in their rifle pits. Finding their shots were being to a great extent wasted, they adopted the policy of trying to exhaust the ammunition of their opponents, by a few cunning devices designed to invite the fire of the troops. The first invitation was to stand as a target, in full view, for a minute, and then drop suddenly out of sight, which they soon found to be a rather dangerous experiment; then they tried the ruse of raising a hat and blanket on a stick or pole, but the soldiers of the Seventh Cavalry had found Indians too often to be deceived by such old-fashioned tactics.

In brief, a continuous fusillade was kept up on both sides, with an occasional volley from the Indians, for the greater part of the day.

Some brilliant sorties were made by troop commanders of Benteen's command, which it would appear was most exposed to the fire of the Indians, who made numerous attempts to run into his lines. At one time Benteen made a bold charge against an aggressive party of Indians, driving them nearly to the river.

At about one o'clock p.m. when the situation was most critical, the ammunition being nearly exhausted, the Indians for the most part withdrew.

Up to this time the soldiers, having been entirely cut off from the river, had suffered intensely with thirst. Their tongues had become parched and swollen, their lips were cracked and bleeding; every drop of moisture in the glands of the body having been absorbed. In the hope of finding relief they resorted to chewing grass roots, but without effect. As a last resort, raw potatoes were sparingly doled out to the famished men, which in small measure lessened their terrible suffering. The sickening stench from the rapidly decomposing dead added to the horrors of the situation. The wounded and the dying—ah, pitying heaven!—lay under the burning rays of a pitiless sun, begging in vain for a drop of water to cool their fevered tongues. Dr. Porter, the army surgeon, never leaving his post of duty, moved like a ministering spirit from one to another of his suffering patients, doing what he could, but without a drop of water with which to cleanse their bleeding wounds.

Numerous attempts had been made by volunteers to reach the water but they were as often driven back by a rain of bullets from the Indians, who were ever on the alert. Capt. Benteen once made a bold charge to the river under the protection of a skirmish line exposed to a galling fire, in response to the piteous appeal of the wounded soldiers, which brave act alone is sufficient to render his name immortal for all time.

At about 2 p.m. the Indians returned to the attack, driving the soldiers again into the trenches. They kept up a kind of desultory firing until about 3 o'clock p.m. when they withdrew altogether.

Later in the afternoon a few horsemen appeared in the valley below and set fire to the grass, and at 7 o'clock they were seen to emerge from behind the cloud of smoke and move in an immense mass across the plateau between the two Horns towards the Big Horn Mountains. Had they abandoned the siege for good, or was it another ruse? Perhaps they were moving their squaws, papooses and non-combatants away to a safe distance, intending to return with all their fighting warriors for a last desperate attempt to drive the soldiers from their intrenchments. Perchance information of the near approach of Terry's and Gibbon's commands with Gen. Custer's battalion had been heralded to them and they were hurrying away to the fastnesses of the mountains to avoid them. These were the various theories suggested in reference to the last movement of the Indians. As the sequel proved, the latter theory was the true one in all save that Custer and his battalion were not of them.

The two days' fight resulted in the loss of eighteen killed and fifty-two wounded.

The commands, doubtful as to the real intentions of the Indians, remained in their position that night. At about 9 o'clock the next morning, June 27th, the third day after the Custer battle, their attention was attracted by a cloud of dust rising in the distance down the valley. The first thought was that the Indians were returning for a last desperate attack. The tired soldiers again began to make hurried preparations for the expected battle. Soon, however, they became satisfied that the approaching forces were soldiers, and not Indians, as their march seemed altogether too slow for the dashing savages.

After nearly an hour of suspense, the cavalcade appeared in sight. No gray-horse troop was to be seen in the column; so it could not be Terry, or Custer would be with him. Then it must be Crook's command. Cheer after cheer was given for Gen. Crook who was coming to their relief. They had not yet learned that Crook's command had been placed hors de combat on the headwaters of the Rosebud ten days before.

They were not long kept in uncertainty, for soon a scout came into their lines bearing a note from Gen. Terry to Custer dated June 26th, which stated that two Crow scouts had given information that his (Custer's) column had been whipped and nearly all killed, but that he did not believe their story and was coming with medical aid. The scout told that he had tried to get within their lines the night before, but could not as the Indians were on the alert.

Let it be understood here that no attack of the Indian village on the 25th was contemplated in the plan of operations nor anticipated by Custer, but finding himself confronted by the enemy sooner than expected, he felt compelled to make the attack on that day, or allow the Indians to escape.

Soon after an officer of Terry's command came into their lines, and the first question asked of him was: "Where is Custer?"

"I don't know," replied the officer, but I suppose he was killed. We counted 197 dead bodies as we passed the battle-ground, and I don't suppose any escaped."

That was the first intimation they had received of Custer's fate nearly two whole days and nights after the battle.

"Gen. Terry and staff, and officers of Gen. Gibbon's command, soon approached and their coming was greeted with prolonged cheers.

"The grave countenance of the General awed the men to silence. The officers assembled to meet their guests. There was scarcely a dry eye; hardly a word was spoken, but quivering lips and hearty grasping of hands, gave token of thankfulness for the relief, and grief for the misfortune," relates Lieut. Godfrey.

On that evening, the 27th, the dead, killed in Reno's two days' fight were buried; the wounded were removed to the camp of Gen. Terry, where they could receive the treatment and care of which they were in such sore need.

On the morning of the 28th the soldiers left the bluffs to bury the dead of Custer's command. Let us precede them, and view the scene where the heroes fell;—the scene of Custer's last battle.

Let us march in sad and silent procession, down the valley two miles (perhaps more) and climb the first considerable bluff on the right of the Little Horn, and about a half mile therefrom and there—ah, what a sickening, grewsome spectacle meets the horrified gaze! All over the battle-ground lay the nude, mutilated bodies of the dead soldiers; officers and men, rider and horse, all lying in promiscuous blending; some with faces upturned to the blue and smiling sky; others with faces prone to the earth, as if biting the dust; some wearing an expression of sweet, restful peace; others a pained, horrified expression; many mutilated beyond recognition. Heaps of exploded cartridges lay thickly strewn over the battle-ground.

On the hill known as "Custer's Hill," where the gallant commander with three of his troops evidently made their last determined stand, we find Custer, victor in many a previous hard-fought Indian battle, with a bullet hole in his temple, and another through his body, but with no other marks of disfigurement. A little distance away—we hardly recognize the face so horribly mutilated, of the brave, large-hearted Tom Custer, and hard by lies the young, inexperienced Boz, (Boston Custer), whom his brother, the General, so much delighted to tease—and the mother's darling. God pity her.

A little to the left of Custer's field is "Crittenden's Hill," where the dismounted troops of Calhoun and Keogh desperately fought and fell—where the same sad spectacle confronts us. Some of the dead are found down near the river; these, it is thought, were trying to make their escape, or, perhaps, had been dispatched as messengers to Reno's command on the bluff above. This, however, is wholly conjectural.

The terrible mutilation of the body of Capt. Tom Custer is laid at the door of the monster Rain-in-the-Face, who had sworn to be avenged on the gallant officer, who had the courage to arrest him for the crime of murdering two defenseless men near Fort Lincoln. Upon an occasion, when Rain-in-the-Face was drawing his ration at his agency, Capt. Custer stepped up behind him, pinned down his arms and manacled him, in the presence of hundreds of Indians; had him taken to Fort Lincoln and placed in prison. He afterwards made his escape, vowing that he would tear out and eat the heart of his brave captor at the first opportunity. That he fulfilled to the letter the first part of his vow is known, and that he fulfilled the latter is believed.

Among those killed on Reno's retreat from the valley was Charlie Reynolds, one of Custer's long tried and most trusted scouts. It is related that the brave fellow sold his life very dearly. After exhausting the cartridges, in both his gun and revolver, he was seen to deal such a fierce blow with the latter, on the head of an Indian, in close combat, that it broke, thus leaving him at the mercy of the enemy. He soon fell shattered by a volley of bullets.

Reynolds was with Custer on his expedition into the Black Hills in 1874, at which time he was sent with dispatches from the Cheyenne river to Fort

162 THE BLACK HILLS; OR,

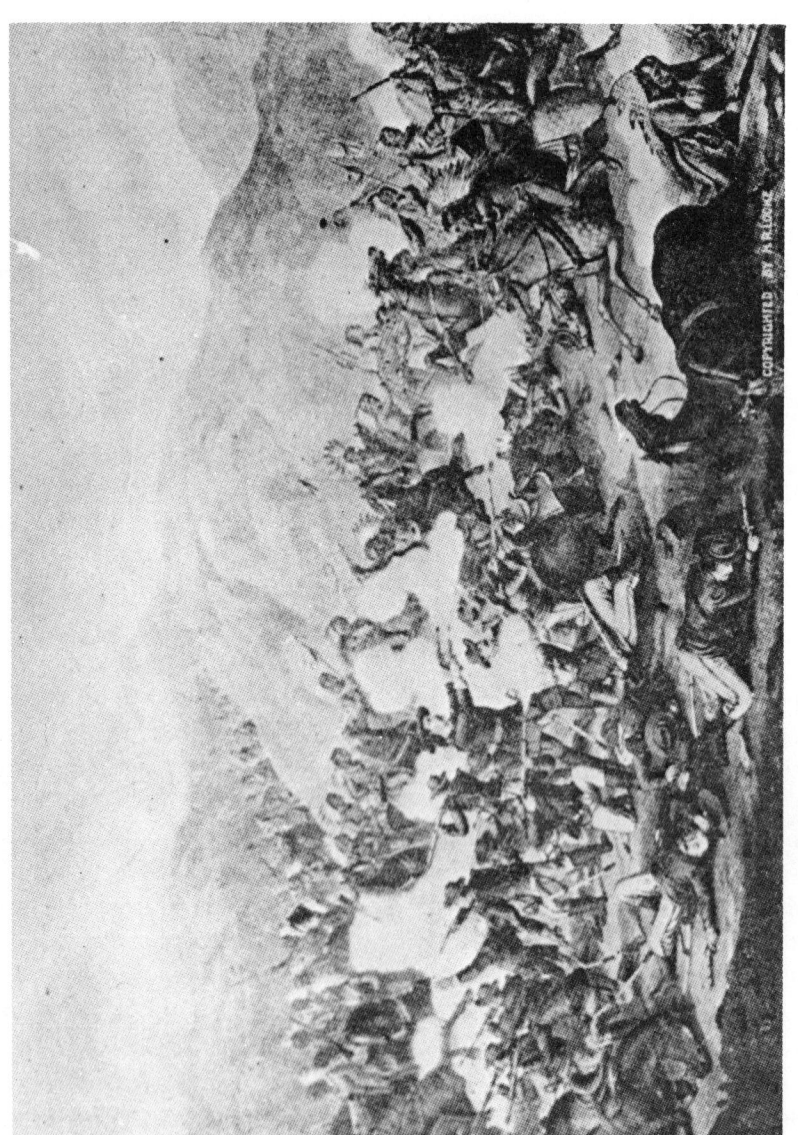

GENERAL CUSTER'S LAST BATTLE. HE AND ALL HIS MEN WERE KILLED—261 IN ALL

Laramie, through the hostile country, enduring hardships and privations, from which he never fully recover.

His early life was wrapped in complete mystery. If he had a secret that darkened his life, as some suspected, he guarded it well, as he skillfully evaded all questions, even from his most intimate friends, referring to his antecedents.

All of the slain were buried on the battle-ground where they fell—ground afterwards (in 1879) set apart by the government as a national cemetery, where an imposing monument was erected to the memory of the dead.

In August, 1879, Gen. Custer's remains were removed from their temporary resting-place and buried with imposing honors at West Point, N. Y., where they now repose, almost in the shadow of the buildings where he was trained in the science and tactics of civilized warfare.

GENERAL CUSTER

Custer's body appears to have been the only one to escape mutilation. Whether the sacrilegious hands of the savages were stayed by a sentiment of admiration for the wonderful bravery of the fair-haired chief, or by a superstitious fear of the wrath of the great Manitou, is a matter for speculation.

It is related that Chief Gall, on being questioned as to the reason why Custer was not scalped, said: "No one knew him from anyone else. His hair was cut short, and we could not tell him from any other."

This statement, however, seems highly improbable, as he had often been seen by many of the Indian chiefs engaged in the battle, and also wore the uniform of his rank, which in itself would distinguish him from any of the others.

Rude stretchers were soon constructed to convey the wounded of Reno's two-days' battle to the forks of the Big Horn—a distance of perhaps twenty miles—where they were placed on board the steamer Far West, which conveyed them to Fort Abraham Lincoln, with the news of the awful disaster to the gallant Seventh Regiment.

CHAPTER XVII

NEWS OF THE TERRIBLE DIASTER REACHES THE BLACK HILLS

News traveled slowly in 1876, before the advent of railroads in the Northwest, and was long reaching the people of the Black Hills. All information of the movements of the forces sent out against the hostiles had then to be carried either down the Missouri by steamer to Eastern points, or across a long stretch of country over the trails west of the Hills, to Fort Laramie, thence by mail to the Black Hills; so, not until about the 10th of July did the awful tidings, that crushed the hearts and blotted all brightness out of the lives of the anxious waiting wives of the slain heroes of the Little Big Horn, reach them at Fort Lincoln; and not till ten days later did the shocking news, that meant so much to the people of the Black Hills, reach Deadwood (the center of population in the Hills in 1876), and other points in direct communication with the outer world.

The intelligence came to the people of the Hills like a mighty blow from an unseen hand—stunning, striking them dumb by its very suddenness. At first, many refused to believe the shocking story. That Custer had met with reverses they admitted was probable, that his entire battalion had been annihilated was not believed possible. However, as the source from which the information emanated left little room for question, soon all doubt of the truth of the story vanished. All were in a state of intense excitement in the city of Deadwood. An extra of the *Pioneer* was speedily struck off, and distributed along Deadwood, Whitewood, and tributary gulches. That great throbbing, busy mining camp, with its thousands of cosmopolitan population, was stirred to the depths, from center to circumference, as the news spread from claim to claim.

The scene presented along the main street of Deadwood, on the evening of that day, when the miners gathered in from all the neighboring gulches, was one not soon to be forgotten. The excited, swaying, jostling masses, surging to and fro on both sides of the long, narrow street; the eager groups of men gathered at the doors of numerous business houses in excited discussion of the terrible disaster, gave evidence of how deeply and universally the people of the Hills of all classes were touched by the unexpected calamity. Even the many gambling resorts that lined the street were silent for the nonce; the roulette tables, the faro banks, and other games had lost their fascination, and the click,click, clicking of the chips fell not for a brief time on the accustomed ear—alas, how brief!

The story of Custer's tragic death soon reached the remote mining camps scattered through the Hills, and no doubt the eyes of many a hardy miner and prospector in their lone huts under the shadow of the Hills, grew moist at the revelation, for many of the early prospectors knew him well, and loved him.

Mingled with the general expression of sorrow and regret at the fate of Custer and his men, were bitter denunciations of the dilatory policy of the government in dealing with the Indians, thereby permitting the lives and property of the people of the Hills to be jeopardized.

The Indian campaign had, thus far, proved barren of good results. Crook's column had been reversed; Terry's column had met with dire disaster; Sitting Bull and his warriors had escaped to the mountains, bearing with them the trophies of victory. The hedge of security that had temporarily been thrown around the Black Hills had been pulled down and torn up by the roots, leaving their borders exposed to the ravages of the savage hordes, who, the people feared, might any day swoop down from the mountains upon the exposed settlements "like wolves on the fold." And our worst fears were in a large measure realized, for soon after, returning bands of the hostiles began again to ply their work of murder and theft in and around the Hills, frequently making bold dashes right into the limits of thickly-settled communities, driving off stock before the eyes of their owners, and killing whenever it was possible. For two months during the summer of 1876, notwithstanding the excellent organizations for protection and defense, the people of the Hills were terrorized by the boldness of their operations, which will be specially referred to further on in this work.

The following verses, couched in the expressive dialect of the plains, from the pen of an early Black Hills pioneer, Capt. Jack Crawford, the "poet scout," to his friend, Buffalo Bill, a brother scout, lamenting the sad fate of Custer, under whom they both served, is well worth preserving, not only on account of its merits, and the popularity of the author, but as a *specimen of real Black Hills literature:*—

1.

Did I hear the news from Custer?
   Well, I reckon I did, old pard.
It came like a streak o' lightning,
   And you bet, it hit me hard.
I ain't no hand to blubber,
   And the briny ain't run for years,
But chalk me down for a lubber
   If I didn't shed regular tears.

2.

What for? Now, look ye here, Bill;
   You're a bully boy, that's true.
As good as ever wore buckskin,
   Or fought with the boys in blue.
But I'll bet my bottom dollar,
   Ye had no trouble to muster
A tear, or perhaps a hundred,
   When ye heard of the death of Custer.

3.

He always thought well of you, pard;
   And, had it been Heaven's will,
In a few more days you'd met him,
   And he'd welcome his old scout Bill;
For, if you remember, at Hat Creek
   I met ye with General Carr,
We talked of the brave young Custer,
   And recounted his deeds of war.

4.

But still, we knew even then, pard,
   And that's just two weeks ago,
How little we dreamed of disaster,
   Or that he had met the foe,
That the fearless, reckless hero,
   So loved by the whole frontier,
Had died on the field of battle,
   In this, our Centennial year.

5.

I served with him in the army,
   In the darkest days of the war,
And I reckon, ye know his record,
   For he was our guiding star.
And the boys who gathered round him
   To charge in the early morn,
War' jest like the brave who perished
   With him on the Little Horn.

6.

And where is the satisfaction,
   And how are we going to get square?
By giving the reds more rifles?
   Inviting them to take more hair?
We want no scouts, no trappers,
   No men who know the frontier,
Phil, old boy, you're mistaken,
   You must have the volunteer.

7.

Never mind that 200,000,
   But give us 100 instead.
Send 5,000 men toward Reno,
   And soon we won't leave you a red.
It will save Uncle Sam lots of money,
   In fortress we need not invest.
Just wallop the devils this summer,
   And the miners will do all the rest.

8.

The Black Hills is now filled with miners,
   The Big Horn will soon be as full,
And which will present the most danger
   To Crazy Horse and Old Sitting Bull—
A band of 10,000 frontiersmen,
   Or a couple of forts, with a few
Of the boys in the East, now enlisting?
   Friend Cody, I leave it with you.

9.

They talk about peace with the demons,
  By feeding and clothing them well,
I'd as soon think an angel from heaven
  Would reign with contentment in hell.
And some day these Quakers will answer,
  Before the great Judge of all
For the death of daring young Custer,
  And the boys that around him did fall.

10.

Perhaps, I am judging them harshly?
  But I mean what I'm telling ye, pard,
I'm letting them down mighty easy,
  Perhaps, they may think it is hard,
But I tell you the day is approaching,
  The boys are beginning to muster,
That day of the great retribution,
  The day of revenge for our Custer.

11.

And I will be with you, friend Cody,
  My weight will go in with the boys,
I shared all their hardships last winter,
  I shared all their sorrows and joys.
So tell them I'm coming, friend William,
  I trust I will meet you ere long,
Regards to the boys in the mountains,
  Yours truly, in friendship still strong.

THE SUMMER CAMPAIGN

    Although the Yellowstone Expedition had, up to that time, met only with disaster and defeat, the campaign was by no means abandoned. The respective commands of Gens. Terry and Crook were soon heavily reinforced, and on the thirtieth day of July—a little more than a month after the battles of the Little Big Horn—an order was received by those officers from Gen. Sheridan to unite their forces and move at once against the hostiles gathered on the Rosebud.

In pursuance of instructions from headquarters in Chicago, on the morning of August 5th, Gen. Crook, with the Second, Third, and Fifth Cavalry regiments in command of Lieut.-Col. Carr, and ten companies of the Fourth, Ninth, and Fourteenth Infantry under Major Chambers, numbering in the aggregate about 2,000 well-equipped soldiers with a force of volunteer and Crow scouts, accompanied by pack trains, set out from his base, on Goose creek, to join Gen. Terry, stationed on the Yellowstone.

The command took up its line of march, down the valley of the Tongue river, thence in a northwesterly direction, over the intervening mountainous bluffs to the valley of the Rosebud, striking the trail over which Custer and his command bravely marched to their Waterloo six weeks before. On the 10th a junction was effected with Gen. Terry about thirty-five miles above the mouth of that stream, but as might reasonably have been expected, the birds had flown—the wary warriors, anxious to avoid a battle with the soldiers, in their somewhat weakened condition, had taken flight. It soon became apparent, from the divergent trails, after leaving the valley of the Rosebud, that the hostile forces had separated into bands, and it subsequently developed that Sitting Bull and his adherents had turned their steps toward the Canadian border, while Crazy Horse and his following had branched out in the general direction of the Black Hills. Without loss of time, Gen. Terry's Fifth Infantry regiment was countermarched to the Yellowstone, for the purpose of patrolling the river and intercepting, if possible, the fleeing savages; but they were not to be caught, as they had made good their escape across the river, and were already on their way towards a place of refuge on British soil.

The next day, August 11th, hoping to overtake the hostile bands that had fled to the eastward, the combined forces crossed the divide, following the trail of the Indians to the Tongue river, then down the valley of that stream, for two days' march, then over the divide and down the valley of Powder river to the Yellowstone, where they arrived on the 17th, without sighting a single Indian.

After their long forced march over the rough divides, and down the valleys of the streams, the command, apparently abandoning all hope of overtaking the enemy, decided to halt for a few days for rest and recuperation on the banks of the Yellowstone.

On the 24th the united forces moved up the Powder river about twenty miles, and on the 26th Gen. Terry returned with his command to the Yellowstone, while the forces of Gen. Crook, fortified with the regular rations of hard tack, bacon, etc., for fifteen days, began their terrible march eastward across the country, in distant pursuit of the fugitive bands. For ten days they plodded along for the most time through rain and mud, bivouacking at night on the sodden ground; enduring, with the soldier's proverbial philosophy, all the trying discomforts of the march without a murmur, reaching the head of Heart river, on the evening of September the 5th. As up this time no Indians had been seen, the conclusion was reached that they had turned their course in the direction of the Black Hills, which conclusion determined the subsequent movement of the commanding general.

In the gray of the following morning, September 6th, Gen. Crook instead of continuing his course east to Fort Lincoln—as some of the weary soldiers hoped he might do, being the most available point at which to replenish their nearly exhausted supplies,—marched his command due south, through a wholly unknown country, crossing the Cannon Ball, the two forks of the Grand and the Moreau rivers towards the Black Hills, under the most inauspicious circumstances. Many of the trails appeared to lead in the direction of the Hills, to whose people Gen. Crook, fully realizing their imminent peril, was anxious to give protection.

Gen. Crook's command was at this time in a truly deplorable condition. Rations were well-nigh exhausted; officers and men being forced to resort to horseflesh to satisfy gaunt hunger. Horses became so jaded that many had to be abandoned altogether; thus compelling cavalrymen to join the ranks of the infantry, who, footsore and weary, had often to wade through mud nearly knee-deep,—the rain being almost incessant during the last week of that memorable march. Mud and water covered the face of the land along the valleys of the streams, and the exhausted soldiers were fortunate indeed if they had not to lie in pools of water at night—not a very delectable bed for a tired body. In short, it may be said that Crook's command suffered hardships, exposure, and privations during the closing days of the summer campaign against the hostiles, rarely paralleled in the annals of military marches. Nothing daunted, however, by the difficulties in the way, the expedition marched bravely on as rapidly as the limitations would permit.

Tiring of the monotony of horse steak straight, on the night of the 7th of August, Capt. Mills, with 150 of the best mounted troopers of the Third Cavalry, was detailed to make a dash ahead to the nearest settlements for the purpose of procuring supplies for the command. On reaching the vicinity of Slim Buttes he surprised a village of Brule Sioux, under Chief Roman Nose, capturing about 400 ponies and other property, including a quantity of dried meat, and making a number of the braves prisoners.

Among the property found in their possession was a Seventh Cavalry guidon, a number of saddles and officers' uniforms, the gauntlets of the brave Capt. Keogh, and three Seventh Cavalry horses—proof that the band were redhanded from the Little Big Horn.

A courier mounted on the swiftest horse was dispatched in hot haste to meet the approaching column, with news of the surprise and capture, and a request from Capt. Mills that a force be sent with all possible speed to his support, as there was danger that the escaped warriors might return with reinforcements, sufficient to overpower him. The news of the surprise and capture was hailed by the soldiers with exceeding delight, and the prospect of having a passage with the hostiles inspired them to a high degree of enthusiasm—for in truth, they would have perferred more fighting and less marching through the rain and mud—besides, they felt that they were owing the savages a big debt, which they were exceedingly anxious to pay.

Without delay the cavalry forces eagerly galloped to the scene of danger, and closely in their wake followed the infantry. Before noon of that day the command had arrived. It was learned from the prisoners that Crazy Horse's village of 300 lodges was only twenty miles away, but owing to the fatigue of the men, and the jaded condition of the horses, it was deemed advisable not to move against the village, but to wait for an attack by the Indians. As was anticipated, about four o'clock p.m. Crazy Horse with his warriors dashed upon the scene, with fierce warwhoop, brandishing their arms and otherwise demonstrating their fell purpose of speedily annihilating Gen. Crook's entire command and recapturing their poines.

This time, however, they reckoned without their hosts. Quickly the command formed into a line of defense around the captured village and property and opened a brisk fire upon the attacking savage forces.

It is part of Indian fighting tactics to stand in solid phalanx to be shot at, as do trained soldiers, so, in the manner peculiar to them, the mounted warriors rode wildly hither and yon for a short time, then circled round and round the environed village, meanwhile returning the fire of the troops, in search of a pregnable point through which they could make a sudden dash and recapture the lost ponies. No such weak point was to be found in the lines, the command standing as firm and solid as a stone wall. The lines stood bravely and unflinchingly facing the shot of the yelling savages, until darkness put a stop to the conflict, when the Indians withdrew, bearing away the dead bodies of a number of their braves, without accomplishing their purpose.

In this fight at Slim Buttes Gen. Crook lost twenty men, while Crazy Horse it was thought lost many more; however, their loss could not positively be ascertained, as Indians always bear away their slain warriors, when they fall, at any personal risk.

By the time the smoke of battle had cleared away, the soldiers again began to realize that remorseless hunger was gnawing at their vitals; to satisfy which fortunately the dried meat, a part of the fruits of Capt. Mills' conquest, was available,—an agreeable change from the horse meat, upon which they had principally subsisted for the few previous days.

The command camped that night on the field of battle, and in the early morning resumed its march Black Hills-ward leaving the First Cavalry battalion, under Major Upham, to destroy the village. Hardly was the rear of the main column out of sight, before the Indians renewed the attack, but being severely repulsed, they withdrew and were not again seen.

The march of Crook's command from Crow creek to Crook City,—which has fittingly been designated the "Mud March," was one long to be remembered by the soldiers. Some of the nearly famished infantry men were disposed to give up the terrible struggle altogether; a few succumbed, and sank down in their tracks from sheer exhaustion, unwilling to make any farther exertion, and only by much urging and persuasion could they be induced to stagger to their feet and renew the struggle. Numerous cavalry horses, worn out by the hard forced march and insufficient feed, had to be left behind.

On the 13th Capt. Mills, who had again, on the night of the 10th, been dispatched ahead to the settlements, started back supplies to meet the command, which had that same day crossed the swollen Belle Fourche and encamped on the south bank of that stream. Relief was near at hand, for soon after going into camp the hearts of the hungry soldiers were made glad by the arrival of a small herd of beef cattle, followed a little later by several wagon loads of supplies, forwarded by citizens of Deadwood to relieve the needs of the soldiers of the command.

In response to an invitation from the Common Council of the city Gen. Crook and staff visited Deadwood, where they were accorded a hearty welcome and generous hospitality, in grateful recognition of the services of the gallant commander in behalf of the people of the Hills. A public reception, at which the polished and genial Gen. Dawson acted as master of ceremonies, was held, when his many friends in Deadwood and surrounding camps had an opportunity of grasping the hand of the brave Indian fighter. On the 27th, in acknowledgment of the courtesies extended on that occasion, Gen. Crook sent the subjoined letter to Deadwood, from headquarters at Omaha:—

Headquarters Dept. of the Platte,
Omaha, Sept. 27th, 1876.

Gentlemen: At this, the earliest moment, I desire to acknowledge the courtesy of the resolutions passed by your honorable body, inviting me to accept the hospitality of your city, and likewise to express, in behalf of myself and staff, a most grateful appreciation of kindness bestowed upon us while with you. To your Mayor, E. B. Farnum, and Messrs. Kurtz, Philbrook, and

Dawson, for the thorough manner in which their duties as a committee were carried out, I desire to make known our feelings of lasting indebtedness.

Your obedient servant,
GEO. CROOK, Brig.-General.

To Mayor and Council of Deadwood.

After a few days of much-needed rest, Crook's command marched from Crook to Custer City, where it remained in camp until the early part of October, when, after a short reconnoissance down the south fork of the Cheyenne river, it returned to Buffalo Gap, thence proceeded directly to Fort Niobrara in Nebraska, where the expedition disbanded October 14th, 1876.

Thus, after nearly nine months of uninterrupted service, ended the Yellowstone Expedition of 1876; and although the great Indian campaign was marked by no signal victories in battle, it resulted in effectually breaking up the gigantic combination of the hostile tribes, driving their standard-bearer, a fugitive, towards the Canadian border, and scattering other hostile bands in the direction of their agencies, whither many of the least warlike soon went, thus accomplishing in great measure the object for which the campaign was inaugurated.

In disbanding Gen. Crook made the following address to his command:—

"In the campaign now closed, I have been obliged to call upon you for much hard service and many sacrifices of personal comfort. At times you have been out of reach of your base of supplies in most inclement weather, and have marched without food and slept without shelter. In your engagements you have evinced a high order of discipline and courage; in your marches, wonderful powers of endurance, and in your deprivations and hardships, patience and fortitude.

"Indian warfare is, of all warfares, the most trying and the most thankless. Not recognized by the United States Congress as war, it possesses for you all the disadvantages of civilized warfare, with all the horrible accompaniments that barbarism can invent and savages execute. In it you are required to serve without the incentive of promotion or recognition, in truth, without favor or the hope of reward. The people of our sparsely settled frontier in whose defense you have labored, have but little influence with the powerful communities in the East; their representatives have little voice in our national councils, while your savage foes are not only the wards of the government and supported in idleness by the nation, but objects of sympathy with large numbers of people otherwise well-informed and discerning. You may therefore congratulate yourselves that in the performance of your military duty you have been on the side of the weak against the strong, and that the few people on the frontier will remember your efforts with gratitude.

GENERAL GEORGE CROOK."

Soon after the disbandment of Crook's command, in October, a detachment of soldiers under command of Major Brown, was sent from Fort Robinson to protect the people of the Black Hills from the depredations of Crazy Horse, who maintained a hostile attitude towards the people until April, 1877, when he surrendered and active hostilities on the part of Indians came to a close.

However, not until about four years later, after having met with several bad defeats at the hands of Gen. Miles, did the Sioux tribes manifest a willingness to surrender and return to their agencies, which they finally did about the 1st of June, 1881, when they came down the Missouri river in steamboats by the hundreds to the Missouri river agencies.

CHAPTER XVIII

1876

The year 1876 may be accounted the crucial period of Black Hills pioneer history. It was essentially the chaotic period; the era of disorder and crime, when, in the absence of civil law, might struggled for the mastery over right; the period when danger followed closely on the trail of the wayfarer, all along the line of march into the Hills, hovering on their flanks during the day, and stalking about their campfires at night; the period when danger lurked behind each cliff and headland along the borders, and peered in at the door of every rude cabin in the mining settlements, near their limits; the year when the pioneers had to do yeoman service in battling with the blood-thirsty Sioux for the establishment of civilization in the Black Hills, many losing their lives, others escaping death by a very narrow margin indeed. In short, the year 1876 was one prolonged tragedy. Ah, what memories cluster around those four simple figures! Even as I write them, many of the scenes of that exciting period come trooping past, in mental review; familiar faces and figures rise up in spectral phalanx like the ghosts of those who were but are not.

SOME OF THE EXPEDITIONS OF 1876

The spirit of dangerous unrest, stirred up by the emissaries of Sitting Bull, at the different agencies, in the early spring of 1876, when immigration to the Black Hills was at its flood, resulted in filling the country with numerous marauding bands of painted warriors, armed and equipped for the Yellowstone, who hung along the lines of travel for the purpose of plunder and theft, incidentally killing all those who interfered with the accomplishment of their purpose. Their early operations consisted principally in running off the horses of the many expeditions making their way over the plains to the Hills. Of course, they were not always successful, but it sometimes happened that an expedition, despite the vigilance of its members, would wake up of a bright morning to find its train of loaded wagons stranded on the broad prairie, minus the major part of the motive power, in which case pursuit of the thieves immediately followed. A posse of plucky men would quickly saddle the few horses that were left, buckle on their cartridge belts, mount and give chase. Following up the trail of the red thieves, they would sometimes over-take them and recover the stolen property, at the cost perhpas of two or three of their number; more frequently, however, the stolen stock was never recovered.

The horse-stealing proclivities of the Indians is exemplified in the case of the Hildebrand party while en route to the Black Hills in the spring of 1876.

This expedition, of which L. F. Hildebrand and family were a part, left Bismarck for the Black Hills, about the last of March, 1876. Mr. Hildebrand had been an old-time prospector and miner in Montana, and was therefore schooled in the successes and reverses of mining camps, as well as the dangers incident to Western pioneer life, and had also doubtless learned something of the natural moral turpitude of the red man. At all events, at the end of the first day's march, the expedition closely corralled their wagons, secured their horses with picket ropes a short distance away, and encircled the camp and stock with a body of armed guards, as a precaution against possible attack. A visit on the first night out was hardly looked for, but contrary to their expectations, at about 3 o'clock on the morning of April 1st, just as the moon had disappeared behind the western horizon, a large band of Standing Rock hostiles made a sudden dash through the line of guards and commenced a

SIOUX INDIANS IN WAR COSTUME

rapid firing on the camp—some of the band, meanwhile, trying to cut loose and stampede the horses. In an instant after the first sound of alarm the whole camp was aroused, and the men were rushing through a storm of bullets to protect and save the stock. Mr. Hildebrand with the aid of his two eldest sons, mere lads at the time, succeeded in securing his individual stock and leading them safely within the circle of wagons. All, however were not so fortunate, as in less time than it takes to relate the occurrence, the Indians, with twenty-two head of horses belonging to the expedition, were riding away with the speed of the wind towards the cottonwoods along the Missouri river bottoms.

Quickly a posse was organized and started in hot pursuit on their trail, overtaking the band about twenty miles distant from camp, and by some lively skirmishing recovering every head of the stolen property. Soon after, however, the Indians surrounded the posse, and in an attempt to recapture the stock a fierce fight took place, resulting in the death of one and the wounding of two of the pursuing party, and the killing of nine of their horses. The battle raged for three or four hours, ending in a victory for the owners of the stock, who then returned to camp with the thirteen head that had escaped the deadly bullets of the red skins.

The Indians were, by no means, always responsible for the many thieving raids made on the herds of expeditions along the lines of 1876. Their white brethren of the craft were not a whit behind them, and, if possible, even more dangerous from the standpoint of actual loss. At a very early date in 1876, regularly organized gangs of white horse thieves—if a horse thief can be called white—began plying their nefarious vocation of stealing and running off stock, regardless of ownership, wherever found and whenever a safe opportunity offered itself; and the operations of these banded robbers were so shrewdly planned, and skillfully carried out, aided and abetted, as they were believed to be, by accomplices under the guise of respectability and honesty, that the stolen property was seldom recovered. Sometimes whole herds would be spirited away in the night and led over devious ways and effectually concealed amid the fastnesses, leaving no clue that might lead to their hiding place.

Perhaps the most serious loss inflicted by these outlaws in 1876 was sustained by Chas. Sasse & Co., in the spring of that year, in Red Canyon, where Persimmons Bill's gang despoiled him of every hoof of the stock belonging to his train, leaving him stranded with his family and loads of valuable merchandise, in the dangerous bloody canyon.

On the 11th day of March, 1876, Mr. Sasse and family, accompanied by a small party of men, left Cheyenne, Wyoming, with a train of 100 mules and twenty-five wagons, freighted with a $10,000 cargo of "Early Times" whisky for the Black Hills market. I say Black Hills market, because it is neither reasonable nor safe to even insinuate that Mr. Sasse was transporting, through a dangerously hostile country, such a quantity of the "fiery fluid" for his sole individual use. Be that as it may, as I first asserted, Mr. Sasse & Co. left Cheyenne with $10,000 worth, in real commerical value, of "Early Times" whisky for the Black Hills, which finally found its way into the Deadwood market.

This was probably the first extensive cargo of that kind of merchandise brought to the Black Hills.

Besides the train of loaded wagons, Mr. Sasse had a team of horses and a wagon for his family and the transportation of their private belongings.

The journey proved devoid of accident or interesting incident until reaching to within a day's march of the Cheyenne river stage station, where his team gave out, and, as no Indians had been seen, he decided to halt for a day's rest. They had not been long in camp before Indians were discovered on the distant bluffs overlooking the trail, when Mr. Sasse, realizing the extreme danger of delay, at once pulled out with his exhausted team to try to overtake the train. On reaching the stage station (the suspected headquarters of the gang, then kept by Persimmons Bill and two brothers, one of whom, a veritable giant, was known as Big John) they were approached by the proprietors and urged to remain at the station that night, as the redskins were thick on the trail.

Viewed in the light of the subsequent wholesale theft, they seemed suspiciously anxious, to their credit be it said, that Mrs. Sasse should not be with the train at the time of the intended raid, as there might be occasion for more or less shooting. However, Mr. Sasse, heedless of their importunities, pressed on and joined the train in Red Canyon. That night while the camp was wrapped in midnight slumbers, all unconscious of the impending calamity, the gang, according to their prearranged plan, stole stealthily into camp and quietly took possession of 100 mules and a span of horses, and noiselessly led them away out of the canyon, then over divergent routes to a secure hiding-place. The next morning an attempt was made to trace up the stolen stock, but all clue being lost in the bewildering mazes of the numerous devious trails, the property was never found. Upon discovering the state of affairs in the morning, Mr. Sasse was forced to return to Cheyenne river station and enlist the services of Big John to transport his family to Custer City.

Perhaps few of our early pioneers had a more thrilling experience with the savage marauders than Capt. C. V. Gardner, who, with others, literally fought their way to the Black Hills through bands of hostile Sioux in the spring of 1876. It was on the occasion of his second visit to the Hills that Capt. Gardner's right of way into their once happy hunting-ground was disputed mile by mile with the red men, his first trip being made over an unmolested trail without "let or hindrance." To all lovers of adventure, the following brief account of Capt. Gardner's first and second journey to the Hills may be of interest.

Capt. Gardner, with whose name all old residents of the Black Hills are familiar, arrived in Cheyenne in the early part of March, or perhaps the latter part of February, 1876, en route for the New Eldorado. During the latter part of the former month, after having purchased the necessary equipments for the journey, including a wagon heavily freighted with merchandise and supplies, he left that early outfitting point for the Black Hills, leaving his goods in charge of his partner, known afterwards in the Hills as "Deaf Thompson." Mounting the stage with his sturdy rifle by his side, he sped on his way to Fort Laramie, thence by mail wagon to old Red Cloud Agency. Here he provided himself with an Indian pony and employed a half-breed Sioux to guide him over the unknown country to Custer at an agreed compensation of $25.00, and all he could realize on the Black Hills mail committed to his (Gardner's) charge by the postal authorities at Red Cloud.

A little after midnight Capt. Gardner and his dusky guide left the agency, and directing their course by the pole-star Black Hills-ward, sleeping nights under the blue starlit canopy without shelter, with lariat ropes secured to their wrists as a safeguard against thieving Indians, reached Buffalo Gap on the third day out from the agency. Traveling up Buffalo Gap Canyon three or four miles, they found on the trail three disabled wagons, from which the horses had been cut and driven off, and lying about, flour sacks and trunks, torn and broken open and contents scattered to the four winds,—the handiwork of the Indians. Continuing their journey towards Custer, when near Point of Rocks, they came upon the party, whose outfit lay demolished and scattered back in the canyon, consisting of about forty persons including families, the latter in the most pitiable state of alarm, some wringing their hands in grief— lamenting the killing of one of their comrades by the Indians. With this forlorn party Capt. Gardner camped for the night, going into Custer on the following morning. After a brief stay of three days in Custer, satisfied as to the prospective outlook for the Black Hills as a gold-producing region, the captain started back on his journey for Cheyenne with a returning empty freight train and about 200 disgusted tenderfeet who were turning their backs upon the Black Hills for all time; no incident worthy of note occurring on the outward trip save that of finding while in camp at Red Canyon, the arrow-pierced body of the colored woman of the Metz-family-massacre.

On reaching Cheyenne Capt. Gardner purchased 60,000 pounds of merchandise, contracted with Chas. Hecht, then of Cheyenne, to transport the goods to the Black Hills at the rate of thirteen and one-fourth cents per pound, and again started for the Hills by stage to Fort Laramie. At the Platte river he joined a large party of gold-seekers, also destined for the Black Hills, among whom were Geo. Boland, Dick Horsford, and Jack King, popularly known in the Hills as the Black Hills rhymist, and brother of "Honest Dick," than whom braver men never crossed the hostile plains to the Black Hills. The party reached Hat Creek Station without molestation and camped for the night. The next morning, however, their tribulations began, for while at breakfast a band of Indians made a dashing raid on the herd and tried to stampede their stock, but, after a brisk skirmish they were driven off without loss on either side. The train then, with an advance guard, preceded by six mounted men dispatched ahead as scouts, traveled on toward the Hills until reaching a point on the route known as "Down Indian Creek," when the scouts were seen riding back toward the train at full speed, followed closely by a half dozen redskins. When within about twenty rods of the advance guard, the scouts took position behind a little knoll where they hoped to be able to defend themselves until the advance guard came to their assistance. The Indians, however, quickly rode around to the opposite side of the knoll and fired, killing one of the scouts and his horse at the first shot, whereupon the others made a dash for the train which had in the meantime corralled their wagons. Soon thereafter the train was attacked by about fifty Indians, who, directing their fire against the weakest points of the corral, kept up a continuous fusillade, which was gallantly returned from behind the barricade of wagons for the space of two hours, when the Indians withdrew, bearing away five dead horses as the result of the battle,—the train losing two horses.

At the close of the battle some of the party, tenderfeet, whose courage was on the wane, concluding that they already had enough of Indian fighting to last them the rest of their lives, proposed that the train return at once to God's own country, and abandon any further attempt to reach the Black Hills. A few demurred, agreeing, however, to leave the question to the decision of the majority. Accordingly, after burying their dead companion, a meeting was held at which every member voted to take the backward trail but six, viz., Jack King, Geo. Boland, Dick Harsford, Capt. Gardner, and two others. In compliance with the decision of the majority, the train then reversed its course and marched back towards Fort Laramie. After traveling all day, continually harassed by the Indians, they were opportunely met by Chas. Hecht's and Street and Thompson's transportation trains accompanied by twenty-five or thirty well-armed men. The situation being explained, the incoming and outgoing trains went into camp together for the night. Thus reinforced, the timid members of the homeward bound party took renewed courage, and at a joint conference held that night, they almost unanimously decided to turn about and fight their way through the hostile lines into the Hills. The next day at about nine o'clock, another unsuccessful attempt was made to run off the stock of the train, shortly after which the camp was surrounded by, as nearly as could be estimated, about 500 yelling Indians. A participant in the fight that followed thought that the whole Sioux nation might have been engaged in the attack, judging from the hailstorm of bullets that came hurtling against the barricades from every direction, many of which went whizzing through the openings between the wagons in unpleasant, not to say dangerous, proximity to their heads. The trainmen, however, returned the compliment by paying the red-skins back in their own coin, to the extent of their ability, from behind their breastworks of loaded wagons. After an hour's fierce battle of bullets, the Indians ceased firing and left, to renew the attack later, with increased numbers, when the train immediately pulled on for Hat Creek Station.

As the prospect for reaching the Hills, against such determined opposition, seemed remote, they decided at this critical crisis to invoke the protection of Uncle Sam's soldiers. Capt. Gardner and Billy Waugh were delegated to go as messengers to Fort Laramie to petition the commanding officer at that post, for a military escort into the Hills. Mounting the fleetest horses belonging to the train, the two messengers started back on their perilous ride for Fort Laramie, but, on reaching Raw Hide Buttes at 3 o'clock in the morning, they providentally found encamped, near the Buttes, a company of cavalry and one of infantry, under Capt. Egan, sent out from the fort on a scouting expedition after Indians.

Capt. Egan, upon learning the mission of the messengers, and appreciating the dangerous situation, readily consented to escort the imperiled train, at least beyond the point of danger. Without a moment's loss of time Gardner and Waugh then returned, with all possible speed, to Hat creek, when the train pulled out for Indian creek where Capt. Egan had promised to overtake them—which he did on the following day. After the arrival of the military, Capt. Gardner was placed in charge of the train, by the commanding officer, who, after establishing a military post at that point, where the infantry remained, started out with his troops to scour the surrounding country for marauding Indians. The train again pushed on, but after traveling about eight miles one of the wagons became disabled, necessitating a halt for repairs. They had hardly got the wagons corralled, and dinner in process of preparation, before again the alarming cry of Indians! Indians! was heard from different points in the camp. The cry came just as Capt. Gardner, who it appears was the breadmaker of his mess, had his hands in the soft dough. Speedily withdrawing his hands from the mixture, without waiting to wash the sticky substance from them, or even to discard his kitchen apron—with face, perchance, artistically flecked with flour, he, with several others, snatched their guns and hastened with all possible speed to the summit of an adjacent hill

ATTACK ON WAGON TRAIN EN ROUTE TO THE BLACK HILLS IN 1876

nearly a half mile distant from where legions of Sioux warriors, in paint and feathers, were seen making directly towards them. Quickly they retreated towards the camp, frequently turning their faces to see if the tufted heads of the savages had yet appeared above the crest of the hill. Upon reaching camp, a messenger was at once dispatched to Capt. Egan's post on Indian creek to notify the command that the train was surrounded by Indians, and in need of speedy assistance. The messenger was a brave lad, not more than seventeen years of age, who had volunteered his services for the dangerous undertaking. Mounting a swift horse, away the courageous boy flew over the backward trail for Capt. Egan's post. He had hardly disappeared from view before hundreds of whooping Indians came dashing over the crest of the hill, soon surrounding the corral at long range. After wildly circling around the train two or three times, after the manner of Indians, they opened a deadly fire against the barricade of loaded wagons, from behind which the boys hurled back cold lead at the red besiegers, as rapidly as they could load and reload their guns. At the end of three terrible hours, the Indians suddenly ceased firing, and disappeared in a twinkling, almost as quickly as if the earth had opened beneath their feet and swallowed them. With marvelous swiftness they sped away over the hills out of sight. With the wonderful keenness, peculiar to these children of nature, they had in the heat of conflict seen or scented approaching danger. Just at the moment of their disappearance Capt. Egan and his troopers were seen riding with the speed of the wind towards the camp, their beautiful white horses panting, with nostrils distended, and flecked with foam. They had ridden hard to the rescue of the imperiled train. In scouting for Indians Capt. Egan's pack mules had got mired, obliging him to return to his post, where he arrived just as the messenger boy put in an appearance, so that no time was lost in going to the relief of the train, and moreover, if the wagon axle had not broken, necessitating a halt for repairs, the train would doubtless have marched right into the deadly embrace of hundreds of hostile Sioux, and have been nearly if not totally wiped out of existence;—thus it would seem that those two mishaps had worked together for the safety of that train. A fatalist would say, that an overruling Providence had interfered to save that brave band of pioneers from utter annihilation.

The following morning, the train once more started for the Hills, this time under military escort, Capt. Egan having consented to accompany the party to Custer, which was finally reached without further trouble.

On nearing Custer the train was met by nearly the entire population of the city, on their way out to the relief of the beleagured freight outfit, rumors of the dangers that had hedged it about having reached the city, whose supplies, by the way, had gotten to low-water mark.

As the story goes, there was a big pow-wow and dance in the pioneer city that night, in celebration of the narrow escape of the 185 gold-seekers, where "all went merry as a marriage bell."

Tradition says that after the ball was over, there was a sort of spectacular performance, in which Doc Peirce, ably supported by Capt. Gardner and Tom Hooper,—the pioneer legal light of the Black Hills—enacted the leading role. Numerous others were in the cast, but taking minor parts. It is said "there was a hot time in the old town that night."

CHAPTER XIX

MONTANA EXPEDITIONS

The great gold-producing State of Montana yielded a generous tribute to the large stream of gold-seekers entering the Black Hills in 1876, furnishing no insignificant proportion of their total population. It has been estimated that nearly one-twelfth of the population of the Black Hills in 1876 came from that State, which is believed to be an overestimate. Howbeit, it was notable that a liberal percentage of those engaged in placer mining operations, on Deadwood and tributary gulches during that year, were old Montana miners.

The most formidable expedition, perhaps, in point of numbers and the magnitude of its equipments, coming to the Black Hills in 1876, was organized in Montana.

In February, 1876, a movement was inaugurated in Helena, Montana, having for its object the organization of the first expedition from that State to the Black Hills. Notices of the contemplated expedition were published in the press, and also, posted in the various mining camps throughout the State, inviting all who desired to join such an enterprise to rendezvous at a designated point on the Yellowstone, by a stated time, for organization. For a few weeks thereafter, all trails led the Black Hills fever-infected Montanians to the recruiting point on the Yellowstone, whither the leaders had preceded them for the purpose of enrolling members. An organization was soon effected, when, on the 20th day of March, 1876, the expedition of 100 pack mules, a long train of supply wagons, and a party of over 200 men, having in its ranks experienced miners, thrifty ranchmen, and skilled mechanics, each animated by the ambition and determination to become speedily rich, if riches were to be found in the new gold region, marched away from the banks of the Yellowstone on the old Bozeman route for the Black Hills.

As they marched along the old trail they passed over the historic spot where nearly ten years before the tragedy of Fort Phil Kearney was enacted, when a wood train with a small military escort was surrounded and attacked by 2,000 Sioux, Cheyenne, and Arapaho Indians almost within sight of the fort. When first attacked Col. Fetterman, commander at the fort, in answer to a signal from a neighboring hill, hastened to the rescue of the train with a force of nearly 100 soldiers, including officers, every one of whom after a hard gallant struggle lasting two hours was lying dead on the battle-ground,—not a white man was left to rehearse the awful story. The wreaked wagons of the demolished wood train were yet lying in a confused heap at the foot of a hill near the trail.

The expedition continued its course across the dry fork of the Powder river, to the Belle Fourche, and down that stream to Bear Lodge, thence across the country to Spearfish valley, which was reached May 20th, 1876. The expedition had two encounters with the Indians in the Bear Lodge mountains, in one of which a member of the party named Geo. Miller was killed.

Among the members of this expedition were R. H. Evans, G. H. Jones, Jas. Ryan, G. W. Read, F. R. Cooper, G. W. Rosenbaum, J. E. Cook, Mike Burton, Hiram Ross, and J. A. Walton, nearly all of whom settled along the broad fertile valley of the Spearfish, where for two score years they have demonstrated the wonderful agricultural possibilities of the valleys of the Black Hills. Any one traveling down the valley of the Spearfish of an early summer's day will not be confronted, every mile of the way, by a scene fair indeed to look upon. Richly cultivated farms—they cannot now be called ranches—for the most part divided and fenced into fields of more or less acreage, according to convenience or the adaptability of the soil for certain crops, some of them covered with waving grain, fast ripening for the sickle, with here and there large patches of the tubers, such as can be grown nowhere in the world outside of the Black Hills; others covered with rich pasturage, dotted over with fat, sleek kine, commodious farm houses, delightfully embowered amid shade trees, many of them planted by the hands of the owners years before; with luxuriant vegetable gardens in the background,—will be found all along the margin of the river from the Queen City to where Spearfish mingles its crystal waters with the red soil stained waters of the Redwater, altogether making a picture of thrift, cosy comfort, and pastoral beauty that is deliciously refreshing, especially to a denizen of the mountains.

On the 26th of May, 1876, this enterprising colony of Montanians took the first step towards reclaiming the virgin soil of the Spearfish valley from the hands of its savage claimants by locating and staking ranches. Commencing at a point a little more than a mile below the site of Spearfish, locations were made for several miles down the stream, when they were numbered and drawn by lot. Ranch No. 1 fell to the lot of R. H. Evans, which he still owns, and where he still lives. On this ranch Mr. Evans built the first log cabin of the colony, where he spent his two years of bachelorhood in the Black Hills, and it was to that log cabin of one room that, in 1878, he brought his bride, a Miss Pettigrew, and the first school-ma'am of Spearfish, where they lived until an increasing family warned them to provide more spacious quarters.

The cabin is still suffered to stand near its present commodious home, within which stands the first stool made in the valley—valued relics of early days. Let the old log cabin stand. Bolster it up and guard it well. Let no desecrating hand touch a single log or chink or a pole of the roof that sheltered an early pioneer. Let no jack-knife fiend whittle a single chip from the old three-legged stool that served him as a chair. At about the same date Joseph Ramsdell located a ranch a little farther up the valley, a part of which is now Ramsdell's addition to Spearfish. Somewhat later, Otto Uhlig from Deadwood, located the ranch that is now, in whole or in part, Uhlig's addition to the city of many additions. J. E. Cook and Mike Burton located ranches on what is known as Centennial prairie, where they soon established the "Montana herd," and built a stockade for the safe keeping of the large amount of stock committed to their charge,—a precaution which, despite the unremitting vigilance and bravery of the proprietors, did not always prove a certain safeguard against the red horse-thieves, as will be shown farther on.

About a month later, a second, but somewhat smaller expedition arrived in the Hills over the same route, from Montana.

About the first of August, 1876, another expedition, composed in part of Western men, and in part of tenderfeet from different sections of the East, reached the Black Hills from Bismarck. Among those comprising the Western contingent of the expedition, were Sol. Star, Seth Bullock, and John Manning, men to whom the exciting shifting scenes of a big mining camp were no novelty, they having already passed through the trying tenderfoot stage of Western life among the booming mining camps of Montana. They had, it is presumed, a few years before, foresworn the luxuries and comforts, and thrown aside the conventionalities, of Eastern civilization, and followed the guiding Star of Empire westward until it stood over the buried treasure among the spurs of the Big Horn Mountains, where they had, doubtless, experienced some of the vicissitudes and encountered some of the dangers incident to a frontier life, and had become what is termed Westernized, in all that the term implies. Well, let us see. From the standpoint of a Western pioneer they must needs have subsisted for several consecutive weeks on bacon, beans, flapjacks, and black coffee, and slept at least a month on the ground floor of a tent. They must necessarily have chased, or have been chased by, Indians a few times, and have been "held up" by road agents a time or two, to entitle them to their credentials from the tenderfoot grade of Western life.

However, having spent some time amid the fascinating excitement of a gold-mining camp, they were unable to withstand the alluring reports from the newly-discovered placer mines of Dakota, and so resolved to go to Deadwood, the pole-star of attraction of 1876. An arrangement of their affairs being completed, they with a party of thirty-five men, left Helena, Montana, for Fort Benton, the head of navigation on the Missouri river, where they loaded their merchandise, supplies, and other equipments on to a steamer, took passage, and sailed down the river to Fort Lincoln. On reaching Bismarck they joined a large party of gold-seeking adventurers from the East; secured transportation on a freight train about to leave for the Hills, and took up their line of march overland for the Black Hills.

Belonging to the party from the East were J. K. P. Miller, Jas. McPherson, and Al. Burnham, names familiar in the business circles of Deadwood for many years. The two first-named gentlemen could not be termed tenderfeet, as they had spent considerable time in different parts of the West. Al. Burnham, on the contrary, was a self-confessed, unfledged tenderfoot, having never before been west of the Father of Waters. However, he was one day siezed by a spirit of adventure, and, being full of daring, he resolved to cut loose from the trammels and narrow environments of the matured East, and enjoy for a time the freedom and breadth of the vague indefinite West, with its dream of grand possibilities.

With this object in view, one bright morning in the early spring of 1876 he, with grip-sack in hand, left his Eastern home in Michigan on his journey to the region of his dreams, the mountains of the boundless West. At Yankton, after a tedious delay of a whole month, awaiting the clearing of the channel of the stream from ice, he boarded a boat and sailed up the river to Fort Buford; but went no farther in the direction of the setting sun. Whether the Far West had lost its glamor, or the hostile attitude of the Sioux had caused him to cut short his journey in that direction, or whether he had lost his reckonings, is not known. At any rate for some occult reason, he changed his mind and took passage on the next boat down the river for Bismarck.

It would appear that Mr. Burnham had a pretty hard experience on his overland trip to the Black Hills. He not only had to pay a good round price for the transportation of his belongings, but had also to work his passage all the way from Bismarck to Deadwood by whacking oxen for the transportation trains. It is told that the master of that outfit, in addition to freight charges, at first demanded ten dollars per capita for the privilege of walking along beside the train,—that, however, may be an exaggerated story. It is inferred that complete harmony and the utmost brotherly love were not distinguishing features of the overland journey of that expedition to the Hills—that is, all did not pull in the same harness, apparently.

On the last day of July, John Manning and a few others of the party arrived in Deadwood, having pulled out from the train at some point on the latter part of the route.

SOL. STAR
Deadwood's Popular Mayor

On the first day of August, 1876, Sol. Star, Seth Bullock, James McPherson, J. K. P. Miller, and Al. Burnham, reached Deadwood just in time to see demonstrated the kind of material Deadwood was in part composed of in 1876. The next day Wild Bill was assassinated in broad daylight.

Continuing the business copartnership entered into before leaving Helena, Montana, Star & Bullock immediately secured a desirable business lot on the corner of Main and Wall streets, by the payment of $1,100.00 purchase money and proceeded at once to prepare the ground for building. A commodious building was soon erected on the site, in which the company, with the keen foresight of shrewd business men, established the hardware business along its various lines and on a scale commensurate with the demands of a large and growing mining community. The business was carried on in this building until the property was destroyed by the great fire which swept away almost the entire business portion of the young city in 1879. Nothing daunted by their disastrous loss the company soon rebuilt a larger and more commodious structure upon the ashes of the old, with the addition of a large fire-proof building of brick, and re-established the business along the same lines, but on a more extended scale than before, where it was continued until removed in 1895 to give place to the handsome stone structure, the Bullock Hotel, now occupying the site. The business was then removed to the building next door west of the Bullock Hotel, where it is still carried on by the later members of the firm. For many years the company of Star & Bullock has stood high in point of reliability and business integrity among the leading business firms of Deadwood, where, as individual members of society, they have ever been wide awake to all that pertained to the advancement and prosperity of their adopted city. Individually they have been honored with various positions of trust and responsibility in municipal and county affairs, during their long continuous residence in the Hills.

Mr. Star has the honor of having been chosen as member of the council of the first city organization of Deadwood in the fall of 1876. On May 24th, 1879, he was appointed postmaster of the Deadwood Post Office by President R. B. Hayes. In 1884 he was elected to the mayoralty of the municipality of Deadwood, and re-elected for every successive term thereafter until 1892 inclusive, and was again re-elected in 1896 for a term of two years, and is therefore now at the head of Greater Deadwood's city government. Mr. Star's long, almost uninterrupted service in the interests of Deadwood, tells more eloquently than can mere words of his executive ability; his skillful management of intricate municipal affairs; his exceeding popularity, and above all his loyalty and devotion to the best interests of the city at the head of whose government he now stands.

Mr. Bullock enjoys the distinction of having been Lawrence County's first sheriff. He was appointed by Gov. Pennington to the shrievalty of the newly organized county and assumed its duties at a critical period in the history of the great mining region of Deadwood, where, for the major part, centered the population of Lawrence County in 1877. It was at a time when valuable mining and other property was frequently in dispute, and whose rightful owners were sometimes dispossessed and kept at bay at the muzzle of a shot-gun or six-shooter; at a time when all kinds of lawlessness, horse-stealing, cattle-rustling, etc., were rampant in the valley north of the Hills, and hydra-headed immorality was in full swing in the highways and by-ways of Deadwood; when desperadoes and crooks galore were prowling about the streets in sheep's clothing, seeking whom they might devour. Deadwood albeit was no worse than all other large new mining camps where outlaws are wont to congregate.

The time had now arrived when law and order must be evolved out of all this seething chaos of iniquity. It was a pretty difficult as well as perilous problem that the first sheriff of Lawrence County was called upon to grapple with. However, Mr. Bullock was well equipped by experience for the work required of him, he having served in the same capacity out among the mining camps of Montana, and was possessed of the nerve and courage to perform his sworn duty; no connivance at wrong-doing, or collusion with wrong-doers, can be laid at his door. He would ferret out and follow the trail of a criminal with all the keenness of a sleuth on the track of a deer, but, when once in his custody, he was equally ready to uphold the law, in protecting his prisoner against a clamorous mob, seeking to mete out summary punishment to the lawbreaker. It is the universal verdict of the early settlers that to Sheriff Bullock was largely due the comparative peace and security prevailing in the county during the term of his appointment.

190 THE BLACK HILLS; OR,

BLACK HILLS TREASURE COACH
The last coach, photographed while going at full speed down the gulch near old toll-gate between Deadwood and Sturgis

John Manning, who succeeded Mr. Bullock as sheriff of Lawrence County, was elected by the popular vote of the county at the election of November, 1877, for a term of one year, and was re-elected to the position in November, 1878, for a term of two years. The conditions confronting Sheriff Manning were similar to those existing during the incumbency of his predecessor. Lawlessness had not ceased to exist, far from it, consequently the duties of sheriff to Lawrence County in 1878 were by no means a sinecure. Arrests requiring plenty of pluck and nerve, and sometimes involving great personal hazard, were of almost daily occurrence, in the execution of which duties Sheriff Manning was never known to show the "white feather."

The extensive litigation, following the establishment of regular courts in the Hills, largely increased the volume of sheriff's business along the line of process serving, during Mr. Manning's terms of office, making the position one much sought after, because of the rapidly accumulating fees. That Sheriff Manning performed the various arduous duties of his office to the entire satisfaction of the majority of the electors of Lawrence County, is fully attested by his re-election for a second term of two years.

J. K. P. Miller and James McPherson will be remembered as two of Deadwood's most prominent business men, for many years. Soon after their arrival in Deadwood, they established jointly the largest wholesale and retail grocery house then in the Black Hills, whose business extended far beyond the locality of the city and the adjacent mining camps, into the remote towns of the Hills. In connection with this business they opened, late in the fall of 1876, the second banking house established in the Black Hills under the firm name of Miller & McPherson. The firm stood high in the commercial circles of Deadwood and were regarded individually as two of its foremost and most valued citizens. Mr. Miller was the head and front of the enterprise for building the little stretch of steam railway, now running hourly between Deadwood and Lead. He carried on a flourishing trade for many years, or until broken health compelled him to throw off the burden and responsibilities of active business life, and seek rest and possible restoration to health in other climes. Finally, however, death claimed him for its own.

Al. Burnham, although coming to the Hills a tenderfoot, certainly possessed none of the average tenderfoot's fatuity in expecting to find a royal road to wealth by picking up golden nuggets along his pathway in the Black Hills. Preeminently self-reliant and practical, he at once took up the pursuit of professional architect and builder, thus compelling brawn and brain to solve the problem. Doubtless many of the finest structures which grace the streets of Deadwood to-day were planned and fashioned by his skillful hands. During his twenty-one years of residence in the Hills, Mr. Burnham has been an esteemed and loyal citizen of Deadwood.

THE CENTENNIAL PARTY

The party bearing the above distinguishing title was organized, for the purpose of exploring the gold fields of Dakota, at Ames, Iowa, in January, 1876. The organization, consisting of only fourteen members, comprised the following names: John Johnston, Hugh Johnston, G. W. Rogers, agent Chicago & N. W. Railway, B. A. Little, R. H. Miller, A. Olson, J. M. Moulton, E. P. Cronen, W. U. Tel. Co., W. H. LaRue, N. Nickson, Lafayette Evans, T. Kinney, W. A. Noland, and a Mr. Otto. Nearly all were residents of Ames and vicinity, none others being eligible to membership according to the regulations. Of the hundreds of applicants for membership from other parts of the State, Dr. Overman alone was permitted to sign his name to the roster of the party. By a suspension of the rules, against the admission of strangers into the organization, Dr. Overman was taken into the exclusive circle on the score of former friendship. However, the doctor failed to complete his arrangements in time and thus did not reach the Black Hills until three months later. John Johnston, the leading spirit of the enterprise, was dispatched to Chicago for supplies and equipments for the party; preliminary preparations were soon made, and on the 1st day of March, 1876, the Centennial Party of fourteen men, with two loaded wagons, left their comfortable homes, in the midst of a wild March storm that reached almost the magnitude of a blizzard, and marched away westward through Sioux City and over the old Elkhorn route for the Black Hills, under the captaincy of John Johnston.

Nothing notable occurred on the journey until reaching O'Neill, the last settlement on the route, where they decided to rest for a day, one of the party being sick. While in camp at O'Neill, a buckskin-clad scout rode into camp with a message from another party of gold adventurers, asking them to delay their journey a day longer, or until the other party could overtake and join them, which was agreed to. "Buckskin," as he was ever after called, went back with the message, and on the following day a well-armed and equipped party of eighty-one men and seventeen teams joined them. Jack Daly, for many years a resident of Lead, was one of the new party. "Buckskin" attached himself to, and was afterwards considered one of, the Centennial Party. On the arrival of the party in Custer little was to be found of an encouraging character; scores of empty houses, a few men scattered along French creek prospecting, and a good many other men doing nothing, was by no means inspiring to the members of this little party, who were mostly tenderfeet, and a feeling of bitter disappointment began to creep over them; in short they began to wish themselves back in their comfortable positions in Ames, Iowa. The sick member of the party was sent back by a returning freight train, and the thirteen left Custer for Hill City, where they found just five men and some more empty houses, which decided them to go no further, as they had already seen enough of the Black Hills to satisfy them that they were by no means what they were reputed to be. A vote was taken on the question of returning to the States, which resulted in twelve to one in favor of going back, the dissenting vote being that of John Johnston, whose wishes in the matter could not be altogether ignored, as he was the largest stockholder in the property of the outfit. After discussing the question into the "wee-sma' " hours of the morning, Mr. Johnston finally agreed to let the twelve take one of the wagons and enough provisions to last them out, and he would take the other wagon and the remainder of the supplies, and continue his journey to the north of the Hills. However, when the division of the property commenced, five of the twelve changed their minds, and joined Mr. Johnston on his trip to the north, the other seven returning to the States.

Of course there is perhaps nothing remarkable, or even unusual, in all of this. It is notable, however, that this Centennial Party gave its name to that large stretch of country around the headwaters of False Bottom creek, known as Centennial Prairie. "Buckskin" and others while out on the prairie cutting hay, one day in July, 1876, christened it "Centennial Prairie," in compliment to the Centennial Party, a name which has clung to it ever since, and will continue to cling to it for a long time to come. To a member of the Centennial Party, John Johnston, also belongs the distinction of having established in connection with Capt. Gardner, the first newspaper published in Spearfish City, compelling its success under conditions which would make the average journalist hesitate. It is notable too that a member of this Centennial Party (Mr. Johnston) was among the first to settle at the head of the Spearfish valley in 1876, and who, ever since the founding of the Queen City of the Hills, has been intimately identified with every movement looking to its growth and prosperity. Mr. Johnston has also been a real force in the promotion of numerous mining enterprises, having spent time and money with a lavish hand in the development of various mining properties throughout the northern Hills during the past twenty years.

OUTWARD BOUND PILGRIMS

While this continuous stream of emigration was making its way over the hostile plains from the North, South, East, and West, in the spring of 1876, many of those who had entered during the previous fall and winter, finding themselves stranded in Custer in the spring without a dollar in their pockets, and no faith in the country, and their little stock of "grub" which they had been economically eking out through the winter diminished to nearly the last pot of beans and the last slice of bacon, disappointed, disheartened and disgusted, went out of the Hills any way to get out, figuratively shaking the dust of the Black Hills off their feet (not gold dust) in testimony against them, and many of them hurling back bitter anathemas as they went. Tenderfeet they were, for the most part, who, lured by the golden reports and buoyed with hope, had left comfortable homes, innocently believing that the coveted treasure was to be picked up along the wayside by the handfuls. Failing to realize their expectations they denounced the glowing reports sent out broadcast over the land as a delusion and a snare. Ah, the poor fellows had yet to learn a lesson—the lesson which teaches that it is only by months, yea, sometimes years, of hard, unceasing toil, under crushing discouragements and disappointments, that even the few of those who dig for gold realize their dreams. Yes, those outward-bound pilgrims were mostly tenderfeet, and as many of them with badly worn shoes, some nearly barefoot, had to walk out, it is easy to believe that their feet were painfully tender ere reaching their homes; that some of them never reached their destination is well known.

CHAPTER XX

CHAPTER OF FIRST EVENTS

The first town-site laid out and platted in the Black Hills was Harney City. The site for the prospective Harney City—the city of such wonderful future possibilities (?)—was regularly surveyed and platted in March, 1875, in the valley of French creek, near the stockade.

The work of laying out the site into streets and blocks was done by Lyman Lamb, Thos. H. Russell, and other members of the party, it being accomplished by the use of a small pocket compass and a picket rope. Harney City, however, was but a dream of its founders, as it never materialized beyond a few foundations on the most desirable corner lots.

The first miners' meeting ever held in the Black Hills, met on French creek, a short distance above the present site of Custer City, on or about the 17th day of June, 1875. There were sixteen persons present at the meeting, among whom were A. D. Trask, now of Pactola, Joseph Reynolds, and Jas. Corneile. A mining district was organized, of which A. D. Trask was chosen recorder.

Custer is entitled to the distinction of being the first town built in the Black Hills. It was laid out and platted on the 10th of August, 1875; the work of surveying being done by Thos. Hooper, aided by a detachment of United States soldiers of Major Pollock's command, the inevitable pocket compass and picket rope being used for the purpose. The first plat of the pioneer city was made by Thos. Hooper on a piece of birch bark 12x12 inches square, as before stated.

The first ton of gold-bearing quartz taken out of the Black Hills for treatment, was mined and transported to Cheyenne, Wyoming, by Joseph Reynolds, in August, 1875. The ore was mined from a ledge about three and one-half miles above Custer City. It was freighted out to Cheyenne where it was sampled and shipped to Georgetown, Colorado, for treatment; the test from best samples resulting in seventeen dollars in gold per ton of quartz.

The first building erected in the Black Hills—barring the seven log cabins within the walls of the stockade—was put in course of construction by Dr. D. M. Flick. The building was substantial hewn-log structure, designed as a home for his family whenever the way was made clear. When this pioneer building neared completion the doctor consented to leave the Hills with the exodus of miners, in obedience to the order of Gen. Crook in August of that year.

Soon thereafter the building was completed by Capt. Pollock and occupied by him as military headquarters during the remainder of his stay in the Hills.

After the withdrawal of the military forces from the Hills, Capt. Jack Crawford, the poet-scout, took possession of and occupied the building undisturbed until one bright morning, about the middle of April, 1876, when Dr. Flick drove up to the door of his residence with his family and household goods, to find it appropriated by somebody who was absent at the time—the doctor didn't know, and didn't care a continental who. In nowise daunted by the unfavorable aspect of the situation, he unloaded his goods, took formal possession of the building, and awaited developments. It is needless to say that the doctor made himself quite generally at home, Mrs. Flick meanwhile making active preparations for dinner.

Just as the family was seated at the table enjoying their noonday meal under their own vine and fig tree, Capt. Jack, with his friend, Attorney T. Harvey, appeared at the door and entered unbidden—doubtless greatly surprised to find what he regarded as a base usurper comfortably domiciled in his snug quarters. The captain, of course, demanded an explanation, as well as an unconditional surrender of the premises, and asked, sternly: "Sir, by what right, and by whose authority are you here?" The doctor replied, defiantly: "By right of ownership, and by my own authority, sir. I need none other. That is good enough for me." Capt. Jack, naturally feeling that his most sacred rights had been ruthlessly invaded, ordered the doctor to "vamoose the ranch" instanter and take all his belongings with him, or take the consequences. Whereupon the doctor, fully conscious of the righteousness of his position, quickly reached for his trusty Sharp's rifle, which stood conveniently at hand, swiftly leveled it at the "poet-scout," and indicating the door, told him to go. The captain, though brave and fearless, having faced many deadly perils in his lifetime, deeming "discretion the better part of valor," wisely withdrew, to appear again in another attitude.

These conflicting claims resulted in the

SECOND SUIT IN EQUITY IN THE BLACK HILLS

Attorney Tom Harvey, in behalf of his client, Capt. Jack Crawford, at once brought action against D. W. Flick for forcible entry and detainer (probably), and in due lapse of time the case was called up for hearing before Provisional-Justice Keifer, and a jury of five miners, good and true. Upon the

DR. D. W. FLICK
The builder of the first cabin erected in the Black Hills in 1875

hearing of the evidence pro and con, Attorney Harvey, in closing for the prosecution, briefly summed his case, in clear, forcible, and convincing language—basing his arguments, we may presume, upon two important points. First, that inasmuch as every square foot of territory, as well as every stick of timber, cut from the trees growing in the valley, or along the mountain slopes of the Black Hills, belonged by virtue of a solemn treaty to the Indians, no title was or could be vested in the defendant.

Second, that the building, as proven by competent witnesses, had been abandoned by the defendant, and was at the time of forcible entry in the rightful and peaceable possession of his client, therefore, in the absence of title, and by virtue of such possession which—he reminded the jury—was, in all civilized communities, considered nine points of the law, but in the Black Hills was at least ten points, or the whole law, he asked that a verdict be rendered in favor of his client, Capt. Jack Crawford, placing him in repossession of the disputed premises. Here the prosecution rested.

In answer, the defendant in his own behalf, rising to the full necessity of the occasion, said, with cutting sarcasm, that he was as fully cognizant of the impossibility of acquiring valid title to property in the Black Hills, as the distinguished counsel for the prosecution, and therefore admitted that point, and did not deny the claim to possession, but that he claimed a title far beyond and above all civil law—an equitable claim, under which every man on God's footstool has the divine right to reap the fruits of his own honest labor.

The doctor waxed eloquent. He told the jury in telling words, and beautifully rounded periods, of how he had procured the timber from the virgin forests that adorned the hillsides hard by, and had them hauled to the ground selected for a home for his family, where they were hewn, fashioned and fitted in their respective places in the structure—all of which was paid for—in part by the sweat of his own brow, but mostly in the true "coin of the realm"—good lawful money of Uncle Sam. He told also, of how, when the fabric was on the verge of completion, he went out of the Hills—like a true patriot, under military escort, with the full determination of returning at the first favorable opportunity. In his closing peroration, it is easy to imagine that the doctor told the jury that he proposed to defend his rights at all times, and would allow no long-haired, buckskin-clad scout—poet though he be—or any other man, to defraud him thereof.

It is needless to state that the jury of honest miners, who are ever on the side of justice and right, rendered a verdict for the defendant, D. W. Flick. Thus ended the second lawsuit (suit in common law) ever tried in the Black Hills.

We are here reminded of a number of similar disputes over property in the Black Hills, which, had they been submitted to the arbitration of a few disinterested parties, would not have resulted, as was sometimes the case, in bloodshed and even death.

FIRST PERSON KILLED IN THE BLACK HILLS

The first person killed in the Black Hills after their invasion by the first expedition was, probably, a man named Kiese, in July, 1875. The particulars of the affair, as far as can be ascertained, are, substantially, as follows: Some time in July, 1875, a party of about forty men, including J. J. Williams, a member of the Collins and Russell expedition, was encamped near the Jenny stockade. While in camp, Kiese and a man named Jackson left the camp together for French creek. After a short absence Jackson returned alone, claiming that they had been attacked by a band of Indians, when a few miles out from camp, and Kiese killed as well as the mule he rode. The story not seeming altogether probable, was not believed by many of the party. Jackson soon after disappeared from camp and was no more seen or heard from. A month later, perhaps, the body of Kiese was found covered with brush, in a ravine, not far from the Jenny stockade and Jackson was strongly suspected of having killed him for a considerable sum of money that he was known to have had in his possession. Be that as it may, he was certainly killed and his body found.

The first hotel in the Black Hills was built in Custer in February, 1876, by a man named Druggeman. The same man also purchased the first town lot ever sold in the Black Hills, the purchase being made of one Jacobs in February, 1876.

The first saw mill in the Black Hills was brought to Custer and operated by J. F. Murphy in February, 1876.

In February, 1876, the first store of general merchandise in the Black Hills, located in Custer on the south side of Custer avenue, between 5th and

6th streets, was opened and kept by Jas. Roberts, who, it is said, died in Deadwood about the year 1890.

The first white child born in the Black Hills was Alvena, daughter of Mr. and Mrs. Chas. Sasse, now of Deadwood. Little Alvena first opened her wondering, though unappreciative eyes, on the marvelous beauty of Custer Park, and expanded her small lungs with the pure bracing air, laden with the grateful aroma of the pines that clothe the rugged slopes, surrounding the park in which nestles the city of her birth, on the 11th of May, 1876. Her life, however, was but a brief span, she was later taken to Deadwood, where, in the following November, she died. Alvena, the pioneer baby of the Black Hills, now lies buried beneath the reckless tread of many busy feet, somewhere on the old cemetery hill, back of the Fourth Ward school building of Deadwood.

A. W. MERRICK
Publisher of the first newspaper in the Black Hills, established in Deadwood, June 8th, 1876

The first newspaper established in the Black Hills, called the Black Hills *Weekly Pioneer,* was published by W. A. Laughlin and A. W. Merrick, under the firm name of Laughlin & Merrick, early in 1876. The proprietors of this important pioneer enterprise, with a faith and courage almost sublime, transported from Denver, Colorado, to the Black Hills, a distance of 400 miles,—in depth of winter, a fully-equipped printing outfit, consisting of a press, a complete selection of type, and all the necessary material for the publication of a daily paper and job office.

The first half sheet of the Black Hills *Pioneer* was printed in Custer in May, 1876, but after one issue, the publishers reloaded their press and other printing equipments, and went with the flood-tide to Deadwood, where it was permanently established as a weekly publication,—the initial number, consisting of a half sheet, appearing on June 8th, 1876. The first number, which was run through the press by Joseph Kubler, now of the Custer *Chronicle,* was struck off under inauspicious conditions and circumstances, indeed, the work being done in an unfinished cabin, which afforded but scant protection from the untoward elements. However, the venture at once proved a great financial success,—a veritable bonanza. The paper was in great demand, thousands of copies being sold every week at twenty-five cents each, many of which found their way to the outer newspaper world, where excerpts from its columns were freely copied.

The Black Hills *Weekly Pioneer* was a wide-awake, newsy sheet in 1876, and made its influence felt far and wide. Not only did it contain information of the rich placer and quartz discoveries and other current news of the great mining camp, but also discussions of many of the important public questions of the day, especially those directly affecting the people of the Black Hills.

It is now recalled that the Indian problem,—in connection with the United States government, was roundly abused for its seeming dereliction in duty to the outlawed people of the Black Hills; the territorial question, the question of county organization,—in which the head of the territorial government of the Dakotas was handled without gloves, for not doing what he really had no power to do, received special consideration. The people of the Black Hills believed in the full and unrestrained liberty of the press in 1876.

The brainy young R. B. Hughes—familiarly called Dick Hughes, was one of the first compositors on the pioneer newspapers, and it is alleged that the way he manipulated the type exceeded all subsequent records in the Black Hills. He was also local reporter for the paper, and is said to be practically the first newspaper reporter in the Black Hills. From this Mr. Hughes drifted into journalism, and in 1878 became connected with the Rapid City *Journal,* as one of its editorial staff, where he demonstrated that he was a clear-cut thinker as well as a polished writer. Dick is now United States Surveyor-General for South Dakota.

Of the brilliant coterie of writers who catered to the Black Hills reading public in 1876, the large-hearted, openhanded Capt. C. V. Gardner alone remains in the Black Hills to-day. Dr. C. W. Myers, Geo. Stokes, Jack Langrishe, and Jack Crawford (an occasional contributor to the department of poetry), having years since left the Hills for other fields. Dr. Myers, a one-time territorial delegate, than whom few wielded a readier pen, is reported dead.

Owing to ill health, W. A. Laughlin soon severed his connection with the *Pioneer,* disposing of his interest in the concern to C. V. Gardner. Mr. Gardner, whose capital and talents gave additional life to the enterprise, made his first literary bow to the newspaper readers of the Black Hills on July 1st, 1876, continuing his connection with the paper for a period of about six months, when it was left to the sole management of A. W. Merrick.

From the date of its establishment as a daily paper on May 15th, 1877, the *Pioneer* had a wonderfully checkered history. It had its ins and outs, its fluctuating periods of prosperity and adversity—like nearly all newspaper enterprises, dependent upon a shifting community for their patronage. Having from that time to share the profits of the newspaper field with another daily paper, the Deadwood *Times,* the question of dollars and cents resolved itself into a serious problem, for what with the competition and the largely-increased expenditures of conducting a daily paper, it was finally found that in reckoning up the monthly accounts, pro and con, the balances began to show—as figures sometimes have the disagreeable habit of doing,—on the wrong side of the ledger. Competition may be the life of trade, but it is financial death to one or the other, if not both of the competitors, in a newspaper business in a narrow field.

The management of the *Pioneer,* during its twenty years of existence, as a daily paper, changed, financially, editorially or otherwise, as many as fifteen times, as will appear from the appended record.

In 1877 A. W. Merrick appears to be handling the craft alone. In 1878 we find R. O. Adams at the helm, the subsequent changes occurring in the following order: In 1879 Merrick & Adams; in 1880 R. O. Adams; in 1880 R. D. Kelly (two weeks); in 1881 Vanocker & Merrick; in 1885 Frank Vanocker; in 1882 G. G. Bennett (six months); in 1883 A. W. Merrick; in 1884 Edwards, Pinneo Bros. & Merrick; in 1884 Edwards & Pinneo; in 1885-6 Bonham, Maskey & Moody; in 1886 W. H. & F. M. Bonham; in 1886-7 Bonham & Kelly; from 1887 to 1897 the Pioneer Publishing Company, under the management of W. H. Bonham. On December 1st, 1887, the name Black Hills *Pioneer,* was changed to Deadwood *Pioneer.*

On May 15th, 1897, the Deadwood *Daily Pioneer* and the Deadwood *Daily Times* were merged into one daily paper, under the proprietorship of the Pioneer-Times Publishing Company, and the editorial and business management of Porter Warner, and W. H. Bonham, respectively.

When W. H. Bonham became connected with the management of the *Pioneer* in 1885, it was found to be heavily incumbered with debt, but, although having a cash capital of only $190 to invest in the concern, he succeeded by wise economy and skillful business management, in rescuing the paper from the financial quicksands into which it was rapidly sinking, and placing it on solid ground, so that when it went into the hands of the Pioneer Publishing Company, in 1887, it was practically free from debt.

The foregoing record makes it very plain, so plain that those who run may read, that A. W. Merrick made a noble and gallant struggle to prolong the life of the first newspaper of the Black Hills.

The first daily newspaper published in the Black Hills was established in Deadwood by Porter Warner in the early spring of 1876.

Mr. Warner arrived in Deadwood from Denver, Colo., with a complete press, well equipped with the needed facilities and ample material for the publication of a daily paper, during the month of March, 1877. He first rented the upper story of the then newly erected bank building of Stebbins, Wood & Post, on the northwest corner of Main and Lee streets, where, on the 7th day of April, 1877, the first number of the Deadwood *Daily Times* was issued. The paper was ably and successfully conducted, under the sole management and proprietorship of its founder, Porter Warner, until May 15th, 1897, when it consolidated with the Deadwood *Pioneer*, under the title of *The Pioneer Times.*

PORTER WARNER
Publisher of the first daily newspaper in the Black Hills, established April 7th, 1877

The Deadwood *Daily Times* is also credited with the distinction of having been the second daily paper published in Dakota Territory.

The first case ever coming up for adjudication before a Black Hills tribunal of any kind, was tried by Justice of the Peace Smith of Custer, in February, 1876. The cause of action originated in a dispute between Wm. Coad and a man named Swartout, as to the rightful ownership of a town lot in Custer City. Thos. H. Harvey appeared for Swartout and Thos. Hooper for Coad. Thus it will be seen that Thos. H. Harvey and Thos. Hooper were the first to practice the profession of law in the Black Hills.

The first authenticated case of murder in the Black Hills was the killing of Boueyer, a half-breed Sioux, by an all-round desperado named C. C. Clayton, in March, 1876. When learning of the affair, a large number of the friends of the murdered man appeared in Custer, to see that even-handed justice be meted out to the slayer of their red brother. Clayton was promptly arrested and tried by a jury, before Police Justice Keifer, of Custer, and found guilty of murder in the first degree, with a penalty of death, by hanging, affixed to the verdict.

When the prisoner was arraigned to receive his sentence, and just as counsel for the defense was laying down the law to the judge, on the illegality of such procedure on the part of a provisional court, a sensational scene occurred in the court room. A large party of the murderer's sympathizers, armed to the teeth, arrived from Deadwood, and filed into the little court room, and there stood, grim and determined, awaiting the decision of the court, prepared to rescue the prisoner in case his life was placed in jeopardy. At this juncture Attorney Harvey demanded the release of the prisoner on the grounds aforementioned, and the judge, concluding that he had no option in the matter, turned him over into the hands of the citizens of the town, who, it is needless to state, escorted him to the limits thereof and turned him loose, with a solemn warning not to show himself again within the limits of the Black Hills.

COL. JAMES M. WOODS

The pioneer banking institution of the Black Hills,—called the Miner's & Mechanic's Bank, was established in Deadwood in the summer of 1876, by J. M. Woods, now of Rapid City. The vault for the safe-keeping of the capital stock, surplus, deposits, undivided profits, etc., of the Miner's & Mechanic's Bank consisted of an ordinary iron safe, which was kept in a frame building, on the east side of Main street, occupied at the time by the store of Boughton & Berry. The principal transactions of this pioneer institution consisted in buying and selling gold dust and shipping same per account of its owners, making collections, etc. It is believed that J. M. Woods was its president, board of directors, and chief stockholder, as well as its cashier, teller, and clerk. That the enterprising firm coined money during those palmy days, when gold dust was lavishly squandered, goes without saying.

J. M. Woods also opened the first harness and saddlery shop in the Black Hills, during the same summer, on the east side of Main street below Wall street.

The first religious service ever held in the Black Hills was conducted in Custer by Rev. H. W. Smith, the martyred Black Hills missionary, on May 7th, 1876. This first service was held in a small log cabin without floor, on Custer avenue, owned by Joseph T. Reynolds, and at the time occupied by Mr. Clippinger. After a short stay in Custer, Rev. Smith, feeling that duty called him to a broader field for Christian effort, left the comparatively moral atmosphere of the pioneer city for Deadwood, where he arrived on or about the 25th of May, 1876, when he at once began to do battle for the right. He opened and conducted a series of outdoor evening meetings in Deadwood, on the corner of Main and Gold streets—using a dry-goods, or some other kind of a box, for a platform, and succeeded, by his intense earnestness and sincerity, in nightly drawing around him large numbers of the crowds of miners, fighters, and tenderfeet, who jostled along the narrow street seeking diversion, despite the many counter-attractions on every hand. It is a notable fact—and to their everlasting credit be it chronicled—that none of the motley crowd, gathered around to listen to his earnest teachings, ever attempted, as far as known, to annoy or disturb him in his work. His labors were not confined to Deadwood alone; he sometimes appointed meetings at distant mining camps, and it was in the fulfillment of one of these engagements that he met his death.

On the 20th day of August, 1876, a day that will long linger in the memories of the then residents of Deadwood, Rev. Smith—notwithstanding he had been warned of the extreme danger of the trip—with his Bible and prayer-book, his only safeguards, under his arm, started confidently away over the old mountain trail between Deadwood and Centennial for Crook City, where he had engaged to hold service, but when near a point on the trail, known by old-timers as the "Rest" he was shot to death in his tracks, by one of the Indian stampeders of the "Montana Herd."

Two hunters, who were at the time engaged in skinning a deer near the spot where Smith was killed, hearing a horseman approaching discovered from their concealed position that the rider was an Indian. Whereupon, one of the hunters, Dan Van Luvin, believing it to be his duty to shoot at anything that looked like an Indian, quickly leveled his gun and fired, killing the horse and badly wounding the Indian. The two hunters then fled precipitately to Deadwood, collected a party and returned to the scene of the shooting where they fully expected to find a dead Indian. The Indian on the contrary was not dead but sufficiently alive to fire a shot into the party killing one of the men, but before he could reload his gun, he was riddled by a volley of bullets. Lo, the poor Indian, was game to the last, it being found that Van Luvin's shot had broken both of his legs and one of his arms.

Rev. Smith was found lying where he fell, with arms folded across his breast, his Bible and prayer-book resting on his bosom. He was not scalped or otherwise mutilated; perchance the savages surmised and respected his calling. He died in the harness, doing his Master's work.

His grave, in the cemetery on one of the hills overlooking Deadwood on the south, is marked by a life-sized figure standing on a square pedestal which bears the inscription. It is cut from native red sandstone and was erected in October, 1891, by his "Black Hills Friends."

The first gold produced from quartz by process of machinery in the Black Hills, was extracted from ore mined from the Chief of the Hills, situated about one mile above the mouth of Black Tail.

In August, 1876, Gardner & Co. and I. Chase purchased from the original locators, California Joe and Jack Hunter, a one-half interest in the mine and at once commenced the construction of a home-made wooden Arastra near the mine for crushing the ore. In the clean-up from the first run made by this crude machine, was found a good-sized nugget, which, in commerical value, was worth about $15.00. The clean-up was made in early part of September, 1876.

The first plant for the manufacture of the popular beverage (beer) in the Black Hills, was established by L. S. Parkhurst & Co., temporarily at Custer, afterward permanently in Deadwood, in June, 1876.

JACK LANGRISHE
The old time Black Hills comedian

It was in July, 1876, that Jack Langrishe, the idol of the early Western mining camps, blazed the way and established the first theater for the "legitimate" in the Black Hills. The Langrishe Troupe, which included Mrs. Langrishe and two other ladies, with a wagon load of stage accessories and an extensive repertory, arrived in Deadwood on or about July 10th, 1876, and as there was no building in the embryo city suitable for the purpose, immediate steps were taken to provide a place of sufficient capacity to accommodate the amusement-loving community of that great mining camp. A large frame theater building was put in process of construction on the south side of Main street on the lots now occupied by Max Fischel and John Herman.

Soon the skeleton structure was inclosed on its four sides by using part canvas, the supply of lumber not being equal to the demand; then covered with a canvas roof and laid with sawdust floor; the internal economy was arranged; a stage with the necessary entrances and exits was hastily constructed and finished by a few skillful sweeps and daubs of the scenic artist's brush; rows and rows of rough hard seats, odds and ends of lumber, were nailed together in the big auditorium, when the pioneer theater building of the Black Hills was ready for the first engagement.

Pending the final touches on the building, the camp was billed for the first show, and indeed it does not seem twenty-one years since the log cabins, sprinkled with a few more pretentious frame business buildings along the narrow street of the embryo city, the trees, the huge boulders and the rocky headlands up and down the gulches, were made radiant by the glaring posters, announcing the first appearance of the celebrated Langrishe theatrical troupe in the Black Hills.

The first performance in the new theater building was given on the night of Saturday, July 22d, 1876, on which important occasion the house was crowded to the doors, and doubtless it will be remembered by many that there came up a heavy sweeping rain during the performance which, penetrating through the canvas roof, soon came pouring down in copious streams upon the devoted heads of the audience and actors alike. Yet despite the dampness of their environments, the enthusiasm of the audience was not dampened to any great extent, as but few left the house. Who could forego the delight of seeing the inimitable Jack Langrishe in one of his funny roles?

By the way, Langrishe was held in high estimation by the play-goers of Deadwood camp, not only for his capability as an actor, but for his sterling qualities as a man, by reason of which he usually played to crowded houses, but it was on Saturday and Sunday nights that the management scooped in the gold dust.

As an all-round actor Langrishe was considered exceedingly clever, but in the arena of old-style comedy he was par excellence, and also a perfect master of the art of facial expression. An occasion is now recalled when his part required that he fail to grasp a point that was plain as noonday to everybody else, and to follow his changing expression which from that of the densest stupidity gradually brightened, as the light of comprehension began to dawn upon his benighted mind, until his broad good-natured face beamed with the effulgence of supreme intelligence, was truly a rare treat. We do not often see his equal as a comedian. Mrs. Langrishe too, as leading lady, was an actress of no small ability, and whether she impersonated an Irish servant girl fresh from the Emerald Isle, a dude, or a red-headed cowboy, she looked and acted her part to perfection.

During the following month, the Langrishe audiences were frequently treated to free shower baths, and usually, as fate decreed it, at the most absorbing stage of the performances. About the middle of August, a waterproof roof was substituted for the canvas, in which condition, it is believed, the building served its purpose until 1878, when a new and larger theater building was constructed on Sherman street, on the lots just south of those now occupied by the B. & M. Railway Depot. This building was destroyed by the disastrous fire of 1879, when Deadwood was nearly obliterated from the map of the Black Hills.

The first masonic funeral services ever held in the Black Hills were conducted in the Langrishe theater building on Main street, in August, 1876, the rites and ceremonies of the order being performed by Sol. Star. The deceased was a man who died at the Woods Hotel, Deadwood.

The first duel fought in the Black Hills took place on a street at Crook City on July 18th, 1875, between Jas. Shannon and Thos. Moore, resulting in the death of the former—the challenged party. The occurrence, although not strictly an affair of honor, and not conducted altogether according to the requirements of the code-duello, was nevertheless a real duel.

The trouble originated in the saloon of C. D. Johnston, and was the result of an altercation over some money matter, the particulars of which are briefly and substantially as follows.

Shannon asked of the proprietor of the saloon a loan of $50.00 to back his horse on a race that was to come off, which was refused. Failing in this he turned and made a similar request of Moore who also refused the accommodation, which so aroused his ire that he proceeded to assault Moore, who, to settle the difficulty, challenged his assailant to a duel. In the absence of seconds, the principals agreed to choose their weapons and shoot each other at sight, and both started for their guns. Moore soon returned but finding Shannon still unarmed, did not shoot in accordance with the terms, but requested his antagonist to go at once and arm himself. Shannon then went for his gun, and in about fifteen minutes put in an appearance, when both fired almost simultaneously, Shannon falling mortally wounded at the first shot. Moore also fell, perhaps shocked by the concussion, but was unhurt. The body of the dead duelist was placed in charge of Dr. R. D. Jennings, now a resident of Hot Springs, who impaneled a coroner's jury to hold an inquest, which resulted in a verdict of justifiable homicide. Preceding the burial, Mr. A. S. Garrison went out a few miles northeast of Crook City and dug a grave, where Whitewood now stands, but the small funeral procession refused to go so far, as the Indians were much in evidence in the locality at the time, so it halted and buried the body on a hill, about half way between Crook City and Whitewood, where the grave may be seen to-day.

The first quartz mill to reach the Black Hills was brought in by Capt. C. V. Gardner & Co., during the early fall of 1876. The machinery of this pioneer quartz mill, consisting of what is known as a Blake Crusher and a Balthoff Ball Pulverizer, was purchased by Capt. Gardner, at Central Colorado, and shipped by rail to Cheyenne, Wyoming, whence it was transported by the May & Appel fast freight line, to its point of destination near Gayville, passing through Deadwood en route on September 25th, 1876. The plant was operated on the rich conglomerate ore taken from the historic Hidden Treasure Mine, on Spring gulch. Before the close of 1876, about $20,000 in gold was produced from the ore, pulverized by the tumbling balls in the cylinder of the crude little plant. The Hidden Treasure Mine was discovered and located by Thomas O'Neal on May 13th, 1876, and later came into the possession of Gardner & Co. by purchase.

CAPT. C. V. GARDNER
Who brought the first quartz mill to the Black Hills on September 25th, 1876

The first stamp mill to make its advent in the Black Hills was brought in by Milton E. Pinney in the late fall of 1876. The mill, a ten-battery plant, was purchased by Mr. Penney at Central Colorado, and shipped by rail to Cheyenne, and from there transported by Wood Foglesong, under contract with the purchasers at $12.50 per 100 pounds to Central, where it was erected on the Alpha and Omega property located near Central. Upon the arrival of the mill on the ground, Woolsey, Jones, and Rowland, owners of the Alpha and Omega mines, conveyed a half interest in their mining property to Pinney & Lorton, in consideration of a half interest in the mill, thus giving to each of the contracting parties an equal proprietary interest in the mines and mill.

J. M. Brelsford and Aaron Dunn, now of Deadwood, and W. E. Jones, of Sturgis, assisted in the work of building the plant, which commenced dropping its ten stamps on December 30, 1876. This mill was operated, with short periods of interruption, on ore taken from the Alpha or Omega Mines,

MILTON E. PINNEY
Who brought the first stamp mill to the Black Hills in the fall of 1876

perhaps it will be more correct to say the Alpha and Omega, until 1885, when the engine and boiler were removed to Sturgis by W. E. Jones to be utilized in a saw mill near that place where they are still in occasional use. The worn-out batteries were thrown aside, having served their day.

The Alpha Mine, a conglomerate crystallized quartz proposition, was discovered and located by Jas. Wolsey, a Californian, W. E. Jones, and M. V. Rowland, on May 12th, 1876. A little later the Omega mine was located by the same parties, in such a way that it overlapped the richer portion of the Alpha location, at which point of intersection the ore pounded out by the batteries of the first stamp mill was mined.

The introduction and successful operation of these two pioneer quartz mills exerted a powerful influence in bringing the Black Hills into public prominence as a gold-producing region; in attracting capital, eager for profitable investment, thereto, and in encouraging new discoveries and future developments. Their operations convinced the world that there was plenty of gold, bright gold, buried beneath the pine-clad hills of the new El Dorado, awaiting similar developments and needing improved and more extensive machinery to convert it into commerical value, and it is thought that those enterprising pioneers who expended their energies, and risked thousands of money in bringing the Black Hills to the fore, are deserving of more credit than the average man or woman in this day and generation think to accord.

It may be proper to state here for the benefit of those who know less about mining than an old Black Hills' pioneer, that there is a distinction as well as a difference between a stamp mill and a quartz mill. Paradoxical as it may seem a stamp mill is essentially a quartz mill, but a quartz mill is not necessarily a stamp mill. In a stamp mill the ore is pulverized by stamp batteries, while in a quartz mill other agencies may be employed for the purpose, as in the case of the Bolthoff and Ball Pulverizer brought into the Hills by Capt. Gardner, which pulverized the ore by the rolling and tumbling of iron balls in a huge cylinder.

The first gold dust to the amount of $1,000, sent out of the Black Hills, was carried from Custer City to Cheyenne, by Emil Faust, now of Lead City, in the early part of March, 1876. The gold was produced for the most part from the placer deposits along the streams of the southern and central Hills, during the late fall of 1875, and was given into the custody of Mr. Faust by several miners, to be invested for their benefit in supplies. As there were no highway robbers on the road, and but few Indians on the warpath at that early date in 1876, the hazard of carrying so much gold was, by virtue of these facts, reduced to a minimum.

The first large shipment of gold dust from the Black Hills was made by the Wheeler Brothers, late in the fall of 1876. Those old mountaineers had, during the summer and fall of 1876, sluiced out thousands upon thousands of glittering gold from claim No. 2 below "Discovery" on Deadwood gulch. Some alleged that they also worked the lower half of No. 1 below; the exact number of thousands is not, and probably never will be, known. The amount has been variously estimated at from $50,000 to $150,000, and even more. At any rate, the boys had made a big stake and were evidently satisfied. After going pretty thoroughly over their claim, they sold out the residue of the gold in the ground and in the tailings for two or three thousand more, when they were ready to turn their backs upon the Black Hills with their pockets filled to overflowing with Black Hills gold.

As the country surrounding the Hills was still filled with depredating bands of the hostile Indians—returned from the battles of the Little Big Horn, and with numerous white desperadoes, who were even more to be feared than the Indians, the question as to the best means by which to ship so large an amount of gold became a matter of grave importance, and one demanding serious consideration. They finally selected and employed a strong guard from among the experienced miners—old mountaineers who, to use a vulgar phrase, had been there before—to escort the train and guard their golden treasure out of the Black Hills, for a consideration of $25 per day, until reaching the railroad. Other miners along the gulches who had a surplus of gold dust, upon hearing of this arrangement for shipment took advantage of the opportunity to ship with them, thus increasing the amount of shipment by about $50,000—a tempting bait for an alert road agent. Fortunately, however, owing to the secrecy with which the arrangements were made, the first large shipment of gold from the Black Hills reached the railway without encountering any serious trouble.

The Congregational Church of Deadwood is, beyond question, entitled to the proud distinction and honor of having formed the first religious society ever organized in the Black Hills. Late in the fall of 1876 Rev. L. P. Norcross was sent by the American Home Mission Society to Deadwood, where he began the work which, after twenty-one years of hard, earnest Christian effort, has culminated in the large and prosperous society of to-day.

Few, perhaps, of those who now worship God under the domes of commodious church buildings of approved church architecture, with stained-glass windows, cushioned seats and richly-carpeted aisles, heated by furnaces and illumined with incandescent lights, fully realize the uncomfortable environments and limitations under which the nucleus of the pioneer church organization of the Black Hills was formed.

At first the devoted and self-sacrificing missionary, sent to bring Deadwood sinners to repentance, and keep others in the straight and narrow path, had, perforce, to conduct his services here and there, wherever a place could be secured for the purpose—in buildings wholly unsuitable for the purpose, whose roofs were not always impervious to rain, furnished with seats of rough boards without cushions or backs, and lighted by a couple of kerosene lamps. In such places Rev. Norcross, from a slightly elevated platform—sometimes a mere box of some kind—read his notes, if it was evening service, by the dim rays of a coal oil lamp, while his listeners sat bolt upright in their backless seats, sometimes shivering with cold. Yes, this is a realistic picture—rather underdrawn.

Rev. Norcross held his first services in Deadwood at the International Hotel on Main street, at the opening of which service only five persons were present, this number, however, increasing to twenty-five or thirty before its close. After two or three Sundays the building was rented for a meat shop, when, for several Sundays, services were conducted in the dining room of the Centennial Hotel.

The Deadwood theater building on Main street was then tendered by its proprietor, Jack Langrishe, which generous offer, owing to the impracticability of heating the building, and the fact that entertainments were frequently held in the evening, was not accepted. The society then commenced holding their meetings in a carpenter's shop in South Deadwood, opposite Boughton and Berry's sawmill, where services were continued for three or four months, the fuel and lights being furnished free of charge by Col. Backus. Occasional services were also held at other places during the fall and winter of 1876 and 1877. About the middle of January, 1877, the church proper was organized, at which time, it is said, nine persons united by letter.

In this connection I am reminded of a very amusing incident that occurred, one evening when I was attending services in a building situated, as I remember it, up toward the point of McGovern hill. I think it was in 1877, and the place may have been the first building erected by the Congregational church. Be that as it may, during the service a brisk shower came up, and soon the rain began to percolate freely through the unfinished roof of the building, when, just as Rev. Norcross began his closing benediction, a shrill childish voice piped out, and fell upon the startled ears of the hushed congregation: "Oh, Mr. Norcross! Mr. Norcross, its a-eaking on me!"—meaning leaking—and no mistake it was a-eaking on the little tot, as well as the rest of us, including Rev. Norcross. It is needless to say that the little congregation was convulsed.

By the efforts of the ladies and private subscriptions, sufficient funds were raised to build a church edifice and purchase an organ, which, on July 9th, 1877, was turned over to the trustees of the organization.

The first settler to avail himself of the pre-emption law in the Black Hills was Mr. Jones, who made settlement on 160 acres of Section 10, Township 6, Range 2 East, on December 5th, 1879, making filing No. 1 on January 27th, 1879, the same day the plat was received at the United States Land Office at Deadwood.

The first settlement in Black Hills under the Homestead Act was made by Joseph Ransdell, of Spearfish, who made entry No. 1 at the United States Land Office on February 3d, 1879, of 160 acres of Section 10, Township 6, Range 2 East of Black Hills meridian.

The first man in the Black Hills to avail himself of the act to encourage the growth of timber on the Western prairies was E. D. Knight, who made Timber Culture Entry No. 1 at United States Land Office on April 16th, 1879.

The government survey of the township and range in which the first entries are located, was made by Charles Scott in the summer and fall of 1878, and the plat filed in the United States Land Office at Deadwood on January 27th, 1879.

The first herd of beef cattle to arrive in the Black Hills was brought in by Mart Boughton and a man called "Skew" Johnston, from Cheyenne, Wyoming. Whether or not "Skew" was his real name, is an open question.

The first minstrel troupe in the Black Hills appeared in Custer on August 18th, 1876, and gave their first performance that night in Long Branch Hall. Admission fee, 75 cents.

The first livery stable in the Black Hills was opened in Deadwood by Clark & Morill, in the spring of 1876.

CHAPTER XXI

CUSTER IN 1876

Custer narrowly escaped achieving a place on the pages of Black Hills history under another name. It may not be generally known that the pioneer town of the Black Hills was once named Stonewall, in honor of the brave Confederate General Stonewall Jackson. Yet it is nevertheless a fact, a fact, however, of which it has no reason to feel ashamed, as it in no way reflects discredit upon Custer's fair fame and honored name, to have once borne the suggestive appellation given to that gallant defender of the "lost cause."

We have it upon authentic authority that as early as July, 1875, a town-site company was organized, and the present site of Custer laid out, and called Stonewall, which name it bore until its reorganization a month later.

On the 10th day of August, 1875, at a mass meeting of nearly all the miners then in the Black Hills, who had gathered there in compliance with the order of Gen. Crook, a new town-site company was organized, and a board of trustees elected, of which Tom Hooper was chosen clerk. On that day a site, one mile square, about two and one-half miles above the stockade on French creek, was surveyed, laid out, platted, and by unanimous choice christened Custer in honor of the brave, intrepid leader of the first military expedition to penetrate the Black Hills, Gen. G. A. Custer. The platted town-site was then divided into lots from one to 1200 and on the 11th day of August, 1875, several hundred miners became (through the medium of a lottery) nominal, if not *de facto*, owners of Black Hills real estate to the extent of a town

THOMAS HOOPER
Judge of the Black Hills Superior Court, established in lieu of regular courts, by the people of the Black Hills, in convention assembled at Custer City, in March, 1876

lot in Custer. As before stated, the survey of the site was made with a small pocket compass, the lines laid by means of picket ropes, and the plat drawn on a piece of birch bark twelve inches square, stripped from a tree growing on the border of French creek.

By permission of Gen. Grook, a detachment of United States soldiers aided in the work of survey. The plat, which has unfortunately been lost, was drawn by Tom Hooper.

Among the first permanent settlers in Custer were D. W. Flick, Sam Shankland, Tom Hooper, and D. K. Snively, whose respective feet trod the ground upon which the prosperous city of to-day stands, even before the site was laid and called Stonewall. In March, 1876, the town of Custer, which then comprised the major part of the population of the Black Hills, asserted itself and assumed the dignity of a full-fledged municipality. A mass convention of the people of the Hills was held, at which all necessary city officers were duly elected. The same convention also organized a provisional government for the entire Black Hills, established a superior court, whose jurisdiction was to extend over the uncertain length and breadth of the Black Hills, which court was constituted a tribunal of last resort for all legal transactions within its jurisdiction until such time as regularly authorized courts should be established by the government. This convention elected Thos. Hooper Judge of the Supreme Court. The municipal officers elected were as follows: Mayor, Dr. Bemis; Justice of the Peace, E. P. Keiffer; City Marshal, John Burrows. Among the twelve members of the Council were: Capt. Jack Crawford, D. K. Snively, S. R. Shankland, Cyrus Abbey, D. Wright, Emil Faust,—Robinson; others not known. In November, 1876, another election was held and the following full complement of municipal officers elected, viz.: Supreme Judge, J. W. C. White; City Clerk, S. R. Shankland; City Attorney, G. H. Mills; City Treasurer, W. H. Harlowe; City Marshal, Michael Carroll; City Surveyor, A. J. Parshall; City Assessor, Joseph Reynolds; Justices of the Peace, I. W. Getchell, W. A. Freeze, and A. B. Hughes; Board of Trustees, G. W. Rothrock, President and ex-officio Mayor, G. V. Ayres, Joseph Bliss, W. H. Bunnell, E. Schlewning, G. A. Clark, W. D. Gardner, D. K. Snively, F. B. Smith, E. G. Ward, M. Woodward, and A. Yerkes.

Custer, which in the marvelously short period of the three months prior to its emergence from its swaddling clothes had expanded from a few prospectors into a population of from six to seven thousand souls, was destined ere many months to become nearly depopulated.

The alluring reports reaching that southern camp of the rich gold discoveries in the northern gulches of Deadwood and Whitewood, quickly

CUSTER IN 1876

emptied the new city of its entire floating population; miners, eager to find richer fields for mining operations; business men actuated by similar economic considerations, soon followed in their wake, until finally, it is said, only fourteen of the thousands remained in the city to direct its future destinies and to lay the foundation of a more enduring prosperity.

Although the blow inflicted upon the aspiring young city was severe, it was by no means vital, it giving only a temporary shock from which with wonderful recuperative powers, stimulated by the push and energy of a few determined men, it gradually recovered. Failing to find a place to drive their stakes in the upper gulches, a few of the deserters soon returned, ready to pin their faith to the pioneer city and the southern gulches.

One of those who stood resolutely by the town was Samuel Shankland, whom no distant enchantment or big stampede ever had power to swerve from his steadfast loyalty to the town he helped to found.

Ever since the day in June, 1875, when he, with one sole companion, stood trembling on a bluff overlooking the valley of French creek, furtively watching from behind a high ledge of micaceous rock, the dreaded blue coats of Col. Dodge's command, he has been true to his first love.

As the government had, in the late fall of 1875, withdrawn all opposition to immigration into the Black Hills, so it had also practically withdrawn all protection to the people, thus leaving them in the spring of 1876 to depend entirely upon their own resources for means of defense against the hostilities of the Sioux, who would, with the opening of the buds and the sprouting of grass, be on the warpath. Realizing this danger, the people of the exposed settlements began early to organize for defensive operations against Indian surprises which were sure to come.

Custer, owing to its location on one of the principal lines of travel into the Hills, occupied an inviting position for Indian raids, so its citizens, wide awake to the peril that menaced their lives and property, about the middle of March, 1876, formed an organization, consisting of 125 men, composed of the best bone and sinew of the city, known as the "Custer Minute Men," to serve as a home-guard. At the head of this organization was Capt. Jack Crawford, the famous government scout, with Chas. Whitehead as his First-lieutenant. The organization was effected none too soon, as early in April hostilities began.

These Indian depredations were directed chiefly against small parties of immigrants, making their way into the Hills, while passing through the gloomy defiles of Buffalo Gap and Red Canyons, springing suddenly out upon them from ambush, capturing their horses, destroying their goods, and often killing the owners who fell bravely defending their property.

Frequently small bands of the red thieves would ride their fleet ponies to the limits of the town, dismount and sneak stealthily to where horses were grazing, cut the lariat ropes, then mount and away with ill-gotten booty like a flash. Occasionally, they even made bold dashes right through the town,— yelling like demons in seeming defiance of the settlers, who, mounting in hot haste, would follow in distant pursuit,—usually too late to overtake the bold marauders. The following extract from a letter, written by a well-known and honored pioneer of 1876, Samuel Booth, now deceased, to the Oskosh *Times*, describing his journey from Sidney to the Black Hills in April, 1876, will pretty clearly illustrate the dangerous environments of the pioneer city at that time. In his closing paragraphs he says:—

"Now we find ourselves in the Black Hills proper. The roads are rough and rocky, and the hills are covered with a thick growth of Norway pine. About noon we came upon three wagons that had been captured by the Indians. Everything in them that had not been

S. M. BOOTH
One of Custer's early settlers in 1876

carried off was destroyed; coffee mills broken, flour scattered about; harness cut into small pieces, and wagons shot full of balls. About a half mile further on we came to another place where there had been a battle;—blood on the stones,—any amount of cartridge shells, and other signs that showed that we were near to business. That night we all stood with our guns in our hands and the next day we drove into Custer—sixteen days from Sidney.

"I had slept only a short nap at noon since I left the Bad Lands, and now that we were safe in sight of a thousand men, and where the sound of axes, hammers, and saws, seemed equal to Oskosh, and miners were turning French creek in every direction, my first thought was to get a little sleep. I accordingly threw a blanket on the ground, dropped upon it, and was soon in the land of 'Nod.' How long I slept I do not know, but I do know that I was aroused by somebody falling over me,—coffee pots and frying pans rattling, women and children screaming, guns rattling, and last, but not least, about a dozen Indians galloping across the valley, yelling like mad. The next minute, and before we could get our guns ready, they had dashed into the timber on the other side of the valley and were gone, taking several head of horses with them. Hurrah, for the 'Custer Minute Men!' Saddle and bridle your poor skeleton horses and give chase. In fifteen minutes they are in motion;—and in an hour and a half they came back leading their poor jaded horses, and thus ended another raid on Custer."

The above is a true picture of the temper of the hostiles in 1876. During the month of April at least three separate parties of emigrants were attacked in Buffalo Gap Canyon, whose outfits were found in the condition described in Mr. Booth's letter. In one case the scene of attack gave evidence that there had been a fierce conflict between the savages and their victims.

Among the first and most atrocious of the bloody deeds committed in the spring of 1876 was the killing of Col. Brown and another of his party, and the massacre of the Metz family in Red Canyon when on their way out of the Hills.

Col. Brown, familiarly known as Stuttering Brown, agent of the Cheyenne & Black Hills Stage Co., and another man, whose name is unknown, were killed, and a man called "Curley" badly wounded, at a point near the mouth of Red Canyon, on April 22d, 1876. Col. Brown was on his way out from Custer to Cheyenne with his two companions, to look up a more practicable route to the Hills, and to establish stations along the line thereof for the above mentioned company, when they met their doom. The Indians (if Indians they were) swooped down upon the little party from behind a projecting headland, at a time and place, perhaps, when they least expected an attack, mortally wounding the two and dangerously wounding the other.

SCENE AT RED CANYON AFTER THE MURDER OF THE METZ PARTY

They were found and carried to the Cheyenne river station, where Col. Brown died that night, the other dying the next day. "Curley," the driver of the team, was taken first to Hat Creek station, where he laid for many days in a little log hut, hovering between life and death. As soon as it was possible to move the wounded man he was conveyed to Fort Laramie, where he finally recovered. Many believe that the deed was not committed by the Indians but by a character called Persimmons Bill and his associates, in an attempt to get possession of the horses belonging to the company. More, however, believe the perpetrators to have been Indians. Be that as it may, the horses were taken, while the wagon, riddled with bullets and bespattered with blood, was found, upturned, near the scene of the attack. The scene of the tragedy gave evidence that the men sold their lives dearly.

MASSACRE OF METZ FAMILY

Two days later, April 24th, the Metz party, consisting of husband and wife, a man who drove the team, and a colored woman, while on their way out from Custer to their home in Laramie City, Wyoming, in passing through Red Canyon were pounced upon by a band of ambushed savages and every member of the defenseless little party brutally massacred. After lying there, scattered along the trail as tempting bait for the hungry vultures for many hours, three of the victims were found, taken to the Cheyenne river stage station, and temporarily buried. After a few days the other victim (the colored woman) was found in a ravine a little distance away, her body pierced with numerous arrows. It appeared that she had attempted to escape, was overtaken in her flight and murdered. Mrs. Metz also had attempted to escape, as her body was found nearly a half mile from the point of attack where the demolished wagon and goods, scattered broadcast, were found. There was one notable feature about those early Indian attacks, viz.: that they rarely took the provisions of their victims, and indeed they had no need to as those graceless wards of the government were amply provided with rations.

HOSTILES RETURNING FROM LITTLE BIG HORN

From the latter part of May until after the battles of the Little Big Horn, the people of the Hills had a comparative surcease from Indian outrages. A little before the middle of July, however, the hosts of Crazy Horse, who had fled from that sanguinary battlefield towards the Black Hills before Gen. Crook's pursuing army, separated into numerous small bands and enboldened by their recent victory and with whetted appetites, renewed aggressive operations against the outposts of the Hills on the north, south, and east. For the two following months those flitting bandits seemed to be omnipresent and there was no telling when nor where they would make their unwelcome presence felt. Scarcely a day passed that did not bring to light some dark tragedy for which they were responsible. Men were way-laid and murdered in almost every part of the Hills; trains were harassed and beleaguered along all the lines thereto; horses were stolen and run off; herds of cattle were driven away, slaughtered and jerked before they could be overtaken; in short, the people of the exposed settlements were kept in a chronic state of horror and suspense. Verily, those were days that tried the souls of the pioneers.

In the early part of July, word came from Gen. Crook to Custer that a large band of 800 Indians was making its way towards the Black Hills, with the avowed purpose of driving out the white settlers from their country, creating no little excitement and consternation,—especially among the women and children, of whom there were a considerable number in the city. On receipt of this alarming information, a meeting of the citizens was called to consider measures for the better defense of the city—when the building of a stockade, large enough to afford a refuge for the population of the city in the event of an attack, was agreed upon. Money and work were liberally subscribed, and the next morning a large force of men was at work upon the building, which was hurried to speedy completion. The immense log structure of 100x150 square feet was built on the north side of Custer avenue, across Seventh street, which point, although central, was not within speedy reach of many residents in case of a surprise.

For this reason two of Custer's enterprising citizens—Joseph Reynolds and H. A. Albion—who lived several blocks away from the stockade, determined to construct private fortifications for the benefit of their own respective families and those of their nearest neighbors, to which they would be able to escape, without encountering Indian bullets, at the first signal of alarm. These two fortifications were planned and constructed wholly along underground lines, and reflected great credit upon the ingenuity of the designers.

An underground passage-way was first dug from their cabins to a distance of about fifteen feet, where a room ten feet square, and just deep enough to permit an average man to stand erect, was excavated; along the top margin of the excavation were laid hewn timbers, into which numerous portholes were bored, and through which all Indians coming within the range, long or short, of their guns, were to be perforated; a board roof covered with a thick layer of earth completed the works—making altogether an ideal underground fort. Fortunately, the people of Custer were never compelled to take refuge within the fortifications, as no formidable force of Indians ever assailed the city. However, small bands were to be seen, almost daily, skulking around the outskirts of the city, stealing horses and killing many of those who ventured outside the city limits.

RAIDS ON CUSTER

On July 24th ten heads of horses were run off while the herder was at dinner. A party of ten mounted men started at once in pursuit of the thieves, and, after a long chase, came, about dark, upon two of the stolen horses, shot through the head, when the chase was given up.

On July 27th two teams belonging to a large freight train, about ready to start to Sidney for goods, was driven out a little distance beyond the city limits, to get better grazing until the train should come along. Just as the horses were unhitched from the wagons and before the harness was removed, seven Indians dashed up with a whoop, captured and drove off the four horses with their harness on, the two men having the horses in charge very wisely running away at the first whoop of the savages. This easy conquest emboldened them to come nearer the city, but they encountered a man the next time who was not so easily frightened, as will be seen.

A man by the name of Welch who had camped for the night in one of the vacant buildings on the outskirts of the city, was letting his four horses graze, watched by himself and son, while his wife was preparing supper within the cabin, when six of the Indians galloped up and attempted to drive off the four horses, at the same time firing their guns at the men, one of the balls just grazing the cheek of the elder Welch. "I'll not run a single step for the whole race of yez," he yelled, making a motion as if brushing it away from his cheek. Quickly his Sharp's rifle came to his shoulder, and be began throwing back lead at the would-be thieves, when one of them sank down in his saddle, badly, if not fatally wounded. In the meantime, Mrs. Welch had rushed in between the two firing parties, caught two of the horses and led them into an empty cabin—the other two following, and then with rifle in hand, came out and joined her husband and son in the battle.

The Indians, finding the plucky Celts more than a match for them, rode hastily away, two of them riding beside their wounded or dead comrade. As they rode away Mr. Welch, Sr., called out to them, at the same time shaking his fist threateningly toward them, "Bad cess to yez, ye thavin' murtherin'spalpeens. By the howly Moses, if oi had a howld of yez, its mesilf would give yez sich a batin' as yez niver dhramed uv." Two boys who had witnessed the whole affray from behind a log, thought they could easily have killed the six Indians, if they had been provided with guns. This raid created intense excitement in Custer. A hundred armed men were in the street in a minute after the alarm was sounded, and in a very brief time twenty-five "minute men," were in their saddles, ready to start in pursuit of the Indians, but were just in time to see them disappear in the thick timber.

SCALPED A MAN ALIVE

During those terrible days, a small party, among whom was a man named Ganzio, left Custer for Fort Laramie. When near Hat Creek Station, Ganzio, while looking for a place to camp, a little in advance of his companions, was fired at by a band of Indians as they rushed out from ambush, and he fell. In relating his experience of what followed, he said: "One of the Indians put his knee on my back, another hit me with the butt of his gun; then they drew their sharp knife and commenced scalping me. It was too much; I died, or thought I died." Hearing his loud cries, several of the party came running up, just in time to prevent the Indians from fully completing the operation. His scalp was laid back, when he was taken with all possible dispatch to Fort Laramie, and placed in the care of the army surgeon. He lived to relate the horrible experience of being scalped alive.

In the latter part of July, a party of four miners with a team and light wagon loaded with supplies, while on their way to one of the northern gulches (I think Potato gulch), where they had been prospecting, were attacked by a band of Indians and the whole party killed. The horses were taken, the wagon riddled with bullets, and their supplies scattered over the ground. Some one who, in passing over the trail soon after, discovered the bodies and the wrecked outfit, carried the shocking news to Custer, when a party of its citizens hastened to the scene of the tragedy, about fifteen miles distant, secured and placed the bodies in their own bullet-pierced wagon and brought them to Custer, where, in a spot set apart for Indian victims, a short distance below the city, they were decently buried.

A few days after the last recorded atrocity, four other men (haymakers) were killed and scalped within a short distance of Custer. The unfortunate men, who were engaged at the time in cutting hay for Ernest Schleuning, Sr., now of Rapid City, went out from Custer on the morning of that fatal day to their work in the hay field, but never returned alive. They had not been gone long before a man came running into the city, breathless and excited, and reported that he had seen Indians out in the direction of the hay field, and that they were up to some deviltry, as he put it. Of course the man did not wait to investigate.

In less time than it takes to relate the facts, nearly all the able-bodied men of the city were armed and on their way to the point indicated; some on horseback dashing over the ground with the speed of the wind, others in wagons rattling along the rough trail, with break-neck speed; many hurrying along on foot, and all willing and anxious to risk their lives to get a shot at the red dare-devils who were daily committing such wanton butcheries. Arrived on the scene, the Indians were nowhere to be seen, but the work of their gory hands was painfully in evidence. The bodies of the four men were found scalped, and curiously enough three of them were scalped in sections of four circular pieces each, while the fourth was removed in one piece. The supposition was that there were thirteen Indians, each of whom desired a piece to exhibit as a trophy of his wonderful achievement.

One of the murdered men was Wilder Cooper, a half-brother of Attorney Cooper of Sundance, Wyoming, another was a young German, name unknown, a stranger in the city, who before leaving that morning, gave to an acquaintance his name, the address of his relatives, etc., indicating that he either felt a presentiment of his coming doom, or realized that no person could in those days leave the protection of the city without taking his life in his own hands. The bodies of the murdered men were interred in the little graveyard a mile or so below Custer, where to-day, may be found among the tangled underbrush and weeds, the sunken graves of numerous victims of Indian savagery, little slabs of crumbling wood marking the spot where repose their ashes.

Custer's first regularly licensed physician was Dr. D. W. Flick, now of Rapid City, who began the practice of his profession in the spring of 1876, and by virtue of priority of residence, was the first in the Black Hills. The climate of Custer, however, proved so deplorably healthy, that the doctor was finally forced to leave that region of perennial health for some more sickly clime.

Its first hotel was built in February, 1876, by a man named Druggeman, who also purchased the first town lot sold in Custer of one Jacobs, during the same month and year.

The first store of general merchandise was opened and kept by Jas. Roberts, on Custer avenue, between Fifth and Sixth streets, in February, 1876. Roberts is said to have died in Deadwood during the year 1890.

The first saw-mill in the Black Hills was brought to Custer and operated by J. F. Murphy in February, 1876.

THOMAS E. HARVEY
One of the attorneys in the first law case ever tried in the Black Hills

The first legal practitioners were Judge Thos. Hooper and Thos. E. Harvey,—both receiving their first retaining fee in the same case.

The first newspaper half sheet printed in Custer was struck off by Laughlin & Merrick in May, 1876—only one issue being printed. The first established newspaper was the Custer *Herald*, first published by J. S. Bartholomew & Co. in October, 1876,—continuing about six months.

Frank B. Smith, for many years identified with the business interests of the Hills, was Custer's private postmaster in 1876, all the mail brought to the Hills by pony express for that point passing through his hands. Prior to the establishment of the pony express, Mr. Smith also handled much of the mail brought to the Hills by trains, purchasing it from the carriers for a safe consideration, then selling the letters for ten cents apiece at Custer, while those addressed to Deadwood were taken there and sold for twenty-five cents each,—making a handsome profit by the transaction.

ELLIS T. PEIRCE
The Black Hills Humorist

Conspicuous among the residents of Custer in 1876, was the versatile Black Hills humorist, E. T. Peirce, familiarly called Doc Peirce, the very "prince of good fellows" among the early pioneers, and their staunch friend. A very interesting character was he in pioneer days, wherever he chanced to pitch his tent. With an acute sense of the ridiculous there was no occurrence so pathetic that "Doc" could not detect, without the aid of a Roentgen ray, a thread of the comic running through its warp and woof. Viewing things from an optimistic standpoint, he ever saw the silver lining behind the darkest cloud. Among the "boys" he gained for himself the reputation of being very fond of and much addicted to practical jokes, to which numerous of his unfortunate victims could testify, if they were so disposed, but it was as a story-teller that "Doc" took the "cake." I know of several who have made for themselves a brilliant record in that line, yet, if I were a betting character, I should be willing to wager a quarter that "Doc Peirce" has spun more yarns than any other man who ever emigrated to the Black Hills.

Possessing an inexhaustible fund of information and boundless resources, he never failed to make his recitals drawing cards, and whether seated outside the door of his cabin of a summer's eve, deftly touching the strings of his guitar, or whether inside around his rude hearthstone, before the glowing blaze of a pitch pine fire of a winter's night, he never failed to draw around him a crowd of interested listeners, who, by their loud merriment, attested their appreciation of the entertainment.

E. T. Peirce arrived in Custer on March 16th, 1876. In June of that year he went to Deadwood, returning on August 16th, to Custer, where he remained until April 1st, 1878, when he went to Rapid City, and with Dan J. Stafford, opened the hotel now known as the International. In the fall of 1880 he was elected sheriff of Pennington County. In 1886 he removed from Rapid City to Hot Springs, where he now resides. Mr. Peirce was also deputy sheriff of Custer County before coming to Rapid City.

Among those who lived in Custer, with their families, during the days of peril, were H. A. Albion, A. B. Hughes, Abram Yerkes, Jos. Reynolds, Dr. Flick, Gen. Scott, Harry Wright and W. H. Harlow, Mrs. Chas. Hayward, Bob Pugh, afterwards issuing clerk at Pine Ridge Agency, and others. Of the above named H. A. Albion and family are still residents of the pioneer city. Mr. Albion was at one time engaged, in connection with S. Booth, in freighting between Sidney and the Black Hills.

CHAPTER XXII

RAPID CITY IN 1876

Rapid City—now just past its legal majority—was founded on the 25th of February, 1876, thus giving it the prestige of being, in point of age, the second city established in the Black Hills. It was on the 23d day of February, 1876, that John R. Brennan, Martin Pensinger, Thos. Ferguson, W. P. Martin, Albert Brown, and Wm. Marsten, arrived on Rapid creek from Palmer gulch, in quest of a desirable place upon which to lay the foundation of a city.

After having spent nearly the entire winter in digging ditches, and delving in vain, in that auriferous gulch, for the glittering flakes and nuggets, for which Palmer gulch afterwards became famous, they finally concluded that founding cities might prove a more profitable enterprise.

Accordingly on that winter's day, they packed their blankets and other equipments,—meanwhile keeping their own counsel, and set out on their new venture, in a northeasterly direction towards Rapid creek,—camping the first night at the point where that swiftly flowing stream comes dashing down from the shadow of the mountains into the broad valley, near what is now known as Cleghorn Springs, about five miles above Rapid City.

The next day, February 24th, the party went down the valley of Rapid creek, a distance of about twenty miles towards its mouth, exploring each graceful bend and abrupt turn of the creek for a suitable place to draw their line, returning at night to the foot-hills, without having found a spot with the essential characteristics of their ideal town-site. That night they established a temporary camp, and planted the banner of civilization, at the point of rocks, the present location of the Electric Light Company's power house on the north side of Rapid creek, where they were joined by a number of men who had followed them from Palmer gulch, surmising that they had left to find new diggings. Among the new arrivals were Sam. Scott, J. W. Allen, James Carney, Major Hutchinson, and Wm. Nuttall.

On the evening of the 24th they went into committee of the whole, and held a meeting under a big tree, at the point of rocks, when it was decided to lay out a town-site near the foot-hills on Rapid creek, at an eligible point, looking to the trade of the Hills, as well as to the rich agricultural country in the valley below. They argued and believed that the valley would, in the near future, become the route of extensive travel to the Hills, and that a town at the grand gateway would become the focus of an extensive trade.

That their judgment was not at fault and their faith well founded, twenty-one years of commerical prosperity has fully shown.

The next day, February 25th, the site was selected, surveyed and laid out along the river to conform to the topography of the valley, and, at the suggestion of W. P. Martin, appropriately named Rapid City, after the stream on whose banks it is located. By the aid of a pocket compass and tape line, the survey was made by Sam. Scott, assisted by J. R. Brennan, James Carney, and J. W. Allen. The ground laid out, covering an area of one mile square, embraced the original town-site of Rapid City. J. W. Allen was chosen recorder.

The six blocks occupying the center of the plat, were divided into lots, and drawn by lottery, each person present being allowed the privilege of drawing five lots, the raffle taking place at the intersection of 5th and 6th streets, that point being the center of the plat. At a meeting held on the evening of the 25th, a town-site company was organized by the election of a board of five trustees, viz.: J. R. Brennan, Wm. Marsten, J. W. Allen, Major Hutchinson, and Wm. Nuttall, whose prescribed duty was to conduct the affairs of the town in a manner to subserve the best interests of its people.

On the day the town was platted, a party composed of Frank Wyman, Fred Edgar, C. Bates, and United States Marshal Ash, arrived at the camp from Yankton *via* Pierre, they being the first ones to reach the Black Hills by that route.

The first enterprise looking to the up-building of the new town-site was a project for laying out a route of travel between Rapid City and Fort Pierre, with a view of encouraging freight and passenger traffic from Eastern points over the line to the natural gateway to the Black Hills. In furtherance of the project, on the eighth day of the following March, J. R. Brennan and Frank Conley accompanied Fred. Edgar, C. W. Marshall and a Mr. Field on a trip of exploration across the country, for the purpose of selecting the most feasible route to Fort Pierre, accomplishing the journey in six days; not, however, without experiencing the exposure and hardships incident to a March journey across the Dakota plains. It is related that during the trip the party encountered a regular Dakota blizzard, lost a horse, and was twenty-four hours without food.

A party of about 100 men, destined for the Black Hills, was found waiting at Pierre, and soon after, another party of equal numbers, led by Gen. Campbell, arrived at Pierre, en route for the same point. By arrangement, Conley conducted Gen. Campbell's party, over the new route to the Hills; Brennan, meanwhile, proceeded to Yankton, for the purpose of filing the plat of Rapid City in the United States Land Office, then, returning to Pierre, piloted the other party, under the leadership of one Dillon, to Rapid City, where he arrived on April 8th, after an absence of one month.

The first cabin built in Rapid City was commenced on the day the townsite was platted, by Sam. Scott, at the corner of 4th and Rapid streets, where it stood an unobtrusive landmark, until 1879, when it was decreed that the little old log cabin must go, to make room for the onward strides of improvement.

The first hotel in Rapid City was built and conducted by J. R. Brennan, on Rapid street, between Fifth and Sixth streets. The structure in which Mr. Brennan entertained his guests in 1876, was a log cabin 12x14 square feet, but, as to whether it was partitioned into two or more apartments, or left in one spacious room of 168 square feet, tradition is silent. Be that as it may, it is safe to record that its guests were served with the best the market afforded,—to say nothing of the extra luxuries of game and fish, for, be it known that "mine host" of Rapid City's first hotel is a successful Nimrod, as well as a devotee of the hook and line.

JOHN R. BRENNAN

By the way, a funny story is told of the way John Brennan managed the cuisine department of that early hostelry, for the truth of which, however, I am not able to vouch, and, to be candid I do not believe a word of the story. It is related that when transient visitors came to the hotel and called for dinner, Mr. Brennan immediately hied him forth to the grocery store and purchased just as much provision as would seem sufficient for their dinners, promising to pay therefor when he secured the money from his customers. He returned, took their orders, and yelled the same into an adjoining room to an imaginary cook, then disappeared behind the scenes and prepared the dinner with his own hands.

The first store of general merchandise in Rapid City was established by Oscar Nicholson in March, 1886.

Rapid City was surrounded by none of the conditions which characterized the abnormal growth of the early mining camps of the Hills. Having no rich placer discoveries to draw the eager rushing throng of gold-seeking adventurers to expand its population, its development depended largely upon its admirable location on the main line of travel from the Missouri river to the eastern gateway to the Hills, and upon its prospective commerical possibilities as a base of supplies for the many mining communities springing up therein. The new town was, however, content to pursue the even tenor of its way, confident of achieving ultimate greatness in a gradual and conservative manner.

The growth of Rapid City was materially retarded in 1876 by the presistent hostilities of the Indians, who, by their frequent murderous attacks upon parties of travelers making their way into the Hills, struck dumb terror into the hearts of many would-be settlers, especially those of the tenderfoot class. Owing to its exposed, position on the eastern limits of the Hills, outside the gate, perhaps some of the early settlements suffered more from the aggressive operations of the Indians along the line of horse stealing than Rapid City and vicinity.

For two months after the middle of March, the few settlers who were determined to stay by the town, were kept constantly on the alert with loaded rifles in hand for the thieving redskins, who were seen almost daily skulking around the outskirts of the town, watching their opportunity to creep stealthily to the limits where horses were picketed, or with a whoop, make a bold dash, capture and run off horses not their own. That they often succeeded and sometimes failed in their purpose, the following cases will show.

On the 14th of March a band of Indians made a bold dash to the limits of the town and succeeded in getting safely away with a herd of twenty-eight horses, belonging to Bob Burleigh, at one time sheriff of Pennington County, Dan. Williams, Jud. Ellis, John Dugdale, and Ben. Northington. Encouraged by their success, they returned on April 12th and and made another attempt to stampede a number of horses, but this time failed in their purpose. After a brisk interchange of shots the Indians made their escape followed by a hail of bullets from the guns of the settlers. During the unsuccessful raid they succeeded in killing a dog belonging to Rufus Madison, and demolish a wagon.

On the 6th day of April, a man named Herman was killed a short distance below Rapid. On the 15th of the same month Capt. Dodge, of Bismarck, was killed near Spring Valley. Capt. Dodge was the leader of a party numbering about 100 men who made their way across the country, from Bismarck to the Hills. When near Rapid City he discovered the loss of a calf from the outfit, and returned alone to look for the missing property, the rest of the party proceeding on their journey to Rapid City. As their leader failed to put in an appearance, and apprehensive that he had fallen a victim to the bloodthirsty Sioux, on the following morning a party headed by J. R. Brennan, organized and went back on the trail in search of the missing man. Their worst fears were soon realized, as the unfortunate man was found at a point near Spring Valley, his body riddled with bullets; his horse lay near by, having shared his master's fate. There was every evidence that the brave man made a desperate struggle for his life, but the odds were against him and he was overpowered.

The next day, April 16th, another man was killed on the Pierre road about two miles east of Rapid City.

On the 6th of May, Edwin Sadler, N. H. Gardner, Texas Jack, and John Harrison, were killed on the Pierre road east of Rapid City, and during the same month S. C. Dodge, Henry Herring, and C. Nelson, were killed and scalped and their bodies burned just above Rapid City.

For a period of about two months, from the middle of May, there was a comparative cessation of hostilities around the Hills, the major part of the Indians having left to join Sitting Bull in the Northwest. However, from the middle of July until Gen. Crook's return from his summer campaign against the Indians in September, they kept the people of Rapid City and other border settlements in a state of constant terror by their murderous work.

On the 22d of August, two men, who were building a cabin on a ranch about two miles below town, were attacked by a band of the hostiles, returned from the Little Horn. The men, under a brisk fire, succeeded in reaching their horses that were picketed near by, and made their escape towards Rapid City, making a running fight for a mile or so, when the Indians gave up the chase without capturing men or horses. As soon as the fugitives reached Rapid, one of its citizens mounted a horse and rode swiftly up the valley to warn wayfarers of the proximity of the savages, which warning, however, was a little too late, as the Indians had preceded the messenger, and had already succeeded in killing two men at a point about two miles west of Cleghorn Springs. The names of the victims were J. W. Patterson and Thos. E. Pendleton.

On the same day, and about the same time, four men who were on their way from Deadwood to Rapid City, were attacked at Limestone Springs, on the Crook City and Deadwood road, and two of them killed. The party consisted of Sam. Scott, I. S. Livermore, G. W. Jones, and John Erquhart. The two latter were killed, Scott and Livermore making their escape into the woods about a half a mile distant, where they lay secreted until dark, when they made their way to Rapid City, arriving at about 10 o'clock p.m.

The next morning, fifteen or twenty men, with one of Volin's freight wagons, started up the valley to bring in the bodies of the murdered men, first going for those of Jones and Erquhart, which were found about one-half mile north of the Leedy springs—from which Rapid City now gets its water supply. They then drove over to the old mill site after the other two victims, one of whom was found lying on his face in the creek, the other on the trail about 100 yards away. The bodies, both of which were scalped and terribly mutilated, were placed in the wagon with the others and taken to Rapid City for interment.

While the party was absent on its humane and self-sacrificing mission, the men who had arranged to leave the country with the Volin train, had become wrought up to a high pitch of excitement, and demanded the immediate removal of the bodies from the wagon, that the train might pull out for Fort Pierre. The proprietor of the outfit expostulated with the terror-striken tenderfeet, to wait until a decent disposition should be made of the dead, but all in vain. Impressed with the feeling that delay meant almost certain death, they insisted that the train must move at once—if not with, without the consent of its proprietor. The bodies were removed from the wagon and laid in ghastly array on the ground beside a log cabin, when the train immediately pulled out for Fort Pierre, and with it went nearly the entire population of Rapid City, fleeing from the terrible Indian-infested country as if a pursuing Nemesis followed closely upon their trail.

Out of a population of 200 only eighteen brave men and one courageous woman had the nerve to stay. The names of the nineteen plucky ones were: Capt. E. LeGro, J. R. Brennan, Howard Worth, N. Newbanks, Charles N. Allen, Charles L. Allen, Jake Dawson, Mart. Pensinger, Andy Griffith, George Boland, Jim Moody, Hugh McKay, Reddy Johnson and wife, O. Nicholson, Pap Madison, Wm. F. Steele, and Bob Burleigh, and one other not remembered.

To the nineteen heroic spirits who, in staying by the town, took their lives in their own hands, the prospect was not a hopeful one. The situation was indeed one well calculated to appall the stoutest hearts. Every day the merciless painted foes of the settlers appeared in sufficient numbers to utterly annihilate them, yet their courage—fortified by trusty loaded rifles, their constant companions—never wavered during those terrible days of peril.

Although hedged about by everpresent personal danger, they did not neglect their duty to the dead. Four rough boxes were made, in which the bodies were laid by strange, yet gentle hands. The boxes were then placed in a wagon furnished by Charles N. Allen, when the funeral cortege, the first in the annals of Rapid City marched to the ground chosen for burial, on the north side of Rapid creek, where, on the brow of a broad, treeless plateau which sloped gently down to meet that swiftly-flowing stream, they were buried in one common grave. Some dug the grave while others stood guard with loaded rifles in hand. John R. Brennan, Samuel Scott, Chas. N. Allen, and Capt. E. Le Gro, buried the men, the funeral services being conducted by Oscar Nicholson. Around the grave stood every resident of Rapid City and many of those brave rugged men who did not hesitate to face the bullets of the Sioux, found it hard indeed to keep back the rising tears.

Erquhart came to the Black Hills from Denver, Colorado, shortly before he met his tragic death. He was well known in Kansas City, Mo., and Fort Scott, Kansas, in both of which cities he had held positions of honor and trust. Jones came to the Hills from Boulder, Colo., Patterson was from Allegheny City, Penn., and came to the Hills as captain of a party of gold-seekers from Pittsburg. Pendleton hailed from one of the New England States, and was a member of the New England & Black Hills Mining Company. Patterson and Pendleton came to the Hills in the same outfit with Lyman Lamb in the early spring of 1876.

After a lapse of twelve years,—long after the blood-curdling war-whoop of the Sioux had ceased to echo in and around the Black Hills, and the old trails that had been freely baptized with the blood of many of our early pioneers had been abandoned, to be overgrown with grass, and when peace, security, and prosperity had settled down upon the lovely city of the valley, with its hundreds of enterprising, thrifty population, a praiseworthy movement was set on foot at the suggestion of J. R. Brennan, to remove the remains of the four murdered pioneers from their common grave on the school section on the north side, and accord them a resting-place with the silent majority in Evergreen Cemetery.

In pursuance of that object, on Saturday, November 10th, 1888, the bodies were exhumed by undertaker Behrens and his assistants, in the presence of a number of those who were present at the burial, twelve years before. The coffins were found to be in an excellent state of preservation, the inscriptions on the lids being plainly legible. Patterson's coffin was opened and, while the clothing and bones were intact, the flesh had resolved itself into dust. Lyman Lamb recognized the boots as a pair he had often seen him wear during his lifetime. On the following day, November 11th, 1888, impressive funeral services were held at Library Hall, which was filled to its utmost capacity,—with an overflow of 200 to 300 people. The Mayor and city council were present, in conformity with a resolution adopted by that body, and also the local post of the Grand Army. Many pioneers from other portions of the Hills were in attendance to pay their last sad tribute to the memory of their murdered comrades. The citizens of Rapid City turned out en masse, in response to the Mayor's proclamation, large numbers from the surrounding country being also present.

At the close of a programme of impressive exercises, consisting of appropriate music, prayer, and touchingly eloquent addresses by R. B. Hughes and Revs. Dr. Hancher and Wilbur, the coffins were borne out, one by one, by their respective pall-bearers, nearly all of whom were early pioneers, and placed in wagons arranged in line in front of the hall. The procession, a full mile in length, then slowly wound its way to Evergreen Cemetery, where, in the four graves previously prepared, the remains were once more consigned to Mother Earth to await the last trumpet call. Revs. Hancher and Wilbur conducted the services at the graves, and when the solemn words, "Earth to earth, ashes to ashes" were recited, John R. Brennan, Sam'l Scott, Chas. N. Allen, and Capt. E. Le Gro—the men who buried the bodies in 1876, threw down the first earth upon their coffins. This time, however, no grim sentinels stood around the graves with loaded rifles, to guard them against a savage foe.

BLOCK HOUSE AT RAPID CITY DAKOTA TERRITORY IN 1876

On the next day after the last recorded tragedy two men from Spring creek reported finding a murdered man on the road about seven or eight miles from Rapid City. A party of ten went out and found the body as reported, which was buried on the spot where found, and so the carnival of blood went on. The perils became so great that all work was suspended in the valleys of Rapid and Spring creeks, and all settlers within a radius of seven or eight miles concentrated for safety at Rapid City.

BLOCK HOUSE BUILT

During the month of August a substantial block house was built on the square, at the intersection of Rapid and Fifth streets, which afforded the harassed settlers a refuge of comparative safety during the remainder of the summer. The building was a two-story structure of logs, with cupola to serve for an outlook, the upper story projecting out two feet on all sides, over the lower story which covered an area of thirty square feet. All extra provisions belonging to the citizens were at all times stored in this block house. That early stronghold of Rapid City was torn down during the summer of 1879, by Frank P. Moulton, then sheriff of Pennington County, and the material used for building a jail.

UPPER RAPID

In the early part of March, 1876, another town, called Upper Rapid, was laid out three and one-half miles above Rapid City, by a party from Bismarck, headed by California Joe. Arthur Harvey, now of Pactola, Thos. Madden and Wm. Browning, were also among its locators. The land upon which the town was laid had previously been located by California Joe while connected with the Jenny Expedition in the summer of 1875, and is now known as the Wm. Morris and Albert Brown ranches. Owing to the persistent hostility of the Indians, the project was abandoned on August 26th, 1876.

LOCATION OF RANCHES IN RAPID RIVER VALLEY IN 1876

Those of the early settlers inclined to rural pursuits, were quick to note the generous agricultural and grazing possibilities of the broad valley of Rapid creek, with its wealth of waters, and were not slow to avail themselves of the golden opportunity to secure a choice of the thousands of rich unoccupied acres lying along the creek from Rapid City to its mouth. Wide smooth acres they were, too, without stumps, or very many stones, or scarcely a tree, save those fringing the margin of the stream, to interfere with the plow in the furrows, or the reaper on the surface. It may well be said that those who had the judicious foresight to possess themselves of a ranch on the fertile valley of Rapid creek, where, with its unsurpassed facilities for irrigation, crops never fail, have to-day a property more to be prized than a gold mine.

CHAPTER XXIII

A TRIP FROM CHEYENNE TO DEADWOOD IN 1876

It was about the time the Sioux Indians, at Red Cloud, Spotted Tail, and the Missouri River Agencies, were rubbing on their war paint, and donning their feathers, preparatory to starting out on the warpath after the scalps of Black Hills gold adventurers in 1876, just as spring was slipping from the lap of winter, and while there were yet banks of snow lying in the bottom of the ravines, and small patches of "the beautiful" lay scattered here and there on the northern slopes of the low sand-hills around the city of Cheyenne, and when the mud lay hub deep in the low depressions along the military highway leading to old Fort Laramie, that a small party of immigrants, six in number, with three two-horse teams, and as many wagons, left that phenomenally windy city for the Black Hills. When I say "phenomenally windy" I speak advisedly—having seen good-sized pebbles lifted from the ground, carried along and toyed with by a fierce "nor' wester," as if they were mere grains of sand, cutting the faces of pedestrians like keen razors.

One of the wagons of the little train was loaded to the guards with merchandise for the Deadwood market—in charge of a man afterwards well known in the Hills as "Deaf Thompson;" another with sundry supplies, camp equipments, etc., of H. N. Gilbert & Son—Sam, than whom, truer gentleman never rehearsed a story around a camp-fire. By the way, I saw Sam a few weeks since, and he does not look a day older than he did twenty-three years ago when we traveled together, and all shared the same tent, from Cheyenne to Custer. The third wagon carried the household belongings of D. G. Tallent, then on his third trip to the Black Hills, and it is needless to state that the writer of this story was part and parcel of said household goods.

Yes, it is twenty-three years since that day in early April, when I bade a reluctant adieu to the wind-swept yet hospitable city of Cheyenne, and, seated in a canvas-covered wagon, behind a span of lean, ossified horses, that had been nearly starved to death during a snowstorm on their way out of the Black Hills two weeks before, resolutely turned my back once more upon civilization and all that it implies, to face the discomforts, hardships, and positive perils of a second journey to the golden "mecca"—a journey which proved to be full of exciting situations.

There is not much in the way of scenic attractions to engage the interest of travelers along the road from Cheyenne to Fort Laramie—as hundreds who have passed over the route will remember—and it was only the superabundance of mud encountered at intervals, claiming our undivided attention, that relieved the journey from the opprobrium of being called disgustingly monotonous—without even the spice of danger.

Several ranches were passed, in convenient succession, where good camping grounds were found, and where accommodations were furnished for man and beast—bearing the unpoetic though perhaps suggestive appellations of Pole Creek, Horse Creek, Bear Springs, and Chugwater—after the creeks upon which they were located. The latter creek, by the way, is deserving of a more euphonious name than Chug, as it is really a beautiful mountain stream, whose valley was already covered with a luxuriant growth of grass, in pleasing contrast to the dreary stretch through which we had just passed.

Nothing occurred to materially change the original status of our little party until it crossed the Platte river, when our numbers began rapidly to augment and our train to lengthen, for, by the time we were well outside the military reservation, we had expended into quite a formidable expedition of about ninety well-armed men, twenty-five or thirty wagons, besides a few horsemen. Among the recruits were Frank Thulen, Wm. Cosgrove, Billy Stokes, Chas. Blackwell, and D. Tom Smith, all well-known early pioneers. I came within one of being the only woman in the outfit, and that one was Mrs. Robinson, now living at Dakota City, on the Cheyenne river.

Although no Indians were encountered on the route, every man in the party, realizing that there was danger all along the line, carried his arms upon his shoulder during the day, and slept with them by his side during the night with his cartridge belts under his hard pillow. Reports came thick and fast of their atrocious deeds near the foot-hills—brought out by returning freighters, and the numerous tenderfeet who were leaving the Hills at the time. On reaching Hat creek these alarming reports received full confirmation, and we came face to face with the perilous situation. Curley, one of the victims of the Col. Brown tragedy, was lying at the time dangerously wounded, in a little log hut, at the station, with but small hopes of recovery. When it became known that a man was lying in a cabin near by, riddled with Indian bullets, excitement and consternation spread through the ranks of the expedition, especially along the rank and file of the two women of the party. The men, however, buckled on their armor and prepared for the worst, scarcely daring to hope to escape a conflict with the redskins. Every precaution being taken to guard against surprise, the train, flanked by a line of armed men, marched boldly on towards the Hills, preceded by an advance guard of six men—and thereby hangs a tale. Now, in view of the tactics peculiar to Indian strategy and attack, an advance guard *per se* may be all right and proper, but, when a body of six armed men persist in marching in advance of me, either at short or long range, with the muzzles of their guns pointed over their shoulders at such an angle that, in case of accidental discharge, their loads would penetrate my cranium just at the point where the gray matter ought to be, it is quite another thing, and assumes an aspect to which I object on purely humanitarian grounds. It is by no means conducive to longevity to sit for hours looking straight into the muzzles of six improved Winchester rifles, shifting uneasily from this side to that, in a vain endeavor to get out of range, and yet that was the exact position I occupied for a while the day we left Hat Creek stage station. At the first halting place our wagon, then near the head of the train, was swung out of line and relegated to the rear, thus causing my vocabulary of adjectives in denunciation of the dangerous practice to become exhausted. As our train neared the Hills we were met every few miles of the way by outward-bound pilgrims, whose forlorn condition stirred me with deep compassion. It would be difficult, indeed, to picture a more pathetic spectacle. Their bright visions of suddenly acquired wealth had vanished as mist beneath the burning rays of a tropical sun, and they were returning from the quest disenchanted, embittered, and many of them destitute. For the major part their clothes were badly soiled and worn; and some there were, alas! whose trousers were literally patched with an old flour sack, with "for family use" to be seen on the back, and a few with sadly demoralized shoes, through which naked protruding toes bade bold defiance to the untoward elements, and nearly all breathing bitter maledictions against the Black Hills, as well as every person who had the temerity to express their faith in them. Every man of them, however, carried a gun, as it behooved him to do. Notwithstanding these discouraging incidents along the line, our belief in the Black Hills remained unshaken, and all believing there was better luck in store for them, pressed gallantly onward, scarcely venturing to look back. I, for one, remembering the example of Lot's wife, was determined to take no chances on the possibility of being speedily converted into a "pillar of salt."

On reaching the Cheyenne river stage station our susceptibilities were still farther harrowed up by seeing two men engaged in exhuming the bodies of Mr. and Mrs. Metz, which were being removed to Laramie City, Wyoming, their former home, for permanent burial. One of the men was a brother of Mrs. Metz.

In passing through Red Canyon, numerous evidences of the terrible tragedies enacted there only a few days before, were discovered scattered along the trail, admonishing us to be on the sharp lookout for ambushed Indians.

While the men manifested no great apprehensions of trouble—though keeping their guns well in hand, I, on the contrary, was in momentary expectation of an attack. Furtively I glanced from side to side of the defile, looking for the plumed heads and cruel beady eyes of the savages peering out at us from behind the rocks. How could we know but at that very time they might be lurking behind the red crags, or in the narrow ravines, waiting to swoop down upon us at the opportune time, "like wolves on the fold"—as they had done twice within ten days before; and, in the light of a subsequent tragedy, it is believed they were on our trail even then.

Just as the train emerged from the canyon the climax came. At a signal from one of the vanguards, the train came to a dead halt. The men marching along in the flanks with guns pointed over their soldiers at the customary dangerous angle, unshouldered their arms, and, grasping them tightly in both hands, rushed precipitately to a bank overlooking a narrow ravine ahead. I thought my worst fears were realized and my days numbered. All my past shortcomings and fast-goings stood up before me in ghostly array, refusing to be laid. Bang! bang! bang! bang! bang! went the guns, until it seemed their magazines were exhausted, when they came back in line, and the train moved on. When asked for an explanation of their conduct, they reported that they had been shooting at a deer! Naturally enough I felt considerably chagrined, at having been caused such unnecessary alarm, but had partial compensation in the knowledge, that the poor deer escaped the terrible fusillade of bullets unscathed. However I breathed freely again and went on sinning as before.

In due time the train arrived at Custer, soon after which it was discovered that one of our number was missing. A small party went back at once, in search of the missing man, who was found lying dead on the trail, surrounded by the imprint of numerous moccasined feet, two or three miles back from Custer. It appeared that he had lingered behind the train as it neared Custer, and was shot down in his tracks by Indian bullets. Lying by his side was a belt, severed in twain, which he had worn around his waist, in which, upon examination, was found concealed about $3,000.00 in greenbacks, which had escaped the scrutiny of the murderers and would-be robbers. The body was conveyed to Custer, where a committee of inquiry made an investigation of the case. Papers were found, which revealed his identity, his former place of residence, and the names of relatives, to whom, at their request, his remains and effects were shipped. The murdered man, whose name was Leggett, was apparently about fifty years of age, and evidently a man of high respectability.

It seems obvious, that this band of red murderers had watched and followed our train, which perhaps they were not strong enough to attack, and pounced upon the unwary pilgrim who had lingered behind, like beasts of prey upon their victim.

I stood again upon the banks of historic French creek; again I looked at the rocky grandeur of the towering granite battlements, surrounding Custer's Park, and once more reveled amid the beauties of the earthly paradise, from which we had been so unceremoniously expelled only a short year before. But how strangely metamorphosed had the scene become meanwhile, to be sure! The dreamy little stream, whose shallow waters were wont to gurgle and murmur peacefully along their pebbly bed, without let or hindrance, is found diverted from its natural channel into numerous prosaic ditches and sluice boxes, and its valley literally turned topsy-turvy,—shorn of all its original attractiveness.

But this was not all. Where no human habitation had existed—not even the most primitive kind of a hut, unless perhaps a deserted Indian tepee—we find a populous city reared; the pine-covered hill-tops had been invaded; the solemn hush that brooded over all had been superseded by the noise and din of many human activities. Change was plainly written upon the face of the whole landscape. The rugged grandeur of the lofty jagged peaks rising up on every side alone remained unchanged and unchangeable.

Impelled by a longing, in which, however, there was but little of sentiment, to have one more look at the old stockade and its familiar environments, one bright morning, soon after the sun had sailed over the naked crest of Calamity Park, I sallied out and strolled down the valley, musing while I strolled, upon the mutability of all things earthly until coming in full view of our old stamping ground.

Then, ascending a low-timbered plateau to the left, I stood upon the very ground where our first permanent camp was made on the morning of December 24th, 1874, when the Black Hills was yet a howling wilderness. It was a beautiful sightly spot, and as I looked around at each familiar landmark, I became inspired, in spite of myself, with something akin to sentiment. I imagine I felt somewhat as did Rob Roy, the Scottish outlaw, on his return to his native haunts, when he exclaimed, "My feet are on my native heath and my name is McGregor."

Although having been divested of much of its crowning beauty—the great pine trees—the topography of the ground was well remembered, and I found no difficulty in locating almost the exact spots where our respective tents had been pitched. Yes, here is the spot where our gorgeous striped tent, a thing of beauty and of pride, went up in smoke; and over there is where the pilfering little donkey turned his vicious heels upon a defenseless woman while heroically endeavoring to rescue from his jaws the "grub" of a comrade,—

thus defeating her noble purpose. That first donkey in the Black Hills, by the way, was a true philosopher, there's no doubt about that. His motto was, "All things will come to those who watch and wait,"—a motto which he lived up to both in theory and practice during his connection with the expedition.

Leaving the "old camp ground" I sauntered down to the stockade on the left bank of French creek, approached the wide-open gate and looked in. After hesitating a few moments to consider the propriety or impropriety of entering the inclosure unbidden, I promptly decided that, inasmuch as I held a sort of proprietary interest in the property, I would be justified, from a moral, if not a legal standpoint, in going boldly in and making myself generally at home. So, acting on what conclusion, in I went, finding, however, no one to welcome me back. Two of the cabins were found tenanted—as evidenced by the padlocked doors—proof positive that their occupants were not at home. After a hasty inspection of the inner works of the fortification, I went the rounds of the vacant cabins, all of which, to a more or less extent, were fast becoming wrecks, more the result of careless tenantry than of time.

The little cabin with a wing had altogether outlived its usefulness, being no longer even habitable; its former glory had forever departed. The picturesque chimney—whose exact counterpart I challenge any one to find in the annals of chimney architecture—built originally of sticks, stones, mud, and things—had become disintegrated, and was fast crumbling into a heap of ruins; the dirt roof in many places let in the snow as well as "the sunshine and the rain." The little square opening for a window was still there, but the flour sack curtain, inscribed with the gaudy legend, was gone. There was the small opening between the wing and the main edifice, through which our next door neighbor was wont to look with intense eyes of aspect of the situation was not pleasant to contemplate, involving, as it did, the alternative of living within the narrow limits of a canvas-covered wagon or out in the open, exposed to the elements and the curious gaze of the motley crowds, without even the shelter of a tent, our tent having been cremated on French creek as before stated. Happily, in this emergency our attention was attracted to a partly finished cabin, whose roof was covered with boards having wide interstices between, and about eight or ten square feet of which was overlaid with shakes (a substitute for shingles) with no floor save *terra firma*. This skeleton structure was located on the south side of the main and only thoroughfare of the new town, in close juxtaposition to—as a matter of fact it was an addition to—a place where various kinds of stimulating beverages were daily and nightly exchanged for an equivalent in gold dust. A very quiet and orderly place of its kind, too, it turned out to be, and the headquarters of Capt.

Jack Crawford, the famous scout, whose occasional presence about the establishment threw around it, in my mind, an atmosphere of respectability.

A little below on the opposite side of the narrow street was another resort, engaged in the same kind of daily and nightly traffic, with the very suggestive name of "The Nugget" printed in the most alluring colors above the door. Notwithstanding the limitations and local environments of this unfinished cabin, which, by the kindness and courtesy of its proprietor, was placed at our disposal for a week, free of rent, as it appeared to be the only alternative, our effects were at once transferred to the small area beneath the shingled portion of the roof, and this is what happened. The morning of the second day found me, with the exception of a small boy of ten years, the sole occupant of this exposed habitation, the result of a stampede to locate a town-site in the valley of the Spearfish. Yet if the elements had not gone on a rampage, all might have been well, but during the day there came up a furious thunder-storm, such a one as used to send me flying to cover in a dark closet or under a smothering feather bed, when a child.

The day had been excessively warm and sultry, presaging the storm which later came in all its fury. Early in the afternoon the dark, threatening clouds began to gather in the west, spreading until the whole visible sky was overcast; soon the chain-lightning began to play fantastic freaks among the black clouds hovering over the mountain crests to the north and west; then in a few minutes, while I was anxiously watching the grand electrical display, hoping against hope that the threatened storm might blow over, there came a sudden blinding flash, followed instantly be a terrific thunderbolt, that shook the earth and burst open the flood-gates overhead, letting the rain come down in vast torrents. Flash after flash, peal after peal from heaven's artillery followed in rapid succession; the wind rose, blowing in great slanting shafts of water through the various openings, until bed, clothing, in fact everything in the inclosure, was drenched. For once, at least, I was not figuratively but literally in the swim. In about an hour the storm came to an end—as all things will—and settled down into a drizzling rain which continued far into the night. Often, and anxiously, during that dreadful afternoon I looked heavenward for a blue rift in the leaden sky, but in vain. Night came on apace, and such a night! Chilled and wet we crept into our damp bed, where, after hours of wakefulness, praying meanwhile, that the clouds might disappear with the night, I finally slept the profound sleep of the just. As if in answer to the secret petition, the following morning dawned bright and clear; the sun beamed down with such cheerful radiance that the misery of the night before was almost forgotten.

CAPT. JACK CRAWFORD, THE POET-SCOUT

Soon after the rising of the sun I slipped out of my wet pack, and by a good deal of active skirmishing around the premises for something combustible I soon had a rousing fire, before which quilts, blankets, wearing apparel, etc., were hung up to dry, and from which clouds of steam floated upward to be condensed for the next downfall. While seated on a dry goods box, enveloped in the ample folds of a bed quilt, watching the interesting process of evaporation, and meditating on the gravity of the situation, I was startled from my reverie by a loud knock at the door. What was to be done? I was truly in an unpleasant dilemma. Of course, I could not receive visitors wrapped in a bed quilt, and without the quilt I couldn't—well, you all know how one feels when inadequately attired. By a sort of dumb alphabet, I enjoined profound silence on the part of the small boy—threatening dire punishment in case it was broken. Another series of raps—louder than before. In sheer desperation, I called out in a high falsetto key, "Yes, in a minute!" Throwing aside my wrap, I hastily and nervously donned a half-dried garment, which took about five minutes instead of one, and called out again, "Come in!" Promptly obeying my mandate they came in, when through the ascending steam I recognized Capt. C. V. Gardner and H. N. Gilbert—the latter our traveling companion on the trip into the Hills. How glad I was to see familiar and friendly faces! How overjoyed indeed was I that I came dangerously near committing the grave indiscretion of falling upon their necks and embracing them then and there. However, resolutely repressing that inclination, I greeted them with tears of joy in my eyes and I fear with rather a sickly smile on my lips. After a hasty survey of the damp premises, and with a look of commiseration in his eyes, Capt. Gardner inquired: "What's the matter here? What does all this mean?" "Oh, it means that we were treated to a generous shower bath yesterday, free of charge; that, and nothing more," I answered.

"Well, well," said he, "this is a d—downright shame." Yes, d—stands for downright. "Of course it is," I assented, "its disgraceful, its dreadful, its worse than a battle with the Sioux Indians." I said I thought it merited the whole category of d—s.

"This will never do," said the Captain, "You must get out of this place as soon as possible." Well, in less than the stipulated time, we vacated the place and moved into a small log cabin at the base of the hill on Williams street, where we remained during the summer of 1876.

Although our temporary abode on Main street furnished but small physical comfort, it had its advantage in that it afforded an excellent point of vantage, from which to see Deadwood in all its early picturesqueness. To be sure, the great rush was not yet at its flood, yet there was already enough excitement to make things exceedingly lively in the big mining camp, and the rush and push of hustling up buildings on every side; the numerous emigrant wagons, and pack animals loaded with blankets, mining tools, etc., that crowded the narrow thoroughfare; and the hundreds of eager jostling fortune-hunters, rushing up and down the street, and in and out between the wagons, contributed no end of amusing diversion, in all of which, however, there was a world of pathos,—in view of the almost certainty, that at least nine-tenths of the expectant throng were doomed to crushing disappointment.

Incidentally, too, Main street was the theater of an occasional farce-comedy, which added spice and variety to the scene, to one of which I was an unvoluntary, though interested witness. One day while at my point of observation, I saw a coatless, hatless, unkempt, red-headed man—with only one suspender—well, I sized him up as a "whacker,"—rush headlong out of the "Nugget" across the way, closely followed by a man of sanguinary aspect, holding a six-shooter in his right hand, and hurling all sorts of billingsgate after the fleeing offender. The red-headed man dodged behind a wagon that providentially stood near by; thus escaping immediate danger. The pursued and the pursuer played a game of hide-and-go-seek around the wagon for several minutes, when some bystanders interfered and put an end to the exhibition. This is only one of many similar exhibitions witnessed in 1876, but one is plenty.

In casting about here and there up and down the narrow auriferous gulches from Gayville to Elizabethtown and below, it was found that every square yard of pay-gravel, from rim to rim, along the entire length of the gulch, was already claimed and staked off by the wide-awake miners, who metaphorically took time by the forelock, and hastened to the new discovery at the first report, thus securing claims from which many reaped fortunes—while the unlucky ones who dawdled away two weeks of precious time waiting for something to "turn up" lost a golden opportunity.

"Of all sad words of tongue or pen
   The saddest are these, It might have been."

CHAPTER XXIV

PLACER MINE IN DEADWOOD GULCH IN 1876

As soon as the alluring notes of the golden tocsin proclaiming the tidings of rich auriferous placer discoveries in the northern Hills, sounded far and wide, and echoed through the remote valleys and gulches of the Black Hills, the news created a furore, such as had not, perhaps, been exceeded since the exciting days of '49. Deadwood then, instead of Custer, became the "Mecca" of gold-hunters from all parts of the land, Montana, Colorado, and even the great gold State of California, contributing their quota to swell the human tide.

All trails through the Hills, lined with pack outfits galore, led to the new diggings in the north. French, Spring, Rapid, and Castle creeks and their tributaries, where, prior to this time, placer mining had been carried on with a fair degree of success, became practically deserted. The nuggets of Bear Gulch and "Nigger Hill,"—in the light of the new discovery, lost their power to dazzle and were temporarily abandoned. And what was the result? Unfortunately, the new diggings were not so extensive as they were rich, consequently hundreds, after a gallant but vain scramble to secure a plum from the plump golden pie, returned to their abandoned claims, presumably well satisfied with making from five to ten dollars per day to the man.

Moral: Let well enough alone.

Soon every claim worth having above Gayville, on Deadwood and tributary gulches, down nearly to Crook City, on Whitewood gulch, was located and staked, cleared of its dead timber and dense undergrowth, ready for operation. From April, through the summer of Fall of 1876, the work of uncovering and washing out the golden product of Deadwood, Whitewood, Gold Run, Black Tail, and Bob-Tail gulches was vigorously prosecuted, from which vast quantities of gold-dust were taken—the aggregate production from these gulches during the year reaching up into the hundreds of thousands of dollars.

It has been impossible to ascertain—as a matter of fact no one has ever known—even approximately the amount taken from these rich placer deposits, and a conjecture would be hazardous, as it might prove very wide of the mark. However, it has been variously estimated, by intelligent, practical

NO. 4, ABOVE DISCOVERY, ON DEADWOOD

miners and close observers of placer mining operations of that day, that from $3,000,000 to $4,000,000 in gold-dust were sluiced from the aforesaid gulches during the years 1876-7, these estimates being based upon the daily clean-ups of certain individual claims. It is stated by those who were in a position to judge that daily clean-ups of from one to two thousand dollars from several claims on Deadwood and a few on Whitewood gulch was no uncommon occurrence, from which it is safe to conclude that the above estimates of the aggregate product of those gulches is not excessive.

That the stories told of those wonderful daily clean-ups were not fairy tales nor the result of an exuberant fancy, but a glittering reality, I am quite prepared to believe, for have not mine eyes often in those days feasted on the great piles of yellow gold mixed with a little black sand, left in the miners' gold-pans after the lighter material was washed off? And did I not as often break the divine mandate written by the finger of God on the tables of stone on the mount: "Thou shalt not covet thy neighbor's goods?" I stand self-condemned.

Among the large producing claims on Deadwood gulch were No. 2, operated by Wheeler brothers; Nos. 4 and 5 below Discovery, owned by Chisholm brothers and sold to Robert Neill for $2,200 after a large fortune had been realized from the claims; Nos. 14 and 15 below, owned by Robert Kenyon; "Discovery Claim," purchased by John Hildebrand from the original locator; No. 1 below, located by Ed. Murphy; No. 9 below, located by Jack McAleer, and numerous others, perhaps equally productive. The largest producing claim on Whitewood gulch was what was known as the Bostwick mines, below Elizabethtown.

Active sluicing operations in those gulches, which began about the middle of April, were at first considerably retarded by the lack of lumber for the construction of sluice boxes, which, in the absence of sawmills, had to be manufactured by hand, by the slow and tedious method of what is called whipsawing. This handicap, however, was soon removed by the establishment of sawmills, three of which were, early in June, in full operation and producing lumber at the rate of 32,000 feet per day—Judge E. G. Dudley's mill, in East Deadwood, turning out about 12,000 feet per day, Street &

CABIN ON CLAIM NO. 2, DEADWOOD GULCH

Thompson's and Boughton & Berry's mills, located below Montana, producing 10,000 feet per day each. Boughton & Berry's mill was later removed to South Deadwood.

"PLACER MINING PROCESSES"

The attention of prospectors on their arrival in a new gold field is at once directed to its auriferous placer deposits: first, because they are a pretty certain index of the richness of the gold-bearing ledges, from which by natural processes they have been liberated; second, because in ordinary operations little capital save that of willing hands and stout arms is needed to remove them from their hiding-places, and by various interesting methods convert them into commerical values. These deposits are found by digging down to the floor or bedrock of the gulch, to which, by virtue of its specific gravity, the gold has sifted, or in bars of gold-laden gravel along the courses of streams, and, strangely enough, in some portions of the Black Hills—notably along the borders of Castle creek—placer gold and wash gravel have been found on the tops of high hills. How they came there, I shall not undertake to explain, not being a geologist.

Some geologists would say, perhaps, that they were carried or pushed along with the rock and *debris* by the early glaciers on their long, slow journey down from the regions of perpetual ice, and left high and dry upon our hilltops; others might advance some other occult theory. However, as it is not the province of history to deal in theories, but in facts, let it suffice to say that the fact remains as above stated, which goes to show that the oft-repeated aphorism that gold is where you find it, is peculiarly applicable to the Black Hills.

After the deposit has been discovered and tested through the medium of the pick, shovel, and gold-pan, the first great requisite for sluicing—which is the method that has been most extensively employed in the Black Hills—is an ample supply of water, without which the richest deposits are comparatively valueless; then comes the construction of a ditch for carrying the necessary supply of water from some point above to the place where it is turned into the sluice. Sometimes a combination of claim owners unite to build the ditch, the water to be used in common, in which case gates are made through which to divert the water from the main canal or ditch to the head of each individual claim; sometimes the water is leased to other miners who have no interest in the enterprise.

In the meantime sluices have been constructed, the sluice consisting of several oblong, open boxes, eighteen inches high and about two feet wide, at the bottom of which are nailed cleats (called riffles) at short intervals to catch the gold, and at the end of the series of boxes a piece of cloth, called an apron, is sometimes attached to save the particles that are washed over the riffles. A little quicksilver is then frequently poured into the boxes above the riffles to attract the gold, when the work of sluicing is ready to begin. The gate is then opened and the water glides through a channel dug for the purpose into the sluice; at first it goes rippling musically over the riffles, then dashes gaily down the slightly inclined plane, and out at the opposite end of the sluice, where it is again turned into the main ditch to be utilized on the claim below, or into the channel of the stream, as the case may be.

A man is stationed at the head of the sluice to shovel the gravel from the dump into the sluice box; another man armed with a many-tined fork is placed at the lower end of the sluice to remove the pebbles and gravel that are washed down, while a third or middle man, also provided with a fork, is employed in removing obstacles from the boxes all along the line. Every night, or at longer intervals, as may seem necessary, there is had what is called a clean-up. The water is turned off, and the accumulation of gold, black sand, and gravel is carefully scraped from the riffles and the apron at the lower extremity of the sluice into a gold pan, and then taken to a stream of water near by, where the gravel and sand for the most part are washed off. This operation requires a good deal of skill and dexterity, and not everyone can do it successfully—the particles of gold being liable to float out with the grosser substances, unless saved by the dexterous hand of an expert. All this done, behold! as a result, $2,000 of gold dust, gold scales, and often gold nuggets in the pan. This is then taken to the miner's cabin and divested of all dross, when it is ready for commercial exchange.

Where the water supply is inadequate for sluicing purposes, the old method of washing out the gold by "rocking" is resorted to. The rocker, though an ancient appliance for washing out gold, is really a very ingenious contrivance, and deserves to occupy a conspicuous niche in placer mining history as well as a warm place in the affections of placer miners. It has been the accommodating agent through which many a stranded miner has secured a "grub stake" when away from his base of supplies. This time-honored affair, which consists of a box mounted on a pair of rockers, is operated on the principle of a child's cradle. A succession of sieves, graduating in texture, are arranged on a slight incline in the box—on the bottom of which are nailed tiny riffles which catch the gold that makes its way through the meshes of the sieves. Two men are required to operate a rocker—one shovels the gravel in at the top, the other dips up the water with a long-handled dipper and pours it on the gravel with his right hand, while with his left he rocks his cradle—not to a lullaby song, but to the music of the water as it percolates through the gravel, from sieve to sieve, and flows out through a spout at the lower end of the incline.

The rocker is a portable concern, and can be easily loaded onto a wheelbarrow and transported from place to place, wherever there chances to be a pool of water, and pay gravel to operate upon. This process was extensively used in washing out the wonderfully rich deposits of Rockerville, where to-day good wages are made through the medium of the despised rocker.

HYDRAULIC PLACER MINES

Another method somewhat similar to ordinary sluicing, but on a far more extensive scale, that has been employed to some extent in the Black Hills, is the hydraulic process. In hydraulic mining, as in sluicing, the first requisite is, of course, the auriferous deposits to be operated upon. These are found as before stated, but the high bar deposit will be taken to illustrate the modus operandi. As these bars are not of a solid rock formation, but accretions of earth, gravel and boulders—mixed with the gold or other mineral that has been liberated, by the action of mountain torrents, and other agencies from veins or ledges above, and washed down and distributed in the soil of the valley or deposited in bars, they are easily broken and disintegrated, when exposed to the action of a sufficient head of water. Then the mining ditches must be built.

These waterways are made by diverting the streams from their natural channels, at some point high enough above the mines to afford the requisite fall, and conveying it by ditch and flume, sometimes many miles along the hill-sides; around or through jutting rocks and across deep ravines, where it is supported by trestle work, to the place where the water is to be utilized. The water is then conducted from the main reservoir or flume through a pipe which connects at the lower end with a strong wooden or cast-iron box, provided with several openings to which are attached smaller pipes, these being again connected with flexible rubber or canvas hose, which can be turned in any direction, terminating in nozzles with orifices from one and a half to three inches in diameter. A wide sluice is then made, which carries off the loosened material from the mine or bar operated upon, into sluice-boxes provided with riffles after the method of ordinary sluicing.

Men are stationed at the nozzle to manipulate the hose, and a very uncomfortable position it seems from my point of view, upon the one and only occasion on which I witnessed the process, then the floodgate, which is usually many miles above, is opened, and the water under a powerful pressure rushes down through ditch, flume, and pipe, with an ever-increasing momentum into the box or bulkhead, then through the distributing pipes into the hose, and out at the orifices with the tremendous force of a battering ram. Continuous streams of water are directed through the nozzles at the base of the bar, undermining it, thus causing the overhanging mass to fall to the base, where by the powerful action of the water it is broken apart and washed down into the sluice; great boulders weighing tons are swept down the slope and toyed with as if they were tiny pebbles. The water flows away down the slope, leaving the larger boulders and the coarser gold on bed-rock, while the finer gold is carried along with the earth and gravel through the sluice boxes, where it is caught in the riffles. It goes without saying that the clean-ups must be something vast, if the deposits are rich, when the amount of material that passes through the sluices is taken into consideration.

In hydraulic mining it would seem to be essential that the men employed should possess wonderful muscle, as well as feel an utter indifference to water and its effects; those stationed along the line to remove obstructions having frequently to lift and throw aside heavy boulders, and are standing or wading around from morning till night in water knee-deep; while the men at the nozzles are in about the condition of the traditional drowning rat, completely drenched by the sheets of spray that are thrown back by the fierce contact of the water with the bank against which it is delivered. To the student of hydrodynamics the whole process from the head of the flume to the foot of the sluices—and the clean-up may as well be included—is one of exceeding interest. To the observer, it presents features that are more than interesting, they are grandly picturesque.

The most extensive hydraulic enterprise projected in the Black Hills was the great Rockerville flume for conducting the waters of Spring creek to the rich, dry placer beds at Rockerville. The flume, which was commenced in 1878, was an immense wooden structure, running from the dam at a point two miles above Sheridan, along a tortuous route, on the side of steep mountains, around abrupt curves, over deep gorges, on lofty trestles to Rockerville, a distance of seventeen miles. It was a gigantic undertaking—requiring the use of hundreds of thousands of feet of lumber and the employment of many men, at a cost of from $250,000 to $300,000.

The operations by this process on the Rockerville gulch deposits continued about five years, resulting in the production of over a half million of dollars in gold.

Hydraulic flumes were also constructed on Rapid creek, near Pactola, by the Estella Del Norte Company at an immense expense, where operations were carried on for a time. Also the Hydraulic Gold Mining Company, on Battle creek, all of which will be referred to farther on.

Placer mining in the Black Hills—as a great mining industry—has long since been abandoned: not because these deposits have been exhausted, by any means. There are to-day, it is believed by miners of judgment and experience, millions of dollars of gold lying buried down deep on the water-washed bed-rock of Spring, Rapid, and Castle creeks, and perhaps other streams, awaiting capital, for the employment of skilled engineers and effective mechanical appliances for exhausting the surplus water on the beds of those streams. That such an enterprise will some day be undertaken, it is believed.

EARLY QUARTZ MINING IN THE BLACK HILLS

In the annals of nearly all mining camps, it is found that their stability and permanency have depended mostly upon the quartz mines. It is shown that not the easy placers, that cost little to operate, and moreover soon become exhausted, but the capital employed and expended in the development and equipment of quartz properties, with engines, steam drills, hoisting plants, mills, and other expensive machinery, and the employment of skilled engineers to set them in motion and operate them, and expert miners to extract the ore from the mine in the most judicious manner for its proper development,—are what build up and maintain vitality in a mining camp; hence in a new camp the chief interest soon centers in its quartz mines, and the history of the great mining camp of Deadwood is no exception to the general rule.

Early in 1876 after the short period of delirious excitement, consequent upon the rich placer discoveries, had given place to calm consideration and sober judgment, the attention of prospectors was directed towards the quartz resources of the camp and soon the hills above the gold-laden gulch were being vigorously exploited—by men who knew gold-bearing rock when they saw it—for traces of the ledges whence the marvelous deposits came. "Float" and "croppings" galore were carried daily to the tents and cabins of prospectors, in bags flung over their shoulders, for testing purposes. Then followed what may appropriately be termed the "mortar and pestle" era, during which the music of numberless of the tiny one-stamp mills was heard from every quarter of the big camp, morning, noon, and night; and one was confronted on every hand, on the street corners, in grocery stores, hotels, and saloons, where men the most did congregate, by the amusing spectacle of men submitting a small piece of innocent rock to the most severe scrutiny, through a magnifying glass, to discover whether it was guilty or innocent of carrying free gold.

A change then came over the silent hills, where erstwhile were heard only the howling of the timber wolf, the solemn hooting of the owl, and kindred sounds, and solitude reigned there nevermore. The clinking of picks and shovels, the creaking of many windlasses, and the roar of dynamite, that tore the rocks asunder, proclaimed the beginning of quartz mining in what was afterwards known throughout the mining world as the great "gold belt" of the Black Hills.

During the year 1876 there were more than 150 quartz mines located and in process of rapid development, within a radius of five miles of Deadwood. Among the earliest discoveries were the Golden Terry on Bob Tail, familiarly known as the Frenchman's Mine, and reputed to be the first discovered quartz mine in the "belt," the Alpha lode, discovered on the 12th of May, 1876, by Messrs. Wolsey, Jones & Rowland, upon which was operated the first stamp mill in the Black Hills; the Homestake, discovered by Emanuel brothers, Alf. Engh, and others; the Hidden Treasure on Spring gulch, discovered by Thos. O'Neal on the 13th of May, 1876, upon which was operated the first quartz mill in the Black Hills; the Chief of the Hills on Black Tail, located by Jack Hunter and California Joe; the Old Abe, discovered by M. Cavanaugh; the Golden Star, located by Smoky Jones; and others located at nearly the same time, or a little later.

The Golden Terry, the Homestake, the Old Abe and the Golden Star have long since lost their identity, having been absorbed with other mines by the capital of the great Homestake Company, that has for the past nineteen years been paying dividends from the product of those early discoveries. Strange, isn't it, and sad, too, when you come to think of it, that the toiling, sweating, powder-begrimed miner rarely reaps the full fruition of his discovery.

The early explorations for gold-bearing quartz were, however, by no means confined to the northern Hills. At a very early date in 1876, some promising discoveries were made among the hills bordering on French creek, and other portions of the southern and central Hills.

A trip through the valleys and gulches of the Black Hills to-day will disclose the fact that a vast deal of prospecting was done during the early years of their history, for both placer and quartz; deserted shafts, with dumps of gravel and rock, broken and decaying windlasses, and ore buckets lying near by; abandoned tunnels, in which sometimes can be found an old pick and shovel corroded with the rust of years, but more frequently filled up with the fallen debris; prospect holes innumerable, and tumble-down log cabins may be seen wherever you go. Nearly every hillside and gulch throughout the length and breadth of the fair domain tell a pathetic story of depleted purses, wasted energies, disappointed hopes, and days, months, yea, sometimes years, of unrewarded toil. Occasionally a piece of expensive machinery will be found going to certain wreck and ruin. Any one who has ever traveled over the road from Rochford to Hill City will perchance have noticed an old wheel lying on the sands on one of the banks of Castle creek, below Castleton, where it has lain for years, a solemn warning to passing miners. That old decaying wheel is the sole representative of a capital of $10,000 in cold cash, expended by H. C. Smith, former County Commissioner of Pennington County, in a futile attempt to exhaust the water from the gold-laden bed-rock of the valley of that stream.

THE PECULIARITIES OF MINERS

Much has been said and more written of the peculiar characteristics of miners as distinct from all other classes of the genus homo that is believed to be erroneous and exaggerated. Their vernacular, their eccentricities, and their personnel have been prolific themes for the pen of the humorist and the caricaturist, ever since the days of "Roaring Camp" and "Poker Flats." The most sanguinary and indefensible murder of the Queen's English has been laid at their doors, and they have been portrayed in garbs that would bring a broad smile to even the face of a stone wall. All this has been told, and more.

Now, perhaps it is not right to aim a deadly blow at a cherished tradition, and try to undermine a fixed belief, but, in justice to the mining fraternity, I want to express the conviction that the popular conception of miners, taking the average Black Hills miner as a type, comes about as near to the truth as that of the traditional Yankee, who sometimes appears on the comedy stage with striped trousers, swallow-tail coat—mostly tail,—high stand-up collar, and a nasal twang and pronunciation, the like of which was never heard by mortal man since the building of the tower of Babel.

Little of what has been said and written about miners is applicable to Black Hills miners, who are an intelligent, and, in many cases, a well-educated class of men. Of course, in a spirit of goodfellowship, they sometimes address each other as "pard," and most wear overalls and rubber boots, as the nature of their vocation requires, but who ever heard of a Black Hills miner talking like this:—

"Look er-har, boys, I'm er goin' ercross ter der s'loon an' ax Bill ter chalk me down fer der drinks fer der crowd. Come er long, boys."

"All right, pard, we've bin kin' er waitin' for yer ter ax us."

CHAPTER XXV

DEADWOOD IN 1876

In among the rugged northern hills, at an altitude of over 4,500 feet above the level of the sea, is situated the city bearing the very unique name of Deadwood, so named because of the chaos of fallen dead timbers which once covered the site of its location. Although the name is a good enough one, and was honestly and appropriately bestowed, there are those who think that the great commerical metropolis of the Black Hills should have been honored with a more euphonious appellation. As a matter of fact, however, in the fitness of things, it could not very well have been called by any other name. But what's in a name, and, indeed, what cared its sponsors what the name of the infant city, when every square foot of its foundation was to yield to them a rich tribute of shining gold? At any rate, Deadwood it was named, and inasmuch as its citizens are satisfied to accept matters as they found them, Deadwood it shall remain.

The site of the original Deadwood was located on the 26th of April, 1876, by Craven Lee, Isaac Brown, J. J. Williams, and others, below the junction of Deadwood and Whitewood creeks, and laid out down the narrow valley of the latter stream, close under the shadow of Forest Hill, and a more picturesque site could hardly have been chosen. The contracted valley, flanked on one side by Forest Hill, which was then clothed with evergreen trees from base to summit, on the other by rugged hills, above which rise the hoary crests of White Rocks, some 2,000 feet above the level of their base, was barely wide enough at points for the laying out of one narrow street. The site was laid out evidently to conform with the topography of the valley, without regard to the points of the compass, the main street, however, trending nearly north and south, and crossed at right angles by Lee, Gold, and Wall streets.

When the howling waste of dead timbers and underbrush was removed from the ground, the work of building at once began. The first structure erected on the platted site was a small log cabin, built by Lee & Brown, at the northwest corner of Main and Gold streets, on part of the ground now occupied by the Nye Block. With the push and energy characteristic of our early pioneers, Lee & Brown had their cabin built and ready for occupancy on the 30th of April, just four days after the site was laid out. Beofre the laying of the

WHITE ROCKS OVERLOOKING DEADWOOD

town-site there had been three other cabins built on the ground, the first by J. J. Williams, on ground afterwards occupied by J. Goldberg's store, the second by John Shive, and the third by W. H. Smith.

The first frame structure erected in Deadwood was built by C. V. Gardner & Co., in June, 1876, on the lot adjoining the one occupied by Lee & Brown. In this frame building Gardner & Co. opened the first completely equipped grocery store in Deadwood. The second is said to have been opened by Furnam & Brown, followed very closely by Browning & Wringrose.

Prior to the opening of these houses, a number of others, among whom were Judge W. L. Kuykendall and Cuthbertson & Young, had carried on a sort of curbstone grocery and provision traffic with freighters, of whom they purchased only in quantities sufficient to meet the existing demand.

The first drug store was established by Julius Deetkin on the east side of Main street, below Lee, in June, 1876. A little later Mr. Deetkin became associated with E. C. Bent, under the firm name of Bent & Deetkin.

The first hotel erected was Gen. Custer House, built by John Scollard, now of Sturgis, on the northeast corner of Main and Lee streets, in June, 1876. This building, a two-story frame structure, was opened to the public as a hostelry in July, 1876, by R. R. Marsh, who retired from the business in December following, and was succeeded by J. J. Sutherland and John Amerman.

But while the Gen. Custer House was the first completed it was not the first opened for business. The Grand Central was built a little later in June of that year, on the west or north side, whichever it may be called—of Main street, and was opened during the same month, first as a restaurant, by C. H. Wagner. Later the building was raised an additional story, after which it was conducted as a regular hotel.

DEADWOOD IN 1876

The first hardware store in Deadwood, and perhaps in the Black Hills, was opened by Boughton & Berry in a building which stood on the ground afterwards occupied by Star & Bullock's hardware store on the east side of Main street.

The first meat shop was opened by J. Shoudy in the spring of 1876; and the first regular restaurant, called the IXL, was opened by J. Vandaniker & McGavock.

The first saddlery and harness shop was opened during the summer of 1876, by J. M. Woods, on the east side of Main street, below Wall, and the first livery barn was established during the same summer by Clark & Morill, who also conducted an auction and commission business in connection with the livery. The first jewelry store was opened by M. N. Gillette.

It is claimed that Judge Miller was the first law practitioner in Deadwood, and Dr. A. W. McKinney the first local physician.

The first school opened in Deadwood was a private school taught by Wm. Commode, during the autumn of 1876. The term was taught in a small log cabin that stood on or near the ground now occupied by the Wentworth Hotel. In November, 1876, a second bank was established by Miller & McPherson, in connection with other lines of business.

Business enterprises followed each other in such bewilderingly rapid succession in 1876, that it is indeed difficult to state positively which was first in the race. Each one speedily reared his structure according to his individual fancy or convenience—with utter disregard to regularity—and opened up his wares for traffic. In four months from the day the first smoke curled up from the rude chimney of Lee & Brown's log cabin, both sides of Main street were crowded with structures of various sizes, shapes, and qualities—log cabins, frame buildings, and tents, in one curious medley bent. Even the cross streets, in defiance of the rules and regulations adopted by the town organization, were appropriated for building and business purposes.

The following are the names of some of the firms conducting business in Deadwood during the initial year of its history: Baer & McKinnis, Janson & Bliss, and Star & Bullock (hardware); J. M. Woods (banker); Miller & McPherson (bankers); D. Hozeman, Browning & Wringrose, Garrison & Dennee (grocers); Bent & Deetkin (druggists); Matheieson & Goldberg, Gardner & Brown, Robinson & Ross (grocers); Garlick Bros. (druggists); A. T. Henzie (jeweler); Cuthbertson & Young, W. L. Kuykendall (commission); Wm. Burton, Vandaniker & McGavock (restaurants); Amerman & Sutherland (hotel); C. H. Wagner (hotel); Matkin & Co. (bakers); Hildebrand & Harding, Phillips & Biddle, Gaston & Shankland, Nye & Co., Samuel Soyster, Knowles & Marshmand, Wm. Le De Moss; and many others.

During that brief period about 7,000 were added to the population of Deadwood, among whom were many reckless adventurers, who scarcely knew for what they came—without other purpose than the possible chance of fleecing unwary and trusting pilgrims. Hotels and other places of entertainment, though numerous, were crowded to overflowing, beds in which to sleep were at a high premium and a chair on which to sit was regarded as a great luxury. As a matter of fact, many had not the price to advance for either, and were forced to slumber in the shadow of the buildings or standing up in saloons and gambling houses.

In the train of the legitimate prospector, came the men of business and professional men—the former with their goods, merchandise, fixtures, etc., and in their wake followed the gamblers and all kinds of crooks and sharps, and with them those fixed facts in the moral or immoral economy of nearly all mining camps and municipalities, those human leeches that remorselessly feed upon the earnings of weak men—the courtesan. By the latter part of August, Deadwood had become a vast seething cauldron of restless humanity, composed of virtue and vice in about equal ratios, engaged each in his own way in the mighty struggle for gold.

Nearly all branches of business were represented in Deadwood in 1876, and the trade along all lines was something immense. Every business man, no matter in what kind of traffic engaged, made money beyond his most sanguine expectations. Hotels and other eating places which fed hundreds every day were veritable gold mines, and the saloons, of which there were scores, grew rich on the reckless expenditures of those who dug for gold.

Profits were large and the demand unlimited; wages were high and gold plentiful. Every miner carried his little buckskin sack, filled with gold dust, which he squandered right and left with reckless prodigality and abandon. An instance of which I chanced to be a witness is now recalled, when a high-stepping, half-seas-over miner, scattered the contents of his well-filled gold sack in the middle of Main street, to see the boys and impecunious men scramble for the shining particles. Let it be understood, however, that all miners were not thus reckless and prodigal of their gold, only the major part of them. As gold dust, whose commerical value was then rated at from eighteen to twenty dollars per ounce, was the almost sole medium of exchange, a pair of gold scales and a blower were indispensable parts of the equipment of every business place.

En-passant, the most unique and perhaps the most profitable load of merchandise brought to Deadwood in 1876, was a consignment of cats. While there were plenty of wild cats among the jungles of the Hills in those days, there were very few of the domestic variety, so taking advantage of the existing dearth, some speculative genius in the East conceived the happy idea of shipping a wagon load of the Eastern surplus to the Black Hills and convert it into gold dust. The load, which was arranged into compartments one above the other, comprised cats of almost every shade and hue, Maltese, black, white, yellow, gray, and spotted.

The average man in Deadwood in 1876 would pay any reasonable price for a "family cat" to keep fresh in his memory "the girl he left behind him," and consequently there was quite an active competition around the wagon in the street as to the privilege of first choice. The Maltese being the prime favorite, commanding the highest price, the maximum being $10.00 in gold dust, and $5.00 the minimum.

Owing to the difficulty and cost, as well as the extreme danger of transportation, provisions of all kinds commanded exorbitant prices, flour, at times of great scarcity, having sold as high as $60.00 per 100 pounds, and other staple articles at proportionate prices. To offset the prevailing high

WITCHER'S FREIGHT TRAIN ON THE STREETS OF DEADWOOD IN 1876

prices of goods, however, wage-earners, both miners and skilled mechancis, received from five to seven dollars per day's work, and mine owners in many cases were making a small fortune every day. Idlers and hangers-on, of whom there were many, of course lived a very precarious existence, oftentimes being forced to go hungry.

SUNDAY IN DEADWOOD DURING PIONEER DAYS

There was no austerity nor solemnity about Sunday in Deadwood during the pioneer days. The current of traffic, like time and tide, flowed on seven days of every week, and Sunday was the maddest business day of all. It was not that its business men had lost their reckoning of the days of the week that Sunday was the busiest of the seven, but because that was the day on which the hundreds of miners and prospectors in the surrounding camps and gulches threw down their picks and shovels and came to Deadwood to replenish their stores of supplies, get their mail, have a jolly good time, and spend their week's earnings. Naturally the business men, not having braved the dangers of a journey into the Black Hills for their health, were nothing loth to exchange their goods and merchandise and otherwise cater to their pleasures for gold dust, hence Deadwood on Sunday presented a scene of extraordinary business activity and excitement, and one not easily forgotten.

Conjure up in your minds one long, rather narrow street, which was practically all there was of Deadwood in the summer of 1876, deeply lined on both sides from one extreme to the other with a dense, dark mass of surging, pushing, struggling, male humanity, every business place open and traffic in full blast. Imagine the arrival upon the scene of several freight trains, heavily laden with merchandise, and the bustle and confusion of unloading the same at the doors of the many hustling dealers along the crowded street. Imagine you hear the oaths of the pitiless drivers accompanied by the sharp crack of their long, cruel lashes, the plaintive "mooing" of the tired, panting cattle, and the loud, resonant braying of many mules, and above all the incessant rasping of numerous saws and the resounding blows of many hammers, and you have a faint mental reproduction of Sunday in Deadwood during the pioneer days, which was but an extreme type of every other day of the week.

DEADWOOD BY LAMPLIGHT

Picturesque and exciting as was the exterior aspect of Deadwood during the day, it presented another even more novel and striking view, which the casual observer could gain only by the rays of numerous kerosene lamps.

By elbowing your way down the street through a jostling crowd of roystering, rollicking miners, noisy "whackers," untutored tenderfeet, and some more kinds of people, when the shades of evening prevailed and the lamps were lighted, you could have had a glimpse of the true inwardness of Deadwood during the early period. You would have seen every store, every saloon and gambling resort, all places of amusement, of questionable propriety, bright and alluringly illuminated by many coal oil lamps. Execrable music, produced from antiquated pianos and cracked violins, mingled with song and hilarious laughter, would have reached your ears from every quarter. By a hasty glance through the wide-open doors of the saloons and gaming resorts, you would have noticed large crowds of men of all classes gathered, eagerly watching as if fascinated, the many games of chance going on, games in which hundreds of dollars were won and lost in a single night, games in which, alas, many a tenderfoot was tempted to stake his all on the hazard of a die, only to lose. The most notorious as well as the most nefarious of the gambling resorts to be found in Deadwood during the early days, was a place on lower Main street called by the musical name of the "Melodeon," but where the melody came in is not understood, unless it might be the mellifluous flow of gold dust into the pockets of the robbers, thieves, bunko men, and general cappers, the "Nutshell Bills," the "Pancake Bills," the "Mysterious Jimmies," and others of that ilk, who were said to have made that unsavory resort their headquarters. There was another popular resort on lower Main street, known as the "Variety Theatre," where under the glare of kerosene lamps the Ella La Rues, the Fanny Garretsons, the Kittie Leroys and the big-voiced Monteverdes, nightly entertained and enchanted hundreds of men with ribald song and dance and wine and smutty jest, until the "wee-sma' " hours of the morning. All this I was told and much more, over which it is better to draw the veil.

In the living panorama surging along the street it was not an uncommon thing to see groups of gaudily-attired, paint-bedaubed creatures—whom for grammatical accuracy we will call women, some from whose faces the bloom of innocence had not yet wholly departed; others whose cheeks evidently had years before forgotten how to blush, boldly parading up and down, amid the jostling crowds, at early lamplight—presenting a spectacle suggestive of a degree of depravity not pleasant to contemplate. Albeit, in view of the fact that the people were outlaws, having no license to control affairs—not even municipal license, for several months, there was a remarkable absence of disorder in the streets of Deadwood during its pioneer days.

HOW WE CELEBRATED OUR NATAL DAY IN 1876

The Centennial Anniversary of our nation's birth was by no means forgotten by the people of the Black Hills, in their eager quest for gold, as was shown by the manner in which the people of Deadwood and its surburban population of miners observed the day. Pioneers never do things by halves, and the fact that they were not regarded by Uncle Sam as citizens, nor accorded any of their rights, lessened not a whit their zeal and patriotism, or their loyalty to the flag they still loved, so the great national holiday was celebrated with a vim and enthusiasm worthy of the important occasion.

To make the necessary preliminary preparations for the proper observance of the day, hundreds of stalwart miners from the adjacent camps gathered in Deadwood on the evening of the third to aid in the erection of a pole of liberty. The tallest and most symmetrical pole that could be found along the mountain slopes was secured and planted in front of the speaker's stand—previously prepared on the north side of Main street, to be ready for the flag at the "dawn's early light."

It is needless to state that the celebrators were on the alert for the hour to begin. I was on the alert too, soon after, for at the last stroke of the midnight hour by the cabin clock, or the last tick of the twelfth hour by the watches in the miners' vest pockets the booming of artillery began. One hundred salutes—anvil salutes—were fired in reasonably rapid succession, which consumed the major part of the time till daylight—as per mathematical calculation; yes, an average of twenty-five booms per hour, in regular sequence, would bring daylight in July, and figures will not lie. It was so soothing to the nerves, you know.

At the rising of the sun the national emblem was raised to its position just beneath the little gilded dome surmounting the pole of liberty, where it unfurled its bright folds, and floated out to the mountain breeze, and it floated none the less proudly in that the red portion of the emblem was composed of a patriotic lady's garment of "mystical sublimity" that was neither "russet, silk nor dimity." Then "pent-up Utica broke forth," and volley after volley of musketry, intermingled with the lusty cheering of the crowd, gave full proof that patriotism was neither dead nor dying in the hearts of the Black Hills pioneers.

There was one notable feature about the Deadwood Centennial celebration, to wit: The ubiquitous boy with the nerve-destroying fire-cracker was not greatly in evidence—a circumstance for which every woman in Deadwood was, no doubt, duly thankful. The crack of small arms, however, could be heard from every quarter from the right and the left, from the front and the rear of you, which, with the singing of patriotic airs and an occasional report from the anvil, continued until nearly noon.

At eleven o'clock a.m. Judge W. S. Kuykendall, having been elected president, mounted the platform and called the assembled multitude to order. After an impressive prayer by the chaplain, Rev. C. E. Halley, the Declaration of Independence was read in his own intimitable style, by Gen. A. R. Z. Dawson. The orator of the day was then introduced in the person of Judge Joseph Miller, who made an eloquent, practical speech—dwelling largely upon local interests, and closing with a stirring patriotic peroration.

The following Memorial to Congress—prepared by himself, was then read by Gen. Dawson and presented for the signature of the people:—

"To the Honored Senate and House of Representatives of the United States in Congress assembled:

Your memorialists, citizens of that portion of Dakota known as the Black Hills, most respectfully petition your honorable body for speedy and prompt action in extinguishing the Indian title to, and the opening for settlement of the country we are now occupying and improving. We have now in the Hills a population of at least 7,000 honest, loyal citizens, who have come here with the expectation of making their homes. Our country is rich not only in mineral resources, but is abundantly supplied with timber, and a soil rich enough to sustain a large population.

"Your memorialists would, therefore, earnestly request that we be no longer deprived of the fruits of our labor and driven from the country we now occupy, but that the government, for which we have offered our lives, at once extend a protecting arm and take us under its care.

"As in duty bound, your petitioners will ever pray.

It goes without saying that every one to whom the memorial was presented, attached his signature.

Celebrations similar to the one in Deadwood were also held in Elizabethtown and Montana City. At the former place Dr. McKinney presided, Dr. Overman read the Declaration of Independence, and Attorney A. B. Chapline delivered the oration. At Montana City, two miles below Deadwood, Judge H. N. Maguire delivered an eloquent oration which stirred his hearers to a high degree of patriotic enthusiasm. In the absence of anvils to emphasize their patriotism, they fired their needle guns into the sides of the mountains and did everything possible with the facilities at hand to make the occasion one long to be remembered.

To still further commemorate the glorious anniversary, a notable event in the annals of the big mining camp transpired on that day. In a little log cabin that stood on the ground now occupied by the Central School building, Revillo F. Robinson, the first child born in Deadwood, made his debut on the tumultuous scene, and having made his advent amid the booming of anvil artillery, the music and cheering of loyal multitudes, and patriotic utterances from eloquent lips, in honor of our Centennial birthday, Revillo should be, and no doubt is, a true and loyal "Young America," and, if he bears out the promise of his early boyhood, Deadwood has good reason to feel proud of her first-born son. Revillo is the son of Mr. and Mrs. J. N. Robinson, now living at Dakota City on the Cheyenne river.

COLLECTION OF TAXES IN THE BLACK HILLS IN 1876

The exercise of the civil functions of the government over the people of the Black Hills, as far as the collection of Federal taxes was concerned, was not long delayed. By an order of April 12th, 1876, this important function was first assigned by the Commissioner of Internal Revenue to the District of Wyoming, but on May 12th, 1876, the order was revoked by the Revenue Department and assigned to the District of Dakota, when Gen. A. R. Z. Dawson was sent to Deadwood as Deputy Revenue Collector.

A. R. Z. DAWSON
First United States revenue collector and first clerk of courts in the Black Hills

Gen. A. R. Z. Dawson—the memory of whose name causes the heart of every old pioneer to thrill with feelings of intense pride—was not only the first to collect United States revenue in the Black Hills, but the sacred words of the great "Declaration" were first uttered by his eloquent lips, and rang out on the Black Hills mountain air on our Centennial natal day; the first memorial to Congress—in behalf of the outlawed people of the Black Hills—was penned by his ready hand; he also served them as first clerk of the first United States courts held in the Black Hills under the new regime in 1877, and his taking away was a sad blow to the people whose stanch friend he ever proved.

The only recognition accorded the people, however, up to 1877, was that of contributing revenue to the government. Bitter protestations were made against what seemed the inconsistent and unjust attitude of the government, and frequent demands were made for recognition, and, if there had been a full-fledged Territory in 1876, Sioux or no Sioux.

Pending the negotiations for the extinguishment of the Indian title to the Black Hills in 1876, the people were in an almost continuous attitude of supplication and prayer. First through a Memorial to Congress—which was conveyed to Washington by C. V. Gardner—they prayed that all disqualifications be removed from the people of the Hills, by legalizing the forced occupancy thereof. In July, 1876, the people of Deadwood sent a petition, with the requisite number of signers, to Gov. John S. Pennington, for county organization.

In July, 1876, they memorialized Congress for speedy action, looking towards the establishment of a separate and distinct territorial government, a government whose enactments would be in harmony with the local interests and requirements of the people. Later, a delegate—in the person of Dr. C. W. Myers—was elected and sent to Yankton and Washington in the interests of the Black Hills, without, however, any immediate effect, though not without its influence. In taking a retrospective view of the then existing circumstances and conditions, it is not seen how the government could have pursued any other policy unless, perhaps, in the matter of giving the people more speedy military protection against the hostile Indians.

PLATTING OF SOUTH DEADWOOD

The necessity for a larger scope of domain, to accommodate the increasing business and rapidly expanding population of Deadwood, suggested to a few speculative individuals the scheme of building a rival town, adjacent thereto, a town which its promoters believed would, in a few weeks, totally eclipse its imperious elder sister on the north side, in point of business enterprise and population. In furtherance of the project, in the early part of July, 1876, a site was selected, laid out and platted on the south side of and up the narrow defile of Whitewood creek, above the original site of Deadwood. A city organization was effected by the election of a mayor, common council, and all other offices necessary to conduct the affairs of a full-fledged city government. By mutual consent the new city was christened South Deadwood, in contradistinction to Deadwood proper.

According to the rules of the organization lots were made subject to location upon specified conditions, and perhaps never in the annals of city building was there a greater scramble for town lots than in the case of South

Deadwood. Squatter sovereignty reigned supreme. At night a man would "wrap the drapery of his couch about him and lie down to pleasant dreams," feeling, secure in the possession of some desirable city property, and wake up the next morning bright and early to find his ground fenced in, or occupied, either with the tent or the goods and chattels of some other fellow. Frequent disputes arose as to priority of location, in the settlement of which six-shooters and shot-guns were potent factors.

The summary manner in which disputes were sometimes settled and lot-jumpers quashed is illustrated by a case of which I was an eye-witness. One morning, on Deadwood street, I was confronted with the alarming spectacle of a woman carrying a shot-gun, engaged in a angry dispute, with an unarmed man, who, it developed, had located her property. Upon his refusal to comply with her peremptory demand to remove his effects from the ground in dispute, she deliberately raised her gun to her shoulder, and aiming it directly at the intruder, said: "I'll give you just one minute, and not a second more, to vacate my property." It is needless to state that the poor man speedily took a vacation. Similar cases were of frequent occurrence in those days.

THE FIRST MURDER IN THE NORTHERN HILLS

The first conspicuous crime committed in the region of Deadwood was the killing of a miner named Jack Hinch, by John R. Carty and Jerry McCarty, at Gayville, on the night of July 9th, 1876. The particulars of the tragic affair, are related to me, are substantially as follows: On Sunday night of the day mentioned, Carty, McCarty and a man named Trainor, were engaged in a game of cards in a saloon at Gayville. Hinch, a friend and mining partner of the latter, while watching the progress of the game, concluded that his partner was being swindled, and persuaded him to abandon the game, which brought about the altercation that culminated in the commission of the crime. About an hour after Hinch had retired to his quarters in Turner & Wilson's saloon, Carty and McCarty entered the place, aroused Hinch, and asked him to get up and drink with them. Believing the proposition to be of a conciliatory nature, Hinch started to get up, when McCarty fired two shots at him, and while in this half-upright position, Carty attacked him with a large sheath knife, together inflicting wounds from the effect of which he died at ten o'clock on the following morning.

Realizing what they had done, the perpetrators hastily disposed of their mining property—a rich hill claim, giving one-half to their landlady and the other half to a friend, procured two horses, and made their escape. A large posse of Hinch's friends started in pursuit, scouring the Hills in every direction, but failed to get any trace of the fugitives. A reward of $500 was then offered for their capture. As subsequently developed, Carty and McCarty made their way to Fort Laramie, near which point they separated, the latter going in the direction of Cheyenne, the former joining the logging train of Coffee & Cuny, about to start for Fort Fetterman.

When the pursuing party reached Fort Laramie the facts were made known to the commanding officer of the post, who assured them that Deputy United States Marshal I. C. Davis would assist them in every way to ferret out the criminals. Davis, on receiving a description of the men, set out in pursuit, overtook the train and captured the man Carty without the least resistance. McCarty, the prinicpal, was never, it is believed, found. On the evening of July 31st, Marshal Davis, accompanied by Mr. Cuny, arrived with his prisoner at Gayville, the scene of the murder.

Marshal Davis drove through Deadwood at a mad pace that day, with Carty wrapped up in a blanket on the bottom of the wagon, and everybody turned out to see the frightful runaway. It appears that he had been notified back at a point known as "Break Neck" hill, that it would be very unsafe to expose his prisoner in passing through Deadwood, as Hinch's friends would surely lynch him; so, after consulting his prisoner, he adopted this bit of strategy, which came very near making farther proceedings unnecessary. It is related that on reaching Gayville the poor fellow was so near suffocated with the extreme heat and want of oxygen, that vigorous measures had to be taken to restore him to consciousness.

In the absence of regularly constituted courts, it seemed necessary, in so grave a charge as murder, that the formalities of a trial be gone through with; so a miners' meeting was called for the next day, August 1st, for the purpose of making preliminary arrangements for trying the prisoner on the charge of murder.

The people were stirred up to a high tension over the affair. By 10 o'clock of the following day Gayville was blocked by a vast gathering of excited, turbulent miners from the camps, and citizens from Deadwood, all eager to witness the sequel to the initial tragedy of the gulch. The respective friends of the murdered man and the prisoner were out in large force, armed to the teeth, the former headed by big Bill Trainor—as he was called—clamorous for summary punishment to be meted out to the accused; the latter led by John Flaherty, who afterwards made a big stake in the sale of the De Smet group of mines—equally determined that he should have a fair trail. For a while the prisoner's life seemed to hang in a balance, with the preponderance of weight against him. "Hang him, hang him!" was the cry of Hinch's friends as they surged threateningly toward the place where the prisoner was held in custody.

"Touch him at your peril!" was hurled back defiantly by his friends. At a critical juncture Marshal Davis—whose nerve never weakened at the threats and curses of the mob that surged about the prisoner, interposed in his behalf. Mounting a barrel he called the attention of the excited mob and thus addressed it:—

"Boys, I have brought this man from Fort Laramie, through a country swarming with Indians, in order that you might try him for his life. When I took him, I gave him his choice to be taken to Yankton and tried by the courts, or to come back to the Hills to be tried by the miners. He chose to come here, and when he did so, I promised him that he should have a fair trial, and by——that he shall have. Try him and if you find him guilty of murder, hang him and I will help you pull the rope. But until he has had a fair trial, the man or men who touch a hair of his head, will first walk over my dead body." This bold and manly stand in the performance of his sworn duty, appealed to the miners' sense of justice and quelled the mob. The prisoner, for the time being, was safe.

In arranging for the trial, the first step was, of course, to find a man with the requisite legal attainments, and some judicial experience, to preside as judge. After casting about for one who would fill these requirements the choice finally fell upon O. H. Simonton, who had just arrived in the Hills, by ox train, over the Fort Pierre route, and who, it was ascertained, had served in the capacity of justice of the peace, in the stock yards of Chicago. From a panel of forty names twelve jurymen were drawn as follows: E. B. Parker, Ed. Durham, J. H. Balf, John Kane, G. Schugardt, George Heinrich, A. C. Lobdell, C. W. Shule, John W. Gill, S. M. Moon, George Atchinson, and—Curley. A. B. Chapline, afterwards a member of the firm of Young & Chapline, was appointed to prosecute the case, Carty securing the services of Mills & Hollis to defend him. The trial of the case, which was held out in the open, continued all through the day, and until 10 o'clock at night, the procedure in legally constituted courts being followed as closely as was possible. Uncomfortably seated on a pile of logs in the vicinage of the court during the long hours of the trial, might have been seen R. B. Hughes (Dick Hughes), with pencil in hand, and paper on his knee, patiently taking notes for "copy" for the Black Hills *Weekly Pioneer,* and by his side, using a part of the same pencil, Rev. Smith, who was waylaid and murdered by Indians about three weeks later.

It was proven at the trial that Carty, although an accessory to the murder, did not inflict the fatal injuries, in accordance with which fact the jury, after a brief deliberation, handed in a verdict of "Guilty of assault and battery." The prisoner was discharged by the court, and given safe convoy out of the country under a strong guard of armed men, who took him to Deadwood, procured a horse for him to ride, escorted him to the limits of the town, where he mounted, and with an exultant whoop rode away, and the Black Hills saw him no more forever.

THE MURDER OF WILD BILL

Late in the afternoon of August 2nd, 1876, the denizens of Deadwood, in the vicinity of lower Main street, were startled by a loud pistol report, immediately followed by the hurried tramping of a multitude of human feet, when the excited cry of "Wild Bill is shot! Wild Bill is shot!" rang out above the wild tumult of the gathering crowd. At almost the same time a man might have been seen backing away up Main street, holding a loaded revolver in each hand to keep at bay a large posse of excited citizens, who were following in close pursuit. After a short chase the desperate man was captured and brought back to No. 10, the scene of the shooting, where he was held in custody to await his fate.

A strong guard was placed around the building to keep the prisoner from the clutches of an excited mob, determined to give him short shrift for his crime. Just at a critical time a force of about fifty well-armed men—the bodyguard of Carty, who had just been acquitted of the murder of Hinch—arrived from Gayville with their charge. After setting Carty free at the lower end of town they consented to aid in protecting the prisoner from the threatening mob.

While Wild Bill was playing cards in Nuttall & Maw's saloon, known as No. 10, wholly unconscious of threatened danger, McCall walked in behind his victim, raised his revolver and fired, the ball entering the back of his head and coming out at the center of his right cheek, killing him instantly.

A meeting of the citizens was called at the theater building, at which Judge W. L. Kuykendall was chosen to preside at the trial of the case. Isaac Brown was elected sheriff, a deputy and twelve guards being appointed by the court. Col. May acted as prosecuting attorney, and Judge Miller defended the prisoner. The only evidence given was by the prisoner himself, who testified that Wild Bill had killed his brother, somewhere in Kansas, and confessed to committing the crime in retaliation. The jury chosen to try the case, after a brief deliberation of about thirty minutes, returned a verdict of "not guilty," much to the surprise and dissatisfaction of hundreds of the people of Deadwood, who declared that trial by jury in the Black Hills was pretty much of a farce, and that in future murder cases Judge Lynch would preside.

McCall, who immediately left the Hills, on his acquittal, was afterwards arrested at Laramie City, Wyoming, by Deputy United States Marshal

Balcombe, and taken to Cheyenne, where he was examined before United States Commissioner Burns, held upon the evidence, and sent to Yankton upon a requisition from the Governor of Dakota, where he was tried, found guilty and sentenced to be hung,—which sentence was promptly executed.

Wild Bill's remains were taken charge of and buried by his friends in the old burying-ground overlooking the Whitewood. His remains were afterwards removed to "Moriah Cemetery," where his ashes now repose. His grave, inclosed by an iron fence, is marked by a rough sandstone obelisk, about six feet in height, surmounted by a bust of the famous scout. This bust has been sadly defaced by relic hunters, by reason of which it to-day bears but a little resemblance to the long-haired, dashing frontiersman of a quarter of a century ago. On the front of the stone beneath crossed revolvers is a carved scroll, bearing, in addition to the ordinary inscription, "Custer was lonely without him."

On the evening of the same day, August 2d, while the excitement consequent upon the killing of Wild Bill was at its height, a horseman— a half-breed Mexican, came dashing furiously up the crowded street with a Sioux whoop, bearing aloft an Indian's head, with its long black hair floating back with the wind, furnishing a weird and most disgusting spectacle, which, as may be imagined, caused the tragic affair of the afternoon to pale into insignificance. An Indian's scalp was just what the average Deadwood citizen had been devoutly wishing for. As the Indians had been making things exceedingly lively by stealing and running off horses from the settlements along the northern border, the people feared that a direct attack upon Deadwood was imminent, and the excitement became intense.

The Mexican's own story of how he gained possession of the ghastly trophy was, that some herders had a brush with a band of red horse-thieves in the vicinity of Crook City, during which one Indian was killed, whereupon he sprang forward under a brisk shower of bullets and attempted to scalp the Indian, but not being an expert at the business, he cut off the entire head.

Another version of the affair was that on the day previous, August 1st, the Indians had rounded up all the loose stock around Crook City, and stampeded them across the country before the surprised inhabitants had time to offer any resistance. Among those who made ready to mount and follow in pursuit was one Felix Rooney, who realizing that pursuit would be useless, dismounted and lay down in the grass—holding the lariat-rope to watch the Indians rapidly disappearing in the distance with the property of the settlers. While there a freighter or cattle "whacker" rode along, dismounted and threw himself on the grass by the side of Rooney—both of whom were well armed. After a short time an Indian in war-paint and feathers dashed up toward Rooney's horse—evidently thinking him picketed. Upon discovering the owner in the grass he immediately seized his rifle, but finding it fast in some way he drew his revolver and fired, whereupon Rooney, instead of firing his gun, threw himself flat on the grass, as he imagined shot.

It developed, however, that Rooney was unhurt, while the Indian lay dead—killed by a bullet from the unerring rifle of the intrepid "bullwhacker." On the next day, August 2d, the Mexican found the dead body of the Indian, and thinking it would be a good scheme, financially, to secure the scalp, he essayed the operation, but finding he could not accomplish the work scientifically decided to cut off the head. This latter version is perhaps the correct one; but whether it is or not, the fact remains that the Indian was decapitated, and the Mexican by fair means or foul, got possession of the head, brought it to Deadwood and paraded it along Main street on the evening of August 2d, on the strength of which he secured from the citizens of Deadwood about seventy-five or eighty dollars, every one of which he "blew in" before the dawn of the following morning.

CHAPTER XXVI

INDIAN RAID ON THE MONTANA HERD

Up to this time the people of Deadwood had felt themselves comparatively safe from Indian attack, not alone because their town was entrenched amid the battlements of the Hills, but because of the cordon of settlements along the northern border, viz., Crook City, Centennial, and Spearfish, whose people were ever on the alert to keep the red marauders at bay. They were rudely awakened one day, however, from their sense of comparative security by the appearance of the painted savages almost at the gates of the city.

During the forenoon of that never-to-be-forgotten Sunday, August 20th, 1876, they were made aware of their proximity by the sight of fifty or sixty badly frightened horses, rushing madly through town on a wild stampede.

The "Montana Herd" as before stated, was established by Burton and Cook on Centennial prairie, where they built a large stockade or inclosure for the protection of the herd at night, the stock for the most part belonging to citizens of Deadwood, and the miners and prospectors of the surrounding camps. As the price of hay and grain was exorbitant at the time, nearly all horses coming to Deadwood were at once sent to the "Montana Herd" where they were kept for a reasonable consideration, Burton and Cook making daily trips across the mountains to Deadwood, a distance of about six miles, to receive and return the stock.

On the 20th of August the Indians made a raid on the herd which resulted in the death of four men, one Indian, and the loss of 100 head of horses. The evening before, the herd was driven into the inclosure as usual, the gate closed and a guard placed on watch, the Indians meanwhile watching the procedure from a near-by bluff. After all had retired for the night, the Indians stole down to the rear of the stockade, and in some way dug out the posts which formed the structure while the guard slept, and succeeded in making an opening large enough for the passage of horses, which it was supposed they intended to stampede early in the morning, while all were profoundly sleeping. If so they failed to carry out their programme.

The next morning the herd was driven out to feed, as was the custom. Cook had gone to Deadwood the evening before and had not yet returned. Burton had just started for Deadwood, with some horses to return to their owners and had reached about half way between the camp and the foot-hills when, hearing a rifle shot, he looked back in the direction of the camp and saw a large band of Indians swooping down upon the herd. The horses becoming frightened at the reports of the rifles and the unearthly yells of the Indians, started on a wild stampede over the Deadwood trail,—the fleetest of them eluding their pursuers, some of whom followed them almost to the limits of the town, and it was when near the "Rest" on the old trail between Deadwood and Crook City, that Rev. Henry Weston Smith met his fate at the hands of the Indians on that day.

About fifty or sixty of the stampeded horses came careering wildly along the main street of Deadwood, causing great consternation and excitement. Some of the horses were caught and in a very brief time about twenty-five well-armed men were mounted on the stampeded horses, and away over the trail to the relief of the herders at the stockade. Meanwhile the Indians had rounded up about 100 head of horses and driven them on towards Lookout Mountain, east of Spearfish, then on across the Redwater to the north.

Finding the herders unharmed, on reaching the stockade the party followed up the trail of the Indians, hoping to overtake them and recover the stock. On riding down Spring creek, Isaac Brown, who was a little in advance of the others, saw skulking along a ravine a lone Indian, who opened fire on the party, which was returned without effect on either side. When the main party came up, it advanced cautiously on the position of the Indian, who from his place of concealment behind a clump of bushes could plainly see his pursuers, but could not be seen by them, his exact position being revealed only when he fired.

Brown and Holland advanced from an exposed point still nearer the ambushed Indian, who then fired, killing Brown instantly; Holland, guided by the direction of the fatal shot, aimed his gun at the Indian's head, as he supposed, and fired, crying out at the same time: "Come on, boys, I've got him," which were his last words, as at that moment he fell pierced through the body by a bullet from the Indian's gun.

All efforts to dislodge him proved unsuccessful; rocks and boulders were hurled down upon him without avail. Night coming on, the party deciding that any further attempt to dislodge him would be useless and might result in the death of others, withdrew out of range of his gun to consider how to recover the bodies of Brown and Holland that were lying within a few feet of the Indian's hiding-place. A reward of $500 was offered by Brown's partner for the recovery of his body, but as no one felt inclined to risk the dangerous undertaking, the party decided to go to Spearfish, and return in the morning for the bodies. The next day they were found—stripped of their clothing, arms, and ammunition—and conveyed to Deadwood for interment.

Papers found on the body of Charles Holland revealed that he was an Odd Fellow, from Sioux City, Iowa. At that time, August 21st, 1876, the first steps were taken towards the organization of a lodge of that order in the Black Hills. A committee of three "past grands," viz., Judge W. L. Kuykendall, Frank C. Thullen, and Green Todd was appointed to examine applicants for recognition, when a temporary organization was effected, by which organization Charles Holland was buried, Dr. Babcock, of Deadwood, reading from their ritual the impressive burial service of the order. Isaac Brown's remains were taken charge of by members of the Masonic order, of which he also was a member, and both were laid to rest in the old cemetery overlooking Whitewood creek.

THE WOLF MOUNTAIN STAMPEDE

During the month of July, 1876, an untraceable rumor of the discovery of fabulously rich diggings somewhere out among the lower ranges of the Big Horn Mountains, was set afloat, causing the maddest of mad stampedes from the rich mining camp of Deadwood. Although the pretended discoverers guarded the secret of the precise spot of their wonderful find well, it got whispered around that a "bald peak" among the Wolf mountain ranges marked the locality, which all believed they would have little difficulty in finding.

Numerous horsemen, and pack outfits galore, surreptitiously left Deadwood—some under the cover of night—and made their way westward over the plains, none knowing whither, each eager to be the first to reach the reputed land of gold and stake off their claims.

After wandering aimlessly for many days over the Western plains and among the mountains—like a ship without rudder or compass—in search of the "bald mountain" that looked down upon the hidden treasure, suffering terrible hardships and exposure, in the face of deadly peril, the quest was finally abandoned. Some turned their steps southward and reached civilization on the Union Pacific Railway; others penetrated the Big Horn Mountains and later made their way to the mines of Montana. One party, after having been severely harassed by the Indians, a few meeting death at their hands, reached and wintered on the Crow reservation. Many found their way back to Deadwood gulch far wiser, if not richer men.

The story of the rich discovery, which turned out to be a cruel fabrication, was circulated, it was suspected, for purpose of profit on the sale of horses, etc.

The following excellent doggerel from the ready pen of the versatile Jack Langrishe, is a good portrayal of the sorry, woe-begone appearance of the badly sold Wolf Mountain stampeders on their return to Deadwood:—

"This is the man of whom we read,
Who left Deadwood, on the big stampede;
He's now returned, all tattered and torn,
From looking for gold on the Big Horn.

He has no malt,
He has no cat,
He has no coat,
He has no hat.

His trousers are patched with an old flour sack,
With "for family use" to be seen on the back;
His bread is shaggy, his hair is long
And this is the burden of his song:
'If ever I hear, if ever I read
Of another great or big stampede,
I'll listen, but I'll give no heed,
But stay in my cabin at Deadwood.'

He paid ten dollars the other day
For a mule to carry his 'grub' away,
He packed his load in half an hour,
Two gallons of whisky, one pound of flour.

He bought a shovel,
And borrowed a pick,
He sported his watch,
And went on tick.

For a side of bacon and a can of lard.
Now look at his fate! My! isn't it hard?
He walked all day and most of the night,
And now he is back a sorrowful sight,
To the cabin he built in Deadwood.

PROVISIONAL CITY GOVERNMENT FOR DEADWOOD

The demand for some kind of municipal government, vested by the concessions of the people of Deadwood with power to enact laws, securing the city against fires, and for the suppression of the reckless discharge of fire-arms within its limits, and other lawless acts placing the lives of its citizens in jeopardy, and also for the more rigid enforcement of the rules and regulations against the use of the streets of the city for building and business purposes, became each day more and more apparent. Realizing the necessity of such an organization, a citizens' proclamation was issued for an election to be held in the City Hall on the 11th of September, 1876. Caucuses were held in due form and several different tickets appeared in the field, the principal contest, however, being for Mayor and City Marshal. I am not informed as to whether the campaign was conducted along political party lines or not; at any rate the election was held as per proclamation. The result as follows:—

For organization, 1,082 votes; against organization, 57 votes. E. B. Farnum was elected Mayor and ex-officio Justice of the Peace, receiving 637 out of the total vote of 1,139. Keller Kurtz, Sol. Star, A. P. Carter, and H. C. Philbrook were elected members of the City Council. Con Stapleton was chosen City Marshal and John A. Swift, Clerk and Treasurer.

To secure revenue for the support of the new municipality, an ordinance was adopted imposing a license for the conduct of each business and the practice of each profession in the city, which license was, it is believed, as a rule promptly paid.

The following were the number of business houses in Deadwood, taken by order of the City Council, about the last of September, 1876:—

Assayers, 1; auctioneers, 4; amusements, 2; bathhouses, 1; butchers, 3; blacksmiths, 2; bankers, 1; breweries, 2; billiard tables, 4; barber shops, 3; bakeries, 6; clothing houses, 11; dentists, 1; doctors, 5; druggists, 4; dry goods, 1; dance houses, 2; fruit dealers, 3; gaming tables, 14; grocer-merchants, 21; hardware, 2; hotels, 5; jewelers, 3; job-wagons, 4; laundries, 8; lawyers, 7; livery stables, 3; miliners, 1; newspapers, 1; painters, 3; photographers, 1; queensware, 3; restaurants, 6; saloons, 27; sawmills, 2; shoemakers, 3; tailors, 3.

Monday, September 25th, 1876, should be chronicled as a real red-letter day in the annals of Deadwood, being made memorable by two very important events; one, the arrival of the first through coach of the Cheyenne and Black Hills stage line, bringing the first lady passenger to Deadwood, in the person of Mrs. R. B. Fay. Among the other passengers on that first trip was Capt. C. V. Gardner, to whom Supt. Voorhees intrusted the grave responsibility of conducting the stage with its load of passengers safely through the hostile lines into the Hills; Mr. David Dickey, an old-time plainsman who had served his apprenticeship on the overland route to California, held the ribbons from Fort Laramie to Deadwood. The running time from Cheyenne to Deadwood was six and one-half days.

On that same day the first quartz mill brought to the Black Hills passed through Deadwood, en route to Gayville, when a large portion of Deadwood's citizens were drawn out on the street to behold its advent.

TELEGRAPH LINE REACHES DEADWOOD

Perhaps the event of most importance to the people of the Black Hills thus far, was the completion of the Black Hills Telegraph Line to Deadwood, on December 1st, 1876. By virtue of the indomitable pluck and the unwavering perseverance of the projector of the enterprise, in the face of multiplied difficulties and dangers, and after months of waiting on the part of the expectant people of the Hills, Deadwood, the terminal point of the line, was on that day placed in direct telegraphic communication with the outside world. The enterprise which promised so much for the success and prosperity of the business interests of the Black Hills had at length reached its fruition, and the citizens of Deadwood were correspondingly jubilant, hailing the event with manifestations of exceeding delight.

As soon as the instrument was put in talking condition there followed an interchange of greetings between Cheyenne and the terminal point of the line. Under the skillful manipulation of James Halley, the operator in Deadwood, the electric current was flashed over the wire to Cheyenne, announcing to the Mayor of that city the completion of the line, and that congratulations were in order, to which came back in response the following:—

JAMES HALLEY
First telegrapher in the Black Hills; sent the first electric current over the wires from Deadwood to Cheyenne, Wyoming, on December 1st, 1876

"CHEYENNE, December 1st, 1876

"To E. B. FARNUM, Mayor of Deadwood:

"Your telegram received. Accept the congratulations of the citizens of Cheyenne, for your people, and our enterprising citizen—formerly—but now your Hibbard. We have reached you by telegraph line, and we have further completed a contract to shorten the road between Cheyenne and Deadwood, sixty or seventy miles, which will be completed in a short time. We hope our efforts will be recognized and appreciated by your people.

"C. R. Bresnaham,
"Mayor of Cheyenne."

In the evening a large crowd of the citizens of Deadwood, and miners from surrounding camps, gathered in front of the telegraph office, on the north side of upper Main street, to celebrate the event in a manner commensurate with its importance. An immense pile of combustible material—consisting of pine knots, brush, etc., was kindled, which brightly illuminated its picturesque environments, throwing its lurid glare far up the rocky hillsides flanking the narrow gulch—presenting a scene which is vividly remembered.

In the exuberance of their joy, and as expressions of their gratitude that they were at last placed in instantaneous communication with home and friends, and the great centers of trade in the East, with anvil and plenty of gun-powder, numerous salutes were fired that would have discounted the most approved artillery. With the booming of anvil artillery, intermingled with the cheering of the crowd, the celebration went gaily on until a late hour, culminating in a ball at the Grand Central Hotel.

At the closing function the creme-de-la-creme of Deadwood society was present. The dining-room of the Grand Central, illuminated by numerous coal oil lamps, brightened by the gorgeous (?) toilet of the ladies and the somewhat incongruous "make-up" of men, presented a fetching scene, but the men couldn't help it, you know, if some of them had to appear in business suits, with white gloves and white neckties, as in those days people were forced to adapt themselves to circumstances, and wear whatever they happened to have on hand. Among the gentlemen who honored the occasion by their presence were the following; Captain Hibbard, the hero of the celebration; Mayor Farnum; Messrs. McPherson, Kehoe, Allen, Adams, Fay; Wagner mine host of the Grand Central; Merrick, of the Black Hills *Pioneer*; Judges Whitehead, Keithly, and McCutcheon; Capt. C. V. Gardner, Doctors Babcock and Myers; Messrs. Berry and Thompson.

It may be proper to note that but few of the wives of the above named gentlemen had yet made their advent in the Hills, which fact in no perceptible way detracted from the enjoyment of the occasion.

The construction of the Black Hills telegraph line was commenced in June, 1876, by William H. Hibbard, for many years superintendent of construction for the Western Union Telegraph Co., but owing to the hostile attitude of the Indians, he was compelled to maintain a large paid armed force to protect the workmen along the line, which, with other untoward circumstances, so nearly exhausted his resources that he was forced either to abandon the project or ask for financial aid from those who would be benefited by the enterprise.

Mr. Hibbard choosing the latter course, came to Deadwood in July and laid the matter before the business men of that city with proposals for a loan, the nature of which the heading of a subscription then opened, will fully explain:—

"We, the undersigned, do hereby agree to purchase from W. H. Hibbard, telegraph scrip to the amount set opposite our names, said scrip being guaranteed by said Hibbard to be redeemed in telegraphing at regular rates for the face value thereof over a line to be constructed between Fort Laramie, Wyoming, and Deadwood City, Dakota, and which scrip we agree to receive and pay for at face value in cash as follows, to wit, one-half the amount subscribed whenever said telegraph line shall have been completed to Custer City, Dakota Territory, and the remaining one-half whenever said line is completed to Deadwood City, Dakota Territory."

The business men of Deadwood, appreciating the advantages of rapid communication with the outside business world, subscribed to the amount of $5,000.00 approximately. Custer also subscribed literally to the loan, secured and guaranteed in the same manner, one-half to be paid when the line reached Red Canyon, the remaining half when it reached Custer City. Aid was also secured in Cheyenne. Thus financially fortified, the construction of the line was pushed rapidly forward, reaching Custer City during the latter part of October and Deadwood on the first of December, every dollar of the scrip being after wards redeemed as per contract.

FAILURE OF THE BILL FOR TERRITORY
OF LINCOLN

The urgent petition presented to Congress in July, 1876, for the formation of a separate and distinct Territory, comprising the mineral region of the Black Hills, supplemented by the continuous earnest efforts of the people to that end resulted in the formulation of a bill, in furtherance of the project. The bill came before the Senate for consideration in February, 1877, and reads as follows:—

"A Bill to establish the Territory of the Black Hills, and to provide for a temporary government thereof:

"Section 1. Be it enacted by the Senate and House of Representatives of the United States of America in Congress assembled, that all that portion of the territory of the United States, described as follows: Commencing at a point where the forty-third parallel of north latitude intersects with the twenty-fifth meridian of longitude west from the city of Washington, thence following a due westerly course along said forty-third parallel to its intersection with the thirtieth meridian west from the city of Washington; thence north along said thirtieth meridian of longitude to its intersection of the Yellowstone river to the center of said channel; thence following the center of said channel to its intersection with the forty-seventh parallel to the western boundary line of Dakota Territory; thence due south along said boundary line to the forty-sixth parallel of north latitude; thence due east along said forty-sixth parallel to the twenty-fifth meridian of longitude west from the city of Washington; thence south along said twenty-fifth meridian to the place of beginning. Be, and the same is hereby organized into a temporary government—by the name of Lincoln Territory.

"Sec. 2. That the said Territory of Lincoln, and the several officers thereof, shall be invested with all the right, powers and privileges, and be subject to all regulations, restrictions and provisions contained in Chapter 1 of Title 23 of the Revised Statutes of the United States, except as herein otherwise provided.

"Sec. 3. That the legislative power and authority of said Territory shall be vested in the Governor and Legislative Assembly. The Legislative Assembly shall consist of a Council and House of Representatives; the Council shall consist of nine members, which may be increased to thirteen members having the qualifications of voters in said Territory.

"Sec. 4. The House of Representatives shall consist of thirteen members, which may be increased to twenty-seven members, possessing the same qualifications as are herein prescribed for the members of the Council; provided, that the right of voting and holding office in said Territory shall be exercised only by inhabitants thereof who are citizens of the United States.

"Sec. 5. That a delegate to the House of Representatives of the United States to serve during such Congress of the United States be elected by the voters of said Territory, qualified to elect members of the Legislative Assembly, who shall be entitled to all and the same rights and privileges as are exercised and enjoyed by the delegates from the several other Territories in said House of Representatives, provided that no person shall be a delegate who shall not have attained the age of twenty-five years, and have the other qualifications of a voter in said Territory.

"Sec. 6. That when the land in said Territory shall be surveyed under the direction of the government of the United States preparatory to bringing the same into the market, sections sixteen and thirty-six in each township in said Territory shall be, and the same is, hereby reserved for the purpose of being applied to schools in the State or States, hereafter to be erected out of the same.

"Sec. 7. That the President of the United States, by and with the consent of the Senate, shall be and is hereby authorized to appoint a Surveyor-General for the said Territory, who shall locate his office at such place as the Secretary of the Interior shall from time to time direct, and whose duties, powers, obligations, responsibilities, compensations, and allowances for clerk hire, office rent, fuel, and incidental expenses, shall be the same as those of the Territory of Dakota under the direction of the Secretary of the Interior, and under instructions as he may deem advisable from time to time to give."

Despite the efforts put forth both at Washington and at home in its behalf the bill failed. When the question of the division of the Territory and its admission into the sisterhood of States as two States came before the people in 1886-9, the question of a separate State for the Black Hills was again agitated by the people of the Hills to no purpose.

CHAPTER XXVII

THE BLACK HILLS OPENED TO SETTLEMENT

With the ratification of the Sioux Treaty of 1876 by Congress, and its approval by the President on February 28th, 1877, we enter upon a new and important epoch in Black Hills history. By the extinguishment of the Sioux title thereto, the stigma of outlawry was removed from the people and they became invested with all the rights, privileges and powers of American citizens, and inasmuch as up to that time they had been, in a great degree, isolated from the rest of the world and entirely outside the pale of the law, they were, as may be imagined, a correspondingly gratified people. The coveted territory was, at last, secured to them for a habitation all their own, where each from the shelter of his own vine and fig tree could watch, unmolested, the coming dawn of a better civilization.

It took not long to set all the complex machinery of civil government in operation, nor for the people to become adjusted to the new order of things.

GRANVILLE G. BENNETT
First Judge of the First Territorial District Court in the Black Hills

Under an Act of the Territorial Legislature, the Governor appointed three commissioners to organize a county government for each of the three counties into which the Black Hills was originally divided; regular United States courts were established by the government, as also United States postal service, at all important points in the Black Hills. In April, 1877, Judge Granville G. Bennett, under appointment by the President, arrived in Deadwood to establish and assume jurisdiction of the courts of the Black Hills, which then formed a part of the First Judicial District of Dakota Territory.

Under the new conditions a radical and salutary change in the material and social economy of the Hills soon became apparent. Capital seeking profitable investment in the many rich quartz mines then in process of development, began to make its way into the country; enterprising business men, fortified with ample means, ventured into the Hills with their families, and identified themselves with their commerical interests; others, who had braved the perils of a journey over the plains at an earlier date, but who had prudently left their families behind until the danger was past, or perhaps to see whether a prize or a blank awaited them, in the then uncertain future of the new El Dorado, sent for their household goods, and founded permanent homes in the towns, or on the fertile valley and plains.

JUDGES OF THE BLACK HILLS DISTRICT AND CIRCUIT COURTS

Appended is a list of the judges who have presided over the District and Circuit Courts of the Black Hills since the first establishment of our regular courts in the spring of 1877 to the present time:—

HON. GIDEON C. MOODY
First United States Senator from the Black Hills, South Dakota

Judge Granville C. Bennett came to the Black Hills under appointment by President Hayes, to establish law and order, in April, 1877. He established courts and assumed jurisdiction on the bench of the First Circuit of the Territorial District Court, which he occupied until September, 1878, when he resigned. Judge G. C. Moody was appointed by President Hayes to fill the vacancy, and presided from 1878 to October, 1882. Judge Wm. E. Church, of Morristown, New Jersey, under appointment by the Garfield administration, occupied the bench from 1882 to 1886, when Judge Chas. M. Thomas of Bowling Green, Ky., under appointment by President Cleveland, succeeded to the bench which he occupied until the termination of the Territorial courts at the close of 1889.

In 1889, when the southern portion of Dakota Territory was admitted to Statehood, the territory comprising the Black Hills was constituted the Seventh and Eighth Judicial Districts of the State Circuit Court, the Seventh consisting of the counties of Pennington, Custer, and Fall River; the Eighth of Lawrence, Butte, and Meade Counties.

At the first election under the State laws in the fall of 1889, Judge John W. Nowlin, of Rapid City, was elected to the bench of the Seventh Judicial District, which he occupied until November, 1892, when, owing to failing health, he resigned, and Judge Wm. Gardner, of Rapid City, was appointed to fill the vacancy for the remainder of the term. In the fall of 1893, Judge Gardner was elected to succeed himself, occupying the bench until January, 1898, when he was succeeded by the present incumbent, Judge Levi McGee.

In the fall of 1889 Judge Chas. M. Thomas was elected to the bench of the Eighth Judicial District, which he occupied until January, 1894, when he was succeeded by Judge A. J. Plowman, of Deadwood, who presided until January, 1898, when Judge Joseph A. Moore donned the ermine.

HIGHWAY ROBBERS AND ROAD AGENTS

Although, with the cession of the Black Hills in 1877, Indian hostilities were reduced to a minimum, and little danger was apprehended from that source, the lines of public travel were still menaced by danger of quite another sort. Instead of being swooped down upon by bands of yelling, whooping savages, passengers were liable at any time and point on the route, to be confronted by the apparition of several masked figures, silently emerging from some shadowy recess near the road, and to find themselves suddenly looking into the persuasive muzzles of several six-shooters, at short range, or shotguns at longer range, and greeted, in sepulchral tones, with the peremptory mandate of "Hold up your hands,"—which discourteous mandate was usually obeyed with the utmost alacrity. While in this helpless attitude of solemn invocation, they were systematically searched, and relieved of all their superfluous belongings, such as money, watches, jewelry, or other valuables found upon their persons. Occasionally, however, a passenger, with more courage than discretion, would reach for his hip pocket, whip out his revolver like a flash, and fire on the masked robbers at first sight, thus precipitating a fight.

Those early knights of the road did their work with a thoroughness worthy of a better cause; indeed they had the profession reduced to a fine art. As some now in the Black Hills who have been put through the course will remember, their modus operandi was as follows: First, after being compelled to dismount and stand in a row, passenger's pockets were emptied of their contents, then the internal economy of the men's hats and women's bonnets and coiffures were carefully examined—they were no respectors of persons, those Sir Knights,—then hands were deftly and caressingly passed over their clothing in quest of any bulges or bumps not accounted for by the average human anatomy, and lastly men's boots and women's shoes were pulled off to secure the possible wad of greenbacks, or some cherished article of jewelry hidden in the toes thereof.

While 1877 began an epoch of material prosperity for the Black Hills, it also began what may appropriately be designated the era of "hold-ups," horse-stealing and "cattle-rustling." In the early years, before the advent of railroads, when passengers were transported and the gold-dust and bullion product of the Hills was shipped by stage over the plains, the country surrounding the Black Hills was infested by as desperate and conscienceless bands of robbers as ever inflicted their unwelcome presence on a new mining camp. As a consequence "hold-ups" and stage robberies were very common occurrences—in fact they were the rule and not the exception.

Perhaps the first attempt at stage robbery within the limits of the Hills was made near Deadwood, on the night of March 25th, 1877, resulting in the killing of Johnny Slaughter, driver of the Sidney and Black Hills stage coach. The stage, it appears, left Custer City on that day with eleven passengers,—ten men and one woman, viz.: Harry Lake, Walter Iler, A. G. Smith, B. P. Smith, Chas. Burns, Angus McMasters, Charlie Ostram, Mattie Ostram, and three other names unknown, and $15,000 in cash, in charge of Harry Lake, for Stebbins, Wood & Co.'s bank, now the First National Bank of Deadwood. When five miles north of Hill City the stage became disabled, causing considerable delay, as it had to travel slowly.

When, at eleven o'clock that night, the lumbering, crippled coach, with its load of tired passengers, reached the mouth of Gold Run, about where the Pluma Mill now stands, five men were noticed marching along the middle of the road ahead, one a little in advance of the others, who, when the stage approached them, separated two on each side, apparently to let it pass. Just as the stage got abreast of them, one of the men on the left suddenly thrust his gun into the stage and fired. Harry Lake quickly grasped the gun with both hands, and held on to it with such desperate tenacity that the robber, in trying to wrest it from his grasp, pulled him out of the stage on the left.

Meanwhile the advance agent had leveled his shot-gun and fired at the driver, who fell dead from the box on the right, the charge grazing the elbow of Iler who was in the act of reaching around to his right side pocket for his revolver. Iler and Burns, who rode on the box, supposing the driver had jumped off the box to avoid the shot, also at almost the same moment jumped and made for a place of shelter and long range. The horses, becoming frightened at the shooting, immediately started on a wild run towards Deadwood with the stage and its five terrified, white-faced passengers, followed by a volley from the guns of the robbers, who then made good their escape without any booty. It all occurred in a much less time than it takes to tell the story. In their mad flight the wheel horses got tangled up in the lines in such a way as to turn the lead team entirely around, so that after running a distance of about a half mile, they came to a dead halt. Soon after, Lake, Iler and Burns put in an appearance, but the unfortunate driver came not.

The passengers, after straightening up the tangled outfit, proceeded to Deadwood, where they arrived at about midnight. The story soon spread over the city, creating intense excitement and indignation that such a bold attempt at highway robbery should be made almost within the shadow of its buildings. A party, composed of A. G. Smith, John Manning, and West Travis, followed by others, hastened to the scene of the encounter in search of Slaughter, whose dead body was soon found where it fell from the box. Upon examination it was found that thirteen buckshot had entered directly over the heart, twelve of them forming a perfect circle. This affair of the road, which occurred just before the establishment of law in the Black Hills, was the only "hold-up" ever attempted within the limits of Lawrence County. Seth Bullock, who about this time received his appointment as Sheriff of Lawrence County, took prompt measures to hunt down the perpetrators of the crime, but, it is believed, without success.

Again, in July, 1877, the Sidney coach was stopped about four miles south of Battle creek and robbed of the treasure box, and the passengers relieved of their money, watches, jewelry, and baggage. The gold shipments were first sent out in an iron or steel treasure box, under guard of armed men.

The officers of the newly-established law in the Hills were ever on the alert for the outlaws, keeping close "tab" on all persons hanging about the town without visible means of support, or suspicious characters lurking in the shadows of public resorts, and their keen untiring vigilance and evident determination to hunt down and drive out the desperate gang from the country made it the part of wisdom and prudence for them to change their base of operations from the Hills to a less torrid clime, where they felt they would be safe from the terrible sleuth-hounds of Black Hills law.

They finally made their stamping ground at Hat creek—a point on the stage route, remote from the settlements of the Hills, where they thought they could ply their avocation of stage robbery with impunity. From this point they continued to hold up and rob stage coaches with great regularity; in fact robberies became so frequent that the driver always expected to be held up when they had treasure aboard, and at certain points on the route looked for a man or men with shot-guns to step out from behind a projecting rock and order him to "halt" and throw out the treasure box.

HOW A DEADWOOD LADY SAVED HER WATCH

Despite their seemingly utter lack of sentiment or moral scruples, those early bandits were not always proof against flattery, as the following episode will illustrate. The story runs thus: A lady, the wife of a well-known Deadwood citizen, was, upon a time, a passenger on one of the stage coaches that was held up on the Sidney route. The lady had a watch on her person that she highly valued, and while the robbers were engaged in securing the property of the other passengers she slyly concealed it among the coils of her back hair. One of the robbers soon approached her and demanded her money and valuables, which she readily yielded up, with the exception of the watch. The robber either accidentally or otherwise espied the watch, reached out and took it, and was coolly transferring it to his pocket, when the lady in imploring accents cried: "Please, Mr. Robber! good Mr. Robber! dear Mr. Robber! don't take my watch." The robber, unable to withstand the stirring appeal, and, perhaps, struck by the humor of the situation, with a hearty laugh handed the watch back to its owner. Such generosity, however, was but rarely displayed.

Another lady, a sister-in-law of W. H. Harlow, now a resident of Spearfish, when leaving the Hills in 1878, took the precaution before starting of concealing the contents of her purse, amounting to $100 or such a matter, among the intricate meshes of her back hair, hoping to smuggle it through without discovery, but, alas! at a point on the road known as "Eagle's Nest," the stage was held up and the passengers robbed of all their valuables, and the roll of greenbacks so carefully concealed in the young lady's hair did not escape detection.

THE DEADWOOD FAMOUS TREASURE COACH

As a last desperate expedient to defeat the purposes of the outlaws, Superintendent Voorhees, of the Sidney and Black Hills Stage and Express Line, had built the historic Deadwood treasure coach, designed expressly for the transportation of Black Hills gold. This famous coach, a familiar object to all old-timers, was a strongly constructed and formidable affair, lined with heavy steel or iron plate, intended to defy the bullets of the desperate bandits. Passengers entering or returning from the Hills by the ordinary passenger coaches frequently shipped their valuables on the treasure coach for greater security, it being regarded as nearly invulnerable.

When completed it was put on the road under the escort of five picked men, unerring pistol shots, with Scott Davis as Chief Messenger—all armed with shot-guns and six-shooters, to guard the treasure on its dangerous way over the line. Brave, intrepid, and nervy men were those messengers who guarded the gold dust and the bullion out of the Black Hills during those early days, and the story of their daring adventures on their perilous trips is by no means the least interesting portion of Black Hills history.

Several trips were made by the new coach without encountering any danger, but a time came later when the true metal of the iron-protected vault on wheels, as well as the nerve of the messengers in charge of the treasure, were put to a crucial test. That occasion was the memorable Cold Springs robbery of 1878.

One day, during that year, the treasure coach with three messengers and a telegraph operator named Campbell aboard, and Big Gene, the driver, on the box, drove up as usual to the stage station at Cold Springs without dreaming that danger lurked about the place. Everything about the premises bore its wonted aspect of security. The stages had never been attacked at the stations. The horses were halted at the door of the station, the driver threw the lines he had held over the six horses to the ground, and was preparing to dismount from the box, when, suddenly, as a thunder-clap from a clear sky, a loud report of fire-arms rang out, and a deadly hail of bullets came hurtling against the side and through the coach, killing Campbell and dangerously wounding Gale Hill, one of the messengers; Scott Davis, Chief Messenger, also slightly wounded, taking in the situation at one glance, jumped to the ground on the opposite side from where their assailants stood, and made for the heavy timber near by, under cover of which he opened a brisk fusillade on the five desperadoes. So fast and furious came the hail of shot from the timber into the ranks of the robbers, that two of them, impelled by the instinct of self-preservation, finally made a sort of breastwork or Big Gene, whom they had captured and disarmed. Placing the poor fellow in front of them, as a protection, they compelled him to walk towards the spot where Davis was concealed, and when within communicating distance, they warned him to stop firing or take the alternative of seeing "Big Gene" killed then and there. Realizing that the driver's life was at stake, he ceased firing and, though wounded, started at once for the nearest stage station for assistance.

After Davis had ceased firing, the robbers compelled the driver to seize a pick and break open the treasure box, when, after taking possession of its contents, $45,000 in gold bullion, they pinioned "Big Gene" to a wheel of the coach, mounted their horses and rode away, leaving their wounded comrade where he had fallen. During all these proceedings the third messenger was lying stretched at full length on the bottom of the coach, apparently dead. He was not dead, however, nor even wounded, but merely acting his part in the tragic drama, and so well did he perform his difficult role, that not even a suspicion of the truth dawned upon the minds of the outlaws. By feigning death he had saved his own life, and also gained some information that afterwards proved valuable when the search for the robbers began. The other two messengers were at the station below, where they intended joining the force upon the arrival of the coach.

The names of the five bandits were Blackburn, Wall, Brookes, "Red Head Mike," and Price, who, it was ascertained, had taken possession of the station and concealed themselves before the arrival of the coach, the stocktenders having been securely bound and gagged, to prevent them giving the alarm. It was several months before the wounded outlaw recovered, from whom a clue was obtained as to the identity of the other members of the gang.

The officers of the law immediately got upon the trails of the robbers and followed them up until they were nearly all captured and most—perhaps all—of the stolen treasure recovered. The vigorous measures taken to hunt down the gang that infested the country had a salutary effect, as no other attempt was made to hold up the treasure shipments on that route.

It is now recalled that a few, at least, of that desperate gang of outlaws who infested the Black Hills region during the late '70s were brought to justice in Deadwood in the summer of 1877, I think it was, and it was this way:—

As I was walking leisurely down Sherman street one Sunday in July of that year, when in the vicinity of the old log jail my attention was attracted to a wild commotion in the street below, and a horseman was seen speeding away over the hills to the right followed by a volley of bullets, the rider turning in his saddle occasionally to fire back at his pursuers. Skipping nimbly away out of the possible range of some stray bullet, I saw no more, but upon inquiry later the following facts relative to the exciting episode were eliminated:—

D. B. May, a ranchman from Lance creek, on the Cheyenne river, thought he recognized among the motley crowd gathered in front of the post-office, one of a gang that "held up" the Black Hills stage coach about four weeks before, robbing him of $70 in money. Upon communicating his suspicion to others, a man named Goldman approached the suspected individual and slapped him upon the shoulder, whereupon he quickly pulled his revolver and fired, the ball grazing the arm of Mr. May, who promptly returned the fire. The stranger then quickly mounted his horse, which was hitched near by, and made for the hills, emptying the chambers of his revolver at the pursuing crowd as he rode. He had not gone far when a well-directed shot by Deputy Sheriff Cochrane brought both horse and rider to the ground. After clearing himself from his fallen horse he tried to make his escape on foot, but was defeated in this purpose by Sheriff Bullock, who, arriving opportunely on the scene in company with Deputy Captain Willard, soon arrested the fugitive and had him conveyed to jail, while he (Bullock) and Deputy Willard started in pursuit of two other men, who appeared to be trying to make their escape and were being pursued by Mr. Gilman. These were also arrested and placed in jail. The prisoners gave their names as Prescott Webb, G. W. Webb, and C. P. Wisdom.

Since the advent of railroads in the Black Hills shipments of bullion from the large mines are made only semi-monthly, and the exceeding precaution taken in making such shipments, has reduced the danger of bullion robbery to a minimum. The gold is molded into bricks, varying in size, but usually about ten inches in length, six inches wide, and five inches in thickness, at the offices of the companies. It is customary, I am informed, for the messenger to receive the bullion at the offices of the companies, where it is receipted for, and then taken under guard to the office of the express company over whose line it is to be shipped, where it is securely wrapped and sealed, then placed in the treasure box and conveyed under guard to the railroad station and placed in the express car. The messenger, armed with loaded shot-gun and six-shooter, accompanies the treasure until it reaches a point of safety. During the early shipments by railroads, messengers have been known to guard the bullion as far as Omaha on its way East. Now, however, the heavy bullion product of the northern Hills is accompanied by the messenger only as far as Rapid City.

Richard Bullock, reputed to be one of the nerviest messengers who ever guarded the gold bullion out of the Black Hills, has been employed for many years to guard the semi-monthly shipments of the bullion product of the great Homestake aggregation of mines, without ever having lost, it is alleged, a single ounce of the millions of treasure intrusted to his care. During the time that Whitewood was the terminus of the first railroad to the Hills, the F. E. & M. V. Bullock guarded the bullion over the stage route between Deadwood and Whitewood, through a mountainous country that was peculiarly inviting to road agents, without ever having encountered a single knight of the road.

CHAPTER XXVIII

CUSTER COUNTY

Custer County originally occupied all that portion of the Black Hills of Dakota, lying between 43° and 43° 50′ north latitude, and between the 103 and 104 meridian of longitude west of Greenwich; besides a small triangular fraction on the northeast, bordering the south fork of the Big Cheyenne river, altogether covering an area of a little more than 3,000 square miles, or one-half of the entire ceded territory.

The county, as first defined, may be divided into two nearly equal portions; the one comprehending the mountainous and mineral-bearing region, in which is included the greater part of the Harney granite uplift; the other the grazing and agricultural lands outside of the foot-hills, in which is included the fertile valleys of the numerous streams draining that area and a considerable extent of prairie land on both sides of the Cheyenne river. The northern or mountainous portion is covered by an abundant growth of pine timber of excellent quality, and interspersed with many charming parks,—half wood and half glade; the middle and southern portion consisting, for the most part, of high prairie table-lands, becoming mountainous toward the south. The whole area is drained by Spring, Battle, French, Beaver, and Fall River creeks.

At the first session of the newly appointed Board of County Commissioners, held in the parlors of the Occidental Hotel at Custer, beginning on the 27th of April, 1877, the county was organized and named Custer, in honor of Gen. Geo. A. Custer, who commanded the first military expedition to the Black Hills in the summer of 1874.

The meetings at Custer were held on the 27th of April, the 4th, 5th, 7th, 8th, 9th, 10th, and 11th of May, 1877, during which the county was temporarily located at Hayward, by a majority vote of the Board, and, by the way, there is a bit of rather amusing history connected with the location of the capital of Custer County, which furnishes an example of a little exceedingly sharp practice on the part of one of the commissioners, and the story runs thus:—

The appointees for Commissioners of Custer County were M. D. Thompson of Yankton, Chas. Hayward of Hayward, and E. G. Ward of Custer City, the two latter places being rivals for county seat honors.

Custer, not having yet fully recovered from the effects of its suddenly arrested growth in the spring of 1876, had at the time but a meager population, while on the other hand, Hayward had developed into a booming, hustling mining camp, of perhaps 300 people.

At the initial session of the Board, M. D. Thompson, the Yankton member, was chosen permanent chairman of the meetings, and when the work of organization, the appointment of subordinate county officers and other preliminary proceedings looking to the establishment of county government, was concluded, Mr. Hayward made a motion to locate the county seat at Hayward, which Ward naturally refused to second, thus blocking procedure in that direction, when, after a short discussion, the Board adjourned to meet on the following morning.

In the interim there was doubtless considerable influence brought to bear on the neutral member, who, after weighing the matter, finally came to the conclusion that the capital should be where it would accommodate the greatest number of the people of the county, so meeting Mr. Hayward he told him to renew his motion at the meeting to be held in the morning. This Hayward did, but, as before, Ward failed to second the motion.

The chairman, who had his bit of strategy all figured out, after waiting a few minutes, pulled a cigar from his pocket, bit off the end, fumbled in his vest pockets for something which he ostensibly failed to find, then, vacating the chair, approached Mr. Ward and asked him for a match. While lighting his cigar, he requested Ward to occupy the chair, which he did, when he (Thompson) seconded Hayward's motion, which, of course, was carried by a majority of one, and thus Hayward was made the temporary county seat. The first meeting of the Board at Hayward was held on May 16th, 1877.

In canvassing the returns of the election held in November, 1877, to elect county officers and permanently locate the capital, there were found, it is claimed, many fraudulent votes. Custer, however, claimed the election, which Hayward refused to concede, and, as a sequence, the contest waxed warm. Tradition says that, to summarily settle the matter, a party of men went to Hayward, took forcible possession of the county archives, and carried them to Custer; and further says, that the party was promptly arrested and compelled to return the county property to Hayward. Not until 1879 was the contest adjusted, and the capital permanently located at Custer City, the last meeting of the Commissioners at Hayward being held on October 7th, 1879, and the first at Custer three days later, on October 10th, 1879.

The first county officers of Custer County were as follows:—

County Commissioners: M. D. Thompson, Chas. Hayward, and E. G. Ward.

Probate Judge: J. W. C. White.
Register of Deeds and *ex officio* County Clerk: Fred. J. Cross.
Sheriff: D. N. Ely.
Treasurer: Frank B. Smith.
Constables: M. H. Brown, C. A. Scott.
Justices of Peace: Theodore Vos. Brough, S. R. Shankland, C. L. Spooner.
Surveyor: Robt. Harvey.
Assessor: A. B. Hughes.

On November 12th, 1881, the boundary line between Custer and Pennington counties was definitely fixed, when Hayward was found to be within the lines of Pennington County, some two or three miles.

Until 1881 courts were held in ordinary buildings. In that year a fine two-story brick structure was erected at a cost to the county of $12,000, for the payment of which county bonds were issued. Up to this time considerable expenditures had been made by the county in improving roads and building bridges across the principal streams, showing a commendable spirit of public enterprise on the part of its 2,000 population.

In 1882 the assessed valuation of Custer City was $363,329; the tax levy thirty mills, and the total indebtedness $29,407.29, at which time county bonds were worth 97 cents on the dollar. In 1883 the county was sub-divided on the boundary line between townships Nos. 6 and 7 south, and the southern subdivision organized into Fall River County, thus cutting off a considerable portion of the grazing lands from the old county, but leaving for the most part the mineral bearing and the most heavily timbered areas to Custer County. This subdivision was made in obedience to the popular verdict of the portion to be segregated.

The county has now (1898) an assessed valuation of $784,564.00; a total indebtedness of $174,188.86, and contained a population of 4,740 in 1896.

THE MINES OF CUSTER COUNTY

From the easily exhausted placer deposits of French creek and tributary gulches, the attention of prospectors was, about 1879, first directed to the discovery and develment (sic) of the other varied resources of that region of the Hills, which resulted in exposing numerous promising mines of gold, mica, tin, and other minerals, but owing to the absence of facilities for dealing with the product, much of the needed stimulus to a vigorous development of mining properties by their owners was lacking during the first years of Custer

County mining history. With the advent of the railroad in 1890, however, a new impetus was given to mining activity in that region.

Among the early discoveries in gold-bearing quartz were the "Grand Junction," "Penobscot," "Salmon," "Atlantic," "Old Bill," "Old Charley," "Lightning," "Mayflower," and "North Pole."

The Grand Junction was located in April, 1879, by Chas. Crary, F. A. Towner, James Friend, and Joseph Summers. This mine is situated about seven and one-half miles northwest of Custer City, near the boundary line of Custer and Pennington counties. In 1880 a company erected a twenty-stamp mill on the property. In 1881 a new company was organized called the Grand Junction Company, which carried on operations for nearly a year, when, in July, 1882, a company of St. Louis capitalists under the name of the Constant Mining Company, purchased the property and erected a forty-stamp mill. This mill was operated on the mine until the winter of 1885, when it closed down, since which time the batteries have been idle.

The Grand Junction is a large vertical vein of quartz, full sixty feet in width, with hornblende on the east and a slate wall on the west side. The ore near the surface was partly free milling, but as depth was attained it was found to be in conformation with base metals, and therefore the gold could not be recovered by amalgamation—hence the suspension.

Unfortunately for that region of the Hills, this failure to extract the gold from refractory ore by the free milling process did not serve as a salutary warning to future mine owners and operators, for, despite this object-lesson they continued to discover mines which yielded rich returns by chemical analysis, upon which they persisted in erecting stamp mills, until nine were erected in Custer County, upon the best mines in the district,—some of which still stand as monuments to the deplorable short-sightedness of the early mine operators.

The Penobscot mine is situated about seven miles northwest from Custer, and was located by A. Wilcox, W. C. Gooch and Joel Mead in 1879. The owners did a small amount of work on the mine, and sold a half interest to Jas. Brodie of Lead City, who was formerly connected with the Old Abe, now the property of the Homestake Co. In 1880 the firm erected a mill on the property and equipped it with antiquated machinery, which was first used in a mill in Colorado, away back in 1860. In 1877, having out-lived its usefulness, it was sold to Messrs. Potter & Powers, who transported it to the Black Hills, and put it in operation on one of the early mines at Central. Proving altogether unsatisfactory for milling purposes, the machinery was sold in 1880 to Gooch, Brodie & Co., who took it down to Custer County, and put it up at the Penobscot mine. The firm tried hard to pound a little gold out of the

Penobscot ore with the condemned batteries, but becoming disgusted with the results they sold the property to Messrs. Fortune, Wilson & Bull, in 1881, the latter selling his interest to Dr. Broughton of Broadhead, Wisconsin. This company ran the mill for a short time, when the worthless machinery was taken down and moved away. Is it any wonder that the ore refused to yield to such treatment? It will be recalled by those whose memories go back twenty-one years, that other obsolete machinery was brought up from Colorado to the Black Hills, and put in operation on some of the early mines around Central, jeopardizing the reputation of the mines, and leaving their owners on the verge of bankruptcy. The Penobscot is a large vein of quartz, which assays $10.00 in gold per ton. A large amount of excavation has been done near the surface, but no great depth has been attained. The property is now in the hands of Edwin Van Cise of Deadwood.

The Salmon mine, situated about two miles north of Custer, was located by Messrs. Peterson and Woodward in 1880. This mine attained early celebrity, for the extraordinary richness of the ore at the surface, and the many free gold specimens it produced. No mill was ever erected on the property, which is owned by the Gold Fish Mining Co., and is now in charge of Joseph Pilcher, of Custer.

The Atlantic mine was located in 1879 by Henry Franklin. This mine, too, was justly famous for its free gold specimens, which were claimed to be the richest ever found in the Black Hills. The mine is now owned by John Wright, of Custer, and Jack McAleer, of Deadwood. No mill has been erected on the property.

The Old Bill mine, situated about four and one-half miles northerly from Custer, was located in May, 1879, by Richard Holiday, Ralph Kenyon, and H. N. Ross, the latter having charge of the mine. The Old Bill is a large, fine vein of quartz, assaying twelve dollars in gold per ton. While there is no mill on the ground, the ore has been milled with good profit. The mine has a shaft sixty feet deep.

The Old Charlie mine was located in July, 1879, by Chas. Holmes and A. Sampson. This property, which consists of three claims, is situated about four miles west of Custer. There are numerous openings on the property, the main working shaft which is about one hundred and fifty feet deep, is a double compartment incline, five and a half by nine feet in ore from the surface downwards. A twenty-stamp mill, and steam hoist are erected on the property, and a great deal of ore has been milled, with excellent results; the ore yielding from five dollars to twenty-one dollars in gold per ton. The property is owned by W. N. Olds and his associates, of New York, and is under the supervision of W. N. Olds, of Custer. When operated on the extensive scale contemplated by the management, the property will doubtless add largely to the gold production of the Hills.

The Lightning mine is another of the famous mines of the early days. This mine, which was located in July, 1879, by Frank Weatherby and J. Juderine, is a fine vein of quartz—true fissure in character, and seven feet in width at the one hundred foot level. Since its first discovery the property has changed hands several times, but is now owned, for the most part, by Leopold Dole, of Omaha, and Henry Schenck, of Custer. The mine has changed its original name, and is now known as the North Star mine. The owners of the property—which is now being rapidly developed—design the erection of complete reduction works in the early spring. The ore is reputed to be very rich.

The May Flower mine, situated about four miles west from Custer City, on a small tributary of French creek, was first located in 1879, by James McShearer and John P. Foran, of Custer. This mine, which has been quite extensively developed, has a large vein of medium grade, and a three-foot vein of high-grade ore. In 1884 a ten-stamp mill was erected on the property, which, after making a short run, closed down, owing to the impossibility of saving the gold by amalgamation. The assay, by Telluride test, runs from $12.00 to $15.00 in gold per ton of ore. The present owners are J. P. Foran, John Durst, and Harry Poland. Among the most promising of the recent discoveries in Custer County are the "Spokane," "Lizzie," "Bonanza," "Granite Reef" and "Union Hill" mines. The Spokane mine, located by Sylvester Judd in 1891, is situated about sixteen miles east of Custer City and twelve miles from Hermosa, on the F. E. & M. V. Railway. This mine has a shaft 100 feet in depth, and a number of connecting drifts. The vein proper, which is about fourteen feet in width, is of medium-grade ore, except four feet of the center or core, which runs quite uniformly twenty ounces in silver and from 35 to 40 per cent in lead to the ton. The property now belongs to the Crown Hill Mining Co., which in addition to this property, is operating extensively in the northern Hills.

The Lizzie mine, located in 1897 by Frank and Ford McLaughlin, of Custer, constitutes one of the claims which comprise a large group, now owned by an incorporated stock company, the greater part of the stock being held by citizens of Le Mars, Iowa. The development consists of a ninety-five-foot tunnel, and 100-foot shaft, at the bottom of which the mine shows a vein of nine feet, incased in walls of quartzite. The ore runs from $6.00 to $40.00 in gold, and two per cent copper to the ton. The company are preparing to ship the product to a smelter for treatment.

The Bonanza mine, situated on Mineral Ridge, three and a half miles west of Custer, has four shafts, the deepest of which is sixty-five feet. This group of claims is owned by H. G. Butterfield & Bro. of Custer.

The Granite Reef mine, situated two miles southeast from Custer, has a fifty-foot shaft, and a tunnel 300 feet in length. The ore of this mine carries two per cent of copper, and from $12.00 to $46.00 in gold to the ton, the vein being nine feet in width. The property is owned by James Demereau, C. W. Robbins, and A. T. Feay, of Custer City.

The Union Hill mine, situated about three miles west from Custer, has a shaft forty-five feet in depth and a tunnel 300 feet in length. The vein is eight feet in width, and assays well in gold. The property is owned by Henry A. Albion of Custer City.

There are numerous other gold mines of bright promise in Custer County, which with the application of proper treatment, will, doubtless, yield handsome profits to their owners. The gold in these veins is readily obtained by the chlorination or cyanide process, but the ore is only to a limited extent adapted to the free milling methods. It only lacks an abundance of capital to transform that region into one of the most productive districts in the Black Hills.

THE MICA MINES OF CUSTER COUNTY

For several years after the beginning of the last decade, the Mica mining industry constituted an important factor in the business economy of Custer County, to which region of the Hills that mineral is principally confined. In fact it is only in the lofty granite mountains of the Harney range, surrounding Custer City, that mica in merchantable form has been found. Strangely enough, although the whole granite region glittered brightly with mica, but little attention was given to it as a commerical commodity until about 1880, when the attention of miners was attracted to the mineral as a possible factor of industrial enterprise, by encountering large blocks, easily separable into sheets, in the development of gold mines.

The first workable mica mine, it is claimed was located as a gold mine in 1879, by Geo. Clark, about three and one-half miles northwest of Custer. Since its first discovery the mine has doubtless changed hands a few times, and has been known under various appellations, but is now known as the Mc-Maken mine. It was at one time owned by Messrs. Offenbacher & Haight, who took from the mine from $75,000.00 to $100,000.00 worth of fine merchantable mica.

Perhaps the most remarkable as well as the most productive deposit of mica discovered is a mine known as the Lost Bonanza, situated about two

CUSTER CITY

miles north of Custer, on the abrupt slope of Buckhorn Mountain, and located by L. C. La Barre, in 1880. Soon after its location, sold to the New Mexico & Dakota Mica Mining Company, composed of Chicago capitalists, which from July, 1881, to March, 1882, took from the mine 24,000 pounds of splendid mica. This may seem a small amount to produce in a period of eight months, but let it be remembered that a vast deal of heavy granite rock has to be removed to reach the mica, and when found only about seven per cent of the whole is merchantable. The market price of the product varied according to quality and demand, ranging from $2.00 to $12.00 per pound. It was hinted about that time, it is recalled, that this corporation so controlled and manipulated the mica market, as to render its production wholly unprofitable to small operators.

A few of the many other mica locations are the "Climax," "New York," "White Spar," "Window Light," "Eureka," "Grand View," "Old Mike," and "Last Find," all of which were more or less developed into very promising properties. The Eureka, six miles northeast of Custer, near Harney's Peak, attained especial celebrity for the large sheets of mica it produced, some of which measured eight by ten square inches, without a flaw or defect.

None of these mines are now being operated, and the reason assigned by those in a position to know is that the market is controlled by a trust in such a way as to bar out all mica that does not pass directly through its hands, thus rendering the production of the mineral unprofitable.

The same is true of the mining of tin, which, according to the expressed opinion of tin experts, exists in paying quantities in the granite hills of Custer County, but which is at present impossible to get upon the market. It is confidently expected by mine owners that changed conditions and a growing demand will revive both of these industries at no distant day.

CUSTER CITY

Custer City, the primary metropolis of the Black Hills—much of whose early history has been hereinbefore recorded,—is finely situated, at an elevation of 5,560 feet above the level of the sea, on the upper valley of French creek, near the center, east and west of what has been designated Custer's Park, than which no spot more alluring and grandly picturesque is to be found in the whole magnificent Black Hills domain.

From the margin of the park, wherein lies the pioneer city, rise bold, lofty mountains, projecting their jagged, naked crests far above the stately pines that clothe their rugged slopes. On the north Buckhorn Peak, covered from base to summit with evergreen foliage, rises up 1,000 feet above the level of the city, and sweeps around its southern spur to within two miles of its outer limits, describing in its curve that peculiar outline to which the name owes its origin. On the eastern margin about two miles away, Calamity Peak extends its bare castellated crest 1,200 feet above the level of the valley, and away ten miles to the northeast Harney's Peak towers in rocky grandeur above all. On the south, near the city, the hills rise to an elevation of perhaps 200 feet, then gradually fall away, disclosing a fascinating view of Prospect Park, while to the east and west widens out the beautiful valley of French creek.

This valley was appropriately designated "Floral Valley" by Gen. Custer, when exploring the Hills in 1874, because of the wonderful variety and beauty of its flora. It is said that in the blossoming season, or during the months of June and July, as many as 160 varieties of wild flowers may be found in bloom.

The region about Custer possesses an ideal climate full of health-giving and health-preserving properties—a climate where epidemics are an almost unknown quantity, The pure, invigorating air circulating through the valley, laden with the grateful aroma of the pines, infuses new life with every expansion of the lungs, causing the weak to become strong, and under its balmy influence the wretched victim of insomnia is wooed to gentle, refreshing slumber. All one has to do is to comfortably adjust his tired anatomy and nature speedily does the rest.

Snow rarely falls to a depth of more than six inches, nor remains more than a few days at a time in Custer's Park, which abounds in pure, cold, crystal springs—leaving nothing to be desired by the tourist in search of health or pleasure.

SYLVAN LAKE

Resting peacefully in among the rugged cliffs of the Harney range, about six miles in a northerly direction from Custer, may be found the crowning attraction of that region, "Sylvan Lake," "a thing of beauty and a joy forever."

This artistic conception was formed in 1882 by the construction of a massive stone dam, near the head of Sunday gulch, to bar the waters of the streams that trickle down the mountain slopes into the basin, thus forming an artificial lake of about sixteen acres in extent.

From Custer this popular resort is reached over a finely constructed driveway, that winds its sinuous way through a region of grandeur, beauty, and picturesqueness not surpassed elsewhere in this "Switzerland of America," and after circling around a labyrinth of hills, near the limits of the

SYLVAN LAKE, AN ATTRACTIVE RESORT NEAR CUSTER

lake, it brings its visitors suddenly in full view, at its upper side, of an exhibition of nature's and art's handiwork combined, that would not willingly be forgotten. On three sides the towering cliffs inclose the miniature lake in their close, rugged embrace, while at the lower margin, the surplus waters dash over the artificial barrier, and go dancing and chattering gaily down the rocky incline. The surface of the lagoon is dotted here and there with white-winged boats, whose small keels are plowing little rippling furrows across its bosom, or, perchance, are rocking on the tiny waves at their moorings. Copious as is the English tongue, it is inadequate to paint the scene in all its lights and shades, and it is only through the eye that one can form a true conception of the enchanting picture.

In a little recession, at the base of the water-laved crags, inclosing the lower end of the lake, at the right of the dam, a commodious veranda-encircled hostelry has been constructed, and provided with all modern conveniences for the entertainment of guests who are there supplied with a cuisine that would challenge the criticism of the most fastidious epicure. It is from the veranda of this hotel that the best view of the lagoon and its environments can be obtained.

CUSTER IN 1877

Custer, on entering its third year of history, found itself prostrate, but purified, in the midst of its grand surroundings. Of the thousands of eager, reckless fortune-hunters, who had departed during the previous year, in pursuit of the "elusive phantom," but few had returned, as the hundreds of tenantless buildings gave pathetic testimony, buildings which were afterward from time to time torn down and converted into fuel.

For the few subsequent years the population of Custer fluctuated, varying from fifty or sixty to 400. On the return of Gen. Crook from his summer campaign against the Indians in the fall of 1876, his command camped at Custer for a time, which brought back a few of the stampeders from Deadwood, and also attracted to that point a considerable number of new-comers to the Hills, increasing the population to about 400, which, owing to new excitements in other portions of the Hills, again diminished, until, on September 5th, 1878, there were, it is said, by actual census, only thirty-seven men, eleven women, and as many children, fifty-seven persons all told, in the pioneer city of the Black Hills. From that time it again began to slowly expand until in 1881 it contained a permanent population of 400, from which date the stability of Custer became an assured fact.

Among those who pinned their faith to Custer for the most time during its early years of vicissitudes and discouraging fluctuations were, first: Thos. Hooper, D. W. Flick, Sam'l R. Shankland, D. K. Snively in 1875, then H. A. Albion, E. G. Peirce, T. H. Harvey, W. H. Harlow, Ernest Schleunning, Sam'l Booth, Frank B. Smith, A. B. Hughes, A. Yerkes, J. C. Saunders, Capt. Haserodt, and others all of whom may be accounted among the first permanent settlers of Custer (let it be remembered that there was little permanency in Custer before 1877)—and the determination and early efforts of these men were largely instrumental in giving Custer its prestige of to-day.

The first postmaster of the U. S. Postal Service in Custer was Thos. H. Harvey; the second, J. S. Bartholomew; the third on the list was Frank B. Smith; the fourth, S. R. Shankland, followed by H. A. Albion.

The first school in Custer, as well as in the Black Hills, was taught during the summer of 1876 by Miss Carrie Scott, who is a daughter of C. A. Scott, of Spearfish. And, by the way, Mr. Scott made the first coffin ever constructed in the Black Hills, at Custer.

The second school taught in Custer was a tuition school opened and taught by Jas. E. Carpenter during the winter of 1876-7. Mr. Carpenter was a partner of Chas. Hayward in founding the town of Hayward on Battle creek, and is now a practicing attorney in Woonsocket, South Dakota, where he has resided for the past seventeen years.

The town was incorporated and a patent was issued by the government for the square mile occupied by the city in 1882.

In 1884 Custer City erected its first public school building, a fine, two-storied brick structure, separated into four rooms, or school departments.

The number of pupils enrolled for the year 1897-8 was 174, and inasmuch as the number of children of school age in the city numbered 265, it seems evident that increased school accommodations will have to be provided in the near future.

Custer's public buildings consist of a handsome brick courthouse and jail, a fine brick public school building, and four churches—the Methodist, Congregational, Baptist, and Catholic.

Since the completion of the Burlington & Missouri Railway to Custer, in 1890, the city has developed rapidly in commerical importance, and its wide streets, its well-filled squares of brick and frame business structures and numerous cosy homes gives ample evidence of thrift and increasing prosperity.

In addition to its complement of business houses, Custer can boast of two flourishing banks—one National and one State—two good hotels, a factory for the manufacture of a mica lubrication from native product, two steam planing mills, and other small industries incident to towns of its class.

What is now the First National Bank of Custer was first established as a private bank in 1881 by D. Corrigan, who owned and managed the same until 1890, when the institution was converted into a national bank, with a capital stock of $50,000. The first officers of the incorporated institution were as follows: D. Corrigan, President; F. A. Towner, Vice President; and W. F. Hanley, Cashier. Both capital and officers have remained unchanged.

The Custer County Bank was organized and opened on April 17th, 1890, with a capital stock of $25,000, with the following officers: S. H. Mills, New York, President; Jos. E. Pilcher, of Custer City, Vice-President; Frank R. Davis, of Rapid City, Cashier; T. W. Delicate, of Custer City, Assistant Cashier.

Subsequently Frank R. Davis died, when T. W. Delicate was promoted to the cashiership, and D. W. Webster succeeded Joseph E. Pilcher as vice-president, so that the present officers of the institution are: Stephen H. Mills, of New York City, President; Daniel W. Webster, of Custer City, Vice-President; Thomas W. Delicate, of Custer City, Cashier.

The press is now represented by the Custer *Chronicle*, a wide-awake sheet, fully abreast of the enterprising community it represents. The paper was established in December, 1879 (the first number appearing on the third of that month), by A. W. Merrick, of Deadwood—the pioneer newspaper man of the Black Hills. At the end of a few months Mr. Merrick sold the paper to Messrs. Clark & Kubler, and it is now conducted by the latter member of the firm, Joseph Kubler. Mr. Kubler is entitled to the distinction of having run through the press the first copy of the Black Hills *Pioneer,* issued in Deadwood in June, 1876.

Custer is supplied with a splendid water service, is well lighted by electricity, and has a present population of from 800 to 1,000 people.

For several years subsequent to the advent of the railroad, Custer was the largest lumber shipping station in the Black Hills—shipping more, it is claimed, that all other Black Hills towns combined. In 1895 there were in that region twenty steam sawmills in active operation, employing an aggragate of 250 men. There were also two steam planing mills in constant operation then as now. Though the stringent restrictions wisely imposed upon the cutting of timber from government lands has inflicted a severe blow to that important industry in the pioneer city, the ever-increasing value of the mining interest, and stock-raising industry in the region about, will buoy it on to the substantial success it so richly deserves.

JOSEPH KUBLER
Who ran through the press the first copy of the Black Hills Pioneer on June 8th, 1876

During the years 1877-8-9, as before stated, the settlements of the Hills were constantly beset by an organized gang of laborers, whose sole occupation was to round up all horses found at the end of lariat ropes or running loose, and they plied their avocation with a zeal and persistency highly creditable to their calling, and they were not in the least particular as to their color, pedigree, or ownership.

Custer's citizens did not wholly escape their vigilance, as the subjoined story will illustrate:—

It was one evening during the month of April, that Wm. H. Harlowe, now a resident of Spearfish, mounted his horse, and just as the shadows began to fall, rode away from Custer City in the direction of Deadwood carrying on his person a considerable quantity of French creek gold-dust for shipment at the latter place,—there being no safe way to ship from Custer City at the time. The gold, it may be proper to state, belonged partly to himself and partly to Samuel Booth of Custer City. After riding seventeen miles, mostly under cover of darkness, he reached what is known as Gillette's ranch, where he picketed his horse and put up for the night, under the hospitable roof of Mr. Gillette. In the morning, to his extreme chagrin, he found his horse missing—lariat and all. He borrowed a horse of the proprietor of the ranch, and after giving an order to be sent to Custer for another horse, to be used on his return, he resumed his journey with his valuable treasure, on the keen outlook for ambushed highwaymen along the way.

On his return from Deadwood, Mr. Harlow found that the horse brought from Custer during his absence had also been spirited away the night before

THE START FOR HARNEY PEAK FROM SYLVAN LAKE

his arrival. He sent word to Custer to have a posse put at once on the trail of the thief or thieves, and the men after following up a clue for two days finally traced the guilty party to the vicinity of Custer at ten o'clock p.m., when sentinels were immediately posted on all the roads leading from the city.

Mr. Harlow and John Halley, a brother of James Halley of the First National Bank of Rapid City (everybody in the Hills knows James Halley, if they don't they ought to),—well, Harlow and Halley, the former armed with a Springfield rifle and the latter with a shot-gun, rode out on the Cheyenne road, in the midst of a terrific thunderstorm, to look for their man. The very blackness of darkness prevailed, save when the lurid glare of the lightning's play illuminated their surroundings. They had not gone more than a half-mile when they discerned through the gloom an approaching horseman, who was ordered to halt when about twenty feet away, but receiving no satisfactory response to the call, Mr. Harlow leveled his rifle at the unknown at the same time ordering him to "hold up his hands." Just at the moment of a brilliant flash of lightning revealed the man with a revolver pointed directly at them. Both fired almost simultaneously, the ball from the revolver inflicting a severe wound on Mr. Harlow's hand, the effects of which he bears to this day. After the interchange of shots, the stranger turned his horse and fled, followed by a storm of shots from Mr. Halley's gun. Five days later the man was buried on Castle creek, about twelve miles north of Custer, having died from the effect of the gunshot wounds received in his flight. The man proved to be a "pal"— that's what they call it, I believe, of the notorious Albert Spears, who was, and perhaps is now, in prison for his complicity in the memorable Cold Springs stage robbery.

HERMOSA

Hermosa is an enterprising little agricultural hamlet situated on Battle creek outside of the foot-hills, on the line of the F. E. & M. V. Railroad. The town was organized in 1888, and contains a population of 125 souls; has three stores of general merchandise, three church organizations, a creditable school building, and a good school separated into an upper and primary grade.

Buffalo Gap, situated on the line of the Fremont, Elkhorn and Missouri Valley Railway, at a point where a branch road leaves the main line for Hot Springs, originated at the time of the advent of that line to the Hills, and was, perhaps is still, an important eating station of the line. The town is noted chiefly for the extensive quarries of different varieties and colors of fine sandstone found in its vicinity, large quantities of which product have found a ready market in some of the Eastern cities. Other places of more or less importance in Custer County are: Fairburn, Folsom, Otis, Spokane, Berne, Mayo, Pringle, Argyle, Wind Cave, Bakerville, and Westford.

CHAPTER XXIX

PENNINGTON COUNTY

Pennington County, the only one of the three counties into which the Black Hills was first separated that has preserved its original territory nearly intact, occupies geographically a central position, extending eighty miles in length east and west, by twenty miles north and south, comprising an area of 1,600 square miles. The base line of the Hills survey on the forty-fourth parallel of north latitude passes through the county at equi-distance from its north and south boundary lines, as defined under an act of the Territorial Legislature, approved in February, 1877. The boundary line between Pennington and Custer counties was not definitely established until November 12th, 1881, as was stated in my treatment of Custer County. Pennington County is divided into two nearly equal portions of mountainous and open country, the western half embracing the entire timbered area, the eastern half comprising the prairie region, and for the most part the broad, fertile valleys of the streams draining the county including some of the great cattle ranges on the south branch of the Cheyenne river. The western or mountainous portion is heavily timbered with an excellent quality of pine timber interspersed with patches of spruce, fir, birch, oak, aspen, and willow, with the exception that here and there within the timber line are found quite extensive areas of open prairie land, elevated from 4,500 to 6,000 feet above the plane of the sea, while the eastern or open portion is almost wholly destitute of trees of any kind, save those fringing the borders of the larger streams.

About one-third of the great granite region of the Hills, including Harney's Peak, is within the limits of Pennington County. This dominant peak of the Black Hills, which is situated about twenty-three miles as the crow flies, southwest from Rapid City, can plainly be seen through the hazy distance from the foot-hills southwest and southeast of the city, proudly lifting its gray coronel into the hovering clouds above the lesser jagged peaks and battlements of the granite uplift. Some of the wildest, grandest scenery of the Hills is to be found among the rugged mountains and along the canyons of the streams in Pennington County—notably the canyons of Box Elder and Rapid creeks. The principal streams draining the area of the county are the Box Elder, Rapid, and Spring creeks. The Box Elder enters the county near the center of the north boundary line, crossing the northeast portion, rarely, however, carrying any surface water beyond the foot-hills.

Rapid creek, the longest stream having its source in the Hills, gathers its headwaters near the boundary line of Dakota and Wyoming, and traverses the entire length of the county in a southeasterly direction to the Cheyenne river, to which it contributes a considerable volume of water throughout the year. Rapid creek is in its entirety a Pennington County stream, running its whole length of 100 miles within the limits of the county.

Spring creek, in the southwestern part of the county, runs for the most of its course parallel with Rapid creek, then passes into Custer County at the southeast corner of Township 2, Range 9 east, its entire course being about eighty miles. It is a copious stream carrying a handsome volume of water beyond the foot-hills.

The upper waters of Battle creek are also in Pennington County. It rises on the northeast slope of the Harney range and after running ten miles through the roughest portion of the county, it passes into Custer County, and discharges its waters during wet seasons into the Cheyenne river, but like Box Elder and Spring creeks its waters disappear in dry seasons when near the foot-hills.

The valley of the Cheyenne river along the eastern border of the county is for the most part narrow with high precipitous bluffs, and includes a portion of the famous Bad Lands of South Dakota.

Pennington County, although the smallest of the three original counties in superficial area, is by no means the least important in point of varied resources. It has been conclusively demonstrated, that in the "mineral belt," within the limits of the county, there exist extensive ledges of rich mineral bearing rock, and, while operations in quartz mining have as yet been limited, there are being developed to-day some of the richest mines of free milling gold ore yet found in the Black Hills, and the county may be ranked as an easy second in the actual gold production of the Hills. While there have been failures in mining operations in the county, there are doubtless millions of gold locked in the natural vaults of its mountains, awaiting capital and judicious management to bring it to the surface.

COUNTY ORGANIZATION

By a provision of the act of the territorial legislature defining the boundaries of Pennington County, the Governor appointed three commissioners to organize county government and locate to county seat. The appointees were: R. H. Vosburg, M. M. Fuller, and Edwin Loveland, the latter not arriving in time to qualify, the office was declared vacant, and Samuel H. Coats was appointed to fill the vacancy.

The whole roster of the first officers of the county were: Commissioners: R. H. Vosburg, M. M. Fuller, and Samuel H. Coats; Probate Judge, E. C. Peters; Register of Deeds, J. R. Hanson; Sheriff, Frank P. Moulton; Clerk of Courts, Leonard W. Bell; Treasurer, ——; District Attorney, F. J. Washabaugh; Superintendent of Public Instruction, John R. Brennan; Surveyor, S. H. Coats.

Strangely enough, important as the office is, there was no Treasurer appointed by the Governor; at least the records make no mention of one—

A DISTANT VIEW OF HARNEY'S PEAK FROM A POINT ON THE BURLINGTON RAILWAY

only stating that on May 9th, 1877, at Sheridan, E. C. Peters resigned as Probate Judge, and on same day was appointed Treasurer, a vacancy existing.

The first meeting of the Board of County Commissioners was held at Rapid City, April 19th, 1877, the second on April 20th, on which date the county seat was located at Sheridan.

The first meeting at Sheridan was held May 7th, 1877, at which session the county was named Pennington, in honor of John L. Pennington, then Governor of the Territory of Dakota.

At the election in November, Rapid City was made the permanent county seat by popular vote, and the first meeting of the Board of Commissioners at the permanent capital was held November 21st, 1877. Large sums were expended by the county in public improvements, such as surveying and improving roads, building bridges, etc., the principal roads laid out being Rapid City to the Cheyenne river, Custer and Rochford, and from the latter place to Hill City *via* Castleton.

In five years from the time of organization, the county had an assessed valuation of $570,000, a total indebtedness of $42,450, and a population of 4,000. In 1897 it had an assessed valuation of $763,000, a total indebtedness of $208,858 and a population of 9,000 approximately.

In 1881 the county built its first courthouse—a fine two and a half story brick structure, at a cost of $12,000, for the payment of which county bonds were issued to run ten years at seven per cent interest, which bonds were fully redeemed on maturity. There were subsequently other quite heavy expenditures in the equipment of the jail, the planting of trees and the improvement of the courthouse square.

Pennington County's first courthouse has an unfortunate, as well as a somewhat singular history. On the night of April 25th, 1897, despite the heroic efforts of the fire department, the handsome brick structure was burned from dome nearly to foundation, only the lower portions of the outer walls remaining. Only by encountering great risk, did the county officials, with the efficient aid of other citizens, succeed in rescuing the valuable records from the flames. The building was covered by an insurance of $10,000.

In the adjustment of damages, the insurance company in lieu of paying the amount of insurance in money, assumed the responsibility of restoring the building to its former condition, and entered into contract for that purpose with Thos. Sweeney, Hugh McMahon, and Mike Whealen, who rapidly pushed forward the work of rebuilding. As if by the irony of fate, on the night of November 10th, when the building was on the eve of completion, it again took fire in some mysterious manner and was consumed to the foundation as before. With admirable pluck and determination, the contractors cleared away the burning debris, and without loss of time began the work of rebuilding though on a somewhat different, but improved plan, the half-story being left off by the consent of the commissioners and an additional ground room added. On the 15th day of May, 1898, the structure was completed and ready for occupancy, and any one visiting the capital of Pennington County to-day will find, delightfully embowered among trees, a handsome two-story brick courthouse, surmounted by a dome, and complete in every detail of its appointments, in the rear of which is a substantial, well-equipped two-story brick jail building in the same inclosure.

THE COUNTY SEAT

Rapid City, the county seat, has more than fulfilled the hopeful predictions of its founders, of whom it may be said that they "builded better than they knew." Its numerous beautiful homes, environed by well-kept lawns and shaded avenues; its many commodious and some even elegant church edifices, and its well-equipped educational institutions; its fine two and three story brick business blocks, and broad well-paved streets; its splendid water service and electric lighting of to-day certainly more than realizes the wildest dreams of the few men who bravely defended their rude log cabin homes from the warlike Sioux in 1876.

While the growth of Rapid City has not been, perhaps, as rapid as the current of the beautiful stream upon which it is situated, and from which it took its name, it has been steady and sure. From the time it was made the permanent county seat in November, 1877, dates its substantial growth. Business about that time began to move from Rapid to Main street where a number of quite pretentious frame buildings were erected during the years 1877-8, among which was Lewis Hall, a two-storied building put up by Wm. Lewis, now deceased, and the old landmark still stands in a good state of preservation—a monument to the enterprise of one of Rapid City's first permanent settlers.

SCHOOLS

The first school in Rapid City was opened and taught by Miss Vena LeGro, afterwards Mrs. Wm. Steele, whose husband was one of the founders of Rapid City.

The first postmaster of the regular postal service in Rapid City was J. R. Brennan, who was also the first Superintendent of Schools of Pennington County.

School District No. 1 of Pennington County was organized in January, 1878, after which schools were taught in rented buildings until 1881, when

RAPID CITY IN 1878

the first public school building of the county was erected in Rapid City. This soon proving to be inadequate to accommodate the children of the growing community, it was decided, at an election held in August of that year, that the district issue bonds for the purpose of raising money to build a more commodious house. Accordingly bonds were issued and in 1882 the present two and one-half storied brick structure was erected at a cost of $12,000. In the plat of the town a large number of lots were reserved to provide a fund which proved ample for current school expenditures at that time.

The old frame school-house stands to-day on Kansas City street between 5th and 6th streets, whither it was removed from its original location, and is now used for diverse purposes, chiefly as a carpenter's shop; and just across the way, on the opposite side of the street, is another old building, badly warped out of all its original symmetry, and leaning reverently towards the rising sun, bearing on its weather-beaten facade the legend, "Felix Poznansky, Dry Goods, Boots & Shoes, &c.," where it has stood bravely defying the elements for lo, these many years. This building, which was removed from the business thoroughfare of the city to its present locality, was one of the earliest and most flourishing dry-goods houses in Rapid City, established and owned by the gentleman whose honored name appears on the legend. Ah, what tales these old landmarks tell of the struggles and aspirations of our early settlers!

The first religious organization in Rapid City was a Union Aid Society, organized in August, 1878 (perhaps a few months earlier) by Rev. J. W. Pickett, who had been employed by the Home Missionary Society in organizing the Rocky Mountain District, in which was included the Black Hills. This society was first composed of members of diverse creeds and religious proclivities, perhaps fifteen in number, the major part of whom subsequently came into communion with the Congregational Church, which society has now a commodious house of worship, and is in point of numbers and financial standing the most flourishing in the city.

The first Methodist Episcopal services were held in March, 1878, by Rev. H. H. Jones; no organization, however, was effected at that time.

In December, 1880, Rev. Jas. Williams and Rev. Ira Wakefield resumed the work begun by Rev. Jones, and in March, 1881, a church was organized and Mrs. C. D. Crandall appointed a class-leader.

A Catholic church was organized in 1881, and soon after their present church building was erected.

The Episcopal church society was formed in the summer of 1886, and their present church edifice completed in 1888, which was followed successively by the Presbyterian, Lutheran, and Baptist churches.

The press is represented in Rapid City by three newspapers, the *Journal,* the *Republican,* and the Black Hills *Union.*

The Black Hills *Journal* appeared on the newspaper stage, and made its initial bow to the Rapid City public, on January 5th, 1878, and has ever since continued to make its weekly appearance with unfailing regularity. In 1886 a daily issue of the paper appeared under the title of the Rapid City *Daily Journal,* since which time both a daily and weekly have been published, the news of the latter being condensed from the columns of the former, for country circulation.

How ably the *Journal* has enacted its difficult role is better attested by its extensive patronage and long continuance, than can be expressed by mere words. For twenty years it has faithfully represented the best interests of the Gate City, ever striving to mould for their betterment the sentiment of its people. The enterprise was established by Joseph B. Gossage, its present proprietor, and George Darrow. At the time, or soon after its establishment, the paper came under the able editorial management of Richard B. Hughes, who is entitled to the distinction of being the first newspaper reporter in the Black Hills, having served in that capacity for the Black Hills, *Weekly Pioneer* in 1876 (see Chapter of First Events). The paper is at present, and has been for a number of years, conducted solely by Mr. and Mrs. Gossage, the latter of whom is a whole voluminous newspaper in herself. The *Journal* has the distinction of being the first newspaper published in Rapid City, and of having had the first contract for the printing of Pennington County.

RICHARD B. HUGHES
Reporter for the Black Hills Weekly Pioneer in 1876 and one of its compositors

The Rapid City *Republican* was established by a corporation of Rapid City capitalists organized by Messrs. Fowler, Halley, Simmons, Henry, Coad, and others, in 1884, since which time the paper has had a somewhat checkered career. The corporation purchased the printing outfit of a "Democratic" paper published by James Boyd, under the title of the *Index*. The first on the roster of the editors of the *Republican* was I. R. Crow—present proprietor of the Bald Mountain *News*—the second was W. H. Mitchell, who was followed in regular sequence by Byers, Simmons, Scott, Bishop, McManus, Williams, and Wallace, all well remembered in Rapid City. The present editors are Messrs. Mills & Wise, former publishers of the Hermosa *Pilot*. The building and plant is still owned by the Republican Publishing Co., the press outfit being leased to the present proprietors. The *Republican* was first issued as a weekly publication, changing to a daily in 1885, and again to a weekly in 1892, but whether daily or weekly, it has always, politically, been published in the interest of the Republican party.

The Black Hills *Union* is an outgrowth of the Black Hills *Weekly Democrat*, published in Rapid City, by G. W. Barrows, in 1887-8. The paper and outfit then passed into the hands of Shelby D. Reed & Co., by which company it was conducted for several years. In 1896 it was published as a political campaign paper, under its present title, by Gird & McManus, the latter severing his connection with the concern at the close of the campaign, leaving it in the hands of its present proprietor, A. W. Gird. The Black Hills *Union* is a spicy little sheet published in advocacy of equal rights and free silver, and what Art. doesn't know about free silver and 16 to 1 is not really worth knowing.

The first marriage in Rapid City was that of Wm. F. Steele and Miss Vena LeGro, in November, 1877. The important ceremony was performed by Judge Granville G. Bennett, the first judge of the first Black Hills District Court.

The first child born in Rapid City was born to Mr. and Mrs. Osceola Chase in the summer of 1877.

LIBRARY ASSOCIATION

An example of the enterprise and progression by which the citizens were actuated, is furnished by the organization, at an early date, of an association having for its object the intellectual and social welfare of its people. The first steps in that direction were taken on the evening of September 22, 1880, by a few socially inclined spirits, who had met to discuss some plan of amusement for winter nights, and the outcome was the organization of the Rapid City Library Association. J. B. Gossage, W. H. Mitchell, and W. F. Manning were appointed a committee to draught a constitution and by-laws, and at a subsequent meeting the organization was perfected. A room was first leased for temporary use and the success of the venture proved so satisfactory that in the spring of 1881, the present Library Hall was designed and built. Land at the northwest corner of Kansas City and Sixth streets was donated by John R. Brennan for a site, and during the summer of 1881 the present structure was completed. The building was designed for a reading-room, library, and theatricals.

The initiation fee to the association was originally placed at $9.00, which entitled the member to the use of the books of the library until 1890, without further dues.

The library contains 500 volumes of biography, poetry, science, and fiction.

Since its building Library Hall has served the people of Rapid City well; not only for the purposes originally contemplated, but for all sorts of functions, political, educational, and social; for the lecture, the concert, and dance. For eighteen years her beauty and her chivalry have gathered there and joined in the "giddy mazes" to enchanting strains. Periodically, for eighteen years the leaders of the opposing political factions have thundered out their respective partisan creeds from its boards; whence the changes have again and again been rung on the whole political gamut, of free trade, protection, free silver, the single gold standard, and other political issues—each uttering prophetic warnings against the dangerous dogmas of their opponents, as tending to undermine and utterly overthrow our free institutions. Yet, strange as it may seem, our "Republic still lives," and old Library Hall stands.

SECRET ORDERS

The preliminary organization of Rapid City Lodge A. F. and A. M. was effected May 16th, 1881, and the first regular communication of the order was held at Masonic Hall, September 2nd, 1882. The organization was soon after perfected, and the lodge is now in a flourishing condition, with handsomely furnished rooms for the meetings of the order. There are now also, large lodges of the I. O. O. F., Knights of Pythias, A. O. U. W., The Eastern Star, Daughters of Rebecca, and perhaps other lodges, with well-fitted commodious rooms.

MANUFACTURING

The first flouring mill in Rapid City was built in 1883 by Lampert & Co., in the gap of the Hills, about a half mile west of the business portion of the city. For several years or until 1890 it was the only plant for the manufacture of flour in the city, when it was supplemented by the plant of the Rapid River Milling Co.

The Rapid River Milling Co. completed its plant on February 1st, 1890, and commenced operations under the directorship of R. C. Lake, D. H. Clark, G. Schnasse, Jas. Halley, Jas. W. Fowler, W. A. Wager and John J. McNamara. The present officers of the company are G. G. Schnasse, President; Jas. W. Fowler, Vice-President; Jas. Halley, Treasurer; John J. McNamara, Secretary and General Manager.

The plant is operated by water power, uses a full roller process, and has a capacity of 150 pounds of flour per day. The plant has established a wide reputation for the manufacture of Superior flour.

CHLORINATION WORKS

The Rapid City Chlorination plant was established in 1890 by the Black Hills Milling & Smelting Co. at an original cost of $125,000. The works were put in operation on ore taken from the Welcome mine in the vicinity of Deadwood, under the management of Robt. Thorburn, but for some reason the enterprise proved a losing venture, as, after running in a kind of intermittent way for a period of perhaps a year, the works closed down, and the property went into the hands of the First National Bank of Rapid City. Whether the ore was not adapted to the process, or the process suited to that particular ore, or for some other reason, is not clear.

After lying idle for five years the plant was purchased by a Colorado company, of which Col. M. H. Day, of Rapid City, is president—under whose management the old works have undergone complete repairs, and other improved machinery added to make the process a success. The plan of the new management contemplates the erection of a smelter to be run in connection with the chlorination works. The smelter is to be of 240 tons capacity, and built of steel, the contract for the construction of which has been awarded to the Colorado Iron Works of Denver, Colorado. The plant, when completed, will operate, in part, on ore taken from the Gilt Edge mine, in Two-Bit gulch, owned by M. H. Day & Son, and in part on custom ore. It is estimated that there are 100,000 tons of low grade ore in sight in the Gilt Edge mine that will average from $16 to $25 per ton. This, however, is said to be the lowest grade of ore in the mine. The success of the enterprise promises a long pay-roll and better times for Rapid City.

THE RAPID CITY WATER SYSTEM

The first movement towards supplying Rapid City with water was made in 1883 or 4 by an organization known as the Rapid City Water Co., of which C. W. Robbins was president, M. Cameron, treasurer, and Sam'l Scott, secretary. The design was to bring the water from what is known as Cleghorn Springs, five miles west of the city, the company having negotiated for their purchase from the owner. An effort was made to secure a franchise from the city without success,—at least there was no binding action taken, the council wisely deciding that the better plan would be for the city to own the system. At a meeting of the council on March 5th, 1895, the city engineer, M. Wiltsie, reported a plan for a system at an estimated cost of $45,000. The council decided to submit the question of issuing bonds and constructing the system to the voters of the municipality. Meetings were held at Library Hall to discuss the question, and present to the people the advantages of the system. At the first meeting on March 20, 1885, Messrs. Simmons, Poznanska, Haft, Hayward, Sweeney, and Clark were appointed a committee to report a plan and estimate cost. At a meeting on March 24 the committee reported, recommending the reservoir system, stating that $45,000 was not an overestimate of cost of such a system, which report was approved. The special election held on the 28th resulted in 200 in favor to three in opposition to the

RAPID CITY CHLORINATION PLANT AND SCHOOL OF MINES

issuing of bonds. At the municipal election, which occurred soon after, the enterprise received the further approval of the voters by the election of James Halley, who had been active in favor of the scheme, to the mayoralty, and Felix Poznansky, L. L. Davis, and F. H. Mohr, to the council, all of whom were in hearty approval of the enterprise.

In July 25th, 1885, the city entered into contract with the Northwestern Water and Gas Supply Company of Minneapolis to put in a system in accordance with the plan, including the construction of the city limits. This reservoir was located on the eastern slope, near the summit of Hangman's

BEECHER'S ROCKS, NEAR CUSTER

Hill, at an elevation of 188 feet above the city, and had a capacity of 375,986 gallons.

By the terms of the contract, which was carefully drawn by Jas. W. Fowler, the system was to be finished for fire purposes by January 5th, 1886, and for all purposes by July 1st of that year, but, owing to delay in the arrival of material, and the failure of subcontractors to complete their work, there was default in both specifications. Not until sixty days after the signing of the contract did the first material arrive on the ground. Lewis Harper, the superintendent of construction, arrived on September 4th, and ground was broken on September 13th, 1885. That was before the advent of railroads to the Hills, and all the heavy supplies for the system had to be transported by wagon across the country from Pierre to Rapid City, a distance of 150 miles.

To provide funds for the construction of the work, the city first issued bonds to the amount of $45,000, payable in twenty years at seven per cent interest. On October 2d, 1885, additional bonds were issued in the sum of $6,000, making the issue to that time $51,000. On December 31st, 1885, the city purchased for $1,000, from Cassius M. Leedy, the springs known as the Leedy or Limestone Springs, the source of the water supply, three miles west of Rapid City.

Seven years later the city decided to make extensive improvements on the system, and on July 27th, 1892, a contract was let for the building of a large reservoir at Limestone Springs, and a conduit line thence to the city, the cost of which was $30,000, paid in city general fund warrants, making the total cost of the system $81,000.

The natural flow from the springs is 540,000 gallons per day. The pressure in the city mains is seventy-five pounds to the square inch, and there are now over ten miles of water mains in the system. No town in the Black Hills can boast of a more complete water system than Rapid City. Hundreds of thousands of gallons of pure, wholesome water, free from all suspicion of disease germs, are daily carried from the inexhaustible fountain head and distributed through a perfect system of main and service pipes to every house and nearly every business place in the city.

RAPID CITY PUBLIC SCHOOLS

Rapid City has good reason to feel proud of her public schools, which in point of educational facilities and general excellence are second to none in the State. From a humble beginning the system has expanded into large and encouraging proportions, with four well-equipped school buildings, filled with an aggregate of from 450 to 500 pupils each year, presided over by a corps of capable progressive instructors. Besides the commodious three-storied brick structure before referred to the city has three comfortable, well-furnished ward school buildings of frame, two of which employ two teachers each, making a total corps of thirteen instructors, including superintendent. The course of study embraces an eight-year course before entering the high school and a four-years' high school course. The high school prepares its graduates for the State University and State normal schools and gives thorough instruction in all the studies included in the courses of the best high schools of the State. The high school was established in 1885 and graduated its first class in the spring of 1886.

The high school building is provided with a library containing 250 volumes of well selected books and more are being added each year. The school population of the city by the census of 1898 was 564, and school expenditures for the term ending June, 1898, was $9,906.62.

SCHOOL OF MINES

With the development of the mineral resources of the Black Hills, facilities for acquiring a technical knowledge of their rock formation, the analyses of their various kinds of ore deposits, mining, etc., became a practical necessity. To supply this demand, and for the purpose of encouraging the production of the precious metals in the Black Hills, the Legislature of 1885, with a wholesome regard for the "eternal fitness of things," passed an act locating the School of Mines of the Territory of Dakota at Rapid City—a central point, equally accessible to the principal mineral-bearing portions of the Hills. This act, however, was coupled with the proviso that, before any steps be taken towards the construction of the buildings, a good and sufficient deed, in fee-simple, be made by Rapid City to the Territory of Dakota, for a tract of land not less than five acres in extent, within, or immediately adjacent to the city limits.

For the purpose of providing funds for the construction of the main building of the School of Mines, the territorial treasurer was authorized to issue $10,000 of territorial bonds, running for a period of twenty years, and payable at the option of the Territory, after a term of ten years, bearing interest at the rate of six per cent annum,—coupous payable semi-annually at the Chemical Bank, New York.

By an act of the Legislature of 1887, additional bonds were authorized by the Territory to the amount of $23,000, bearing interest at five per cent per annum, payable semi-annually as in the first issue. The fund provided by this last issue was appropriated as follows:—

For constructing a metallurgical laboratory on the grounds of the School of Mines and furnishing the same, $10,000; for machinery for laboratory,

$10,000; for engineering instruments, $1,000; for completing chemcial laboratory, $2,000; making a total aggregate of $33,000 of territorial bonds issued on account of the Dakota School of Mines.

Upon the division of the Territory, in 1889, all of these bonds, with some of the coupons detached, came as a legacy to South Dakota, together with nearly $700,000 other territorial bonds issued on account of public institutions. The School of Mines is maintained by the State. Appropriations—more or less liberal, according to the effect of the influence brought to bear upon our legislators—are made for the maintenance of the institution at each biennial session of the Legislature.

The experimental work done by the school in the direction of determining the character and value of the ores of the Hills has proved invaluable to their mining interests, and in the departments of mineralogy and metallurgy, few institutions of the kind anywhere are better equipped for the work.

The school is located about one mile east of the business portion of the city, at the foot of a range of hills forming a semi-circle around the town, and overlooking the valley of Rapid creek.

The first building erected is a three-story brick structure, on the first floor of which is the chemical department, completely equipped and perfectly arranged for chemical laboratory work, and capable of accommodating about thirty students at one time, each provided with all the necessary facilities for thorough chemical tests. The second floor consists of two lecture rooms and dean's office, in which is kept the library of the institution. The third floor is devoted exclusively to the mineralogical and paleontological cabinets, in which there are extensive and valuable collections.

The second building, 200 feet to the eastward, contains the assay and metallurgical laboratories. This building, the front portion of which is two stories in height, is also built of brick. On the first floor of this portion are the assay rooms for the students, provided with a number of crucible furnaces built of fire-brick and set in the wall. The rear portion of the building, which is only one story high, contains a complete 3-stamp gold mill, a 5-stamp silver mill, concentrating machinery, and other approved appliances for the treatment of ores. In short, every facility is afforded the student for acquiring a thorough practical knowledge of the art of separating and refining the various kinds of metals.

INDIAN SCHOOL

A recent addition to the educational institutions of Rapid City is the government Indian school. This establishment of this institution at Rapid City and the appropriations therefor were secured mainly through the efforts of

Senator Pettigrew and Representative Gamble of South Dakota. At the last session of the Fifty-first Congress the bill was passed, appropriating the sum of $25,000 for the purchase of a tract of agricultural land, and the construction of suitable buildings for the education, industrial and otherwise, of Uncle Sam's youthful wards in South Dakota. A fine farm of 160 acres situated in the valley of Rapid creek, about one mile west of Rapid City, was purchased of Geo. P. Bennett, at a cost of $2,000, and a site for the buildings selected on an elevated plateau adjacent thereto.

An additional appropriation of $18,000 was afterwards made for the cost of heating, sewerage, industrial shops, laundry, etc. The main building, which is now completed, is a commodious, two-story brick structure, suitably arranged for the purpose for which it is designed. The other buildings appertaining to the institution are nearing completion, and will soon be equipped for the opening of the school.

RAPID CITY INCORPORATED

On October 11th, 1882, the town of Rapid City was incorporated as a village and divided into four wards with John R. Brennan as President of the Board of Trustees, which consisted of one member from each of the four wards.

The village was incorporated as a city under a special charter granted by the Legislature in February, 1883, with Fred E. Stearns as the city's first Mayor and one member of the City Council from each ward.

It was again incorporated under the general laws on November 16th, 1888, with David H. Clark as Mayor of last incorporation, the Council consisting of two Aldermen from each ward.

Several additions have from time to time been attached to the original plat, and incorporated into the city until now it covers an area of two miles square, and, basing the estimate upon the school census of 1898, contains a population of 2,000.

THE FIRST RAILROAD

Rapid City enjoys the distinction of being the first city in the Black Hills to be connected by railway with the outside world. On the 4th day of July, 1886, the first steam locomotive to invade the solitude of the Hills,— heralding its approach by the shrill tooting of its whistle, arrived at Rapid City with five passenger cars, gaily decorated with flags attached, amid the loud acclamations of the throng that had gathered at the station to welcome its advent. It is needless to say that the event was celebrated by the people in a manner commensurate with its importance. On the strength of the prevalent belief that it might be the terminus of the F. E. & M. V. Railway line Rapid City had the nearest approach to a veritable boom that that sober city ever experienced. For the month that it remained the terminus all freight for other points in the Hills was unloaded from the cars and shipped by wagon to its destination,—making times exceedingly lively; so when the grading began along the line northward, the bubble began to collapse, much to the disgust of the average Rapid City citizen.

During the inflation of the bubble several important railroad projects were inaugurated, which promised to make Rapid City a great railroad center. A survey for a narrow-gauge line to connect with the mineral and lumber regions of the Hills was made, and the projector of the scheme, Mr. E. B. Chapman, agreed, in consideration of a liberal bonus by the people, to have thirty miles of line completed and in operation by the beginning of the year 1888.

Another survey for a narrow-gauge railroad was made from Rapid City to the tin districts of Harney Peak and Hill City, to extend into Wyoming. This was a project of the Harney Peak Tin Mining Co.

Another survey was made from Chamberlain to Rapid City by the Chicago, Milwaukee & St. Paul Railway Co. with the purpose of constructing a road soon after the opening of the Sioux reservation. While none of these projects have yet been carried out, it is believed that, owing to its inviting location at the natural gateway to the Hills, and by virtue of the enterprise and liberality of its citizens, Rapid City will, in the not distant future, become the focus of several converging and diverging lines of railway.

In the summer of 1886 the Rapid City Street Railway Co. was formed, which constructed a street line of about one mile in length along the center of Main street from West boulevard to the Fremont, Elkhorn & Missouri Valley Railway station, which line was afterwards extended to the School of Mines to accommodate the students and faculty of that institution. The company was incorporated and stocked in the sum of $10,000, and the cost of the line is estimated at about $7,000. The enterprise is yet a living, moving reality, operated under the management of Howard Worth, of Rapid City.

THE ELECTRIC SYSTEM OF RAPID CITY

The Rapid City Electric and Gas Light Company was organized in September, 1886, by O. L. Cooper, of Rapid City, and at once incorporated with a capital of $20,000. The first officers of the company were: G. S. Congdon, President; O. L. Cooper, Secretary; and H. S. Hall, Treasurer. The plant, which is operated by water power, had an original capacity of only forty-seven lights of 1,200 candle power, since, however, the capacity of the

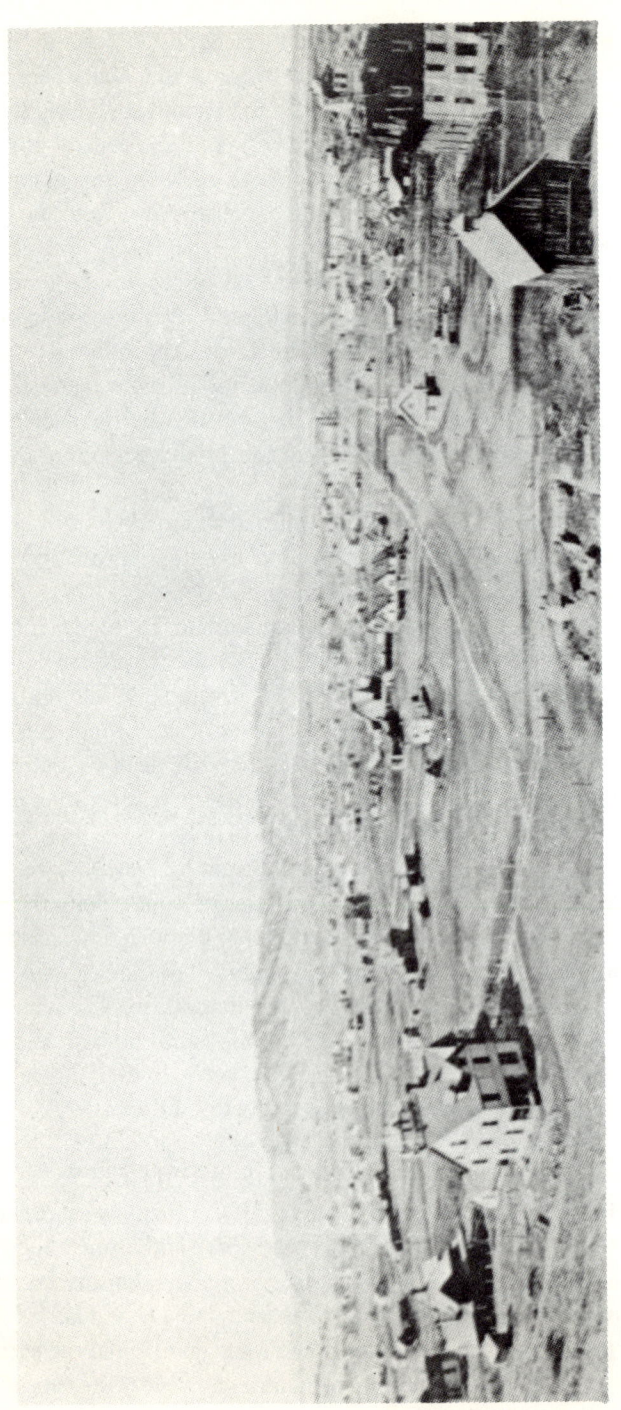

RAPID CITY, S. D., LOOKING NORTH, IN 1899

dynamo has been greatly enlarged. For the first five years only the arc light system was used, to which, in 1892, the incandescent light was added. While the plant is owned by the same corporation, none of the original incorporators are now connected with it.

THE RAPID CITY FIRE DEPARTMENT

The present efficient Fire Department of Rapid City was organized in 1887, at which time it was composed of the following companies with their respective officers:—

Gate City Hose Company, No. 1; D. G. Ferguson, Foreman; Mel. Miller, First Assistant; Frank McMahon, Second Assistant; Jack Taylor, Secretary; W. L. Carr, Treasurer.

Rapid City Hook and Ladder, No. 1: Chas. N. Spencer, Foreman; Cassius Price, First Assistant; J. J. Sharp, Second Assistant; J. J. Rockford, Secretary; Lem Fall, Treasurer.

Tom Sweeney Hose Company: A. L. Overpeck, Foreman; R. E. Grimshaw, First Assistant; A. H. Smith, Second Assistant; Jas. W. Post, Secretary; John S. Kelliher, Treasurer.

There was a partial organization of the first two companies mentioned in 1886, which was completed in 1887.

BANKING INSTITUTIONS

The business interests of Rapid City at present support two banking institutions, both strong, well managed organizations, having a fine prestige in financial circles throughout the country.

The oldest of these, and the pioneer banking institution of Rapid City, was first opened for the transaction of business on December 1st, 1879, by Lake, Halley & Patterson, with a capital of $10,000.00.

In 1881 Lake & Halley bought Mr. Patterson's interest in the concern, and the bank was then conducted under the name of Lake & Halley until September 1st, 1884, when the bank was merged into the First National Bank of Rapid City, with Richard C. Lake as President, and Jas. Halley as Cashier, with a capital stock of $50,000.00. The present officers of the bank are: Jas. Halley, President; Charlotte Gardner, Vice-President; H. H. Somers, Cashier. Its capital is $50,000.00; surplus $10,000.00; deposits, $300,000.00. The bank has paid in dividends to its stockholders $119,500.00. The First National Bank conducts all the departments of a legitimate banking business—including the negotiation of loans, the reception of deposits, the issuance of notes, drafts, and letters of credit, and has been a successful institution from the first.

The Pennington County Bank of Rapid City began business on the 22d day of April, 1888, under the laws of the State of South Dakota, with a paid-up capital of $50,000.00. The bank was established by Capt. Frank R. Davis of Rapid City; Stephen H. Mills of New York City; Jesse Carll of Northport, New York, and other associates of Mr. Davis. The first officers of the bank were: S. H. Mills, President; Edward Oakes, Vice-President; Frank R. Davis, Cashier; Geo. F. Schneider, Assistant Cashier. In 1892 Jas. M. Woods was elected vice-president to fill the vacancy caused by the death of Mr. Oakes. In 1893 Mr. Davis died, when Geo. F. Schneider was elected cashier. The present officers of the bank are: Stephen H. Mills, President; Jas. M. Woods, Vice-President; Geo. F. Schneider, Cashier; Paul S. Woods, Assistant Cashier. The Pennington County Bank is a State bank organized under the laws of the State of South Dakota; and enjoys the distinction of being the largest State bank in South Dakota. Its capital stock is $50,000.00; a surplus of $10,000.00; undivided profits, $5,076.00; average deposits, $225,000, and pays a semi-annual dividend of five per cent to its stockholders. The Pennington County Bank is the county depositary of Pennington County.

Rapid City sustains four hotels, between fifty and sixty business houses of various kinds, among which are a number of mammoth establishments, conducting several distinct lines of business, fourteen lawyers, six doctors, one dental surgeon, and several real estate and insurance offices.

Of the four hotels, the International, now kept by P. B. McCarty, is believed to be the oldest. Around this venerable hostelry clusters memories of the hustling, bustling days of early stage travel and road agents, when sleeping accommodations for the bruised and battered passengers was at a premium, and when the rumbling of the old tallyhos, as they dashed up to their respective headquarters on opposite corners, was a familiar sound. During those days the International was the headquarters of the Northwestern Stage & Transportation Line running between Deadwood and Pierre, while its rival on the opposite corner, first kept by John R. Brennan, furnished accommodations for travelers over the Deadwood & Sidney Express Line.

Hotel Harney, a fine three-storied brick structure, containing fifty rooms, with a capacity for entertaining seventy-five guests, was opened in 1878 and is still conducted by John R. Brennan,—mine host of the 12x14 log hotel of 1876.

Among the present firms that began business when the town was very young, and when goods and merchandise had to be brought in by mule and ox-teams, are the following: Perhaps the oldest is that of Grambery & Co., established by Schnasse & Grambery in the fall of 1877. The oldest dry goods firm is that of Morris & Co., established in Rapid City in the spring of 1878. Mr. Jacob Morris brought his stock of clothing and furnishing goods down from Deadwood in the early part of May, and opened business on Main street where he is located to-day. The longest established of the drug stores of Rapid City was opened by Chas. D. Matteson in 1878, and oldest hardware store by Thomas Sweeney.

It is cruelly related of Tom that he came over the trail alongside of an ox-train with his hat in his hand and arrived in Rapid City in 1877, without a dollar in his pocket and destitute of "grub," but being a business man and a born "rustler," he soon devised ways and means to put himself on a paying basis. He rented a small room, borrowed a razor, and opened a barber shop. His first customer was Fred Evans, who paid him the liberal sum of fifty cents for the shave. This half dollar was the capital stock which started him in business, and put him on the high road to wealth. It is believed, however, that this story is an exaggeration. Be that as it may, Thos. Sweeney is now conducting one of the largest business establishments in the Black Hills.

Of the present bar, Chauncey L. Wood has the distinction of being the first to establish himself in the practice of his profession in Rapid City, where he arrived in the spring of 1877, and soon after opened an office. In the spring of 1878 he became associated with his old-time friend and college chum, John W. Nowlin, whose interesting career will be referred to further on. For the past twenty years Chauncey L. Wood has been a conspicuous figure in the political history of the Black Hills, and a leader in the Democratic party of Dakota. He is a profound lawyer, a powerful and eloquent pleader, and his name stands high among the leading attorneys of the State. Because of his knowledge of constitutional law he was selected as one of the delegates to represent the Black Hills at the constitutional convention held at Sioux Falls on July 4th, 1889, to help frame a constitution for the new State of South Dakota, as provided for in the bill, admitting it to Statehood.

The history of Rapid City would scarcely be complete without a brief sketch of the Black Hills career of John W. Nowlin, who for a number of years was intimately identified with its municipal affairs, and whose name, a synonym for all that is admirable in manhood, is still honored by its people. Early in the spring of 1876, Judge Nowlin, then a young law graduate from the Iowa State University, left his native State (Iowa) to seek his fortune and fame amid the more generous possibilities of the boundless West. In the spring of 1877, the ambitious young adventurer, after having spent a year on the threshold at Yankton, purchased an outfit and established a freight line between Pierre and Deadwood, but during the summer of the same year sold

JUDGE JOHN W. NOWLIN

his line and opened an office for the practice of law in Crook City, then on the wane, where he remained but a short time.

In April, 1878, he entered into partnership with Chauncey L. Wood, which firm opened practice in Rapid City under the firm name of Nowlin & Wood. In the fall of 1878 he was elected Judge of Probate for Pennington County, and re-elected in 1880, and it was during his imcumbency as Probate Judge that he did such valuable service for Rapid City. Against strong opposition he secured the patent for the town-site in 1881, and also drew the first charter under which it was incorporated as a city in 1883. In the fall of 1884, he was elected to the Territorial Legislature, at which session he drew, and was largely instrumental in securing the passage of the act, establishing the school of Mines at Rapid City. In 1885 he was appointed Judge of the first Circuit Court, by the executive of the provisional State government formed during that year.

About this time his health began to fail, when he suspended practice, and journeyed away off to the sunny slopes of California, visiting Arizona and New Mexico, with the vain hope of arresting the malady that was sapping his existence. In 1889, when South Dakota was admitted to Statehood, he was elected to the bench of the Seventh Judicial District of the Circuit Court, which position he resigned in November, 1892, and in March, 1893, when in the prime of life, as told by years, he died.

CHAPTER XXX

HORSE-STEALING AROUND RAPID CITY IN 1877

Perhaps none of the early settlements were more persistently harassed by horse-thieves in 1877 than Rapid City, for which reason its citizens were disposed to give them short shrift for their moral and mental obliquity, so one dark night in the month of June, 1877, three suspected men who had been caught were suspended from the limb of a pine tree standing on what has since been known as "Hangman's Hill," a half mile west of the town. This grewsome act of speedy retribution recalls a story related by one of the early settlers, of how a small party of the citizens of Rapid City, for about an hour, dodged bullets from 45-caliber rifles fired by four horse-thieves and all-around desperadoes one day in 1877, viz: Dunc. Blackburn, "Billy the Kid," "Laughing Sam" and one other, thus: The four outlaws had been committing frequent depredations in and around Rapid City, so hearing that they were seen a few miles from town, John Brennan organized a posse to ride out in pursuit and capture them if possible. The outlaws were found near the outskirts of the town when the exciting chase began. The road agents were mounted on swift-going steeds (stolen, doubtless), and, consequently, with the exception of John Brennan, Wm. Steele, and a stock tender, left the pursuing party far in the rear. Brennan was the only one of the three armed with a rifle, the others having only six-shooters. However, that made no difference, they followed up the chase, and got within shooting distance just as the outlaws were crossing the Box Elder, when they opened fire on them, receiving no reply. Crossing Box Elder the pursuit was continued and the last seen of the outlaws they were disappearing over a little elevation about 880 yards distant on Elk creek. Putting spurs to their horses they hurried on to overtake them, and when within seventy-five yards of the summit of the hill they were greeted with a hail of bullets, one of which penetrated the breast of Steele's horse; whiz, whiz, went the leaden missiles past the heads of the pursuers; thick and fast they came. "Great, Scott! but they are big ones; hear them sing," exclaimed Brennan. The party dismounted and returned the fire, but the outlaws, being under cover of the hill, had them at a disadvantage, until Brennan, at a great personal risk, made a detour to the right and succeeded in outflanking them and with a few well-directed shots from his rifle, soon put the desperadoes to flight. It was afterwards learned that two of them were slightly wounded.

MINING STAMPEDE IN RAPID CITY

Strange and incredible as it may seem to those who know them, Chauncey Wood, with all his profundity and legal acumen, and Thomas Sweeney, with all his business shrewdness, were once upon a time led away on one of the most exciting stampedes known in the history of the Black Hills. Of stampedes in general, and this one in particular, Doc. Peirce, himself one of the victims, gives the following amusing account. Dr. says: "Stampedes create more excitement in a mining camp than any other cause, and in ninety-nine cases out of 100 they are as delusive as a man's word on election day. I made just two of these nocturnal excursions, on foot, and ran most of the time to keep up with the horsemen, falling over logs and rocks, and snagging myself on dead limbs.

"When I returned from the second one, the 'Box Elder' stampede, I took an inventory of myself and discovered that I did not have clothes enough on to flag a hand-car. My epidermis needed repairing badly, and as my stomach was not built on the same liberal plan as the one Dr. Tanner was using, so I subsided and went out in the woods in the daytime and ate berries, and would return to town at night to slumber. I found this mode of living gave me the necessary exercise for health, and as even dried-apple pies at that time sold for $1 each, and as I was never known to have a dollar, time proved that my system was the cheapest."

The most cruel stampede ever concocted in the Hills was the one to the Bear Paw mountains, gotten up, it was claimed, by "Red" Clark and others, for the purpose of unloading some old-worn-out saddle and pack-ponies. If that be true their scheme proved a glittering success, but not so with the poor boys who made that trip, for they suffered untold misery, and more than one never lived to get back to Deadwood.

But the most comical thing in the way of a stampede happened at Rapid City, in 1889. The lawyers there, in those dull times, were suffering from ennui, so they got up a stampede just for excitement. A committee was appointed to get some gold dust and go out on the Rockerville road and plant it. The committee was ignorant of formations, and as they did not like to exert themselves in walking out very far, they stopped in the "red hills" back of town and salted a gypsum bed. Old Bart Henderson, the veteran prospector of the Rocky Mountains, came along where they were working, and, taking in the situation, requested to be let in on the deal. The boys, knowing that Bart knew all about the chloride of sodium act, took him in the conspiracy, thereby greatly disturbing the peace and dignity of the other peaceable citizens of Rapid City.

After performing their nefarious work the boys separated and meandered back to town, and commenced to agitate the subject of mining. Some thought the only way to save Rapid City was for the citizens to employ competent prospectors and send them out with plenty of grub and mining utensils, and see if they could not find another Rockerville district closer to town, and after considerable talk this plan was finally adopted.

Committees were appointed to raise funds to pay expenses, men were chosen to go prospecting, and, of course, one of the boys insisted on going who knew where the plant was. In a short time he came back all out of breath, with a panful of decomposed gypsum, and appearing very excited. "I think I have struck it right up there in that hill back of town; here is some of the dirt, let us go to the creek and wash it out." Everybody followed; even Tom Sweeney took a lay-off and went along. They panned out the dirt, and when the gold dust, which was very fine, commenced to show up in the pan, everybody went wild with excitement. Sweeney ran around with his hat in his hand, exclaiming, "Isn't she a bird, boys; I tell you, old Rapid is a hummer; she is all right!" And during the excitement, Bart Henderson, who always kept on hand a few choice nuggets for specimens, asked permission to pan a while, and as he was the chief in that line, the boys readily assented, and that was where they let the bars down, for Bart had a nugget in hand about the size of a hickory nut, and while he was splashing the water around in the pan, he gently let the nugget slide in with the other gold. It was not long before old man Chase discovered the big chunk, and such a yell as went up from that crowd! Henderson claimed the nugget, as he had panned it out. The boys who had put up the job drew off to one side and spoke low. "Boys," whispered Chauncey Wood, "we never put in that big chunk, she is there as true as gospel, let us get up there quick before the mob goes, and stake our claims." "I'll go you," says Sweeney; and they started on the run, and such a scramble was never seen before or since in the Black Hills. Men, women, and children went daft. Chauncey was not in condition to run over a quarter of a mile, but Sweeney urged him on by saying: "It is the chance of a lifetime, old son, hurry up."

When they arrived at the place where the plant was, Chauncey got a stake and commenced writing a mining notice. Sweeney had never been in the mines, so he was not acquainted with the form used, but stood looking on, and when he read the words: "I claim 300 feet up this hill for mining purposes," yelled out, "For God's sake don't take it all." Chauncey arose very dignified and stroking the proper attitude for effect said, "Tom, if you say another word, I will take 160 acres." "Fire away, old son," replied Sweeney. "Take all you want but leave me a slice of this melon." By this time the crowd had arrived, and they soon staked the whole country. A wag in the party, who did not find anything else to stake, blazed a large pine tree, and wrote the following notice upon it: "I hereby claim 300 feet up this tree for climbing purposes,—also claim all knots, limbs, woodpecker holes, etc., for working purposes, and all jumpers are hereby warned not to meddle with this claim in any manner, for if they do this tree will be used for a headstone." That last line settled it, for it is safe to say that at least a dozen of otherwise intelligent men stopped, read that notice and rode on, and don't know to this day that it was meaningless. Thus the salter was salted.

CHAPTER XXXI

HILL CITY

The story of the rise and decline of the many early booming camps of Pennington County, in which there is something almost pathetic, may be briefly told. Hill City, the first of these and the second oldest mining camp in the Black Hills, Custer antedating it by only a few months, was laid out by Thos. Harvey, John Miller, Hugh McCullough, and others, in February, 1876. Good prospects had been found in the gulches and bars along Spring creek during the summer and fall of 1875, when the miners were being harassed to the point of desperation by Uncle Sam's blue coats, and on the opening of placer operations in the spring of 1876, the camp suddenly grew into a booming town. About two score of substantial log cabins were hastily erected and numerous tents were sandwiched in between or scattered thickly over the site.

About the first of May, when Hill City's future seemed assured, glowing reports of the rich diggings in Deadwood gulch came floating down with the north wind, when the miners on Spring creek individually and in groups hastily packed their burros with blankets, mining implements, etc., or shouldered them according to circumstances, and made their way over the hills to the new golden Mecca, leaving Hill City by the middle of May as deserted as a graveyard—only one man and a dog remaining to tell the story of its desertion. This closes the first short chapter of its history.

Subsequently, some returned to their first love, others came, and considerable placer mining was done on Spring creek, Newton's Fork, and other branches of Spring creek, and a number of ranches were located in its broad fertile valley. During the few succeeding years much prospecting was done for quartz within a radius of five or six miles of Hill city, and a number of exceedingly rich gold ledges were discovered, and to a more or less extent developed, among which were the Grizzly Bear, the St. Elmo, the Bengal Tiger, the King Solomon, The Golden Summit, and others.

The Grizzly Bear mine, situated about four miles southwest of Hill City and within a short distance of Harney's Peak, was discovered in 1879 by Messrs. Cook, Rogers, and Barber. The discoverers afterwards sold to Messrs. Miller and Mather, of Deadwood, who erected a twenty-stamp mill on the property, which finally came into the possession of Louis Florman, of

HILL CITY IN 1876

Hill City. The property is now leased to Geo. Bertchey, of Sheridan. The Grizzly Bear has since the erection of the mill been a producing mine, and is considered among the best in that region of the Hills.

The St. Elmo gold mine is located in Sunday gulch, a branch of Spring creek, about four miles south of Hill City. This mine was discovered by B. Wood and J. Bishop in 1880. In 1881 the property was purchased by G. Kimball and O. B. Elliott, who commenced the erection of a five-stamp mill. In 1883 a third interest in the mine was sold to J. C. McDonald and Wm. T. Jewett, when the mill was completed and put in operation, but during the same year was sold to Deadwood parties, who have operated the mill, though not continuously, since. The mine is regarded by experts as a first-class mine; the ore, which is for the most part free-milling, assays an average of $11.50 in gold per ton.

About two and one-half miles northwest of Hill City is located the Bengal Tiger gold mine, discovered about 1878 by B. Gibson, and later owned by a Mr. Long of Philadelphia, Penn. This mine developed a wonderfully rich streak of gold-bearing quartz, which was soon lost in the larger deposit of low grade ore. Hoisting machinery was operated at the mine, but no mill was erected. About twelve years ago the Bengal Tiger withdrew to his native jungles, and has not since been heard of.

The King Solomon, situated about six miles northwest of Hill City, was located in 1878 or 1879. The King Solomon Company erected a fifteen-stamp mill on the property, which, after running a few months, was closed down, and later the machinery was moved away. The mill and other buildings erected on the property were also torn down and the lumber sold to different parties. A little hamlet of log cabins grew up near by on the strength of these operations, and was christened Tigerville, after the great Bengal Tiger mine. It is to-day only a memory.

Among the men who figured prominently in connection with the King Solomon mine was Prof. A. L. Dickerman, who superintended operations, and was regarded as a very competent geologist and mineralogist. The mine is yet believed to be very rich.

The Golden Summit mine discovered about 1879 by Henry Schenck of Sheridan, but is now owned by a Cedar Rapids company. A thirty-stamp mill was erected on the property, which ran about three years, when operations closed. This mine also produced some marvelously rich specimens of free gold.

Although these mining enterprises resulted in the building up of a settlement at Hill City, its fortunes were extremely vacillating until 1883, when the discovery of tin in the vicinity brought it into sudden and wide prominence. From that time the history of the tin industry and Hill City—its base of operations—are closely interwoven.

Every one, at least almost everyone, knows that, up to that time, the mineral known as tin was exclusively a foreign product, while its use in the United States was very extensive, and the commodity expensive, consequently its discovery in the Black Hills caused a furore of excitement in the region round about the great granite uplift, where it was found, and a widespread interest throughout this and other countries.

The revelation of the existence of tin in the Hills, as great discoveries oftentimes do, came accidentally,—or perhaps it were better to say, incidentally. The first discovery is claimed to have been made by Dr. S. H. Ferguson in what is known as the "Etta Mine," which is situated near the summit of a granite uplift, rising some 200 feet above Grizzly creek, which discharges its waters—when it has any—into Battle creek—six miles east of Harney Peak, in Pennington County. The Etta mine was located by Dr. S. H. Ferguson and L. W. McDonald in March, 1883, as a mica mine. In working the mine, they discovered in the black ore, the presence of a mineral, the nature and value of which they were unable to determine; so finally a test was made by melting a small quantity of the ore in a common forge, which resulted in producing a substance which was at first supposed to be silver. To determine more fully, a piece of the ore was sent to Prof. Hubrecken, of Quincy, Ill., who at once pronounced it tin. It will be remembered that Prof. Jenny stated in 1875 that the Black Hills showed the best indications of tin he had seen in this country, and that it ought to be found there.

According to reliable information, the first public announcement of the discovery of tin in the Hills was made by Major A. J. Simmons, then of Rapid City, but now of Deadwood, in an article on the subject, published in the Rapid City *Journal* of June 7th, 1883, in which he says: "The indications already point to the existence of an extensive district of the mineral." In reference to the discovery Prof. Wm. Blake says: "The discovery of tin ore in the Black Hills of Dakota Territory may be said to have been complete on the 7th of June, 1883, when a sample, which had been forwarded by Capt. A. J. Simmons, of Rapid City, to Gen. Gashwiler, of San Francisco, was submitted to me for determination."

In July, 1883, Prof. Blake visited the Hills and made a careful examination of the deposit, taking specimens of the rock away for assaying purposes, and, in view of the suspension of the tin mining industry in the Black Hills it may be interesting to note his opinion of the value of the deposit at the time of its discovery.

In a series of articles, published in the *New York Mining Journal,* Prof. Blake says: "The showing of tin in the Black Hills is remarkable, exceeding anything I have ever seen, giving a far better percentage of pure tin than any other mines in the world;" and, further, says: "The assay shows results varying from five to forty per cent, and there seems to be a vast body of tin-bearing rock in sight."

Indeed, a look at the Etta mine in 1883, would indicate an inexhaustible body of that precious mineral. The walls in the cut in the mountain side, which was about twenty feet vertically and horizontally, showed a vast body of the blocks of mica of various colors, mixed with quartz, and the whole slope of the hill glittered with mica, thrown out from the excavation.

In August of the same year, the "Nickel Plate" mine, situated about eighty rods east of the Etta, was discovered. This mine showed assays of forty-one and two-thirds per cent tin, and seven and one-half per cent nickel and cobalt; the nickel crystals in the mine giving twenty-five per cent pure nickel.

The Etta mine was first owned by Dr. S. H. Ferguson, B. W. McDonald, A. J. Simmons, and Alexander Medill, and the "Nickel Plate" by Dr. S. A. Ferguson, B. W. McDonald, and Messrs. Cunningham and Smith.

About the same time another promising discovery was made on the north slope of Harney's Peak, by R. P. Wheelock and Rob't Florman. At the base of the mountain on which this discovery was made, on Palmer's gulch, splendid specimens of stream tin were found.

In the fall of 1883, a stock company was formed for working the mine, of which Rob't Florman was president; J. S. Gantz, secretary; Milton Frease, treasurer; and R. P. Wheelock, A. P. Sterling, Wm. Lewis, Wm. McMurtrie, Richard B. Hughes, Rufus Madison, J. H. Lewis, and Wm. Rosenbaum, members.

In the fall of 1883 a representative of English capitalists visited the Hills, and made a thorough examination of the tin deposits around Harney's Peak, reporting to his employers in glowing terms of their abundance and richness. Subsequently, a powerful corporation of American and English stockholders was formed under the name of the Harney Peak Consolidated Tin Company, which proceeded at once to buy up nearly everything looking like tin in sight, until the combination controlled a large per cent of the tin deposits in the Black Hills. It is stated that the company have on record in Pennington and Custer Counties, over 1,100 mining locations, nearly 5,000 acres of placer ground, and a number of valuable water rights along the line of the tin belt. It is estimated that the company has expended $2,000,000 in the purchase and development of properties, and the erection of plants for the reduction of ore.

In 1891 the company commenced the erection of a large plant for the reduction of ore near Hill City. This plant, which was finished in 1892, was provided with the most approved machinery for the treatment of ores, and is conceded by those competent to judge to be, both in construction and equipment, the most complete plant of the kind ever erected in the Black Hills. In November, 1892, the machinery was set in motion and continued to run without friction, and with satisfactory results as far as known, for a period of two months, when the works were temporarily (?) closed down, pending the adjustment of certain complications between the American and foreign stockholders. Why it has taken more than five years to adjust these differences, is a problem which the people of the Black Hills at large would like to see solved.

The natural depression caused by the closing of its chief industry was severely felt by Hill City, but its people have never yet lost faith in its ultimate revival, and the consequent prosperity of the town. However, Hill City is by no means wholly dependent upon tin for its continuance as a town, as there are numerous promising gold ledges in the vicinity that are being rapidly developed, among which are the "Tea," "Dolcode," "Golden Slipper," "New Eldorado," and other lodes where ores have been treated at the J. R. Mill, about three and one-half miles northeast of Hill City and found to be rich. About three miles north of Hill City on Newton's Fork is the Sunny Side mine which has proven to be a veritable bonanza. This mine was discovered by Geo. Coats of Hill City in 1895 or 1896, but is now owned in whole or in part by the Holy Terror Gold Mining Co., which runs a night and day shaft, employing about thirty men. There are hoisting works at the mine, and the company contemplate the erection of reduction works in the near future. The ore is claimed to be very rich.

QUEEN BEE

Queen Bee, a small mining camp, situated about four miles north of Tigerville, on a branch of Slate creek, dates its origin from the discovery of what is known as the Queen Bee gold mine, which was located by F. H. Griffin in 1879. Later, other locations were made known as Queen Bee No. 2, New Holland, and New Holland No. 2—extensions of the original claim.

In the spring of 1880, Mr. Griffin bonded the property for $125,000.00 to J. I. Case of Racine, Wisconsin, who developed the property for about two months, when the work was discontinued. Subsequently Mr. Hall became interested in the property with Mr. Griffin, when they purchased machinery for a ten-stamp mill, of Fred Evans and E. Loveland, and built the Queen Bee mill which was operated for two months, when it closed for the winter. During the winter the property was bonded to Chicago parties for $55,000, but nothing came of the transaction. In 1881 it was sold to Col. D. Boyce of Chicago, for the Michigan Southern Railway Co., which after expending several hundred dollars on the property, deeded it back to the original owners. In 1882 a two-third interest was sold to Edwin Loveland and Jas. Jacoby of Rapid City, who added five stamps to the mill and built a tramway from the mill to the mine.

SHERIDAN

A half-dozen dilapidated log cabins, in various stages of decay, relieved by two or three comfortable farm-houses and a little log schoolhouse, is all that remains of the once flourishing town of Sheridan. Beautifully located in a wide basin in the valley of Spring creek is Sheridan, the first capital of Pennington County. In point of age, it enjoys the distinction of being the third town located in the Black Hills, it having been laid out in the fall of 1875, and first called "Golden," which was afterwards changed to its present name, given in honor of the famous cavalry officer, Gen. Phil. Sheridan.

Among the first to reach the site of Sheridan were Andrew J. Williams, Ernest Barthold, John W. Allen, A. J. Carlin, Ed. Flaherty, Frank Bethune, Wm. Marsten, Ezekiel Brown, and Deacon Willard, who reached that point in July, 1875, about the time of the arrival of the exploring party under Professor Jenny.

The first gold discovery was made on July 18th by A. J. Williams who, it is claimed, washed $2.00 from one pan of gravel taken from Stand-off bar.

On the morning after his rich find he staked his claim and then rode away post-haste to Custer to notify his partners, who were washing out gold on French creek, of his good fortune. On his return with his five partners he found his claim jumped, and moreover nearly the whole bar staked off and taken. At a subsequent miners' meeting, however, his claim was restored to him. In August the miners were ordered out of the Hills by Gen. Crook but, before the middle of October, they were all back working on their claims.

Soon after a party from Montana arrived and staked off the lower end of the bar, and called it "Montana" bar, from which, during the first week, they washed out $3,000 in gold, including a nugget valued at $23.00. On finding bed-rock pitching into the channel of the creek, the ground was soon after abandoned. Among this Montana party were Fred Cruse, E. Davis, Chas. Spencer, Jas. Hayward, and John Norton.

During the summer of 1876 the population of Sheridan grew rapidly and log cabins went up on every hand. To keep the Indians, who were very troublesome in that locality, at a respectful distance, many of the cabins erected were provided with portholes, after the style of frontier block houses. Very few settlements, no matter how secluded the spot, escaped the keen vision of the redskins in 1876, especially if there chanced to be any horses picketed around. The noble red man had a wonderful penchant for the horses of the pale-faces in those days, to gratify which they one day captured and run off thirty-two horses belonging to the settlers in Sheridan at one fell swoop.

As Sheridan gave promise of being the future town of the Central Hills, the county commissioners at their first session held at Rapid City in April, 1877, made it the temporary county seat of Pennington County. It was also designated as the location of the United States Land Office in March, 1877, which, however, was removed to Deadwood in the following May. In October, 1877, the first term of the Black Hills Circuit Court was held at Sheridan, the Hon. Granville G. Bennett presiding. The court convened in a large log building, which stood until 1895, when the old landmark was burned to the ground. It is told that several attorneys from Deadwood were present at the opening session of court, and that sleeping accommodations being scarce, they were compelled to sleep upon the floor of the log courthouse, which really was nothing remarkable in those days. As a matter of fact, they should have thought themselves fortunate in being able to secure even floor space for sleeping.

Near Sheridan, on the south side of Spring creek, is located the one-time famous Blue Lead quartz mines, four in number, formerly known as the Blue Wing, Gray Eagle, Strader, and Fraction Lodes. These mines, which were at one time considered very valuable, were bonded to an English syndicate for $100,000, but the deal fell through because the ore was thought to be refractory. It is believed that for several years nothing has been done with the property further than legal development work.

About three and a half miles above Sheridan, on Spring creek, is located the J. R. Mine, owned by F. C. Crocker. A 300-foot shaft has been sunk on this mine, and the ore is reputed to be exceedingly rich. A stamp mill has been in successful operation on the property for several years.

ROCHFORD

In between exceedingly wild and rugged hills, that rise far above the ocean's level, about twenty-five miles by the traveled road, northerly from Hill City on the line of the Burlington & Missouri Railway, may be found the town known by the musical name of Rochford. It contains about two score or more tenantless and sadly demoralized structures of various patterns, log and frame, dotted here and there with less than a baker's dozen of the comfortable homes of a few who tenaciously adhere to the belief that Rochford and the region round about has a bright and glorious future.

Rochford has two hotels, supported mainly by the traveling public; two stores of general merchandise, and one saloon. It also has one disciple of

Esculapius, who, as occasion requires, administers to the physical ailments of the little community; and a good school. Rochford was not always as it is now. There was a time when its narrow streets were thronged with excited miners; when, instead of two score, there were two hundred or more structures lining the street, and a population of more than five hundred souls.

Rochford owes its existence on the map of the Black Hills wholly to the discovery and development of its quartz mines, and this is the way it was brought about:—One day in August, 1876, M. D. Rochford, Richard B. Hughes, and Wm. Van Fleet, left Deadwood for the central hills on a hunting excursion, and while looking for game one of the party picked up, on Montezuma hill, what proved to be a fine specimen of gold-bearing rock. Nothing was done towards development, however, until February, 1877, when Messrs. Rochford and Hughes again visited the valley of Little Rapid creek, Joe McKirihan, afterward the owner of the Evangeline mine, on Irish gulch, accompanying them. In the meantime a couple of men had been at work in the vicinity during the winter.

In March, 1877, a party of miners from Castle creek arrived, and numerous locations were made in the vicinity of the first discovery, when a mining district was organized, of which Jas. Morrison was elected recorder. During the year 1877 many locations were made in the hills bordering on Little Rapid creek by prospectors from Lead and Central, among which was the "Stand-by," by Rochford, Nyswanger & Co., and the "Fort Wayne," by A. P. Reppert.

The first building on the site where Rochford stands was erected by M. S. Hughes. The meeting for the town organization was held in Hughes' cabin in May, 1878, when the town was named Rochford, in honor of M. D. Rochford, one of the first discoverers of gold in that region. From that time there was such a great rush to these quartz mines that Rochford, in the fall of 1878, was a booming camp, one of the liveliest in the Hills. In December of that year Rochford contained five hundred people and the camp a population of one thousand.

In 1879 two twenty-stamp mills were erected in the district, one at the Evangeline, on Irish gulch; the other at the Minnesota mine, on Silver creek, both within the lines of Lawrence County.

About the same time a company was formed which purchased the Stand-By mine, and expended large sums in the construction of a ditch and flume, and what was at the time considered a fine dwelling, called "The Mansion," for the use of the officers of the company. Subsequently a forty-stamp mill was erected and put in operation at the mine, under the management of A. J. Simmons, one of the stockholders, but after running for a short time the mill closed down, first for farther development of the mine, and finally for good, because the ore failed to pay. It has clearly and often been demonstrated that no lower grade ore will pay unless operated on a large scale.

ROCHFORD AT THE BEGINNING OF THE BOOM IN 1878

The subsequent history of that once famous mine is a complex one, frequently changing management, and running spasmodically. The mill and machinery were once sold for taxes levied by Pennington County, when the property fell into the possession of John Rochford on tax sale. It is now controlled by the Apex Consolidated Mining & Milling Co., a corporation composed mostly of Rapid City gentlemen.

Another mine that failed to pay was the Alta Lodi mine, situated at the head of Smith's canyon about three miles southwest of Rochford. A company organized in Red Oak, Iowa, erected a twenty-stamp mill on the property which, after running a few months, permanently closed operations. In 1883 the mill was purchased by Messrs. Robinson, Hawgood & Hoskins of Lead City, and removed by them to Lookout, about six miles south of Rochford, where it was operated for a time on the Lookout mine. In 1887 it was bought by Col. M. H. Day, and operated by a company known as the Blossom Mining Co. on the Lookout and Spread Eagle mines, owned by Hooper & Ayers. The stamps of the Alta Lodi mill have for several years been hung up.

Strangely enough, a five-stamp Huntington mill is now being operated on the old Alti Lodi mine by Jas. Cochrane, who is taking out good ore and making money. Another speculation that failed in the Rochford district is the Montana mine, situated above the head of Irish gulch, discovered by Chas. L. Dunphy. In 1890 a forty-stamp mill was built at the mine by Geo. G. Smith and others of New Hampshire, under the name of the Gregory Gold Mining Co. at a cost of $160,000 on mine and mill, but after running about two months the mill closed and has since been idle. Despite all these failures, there are millions of gold hidden in the rugged hills of the Rochford district, awaiting development and discreet management.

Now while it may seem unnecessary to record these many failures of mining enterprises in the central and southern Hills, let it be remembered that the province of history is to relate facts, and the real facts are, that nine-tenths of the stamp mills erected throughout the Hills during the early years of their quartz-mining history were failures and a detriment to the reputation of the entire Black Hills, and more, their erections were stupendous blunders on the part of mine owners and mine operators.

Let it not be inferred, however, that because of the failure of these stamp mills, the mines upon which they operated are worthless, as quite the reverse is the truth. It has been ascertained, upon inquiry, as well as upon unquestionable authority, that the ores of the major part of the mines where failures have occurred, when submitted to scientific chemical tests, have assayed from five to fifteen and twenty dollars per ton of ore—else no stamp mills would have been erected. Then, why did they fail to pay? The reasonable and logical deduction is that the ores being only in part free milling, refused to yield to the amalgamating process, and therefore could not possibly pay operation on a small scale. Could the great Homestake mine be made to pay if operated upon with a twenty or forty-stamp mill without even concentrating machinery attached? And indeed, what would the numerous other properties in the northern Hills that are paying so richly to-day amount to without their smelting, chlorinating, and cyanide plants? When capital is willing to invest several hundreds of thousands of dollars, in similar enterprises, in the central and southern Hills, these abandoned properties will also pay. Moral. Never erect a small stamp mill on a low grade mine.

PACTOLA

Few of the early settlements of the Black Hills have a more interesting history than Pactola, on Rapid creek. When Gen. Crook encamped with a force of cavalry in that wide, beautiful basin in the valley of that swiftly flowing stream in the summer of 1875, it was named "Camp Crook," in honor of that gallant officer. Camp Crook was one of the earliest mining camps of the Hills, gold having been discovered there in July, 1875, shortly after the settlement of Custer. The discoverers at once organized a mining district, calling it the Rapid Creek Mining District, and elected as recorder a Mr. Watts, who, when the miners were removed from the Hills in August, was left to look after the claims during the absence of their owners. These soon returned, and many others with them, but in February, 1876, when the great hegira began to move toward Deadwood, Camp Crook lost a large percentage of its population. However, many remained, else those who left soon returned, as when Jas. C. Sherman, one of the founders of Pactola, arrived with his party in March, 1876, a large number of miners were found working on claims on Rapid creek in that vicinity.

Mr. Sherman, to whom more than to any other person Pactola owes its existence to-day, left Yankton with a train of eighty men and twenty teams on the 22d of February, 1876, and, after encountering storms, such as the plains of Dakota at that season of the year only knows, and many hardships, arrived on March 19th, at Custer, where the party broke up and scattered through the Hills.

Mr. Sherman with nine of the party, among whom were B. B. Benedict, L. Smith, P. Davis, W. S. Lent, and four others, started for Deadwood, but were caught in the icy teeth of a terrific snowstorm at Camp Crook, where, upon being assured that the indications for placer diggings were excellent on Rapid creek, equal to those farther north, they decided to remain, and, as far as Mr. Sherman is concerned, he did remain and is there yet.

Nearly all the ground for quite a distance up and down Rapid creek was found taken, and great excitement prevailed in the camp among the miners, who considered their ground very valuable, some estimating their worth at $50,000 for a single claim. It was nothing uncommon to have from 250 to 300 miners present at a miners' meeting.

During the summer of 1876 Camp Crook was one of the busiest points in the central Hills. Two stages passed through the camp, one from Sidney, whose route was afterwards changed from the Hills to the foot-hills *via* Rapid

City to Deadwood; the other, the Cheyenne, which took the old telegraph road from Custer to Deadwood.

In the early spring of 1876, a store of general merchandise was opened at Camp Crook by Wm. Keeler, who, in the fall of the same year, sold his establishment to Arthur Harvey and Chas. Seip. This was the first store, and perhaps the only one, opened at Camp Crook.

A post-office was established at Camp Crook, with Arthur Harvey as its first postmaster, in the spring of 1877, when the name was changed to Pactola.

During the same spring Jas. C. Sherman built the Sherman House—the first hotel in that region. In January, 1878, Mrs. Sherman, with her two children, arrived at Pactola, where the family have resided ever since.

Several important mining enterprises were set on foot in Pactola during the first years of its history, first among which was a scheme to bring water by ditch and flume from above to operate on the placer deposits below town. To carry out the scheme, a company composed in part of Judge Maguire, B. B. Benedict, and Col. Stockton, was organized under the name of the Rapid Creek Mining & Manufacturing Company, which built a sawmill to furnish lumber, and employed a large number of men to construct a flume from a point six miles above, on Rapid creek, to the point of contemplated operations below, expending large sums of money in prosecuting the work. By the time three miles of the flume were completed, the company had exhausted its capital and went to pieces.

In 1880 the Estrella Del Norte Company commenced the construction of a new flume to Swede Bar, three miles below, where operations were carried on for several years with varying success, when the work was abandoned. This same company also constructed four miles of flume above Pactola at heavy cost, which was also abandoned. Rapid creek and its small tributaries in the vicinity of Pactola have been worked for placer ever since the discovery of gold, and much work has also been done in the development of the quartz mine in that region, where there are numerous promising locations whose owners are hopeful will in the near future be brought into prominence.

HARNEY

Harney owes its origin to the discovery of placer gold at that point on Battle creek, in 1876, and takes its name from the lofty peak under whose shadow it lies. For two years after the first discovery of gold it grew rapidly, and soon became an important and populous camp. Yet, although placer gold was known to exist in abundance on the bed-rock of that stream, the great depth of the gravel deposit, and the consequent difficulty of reaching it with bed-rock flume, rendered their operation almost wholly impracticable; hence, after two years, placer mining at that point was comparatively abandoned, a few miners only continuing to work the gravel on a small scale along the rim-rock.

In 1883, however, with the object of trying to reach the deep gravel beds by hydraulic process, a company called the Harney Hydraulic Gold-Mining Co. was organized and incorporated under the general laws of Dakota Territory, with A. J. Simmon, Wm. Claggett, and T. H. Russell, as incorporators; with the immense nominal capital of $2,000,000, divided into 200,000 shares of the par value of $10 each. The plan of the company contemplated a complete system of hydraulic mining on a gigantic scale on their extensive property, which consisted of six miles along the bed of Battle creek. Two flumes were built, one bringing water from Grizzly gulch, the other from Battle creek, the two meeting at the mouth of the former stream, thence the combined water was carried to the bar deposits in a main flume which crossed the gulch on a marvelous trestle over 200 feet high and 700 feet long. Large sums were expended in the construction of flumes and other works, and it bade fair to become one of the most profitable enterprises in the Black Hills.

Work continued for one and a half years, and considerable gold was taken from "Mitchell's bar," just below where Keystone now stands, when operations were suspended. The stock is now held by Milwaukee parties.

The first officers of the company, which was for the most part composed of Deadwood men, were: Hon. Wm. Claggett, President; Henry Jackson, United States Army, Vice-President; Edward W. Johnston, Secretary; E. G. Spilman, Assistant Secretary; E. F. Kellogg, Treasurer; James Halley, Rapid City, Assistant Treasurer; Richard P. Wheelock, General Superintendent and Engineer.

Placer mining in a limited way has since been carried on along the creek, and much prospecting and development work has been done on quartz in the vicinity, by reason of which a little hamlet with post-office and school continued to exist for many years. However, Harney has now almost lost its identity as a town, being so completely overshadowed by the importance of the rich mining camp of Keystone, about two miles up the stream, that it has neither post-office nor school to-day.

HAYWARD

Hayward, situated about six miles below Harney, on Battle creek, also grew up as a result of the discovery of placer gold on that stream.

The first discovery of gold at that point was made by Chas. Phillips, Phillip Brown, and Judge Willis in the early fall of 1876, but by whom, owing to the appearance of Indians in the locality, it was temporarily abandoned. It is told that one day shortly after their arrival, a small band of the ubiquitous red men manifested their unwelcome presence in the vicinity by firing a volley of bullets into their camp from the summit of an adjacent hill, perforating their frying-pan, but doing no other damage, and that the party then at once packed their belongings and hastily left the rugged hills to their primitive solitude. Now, if such was the case, the abandonment was only temporary, as the men were found there a little later by the next party to arrive. However, the fact remains that the above mentioned men made the first discovery of gold in that locality.

The next to reach that point was Chas. Hayward, Jas. E. Carpenter, and six miners who hailed from Montana. This party left Custer with a wagon-load of supplies, which, tradition says, overturned seventeen times while en route over the rough granite hills to Battle creek. However, they finally reached their objective point, where they found the first discoveries in November, 1876.

The day after their arrival a town was laid out and named Hayward, in honor of Chas Hayward, the leader of the party.

The town grew rapidly, soon becoming the most populous camp in that region of the Hills. Within a period of six months after the first discovery of gold, there were about 300 miners engaged in placer operations along Battle creek, in the vicinity of the newly-founded town. In April, 1877, Hayward—outrivaling Custer City in population—was made the temporary county seat of Custer City, particulars of which are told in the history of that county. For several years Hayward continued quite an important mining camp, and indeed a few are yet working claims along the creek with more or less success. A large amount of quartz development has been done in the region around Hayward, exposing a number of very promising gold-bearing ledges, which will, doubtless, ere long attract the attention of capitalists.

To-day, a little straggling hamlet, hemmed in by exceedingly lofty and rugged hills, containing some half dozen or more families, a post-office and schoolhouse, represents the once flourishing mining camp and the erstwhile judicial seat of Custer County.

ROCKERVILLE

The history of Rockerville, in which there is a tinge of the romantic, began with the discovery of the wonderful placer gold deposits in what was afterwards called Rockerville gulch, a branch of Spring creek, late in the fall of 1876. This extensive deposit, which covered an area of about six miles square, was, next to Deadwood and Whitewood gulches, the richest placer deposit found in the Black Hills; consequently, soon after the discovery, an eager, feverish, maddened throng of gold-hunters was drawn thither in pursuit of the beckoning phantom that had, till then, eluded their grasp. During the first few years, therefore, the old camp of Rockerville was the scene of mad excitement and reckless expenditure that would have done credit to Deadwood during the palmy days of '76. Gold dust and gold nuggets were plentiful, speculation was rife, and if tradition is to be relied upon, "high jinks" generally ruled the day as well as the night—especially the night.

The discovery of this marvelous deposit was made by Wm. Keeler in December, 1876, and this is the way it happened: Mr. Keeler was on his way down the valley of Spring creek, or over the hills by a short cut from Sheridan, with a couple of burros laden with a camp outfit, when he was overtaken by a severe snow-storm which compelled him to go into camp, and while in camp waiting for the storm to abate, true to the instincts of an old miner, he prospected a little and found the first gold in that locality, taking out an encouraging little sum. The next to arrive was the old-time prospector and miner, Bart Henderson, and D. G. Silliman. Others soon followed, and the work of washing out gold began under somewhat unfavorable conditions.

Owing to the extreme scarcity of water, no sluicing operations were possible in the immediate locality of the deposit, so the gold for the most part had to be washed out through the medium of the primitive rocker, but only at favorable seasons of the year could sufficient of the essential fluid be found for even the rocking process. At times of greatest scarcity, many of the miners transported their pay gravel and cradles in small handcarts to wherever a pool of water could be found, and rocked out their loads, often realizing $100.00 from a single cartload. It was during the springtide, however, when the snow began to melt in the mountains and the water therefrom flowed in copious streams down the slopes into the gulch, that miners reaped their richest harvest.

During the spring flood, every miner who owned a rocker, wisely "taking the current when it served," kept it in constant and active operation early and late, and it is easy to imagine that the gulch, with its hundreds of cradles rocking along the line, presented a very remarkable, as well as an exceedingly ludicrous aspect. It is estimated that during the first two or three years of placer operation in Rockerville gulch, over $500,000 in gold was washed out by the slow rocker process alone. To this extensive use of the rocker, the town of Rockerville owes its very unique name.

To supply water to operate these dry deposits on an extensive scale, the Black Hills Placer Mining Co. was organized and it was during the building of the great Rockerville flume, completed in 1880, that the excitement in the camp was at its zenith. This flume was an immense wooden structure, with a capacity of 2,000 miner's inches of water running from the dam at a point about two miles above Sheridan, by a meandering route along the steep mountain slope over deep gorges on lofty trestles, through which was carried the waters of Spring creek to the rich placer beds below, a distance of seventeen miles.

Pending the building of this flume a portable steam sawmill was put in operation along the line to furnish lumber for its construction, presenting a scene of great activity along the entire route.

Operations were carried on for about two years when, after having produced about $500,000 of gold, litigation put a stop to the gigantic enterprise, and mining was for a long time at a standstill.

In 1881 a company called the Rockerville Gold Mining Co. was formed for the purpose of constructing a bed-rock flume, and 1,100 feet of flume was built below town at a cost of thousands of dollars, but the expectations of the company were never realized.

Like nearly all mining camps, Rockerville had its Don Quixote, in the person of a prospector named Spicer, who besides being an enthusiastic geological theorist was also a dreamer, and the appended story will illustrate how one of his dreams was verified.

This man Spicer, as he lay in his bunk one night building airy fabrics, finally fell asleep and dreamed, and in his dream he was led to a spot about two miles down Spring creek where, with a pick and shovel, he dug a prospect hole, in which he found a pile of glittering gold. So vivid was his dream upon awaking the next morning, that he hastily dressed and with a companion started out in quest of the place where he had seen the golden treasure in his dream. Upon reaching the spot, which he had no difficulty in finding, he dug a hole, and about two feet below the surface, found a nugget worth in commerical value $38.00 and, as the boys say, no fooling. This remarkable find completely upset poor Spicer's mental equilibrium. He proceeded at once to form a company to put in a flume for the purpose of draining Spring creek near where he had found the nugget. The company spent several thousand dollars in constructing a dam and flumes, which the first high water in the spring washed entirely out of existence, and, strangely enough, there was never a trace of gold found there after.

During its flourishing days Rockerville—in addition to its numerous business places, had a banking house which furnished exchange and bought gold dust from the miners. It also had at least one shrewd lawyer, as the following bit of sharp practice will show:—

One day a man claiming to be a member of that profession arrived in camp, and after looking over the situation, and carefully summing up its possibilities, decided to locate in his profession. He had no money, but, as the sequel proves, he had considerable native shrewdness, and a vast amount of what is vulgarly called "cheek" which served him in good turn. Money or its equivalent he must have, with which to build him an office and start himself in practice, and this is the way he managed to secure it: He struck up an acquaintance with a man, whom he persuaded to believe that it was his patriotic duty to sue a lumberman for cutting timber on the public domain. He then offered his services to the defendant, whom he had caused to be sued, and was retained, getting for his fee lumber enough to build him a small office.

Another case will still farther illustrate the shrewdness of the Rockerville lawyers, when the camp was young—not the same lawyer, however. A mining case was on trial before a justice of the peace and a jury. The defendant in the case, who was in possession of the placer ground in dispute, which was exceedingly rich, was advised by his attorney to smuggle into the jury room, enough Black Hills whiskey to keep the jury drunk for several days, to stave off an agreement. Consequently, when the verdict was finally handed in, the ground had all been worked out by the defendant, and the gold safely tied up in a buckskin sack. This case is typical of many lawsuits, in which the meat of the nut is gone before the contest is finally decided. These stories are both founded upon fact.

Ever since the first discovery, miners have rocked and are still rocking out gold in Rockerville gulch, and making good wages.

Around Rockerville there exists a vast deposit of cement containing gold and silver, which, by systematic, intelligent operations, may yet be made to yield a fortune to the operators. In this deposit is included the once famous "Mineral Hill" property, upon which at an early date a ten-stamp mill was erected and unsuccessfully operated for a short time.

The town now contains about a dozen resident families, has a good hotel, a post-office, and a flourishing school. The Rapid City & Keystone stage line passes through the town, giving it additional vitality.

CASTLETON, SITTING BULL, AND SILVER CITY

There are a few other mining camps in Pennington County that figured more or less prominently in the drama of its early history—notably, Castleton and Sitting Bull on Castle creek, and Silver City on Rapid creek. The two former both owe their origin to the discovery of placer gold on that stream in 1876. The site of Castleton was laid out in July of that year, and considerable money was expended in a futile attempt to put in bed-rock flumes, which enterprise had to be abandoned on account of the depth of the deposit and the impossibility of obtaining sufficient fall for dumping purposes. However, thousands upon thousands of placer gold have been taken from the hills and bars along that stream, some of which are still profitably worked. Some of the most promising quartz mines in the Black Hills are located on Castle creek in the vicinity of Lookout, which will, by the application of scientific treatment to their ores, become rich gold-producers. Silver City was early brought into prominence by the discovery of wonderfully rich silver as well as gold-bearing ledges in its vicinity, which are to-day attracting the attention of capital seeking profitable investment.

KEYSTONE

Keystone, the youngest and now richest of the mining camps of Pennington County, is situated in among the rugged hills bordering on upper Battle creek, about seven miles southwest of Rockerville. It dates its short history from 1891, and owes its present prosperity mostly to the successful operations of the Holy Terror Gold Mining Co. The following is a summary history of the mines to which Keystone owes its origin and present prestige:—

The Keystone mine was located in December, 1891, by Wm. B. Franklin, Thomas C. Blair, and Jacob Reed, who in 1892 sold the property to a number of St. Paul capitalists organized under the name of the Keystone Gold Mining Co. In the fall of 1892 the company erected a twenty-stamp mill and put it in operation on the mine first with Major A. J. Simmons as superintendent and general manager, and later under the management of Col. L. R. Stone, of St. Paul.

This company operated the mill with more or less continuity until the property was bonded by the Holy Terror Gold Mining Co. in the fall of 1897. During its operation it is claimed that the ore of the mine averaged $7.50 per ton.

The Holy Terror Lode was located by Wm. B. Franklin and Thos. C. Blair, on June 28th, 1894, and was subsequently sold to John J. Fayel of Keystone, John S. George, and other Milwaukee capitalists, organized under the name of the Holy Terror Gold Mining Company. The company erected a ten-stamp mill at the mine, which has since been operated under the supervision of John J. Fayel, one of the owners of the property. The ore from the Holy Terror is mostly free milling and of high grade, averaging, it is asserted, from $15 to $20 per ton of ore, which, judging from the monthly dividends already paid to its stockholders, is not an overestimate. Since September, 1897 when the first dividend was paid, the company has issued checks in the sum of $108,000 in payment of dividends, which, considering the heavy expenditures for machinery and the loss resulting from a large amount of dead work on the mine, is a remarkable showing for a ten-stamp mill.

The two mines, which are only 500 feet apart, are being connected by cuts from the lower levels of the respective mines, and when the option of the Holy Terror Company on the Keystone property matures, and the deal is consummated, the consolidated mines will include under one management the richest vein of permanence yet discovered in the Black Hills. With the additional twenty stamps to the Keystone battery contemplated, the two mills will have an aggregate of fifty stamps, which, when put in operation on the property, should, according to the rules of simple proportion, make it no mean rival to the great Homestake in the payment of dividends. It will certainly disprove the erstwhile claim that no rich gold ledges existed outside of the great northern "belt."

In the vicinity of Keystone there is also a ten-stamp custom mill, owned by D. B. Ingram & Company, which runs on ore from the "Big Hit," "Bismarck," "Bullion," "Lucky Boy," and "Tom Austin" mines, all of which have proved to be rich producing properties.

Keystone contains a present population of 1,500, and has two church organizations, the Congregational and Methodist, a large school, but as yet no school building. The camp has one newspaper establishment, three hotels, two assay offices, and about twenty-five other business places of various kinds. The site of Keystone is patented for placer ground and owned for the most part by the Holy Terror Mining Company.

One of the first permanent settlers in the vicinity of Keystone was Fred. J. Cross. Mr. Cross came to that locality early in 1877, long before the Keystone, Holy Terror, or any other of the promising mines thereabout, saw the light of day. In his cosy cabin, among the spruces and the pines of Buckeye gulch, he has lived ever since, and moreover, during the years he has gathered in his cabin a collection of rich ore specimens and rare curios, that is worth going a long journey to see. Mr. Cross was Custer County's first Register of Deeds, having been appointed to that office by Governor Pennington in the spring of 1877. He was also twice elected County Commissioner of Pennington County, and is a member of its present Board.

The other small hamlets and post-offices in Pennington County are Silver City, Merritt, Lookout, Redfern, Mystic, Laverne, Moulton, Dakota City, Creston, and Farmingdale.

CHAPTER XXXII

LAWRENCE COUNTY

Lawrence County originally extended from the two branches of the Cheyenne river on the east, to Wyoming Territory on the west, and the Belle Fourche on the north to Pennington County on the south, measuring eighty-seven miles in length from east to west by an average width of about twenty-four miles from north to south, comprising an area of a little more than 2,000 square miles, but by reason of subsequent encroachments upon its original domain, it has been cut down to its present limitations. In running the line of Butte County in 1883, a strip of nearly six miles in width was cut off, along the northern boundary, and when in 1889 Lawrence and Meade counties came to the parting of their ways, the latter took with it the eastern portion comprising more than one-half of its original territory.

The county of Lawrence is now bounded on the north by Butte County; on the east by Meade; on the south by Pennington County; and on the west by Wyoming, measuring in length from north to south twenty-four miles, by thirty miles in width from east to west, making an area of 720 square miles.

While Lawrence County is the smallest in superficial area, in point of wealth and population it is the most important of the Black Hills counties, containing over half of their entire population, and a proportionate amount of their accumulated wealth.

The gold-bearing region of the county, which lies mostly within a radius of six miles of Deadwood, consists of extremely bold and rugged hills, which descend abruptly to the plains on the north, the streams having a descent of from 150 to 200 feet per mile until reaching the open plains, while the region around their headwaters on the southwest is comparatively level. The principal streams draining the area of Lawrence County are the Redwater, Spearfish, False Bottom, and Whitewood creeks, the Spearfish being the longest and largest stream wholly within the county, carrying a large volume of water throughout the year to the Redwater river. Along the valleys of these streams and Centennial prairie are the richest and best developed agricultural lands in Lawrence County. Here and there through the county are considerable areas of elevated prairie land, notably Boulder Park, which contains hundreds of acres of fine grazing land,—portions of which are adapted to agricultural purposes.

The first meeting of the commissioners, appointed to organize Lawrence County, was held at Crook City in April, 1877, from which it appears to have been the original intention of the board to locate the county seat at that point, which was then thought by some to be the coming town of the Black Hills. Contrary to their original intention, however, although large inducements were offered in the way of town lots, by the people of Crook City, the board adjourned to Deadwood without, it is believed, transacting any business. At the adjourned meeting the county was organized and named Lawrence, in honor of Col. John Lawrence, the county's first treasurer, at which time the temporary county seat was located at Deadwood, which, in the following November, was chosen the permanent capital by the popular vote of the county.

The first officers of Lawrence County were as follows:—

Commissioners, Fred. T. Evans, John Wolzmuth, and A. W. Lavender; Sheriff, Seth Bullock; Treasurer, John Lawrence; Register of Deeds, Jas. Hand; Probate Judge, C. E. Hanrahan; Prosecuting Attorney, A. J. Flanner; Superintendent of Public Instruction, Chas. McKinnis; Assessor, ——— James; Coroner, Dr. Babcock.

During the following May a change was made, and Chas. McKinnis was appointed Judge of Probate and C. E. Hanrahan, Superintendent of Public Instruction.

Judge Granville G. Bennett was appointed first Judge of the Black Hills Circuit Court and Gen. A. R. Z. Dawson, first Clerk of Courts.

Prior to the election in November, 1877, the commissioners divided the county into four voting precincts, viz.: Deadwood, Gayville (changed to Troy), Crook City, and Spearfish, and at the election the following county officers were chosen for one year:—

Commissioners, Jas. Ryan, B. Whitson, and Geo. Gates; Sheriff, John Manning; Register of Deeds, Chas. McKinnis; Treasurer, ——— Brigham; Judge of Probate, L. W. Kuykendall; Prosecuting Attorney, Joseph Miller.

Large expenditures were made by the county during the first two years after its organization, in the construction of roads and bridges throughout the county, many of which were badly damaged or entirely washed away by the disastrous flood of 1883. The damage, however, was soon repaired and put in better condition than before.

During the first year after the inauguration of the public school system, fourteen schools were established in Lawrence County, the first of which is claimed to have been taught at Central City.

The courts of Lawrence County were held in a rented building on Main street, until 1879, when the commissioners purchased of Fred. T. Evans a two-story brick structure, designed for a business house, which was converted into the present courthouse of Lawrence County at a cost of $12,000.00.

The assessed valuation of Lawrence County in 1898 amounted to $4,442,628.00, its total indebtedness to $431,250.00, and its population in 1896 was 27,000, which constitutes more than one-half of the entire population of the Black Hills.

DEADWOOD

Deadwood entered upon the second year of its history with increased assurances of permanency and prosperity. The rich placer deposits of Deadwood, Whitewood, and other gulches, were supplemented by new discoveries of extensive areas of deep gravel and rich hill diggings, from which multiplied thousands were later mined; the quartz ledges in the vicinity, too, were beginning to yield their tribute of gold, all of which found its way to the great center of trade, Deadwood. During its second year, capital began to make its appearance, and here and there, a number of two-story substantial business blocks reared their imposing individualities above the medley of one-story structures, thrown up at haphazard during the excitement of the first year, and several new and important enterprises were inaugurated.

Early in 1877 two daily newspapers were established in Deadwood, to reproduce the strange sights and sounds, and chronicle the comedies and tragedies of the thronged city and the mining camps round about. Of these the Deadwood *Daily Times* was the first, the initial number appearing on April 7th, 1877, under the editorial management and sole proprietorship of Porter Warner, who has ably conducted the enterprise, and alone controlled its destinies through the vicissitudes of a little more than twenty years.

On the 15th of May following, the Black Hills *Weekly Pioneer,* whose history has already been told, was converted into a daily paper.

In the early part of 1877, two new banking institutions were opened in Deadwood, to aid those previously established in furnishing exchange for the immense gold dust production, and a safe deposit for the surplus earnings of the miners. The first of these was opened by Stebbins, Wood & Post in a building erected on that part of Lee street now occupied by the First National Bank building. It may be remembered by then residents of Deadwood, that while this building was in process of construction, in the latter part of March, 1877, several armed men were stationed around the site to protect the workmen from expected interference by the city marshal, or the owners of the corner lot on the north.

Be it known that the public street was being appropriated for building purposes contrary to the letter and spirit of the rules and regulations governing the city—hence the precaution. Among those defiant guards who stood grim and determined, with guns well in hand, were Noah Siever and the unfortunate Ed. Durham, both of whom will be well remembered by all old-timers of Deadwood. No physical force was used, however, but whether through fear of the threatening attitude of the builders, or indifference as to the blocking of the street, which runs plump into a steep hill directly in the rear, is a matter of conjecture. At any rate the building was rushed to a speedy completion, taking but three or four days to finish the structure from foundation to roof, and was immediately let to W. R. Stebbins, who associated with Wood & Post, opened its doors for business on April 6th, 1877, with a cash capital of $10,000.00. This important event in Deadwood's history was inaugurated by a grand ball that night in the Grand Central Hotel.

The building, a two-story frame shell, was owned by Messrs. Siever, Durham, Hamilton, and Scott, and was let by them to the banking firm at an annual rental, it is stated, of $3,000.00, the upper story being subrented by Porter Warner for the office of the Deadwood *Daily Times,* established something more than a month later. An exceedingly tragic event is recalled at the mention of the name of one of the owners of this building—a tragedy which sent one man swiftly into eternity, and another through the portals of a gloomy prison.

It was one Sunday in earlyApril, 1878, that the unfortunate Ed. Durham entered a place called "Progressive Hall," located a few doors below the corner of Lee and Main street on the north, for the last time. He had been there before, it appears, on the same mission, and demanded the immediate settlement of an account which he held against the proprietor, Chris. Hoffman. A quarrel ensued, during which Durham, goaded and desperate, quickly and with true aim, leveled his six-shooter and fired, killing Hoffman instantly. Notwithstanding the fact that civil law was in force at that time, the friends of the murdered man made an active effort to work up a sentiment among the people, in favor of meeting out summary punishment to the guilty man, which, however, was frowned down by their better sense and the law was permitted to take its course.

Durham was tried by Judge Alanson H. Barnes, who at the time was holding court for Judge Bennett, and by him sentenced to twelve years in the Yankton penitentiary, but after serving eight years of his sentence he was released on the petition of the people of the Hills, to which he never returned, that being a condition of his release.

STAGE COACH, MAIN STREET, DEADWOOD

 The second to establish a bank in 1877 was the firm of Brown & Thum, who erected a bank building on the northwest corner of Main and Lee streets, and opened its doors for business in the latter part of May of that year. Who, of the then residents of Deadwood, will not remember the two-story structure, whose marble-blocked facade loomed up so conspicuously above its less pretentious neighbors on the left of the bank of Stebbins, Wood & Post? It may be recalled, too, that the opening of the bank was made the occasion of a grand social function gotten up by prominent gentlemen of Deadwood for the night of May 24th, 1877, in compliment to the enterprising firm; and perchance there are some yet in Deadwood who, on that occasion, were prominent figures on the floor of the gaily decorated and brilliantly lamp-lighted building, where about fifty couples of Deadwood's fair women and brave men trod the "giddy mazes" to the enchanting strains of a six-piece orchestra. The decorations, menu, etc., of that old-time social affair were under the especial charge of Messrs. Amerman & Sutherland, of the General

Custer House, who acquitted themselves with honor to themselves and credit to the occasion.

POST-OFFICE

In April, 1877, a regular United States post-office was established in Deadwood with R. O. Adams as its first postmaster, the first office being opened on Sherman street, South Deadwood. Mr. Adams continued in office until May or June, 1879, when he abdicated, and was succeeded by Sol. Star, who occupied the office until 1881, when he was succeeded by J. A. Harding. In 1882 the office was removed from Sherman to Main street, where it has since remained. The Deadwood post-office, from the standpoint of receipts and disbursements through the office, is one of the most important in South Dakota to-day.

CHURCHES

The first religious organization in Deadwood was formed by the Congregational Society in the fall of 1876, and their first church edifice was built during the early part of 1877, the first service being held in the building in July of that year (see Chapter of First Events).

The second was formed by the Methodist society, which was organized in the fall of 1877, by Rev. Jas. Williams, who was sent to the Black Hills missionary field from the Northwestern Iowa conference. In December, 1880, the society was incorporated under the name of the First Methodist Episcopal Church of Deadwood. A lot was purchased at the corner of Pine and Water streets at a cost of $1,000, and subsequently a church building erected thereon. Despite the bulkhead that had been erected to protect the property against the annual high tides of Whitewood creek, the building and lot, from spire to bed-rock, was remorselessly swept away by the disastrous flood of 1883.

The Roman Catholics, too, were early in the field. Father John Lonegan, who was sent to the Black Hills by Bishop O'Connor, of Omaha, said his first mass in a shop belonging to Mr. Webster, on Sherman street, on the 22d of May, 1877. During the summer of 1877 a small church building was erected on the site now occupied by the Catholic church of Deadwood, on Williams street.

The society which formed the nucleus of the now flourishing Episcopal church of Deadwood was organized during the summer of 1878. Rev. E. J. K. Lessell was appointed missionary to the Black Hills in July of that year by Bishop Hare, who made his first visit to the Hills in the following October. In September, 1880, he again visited Deadwood, and on the 12th of that month laid the corner-stone of the church. On Easter Sunday, April 17th, 1881, the first service was held, with Rev. Geo. C. Pennell as minister.

The first public school building in Deadwood—a two-story frame structure—was erected near the corner of Pine and Water streets in the fall of 1877, and later, in the fall of the same year, Prof. Dolph Edwards, assisted by Miss Eva Deffenbacher, opened and taught Deadwood's first public school.

The first company of the Deadwood Fire Department to organize was the Pioneer Hook and Ladder Company, in June, 1877, which was also, doubtless, the first organization of the kind in the Black Hills. The preliminary meeting for the organization of this company was held on June 19th, 1877, at which time the kind and name of the company to be organized was decided upon, and a committee on organization, consisting of W. J. Thornby, John Manning, and Robert Chew, was appointed. On the 25th of June the organization was completed with John Manning as Foreman; H. B. Beeman, First Assistant; John Worth, Second Assistant; and James McPherson, Treasurer; and on the roster of members appeared the names of sixty-four of Deadwood's business men. A hundred canvas buckets and the running gear of an old wagon fitted up as a hook and ladder truck, constituted the equipment of this pioneer fire company.

In January, 1879, the first hose company was organized, but disbanded before the great fire in September of that year.

In December, 1879, the South Deadwood and Homestake companies were organized, and joined the department. According to the annual report of Chief Frawley to the Mayor and City Council, the Deadwood Fire Department in 1898 consisted of five companies, with an aggregate of 156 energetic firemen, the equipment of the department consisting of eight hose carts, 4,200 feet of good hose, a hook and ladder truck, a fifty-five gallon chemical engine, banners and regalia for service and display.

During the two succeeding years, the major part of the nondescript shacks that had sprung up in a day, were torn down, and in their stead appeared more solid business structures, and banking, mercantile, and other kinds of legitimate enterprises multiplied in proportion.

On September 1st, 1878, the First National Bank,—believed to be the first legitimate banking institution in the Black Hills, was organized with L. R. Graves as President, and S. N. Wood as Cashier, the original institution changing hands in August, 1879, when O. J. Salisbury became President; D. K. Dickinson, Vice-President; and D. A. McPherson, Cashier. The first building occupied by this bank, which was identical with the structure erected on Lee street, and rented, but subsequently purchased, by Stebbins, Wood & Post, in 1877, was destroyed by the fire of 1879, but the books, papers, etc., were preserved in the vault and the business was continued in a new building of brick and iron, soon after constructed, which is occupied by the First National Bank of Deadwood to-day.

The next was a private bank opened by Stebbins, Post & Mund, in March, 1879, with a capital stock of $20,000.00 which it was soon found necessary to increase to $50,000.00. In November of the same year the private concern was merged into the Merchants' National Bank, which opened with a capital stock of $100,000, and was officered as follows: W. R. Stebbins, President; Seth Bullock, Vice-President; and Alvin Fox, Cashier. A new brick bank building, when on the verge of completion, was destroyed by the great fire of 1879.

On the day succeeding the fire, work was commenced on a new structure which was completed in 1880, the bank meanwhile continuing business in a temporary building.

Those early banking establishments were prosperous institutions, their aggregate business reaching up into millions of dollars annually. The early bullion product of the Hills which was handled by these banks was in itself no small factor in making up the sum total.

THE GREAT FIRE

There being but scant room for expansion in the contracted valleys below, the rapidly increasing homes, unable to find a respectable foothold on the lower levels, began to climb higher and higher up the steep slope of Forest Hill and also to extend up the forking defiles of Whitewood and Deadwood gulches, and on to the low plateaus of the former stream. In fact Deadwood had nearly outgrown the fortuitous conditions of its origin, when the first great calamity befell the ambitious young city.

On the night of September 25th, 1879, a little fire was accidentally kindled which spread with the rapidity of a race-horse over nearly the entire business portion of the town, leaving nothing in its wide pathway but heaps of ashes and masses of smoking ruins. The destruction was speedy and complete.

The next morning's sun that had last set upon a prosperous business community rose upon a widely different scene. Hundreds of people,—men and women,—many of the latter who had fled precipitately up from the pursuing flames, in scanty attire, lined the slope of Forest Hill, and looked helplessly down upon the smouldering ruins of their property and in many instances their homes.

The fire originated in the Empire bakery, a frame building located in a well-built-up portion of Sherman street, kept by Mrs. Ellsner. The fire quickly spread and communicated with the hardware store of Jensen & Bliss in the same block, in which kegs of black powder were stored. The fire spreading rapidly, soon after the building was wrapped in flames and the powder ignited, when there occurred a terrific explosion which sent a shower of burning cinders broadcast over the doomed city. In a few moments the Welch House on Lee street was ablaze, thence the fire leaped onto Main street, down which it sped from one inflammable structure to another, until the whole of that portion of the town from the old courthouse north, to Williams street and to Chinatown on the south, was in one continuous blaze. As the various explosives were reached on its swift pace down Main street explosion after explosion took place, expediting the work of destruction and adding to the terror of the already stricken people.

As Deadwood at that time had no perfected water systems for fire purposes nothing could be done to stay the progress of the fire, it only stopping at last for lack of material to feed upon. Every building, brick and frame, from Pine and Sherman streets to Chinatown, covering an area of about one-half by one-quarter of a mile, was consumed with their contents; the bank vaults and a few fire-proof store houses alone withstanding the destructive element.

The fire of 1879 was to Deadwood what the great fire of 1871 was to Chicago, only the blow fell more heavily on the former, in that it was hundreds of miles by wagon road away from its base of supplies.

By a singular coincidence a woman was innocently at the root of both disasters, and, moreover, there is another point of similarity.

The business men of Deadwood, with the same Western pluck and determination, proceeded without delay to rear upon the ruins a far more beautiful and enduring city.

The business men of Deadwood believed in the old adage which says: "There's no use in crying over spilled milk," so, putting their convictions into practice instead of folding their hands and shedding unavailing tears over the dreadful calamity, they at once buckled to the work of rebuilding new structures upon the ashes of the old, and starting anew. They immediately, by telegram, ordered new stocks of goods to be forwarded by express to Deadwood, procured lumber from the nearest sawmill, and proceeded to rake away the smoking ruins from the hot foundations upon which the temporary buildings were erected and opened for business within twenty-four hours after the burning. Within forty-eight hours thereafter, foundations were laid for several brick blocks, which in ninety days were finished and ready for occupancy. The work of rebuilding was continued until the entire burnt area was covered with substantial structures, of material capable of resisting to a great degree the action of the destructive element.

It may be said that Deadwood practically dates its permanency from the great conflagration of 1879. A better order of affairs, such as could not have been hoped for under its former regimé, was soon established, placing the town upon a more progressive basis as well as a more dignified plane.

DEADWOOD'S WATER SYSTEM

On the 30th day of June, 1879, the commissioners of Lawrence County in behalf of the city of Deadwood, entered into contract with the Black Hills Canal & Water Co. to supply the city with water for a period of twenty years, and on the 29th day of October of the same year the system was completed. The supply of water for the system is obtained from mountain springs on City, Spring, and Elk creeks, and conducted through about eight miles of bed-rock flumes and pipes to large reservoirs, situated on a hill overlooking City creek, over 200 feet above Main street, and thence distributed through pipes to every part of the city. From this elevation the pressure of the water is great, obviating the necessity of engines for fire purposes. All that Deadwood's efficient fire laddies have to do, in case of fire, is to remove the plugs, attach the hose, when the water rushes through them with the force of a catapult. When the contract with the Black Hills Canal & Water Co. expires in October, 1899, Deadwood will, perhaps, establish a water system of her own.

In the spring of 1882, the Black Hills Telephone Exchange was established in Deadwood, by W. M. and J. L. Baird, and the system now, with its 300 or more miles of wire outside of the city, puts its citizens in convenient speaking communication with every city and camp of importance in the Black Hills.

DEADWOOD INCORPORATED

In 1881 Deadwood was incorporated as a city, by act of the Territorial Legislature, and separated into four wards, each ward being represented by two members to the Common Council. By this act, Deadwood, South Deadwood, Cleveland, Ingleside, Elizabethtown, Chinatown, Fountain City, Montana City, and other hamlets clustering around Deadwood, were incorporated into one city. From the time of this union of municipal interests, the rivalry and strained relations which had from the first existed between Deadwood and South Deadwood were reduced to a minimum. Judge D. McLaughlin was first Mayor of Greater Deadwood.

BOARD OF EDUCATION

In March, 1881, a Board of Education was provided for by act of the Legislature, and the consolidated city was constituted an independent school district, subdivided into four wards, each ward being represented by two members of the Board of Education.

During the same year, the city voted to issue bonds for school purposes to the amount of $12,000; and two school buildings were erected, one in the first ward (Elizabethtown), and a large central brick building, in the third ward, which building was swept away by the flood of 1883.

MANUFACTURES

In 1881, the Deadwood Flouring Mill Company, consisting of Sol. Star, Seth Bullock, and Harris Franklin, was organized, and a fine steam plant, with a capacity of 150 pounds of flour per day, was erected during the same year, at a cost of $60,000 for building and equipments. The grain used by this mill, when in operation, was grown exclusively in and around the Black Hills, and no better wheat is produced in the world than is grown in the fertile valleys of the Hills, and no better flour was ever manufactured than the old Board of Trade flour, turned out by the Deadwood Steam Flouring Mill. The industry is now at a standstill, owing, it is alleged, to a lack of a sufficient supply of native grain.

Several other important manufacturing industries were established in Deadwood about that period of its history, such as brick, sash and door manufactories, iron foundries, wagon factories, planing mills, etc., the latter turning out millions of feet of dressed lumber annually from timber cut from the surrounding forests.

The usual secret orders and benevolent associations common to cities of its class were early organized in Deadwood, viz.: Masonic, Odd Fellows, Knights of Pythias, Miners' Union, Liberal League, etc. The first steps taken toward the organization of Masonic and Odd Fellow lodges were away back in 1876, on the occasion of the funerals of Isaac Brown and Chas. Holland, as before recorded.

THE GREAT FLOOD

In the midst of its prosperity, however, Deadwood's progress was rudely arrested by the great flood of 1883. As it has been written, and graphically written, too, doubtless every one in the Black Hills is already familiar with the story. Yet, realizing that no history of Deadwood will be quite complete without, at least, a brief record of an event which caused such incalculable destruction of property coupled with loss of life, a condensed account of the cause and disastrous effects of the great deluge is appended.

It may not be out of place to preface the account with a brief reference to a previous, but far less disastrous, flood, which visited Deadwood in 1878, and which might have served as a warning to its citizens of the dangerous possibilities of the situation. This flood occurred it is thought soon after the phenomenal snow-fall in the spring of 1878, which no one living in the Hills at the time is liable to forget. Yet it may have been somewhat later in the year.

It was in 1878 that the swollen streams of Deadwood and Whitewood rushed down the gulches and, after uniting their waters below, carried from their foundations a number of small structures that had encroached too closely upon the borders of the latter stream. It would not have been quite so damaging, perhaps, had not a dam that had become gorged above on Whitewood creek given way to the pressure, letting or rather precipitating an avalanche of water which swept in great waves ten or more feet deep down the valley, flooding the buildings on the lower levels, and undermining the Welch House on Lee street to such an extent, that there was imminent danger of its toppling over into the turbulent stream.

In connection with this flood an act of heroism is recalled which is worthy of record. When the avalanche of water came, a rather slightly built man was seen struggling bravely through the water nearly waist deep towards a building near a Deadwood street bridge, in the door of which stood knee-deep in water, a stout woman of 200 pounds avoirdupois, calling lustily for help. Upon reaching the imperiled woman, he clasped his arms around her ample waist, and gallantly but pantingly bore her safely to higher ground, I meanwhile standing on the opposite side of the street in two feet of water laughing heartily at the ludicrous spectacle. That man was a hero, and his name was John Meade, of the firm of Robert Chew & Co., located on Lee street, whom doubtless many of the old-timers will remember. As the incident is not essential to this history the name of the rescued woman is withheld. But I have digressed and will now return to the more important story of the flood of 1883.

It was in the early part of May, 1883, about the usual time for the final breaking up of winter in the Black Hills, that a heavy snowstorm broke over the northern Hills which, supplemented by a warm protracted rain, accelerated the melting of the unusually heavy snows that had accumulated in the mountains during the previous winter, bringing down small rivers of waters through hundreds of gulches and ravines into the main streams, which went coursing madly on down the narrow valleys to the doomed city, sweeping everything in its pathway and leaving devastation and death behind.

About the middle of May the situation became alarming but nothing could be done to avert the impending calamity, more than to remove valuable property to places of safety. All that day the ever-increasing volume of water came rushing down from above, piling up its freight of trees, roots, branches, lumber, logs, sluice boxes, cordwood, and all sorts of debris against the Lee street bridge, despite the herculean efforts of the citizens of Deadwood to clear the way of obstructions. Towards evening the irresistible current turned and found for itself a new channel through the city. By order of the city authorities a number of buildings that stood in the track of the water were speedily torn down and removed to prevent its further spread. All the night through, with the appalling roar of the mighty torrent sounding in their ears like a veritable Niagara, the firemen and numerous citizens struggled valiantly to relieve the gorged condition of the channels, while others were engaged in removing valuable property from such buildings as seemed destined to destruction. That was a terrible night, the like of which the people of Deadwood would not care to have repeated.

DEADWOOD AFTER THE GREAT FLOOD IN 1883

Comparatively little damage was done by the flood on Whitewood creek until reaching the toll gate below the mouth of Gold Run, where the toll house was carried from its foundation, and its three occupants, Mr. and Mrs. G. W. Chandler, and Gustave Holthausen, drowned. These unfortunate people had left the building but had returned to save some household goods, when the house with its inmates was suddenly swept into the boiling flood. At Cleveland, the waters overleaped their natural barrier, carrying away a number of residences that stood in their course, then on down the street rushed the torrent, which soon cut its way around the bulkhead that had been erected to protect the public property and with one mighty sweep struck first the public school building, then the Methodist church, picking them up as if mere toys and carrying them with their foundations in broken fragments down the swift current.

Meanwhile Deadwood creek on the opposite side of the narrow divide came rushing frantically down the gulch, bearing on its turbulent bosom all kinds of flotsam from the upper camps, as if eager seemingly to join its twin sister in a mutual work of destruction below.

Although the several little hamlets clustering around Central City suffered greatly by the flood, the greatest damage was sustained by the placer mines along Deadwood gulch; especially heavy was the loss to Messrs. Allen and Thompson, whose extensive and expensive bed-rock flume and bulkhead was either entirely washed away or irrecoverably buried beneath an accumulation of sand, gravel, and boulders.

After the subsidence of the flood, Deadwood and its environments presented a very sorry aspect, in fact all of the gulches from the sources of the streams to the plains was a scene of complete wreckage and destruction. The loss to Deadwood as a city, and to its individual citizens, was enormous, as besides those destroyed by the authority of the city, many buildings, as well as other valuable property, were entirely swept away, and many more were badly damaged by the flood—amounting, it is estimated, to an aggregate loss of from $250,000 to $300,000.

The blow was a telling one to the business men of Deadwood, but, with wonderful recuperative powers they soon rallied to the work of repairing damages. Bridges were rebuilt, streets were repaired and graded up, and business buildings were placed upon a more substantial foundation than before the flood, and moreover, to guard against any future escapades, the unruly streams were curbed with an enormous bulkhead or crib, which was first constructed from Deadwood street to Wall street, but afterwards extended at each extremity, until now it is over a mile in length.

The structure is built up from bed-rock of heavy timbers in the form of cribs or sections, and solidly filled in with heavy boulders and coarse sand, forming a perfect safeguard to the city against future floods.

A new two-story school building of brick was soon after erected, far above high-water mark, beyond the possible reach of floods. Since, another school building has been erected at Ingleside, in the third ward.

CHAPTER XXXIII

NEW DEADWOOD

Deadwood has largely expanded, both in material growth and commercial importance, since its recovery from the overwhelming disaster of 1883, and all evidences of the terrible baptism of fire and flood through which it has passed have long been obliterated. The narrow valley has been widened, fine brick and stone blocks have been erected along the main thoroughfares of the greater city, indicating the prosperity of its merchants along the different lines of trade, extensive commercial enterprises have been established within the city limits, which justly entitle it to the distinction of being the commercial metropolis of the Black Hills; as a matter of fact it could not, in the nature of things, be otherwise. Its advantageous situation in the practical center of the great northern gold belt, surrounded by hills whose product comes to the valley as naturally as comes the water from their slopes, and the superior facilities afforded for the treatment of all kinds of rebellious ore, with which they abound, makes Deadwood a commercial necessity.

DEADWOOD'S REDUCTION PLANTS

To its finely equipped reduction plants, more than to any other factor, Deadwood owes its present commercial prestige and importance. As is well known, prior to about 1890 the greater part of the bullion product of the Hills was derived from the low grade deposits of the free milling belt which yield readily to the ordinary treatment of stamp mill and amalgamation, while vast bodies of rich gold ore, carrying metals difficult of separation, were lying practically valueless in the ground for lack of proper facilities, or perhaps, it would better be said, want of knowledge of their correct treatment. Science at last solved the problem.

By the continued and persistent experiments of metallurgists, with the refractory ores of the Hills, two processes were finally discovered, which proved satisfactory—the chlorination and pyritic smelting—later experiment adding a third, known as the cyanide process. These invaluable discoveries, the credit for which is largely due to Prof. Franklin R. Carpenter, of Deadwood, resulted in the immediate erection of the Golden Reward Chlorination, and the Deadwood & Delaware Smelting plants.

THE DEADWOOD AND DELAWARE SMELTING WORKS, DEADWOOD, S. D.

In 1887 the Golden Reward Company built their first plant, at an approximate cost of $200,000, which soon after its completion was destroyed by fire. The works were at once rebuilt, and put in operation, with a reducing capacity of 125 tons of ore per day.

The Deadwood & Delaware Smelting Company built their first plant in 1888, at an expenditure for buildings, equipments and mines of some half million dollars, and put it in operation, with a running capacity of 175 tons of ores per day.

On the night of March 10th, 1898, as if by the irony of fate this costly plant was also destroyed by fire, but was immediately replaced by one of largely increased capacity, built entirely of steel, with greatly improved facilities for the handling and treatment of refractory ores. This immense pyritic smelting plant, which operates largely though not exclusively on custom ores, the company having numerous valuable mining properites of its own, produces, it is estimated, about $2,000,000 a year in gold. The institution, including smelter and mines, is under the general management of Prof. Frank R. Carpenter, of Deadwood.

The third reduction works established within the limits of the city were built by the Gold and Silver Extraction, Mining & Milling Company, and employs the cyanide process, the plant having a capacity of seventy-five tons per day. These three plants, each employing different methods of treatment, together with the Kildonan Chlorination works, erected in 1896 at Pluma, a short distance above Deadwood, brings the aggregate daily capacity of reduction to about 1,000 tons per day of ores which assay all the way from $15.00 to $500.00 in gold per ton,—ores which, prior to the establishment of these great enterprises, were permitted to lie idle where nature's processes placed them.

An intricate network of narrow-gauge railroads brings the refractory ore product of the prolific districts of Bald Mountain, Ruby Basin, and Garden City, some miles away, and Spruce and Two-Bit gulches, near by, to these works for treatment, taxing them to their full capacity, with an ever growing demand for increased facilities. The comparatively new business has been estimated at a monthly aggregate of a half million dollars.

DEADWOOD'S FIRST RAILROAD

Up to 1890, Deadwood notwithstanding its local advantages, lacked one of the chief requisites of complete commercial success,—outside railway communication. Until that time, barring the inter-urban, narrow-gauge short line, built between Deadwood and Lead, it had no railroad, and for two years after the advent of the first railroad in the Black Hills it seemed somewhat problematical, owing to its geographical inaccessibility, whether the line would be extended to Deadwood or not. After two years of indecision, however, when the "Burlington" Railway Company turned its wonderful line in the direction of the Black Hills, and was making rapid strides through the mountain fastnesses, towards Deadwood, engineering skill speedily solved the difficult problem. A branch road of the F. E. & M. V. Railway was built from Whitewood, and the first locomotive with passenger car attached, came steaming down the incline, through the long tunnel into Deadwood, on the 29th day of December, 1890. The line was later extended to the refractory ore district, around Bald Mountain, about nine miles west and south of Deadwood.

On the 28th day of January, 1891, nearly a month later, the first passenger train of the Burlington & Missouri road, arrived over their line at Deadwood. Subsequently the Burlington & Missouri Company constructed a branch road from Englewood, on the main line, to Spearfish, about fourteen miles northwest from Deadwood, and perhaps no more wonderful feat of engineering skill was every accomplished. A trip over this marvelous piece of mountain railway—up the dizzy heights to the extreme summit of Bald Mountain, around through a labyrinth of lofty crags in perfectly bewildering curves, and a plunge down into and through the most beautiful canyon in the world (the Spearfish), is a revelation of grandeur and beauty unsurpassed, and the treat of a lifetime. The road winds its sinuous way through some of the most enchanting scenery to be found even in this land of scenic wonders,— sometimes doubling on its track, over a route nearly forty miles in length to reach its terminus, only fourteen miles away, by the traveled highway. As one looks down from the summit of Bald Mountain on the mines far below, and the numerous narrow-gauge railways winding around the bases of the hills, it is difficult to conceive that but a few years ago, the whole visible expanse was an unbroken solitude, into whose wild depths it seems a mystery that man should penetrate.

The inter-urban narrow gauge short line connecting Deadwood and Lead, was built and equipped in the fall of 1890 at a cost of $300,000 and is believed to be the first piece of strictly commercial railway constructed in the Black Hills.

The promoter of the enterprise which brought the two most important towns of the northern Hills into speedy communication was a company composed of J. K. P. Miller Joseph Swift, W. H. Swift, Joseph Ogden, C. H. Graham, and V. P. Sweetman. Deadwood, though the last of the early towns of the Hills, except Spearfish, to be reached by outside railway, is to-day the railroad center of the Black Hills.

The public spirit of the municipality has kept swift pace with its commercial growth and prosperity, as its well graded streets, its complete system of sewerage, and excellent electric lighting system fully attest. Besides its five churches, its central and ward school buildings, its two-story brick Courthouse, and three-storied City Hall, it has the distinction of being the location of a two-storied U.S. Government Assay building.

Moreover, the private enterprise of its citizens has kept fully abreast of its public thrift. Two daily newspapers, the *Pioneer Times* and *Independent,* and one weekly publication, the *Mining Review,* represent the press. It is interesting to note that the Deadwood *Daily Pioneer Times* enjoys the proud distinction of being a consolidation of the first weekly and the first daily newspapers ever published in the Black Hills, the *Pioneer* having been established as a weekly on June 8th, 1876, and the *Times* as a daily on May 7th, 1877, the consolidation being effected on May 15th, 1897. The paper is now conducted under the judicious and capable business management of W. H. Bonham, and is edited by Porter Warner, who had been editor and proprietor of the *Daily Times* from the date of its birth to that of its dissolution as an independent publication.

The *Independent* was established in 1889 by Freeman Knowles, but the enterprise is now under the control of a company, of which W. O. Temple, of Deadwood, is President; Judge Joseph B. Moore, Vice-president, and M. L.

Fox, Secretary. The paper is now under the editorial management of M. L. Fox, with G. T. Jameson as Business Manager.

The Mining Review, a paper devoted to statistics and other information relating to the mines and mining industries of the Hills, is published by A. W. Merrick, the first newspaper man in the Black Hills. (See Chapter of First Events.)

BANKING INSTITUTIONS

Deadwood now sustains two National banks—both flourishing institutions, whose business reaches up into the millions annually. The oldest of these is the First National Bank, whose history dates from away back in 1878. This bank, which is entitled to the distinction of being the first legitimate banking institution established in the Black Hills, received its charter, and opened its doors for business, on the site which it now occupies, on the first day of September, 1878, with L. R. Graves as its first President and S. N. Wood, formerly of the private banking firm of Stebbins, Wood & Post, as its first Cashier. In 1879 it changed management. The building first occupied was destroyed—all save the vault, by the fire of 1879, and was replaced by the two-story brick structure occupied by the First National Bank to-day. It now has a capital stock of $100,000.00, a surplus of $150,000.00, and undivided profits to the amount of $11,277.64 and is officered as follows: O. J. Salisbury, President; T. J. Grier, Vice-President, and D. A. McPherson, Cashier. The ability of its management is evidenced in the large amount of surplus held, exceeding by one-third its capital stock.

The American National Bank opened for business on January 2, 1895. It has now a paid-up capital of $50,000.00, a surplus of $10,000.00, and resources, totaling $689,382.46. Its present officers are: Harris Franklin, President; John Treber, Vice-President; Ben Baer, Cashier. Although a young institution, its property rests upon a solid foundation, and the success it has recorded thus far is a guarantee for the future under its conservative supervision.

On February 14th, 1898, "The Deadwood Labor Union," was organized with the following officers, viz.: James Tuley, President; Thos. Brown, Vice-President; Thos. Carroll, Financial Secretary; Andrew Oleson, Recording Secretary; Frank Irons, Treasurer; and a membership of forty.

The Deadwood Labor Union building, a commodious two-story and basement structure, with stone foundation and press-brick front, covering an area of eighty by thirty feet, was completed in the early part of 1899, at a cost of $7,000 to the Union which owns the property. The growth of the organization has been phenomenal, having increased within the limits of a year from forty to four hundred and thirty-six members.

In a volume like this it is plainly impracticable to note in detail the many and various kinds of business—professional, mercantile, etc., with which Deadwood is supplied; but well appointed and well patronized hotels indicate their popularity, and the tasteful display of all kinds of goods in the windows of dry goods, clothing, grocery, drug, fruit, and other stores bespeak the prosperity of its merchants, and the quality of trade along the different lines of traffic.

The bar of Deadwood, numbering about eighty, is composed of some of the ablest and shrewdest lawyers in the Wide West, where legal acumen is the almost universal rule and not the exception, among whom are such eminent jurists as Hons. Granville G. Bennett and Gideon C. Moody, who have both balanced to a nicety the scales of justice from the Black Hills bench, or eloquently pleaded for even-handed justice at the Black Hills bar, ever since the first establishment of law in 1877, and who have been intimately identified with its subsequent history.

Judge Bennett came to Deadwood from Yankton, under appointment by President Hayes to establish regular courts in the Black Hills, and assume jurisdiction thereof, in April, 1877. He occupied the bench of the First Circuit of the Territorial District Court, of which the Black Hills then formed a part, until September, 1878, when he resigned to accept the nomination as representative of the Black Hills to the United States Congress, to which position he was elected. At the close of the session, Judge Bennett returned to Deadwood, where he has since devoted himself to the practice of his profession, an honored member of the Deadwood bar.

Judge G. C. Moody, then engaged in the practice of law in Yankton, Dakota Territory, was appointed to the bench made vacant by the resignation of Judge Bennett, by President Hayes, in October, 1878, which he occupied for his full term of four years. In 1885 he was chosen United States Senator by the Legislature of the provisional State Government of South Dakota, but, while himself and colleague, Alonzo J. Edgerton, were accorded especial consideration in Congress, they were not admitted to the full privileges of members of that body. On October 17th, 1889, he and R. F. Pettigrew were chsoen United States Senators by the first State Legislature of South Dakota, which convened at Pierre on the 15th of that month. About 1883 or 1884, Judge Moody succeeded Judge A. D. Thomas, as attorney for the great Homestake Mining Company, which important position he still holds.

Among other members of the present Deadwood bar, who have practiced in the Black Hills courts since their establishment in 1877, are Frank J.

Washabaugh and Edwin Van Cise, whose names have been familiar to the people of the Black Hills ever since they became an entity.

Frank J. Washabaugh has many times represented the people of the Black Hills, both in the Territorial and State Legislatures, and it will perhaps be conceded that no man in the Hills to-day has been more intimately identified with every public movement for the advancement of the Black Hills and the State. First, Mr. Washabaugh is, in a double sense, a pioneer, having come, a young law graduate from Lafayette College, Easton, Pennsylvania, to Yankton, the then capital of Dakota, in the early territorial days, where he was admitted to the bar and began the practice of his profession. In 1876 he was allured to the Black Hills by the reported gold discoveries, settling first in Pennington County, where he engaged in placer mining on Spring creek, meanwhile practicing his profession before miners' meetings, the only recognized courts in those days and from whose findings there was no appeal. Mr. Washabaugh held the positions of First Prosecuting Attorney for Pennington County and Clerk of the United States and Territorial Courts.

FRANK J. WASHABAUGH, DEADWOOD, S. D.

He was elected as a member of the Territorial Council and State Senate from the Black Hills for seven consecutive terms, during which time he was largely instrumental in securing the passage of several bills of importance to the people of different localities in the Hills. He was the author of the bill introduced and passed by the Territorial Legislature, calling a constitutional convention for the southern half of the Territory, and the memorial to Congress for the admission of that portion of the Territory to Statehood. Mr. Washabaugh is the present County Judge of Lawrence County.

Edwin Van Cise came to the Black Hills from Mount Pleasant, Iowa, where he had practiced law, reaching Deadwood on May 11th, 1877. He was admitted to practice in the Black Hills courts, at the first term held by Judge Bennett, in the temporary courthouse on Sherman street, and at once opened an office for practice on that street. In August he became engaged in a mining enterprise that took him to Pactola, Pennington County, where in October of that year he was chosen County Attorney of Pennington County. In January, 1878, he qualified and opened an office in Rapid City where he remained until March, 1879, then returned to Deadwood and formed a partnership with John R. Wilson, under the firm name of Van Cise & Wilson. This partnership continued until 1892, when it was dissolved, since which time Mr. Van Cise has been in practice by himself—a conspicuous figure in the bright galaxy composing the Deadwood bar.

Of the present medical fraternity of Deadwood, the longest established practitioner is Dr. L. F. Babcock, who first opened his office for practice about August, 1876, since which time he has been in continuous practice. Dr. Babcock was selected as first coroner of Lawrence County in the spring of 1877, and was subsequently elected to the same position at various times. In 1879 he was made examining surgeon for pensions, in which capacity he served for several years. It is now recalled that Dr. Babcock rode away from Deadwood more than once during the years of 1876 and 1877 in the capacity of surgeon, with parties in the pursuit of Indians, to care for those who might be perforated by Indian bullets.

The offices of several mining companies, which make Deadwood their headquarters; the real estate and insurance offices, etc., form no insignificant factors in the whole business economy of the commercial metropolis of the Hills. The municipality in 1897 had an assessed valuation of $1,241,420.00 and contained a population of 6,290 souls.

In the whirl of business, and the almost universal devotion to monetary pursuits, the citizens of Deadwood have by no means lost sight of the amenities of life, as is demonstrated by its numerous clubs of various kinds.

It has literary clubs for the women; commercial clubs, athletic clubs, and gun clubs for the men; and musical and social clubs for both. Of the former there are at least three, to wit: The Thursday, "Round Table" and Culture clubs, composed of some of the city's most cultured and advanced women, who, it is said, were among the first in the Black Hills to catch the infection of the almost universal, shall I call it mania?—for club organization and federation among women. These women's clubs and associations are doing much in cultivating a taste for what is best in our literature, among those who come within the influence of the charmed circles, in lifting the woman of this last decade of the nineteenth century up to a higher intellectual plane, and, doubtless, the world at large is happier and better for their efforts. But oh! my dear club women, what would your grandmothers and great-grandmothers have thought and said of this utter disregard of their teachings and cherished traditions, of all this "fuss" about "letters?" What, indeed?

While there are many charming homes on Forest Hill and Ingleside, Deadwood is not what can, by the most liberal stretch of the imagination, be called a beautiful city. Its irregular outlines, its angular streets, its narrow valleys, traversed by the muddiest of muddy streams, and its gold-reduction plants, place it outside the limits of the beautiful and lovely. On the other hand, the terraced slope of Forest Hill, which affords pleasant, though seemingly precarious home-sites amid its native pines, far above the busy haunts of traffic; its romantic drives, leading out in different directions into the Hills, and the lofty lookout on its outer barriers, gives it an aspect that is delightfully picturesque.

Deadwood has not yet wholly outgrown the cosmopolitan characteristics of its youth, as a stroll along its business thoroughfares on any pleasant day will make obvious to the least critical observer. Included in its population is a considerable element of Chinese, who are rapidly becoming assimilated in dress, manners, etc., with American customs. Besides their usual occupation as laundrymen and restaurateurs, there are merchants and doctors who conform to American fashions, speak the English tongue fluently, and send their children to the public school. However, while the men modify their style to conform with American fashions—in all their "cues," to which they religiously cling, the women and girls tenaciously adhere to their native costumes. Dignified, demure little almond-eyed, olive-skinned maidens, in

DEADWOOD FROM FOREST HILL

the very acme of Chinese fashions, may be seen decorously making their way to school, in striking contrast to their rosy-cheeked, buoyant, frolicking "Melican" sisters.

Across the valley, on a broad shelf about 800 feet above Whitewood Creek, is "Mount Moriah" Cemetery, where, mid rocks and rills and shaded dells, repose the city's dead; where lie buried not a few of the brave men who bore the brunt of the hard battle for civilization against the murderous foe; where also, mute witnesses of two of Deadwood's early tragedies, are the graves of "Wild Bill" and Henry Weston Smith—first Black Hills missionary.

Back of the cemetery, like a faithful sentinel keeping guard over the abodes of the dead, stands White Rocks, from whose bald summit, 2,000 feet above the levels of its base, may be obtained a comprehensive view of the environing camps, and the mysterious hills and vales for miles around.

CHAPTER XXXIV

HISTORY OF HOMESTAKE MINES

Near the head of Gold Run, a tributary of Whitewood creek, about three miles, as the crow flies, southwest of Deadwood, at an elevation of over 5,000 feet above the ocean's plane, is situated Lead, the home of the most extensive gold mining industry in the world. It had its auspicious birth twenty-two years ago in the discovery of gold-bearing quartz in the great "lead" from which it derived its name, and though but one year past its legal majority, it has already become the most populous city,—not only of the Black Hills, but of South Dakota, west of the Missouri river.

Early in the spring of 1876, soon after the discovery of placer diggings on Gold Run Gulch, which did not uniformly pay, the attention of miners was turned to prospecting for quartz, and a number of promising mines were discovered. Among the first of these was the Homestake mine, which was discovered and located by Fred and Moses Manuel or Emanuel, Alex. Engh, and Henry Harney, becoming, either by location or purchase, joint owners in the property. A little later, the Highland was discovered by M. Cavanaugh, and the Golden Star by Smoky Jones.

Soon after the location of the Homestake, the Emanuel brothers located the "Old Abe" mine, which, according to the statement of those familiar with the early history of the mines, was previously discovered by J. B. Pearson, making it probably the first quartz mine discovered in that locality.

During the summer of 1876 the original owners of the Homestake mine prosecuted a vigorous development of their property, which improved in strength and value with every square foot of development work done, and to still farther test the value of their mine, the Emanuel brothers erected an arastra a short distance below, near Pennington, and put the crude pulverizer in operation on the ore, which proved to their complete satisfaction that they were the possessors of property of immense value. In the fall of 1876 Engh and Harney sold 100 linear feet of their divided interest in the mine to H. B. Young for $300.00, after which each continued active development work on their respective holdings until the fall of 1877.

During the spring and summer of 1877 two custom mills were put in operation on the ores of the quartz mines in the vicinity with highly satisfactory results. The first was a ten-stamp mill, later increased to twenty stamps, built by the Racine Mining and Milling Company on a site near where the Deadwood Central Depot now stands. The Racine Mill, which was built for the aforesaid company by Geo. Beemer, commenced dropping its twenty stamps on April 15th, 1877.

The second, called the Enos Mill, after its owner, was built by Mr. Enos in July, 1877. Mr. Enos had acquired Harney's interest of 325 feet of the Homestake mine, the ore from which, in part, supplied his mill. Subsequently, when the Homestake company absorbed the most valuable and productive mines in the vicinity, both of these mills were torn down and the machinery sold and removed to other regions of the Hills.

Meanwhile glowing reports had reached and attracted the attention of prominent California capitalists, among whom were J. B. Haggen and Geo. Hearst, who with the object of investigating the matter, decided to dispatch an expert to the Black Hills for that purpose. Accordingly about June, 1877, L. D. Kellogg, a practical miner, was sent to examine the gold-bearing region in the vicinity of Lead, clothed with discretionary power to negotiate for the purchase of such property as proved satisfactory to him.

After a careful examination of the mines he was so well satisfied with the result of his investigation that he secured a short option on the portion of the Homestake owned by the Emanuel brothers and Engh, and, it is alleged, the Deadwood Mine, for $50,000 and $80,000 respectively, and immediately returned to San Francisco to report to his employers. On the following day he started on his return to the Hills accompanied by Mr. Hearst, who at once purchased the property for the aforesaid sums according to the terms of the option.

Subsequently, Mr. Young sold his 100 feet to the company for $10,000, and Mr. Enos, who had purchased Mr. Harney's interest, sold to a Davenport, Iowa, mining and milling company, which, in turn, sold to the Homestake Company for $45,000, making the price paid for the Homestake Mine No. 1, $105,000.

Mr. Hearst returned to San Francisco well pleased with his venture, and in connection with J. B. Haggan and Lloyd Tevis, without unnecessary delay purchased an eighty-stamp mill, hoisting machinery, etc., and shipped the same by rail to Sidney, Neb. The contract for freighting the mill and machinery from Sidney to Lead City was awarded to the firm of Cuthbertson & Young, at the rate of six cents per pound, which amounted to a total of $33,000. The greater part of the machinery was landed safely on the ground by the first of January, 1878. A portion, however, which was freighted in by ox train, was caught in the great snowstorm of March, 1878, near Crook City, where every poor bovine perished, and did not reach its destination until well on toward the first of April. The mill was built, the machinery placed and the eighty stamps were put in operation about the first of July, 1878, and that was the beginning of the great Homestake consolidated company's operations.

The Homestake Company was soon after organized, with a nominal capital of $2,500,000, when other valuable mines were added to the original purchase made by Mr. Hearst. The Golden Star, the Highland, and Old Abe mines were successively acquired by the company, the first named in December, 1877, the second in May or June, 1878, and the Old Abe during the latter part of the same year. Early in 1880, the Deadwood Terra Company was absorbed, and the De Smet Company later. From time to time since, additional mineral lands have been purchased, until to-day the major part of the gold-bearing area in the vicinity of Lead is owned and controlled by the Homestake Company.

The chief element of success in all gold-reduction operations is a bountiful supply of water, without which the richest mines in the world are practically worthless. Recognizing this fact, the company and its stockholders directly or indirectly shrewdly secured, at an early date, every available miner's inch of that essential fluid, capable of being utilized in its operations or in supplying the outside demand. From the headwaters of nearly all the principal streams in the region round about, their waters were conducted through many miles of ditch and flume at enormous expense, to vast receptacles, convenient to the points where the water was designed to be utilized,—receptacles from which the principal towns in the vicinity have, for nearly two decades, received their main water supply.

Availing itself to the fullest extent of its privileges under the mining laws, the company selected a large area of fine timber land lying to the southward of Lead City, and, for the purpose of transporting the vast amount of timber required for the mines and fuel for the mills, constructed a narrow-gauge railway across the deep ravines, over the streams and up the deep slopes, a distance of perhaps fourteen miles, to a point where a station was established called Woodville. As the land was stripped of its timber, the line and army of woodchoppers pushed farther and farther into the heavily timbered territory, leaving behind a forest of unsightly stumps. Subsequently the line was extended from Brownsville—the last wood station—to Piedmont, to connect with the F. E. & M. V. R. R. and called the Fort Pierre & B. H. Railway. This line, constructed by the Homestake Company, was the first piece of steam railway built in the Black Hills.

Since the building of the Homestake eighty-stamp mill in 1878, the operations of the company have increased to vast proportions. The acquisition of new mines was speedily followed by the construction of extensive mills, whose original capacities have been from time to time increased until today the Homestake Consolidated Company own seven enormous plants of the following respective capacities, to wit:—

At Lead the Homestake, or old eighty-stamp mill, 200; Golden Star, 140, and Highland, 200 stamps; at Terraville, the Deadwood Terra, two mills of eighty stamps each, 160; the Caledonia, eighty stamps; at Central, the DeSmet, 120 stamps, making a total of 900 stamps, which produce an annual output of over $4,000,000 of gold bullion for the company, or, at a conservative estimate, $75,000,000 since operations began in 1878.

THE GREAT HOMESTAKE WORKS AT LEAD

The product of the Homestake Mines, so far, has been from what is regarded in the Black Hills as low grade ore, averaging from four to six dollars per ton of gold, which demonstrates that a mine does not necessarily have to be high grade to be an enormous producer of net values. It is not, therefore, because of the richness, but because of the vastness of the ore body, and the gigantic scale upon which it is operated, and upon the systematic, economic and strictly business principles upon which these operations are conducted, that the Homestake mines have been the largest and most continuous dividend-payers in the world.

Notwithstanding the fact that for the first ten or twelve years of their operations, not an ounce of the concentrates contained in the ore was saved, not a single non-payment of dividend by the company has been recorded from the first. Strangely enough, no attempt was made to recover the gold in the concentrates until about 1890, by reason of which, it is reasonable to conclude, that not less than a half million of dollars of gold was carried down with the current to the Gulf, or caught on the bars along the way.

Although a liberal scale of wages has been adopted by the company, every department of the vast industry is conducted on such a plan of economics as will insure the most profitable results. While the whole complicated machinery is under the supervision of a general superintendent, each branch of the business, the offices, mills, mines, stores, and shops, is under the immediate charge of an expert in his line, to whom a princely salary is paid, who looks after all the minute details of the branch under his supervision. Every cog and every wheel in the vast human machinery of the great industry, is thus compelled to perform its assigned function with the punctuality and regularity of clock work.

Of the various branches of the Homestake industry not the least important and responsible is that of timbering the mines. It requires the skill and genius of a master mechanic, to so adjust the timbers as to preclude the "awful" possibility of their giving way and letting the whole superincumbent mass of rock down upon the army of miners working beneath.

When you are told that 2,000,000 running feet of timber are used annually in timbering the Homestake mines, you may, perhaps, feel inclined to doubt the accuracy of the statement. If so, make your last will and testament; bid a solemn good-bye to your friends, then take a seat in the "cage" and descend down, down 700 feet into the blackness of the mysterious underworld, where the light of day never reaches; visit the long tunnels which penetrate far into the mountain in every direction on the different levels, and see the great high cavities built up and supported by a forest of heavy solid timbers, skillfully braced, and you will be convinced. It will be interesting, too, to watch for a while the hundreds of grimy miners, who, faintly discernible by the glimmering lights in the dark tunnels, are busy with pick and shovel, and drill and hammer, blasting and breaking the ore into pieces and loading it on the train of small cars to be transported to the mills outside. By this time you are, doubtless, satisfied and glad to ascend into the glorious sunshine of the upper world.

The mills of the combined company have an aggregate milling capacity of from 2,500 to 3,000 tons of ore per day. The ore is submitted to daily tests by assay, so that the management knows to a nicety the average daily production per ton. The mills for the greater part are connected with the mines by narrow-gauge railways which carry the ore in small cars, of the capacity of about one ton each, to the upper story of the mill, where it is dumped into the crushers, which, in turn, discharge the crushed ore through chutes into the ore bins, from which it is fed into the batteries.

To carry on the various branches of the vast enterprise requires that a large force of men be kept on the company's pay-rolls. Besides the men in the mills and mines, a local engineer is employed, whose duty it is to make all the plans and surveys for the mines, an expert assayer, to keep the management informed as to the value of the ores milled, and numerous clerks, carpenters, machinists, blacksmiths, etc.

There are now about 1,500 men employed by the Homestake Consolidated Company, who receive wages ranging from $3.50 to $2.50 per day.

The wages paid underground employees are $3.50 for miners, $3.00 for mine laborers, and $2.50 for surface laborers. Exceptionally skilled miners who supervise the work are paid much more, and perhaps poor workmen receive less. However, it is believed that the management regards a poor workman dear at any price and prefers paying good workman good wages to skilled men in any capacity. A good, faithful employee can hold his position all the year round, and, what is better still, the company never misses a payday,—never.

Improved facilities in the way of machinery are added by the management as the business of the company demands. The most notable, as well as

THE HOMESTAKE HOISTING-WORKS, 2,000 HORSE-POWER ENGINE USED, LEAD

noticeable, improvements of recent date are the magnificent steel building and steam hoisting works, erected over what is known as the Ellison shaft, on the south side of Gold Run gulch, opposite the mills; and the fine steel viaduct, 900 feet in length, connecting the works with the mills on the north side. A three-compartment shaft was sunk to the depth of 400 feet, and the 200, 300, and 400-feet levels of the mine connected therewith. The gold-laden ore is lifted by a powerful pair of hoisting engines from the unseen depths below, then loaded onto small cars and carried across the viaduct to the mills.

During the year ending June 1st, 1897, 100 stamps were added to the old Homestake mill, and a powerful twin compound condensing engine to run the enlarged establishment.

According to the statement of Financial Secretary F. G. Drum, in his annual report to the President of the Homestake Company, the net proceeds for the year ending June 1st, 1897, from ore milled at the mills at Lead were: Bars, 878 to 940 inclusive, $1,843,501; net proceeds concentrates, $45,938.16, amounting to a total of $1,889,439.41. The amount of ore milled was 395,530 tons, yielding at the rate of $4.77 in gold per ton, and a small percentage of silver.

The Homestake and associate properites are sending out into the commercial world $4,000,000 annually, and according to a conservative estimate by Superintendent Grier, there is ore enough in sight, even with the increased facilities, to keep the mills running for twenty years to come. Since the mines began producing in 1878, the company has paid to its stockholders in monthly dividends the handsome sum of $12,000,000 approximately.

DURANGO LODE

Outside of the Homestake mining properties in the vicinity of Lead, there is at least one individual holding, from which its fortunate owners are realizing vast wealth. This is what is known as the Durango Lode, which has something of a history. The mine was discovered in 1877, and patented by the Durango Gold Mining Company, which, after working out a few pockets of rich free gold ore, practically abandoned the property as worthless. It was finally sold for taxes to James Cusick, Tim Foley, and John L. Sullivan. The Durango Company brought suit to set aside the tax deed, resulting in a compromise by which the owners paid $1,000 for the company's title. The mine is an immense siliceous ore deposit, running from $75 to $100 in gold per ton. The property is being worked, and regular shipments of the refractory stuff are made to Kansas City for treatment.

LEAD CITY

The history of Lead City dates back to the early spring of 1876, when placer operations began on Gold Run Gulch, and is co-extensive with the great mining industry of the Homestake Company, growing with its growth and strengthening with its strength. The first discovery of placer gold in that gulch was made by Thomas E. Carey, who came over the divide from Deadwood gulch in February, 1876, and found the first shining particles in the creek just below the large settling dam of the Homestake Company. Mr. Carey also built the first structure on the gulch, a small log cabin which stood—a venerable landmark of the early days—for twenty-two years, when it was torn down to make room for a more modern and pretentious edifice.

Shortly after the discovery of gold in the gulch, a prospector, who passed current among the miners by the suggestive sobriquet of "Smokey Jones"—"Smokey" presumably was not his baptismal name—made a preliminary, or pocket compass survey, and with the aid of others, laid out a town-site along the gulch, and named it Washington, in honor of the little boy who could not tell a lie (?)

The first grocery store erected on the site was built, tradition says, by Antoine Weber, who a few years later carried on business at Rochford in the central Hills, where the writer knew him well. Among the very first to open business in this birth-place of Lead City was P. A. Gushurst, now the efficient mayor of the flourishing municipality, and one of its most influential and enterprising citizens. The town grew but slowly at first, only a few scattered log cabins, occupied by the miners and prospectors of the vicinity, being built during the first year of its existence.

In the spring of 1877, however, when the first attempts at gold quartz reduction were made, the town received a new impetus and began gradually to expand. A new survey was made by a local surveyor, J. D. McIntyre, by which the lines of the old site were extended farther up toward the head of Gold Run, when the business for the most part left the narrow confines of the gulch below, to build along the bases of the adjacent hills above, and the homes soon began to climb the dizzy heights. Higher and higher up the steep slopes they climbed, year by year, until to-day the environing hills are densely covered from base to summit with the homes of thousands of thrifty, prosperous people—homes, in good part, of the hardy, muscular men, who are daily and nightly busy with pick, shovel, and hammer, in the miles of stopes and tunnels of the different levels, reaching down 700 feet beneath the surface. The name given the new town was Lead City, so called because of the great leads traversing the surrounding hills.

The first frame building in Lead City was erected on the corner of Main and Mill streets, by Geo. Beemer, in the spring of 1877. The building was afterwards owned and occupied by John Daly as a blacksmith shop, and was, a few years since, and perhaps is still standing. The second frame structure was a building known as the Jentes' Corner, where, tradition says, the first dance in Lead City was had on the night of July 4th, 1877. At this initial dance there were seven women in attendance, who constituted the total adult female population of Lead City at that date.

The first brick structure in Lead City, known as the "Brick Stone," was built by the Homestake Co. in 1880. This was followed successively by E. May's store, Dr. Lowie's drug store and the Masonic and Odd Fellows' Hall, constructed at the corner of Main and Bleeker streets. This substantial brick structure is still used for the lodge meetings of the two orders.

The first school opened in Lead City was a tuition school taught by a Miss Graham, in a small log cabin located on North Bleeker street, in the fall of 1877.

From early Black Hills chronicles, which are verified by living witnesses, the following items have been gathered:—

The first hotel in Lead City was the Miners' Hotel, a frame building erected by Jas. Long, in June, 1877.

The first exclusive grocery store was opened by Mealy & Smith in 1877; the first dry goods by Silver Bros.; the first meat market by Thos. Jones; first express and delivery by Wesley Alexander; first millinery by Mrs. John Bragg; first clothing store by P. Cohen; first furniture and undertaking by S. R. Smith. The first woman was Mrs. Carter, the first child Josie Carter; first baby born, Pearly McCoy; first newspaper, Lead City *Telegraph.*

The first justice of the peace was Henry Hill, who was elected in June, 1878, and the first case tried by him was a criminal one, June 25th. The first bank was established in 1878, in charge of Hy. John Ainley.

The first church erected in Lead City was built by the Catholic society during the spring of 1878, with Rev. Father Mackin as its first pastor. This church was followed successively by the Congregational society organized August 27th, 1878, and the Methodist society organized on the 15th of November, 1880, by Rev. W. D. Phifer. The latter first held services in the old opera house, afterwards in the old school building and later in the first Miners' Union Hall. In 1881 the society began the erection of a church building, which, when nearing completion, was blown down by a violent storm. A new building was soon constructed out of the ruins, which, on the 11th of August, 1881, was dedicated by Bishop Foss.

The Episcopal and Presbyterian societies were next organized, both of which have rapidly increased in membership. The former, it is alleged, has now the largest church edifice in the Black Hills.

Lead City's first opera house was built by John Brooke on Main between Mill and Bleeker streets, in 1878, and the Langrishe Comedy Company gave the first theatrical performance in Lead City in this "house" during the same year. The lower floor of the building was and is still used as a saloon, but the old hall on the second floor, where once rang the plaudits of the appreciative crowds, is now utilized for lodging rooms.

In the spring of 1877, soon after quartz mining operations began, the miners of the camp combined for mutual protection and for the purpose of securing for the men engaged in the hazardous occupation of mining for wages, a just compensation for their labors, and the right to use the fruits of their toil, without let or hindrance, or dictation from their employers, and to otherwise protect their mutual interests a union of miners was organized with Pat O'Grady as its first president.

In 1878 the brotherhood erected their first Miners' Union Hall, which served its purpose for fifteen years, or until the organization grew beyond its capacity. The first floor of the old hall, which still stands on the northwest corner of Main and Bleeker streets, is now occupied by two stores, while the second floor is the present headquarters of the Salvation Army.

In 1894 the new Miners' Union building or block, situated at the corner of Main and Walnut streets, was erected at a cost of $68,000.00 and is owned by the Lead City Miners' Union. It is a fine three-story building constructed of variegated sandstone, cut from the quarries of the hills adjacent to the city. On the second floor of this immense structure is the present Lead City Opera House, which is the largest in the State, having a seating capacity of 1,500. The third floor is separated into two commodious rooms, one for the Miners' Union Meeting, the other for the use of the Ancient Order of United Workmen and Knights of Pythias orders, while the lower floor is let for business purposes. The "Union" has a present membership of 750.

The first fire company of Lead City was organized in 1878. Hose Company No. 1 was formed in 1879, and No. 2 was added in 1888. The department was organized in 1889 with David Morgan as Chief.

The present department is composed of Lead City Hose Company No. 1, Lead City Hose Company No. 2, and the Albert Hose Company, which organization for efficiency is second to none in the Black Hills.

In 1878 the Lead City water system was established by the Black Hills Canal and Water Supply Company under contract with the town corporation, the exact terms of which agreement were not obtainable. The water supply is drawn from the headwaters of Whitetail, Little Rapid, and Castle creeks, and carried, at a tremendous cost, through many miles of underground, ditch and pipe to vast reservoirs, constructed on the hills north and south of the city, and thence distributed by pipes to its consumers. While the volume of water is sufficient to supply the demands of the people, and for amalgamating use at the mills, there appears to be no supply for sewerage purposes, except an occasional "flush," as it is called.

In June, 1878, the first district school meeting in Lead was held and the following officers elected, viz.: Henry Hill, clerk; Thos. Pryor, treasurer; F. Abt, director. The first public school was taught during the summer of 1878, in a room over Belliveau's store, by Prof. Dean, with an attendance of thirty-two pupils,—sixteen girls and sixteen boys. The September term of 1878 was taught by Prof. Wheeler, assisted by Julia B. Snyder, in a house on Pine street, opposite the old hose house. The school of 1879 and 1880 was conducted by Prof. Darling, assisted by Miss L. Chapman, in a house located on Bleeker street, where J. R. Searles' residence formerly stood.

The schools were held in rented buildings until 1881, when the Sister's Hospital, located on the ground occupied by the Lead school building of to-day, was purchased by the school board, and transformed into a suitably arranged schoolhouse, which served the purpose until the completion of the new building in 1896.

The teachers in the first public school building were: J. S. Thompson, principal, and E. J. Bishop, Miss Anna Graham, and Miss Burnham, assistants. In 1882 Mr. Thompson was re-elected principal and Ed. Darling and Misses Rogers and Barry, assistants. In 1883 E. J. Bishop was elected principal, but shortly after resigned, on account of sickness, when Miss Rogers was appointed to fill the vacancy, with Miss Kate Barry and Pauline Pincus as assistants.

From 1884 to 1891 the schools were successively conducted by R. H. Driscoll for 1884-5; C. J. Green for 1886-7; L. A. Fell for 1887-8, and Prof. Frazee from 1888 to 1896. From 1891 to 1896 the schools were under the supervision of Prof. Kimmel, who was succeeded by the present incumbent, Prof. C. M. Pinkerton.

Since the opening of the first public school in 1878 the number of pupils has increased from thirty-two to an enrollment of 1,103, for the term beginning September, 1898, and from one teacher to a corps of twenty-three instructors including superintendent.

In 1896 the present elegant two-storied brick school structure which is conceded to be the finest and best equipped building of the kind in the Black Hills, was erected on the site of the old building on west side of south Wall

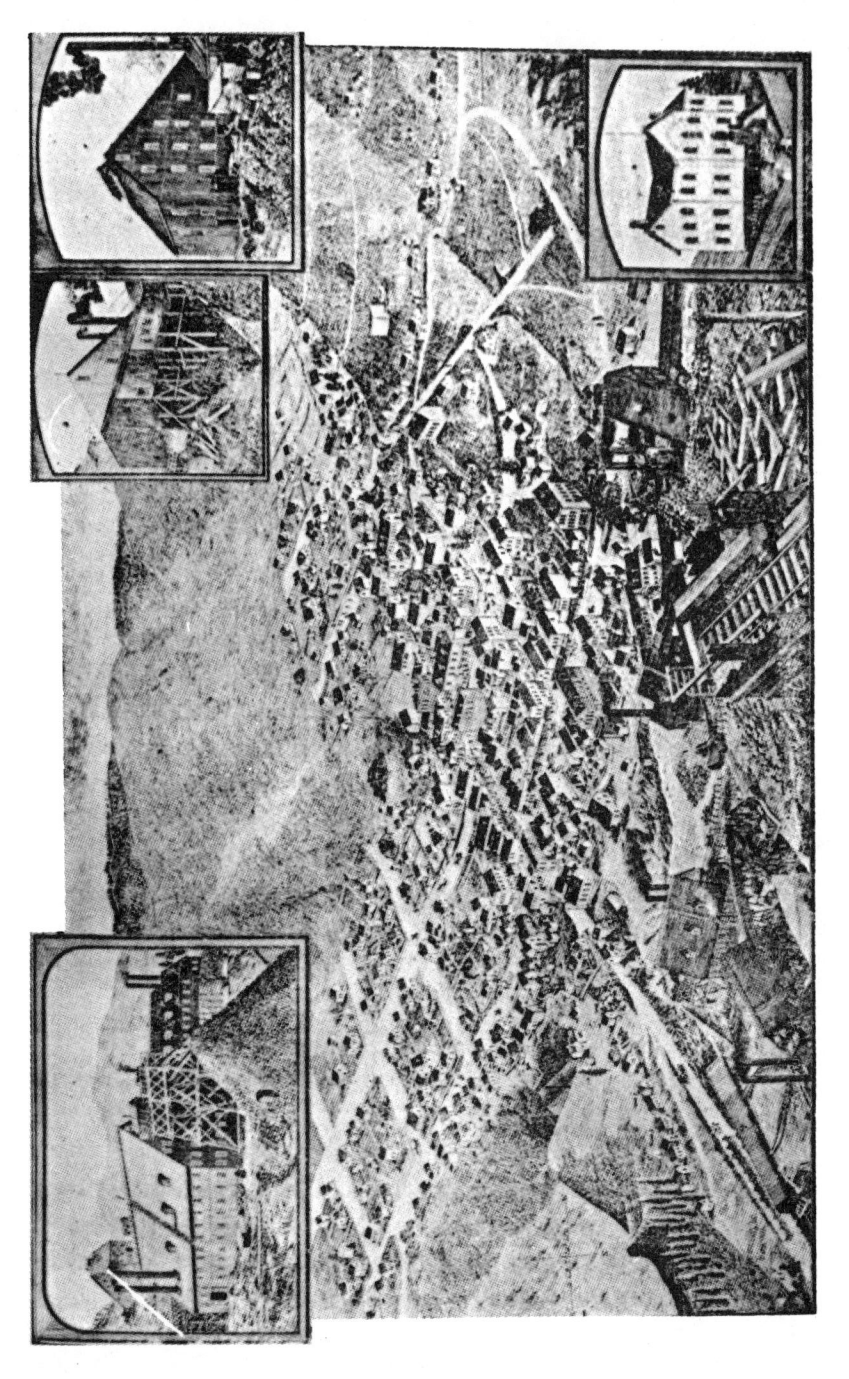

LEAD CITY, BLACK HILLS, DAKOTA

street, at a cost of $31,000.00 for which bonds of the district were issued by the Board of Education. The old structure which yet stands in the rear is still used in connection with the new building. Besides the Central building there is what is called the "Washington School House," in the Fourth Ward.

In 1890, after an eventful career of nearly fourteen years as a private corporation, Lead City came to the conclusion that it was high time to assume the dignity of a municipality, even if it did impose some new responsibilities. In justice to herself, as the greatest gold reduction camp in the world, she felt—and justly so—that she was entitled to recognition as something more than a mere town on the map of the Black Hills. So, in the year aforesaid Lead City, by general consent, was incorporated under the general laws of the State of South Dakota, and became a city *de facto* as well as in name. At this time the appendage "City" was dropped, and the new organization called simply Lead. The city was divided into four wards, each to be represented by two members in the City Council. The personnel of the first City Council was as follows:—

Cyrus H. Enos, Mayor; Charles Barclay, Ernest May, P. A. Gushurst, Daniel J. O'Donnell, John K. Searle, Frank Abt, Jr., Thomas Connors, Michael Cain, Aldermen. Lead has eight religious organizations, viz.: Catholic, Congregational, Methodist, Episcopal, Presbyterian, Lutheran, Baptist, and Seventh Day Adventists.

In the line of secret societies, it is believed that Lead breaks the record in the Black Hills, and if there are any who doubt the statement, a glance over the following roster will convince the most incredulous. I shall merely give the initials and leave it to the reader to decipher the puzzle: A. F. and A. M.; R. A. .M; O. E. S.; I. O. O. F.; K. of P.; R. S.; A. O. U. W.; D. of H.; M. W. A.; R. N. of A.; S. of St. G.; G. A. R.; W. R. C.; H. F.; W. of W.; I. O. R. M.; O. S. C.

Since its first formation in 1877, the Miners' Union of Lead has grown into a formidable combination of members, yet it is gratifying to note that we never hear of "strikes" and "lockouts" or any kind of friction between employers or employees in Lead.

EMERGENCY HOSPITAL

Doubtless the finest and best equipped institution of its kind in the Black Hills, and in fact west of Omaha, is Emergency Hospital at Lead. Emergency Hospital, which was built and equipped by the Homestake Company, was designed, as its name implies, as an asylum where skillful medical and surgical treatment and careful nursing could be speedily administered to the sick and injured employees of the company. The hospital is provided with complete clinical appurtenances, and a number of experienced nurses to look after the needs of patients under the directions and advice of the hospital physician. However, any person seeking admission for treatment is taken in upon the payment of fixed rates.

To provide funds for the maintenance of the institution an assessment of $1.25 per month is levied on the wages of each employee of the company, which entitles him to the full privileges and benefits of the hospital without additional cost.

HEARST FREE LIBRARY

Another institution, worthy of especial note, is the Hearst Free Library. This institution, which is highly appreciated by its people, was established in Lead in 1894, by Mrs. P. A. Hearst, widow of the late United States Senator Geo. Hearst of California, for the especial, though not exclusive, benefit of the employees of the Homestake Company, of which Mr. Hearst was one of the organizers.

The library was first installed in the new Miners' Union Opera House, where it was kept until the completion of the present two-story brick and stone library building, adjoining the company's brick store on the north in 1896. The upper floor of this building is elegantly fitted up with handsomely ornamented iron and easy chairs, piano, tables, etc.,—in fact, nothing has been omitted by the generous founder, to make the room an attractive resort where the company's employees and others can spend their leisure hours in pleasant companionship with entertaining authors. One side of the long room is lined with glass covered cases, containing 4,000 volumes of standard literature—comprising history, biography, science, art, poetry and fiction; besides which a large number of our best periodicals are regularly found upon the tables. An average of about 175 books are daily drawn from the library, and an equal number of persons daily visit the room,—and indeed it is a pleasant room to visit.

One of the conditions imposed by Mrs. Hearst, is the holding of monthly musicals for the entertainment of the employees, to whom tickets, limited in number to the capacity of the room, are alternately issued, thus insuring to all equal opportunities. These delightful functions are conducted under the directions of the librarian, who must needs be, not only a connoisseur in music, but himself gifted in the glorious art of song.

NEWSPAPERS

Two enterprising daily newspapers, but, by the way, of radically different political creeds, the *Tribune* and the *Call,* at present reproduce the important daily happenings in and around the metropolis of the "belt." The oldest of these, the Lead *Daily Tribune,* is something of a veteran, having been first established by Messrs. Edwards and Pinneo, away back in 1881. It is now under the management of Henry Schmitz, and is a staunch Republican sheet in politics. The Lead *Daily Evening Call* was established by John W. Jones, in August, 1893, and is now owned and edited by A. C. Potter, who conducts the publication politically, in the interest of the fusion party.

The first National Bank of Lead was first established as a State bank, under the laws of South Dakota, in 1890. In 1891 it was converted into a National Bank, numbering 4,631 on the official roster at Washington. The bank has a capital stock of $50,000; surplus and profits, $18,679.30; circulation, $11,250; deposits, $430,644.95, with total liabilities and resources of $510,574.25, and is officered as follows:—

T. J. Grier, President; Ernest May, Vice-President; R. H. Driscoll, Cashier; J. E. Corcoran, Assistant Cashier; Directors, W. E. Smead, P. A. Gushurst, Dr. J. W. Freeman, Ernest May, T. J. Grier. The names of these gentlemen are held in the highest honor in financial circles, and the fact that they are representative business and professional men, well acquainted with baking methods, is a guaranty of the success of the comparatively young institution.

Besides the buildings already referred to, Lead has a a large number of handsome business blocks; every kind of business common to cities of its class, as well as the different professions, are well represented, in short, public thrift and private enterprise appears to have kept even pace with the growth of its great mining industry.

Notwithstanding the fact that for a time the growth and general development of Lead was greatly retarded by the doubt cast upon the validity of the corporation's title to the ground upon which it stands, it has increased, until to-day it ranks second in wealth and first in population in the Black Hills, having an actual valuation of $787,262, and a population numbering 8,000 or more people.

Ethnologically Lead, like all great mining centers, is composite, nearly every nationality under the sun being represented in its population. There are English, Swedes, Norwegians, Finlanders, Italians, Slavonians, French, Germans, Irish, Scotch, and perhaps a sprinkling of other nationalities—Irish-Americans predominating. Of the voting population 300 are English; 300 Swedes, Norwegians, and Finlanders; 150 Slavonians, and perhaps 150 other naturalized citizens, making a total of 900 voters of foreign birth, or on that basis, over one-half of its entire population. Perhaps no town in the State has so large a proportion of foreign born residents, the majority of whom, however, are pretty well Americanized both in habits and sentiment, and the rising generation are Yankee to the core.

Many of the foreigners are born musicians, for which reason Lead is a pre-eminently musical city. Cornish, Swedish, and German choral and glee clubs, and brass bands are numerous. The Cornishmen are especially accomplished musicians, have superb voices, and know how to use them, and much the same may be said of the German, Swedish, and Italian element.

Moreover these muscular men are extremely fond of all kinds of athletic sports, foot ball, base ball, horse-racing and wrestling—Cornish wrestling being an especially favorite pastime. In short the employees of the Homestake Mining Company are a thrifty, prosperous class. They for the greater part own their own homes, receive good wages, live lavishly, and altogether make the most of life.

CHAPTER XXXV

CENTRAL CITY

Situated about two miles southwest of Deadwood, near the geographical center of a cluster of some half dozen small mining camps, which form an almost continuous town, is Central City, the once booming mining center of upper Deadwood gulch. The town comprises Gayville, the oldest of the group, where, it is alleged, the first cabin in the gulch was built by Alfred Gay in the fall of 1875. South Bend, Central, Anchor City, Golden Gate, and Blacktail, each of which were more or less potent factors in the economy of the whole.

In the vicinity of Central is located the DeSmet 120-stamp mill belonging to the Homestake Company; and the famous DeSmet mine, from which tradition says, the Indians procured the handfuls of glittering metal, shown the reverend missionary, in whose honor it was named.

The first cabins erected in Central are said to have been built by Wm. Lardner and E. McKay in December, 1875. The earliest quartz mines discovered near Central were the Giant and Erin, one located in November, and the other in December, 1875; the discoverers being John B. Pearson and Frank Bryant. The history of the first placer discoveries in the gulch has been already recorded.

It appears that a large mining community had settled on the site before a name was selected for the town. At a public meeting held on January 20th, 1877, the town asserting its individuality was formally christened Central City, I. V. Skidmore, of Central City, Colorado, standing, sponsor. At this meeting Wm. Lardner presided as chairman, A. H. Loudon acted as secretary, and Geo. Williams was chosen city recorder.

The first newspaper established in Central was the *Herald,* a daily paper published by J. S. Bartholomew from 1877 to 1881. About the same time the *Champion,* a weekly paper, was established by Chas. Collins, and published until 1878. The *Enterprise,* also a daily paper, was published by T. J. Webster from 1881 to 1882.

CHURCHES

The first religious services held in Central were conducted by Judge David B. Ogden, of Anchor City, in 1877, the meetings being first held at

CENTRAL CITY IN 1878

Golden Gate. In 1878 the Reverend Judge, assisted by other gentlemen of the camp, conducted a religious revival in a school building which stood on the lot afterwards occupied by the American Hotel. Soon after the sale of the schoolhouse compelled them to find another place, when the meetings were held in the Opera House. In November, 1878, Rev. Jas. Williams, of the Northwest Iowa Conference, was sent to the Black Hills, at which time the first quarterly meeting of the Methodist Church was held. In 1879 a Congregational society was organized and soon after a church structure was built by Rev. B. F. Mills. A Catholic society with a large following was organized, and a building erected at an early date.

Central has been credited with being the first town in the Hills to establish a school under the public school system of Dakota Territory, having opened a term in the early fall of 1877, with Dolph Edwards as teacher. It is claimed by some, however, that the opening of the school at Crook City antedated it by about two weeks. Be that as it may, there can be no doubt that Central was in the van in the establishment of public schools in the Black Hills.

In passing through the cluster of hamlets on upper Deadwood gulch, some of which are now nearly deserted, one can hardly realize that once the region thereabouts was thickly dotted with stamp mills in active operation, but such is the fact, as the following partial list of mills that were kept in more or less continuous operation during the years 1877-8 proves:—

The Black Hills Gold Mining Company, twenty stamps; Alpha Mining Company, ten stamps; Pearson Mill, twenty stamps; Sheldon Edwards Mill, twenty stamps; McLaughlin & Cassel's Custom Mill; Thompson's Custom Mill, twenty stamps; Brown & Thum's Mill; Central Gold Mining and Milling Company's Custom Mill; Lancaster Mill, twenty-five stamps; Wolzmuth & Goewey's Mill, fifteen stamps; Franklin Mill at Golden Gate; Badger Mill; Ledwich Brothers' Mill; Union Mill Company; A. P. Moon & Company's Mill, Lower Central; Girdler & Orr's Mill.

In this cradle of gold quartz reduction in the Black Hills there is now—barring the DeSmet mill—but one twenty-stamp custom mill, called the "Deadbroke," in operation. The powerful Homestake Company, with its 900 ponderous stamps which are causing the whole free gold region thereabouts to throb from center to circumference, leaves but small chance for small operations. It is believed, however, that the old-time activity will soon return to Central and her sister hamlets, as, at this writing, it is currently reported that marvelously rich discoveries have been made in their vicinity.

Central, though it has declined somewhat in material importance, is still exceedingly rich in unwritten tragic history. It was not only the scene of the first gold reduction operations in the Black Hills, but was also the scene of numerous dark tragedies, a few of which yet stand out in bold relief against the background of memory.

During the early years, when excitement ran high, "claim-jumping" was a common occurrence, in consequence of which frequent disputes arose, in the settlement of which a number of valuable lives were blotted out. One case is now recalled, which has in it a world of pathos, where two men fought to the death over the possession of a mill-site near Central. It was on October 6th, 1877, that the double tragedy occurred, in which John Bryant and a man named Adams lost their lives. It appears that Bryant had sold the ground in dispute to a Mr. Bogle for a mill-site, after which it was taken possession of by the other claimant. Mr. Bryant feeling in honor bound to protect the purchaser in his rights, ordered off the intruder, who, instead of complying, leveled his gun and fired at Bryant, shooting him through the body. Notwithstanding he had received his death wound, Bryant approached, emptying the magazine of his gun, meanwhile, at his adversary, who fell dead, when Bryant too, fell dead across his body.

Who of the early residents of the upper camps will not remember the tragedy of Hidden Treasure gulch? In this gulch, which makes out from Deadwood gulch in the vicinity of Central, there is, or rather was, a sort of conglomerate cement deposit, rich in free gold, which early attracted the attention of prospectors and investors. On this blanket deposit, which, though rich, was not very extensive in superficial area, several claims had been located and relocated in such a way that the lines of the respective claims crossed each other at various angles, forming all kinds of geometric figures, and thereby hangs the tale.

Among the first to secure property on this historic gulch was Capt. C. V. Gardner, who, it may be remembered, finally vindicated his right to the famous Hidden Treasure mine by due process of law. Subsequently, in 1876, Mr. Henry Keets, member of a company formed in Cheyenne, Wyoming, located the Comstock, which was afterwards known as the Keets mine.

In the spring or early summer of 1877, Cephas Tuttle located the Aurora mine, so that its lines overlapped the ground previously located by Mr. Keets, resulting in a conflict of interests and the consequent bitterness which led up to the tragedy of Hidden Treasure gulch. It is not the province of the writer to discuss the merits or demerits of that unhappy contest, but simply to record the facts, as far as known, relating thereto, which are in substance as follows:—

It was one day in August, 1877, and Mr. Tuttle, who, in company with C. H. Deitrich and Senator Thos. C. Platt of New York, was interested in the Aurora mine, perfected his plan and carried out his fell purpose, according to his own declaration, of exploding the whole conglomerate proposition with dynamite.

When seen laboriously pushing a wheelbarrow loaded with boxes of powder towards the air shaft on his mine, Mr. Keets inquired, "What under the sun are you intending to do with all that powder?" "I am going to blow the entire works to—to the realms of Pluto," promptly replied Tuttle. He was as good as his word—he did.

It appears that the two mines, each of which had a shaft, were connected by a long tunnel, which at the time was in the possession of the Keets employees. When reminded that there was a large number of men in the tunnel, some of whom might get killed, in case he carried out his threat, he said "Get your men out of the mine, for I shall certainly blow it up. I am a Napoleon and was never yet outgeneraled." This he said, and more, in the way of embellishment. Finding that he was determined to execute his threat Mr. Keets hastened into the tunnel and told the men to get out quickly as Mr. Tuttle was about to explode the mine. All of the men except one named Norris, who regarded the threat as a mere bravado, left the tunnel and repaired to the Keets' cabin, or a blacksmith shop on the ground.

Tuttle tied a rope around the boxes of powder, lowered them into the shaft; lighted the fuse attached to the boxes, and was about to lower it into the shaft, when a well-directed shot from some quarter extinguished it. "Good shot!" exclaimed Tuttle admiringly. Nothing daunted, he at once relighted the fuse, let it down into the shaft and left the spot, shortly after which the explosion occurred. Then followed an interchange of shots between the Keets men in the cabin, and the Aurora men from behind a barricade, slight wounds being inflicted on several of the men. In the midst of the general confusion an unerring bullet found its way to the heart of Mr. Tuttle, killing him, it is believed, instantly. The man Norris, who remained in the tunnel, was knocked into insensibility by the concussion, and was afterwards deaf.

A posse of armed men was stationed around the cabin in which the Keets men had taken refuge, to keep guard until the arrival of the sheriff, who placed several of the Keets men under arrest, took them in custody to Deadwood, where they were arraigned in Justice Baker's court for preliminary trial, on the charge of murder. A prolonged examination of witnesses, pro and con, failed to fix the crime, and they were released. The names of the prisoners were Geo. H. Fullerton, J. S. Hubbell, Joe Maxwell, C. L. Torbet, J. S. Goddard, E. C. Smith, and H. F. Paslin.

Hidden Treasure gulch was the scene of an amusing comedy as well as a tragedy during the same year. By some injudicious management on the part of the superintendent of the Keets' works there was a default in the payment of the wages of the employees, who, to secure themselves, took formal possession of the property. It was in November, 1877, that the Keets employees set up housekeeping in the tunnel of the Keets mine. They removed their cabin belongings, supplies, beds and bedding, cook utensils, etc., into the tunnel, set up the cook stove near the air shaft, which was utilized for a flue, and made all needful preparations for an indefinite stay. No persuasion by mere promises to pay could lure them from their chosen vantage ground.

The owners of the mine then called into requisition the services of Sheriff Bullock, who, upon reaching the ground armed with due process of law, peered down through the smoke of the air shaft and in stentorian tones read to them the "riot act;" but for once the potential influence of that efficient officer of the law failed, as threats availed nothing.

As a last resort the aid of the military arm of the government was invoked, and Lieut. Edgerly, in response to a requisition from Sheriff Bullock, rode to the scene of trouble with a detachment of United States cavalry from Camp Sturgis. The lieutenant, upon his arrival, communicated formal notice to the occupants of the tunnel that unless they surrendered the fort unconditionally within a specified time he would bombard the works. "Bombard away," replied the plucky miners, "we will die in the last ditch before we surrender." Uncle Sam's troopers had no terrors for the men comfortably domiciled in the tunnel. All efforts to dislodge them proved ineffectual until someone hit upon the happy expedient of throwing burning sulphur into the tunnel, which brought them to a speedy capitulation. To the fumes of fire and brimstone they were finally forced to succumb.

SETH BULLOCK
First Sheriff of Lawrence County

TERRAVILLE

In a small gulch, between Central City and Lead, at an elevation of about 200 feet above the former place, is Terraville, the location of the Deadwood, Terra, and Caledonia mills, to whose operations it owes its present existence. The camp had its origin in 1877, in the discovery of the several mines comprising the properties of the two companies respectively, the earliest of which were the Caledonia and the Deadwood and Terra mines. The Deadwood Terra Company has tow mills of eighty stamps each, and the Caledonia one mill of eighty stamps, making a total of 220 stamps, which are kept in constant operation, employing an aggregate of 150 men.

These two companies, which are now included in the Homestake combination, own the major part of the mineral-bearing territory in the vicinity of Terraville. Among the mines belonging to the Caledonia group on

Bobtail gulch are the Caledonia, Grand Prize, Clara Nos. 1 and 2, Queen of the Hills, Cornucopia, Monroe, besides placer ground on the gulch.

In these mines, as in the Homestake properties at Lead, there is a large amount of pay ore in sight, which is mined at a great saving of expense, pillars of the ore being skillfully left to support the roof, thereby saving the expenditure of thousands of dollars annually for timber and labor. In all other particulars the same methods are employed as in the mills and mines at Lead.

TERRAVILLE, GOLD MINING CAMP

Although Terraville has a present population of 600, very little traffic is carried on owing to its close proximity to Lead, the trade center for that region.

CROOK CITY

Crook City, one of the oldest towns in the northern Hills, is situated on Whitewood creek, about seven miles by the traveled highway northeast of Deadwood, at the foot of the hills where the creek debouches into the open country. It was originally called "Camp Crook" in honor of Gen. Crook, who encamped on the ground with several troops of cavalry in 1875, and again in 1876, on his return from his memorable summer campaign against the hostile Sioux. Early in 1876 a large population gathered at that point for the purpose of catching the float gold, with which Whitewood creek was believed to be teeming, as it was washed down with the tide. It grew so rapidly in population and importance during the year, that, in the spring of 1877, upon the formation of Lawrence County, it was considered a worthy rival of Deadwood in the race for capital honors. As a matter of fact, the first meeting of the county commissioners was held at Crook, but for some reason best known to that board, the meeting adjourned to Deadwood, which later secured the plum, despite the liberal bonus offered by the people of Crook in landed property.

The town was laid out in the spring of 1876, when it received its formal christening, each of the original settlers being given the privilege of drawing a town lot. At that time town lots in Crook City were in active demand, selling readily at $500.00 each. Among the first settlers were Wm. Cable, L. W. Valentine, Henry Ash, Joseph Sparks, A. H. Burke, H. M. Vroman, Wm. Wigginton, E. R. Collins, W. D. Wakeman, Major James Whitewood, Benjamin Hazen, Sam. Jackson, John Gallinger, Wm. Wade, Geo. Mattox, Ed. Wolf, Ed. Donahue, Thomas Moore, Thomas Shannon, and many

CROOK CITY IN 1876

others, the majority of whom were soon drawn away to Deadwood. The two last named fought a duel in 1876, in which T. Shannon fell (see Chapter of First Events). Aunt Sally, who claimed the distinction of being "de fustest culled lady in de Brack Hills," was also one of the early settlers of Crook City.

Among the first to establish business in the town, were: Joseph Sparks, hotel; Henry Ash, grocery; Wm. Wigginton, meat shop; Mike McMahon, restaurant,; Clark & Wilson, bakery; Homer Levings, general merchandise; A. Jackson, saloon.

The first school in Crook City was taught by Mrs. J. S. Bennett, in June, 1877. It is claimed that District No. 1 of Lawrence County was organized there at that time with H. M. Vroman, treasurer, W. D. Wakeman, director, and W. M. Anderson, clerk. That being the case it was the first school district organized in the Black Hills. The school was first taught in a rented log cabin, but soon after a comfortable school building was erected.

The Crook City *Tribune,* the second newspaper in the Black Hills, was established at Crook City on June 10th, 1876, just two days after the first issue of the Black Hills weekly *Pioneer.* The paper was published by H. S. Burke.

A regular post-office was established at Crook City in 1877, with William Logan as first postmaster. Prior to that time the people of the town received their mail through the same uncertain and dangerous channels as did other early settlements of the Hills.

Situated as it was, on the outer environment of the Hills, Crook City was particularly exposed to Indian depredations in 1876, and a number of persons were killed in its vicinity during that year, among whom were three members of a family named Wagnus, who were encamped near the town, an intrepid mail carrier named Herbert, and several other parties. Stealing and running off horses and cattle from the vicinity was an almost daily occurrence, and the settlers were consequently kept in a constant state of alarm. It was while on his way to Crook City to fulfill an engagement to hold religious services that Rev. Smith was killed by the Indians in 1876, the particulars of which are related in Chapter of First Events.

In the early eighties the town-site, comprising about 400 acres, was pre-empted by L. W. Valentine and J. L. Denman, who deeded lots to occupants at a mere nominal figure. Although liberal inducements were offered, all attempts to secure for Crook City a railway station have so far failed, and while a small settlement of ranchmen is still there, as a town it is but little more than a memory. A rich agricultural and grazing region surrounds the old townsite, including Whitewood, Spring, and False Bottom valleys, and the eastern portion of Centennial Prairie, and it has doubtless proved more valuable as a ranch than it ever did as a town.

CHAPTER XXXVI

SPEARFISH

Situated in the valley of Spearfish creek, about seven miles above its confluence with the Redwater, and fourteen miles northwest of Deadwood by wagon road, and thirty-one miles by the winding railway, may be found Spearfish, the Queen City of the Black Hills, and a delightfully attractive picture indeed it presents to the vistor. Its broad, clean, well-shaded streets; its cosy, tree-embowered homes—bespeaking the prosperity and thrift of their owners—and the broad, green valley in which it stands, form a magnificent setting to the rugged grandeur of the surrounding hills and mountains which shield the confiding city from every stormy wind that blows.

The mountains rear their protecting battlements on every side. Crow Butte with its flanking cohorts, on the south, Spearfish Peak on the east, and on the west Crow Peak towers up about 6,000 feet above the tide, and 2,500 feet above the town, while, near its limits on the east, rises up the encroaching barrier of Lookout Mountain, from whose lofty summit the early settlers of the valley were wont to eagerly scan the different approaches thereto, in the days of the country's peril.

In the beauty and harmony of its scenic environments, Spearfish stands unexcelled by any other town in the Hills, Custer alone excelling it in grandeur. The quiet peaceful village, Spearfish creek, clear as crystal, fringed with a thrifty growth of forest trees, traversing the wide verdant valley, and the embracing mountains combined, form a landscape that would delight the artistic eye of a painter. The peculiar features of the valley of the Redwater are also conspicuous around Spearfish, the white of the gypsum and the vermillion of the Red Beds contrasting with pleasing effect.

The varied attractions of the valley of Spearfish and the wide "Centennial Prairie" on the east, did not long remain unnoticed by those seeking homes in the Black Hills. Professor Jenny who encamped on the valleys, during his exploration of the Hills in 1875, spoke in glowing language of its beauty and fertility which first brought it into notice. It was not albeit until about the time that the valley began to grow green in the spring of 1876, soon after the Sioux in fresh paint and plumage had started out on the trail of the pale-faces, that attention was first attracted to that region with a view to settlement.

It is claimed by some that Jas. Butcher, who later settled on Centennial Prairie, was the first actual settler on the northern frontier, having located and built a cabin, prior to the location of the town-site, on ground afterwards occupied by J. C. Ryan's store, which was soon abandoned, owing to the appearance of Indians. The next to arrive, according to pretty well authenticated statements, was a company formed in Deadwood in the early part of May, 1876, for the purpose of locating lands in the valley of Spearfish creek—which, too, by reason of the hostility of the Indians, was compelled to beat a hasty retreat, without fully accomplishing its object. It appears, however, that Otto Uhlig, the prime mover in the scheme, soon after returned and joined the Montana colony, which arrived in the valley on the 20th of May, 1876, and located a homestead adjoining the original town-site on the east,—a part of which is now Uhlig's Addition to Spearfish.

Colorado Jack had, prior to this, according to tradition, verified by living witnesses, pre-empted the town-site, but was soon driven off by the Indians, abandoning his claim. On the 22d of May, 1876, it was relocated by Thomas Jefferson, who subsequently relinquished his right to the Town-site Company. About the same time, perhaps a little before, John Johnston, leader of the "Centennial" party from Ames, Iowa, arrived in the valley, where he has since, for the most time, remained.

On the 26th of May the Montana colony began to locate ranches down the valley, beginning at the ranch now owned by R. H. Evans, which he drew at that time. Joseph Ramsdell, at the same time, located the ground which is now in part Ramsdell's Addition to Spearfish.

It appears that there were two adverse claimants to the town-site, designated as the Gay and Smith parties respectively, each claiming priority of location, but, after a heated discussion, a compromise was effected, by which the two parties were to unite in forming a large town-site company. Accordingly on the 29th of May, 1876, Spearfish was laid out on the banks of the beautiful stream from which it derived its name. The site was surveyed and platted by H. S. Burke,—who established the first newspaper at Crook City, and was afterwards Justice of the Peace at Deadwood—with the aid of the traditional pocket compass. The original stockholders of the Town-site Company were: Alfred Gay, A. J. Arnold, J. E. Smith, T. K. Bradley, J. F. Bradley, Wm. Gay, W. L. Kuykendall, E. B. Farnum, H. B. Young, Thos. Jefferson, R. H. Evans, J. H. Bigler, C. L. Craig J. Fitzsimmons, J. McHenry, J. R. Frost, H. S. Burke, D. G. Tallent, A. F. Wood, T. G. Murphy, J. J. Crawford, E. F. Slater, C. F. Thomas, C. C. Spades, J. J. Bump, J. Laham, M. Gearney, Wm. Plaudney, S. S. Peters, P. O. Mill, M.

B. Goodsell, and R. Holt, thirty-two in all. J. E. Smith was chosen president of the company.

The organization was effected under the provisions of a law of the United States authorizing the location of town-sites on government unsurveyed lands which provided that all unclaimed lots after a specified period should revert to and become the property of the school district. A preliminary survey of the original plat, which contained 640 acres located on government unsurveyed lands was made by members of the Town-site Company in 1876. In 1877 the 640-acre tract was resurveyed and platted by E. E. Fine, for which service the company paid him $350 in good, lawful money. The streets were laid out and numbered from one to twenty-seven north and south, and from A to S east and west, and as there was ample room for expansion in the tract they laid out veritable boulevards, with alleys twenty feet in width.

In 1878 the government survey by Scott was made, by which the town-site tract was found to be parts of sections 10 and 15, township 6, range 2 east of Black Hills meridian. It then developed that the population of the town did not entitle it to more than 320 acres, consequently that area was surveyed and platted, and on January 27th, 1879, was recorded in the United States Land Office at Deadwood. Since then several additions have been made largely increasing its original area. Subsequently the company became involved in prolonged and expensive litigation with those to whom lots had been sold and squatters who settled on the site prior to its cession by the government; consequently, becoming weary of the struggle, the company finally abandoned the scheme.

The first structure erected on the plat was a log cabin, built by the Town-site Company, the logs for which were cut by Jas. Bradley and Thos. Jefferson. The second house was built by James and Kellar Bradley, at the southeast corner of 7th and H streets, on the ground afterwards owned by Robinson & Ripley.

J. E. Smith, Jas. Ryan, Henry Folsom, and Geo. Reed broke the first ground in Spearfish valley in June, 1876, and J. E. Smith sowed the first acre of oats on the ranch now owned by M. G. Tonn. While, despite Indians, numerous small improvements were made on the ranches along the valley, the town grew but slowly during the first year of its history.

Early in September, 1876, it having become imperative that a haven of refuge be provided for the settlers, in the event of an attack by the Indians, who were at the time boldly raiding the surrounding country, even to the limits of the town, a stockade was built. The plan of the structure, through something unique in the annals of defensive works, was yet quite creditable to its designers. Four separate cabins, occupying the four respective corners of

SPEARFISH IN 1876, WITH LOOKOUT MOUNTAIN IN THE BACKGROUND

the area, laid out for the inclosure, were provided with embrasures on all sides, thus commanding the situation form every point of the compass. On the northeast corner, afterwards occupied by Court & Bulf's building, stood John Ward's cabin; on the southeast corner, on the ground now occupied by Gammon's livery stable, stood P. C. Riley's cabin; the two 100 feet apart. On the northwest corner, now occupied by Nutt's core, stood John Spaulding's cabin, and Henry Folsom's cabin occupied the southwest corner of the inclosure. All munitions of war, provisions, etc., were stored in these four log cabins, where the few settlers took up quarters and successfully defended themselves during the winter of 1876-7, and where, it may be imagined, they reposed upon no downy pillows.

All through the year of 1876 and up to July, 1877, the settlers in the valley held their possessions by a very hazardous and uncertain tenure indeed. They were perpetually harassed by the aggressions of the Indians who were especially active along the northern border, around the exposed settlements of Spearfish, Centennial, and Crook City. Often during that terrible period did they climb the slope of Lookout Mountain and stand upon its commanding summit to scan the wide scope of valley and prairie to the north and east, anxiously watching for the ubiquitous redskins, who came and went like a flash—and there was no telling whence nor where. Large bands were liable on any day or at any hour to swoop down upon a herd of horses or cattle or sheep and with wild unearthly yells and whoops and frantic gesticulations stampede the whole herd away out of sight, before their keepers could hardly realize what had been done. Not that the herders were lacking either in vigilance or bravery—quite the reverse. What availed two or three men, pitted against a band of fifty or more well-mounted and well-armed Indians?

Strange as it may seem, there were hundreds of horses and cattle feeding on the rich grazing lands lying north of the Hills even as early as 1876. It is related that at one time a large band of red marauders drove away from the vicinity of Crook City 400 head of cattle belonging to Capt. Dodson and slaughtered the entire herd except one lame ox, converted the same into jerked beef and made their escape from the pursuers. A party from Crook City accompanied by the Montana hay-makers followed in pursuit but they were too late.

That the Indians did not confine themselves strictly to horse and cattle stealing, but, when opportunity offered, dabbled in other kinds of stock, will be shown by the following. In the fall of 1876 a man named Ames, who had located a sheep ranch on the Redwater, near the mouth of False Bottom, brought in from Wyoming a flock of sheep to be disposed of to meat dealers during the winter and but for the interposition of a force of United States troops he would have been robbed of his entire flock.

Lieut. Cummings, it may be remembered, was sent with a force of cavalry to guard the northern frontier against the incursions of the Indians in the fall of 1876. On one occasion the lieutenant and his command, accompanied by a number of settlers, among whom were Mike Burton and Joe Cook of "Montana Herd" fame, went out north of the Belle Fourche river on a scouting expedition after Indians. On their return trip, when at the point where the town of Belle Fourche now stands, they were met by Mr. Ames' flock of sheep, behind which were a small band of Indians, urging them forward with all possible speed. The officer in command ordered a charge on the Indians, who, taken by surprise, fled precipitately to a high bank overlooking the river, pursued by the soldiers. Finding themselves surrounded they urged their ponies down the steep bank into the stream, reached the opposite side and took shelter in the timber. The sheep were recovered and returned by the soldiers to their owner, Mr. Ames.

That night they went into camp at the Boughton and Giles stockade, where on the following morning a message arrived, from "Skew" Johnston's ranch asking immediate assistance. A large band of Indians had dashed down upon their herd of cattle, and driven them off in a northwest direction towards the Little Missouri river. "Boots and Saddles" was ordered and the soliders and citizens were soon mounted and on their trail, which was followed as far as the Belle Fourche river. They found stragglers from the herd along the trail, exhausted by the long rapid drive, and as they neared the Belle Fourche river the lowing of the cattle could be heard in the distance, evidencing that the Indians, with their booty, were not far in advance. Believing that the Indians were in overpowering numbers and fearful of being drawn into ambush, Lieut. Cummings, deeming "discretion the better part of valor," ordered the return of his command to Centennial Prairie. The Indians drove the entire herd, except the few stragglers, to their rendezvous northwest of the Hills.

These are but a few of the many losses suffered by the early settlers along the northern frontier, but sufficient to illustrate some of the difficulties with which they were constantly beset during the period of its early settlement. Would it could be recorded here that large herds of horses and cattle and sheep had been sufficient to satisfy the rapacity of those graceless savages! But no, whenever opportunity offered they, too, stained the green of the beautiful valley with the blood of the settlers. Every day and every hour deadly peril menaced them, and any man who ventured far beyond the protecting walls of his log cabin, virtually courted death, as he was liable to become the target for the skillful marksmanship of a band of concealed Indians. Especially was this the case after the return of the Sioux from the battle of the Little Horn in the late summer and early fall of 1876, during which time a number were killed.

One of these was a young man, who hailed from Louisville, Kentucky, Jimmy Irion by name and a printer by trade. "Jimmy," as he was familiarly called, was employed as a "lookout" by a party of hay-makers in the valley of False Bottom creek, and one bright, fatal morning in early September, he mounted his horse, placed his gun across the pommel of his saddle, as was his wont, and rode away from camp to his doom. Poor fellow, when climbing the hill to his accustomed point of observation, he fell, pierced and shattered by a volley of Indian bullets. His mutilated body was found soon after, and later taken to Deadwood for interment. Upon examination it was discovered that one of the balls had struck a cartridge in his belt, which he wore over his left shoulder across under his left arm, and exploded it, the concussion shattering his body frightfully.

A somewhat peculiar case now recalled, was the killing of a man named Hayward, a few miles north of Spearfish, in the summer or fall of 1876. Hayward, who was the owner of a team and wagon, was engaged by a party of some half dozen Deadwood coal prospectors to take them to the newly-discovered Hay creek coal-beds, about forty miles northerly from Deadwood. It was a dangerous trip, and one that few cared to take in those days. Hayward, a tenderfoot of the tenderest type, was just from the East, and had a morbid fear of being killed by Indians that was pitiable in the extreme. Indeed he had a premonition which presaged his certain death at their hands, and he was not to be shaken in that belief.

However, by dint of much persuasion, and the promise of large emoluments, he was finally induced to undertake the journey which, although there were plenty of Indians flitting about all over that region of the country, was accomplished without encountering a single redskin. After spending a few days in exploring the coal deposit without molestation, the men started on their way homeward, and when about half the distance to Spearfish had been covered, a band of mounted Indians was discovered in the distance, following swiftly on their trail. The horses were urged forward at their utmost speed, and the Indians gave chase. After running two or three miles or such a matter, finding that their pursuers were gaining rapidly upon them, the panting, foaming team was swiftly switched in behind a low embankment, where they prepared to defend themselves as best they could. For hours they stood off that band of bloodthirsty savages, who largely outnumbered them, leveling and firing their guns over the embankment whenever an Indian came within range; they in turn firing back as often as the top of a head appeared above the natural parapet. Hayward, who meanwhile was in a mad frenzy of exictement, persisted, in spite of repeated warnings, in standing up every few minutes in full view of the Indians, as if inviting his fate, to see if they were still there. Poor fellow! he exposed himself as a target once too often, for at last, as night was approaching, the fatal ball went true to its mark, and he fell dead, as he predicted he would. Shortly after the Indians withdrew, when the body was placed in the wagon and conveyed to Spearfish, where it was laid to rest in a spot set apart for the burial of Indian victims.

On the 23d of July, 1877, David Abernethy and Deputy-Sheriff Wilson left Spearfish in pursuit of two men who had run off with a wagon belonging to the former. On reaching Montana Lake, two miles east of Beulah, close on the trail of the thieves, they halted for a brief rest, when suddenly a band of Indians rushed out from ambush and killed them both, then took horses, saddles, and guns, rifled their pockets, and rode away with their booty. Information of the murder reached Spearfish, when a party of armed men went out to the lake, found the bodies and brought them back to Spearfish for burial.

During the same month and year a party went out from Spearfish to the rescue of a party of immigrants who were surrounded and held by the Indians on the Redwater. They brought them safely in, also the bodies of four men who had been killed and scalped not far from town.

The last hostile appearance of the Sioux in the vicinity of Spearfish was in July, 1877, when what was known as the "Pettigrew" party was beleagured for three days on Sand creek, while en route overland for the Pacific Coast. This party, which was partly recruited at Spearfish, was composed of about fifty men, women, and children, including the family of the leader, Charles W. Pettigrew. On reaching Sand creek they went into camp on a little eminence near where the Beulah bridge now stands, and while waiting there to secure additional recruits at that small settlement two members of the party were run in by a small force of Indians, who fired a volley after them into camp, at long range, causing no small panic among the women and children. To defend the camp against an expected attack, they at once corralled their wagons, placed the women and children inside the barricade, dug rifle pits outside for the men, and, thus entrenched, awaited events.

The next morning a large force of Indians, numbering from sixty to seventy braves, in detached squads, surrounded the camp on all sides, and opened a brisk fire at long range, on the defenses, the men in the pits returning the fire whenever an Indian came within range of their guns. This intermittent interchange of bullets continued for three days, during which time two futile attempts were made to stampede the stock of the besieged party.

Meanwhile, information of their perilous situation had reached Spearfish and Deadwood, when a body of armed men from each of these places mounted their horses and rode swiftly to their relief. Near the close of the third day they arrived at the seat of hostilities, when, it is needless to state, the braves suddenly disappeared and were seen no more.

Among this party was Mr. Deffebaugh, of Spearfish, who two years later was killed by Indians at Devil's Tower. Unanimously deciding not to continue their journey farther towards the setting sun, the party returned with its rescuers to Spearfish, where the leader, Mr. Pettigrew, settled with his family and has since made his home.

The first public enterprise planned by the Town-site Company was a scheme to bring travel from Bismarck to the Hills *via* Spearfish. In furtherance of the project, Jas. Bradley, who was regarded as something of a "Kit Carson" by the early settlers, was selected to conduct a party of exploration to the north and east, for the purpose of laying out a feasible route from Spearfish, to intersect the old road from Bismarck to the Hills laid out in 1875.

Accordingly, on July 2, 1877, Jas. Bradley, W. W. Bradley, Gus. M. Wood, Jas. H. Madding, and a teamster named Paste, started from Spearfish in a northwest direction across the Belle Fourche three or four miles below the mouth of the Redwater. After traveling about 200 miles over an almost impenetrable country, frequently changing their course, and enduring a good deal of hardship, they at last came upon the old Bismarck wagon trial. On their return an estimate based upon their report was made, when it was decided that the cost of constructing the road would be too great, and the enterprise was abandoned. Strangely enough, though marauding bands of Indians were still roaming over the country, not a single redskin was encountered during the trip.

With the quieting of the Sioux title, and the subsequent cessation of Indian hostilities along the northern border in the summer of 1877, and the consequent influx of immigration and freedom to develop unmolested the resources of the fertile valley, and to utilize the vast areas of rich grazing land lying adjacent to and extending far to the north and west, began the growth and prosperity of Spearfish. These with its advantages of location on one of the never-failing streams of the Hills, affording unsurpassed water-power facilities, made its permanence an assured fact. Fully alive to these advantages and confident of its future success, business at that time began to expand.

The first store is said to have been opened by John Arrington and H. M. Jorgans in 1877, in a building afterwards occupied by M. V. Walk as a blacksmith shop. In this same building was kept the first post-office of Spearfish, established in 1877, with H. M. Jorgans as first postmaster, and Jas. Rogers as first United States mail carrier.

SPEARFISH TOWN IN 1877

The second merchant was J. C. Ryan, who, in the fall of 1877, erected a one-story frame building twenty by forty feet, and opened a stock of general merchandise. In 1883 Mr. Ryan erected a two-story frame building twenty-six by fifty feet with fire-proof cellar underneath. The second floor of this building was designed and occupied as a Masonic Hall.

The first regular hostelry in Spearfish, called the Spearfish Hotel, was built by P. C. Riley, Jas. Ryan, and Tony Gerig, in the fall of 1877, on the ground now occupied by the Spearfish House. After a few months, Riley bought the interests of his copartners and conducted the business alone during the winter, when he in turn sold the establishment and its partronage to Jas. Rogers. Prior to the building of this hotel, however, a sort of a lunch-room was kept for a short time in a log cabin by the same gentlemen, one of whom superintended the culinary department, and did the cooking.

The first sawmill was built and operated by M. B. Goodsell, in the spring of 1877, on the site now occupied by the Spearfish Milling Company.

The first blacksmith shop was opened by Kellar Bradley in 1877 on the site now occupied by Tom Mathews, and the first livery stable was established by P. C. Riley during the same year.

The first to establish the practice of law in Spearfish was W. W. Bradley, early in 1877, and moreover Mr. Bradley is also entitled to the distinction of having performed the first marriage ceremony—if ceremony it can be called—in June, 1877. This first marriage was solemnized under somewhat peculiar circumstances. When John Henry Skinner and Jessie Edwins decided to be "spliced" and made one, they were confronted by a grave difficulty. There was no one in Spearfish at that date, endowed with legal authority to perform the sacred ceremony, so, in their dilemma, they appealed to Attorney Bradley, then the only lawyer in the town, to help them out of the difficulty. He advised that he could tie the "nuptial knot," so that it would hold through sunshine and shadow, through evil as well as good report. He argued with himself that marriage was a civil contract, and, in that belief, he proceeded to draw up a contract for their signatures. Appended is the contract verbatim et literatim:—

This agreement, made and entered into this first day of June, 1878, by and between John Henry Skinner, party of the first part, and Jessie Edwins of Spearfish, Lawrence County, South Dakota, party of the second part, witnesseth: That whereas the said first and second parties have by these presents, agreed and contracted in good faith and virtue to become man and wife, and that there being no officer of the law or minister of the gospel to perform the ceremony of marriage, therefore we, the said parties above mentioned, in presence of two witnesses, do hereby bind ourselves in all law of any State or

Territory, both moral and equitable, to be henceforth husband and wife, in the true legal and equitable and moral sense of the term.

The said first party agreeing to do and perform all acts towards said second party that are required by law, and that I, the said John Henry Skinner, do by these presents, agree to take the said Jessie Edwins as my true and lawful wife, her to love, defend and care for, in sickness or in health, and forsaking all others until death do us part. And the said Jessie Edwins, party of the second part, agrees to take the said Henry Skinner as her true and lawful husband, him to love, cherish and defend, in sickness and in health, forsaking all others as long as we both do live.

Witness our hands and seal, this the day and year above mentioned.

JOHN HENRY SKINNER
JESSIE EDWINS

Witnesses:
JAMES FORTUNE,
FLORA OSBORNE,
R. H. EVANS.

What fee he received for the important document tradition sayeth not.

The first school in Spearfish was a private school opened in the fall of 1877, and taught by Miss Pettigrew—now Mrs. R. H. Evans—in a private house owned by John Ingersoll.

The first religious services are said to have been held by Rev. George Reed—Methodist—in 1878, though no church building was erected until years later.

During the same year a Congregational society was organized, and in 1879 a frame church building was erected and used jointly for church and academic school purposes until 1882, when the society began the erection of a handsome Gothic church edifice north of the city on ground donated by Joseph Ramsdell. The building was completed in 1883 at a cost of about $4,000. Much of the credit for its accomplishment is said to be due to the efforts of M. F. Connors, who contributed liberally to the building fund.

The first flouring mill was built by C. V. Gardner and Porter Warner—then proprietor of the Deadwood *Daily Times*—in 1879. The mill, which employed the grinding process, was propelled by water-power furnished by Spearfish creek, and operated exclusively on home-grown wheat.

In 1883 a new mill, upon the roller plan, with a capacity of 100 barrels per day, was erected by the Spearfish Milling Company, composed of Spearfish and Crook City capitalists. The motor power for these enlarged operations was furnished by an immense flume bringing water from the creek to the mill, with a fall of seventeen feet.

The first drug store was opened in June, 1878, by Dr. J. M. Louthan and George Stotts, in a building located on the corner of Sixth and I streets. Dr. Louthan was also the first to start the practice of medicine; in fact, he was the only physician in Spearfish for a number of years.

It appears from data obtained that the Spearfish *Valley Gazette*—edited by John M. Elliott—was the first newspaper published in Spearfish, the first sheet appearing on May 7th, 1881, and John Cashner is entitled to the distinction of having taken the first paper from the press.

The Dakota *Weekly Register,* an eight-column folio, was established less than a month later by Messrs. C. V. Gardner and John Johnston, the initial number appearing on June 4th, 1881. In 1883 Mr. Gardner retired from the firm, leaving the enterprise under the sole proprietorship and management of Mr. Johnston. On the 1st of December, 1885, Henry & Grant took charge of the paper, which, on November 1st, 1896, passed into the hands of A. C.

PICTURE GALLERY IN SPEARFISH IN 1877

Potter, under whose management it continued until December 3d, 1898, on which date it went into the hands of its present proprietor, F. B. Corum.

The first bank opened in Spearfish was a private institution established by Stebbins, Fox & Co., in November, 1882, with J. F. Summers as its first cashier. The bank building of Stebbins, Fox & Co. was the first brick structure erected in Spearfish. This private concern was organized under the territorial laws in 1887 under the title of the Bank of Spearfish, with L. W. Valentine as president and J. F. Summers as cashier. The bank organized in 1887 is identical with the present bank of Spearfish.

The first furniture store in Spearfish was opened by John Johnston in 1882, on H street between Fifth and Sixth streets.

The first exclusive dry goods store was opened by M. Liebman, on the site now occupied by W. L. Graham on Sixth street between H and I streets, and the first clothing store by Zoellner Bros. & Co., on H street between Fifth and Sixth streets, in September, 1891.

In 1883 an association, which, although essentially a Spearfish institution, was called the Lawrence County Agricultural Association, was organized with the following officers: J. C. Ryan of Spearfish, President; L. W. Valentine, of Crook City, Vice-President; W. P. Lindley, Secretary. The first fair of the association, held on the grounds adjacent to Spearfish, on October of that year, is pronounced to have been a decided success, the exhibition of stock, grain, vegetables, poultry, etc., having been exceedingly fine.

Speaking of this association brings to mind a combination formed at an early date by the producers of Spearfish valley, called the "Farmers' Club." This organization which, in view of the convictions of the average farmer of to-day, was, to say the least, remarkable, was in the nature of a "trust," formed for the purpose of controlling the price of grain in the markets of the Hills. One of the sections of the constitution of the "club," which embodied rules as binding as the laws of the Medes and Persians, is as follows, and is well worthy of preservation:—

Preamble: "Whereas the farmers of Lawrence County, Dakota Territory, believing that they can better regulate and control the prices of their produce of all kinds, by a more perfect organization, do by these presents, agree to adopt a constitution, by-laws, and rules, as the laws of said organization."

Section of Constitution: "The members of this 'club' hereby agree not to sell oats or barley for a less price than two and one-half cents per pound, at any of the mining or gulch towns, including Crook City, and two cents per pound in all the valley towns and valleys where the same is raised, and the penalty for violating any part of this section, by any member of this 'club' shall be a forfeiture by such member of the sum of $100.00, to be paid to this club immediately upon ascertaining that a violation has been committed, and the officers of the club are hereby authorized to sue and recover the same from any member violating the provisions of this section.

"The above shall be binding by law upon all members until the first day of June, 1880."

How long after that time this peculiar organization was continued is not known, but perhaps it was merged into the Farmers' Alliance in 1888 or 1889.

CHAPTER XXXVII

HORSE-THIEVES AND CATTLE-RUSTLING ON THE NORTHERN FRONTIER

Perhaps the most flourishing and profitable industry carried on in the region lying north and west of the Hills during the years extending from 1877 to 1883, was horse-stealing, and what is termed, in the vernacular of the ranges, "cattle-rustling." During those years, regularly organized bands of professional thieves and rustlers, the record of whose crimes, followed sometimes by speedy retribution, fills not a few tragic pages in the history of Spearfish, under the guise of ranchmen and hunters, made their sole living by appropriating the stock that roamed at large over the northern plains.

The modus operandi of these banded outlaws, many of whom claimed ranches in remote and out-of-the-way localities, was to run off the stolen horses to these hidden places until a sufficient number were secured, when they were taken into Wyoming, or some other market, and sold for good prices, while the cattle were driven singly or in numbers to some secluded spot, slaughtered, their hides burned, and the meat sold in the markets of the Hills. It was difficult to detect them, as they were ostensibly disposing of their own property, and even if cattle, bearing the brand of their owners, were traced and found on the premises of the thieves, it furnished no proof that they had been stolen, as the wide expanse of prairie was their legitimate range.

Thus it will be seen that the law was practically powerless to protect private property and the thieves were suffered to continue their nefarious traffic, unwhipped of justice for years. Receiving but little protection from the courts, the settlers and stock-owners, exasperated beyond the point of endurance by their frequent losses and the boldness of the thieves, finally resolved to take the law into their own hands. So one night, early in 1877, a few determined men met in secret conclave, bound themselves together by an iron-clad oath, and issued forth, sworn to mete out summary justice to every "rustler" upon whom they could henceforward lay their avenging hands; perchance the innocent sometimes suffered with the guilty. They had not long to wait.

One balmy night in August, 1877, it was whispered around that a party of horse thieves was encamped in the brush east of Lookout Mountain, and as it approached the midnight watch a small band of masked men—vigilants they were—armed to the teeth, carrying a rope, stealthily made their way round the base of the mountain, crept up to the camp, captured two men named Bean Davis and George Skeating, slipped a noose over each head, and swung them from the limb of a near-by pine tree, and no other, save the eye of Omniscience, witnessed the tragedy. It was thought two others, detecting their guarded approach, made their escape. The vigilants then silently separated, and each retired to his respective home and bed to sleep, perchance to dream—of what?

Another, who died with his boots on because of his natural or acquired penchant for other people's horses, was Jack Cole, a local celebrity known around Spearfish as "Buckskin Jack," and, by the way, I wonder if he was the same "Buckskin" who joined the "Centennial Party," while en route to the Hills early in the spring of 1876. If so, he became short on moral scruples, went north on the range, joined the gang, was finally caught and given free passage *via* the suspension route to his last account. Poor Buckskin!

The most notorious as well as the most nefarious of the outlaws who for years infested the region northeast and west of the Hills were what is widely known as the Exelbee gang, composed of such names as John Campbell, Billy McCarthy or the "Kid," Chas. Brown or "Broncho Charley," and Alex. Grady, with George Exelbee as chief. Members of the gang frequently visited the settlements in the garb of hunters or cowboys, for the purpose, so to speak, of spying out the land, and even men engaged in legitimate business were sometimes, under the cloak of respectability, found aiding and abetting the gang and sharing in its profits.

In 1878 some of the citizens of the town were suspected, their movements watched, and finally after a good deal of detective work on the part of the citizens, were caught. One night, long after the shadows fell, two of the suspects were discovered driving off cattle not their own, and were followed. About midnight they halted to rest, went into camp, and while sleeping were surrounded by the grim avengers and captured. No explanation was asked of the trembling culprits, and one was needed. They had been caught in the commission of the crime, to expiate which they were soon struggling in midair from the limb of a tree, where the bodies were left and afterwards found.

Another man who was strongly suspected of being secretly connected with the notorious Exelbee gang, now recalled, was J. B. Pruden, mail contractor, express agent, and stage owner on the route from Miles City to Spearfish. Pruden was finally arrested at the former place by a Deputy United States Marshal, who telegraphed to United States Marshal A A. Raymond at Deadwood to send an officer for the prisoner. Fred A. Willard, who was deputy at Spearfish, deputized J. W. Ryan to go to Miles City and bring Pruden to Deadwood to be tried by the courts.

In the winter of 1883-4 the curtain finally dropped on the long wicked career of the Exelbee gang, at Stonewall, Montana. The story of the closing scenes of the tragic drama, is, shorn of tedious details, about as follows:—

The outlaws in their extended raids had visited the Indian reservations on the Missouri river and stolen a lot of Indian horses. Complaint was made by the agent to the United States District Attorney at Deadwood, and a warrant was issued for the arrest of the thieves and placed in the hands of Deputy United States Marshal A. J. Raymond, of Deadwood, who at once put officers on the trail. The outlaws, having doubtless been forewarned of the danger of their being caught in the meshes of the law, had packed their personal equipments, and moved out westward for Miles City. Officers Fred. A. Willard and Jack O'Harra, of Spearfish, and Capt. A. M. Willard, of Deadwood, armed with due process of law, as well as trusty guns, mounted their horses and started in hot pursuit of their game, like sleuths on the track of a murderer.

Dr. J. M. Louthan, O. F. Howard, Dan Stout, Osman Onge, J. Talbot, D. Scoop, H. Hood, Billy Howe, John Bell, and Bill Gay, from Spearfish, and Deputy United States Marshals A. A. Raymond, J. C. Duffy, E. P. Jackson, and Fred Bartlett, accompanied by Dr. Babcock, as surgeon from Deadwood, followed, but did not arrive in time to participate in the battle.

The five mounted bandits with three pack horses were overtaken at a place called Stonewall, Montana, where a desperate fight occurred, resulting in the death of one of the officers, Jack O'Harra, and the mortal wounding of each member of the gang, except "Billy the Kid," who escaped unscathed. Upon discovering their game, the officers circled around to the northward and climbed a little eminence where they could command the situation, when Willard, taking position with O'Harra on the right, called to the leader, Exelbee: "I have a warrant for your arrest;" whereupon the outlaws turned and faced the officers, when the shooting began on both sides. Willard's first shot struck Campbell, who threw up his hands and fell from his horse, and at about the same moment O'Harra was heard to exclaim: "I guess I am killed!" Willard threw his arms around him as he was about to fall, when a shot from the rear penetrated his left shoulder, glanced across and came out at the right, causing a serious though not dangerous flesh wound. O'Harra lived about ten minutes. About the fourth shot Exelbee was seen to throw up his hands and fall from his horse. By this time the officers discovered that they were being fired at from the rear by "Kid," who had taken refuge behind a pile of lumber, from where he had shot the two officers. During the fight two more of the outlaws were wounded, the three pack-horses, and two saddle-horses killed, and two saddle-horses captured by the officers, leaving them only one horse, with which to make good their escape.

Exelbee and his men then retreated into the brush, made a circuit and came out on the opposite of the officers, from where they fired at a lot of cowboys who chanced to be in the vicinity, killing one Billy Cunningham and wounding another, named Jack Harris, who later died as a result of the wound.

SEQUEL TO THE FIGHT

That night Exelbee, the wounded chief, came to Sheldon's ranch, five miles above, with three of his comrades, and begged for bread, bandages, and money,—saying he was going to leave the country as it was becoming too torrid for him. The next day, Campbell, who had gotten separated from the others, sent to Humphrey Hood, foreman of the Hash-knife cattle ranch, by a stage driver named Chase, the following pleading note which tells its own story:—

DEAR HOOD: "I was badly wounded in the head during the fight yesterday and my horse was killed. The boys were all shot to pieces and scattered. For God's sake send me a horse by bearer as soon as it is dark enough to get away from the officers."

Hood, not wishing to be implicated, sent the note to Officer Willard, who detained the bearer, Chase, until dark, when he and Chas. Conley went with Chase to the cabin where Campbell was hidden, five miles away. Upon reaching the place Chase was ordered to take one of the horses and fasten him at the gate, then go inside and tell Campbell that there was a horse for him outside. Campbell soon came out with a pistol in his right and a rifle in his left hand and when half way to the gate Willard called to him to throw up his hands. Instead of complying he commenced shooting in the direction of the voice, whereupon Willard and Conley both fired at the desperate man and he fell dead. On the Friday following, February 22d, Tuttle was brought to Spearfish and placed in the county hospital, where Dr. Louthan examined the wounded arm and found that amputation would be necessary. The operation was never performed, for, as the tragic story goes—Ah, pity, 'tis, 'tis true—during the silent hours one dark night a band of six masked men entered the hospital where the sufferer slept, gagged him, and carried him away groaning with pain, the inmates of the hospital meanwhile not daring to make any outcry against the procedure. The next morning, the 27th, his rigid body, clad only in a thin cotton shirt, and a bandage around his neck, supporting his wounded arm, was seen swinging like a pendulum from the limb of an oak tree in the cold winter wind, bearing every indication that he had slowly choked to death. Poor, misguided man, even now I brush aside a tear at the remembrance of his unhappy fate.

Tuttle was born and reared in the lap of luxury,—a father's pride and a fond mother's joy, doubtless. He had been educated in the best schools of this country, and was then sent abroad to complete his studies. His father died leaving him a fortune of $40,000, or $50,000, when he left New York City and came to the "wild and woolly" West, landing in Minnesota where he opened the drug business with a partner. Inexperienced in the ways of the untrammeled West, and susceptible perhaps to evil influences, he soon squandered his heritage, and was left penniless. After wandering from one point to another for a time he came to the Hills and went onto the cattle range, joined the gang, as an easy way to make a living, and finally ended his once promising life, as stated.

The breaking up of this notorious gang had the effect of putting a final quietus on the several bands of horse and cattle thieves who had infested the Black Hills for many years and stock-owners were after that left to their pursuits unmolested.

HOW SPEARFISH CAME TO BE CALLED THE QUEEN CITY

Perhaps there are some in the Black Hills who do not know how Spearfish came to be honored with the appellation of "The Queen City of the Hills," therefore it may not be out of place to relate the circumstances under which it received that distinction. This is the way it originated: at its first public celebration of our great national holiday, July 4th, 1878, Judge Bradley of that city—brimming over with patriotism, as well as admiration for and loyalty to his adopted city, in his address of welcome gave eloquent expression to the following truly poetic sentiments:—

"We throw wide open the gates of the city and bid you welcome to the land of the wild rose, and the home of the golden grain. Come and kiss the gentle zephyrs mid the wild flowers—sweeter than Eros ever sipped from the lips of Psyche. We lay upon the altars of our homes our hearts and our hospitality, and again we bid you welcome, yea, a hundred times welcome, to Spearfish, 'The Queen City of the Hills.' "

This fitting title has clung to Spearfish since that time, and probably will continue to cling to it for all time to come. At that first public celebration of the day of our nation's birth at Spearfish, Lorin E. Gaffey, now Judge of the Sixth Judicial District of South Dakota, delivered the oration.

PUBLIC SCHOOL

The Spearfish public school district was first organized in the fall of 1878, R. H. Evans, J. B. Black, and L. W. Stone, constituting the first board of the district, and the first term of the public school was taught by Miss Pettigrew, now Mrs. R. H. Evans, in a log cabin that stood on the ground now occupied by the Burlington & Missouri Railway depot, with an attendance of fourteen pupils. For a few years the schools were taught in rented rooms, which, proving inadequate, a commodious public school building was erected in 1881, at a cost of $5,000.00. On the first of November of that year the building was dedicated, since which time the school has grown and flourished. From the time of the opening of the first term in 1878 with one teacher and fourteen pupils, the school has increased to an enrollment of 230 pupils, separated into four departments requiring the employment of five instructors.

In April, 1897, Spearfish was organized into an independent school district, and a Board of Education provided for by special act of the Legislature to consist of two members from each of the three wards of the city and a member at large. The members of the first board were: P. J. M. Burgess, President; Hiram Dodson, J. T. McConachie, Hugh Gibson, Mrs. Viola Smith, W. A. Zink, and J. H. Russell; Henry Court, Clerk.

SPEARFISH NORMAL SCHOOL

On a commanding site on the northwestern limits of the city is located the State Normal School—the especial boast and pride of the Queen City of the Hills. The edifice is a handsome three-storied structure, in full Romanesque style of architecture, surmounted directly over the main entrance by an imposing tower, which is almost the first object to attract the attention of the visitor entering the city from any direction. The superstructure, which rests upon a half-story basement of stone work, is constructed of brick, ornamented with light gray sandstone, roofed with metallic shingles, and presents with its environments of shade trees and cultivated acres of luscious small fruits, a very attractive, and, I might add, an exceedingly tempting appearance.

The interior arrangements of the building, which nearly approach perfection, compare favorably in design, finish, and equipment, with the best institutions of its kind in the West. It is provided with a commodious assembly room, study and recitation rooms, laboratory, library, gymnasium, etc., each of which is handsomely and appropriately furnished, and fitted with hot and cold registers, thus placing the temperature of the rooms under the complete control of the occupants. The library is well filled with works of the best standard literature, but is especially developed along the line of science and applied mechanics, and the museum contains an extensive and valuable collection of minerals, fossils, and curios. In the basement are the furnaces, the manual training rooms, carpenter shop, gymnasium, and fuel rooms.

The curriculum of the institution embraces a wide range of studies, including music, drawing, bookkeeping, stenography, physics, chemistry, natural science, Latin, history, and pedagogics. The course of instruction in these branches is thorough and complete, especially so along the line of pedagogics, and some of the best equipped teachers in the Black Hills have received their training within its classic walls. Under the efficient management of its principal, Fayette L. Cook, aided by a corps of competent instructors, the institution has acquired an enviable reputation throughout the State, and attracts a large attendance, some from remote localities, and is a monument to the enterprise of the men through whose unflagging and untiring efforts the institution was made possible. The inception of the enterprise appears to have been hedged about by many discouraging difficulties and failures, as the following brief account will illustrate:—

The first steps towards the establishment of the school were taken in 1881, when a bill introduced by Frank J. Washabaugh passed the Territorial Legislature, authorizing: "That a Normal School for the Territory of Dakota be established at Spearfish, Lawrence County, the exclusive purpose of which shall be the instruction of persons both male and female in the art of teaching, and in all the various branches that pertain to a good common school education, also to give instruction in the mechanical arts, and in husbandry and agricultural chemistry, in the fundamental laws of the United States, and in what regards the rights and duties of citizens; provided, that a tract of land not less than forty acres be donated and secured to the Territory of Dakota, in fee simple, as a site for said Normal school, within six months from the taking effect of this act; and the Governor of the Territory is hereby empowered, and it is made his duty to see that a good and sufficient deed, so far as can be, be made to the Territory for the same."

Through failure to comply with the requirements of the act, in the matter of securing a site within the specified time, the law became null and void. At the legislative session of 1883, the same bill was again introduced by Mr. Washabaugh, and again passed through both branches of the Legislature. Messrs. Joseph Ramsdell of Spearfish, R. D. Millett of Lead, and F. P. Bass of Central, were appointed on the Board of Directors, who, upon receiving their credentials, at once proceeded to secure the requisite ground. Various eligible sites were offered at prices ranging from $3,000.00 to $800.00, the latter offer being made by Mr. John Maurer, for the ground on which the Normal building now stands, consisting of forty acres of land traversed by two irrigating ditches, which, being the cheapest eligible site, was favored by the board. Before entering into arrangements for the transfer of the ground, however, a citizens' meeting was called, at which two of the citizens of Spearfish, M. C. Connors and W. F. Powers, offered to donate the ground jointly—the latter to give twenty acres from his ground on the plateau south of town and the former to purchase an equal number of acres from the Bradley farm adjoining. The board readily accepted the offer, and agreed to build the school on the donated ground.

Accordingly Messrs. Connors and Powers executed a deed to the aforesaid grounds to the Territory and had it recorded, but contrary to the letter and spirit of the act, it contained the proviso that the said premises are to be used by the said Territory for the said purpose within two years from the date thereof, and if not so used by the said Territory, the said property shall revert to said M. C. Connors and W. T. Powers, respectively. The deed was forwarded to Gov. N. J. Ordway in August, within less than a month of the time when the law would again become inoperative.

Upon receipt of the document the Governor sent the following dispatch:—

BISMARCK, D. T., August 28th, 1883

JOS. RAMSDELL, Spearfish:

Acts of 1883 provide bond must be secured to Territory, in fee simple. See chapter 20, special act session laws of 1883. I cannot accept any other form of title.

(Signed)   N. J. ORDWAY,
Governor

Upon receipt of dispatch Mr. Ramsdell appealed to the donors, who refused to amend the deed to confrom to the requirements of the Act, when the board renewed the effort to secure the Maurer site, which was successful. The ground was purchased at the terms aforementioned, and a deed in fee simple made to the Territory therefor just in time to save the Act from going a second time into the Governor's waste basket. The purchase fund for the site was secured by subscription among those friendly to the enterprise.

On the strength of the meager appropriation of $5,000.00 for building, and $2,000.00 for first year's running expenses, the enterprise was launched. By dint of economy, an apology for a building was erected, and by renting the school furniture of the Congregational Academy, which had been discontinued, it was made possible to open the school on the 14th of April, 1884, with Prof. Van B. Baker as first principal and an attendance at the opening of term of twenty students, which soon increased to forty. The opening year of the school under the principalship of Prof. Van B. Baker appears not to have proven a glittering success. His mismanagement and general defalcations along the line of his school duties became so unsatisfactory to the students and distasteful to the patrons and the board that he was compelled to surrender the helm in January, some months before the close of the first school year, to more judicious and capable hands.

The $2,000 appropriated for first year's running expenses having become exhausted, the school remained closed until the following fall. In the interim, Mr. Harry M. Gregg, assisted by Mr. Washabaugh, succeeded in securing from the Legislature of 1885 an appropriation of $5,000 for the purchase of needed furniture and the maintenance of the school for the two succeeding years. In March, 1885, Gov. Pierce appointed a new board of directors, composed of Messrs. H. M. Gregg, Samuel Cushman, and Albert Powers, who were fortunate in securing Fayette L. Cook, the present incumbent, to take charge of the school.

On the 14th of September, 1885, Prof. Cook opened the school for its second term with seventeen students, which number, under his superior management, increased to thirty-seven before the close of the first term. The next term the attendance increased to seventy, when it became necessary to employ an assistant, for which position the services of Miss Zella Busian, a graduate of the Winona Normal School, Minnesota, were secured.

The third year opened September 6th, 1886, with over ninety students, while the seating capacity of both rooms of the school was only seventy-eight, which, before the close of the term, increased to an enrollment of 104, besides a number were refused admission for lack of capacity. During the third year three assistants were employed, viz.: Miss Busian, Miss W. A. Thompson, and Miss Bertha Youmans, the latter having charge of the primary department of the public school, which had, by permission of the district school board, been converted into a model school for the Normal.

On June 28th, 1887, the first graduating class, consisting of Misses Nettie M. Pratt, Maude A. Gardner, Jean Cowgill, Cora Grubbs, May Chase, Kate M. Kemper, Sallie R. Pryor, and Masters Harry M. Jones, Richard G. Whitney and Eugene T. Pettigrew, received their diplomas, 'mid the perfume of potted plants and bouquets of flowers.

At the legislative session of 1887 Mr. John Wolzmuth by untiring and unremitting effort, assisted by Messrs. Patton and Stewart in the House, and Washabaugh and Wells in the Council, succeeded in securing the passage of a bill authorizing the appropriation of $25,000.00 for the construction of a suitable building, and $21,400.00 for the current expenses of the ensuing two years. The newly appointed board of directors, Mr. Wolzmuth, J. F. Summers, and A. Powers, under the advice of the principal, set about perfecting plans for a structure, worthy of the school, which resulted in the construction of the building already described. Under the experienced and skillfull guidance of Professor Cook, who is still at the helm, the institution year by year has grown in popularity until it is to-day the pride, not only of the "Queen City," but of the entire Black Hills.

ORGANIZATION

On March 31st, 1885, the town organization was completed, with J. F. Summers, Frank Welch, Henry Keets, Jas. Rogers, and J. A. Bishop as Board of Trustees, of which J. F. Summers was President, and Frank Overman, clerk. On June 7th, 1888, the town was organized under the general incorporation laws into the "City of Spearfish" and divided into three wards to be represented in the City Council by two members from each ward. The first officers of the city were M. C. Connors, Mayor; John A. Clark, Clerk; Henry Keets, Dr. J. M. Louthan, Henry Court, W. H. Harlow, H. A. Miller, and Frank Welch, Aldermen.

The Spearfish water system, which is owned by the city, was established during the summer of 1887. An abundant water supply is drawn from mountain springs, known as "Clemmons Springs," some two or three miles away, and poured into a reservoir one hundred and sixty feet above the level of the street. This is distributed through the city, and for defense against fires is supplemented by an excellent fire department.

The Spearfish Fire Department consisting of Hose Companies Nos. 1 and 2, Alert Hose Company, and one Hook & Ladder Company, was first organized on April 15th, 1888, with John A. Clark as its first Chief. The present department is represented by the same companies.

The first daily newspaper published in Spearfish, called the Spearfish *Evening Bulletin* was established by J. H. & E. H. Warren, the first issue appearing June 3d, 1889. The Spearfish *Mail*, a weekly publication, was established by the same firm, on January 29th, 1889, and is identical with the Spearfish *Mail* of to-day. The paper, a wide-awake, readable sheet, is under the present control and management of E. H. Warren, now member elect to the House of the South Dakota Legislature.

The Spearfish Electric Light system was established in 1893 by the Spearfish Electric Light and Power Co., composed of Chicago capitalists. The lights are maintained by a plant located on Spearfish river some two and half miles from the city, at a cost to the municipality of $1,260 per year. The system is managed by G. C. Favorite, an expert electrician.

430   THE BLACK HILLS; OR,

SPEARFISH IN 1895—LOOKING WEST

The manufacturing industries of Spearfish consist of a fine flouring mill, stucco works, a planing mill and two saw mills. Moreover, among its industries may also be listed a cyanide gold-reduction plant which is now in course of construction, if, indeed, it is not already finished and in operation. The enterprise was projected and established by an organization known as the Spearfish Cyanide Co., composed chiefly of "Ragged Top" mining men who design putting the plant in operation on the refractory ores of the Ragged Top Mining district where a group of claims designated the Metallic Streak, located on Calamity gulch, has been leased. With commendable economy the company leased an old disused stucco mill at Spearfish, which was remodeled, enlarged, and equipped with the requisite machinery to the capacity of twenty-five tons of ore per day. It is claimed that the ore deposit which crosses the claims is three feet in thickness carrying an average of $10.00 per ton of gold. This with the fact that the claims are located within easy hauling distance of the B. and M. Station, reducing the cost of transportation to a minimum, should insure to the projectors of the enterprise profitable returns from their investment.

Besides the State Normal and public school building, Spearfish has three places of public worship, viz., the Congregational, Methodist, and Episcopal Churches. There are also Catholic and Christian societies which have no church buildings. Among the secret orders are the Masonic and Odd Fellows' societies, established in 1880, the Knights of Pythias, A. O. U. W. and Modern Woodmen of America.

With the advent of the Burlington Railway in December, 1893, Spearfish was brought into more vital commercial relations with the trade centers of the Hills, since which time its growth, if not phenomenally rapid, has been sure and steadfast. That its stimulating influence has been felt through every avenue of enterprise is indicated by its long array of business establishments of various kinds. Besides its two newspapers and a flourishing banking institution, it has two hotels, three stores of general merchandise, one exclusive grocery store, one store of dry goods, boots and shoes, one store of groceries, boots and shoes, two drug stores, one clothing store, one hardware store, three confectionery and stationery stores, two variety stores, two millinery shops, three blacksmith shops, three livery barns, three barber shops, one photograph gallery, one tailor shop, three real estate offices, three doctors, three lawyers, and claims a present population of 1,500 souls.

While Spearfish depends largely upon the agricultural products of the broad fertile valleys, which spread out in all directions, it derives no inconsiderable volume of its trade from the numerous cattle ranches, occupying the foot-hills and uplands bordering the valleys, of which it is the headquarters. Moreover, the valley of Spearfish river is the natural outlet of several promising mining districts, some of which have been systematically developed in past years, and which with needed facilities will become important factors in the future business economy of the city to which they are tributary.

Only twelve miles away to the southwest is the once famous "Nigger Hill" tin district, whose extent and richness has been long since demonstrated, and which experts declared produced five per cent pure tin. When that important industry is revived in the Black Hills, as it doubtless will be with changed conditions, "Nigger Hill" will doubtless rival in production any other portion of the Hills. At the foot of "Nigger Hill" are the Bear gulch placer diggings, which in the early years produced some of the richest specimens of wash gold found in the Black Hills, indicating the existence of valuable gold ledges, within the drainage area of the stream. Near at hand is the erstwhile booming silver-lead carbonate camp, the scene of the great "Iron Hill" excitement which in 1886 completely overturned the mental equilibrium of even old miners and prospectors, to say nothing of inexperienced tenderfeet. The great bubble collapsed, it is true, but did not burst and may again be inflated. Considerable work is now being done on the property, and its production may yet prove a tangible quantity in the mineral wealth of the northern Hills. Then there is the Ragged Top district, whose siliceous gold ores will soon be carried to the doors of the city over the steel rails of the Burlington Railway for reduction. These, with the extensive quarries of marble, limestone, gypsum, etc., in the surrounding hills, and last, but not least, its proximity and accessibility to the extensive coal fields of Hay creek, give Spearfish no insignificant portion of the mineral wealth of the Black Hills. Albeit, those who expect to see in the Queen City a booming town like Deadwood and Lead will be greatly disappointed, for instead they will find a sober, serious community pursuing the even tenor of its way, in an unostentatious, yet thoroughly business-like manner.

CHAPTER XXXVIII

GALENA SILVER CAMP

In a deep gulch, surrounded on all sides by lofty pine-covered hills, about six miles in an air line southeast of Deadwood, on Bear Butte creek, is situated Galena, the center of the chief silver mining industry of the Black Hills.

Early in March, 1876, a number of prospectors in search of gold, penetrated the region along that stream and discovered the silver mines, which have since made that district famous. Among the first settlers in Galena were James Conzette, E. R. Collins, David Dusette, Wm. Ferguson, W. H. Wood, David Galvin, Arthur Finnegan, and an Italian named Esperando Feri. Among the earliest mines discovered were the Florence, and Merritt Nos. 1 and 2, by H. N. Merritt & Brother; the Sitting Bull, by Frank Cochrane; the Emma, by James Conzette; the El-Refugio, by W. H. Franklin & Cook; other locations, both gold and silver, soon following. While developing these mines, a vein of almost pure galena was exposed in the Florence and Sitting Bull ledges—from which discovery the town derives its name.

In September, 1876, Robt. Florman, the veteran miner and prospector, arrived in the new silver camp and purchased the Florence mine, which he owned and developed until 1878, when the property was absorbed by the "Florence Mining Company," an organization of St. Paul capitalists, who erected a ten-stamp mill on the property and operated them until about 1880, during which time the town had grown into considerable prominence. It received its first real importance, however, from the subsequent silver mining operations of Col. J. H. Davey, an expert in the treatment of the white metal, who arrived in the camp in 1880. Mr. Davey secured a lease on the Florence mine and mill which yielded such an encouraging profit that in 1881 he purchased the property, secured other mineral and timber land, and at once began the work of increasing and improving the facilities for operating the same. He built an extensive and completely equipped smelting plant, which, it is believed, was the first of the kind erected in the Black Hills, enlarged the capacity of the mill to twenty stamps, and put the wheels of the silver reduction industry in motion. After operating the property successfully for something less than a year, a process of injunction was served on Mr. Davey by the Richmond Mining Company, which had the effect of closing down and silencing the works for many years. Long and expensive litigation ensued, the question involved being the right of the enjoined to follow the trend or dip of his ledge beyond the side lines of his claim which joined that of the Richmond Company on the north.

For several years the case was exploited in the courts of Deadwood, from where it was sent on appeal to the Supreme Court of the Territory of Dakota, where a decision was handed down in favor of the enjoiner. It was then appealed to the Supreme Court of the United States where the case was still pending, when Col. Davey, impatient of the law's delays, gave up the battle, disposed of his property, and left the Black Hills for a new field of enterprise in the Far West. Subsequently the case was settled out of court by a compromise between Mr. Davey's successors and the Richmond Mining Co.

Notwithstanding the discouraging conditions resulting from the temporary closing of the silver industry, a faithful few stayed by the camp during its period of depression, and the town remained a tangible reality until it was revivified by the operations of the Union Hill Mining Co. in 1897. On the 22d of March of that year, the Union Hill Mining Company, a New Jersey corporation, filed articles in the office of the Secretary of the State of South Dakota with Francis C. Grable of Omaha, Neb., Herbert F. Hatch of East Orange, N. J., and Jacob Sterner of Jersey City, N. J., as incorporators.

Included in this company's properties were the Florence mine, stamp mill and smelting plant, the Richmond, Sitting Bull, Emma, Alexander, Union Hill, Hoodoo, Gold Bug and the Calumett and Colletta groups of mines. Under the management, or perhaps it would better be said, mismanagement of Francis C. Grable, extensive preparations, involving large expenditures, were at once begun, to operate the company's properties on a gigantic scale. The mill and smelting plant were overhauled and put in complete repair, sumptuous officers' quarters were provided; assay and chemical rooms, and a mammoth building for a 200-stamp mill—in which, however, the machinery was never installed—was built, but, at the expiration of about one year of "pernicious activity," the further progress of the promising enterprise, like a thunder-clap from a cloudless sky, was suddenly arrested,—the manager had ventured beyond his depth, and was lost amid the breakers.

Despite this failure, the future prospects of the camp are exceedingly promising. It has been satisfactorily demonstrated that there are numerous very valuable silver as well as gold mines in the district, which, with judicious management, will develop into extensive, paying properties. A few miles farther up, on the headwaters of Bear Butte creek, there were also discovered valuable gold and silver mines at an early date. Notably the Oro Fino gold mine in Strawberry gulch. The Oro Fino Mining Company operated a twenty-stamp mill on the mine for a number of years, but the ore body, though rich, was not altogether free milling, for which reason it proved unprofitable. With the proper method of treatment this, with other locations in the vicinity, will doubtless become paying properties.

TERRY

Lying almost directly under the shadow of the lofty peak from which it derives its name, about nine geographical miles southwest of Deadwood, is Terry, the mining center of the great siliceous ore district of the northern Hills. In view of the difficulty found in ascertaining just when the town was laid out and platted, the conclusion is reached that perhaps Terry, like "Topsy," "never was borned, but just growed." At a venture, however, it may be said that it probably drew its first embryotic breath as a town back in the late 80's, about, or perchance a little after, the time when Prof. Carpenter of Deadwood, and other expert chemists and mineralogists, were, metaphorically speaking, lying awake o' nights, puzzling their brains in trying to discover some occult process by which to classify and separate the new character of ore that had been encountered in the region of the Bald

TERRY, MINING CENTER OF THE GREAT REFRACTORY ORE DISTRICT OF
THE BLACK HILLS

Mountain. At any rate the town exists, and owes its present importance, to the final successful treatment of the rebellious ore product of that now famous district.

Prior to this time there had existed small temporary mining camps on "Squaw creek" and "Nevada" gulches, but as soon as the district proved to be a productive field, the rush of prospectors, miners, and speculators made the demand for a general center a necessity, and the site at the northeastern base of Terry's peak was selected for such center but, whether by design or mere tacit consent, or whether laid out and the lots sold by an organized company, or whether taken under a "squatter's" rights, remains unfortunately a matter for speculation. Howbeit, no more desirable spot could have been found within the limits of the refractory ore belt.

By reason of its advantageous situation, in the heart of a rich mining district, enhanced by the progressive spirit of the community, the town has forged rapidly to the front, and is to-day no insignificant power in the business as well as political economy of the northern Hills. It has schools, religious societies, newspapers, and secret organizations galore.

In July, 1891, school district No. 76, of Lawrence County, was organized, with M. A. Wilcox as president, Joseph Congdon, clerk, and Geo. M. Glover, treasurer. The first school was taught in a small log cabin in Nevada gulch, by Miss Atlanta Fuller of Lead, with an attendance of ten pupils.

Subsequently a small school building, consisting of one room, twenty-four by forty feet, was erected at Terry, which, to accommodate the increased attendance of pupils, was soon enlarged by an addition of equal dimensions, and in 1897 a second addition of a room, twenty-eight by thirty feet, was made, at a cost of $1,000.00. The school is now composed of three departments, under the efficient principalship of L. P. McCain, with an aggregate attendance of 217 pupils.

Terry has three religious organizations, the Methodist, Congregational, and Catholic, the latter being the only one having, as yet, a church edifice erected.

Terry, being essentially a mining community, at an early date in its history, August, 1891, organized a Miners' Union society which has since increased to 650 members, more than three-fifths of its entire population.

The secret societies are: the Ancient Order of United Workmen, organized December 24th, 1894, now numbering 110 members; the "Home Forum," organized October 1st, 1897, fifty-four members; "Knights of Pythias," organized June 8th, 1898, sixty-five members;

"Odd Fellows," organized November 10th, 1898, forty members; "Woodmen of the World," organized October, 1898, twenty members.

The fire department, consisting of Terry Hose Company No. 1, was organized November 14th, 1898, and doubtless the department makes up in efficiency what it lacks in its number of companies.

Terry can also boast of two newspapers, the *Bald Mountain News* and the Terry *Record,* both weekly publications. The *Bald Mountain News* was established on March 2d, 1895, by John H. Skinner, who conducted the *Enterprise* until August, 1898, when it was purchased by I. R. Crow, its present editor and proprietor. The Terry *Record* was established on June 5th, 1896, and is now published by Messrs. Wilcox and Monkman. The fact that each of these newspapers has a bona fide circulation of 500 copies, evidences the estimation in which the publications are held by the reading and news-loving community of Terry. The professions are represented by two lawyers and two doctors.

The business houses of Terry consist of one store of general merchandise, one exclusive grocery store, one hardware, two drug, one clothing, one jewelry, two confection and stationery stores, two bakeries, three barber shops, two blacksmith's shops, two livery barns, one meat market, five hotels, three restaurants and four saloons. Population, 1,000.

THE BALD MOUNTAIN REFRACTORY ORE DEPOSIT

Not having made a special study of the subject, I dare not venture or presume, of my own knowledge, to describe the peculiar rock formation and characteristics of this remarkable deposit but geologists who know whereof they speak would call them "contact deposits" found in Palaezoic rock formation, the ore bodies occurring in long "shoots," instead of continuous veins. These "shoots" usually vary from fifty to sixty feet in width and from two inches to ten or twelve feet in thickness, but in exceptional cases are much wider, as in the great Tornado mine, whose ore body is 300 feet in width, extending from Nevada to Whitetail gulches, and very rich. The ore found throughout the Bald Mountain region, including Ruby Basin, Garden City, and Ragged Top, is what is termed by scientists, "refractory"—a generic name applied to all ores, not separable by amalgamation or the stamp mill process.

The history of this wonderful region furnishes a splendid illustration of the mystery of nature's processes in mineral formations, and of how millions of gold may lie for years, practically worthless, under foot, until through equally mysterious chemical agencies, the component parts of the mass are disintegrated.

The attention of the ever-searching prospector was first turned to this rebellious ore district early in 1877, during which year numerous locations were made on Squaw creek, Nevada and Fantail gulches, in the immediate vicinity of Bald Mountain, to which locality the earliest discoveries were principally confined. Among the first locations that are now producing mines were the Portland, Empire State, Clinton, Double Standard, Rebecca, Big Bonanza, "Willie Wassel," now the Tornado, and others. The Portland is claimed to be the first mine in the district in which the ore body, after repeated chemical tests, and stamp-mill process, was found to be "refractory."

At an early date a twenty-stamp mill was erected on the property by the original locators by which the ores of the Portland and several other mines in the vicinity were tested and although submitted to the "roasting" and "bleaching" process before being run through the mill, the ores uniformly refused to yield their rich product of gold. In 1878 a thirty-stamp mill was built on the Lackawana mine, now known as the Snowstorm, which also proved a failure. As a consequence many of the mines which are to-day the best gold-producers in the district, after absorbing the contents of many voluptuous pocketbooks in vain experiment, were practically abandoned by their owners and Bald Mountain became, for a few years, a by-word and a reproach.

"No paying mines will ever be found in the Black Hills outside the 'Belt,' " was confidently asserted by many. Notwithstanding, some clung tenaciously to their claims with a sublime faith in their intrinsic worth, doing their legal development work each year, while others turned their backs forever upon the—to them, novel formation. Science, however, applied by men, skilled in the use of chemicals, and the nature of the affinity, existing between different metals, after long and patient experiment with the rebellious stuff at last solved the perplexing problem, that took away the reproach from Bald Mountain. Eureka!

The real value of these ores was not fully demonstrated until about 1887, when renewed interest was awakened in the district. Abandoned mines were relocated, new ones were discovered, and the boundaries of the limited territory began to widen and the mines to multiply, until to-day there are more than a hundred rich producers in the gulches centering around Bald Mountain. New probabilities opened up before the eyes of the ever-alert prospector, and sent him post-haste into adjacent fields in search of the erstwhile despised deposit. Ruby Basin, "Garden City," and finally the "Ragged Top" district, all of similar formation and character, were added to the siliceous ore territory, which now comprises, including the latter, an area of perhaps twenty-five or thirty square miles, with producing mines scattered over the entire area.

The major part of the ores from these districts are treated at the Golden Reward Chlorination plant, the Deadwood and Delaware Pyritic Smelter and the Cyanide reduction works at Deadwood, and the Kildonan plant at Pluma, and some are shipped to Omaha, Denver, and Kansas City. The gold-laden product is transported from the various mines to these plants, over the "Elkhorn" and "Burlington" narrow-gauge railroads, each of which, from opposite sides, extends its ramifications through the gulches to all the productive mines in the district.

Among the productive mines around Bald Mountain, are the following:—

The Portland, on Squaw Creek between Deadwood and Nevada gulches, located in 1877 by a Mr. Brown, but now owned by the Portland Consolidated Mining Co.

GOLDEN REWARD GOLD MILL, DEADWOOD S. D.

The Tornado Mine, on Nevada gulch, originally located in June, 1877, by Joseph L. Orr and Wm. Richmond, and first called Willie Wassel Lode. In 1882, it was relocated by Jos. Orr and Andrew Hanson, a Mr. Schlittenger afterwards becoming interested in the property, when the name was changed from Willie Wassel to Tornado. During the same year it was transferred, in whole or in part, to James Schultz, when the mine was incorporated. Subsequently, it was sold to Martin Chapman, Earnest May and Seth Bullock, who stocked the property and sold to the Golden Reward Company.

The ore body of the Tornado mine is by far the largest in the district, the deposit extending from Nevada to Whitetail gulches, 300 feet in width and from ten to twelve feet in thickness.

The Double Standard mine, now one of a group, was located in 1877 by Thomas Edwards. The "Last Chance," now known as the Liberty Lode, belonging to the Double Standard group, was located in 1877 between Nevada and Fantail gulches. The Big Bonanza, situated on Fantail gulch, was located by Martin Chapman, in 1877. The Clinton on Nevada gulch was located by Ankeny Brothers in 1877. The Rebecca, also on Nevada gulch, was located by John Strobe and William Dirkin in 1877.

The Empire State Lode and the Decorah Lode on Green Mountain were both located in 1877 by Messrs. John Greenough, Holloway, and McHenry.

The Ross Hannibal, located in 1877, is now owned by the D. & D. Smelting Co. The Buxton, now belonging to the Buxton group, situated between Nevada and Fantail gulches, was located in 1878 by Messrs. Molliter and McAllister. The Welcome, now one of the Welcome group, at the base of Terry's Peak, was located in July, 1878, by G. F. King and Mattiner, who bonded the property to Cephas Waite, who built the chlorination plant at Rapid City. The property now belongs to the Horseshoe Company, and the ores are treated at the Kildonan plant at Pluma. The Horseshoe mine, at the base of Terry's Peak, belongs to Horseshoe Company.

The Harmony group, on south side of Fantail gulch, was located in July, 1879, by G. F. King and Desire La Chapelle, who also during the same year located the Rebecca, afterwards incorporated and called the "Retreiver." The Bascobell or Smiley Lundt group, situated same as Retreiver, was located by Messrs. Lundt and Toney in 1879.

The Baltimore and Richmond, originally called the Maryland and Virginia, on Nevada gulch, was located by Col. Muse and J. J. Goff in 1878.

The Dark Horse, Grant, and Lackawana, the latter now known as the "Snowstorm" were located on Nevada gulch in 1877 or 1878 by Messrs. Collins and O'Leary. The two first named mines are now owned jointly by the Golden Reward Company and the original locators, the latter still owning the Snowstorm. In 1878, as before stated, a thirty-stamp mill was built on the Lackawana, which proved a failure.

The Trojan Enterprise group, between Deadwood and Nevada gulches, was located in 1878 by Messrs. Greenough and A. J. Smith, but it is now owned by the Portland Consolidated Mining Company.

The Apex group, on Nevada gulch, was located in 1878 by Hugh and Thos. McGovern. The property, which is now in litigation, is owned by the McGovern heirs.

The Leopold mine, between Deadwood and Nevada gulches, was located in 1890, and is now owned by the Golden Reward Company.

The Golden Reward and Maggie claims, on Fantail gulch, were originally located by Wm. Wilson and Martin Chapman, but are now owned and operated by the Golden Reward Company. The Bottleson group, located by Eli Bottleson in 1890, and the Little Bonanza, on Fantail, are owned by the same company.

The Golden Sands mine, on Deadwood gulch, was located in 1886 by the McGovern brothers, and is now owned by the Horseshoe Company.

The Mark Twain, on Nevada gulch, was located in 1884 by Street Brothers, and is now owned by the Horseshoe Company.

The Dividend, between Deadwood and Nevada gulches, was leased from the original locators, whose names are not known, by Messrs. Greenough, Mosier, and Harris, but is now owned by S. M. Kane, of Chicago.

The Ben Hur, on Nevada gulch, was located in 1886 by Alex. Patterson, but is now owned by Messrs. Faucett & Dalahaut, Earnest May, and S. M. Kane of Chicago.

The Gunnison group, on Square creek, is now owned by Seth Bullock, of Deadwood.

The Plutas, between Nevada and Fantail gulches, located in 1883, by Henry Lundt and Lewis Toney, and sold by them to Martin Chapman and Earnest May in 1886, is now the property of the Golden Reward Company.

The Hardscrabble was located in 1884 on Fantail gulch by Hug Carr and Albert Moliter.

The Ryan Fraction, on Nevada gulch, was located in 1887 by Messrs. Hawgood, Chambers & Workman.

The Stuart Lode, located in 1887 by A. D. Clark.

The Wm. Sherman group, located in 1884 by Joseph L. Orr.

The Calumet, location not known, but is a rich producer and is owned by the Deadwood & Delaware Smelting Company.

The Isadora group, located by W. A. Wilson in 1884.

The Little Bonanza, on Fantail gulch, was located by Chas. Schrader, in 1886.

Besides those mentioned there may be many other producing mines in the district which have not come to the knowledge of the writer, but those named will show something of the extent and richness of the refractory ore belt of the northern Hills. The output from these mines, which has already been something immense, is increasing in volume year by year, and making many of their fortunate owners correspondingly rich. Not all are fortunate, however, as digging for gold under the most favorable conditions is a good deal of a lottery.

The largest unproductive mines in the district and perhaps in the Black Hills are what are known as the Snowstorm group, situated on Nevada gulch. The property was located by John Hawgood in 1888, but is now owned by Messrs. Hawgood and Wilcox. It has a shaft down over 342 feet in depth and is traversed by 2,700 feet of tunneling which development has cost the owners $100,000.00. The future output of this group of mines may soon be the wonder of the world.

KILDONAN CHLORINATION PLANT AT PLUMA, BETWEEN DEADWOOD AND LEAD

WHITEWOOD

Whitewood, one of the youngest of the important towns of Lawrence County, is handsomely located on Whitewood creek near the foot-hills, about seven miles north of Sturgis. The original plat of the town was laid out on

December 8th, 1887, by the Pioneer Town-site Company and the Chicago & Northwestern Railway Company, and owes its origin to the arrival of the F. E. & M. V. R. R. at that point. This extension of the Northwestern Railway line reached the point where Whitewood stands, in November, 1887, and remained the terminus until 1890, during which years the town forged rapidly to the fore. In May, 1888, it was incorporated with Enos Lane, J. C. Jones, and Patrick Cusick, as members of the first Board of Trustees.

In the fall of 1888 two church societies were organized, viz., the Methodist and Presbyterian, both of which now have neat houses of public worship. During the same year School District No. 66 of Lawrence County was organized, J. C. Calihan, Elijah Fowler, and H. S. Grant, constituting the first school board. The town has now a commodious two-story frame school building separated into three departments, affording ample accommodations for the children of the town. The school has a present enrollment (1898) of 136 pupils, which are divided into three grades—grammar, intermediate and primary, conducted under the present supervision of Prof. Arthur Reynolds.

In 1889, the first flouring mill, having a capacity of fifty barrels of flour per day, was erected by Christopher Crow, and operated until 1892, when the plant was destroyed by fire. This mill was supplemented by the erection of the present Whitewood Flouring Mill, by Messrs. Mitchell & Thompson in 1894, which is a forty-five horse-power steam mill, having an easy daily capacity of fifty barrels of flour per day. The plant is equipped with the most approved machinery, uses the full roller process, and has the reputation of manufacturing flour of a superior grade.

The Whitewood Water System was constructed during the year 1890, by H. T. Cooper, of Whitewood, at a cost of $15,000. The supply is drawn from Oak Grove Springs, situated one mile from the limits of the town and conducted through pipes to two separate reservoirs, located at the requisite elevation above the streets, having a capacity of 50,000 gallons each, whence it is distributed through six-inch mains, provided with hydrants for fire purposes, to all parts of the town.

The Whitewood Fire Department is composed of Rescue Hose Company, No. 1, which was organized in September, 1891, supplemented by a Juvenile Hose Company, and is officered as follows: H. T. Cooper, Chief; H. H. Broman, Foreman; G. B. Adams, Secretary; and H. B. Tremble, Treasurer. The Whitewood A. O. U. W. society was organized in May, 1892, and has a present membership of eighty-five.

Whitewood sustains a weekly newspaper, the Whitewood *Plaindealer,* which was established by DeKay Brothers at an early date in the history of the town, and also a flourishing banking institution.

444 THE BLACK HILLS; OR,

In addition to these it has three hotels, two general stores, two grocery, one hardware, one drug, one confectionery, and one millinery store, two implement houses, two livery barns, two blacksmith shops and one saloon.

The other towns and small settlements of Lawrence County are St. Ange, situated on False Bottom creek, and a station on the Elkhorn Railroad, where is settled a community of French Canadians—Englewood, Dumont, Nasby, Nemo, Brownsville, Perry, Nahant, and perhaps others.

CHAPTER XXXIX

OUR PIONEERS

To those who are fond of adventures, there are perhaps no more interesting characters portrayed on the pages of American history than those of our pioneers, who conquered this great American wilderness from the dominion of the red men. Ever since the time, more than four centuries ago, when the great Venetian navigator anchored his small fleet off the bleak coast of Eastern Labrador, and planted the English flag on its sterile soil, taking possession thereof in the name of England's king, there have been pioneers and pioneers, whose daring deeds and heroic exploits have been prolific themes for the pen of the historian whose praises have been rung in song and story,—brave, adventurous men, who from various points and at different periods, resolutely pushed their way towards the setting sun, until it may be said that nearly every portion of the American Continent, from the Atlantic to the golden shores of the Pacific, has witnessed the struggles, the hardships, the sufferings, and been freely baptized in the blood of our pioneers. The last, but by no means the least, on the long list are our own Black Hills pioneers, than whom, in all that pertains to undaunted courage, no truer heroes have appeared on the pages of our history.

In this connection the question: "Who are our pioneers?" seems pertinent, as there are several grades of Black Hills pioneers.

When, in 1874, the little band of twenty-six men shouldered their guns and marched away over the unknown, trackless plains through the entire length of the hostile Sioux domain into the wilderness, and planted the banner of civilization amid the mountain fastnesses of the Black Hills and erected their comfortless homes under the shadow of their loftiest peak in the depth of winter, they were pioneers. When, in 1875, the Black Hills having lapsed for a brief time into their original solitude, other brave spirits blazed their way over new routes into the wilderness in the teeth of the most active military opposition, and built the first town in the Black Hills, they were pioneers. When, in 1876, heroic hundreds hewed their way through the most bloodthirsty and warlike of the Indian tribes, built towns, established newspapers, schools, stage lines, banking institutions, telegraph lines, mined gold-dust by the millions, discovered quartz ledges, imported mining machinery, etc., etc., they were pioneers. And moreover, when in 1877 hundreds of others ran the gauntlet of as villainous a lot of desperadoes and highway robbers as ever infested a new mining country, and helped to chisel out and lay the first blocks of our present grand superstructure on the foundation already built; who put their shoulders to the wheel of progress, by risking the investment of large capital, at a time when business enterprises were yet but an experiment; who helped to evolve order out of chaos, in the doing of which they reposed not at all times on beds of roses, were they not also pioneers? Who shall draw the line?

THE SOCIETY OF BLACK HILLS PIONEERS

At a meeting of Black Hills pioneers held at Deadwood on January 8th, 1889, in pursuance of a call of a previous preliminary meeting, the permanent organization of The Society of Black Hills Pioneers was effected by the adoption of a constitution and by-laws, and the election of the following officers:—

President: Thomas H. Russell, Deadwood; Vice-Presidents: Jack Gray Terraville; R. B. Hughes, Rapid; Sam'l Shankland, Custer; E. G. Dudley, Hot Springs; Frank Thulen, Minnesela; Jas. Ryan, Sundance; Secretary: L. F. Whitbeck, Deadwood; Treasurer: John R. Brennan, Rapid; Marshall: A. R. Z. Dawson, Deadwood; Directors: C. V. Gardner, Spring Valley; John Belding, Deadwood; Noah Newbanks, Whitewood; George W. Cole, Sturgis; S. M. Booth, Custer; Historian *ad interim,* C. V. Gardner, Spring Valley.

The aims and objects of the association are clearly set forth in article first of its constitution, which says:—

"This association shall be called and known as 'The Society of Black Hills Pioneers.' It is designed to be, and is, a moral, benevolent, and literary association, and its objects are: To cultivate social intercourse, form a more perfect union among its members, and create a fund for charitable purposes in their behalf; to collect and preserve information, connected with the early settlement of the country, to perpetuate the memory of those whose sagacity, energy, and enterprise induced them to settle in the wilderness, and become the founders of a new State.''

By the rules governing the organization, only those who came to the Black Hills prior to the 31st of December, 1876, are admitted to membership. At the first annual meeting of the society held at Deadwood on October 9th, 1889, the names of 153 members had been enrolled, which number gradually increased until 1891, when there were 220 names on the roster of the society. From that time the membership fluctuated, some leaving the country, when in due time their names were stricken from the roll; other places were left vacant by death. At the last annual roll-call the secretary reported 213 members in good standing on the roll, five of whom were honorary members.

At each annual roll-call on the 8th of January, the date fixed by the Board of Directors for the yearly banquet and election of officers, some, whose lips are forever silent, fail to respond to the call, some seventy members, having joined the silent majority since its first organization in 1889. Appended is the death list, as shown by the records of the society: —

1889 August 12th, E. McVey.
1890, May 5th, E. Rainwater.
1890, June 25th, S. M. Booth.
1890, June 25th, W. H. Collins.
1890, November 25th, John A. Swift.
1891, February 19th, Hugh McGovern.
1891, February 19th, Phil. McGuire.
1891, April 1st, F. M. Allen.
1891, April 3d, Chas. Dumphy.
1891, April 8th, C. H. Moulton.
1891, —— —, Henry Benns.
1892, —— —, Singleton Kimmel.
1892, —— —, T. Hopkins.
1892, March 31st, C. F. Thompson.
1892, May 24th, Jas. Carney.
1893, March 16th, J. A. Gaston.
1893, June 2d, R. McLaren.
1893, June 8th, Chas. ——.
1893, October 15th, Wm. F. Steele.
1893, —— —, Geo. Hacker.
1893, —— —, H. J. Fuller.
1893, October 16th, Peter Hann.
1894, January 2d, Nicholas Sands.
1894, January 2d, David Wolzmuth.
1894, March 9th, Peter O'Neill.
1894, March 24th, Ed. Farnum.
1894, July 3d, Wm. Howard.
1894, December 12th, Peter Koppleton.
1895, January 12th, D. L. Mitchell.
1895, March 10th, Andrew Farrell.
1895, September 6th, P. S. Tetrault.
1895, November —, Wm. B. Franklin.
1895, December —, John Stannus.

1895, —— ——, W. L. Dunn.
1895, —— ——, John Haltner.
1896, January 22d, R. A. Bailey.
1896, February 15th, J. Scott.
1896, April 15th, E. J. Crawford.
1896, July 19th, A. R. Z. Dawson.
1896, August 7th, Mrs. John Manning (Honorary member).
1896, September 29th, W. Foglesong.
1896, October 18th, Luke McDon.
1896, November 10th, Ed. Murphy.
1896, —— ——, J. B. Cheney.
1896, November 17th, B. C. Wood.
1897, April 1st, J. H. Flynn.
1897, April 19th, Jas. Culp.
1897, May 5th, Pat. Casey.
1897, June 13th, Desire LaBesch.
1897, November 19th, W. M. Flanegan.
1897, November 21st, Jas. Rossiter.
1898, August 11th, John Wiek.
1898, August 24th, Le R. Graves.
1898, September 9th, Thos. Bentley.
1898, January 29th, John Theins.
1898, —— ——, Mrs. John Gray (Honorary member).

This list tells us that the ranks of the early pioneers are becoming rapidly depleted; the links which bind them together by ties of common hardships, are being severed and removed one by one, and before very long, the last burnished link of the golden chain will be rudely broken.

From the annual report of the secretary for the year 1898, it appears that, during that year, there were $360.26 disbursed from the funds of the society, for various purposes, the expenditures being for the most part for the care of the sick, and the funeral expenses of members, which bespeaks the benefits of the organization.

The annual banquets of the society which are given at Deadwood on the 8th of January of each year, when, under the influence of the good cheer, members become delightfully reminiscent, as also the yearly picnics, held on the 8th of June, alternately at different points throughout the Hills, are both pronounced exceedingly enjoyable affairs.

In 1890 Thos. H. Russell was succeeded in the presidency of the society by Seth Bullock, who was elected for two consecutive years, with J. H. Flynn as secretary and J. A. Gaston as treasurer for both years. A. R. Z. Dawson presided from 1892 to 1894; Jas. W. Allen, of Deadwood, from 1894 to 1896; John Gray, of Terraville, from 1896 to 1898; J. H. Flynn and D. W. Gillette occupying the respective positions of secretary and treasurer for the six consecutive years. In 1898 P. A. Gushurst, of Lead, was elected president; Paul Rewman, secretary, and D. M. Gillette, treasurer. In 1899 Geo. V. Ayers, of Deadwood, the present incumbent of the chair, was elected, with Paul Rewman, secretary, and D. M. Gillette, treasurer. These officers, who are representative pioneers of 1874-5-6 stand for the rank and file of the members of the "Society of Black Hills Pioneers."

In explanation it may be proper to state that the first three presidents of the "Society of Black Hills Pioneers" have been omitted from the accompanying group, for a reason which will be easily made apparent. When it was found that in making cut for the group the originals would have to be more or less mutilated, one of the number had to be left out, because my word of honor had been given to return the same intact to the owner. Thus having to omit one, it was deemed best to omit the three, whose portraits and sketches appear elsewhere on the pages of this work, in another connection.

Jas. W. Allen, fourth president of the association, came to the Black Hills during the latter part of December, 1875, too late to meet with opposition from Uncle Sam's blue coats, and too early to encounter the hostile Sioux along the line shortly before they entered upon the sensational stage of mining development. Mr. Allen, although born and reared, to almost the verge of young manhood, in the staid old Keystone State, was by no means a stranger to the hap-go-hazard phases of frontier life, having spent years before coming to the Hills in each of the now great Western Territories and States of Idaho, Montana, Colorado, and Wyoming, while they were yet very young, and may therefore be accounted a typical pioneer. Upon his arrival in the Black Hills, he first went to Spring creek, in the vicinity of "Stand-off Bar," where he remained but a short time, going from there to Rapid Valley, about the time the Gate City was laid out and platted. For some reason he was not at all enthusiastic over the future prospects of the Denver of the Black Hills, for, although corner lots were to be had at a bargain, he emphatically refused to take a dollar's worth of stock in the enterprise. He subsequently went to Deadwood, of which he became a permanent resident in 1877, since which time he has been intimately identified with the business interests of his adopted city, in whose future greatness, as well as the entire Black Hills, he has the most implicit and abiding faith. Mr. Allen was one of the charter members of the Society of Black Hills Pioneers, and has, since its organization, been a faithful and interested worker in its ranks. The Black Hills has dealt generously and kindly with James W. Allen, both from a financial and physical stand-point—especially the latter, as a glance at the accompanying cut will attest.

John Gray, fifth on the roster of presidents of the Society of Black Hills Pioneers, emigrated to America from the north of England—the land of his nativity, when a young man in his early twenties. Upon landing on the shores of the ''land of the free and the home of the brave,'' he turned his steps towards the setting sun; sojourning for one year in one of the States of the Middle West (Ohio), when he followed the Star of Empire westward to Wyoming, where he remained until 1873. He then decided to try his fortune in South America, and journeyed thither, but, after spending a year among the pampas and silvas, the boa-constrictors and anacondas of that tropical, volcanic region, he returned to Carbon, Wyoming, in 1874, when the Black Hills first began to attract public attention. In 1876 he came to the Black Hills from Cheyenne, Wyoming, with a large party of gold seeking adventurers—among whom was Wild Bill, who had outfitted at that point. Although Indians galore were seen along the route, the train was not molested, the Indians, doubtless, being afraid to encounter so large an aggregation of well-armed white men, as well they might be, if there were many of the Wild Bill stamp in the outfit. Mr. Gray went directly to the northern Hills, where he has since been extensively engaged in mining operations on or near the great northern ''gold belt,'' making Terraville his base of operations. Mr. Gray has also been identified with the Society of Black Hills Pioneers since its first organization, and is regarded as one of its most efficient members.

Next, and sixth on the list of presidents of the Society of Black Hills Pioneers, is P. A. Gushurst, a son of the great Empire State, who was born in Rochester, on the banks of the famous Genesee, whose valley became celebrated for the production of the best wheat in the wide world. By the way, the writer of this sketch was born and bred within twenty-five miles of that great flour manufacturing city, and it is now recalled with a thrill of amusement that, more than once did she, with a gay bevy of equally crude and unsophisticated village maidens, take a trip down through the locks of the Genesee Valley Canal, on a towboat, to the metropolis and trade center of Monroe County, to see the Falls, and the ''Elephant,'' before the advent of a

1. GEORGE AYERS 2. JAMES W. ALLEN 3. JOHN GRAY
4. P. A. GUSHURST 5. PAUL REWMAN

railroad in that region—but this is a digression and difficult though it is, I must refrain from indulging farther in impertinent personal reminiscences.

With a good deal of daring and enterprise for one so young, and doubtless filled with boyish dreams, P. A. Gushurst, when a lad of only sixteen, left his native city to seek his fortune amid the then unmeasured possibilities of the "Great West." The young adventurer stopped first at Omaha, then a border town, and the chief supply depot, for the Rocky Mountain region to the West, at a time when prairie chickens and quails were plentiful thereabouts and deer and antelope were yet to be seen among the adjacent timbered bluffs, where, having secured lucrative employment, he remained six years: one year in a grocery store, one year as time-keeper and four years in the machine shops of the Union Pacific Railway.

On May 1st, 1876, he left Omaha, and came via Cheyenne and Fort Laramie over the dangerous trail to the Black Hills, arriving at Custer, on May 24th, and Deadwood, June 1st, 1876, since which time he has been an exceedingly and uncommonly active business man. He first started business in Deadwood in a tent, then purchased the lot on Main street, now occupied by J. Goldberg's store, and built the frame store building known as the Big Horn Store. In August of the same year he moved to Lead where he has lived and carried on business since, during which time he has occupied numerous positions of honor and trust.

He was elected Recorder of the Gold Run Gulch, succeeding Thos. Carey, the discoverer of placer gold on that stream; was elected one of the three trustees of Lead, at the first Citizens' Meeting held in 1877; was elected School Treasurer, and served six years as a member of the Board of Education; was a member of the first Council of the Municipality of Lead, and was elected as its Mayor in 1898. For many years Mr. Gushurst has been a director in the First National Bank of Deadwood, also in the First National Bank of Lead. He was chairman of the Lead Town-site Company in the litigation with the Homestake Mining Company on the question affecting the validity of the title of the city to the surface of the ground which it covers, and after its amicable settlement was appointed with Earnest May and Cyrus H. Enos, trustees to deed the property to the citizens.

Besides his extensive mercantile business, Mr. Gushurst has been, and is, largely engaged in mining enterprises and was at one time an owner in the Little Bonanza, the now famous Tornado, and other mining properties in the great refractory ore "gold belt." Later, with John Wolzmuth, he purchased the Squaw creek mining claims and was the first to ship ore from that section of the country for treatment. In his business and mining ventures Mr.

Gushurst has been eminently successful, and deservedly so, having by industry, perseverance, and sagacity, acquired a handsome fortune.

It is interesting to note that the marriage of P. A. Gushurst to Miss Josephine Ackey, in 1877, was the first marriage solemnized in Lead.

BUILDING ERECTED AT LEAD BY P. A. GUSHURST IN 1877—now being torn down to make room for new brick and stone structure now (1899) in course of construction—and a group of early pioneers

The picture accompanying this sketch is a reproduction of a portion of the old store building in which Mr. Gushurst opened business in Lead in 1877, and a group of early pioneers. The venerable landmark is being torn down by its proprietor, to make room for a large brick and stone block, which is to cover an area of 50x95 feet.

During the winter of 1876-7 Mr. Gushurst cut the trees and made the shingles for the roof of the old structure, many of which, after having been exposed to the elements for twenty-two winters and summers, were found to be in a good state of preservation, some of them being carried away by the citizens to be preserved as relics.

The group, for the major part, is composed of pioneers of 1876, among whom will readily be recognized P. A. Gushurst, standing in the center at the left of the upright post, holding in his right hand something that looks wonderfully like a glass of the foaming beverage, while leaning against the same post on the right, without any of the beverage, is Emil Faust. The second figure to the left of Mr. Faust and to the right of the picture, holding his hat in his left hand, is recognized as Jack Daly; next, holding a bottle in his left hand, is George Beemer; next comes Frank Abt, also holding a bottle of the beverage, and at his left is Earnest May with a glass of the frothy fluid in his left hand. The lady in the group is Miss Maude Faust, and an honorary member of the "Society of Black Hills Pioneers." The other figures composing the group will doubtless be easily recognized by all of the early pioneers as well as by many who are not pioneers.

George Vincent Ayres, seventh president of the Society of Black Hills' Pioneers, was born among the rugged hills of the old Keystone State, on November 1st, 1852, and when a boy of five years, was taken by his parents to Illinois, from whence they moved to Missouri in 1858, and thence to Kansas in 1859. In 1860, they removed to Nebraska, locating on a farm about sixteen miles from Beatrice, where they remained until 1866 when they moved into the town of Beatrice to give their family of growing children the benefit of a school, where George received the first rudiments of education.

In 1870 George Vincent, at the age of eighteen years, first asserted his individuality and became a factor in the business world, by entering a drug store at Beatrice, where he remained six years and became an adept pharmacist. Early in 1876, when the Black Hills gold excitement was prevalent throughout the land, he caught the infection, resigned his position in the drug store, and on March 1st, 1876, embarked viz Cheyenne and Fort Laramie for the new gold fields, arriving on the 25th of March at Custer, where he remained until May, when he went with the tide of Deadwood, where was taken sick with the mountain fever.

Upon his recovery in July he returned to Custer where he remained until the fall of 1877, when he returned to Deadwood. Although coming to the Hills a tenderfoot, he had none of the tenderfoot fatuity. Becoming readily assimilated with the conditions of the new mining camp, he at once entered extensively, into the hardware business, which is still carried on under the name of the Ayres & Wardman Hardware Co., of which he is president and general manager. He has also occupied various other important positions, both civil and political, during his residence in the Hills. He was Receiver of Public Moneys of the United States Land Office at Rapid City during the Harrison administration; has been president of the Business Men's Protective Association of Deadwood; was chairman of the Lawrence County Republican Central Committee, and is now president of the Society of Black Hills Pioneers.

Mr. Ayres has a long and honorable record as a member of the Order of Free Masons, but not having a key to the sublime mysteries of that ancient order, I am utterly unable to trace intelligently the various degrees by which he has risen to his present high standing among the fraternity. I am told, however, that he became a Master Mason in Beatrice Lodge No. 26, located at Beatrice, Nebraska, on June 27th, 1874, and affiliated with Deadwood Lodge No. 7 on November 27th, 1882; was elected Grand Master of the Grand Lodge of South Dakota on June 12th, 1889. He became a Royal Arch Mason in Livingston Chapter No. 10, located at Beatrice, Nebraska, on July 13th, 1885, and affiliated with Dakota Chapter No. 3, located at Deadwood, October 8th, 1880; became a Knights Templar and Knight of Malta in Dakota Commandery No. 1, located at Deadwood, on February 2d, 1881; received the degrees in the A. & A. S. R., Southern Jurisdiction of the United States, in the Golden Belt Lodge of Perfection No. 5, April 11th, 1893. He crossed the burning sands of the A. A. O. N. M. S. in the Naja Temple located at Deadwood, April 14th, 1893, and was anointed High Priest in the Grand Council of Anointed High Priests of South Dakota on June 11th, 1896,—all of which is a sealed book to the writer.

During his term of Grand Master he enforced a resolution adopted by the Grand Lodge, and drove the so-called "Cerneau Rite"—whatever that may be—out of the State, and also founded the Grand Charity and Widows' and Orphans' Funds.

Paul Rewman, now secretary of the Society of Black Hills Pioneers, was born in England, of German parentage, in 1855.

In 1870, when a boy of fifteen, Paul left his native land, and crossed the billowy deep to New York, from whence he journeyed to the Southwest, and engaged in the stock business for several years on the great cattle ranges of New Mexico, Texas, and Arizona.

In 1874, he went to Colorado, where he remained until stricken with gold fever in June, 1876, when he started with a party via Cheyenne, Wyoming, for the Black Hills, arriving in Deadwood on July 20th of that year, when the gold excitement was at its zenith, where he has continuously resided since.

Although young on coming to the Hills, Mr. Rewman was not altogether an unfledged tenderfoot, having already mastered the rudiments of Western life on the plains of the southwest and profited doubtless by his experience. At any rate he cautiously avoided the pitfalls of the big mining camp, and made the most of his opportunities. He was made Deputy Sheriff of Lawrence County under John Manning in 1878 or 1879, serving in that capacity two years.

He carried the first mail from Deadwood to the Belle Fourche river at a time when Indians were infesting the northern border, and when his personal safety depended upon the utmost caution.

From 1881 to 1891, he was in sole charge of the affairs of the Black Hills Telephone Company, since which date he has had the full management of the Deadwood Electric Lighting System, in which he owns a large interest.

With no original capital, but plenty of vim and push, Mr. Rewman has acquired a handsome competence, far beyond that attained by the average of our early Black Hills pioneers. By mathematical calculation, basing the estimate on his probable actual weight at the time, he had, on reaching Cheyenne en route for the Black Hills, about $40.00 in his pocket, to outfit, take him to Deadwood, and start him on the high road to fortune. Let us see. One hundred and sixty pounds at twenty-five cents per pound produces just $40.00. Mr. Rewman has been a member of the Society of Black Hills Pioneers since its organization, and the secretary of the association for the two years last past.

BLACK HILLS PIONEER AND HISTORICAL SOCIETY OF 1877

Having in view the organization of the above named society, an informal meeting was held in Deadwood on January 26th, 1895, at which about forty of those who arrived in the Black Hills during the year 1877, and a few who arrived prior to that year but were interested in the organization of the society, were present. Hon. Granville G. Bennett was called to the chair, and H. J. Ainley acted as secretary. After the object of the meeting was explained by Col. Hiram F. Hale, who, with Porter Warner and F. J. Washabaugh, earnestly advocated the organization of the society, a motion prevailed for the appointment of a committee to draft a constitution and by-laws, to be submitted to a full meeting called for January 30th, 1895.

At the meeting of January 30th, 1895, a permanent organization was effected by the adoption of a constitution and by-laws, and the election of the following officers, viz.:—

President, Hon. Granville G. Bennett; Vice-President, Col. Hiram F. Hale; Secretary, H. J. Ainley; Treasurer, Frank J. Washabaugh; Historian, Wm. Warner; Marshal, Homer E. Moore; Directors, Wm. Allinson, John Herman, and Willis H. Bonham, with an original membership of 124.

This society was organized, as indicated by its name, for the double purpose of perpetuating a bond of union between those who first came to the Black Hills during the year 1877, for the mutual benefit and enjoyment of its members, and collecting facts and events relating to their history, and doubtless as 1877 was the beginning of an important history-making epoch, much invaluable information will be gathered and preserved through its efforts, which otherwise would be lost and forgotten.

Among the pleasant features of this society are its annual picnics, which, it is believed, are held during the early summer months, whenever the weather is auspicious without regard to a fixed date.

There have been eleven deaths of members of the society since its organization, among whom are Porter Warner, who was Vice-President of the association at the time of his death in February, 1899, and John Herman, a director.

The original officers chosen have been retained from year to year, with but few exceptions. The present chief officers of the society are: Hon. Granville G. Bennett, President; Frank McLaughlin, Esq., Secretary; Frank J. Washabaugh, Treasurer; Dr. H. Stein, Historian.

CHAPTER XL

MEADE COUNTY

Prior to 1889 all that portion of the Black Hills now embraced within the boundary lines of Meade County formed a part of the original territory of Lawrence County, whose lines extended nearly ninety miles from east to west, but by an act of the Territorial Legislature of that year the unwieldy organization was cut in twain from north to south near its geographical center, and the eastern subdivision created into Meade County. By this subdivision Lawrence County was separated into two sections differing widely in topography and material resources—the one comprising the major part of the open prairie land of the county, stretching away eastward to the North Fork of the Cheyenne river; the other, all the rich mineral-bearing and heavily timbered region of the west.

The new county created by the Act contains some of the finest agricultural and grazing land to be found in the Black Hills. It is well watered by numerous streams whose headwaters are gathered from multitudes of springs which issue forth from the granite and metamorphic rock high up among the mountains on the west, and traverse the county to its eastern limits on the Belle Fourche river. Chief among these streams are the Bear Butte, Alkali, Elk, Box Elder, and their numerous small tributaries. These, supplemented by a bountiful precipitation—caused, in part, doubtless, by the proximity of the heavily timbered region of the Hills along its western boundary—render the soil peculiarly adapted to farming and stock-raising.

With an unlimited range covered with rich grasses which cure readily where they grow and retain all their nutritious qualities for winter feeding, together with the mildness of the climate, make the raising of stock on a large or small scale a profitable industry in Meade County, which, it is conceded by stockmen, produces some of the fattest, sleekest cattle to be found on the ranges of the Black Hills.

The streams draining the area of Meade County are heavily fringed with several different varieties of timber—elm, box elder, and other trees—while along the foot-hills is found an abundant growth of spruce and pine, furnishing an ample supply of timber for fuel and other purposes. There are several large sawmills located in Meade County which produce hundreds of thousands of feet of lumber annually from the pine timbers cut from the Hills along its western limits.

Primarily the cause of separation appears to have been the expense and hardships imposed upon the people of the eastern portion of the original county, by the extreme remoteness of the seat of county government, where all legal business had necessarily to be transacted. A secondary cause perhaps was the accretion of taxation for the maintenance of the courts, whose time was for the most part employed in adjucating mineral cases, in which the people of the agricultural districts had no interest, and from which no benefit accrued to them.

For several years prior to the segregation, they labored hard to bring about a division, leaving no stone unturned to accomplish that result. Finally, having the requisite population to entitle them to such action, they left the home roof, at the time, and in the manner before stated, and set up a county government of their own, burdened with a heavy legacy of debt. Naturally when they came to the parting of the ways, Lawrence County was loth to have her rebellious people go, but, smarting under the accumulated burdens of taxation, without representation, and, perhaps, an unequal distribution of the spoils of office, they would not be stayed, and the outcome was the creation of Meade County—thus named after Fort Meade. To the untiring and indefatigable efforts of John D. Patton, who was a member of the Legislature at the time, more than to any other person is due the credit for the passage of the Act creating Meade County.

STURGIS IN 1899

The first commissioners of the county, appointed by the Act, were Max Hoehn, Daniel P. Flood, and W. C. Burton, who were charged with the especial duty of making all necessary provisions for holding an election, for choosing county officers and selecting county seat by popular ballot. On May 7th, 1889, the election was held at the different voting precincts of the county, resulting in the election of the following officers:—

Commissioners, Samuel H. Martin, Chairman; Bland Herring, Elliott Nichols; Sheriff, W. F. L. Suter; Treasurer, E. F. Huffman; Register of Deeds, Fred Dunham; Auditor, E. C. Lane; States Attorney, C. C. Polk; Superintendent of Schools, Lulu Schell; Surveyor, H. E. Palmer; Coroner, Dr. J. B. Cheney; County Physician, Dr. W. G. Smith; County Judge, Wm. Cable; Clerk of Courts, Max Hoehn, appointed by court. These officers were to serve until the next general election or until their successors were elected and qualified.

The rival candidates for capital honors were Sturgis and Tilford, the former capturing the plum by a handsome majority of the popular vote, in consideration of which the city guaranteed to the county the sum of $15,000.00 towards the erection of a courthouse. In partial fulfillment of this obligation, the Meade County Land and Improvement Company, of which J. J. Davenport was president and Max Hoehn, secretary, purchased an entire block of ground on the elevated plateau in the western part of the city and deeded the same to the county for a courthouse site.

In the adjustment of the credits and debits of Lawrence County, at a joint meeting of their respective commissioners there was apportioned to Meade County twenty-two and one-tenth per cent of the entire indebtedness of Lawrence County, said apportionment being based upon the assessed valuation of the county in 1878. To guarantee the payment of its obligations, Meade County issued to Lawrence County the following bonds, to wit: $107,500 five per cent bonds, and $24,500.00 ten per cent bonds, upon which the interest coupons have been regularly paid since their issuance. In this connection it appears that, in issuing bonds to refund the indebtedness of Lawrence County, its commissioners had overstepped the limits prescribed by law, which excess the county subsequently sought to repudiate.

Litigation ensued, and, after pending in the courts for several years, the question was finally settled by a decision of the United States Supreme Court, holding Lawrence County for the full face of the bonds. Meade County meanwhile had refused to pay its proportion of the questionable bonds until the matter was settled by the courts.

Soon after the complete organization of the county, its commissioners directed their attention to the adjustment of the school districts to the new order of things; the repairing of old, and the laying out and building new roads and bridges throughout the county, for which considerable sums were expended. Finally in 1896, the courthouse, the crowning glory of the county and its capital city, was completed at a cost for grounds, building, and equipments of nearly $26,000, of which Sturgis paid $15,000 as per agreement.

The building, which stands conspicuous on the elevated site chosen for it, is an imposing three-storied structure of white cut stone, handsomely ornamented with pink sandstone, and, from the iron-barred windows of the basement (which is used for a jail), to the top of the rounded dome, is a model of substantial and dignified architecture, strongly suggestive of the immutability of the "blind goddess," who is supposed to preside within. In internal arrangement and finish it is perfect, and its appointments complete in every detail. The building is heated by furnaces in the basement, and every office and room throughout is provided with telephone, water, and electric service, in short, it is conceded to be the most complete courthouse in the Black Hills, as well as the most costly.

Exclusive of the bonds inherited from Lawrence County the total indebtedness of Meade County is $50,000, its assessed valuation $1,600,000, and its population in 1898, 5,000.

MEADE COUNTY COURTHOUSE

STURGIS

Sturgis, the administrative center of Meade County, is admirably located in a wide basin in the valley of Bear Butte creek, snugly embraced by two confluents of the stream, a mile and one-half west of Fort Meade, and about fifteen miles by railway northeast of Deadwood. The bustling, enterprising young city had its origin twenty years ago, soon after the location of Fort Meade in August, 1878, on the spot where it has since grown and flourished.

Among its founders were Major J. C. Wilcox, J. W. Rodebank, B. G. Caulfield, Judge Dudley, Arthur Buckbee, J. W. Caldwell, and Major H. M. Lazelle, then in command at Fort Meade, who, anticipating fabulous values in corner lots, as soon as the location of the post became a fixed fact, appeared with compass and chain, selected and laid out a town-site, and named it Sturgis in honor of Col. S. D. Sturgis, later in command of the garrison at Fort Meade.

The original plat, containing eighty acres, was covered with what was called "Valentine Scrip," through the agency of Barney G. Caulfield, on October 25th, 1878. Subsequently, this questionable title to the public lands resulted in a conflict of interests, which caused considerable litigation and much friction between the town-site company and lot-holders, which difficulty was, however, ultimately settled by the Secretary of the Interior in favor of the company.

To the original plat of eighty acres numerous additions have since been made, providing ample space for future expansion, viz.: The Fort Meade addition of forty acres, platted by Col. S. D. Sturgis, August 16th, 1880; the Ash Extension of 120 acres, on July 7th, 1883; the McMillan Extension of 160 acres, on October 20th, 1883; Bosworth's Addition of forty acres, platted by C. C. Moody, July 9th, 1884; the Rodebank Addition of forty acres, platted by J. W. Rodebank, November 11th, 1884; Dudley & Caldwell's Addition of forty acres, in February, 1885; Patton's First and Second Additions of forty acres each, on July 15th and July 16th, 1886, respectively; Comstock's Addition of forty acres, July 19th, 1886; Fairview Addition of sixty acres, June 11th, 1887; Rodebank's Second Addition of forty acres, June 15th, 1887; Schnell's Addition, July 16th, 1887; Mc-Millan's Southwestern and Southern Addition of eighty acres, August 2d, 1887; Franklin's Addition; and perhaps others.

The first to settle on the site of Sturgis was Geo. Bosworth, who, in the summer of 1877, settled on the ground which is now in part Bosworth's Addition to Sturgis. A Mrs. Beck, also, prior to the location of the town-site, took up a piece of ground, which was subsequently purchased by Wm. McMillan, on a part of which his residence now stands.

The first settlers in the valley of Bear Butte creek, in the vicinity of Sturgis, were Wm. Fletcher and Wm. Myers, both of whom came to the valley in July, 1876, and located the ranches upon which they now respectively reside, the former a mile and a half below Fort Meade, the latter an equal distance further down the creek. Until the summer of 1877 these two men were the only settlers in the region for miles around, and were constantly exposed to the scant mercy of the roving bands of Indians, who were, at that time, depredating the Hills from center to circumference, and Bear Butte valley did not escape their notice.

In August, 1876, a pony express rider, while en route from Fort Pierre to Crook City with the mail, was murdered by the savages, who cut open the mail pouch, mutilated and threw its contents to the winds, then rode away with the horse of their dead victim. Mr. Fletcher, who was attracted to the spot by the unusual spectacle of a profusion of white papers lying scattered about under a tree, discovered the body, which he buried as best he could on a spot near the present residence of H. Carroll, where his ashes still repose. Although Mr. Fletcher kept an experienced scout constantly employed at a salary of fifty dollars per month in patrolling the surrounding country to warn the two lone men against surprise, the Indians stole in one morning, in March, 1877, just at the glimmering of the dawn, while Mr. Fletcher, Mr. Myers, and the scout were profoundly sleeping in their tent, and applied the torch to forty tons of hay stacked a short distance away.

On emerging from his tent a little later, Mr. Fletcher proceeded to a slight elevation of ground and scanned the valley up and down, to make sure that all was well, when he beheld the fruits of his toil going up in flame and smoke and about a dozen Indians circling and dancing gleefully around the burning pile. He prudently retreated to the tent, when the three inmates hastily put themselves on a defensive war footing, and awaited the denouement, but they were not molested. The band then rode off down the valley and burned eighty tons of baled hay stacked on the Myers' ranch below.

It is also related that during the same year Major Wilcox employed men to cut hay north of Bear Butte, where he had located a temporary ranch, which one day was raided by a band of Indians, who killed his cattle and two men and a woman, emigrants who had taken refuge at the ranch. Another man fled for safety to a dugout, in the face of a bluff near by, and kept them at bay with his trusty Sharp's rifle.

The first store on the site of Sturgis was built and opened by Capt. Harmon, in September, 1878, in the building which yet stands on the northwest corner of Main and First streets, now occupied by John Scott as a second-hand store. Mr. Harmon opened business with an extensive stock of general merchandise, including everything from a glass of "Early Times" whisky to a paper of pins, and, it goes without saying, that he transacted a flourishing business. The second store was opened during the same fall by Wm. McMillan, who followed closely upon the heels of Capt. Harmon with a general stock of dry goods, groceries, boots and shoes, clothing, etc. As a matter of fact Mr. McMillan might have been the pioneer merchant of Sturgis had he not unselfishly aided Capt. Harmon in the erection of his store instead of first building his own.

The first hotel, in the common acceptation of the term, was opened by Chas. Elsener in the veritable building now known as the Charles Hotel, on the south side of Main street, in the early part of October, 1878. However, on the 26th of September, 1878, Mr. John Scollard opened a restaurant and lodging rooms in a building which stood on the ground now occupied by Benevolent Hall, on the southeast corner of Main and Second streets, which he conducted as a house of entertainment pending the construction of his hotel. On the 21st of January, 1879, he opened the Sheridan House, a commodious two-story structure, on the north side of Main street, where, for the past twenty winters and summers, he has enacted the role of "genial host."

In the winter of 1878-9, a regular post office was established at Sturgis with Charles Collins as first postmaster. Mr. Collins was succeeded by Major J. C. Wilcox, who held the position from 1879 to 1883.

While these business enterprises were soon supplemented by other kinds of trade and traffic, perhaps equally worthy of note, this especial reference is made to the first ventures because they led the procession out on the broad highway to the city's present prosperity. Owing to the comparatively unsettled and undeveloped condition of the rich agricultural lands, comprising the eastern portion of what was then Lawrence County, the growth of Sturgis, during the first few years of its history, was somewhat discouragingly slow, much of its trade being derived from the garrison at Fort Meade.

In 1883, however, the memorable year in which the great flood laid waste the valleys of the north, and nearly blotted Deadwood from the map of the Black Hills, the town shot up like a sky-rocket, nearly doubling its population and number of business houses within a year. Sturgis, though not in the least rejoicing at, yet hoping to profit by, the terrible disaster to the capital city, which, it was thought, could never recuperate in its native contracted valley, expected, yea, longed to embrace within her expansive arms, a large percentage of the businessless and homeless population of the stricken city, and to that end, opened wide her hospitable gates. But, alas! "the best laid plans o' mice and men,"—you know the rest. Sturgis did not properly estimate the metal of which Deadwood was composed, nor the strength of its attachment to the gold-laden hills and valleys of its birthplace. Pure air and plenty of space counts for little in the balance against gold.

Although the influx of population did not materialize to any great extent at that time, Sturgis maintained its status, and pursued the even tenor of its way, until it received a new impetus in 1888 by the arrival of the F. E. & M. V. R. R., which, although its station was built at a provoking distance from the center of business, added much to its commercial importance, since which time its growth has been steady and permanent.

On March 15th, 1886, the town was reorganized, and the following officers duly elected: Board of Trustees, Max Hoehn, President, J. J. Davenport and John Farley; Marshal, W. F. L. Sonter; Clerk, Treasurer, Assessor and City Justice of the Peace, O. W. Jewett.

This organization continued in force until June, 1888, when the town was incorporated into a city by an Act of the Territorial Legislature, and separated into three wards, each ward being represented by two members to the Common Council, whose first meeting was held on June 22d, 1888. The first officers of the new municipality were: Mayor, John T. Potter; Aldermen, J. C. McMillan, W. W. Sabin, Max Blatt, Lewis Abrams, W. G. Smith, and Wenkie; City Auditor, Max Hoehn; City Attorney, C. C. Polk; Treasurer, J. J. Davenport; Chief of Police, Pat Flavin; City Justice, B. F. Stearns.

PUBLIC SCHOOLS

Early in the spring of 1879, a district of the public schools of Lawrence County was organized for Sturgis, and in April of that year the first public school was opened by Mrs. Nellie Rodebank with an attendance of ten pupils. This first term was taught in a small, unfinished board shanty that stood on Lazalle street opposite Second avenue. During the summer of 1879 a log cabin that stood almost directly opposite the board shanty was secured for school purposes, in which the following teachers were successively employed: Miss Ada C. Hall of Bear Butte Valley, for the fall term of 1879; Mrs. Robt. Neill, the spring and summer term of 1880; and Mrs. Bartholomew, wife of a Methodist minister, for the fall term of that year.

During the year 1881 the first public school building of the district, a small one-story frame structure, was erected on or near the site now occupied by the courthouse. The first teacher in the new building was Miss Clara Barber, who was succeeded by Miss Kate Doyle (now Mrs. C. B. Harris of Galena). In 1882 the frame building was moved from the hill to a site secured by the board on Sherman street, nearly opposite the present home of Wesley

A. Stuart, when, to accommodate the rapidly increasing attendance of pupils, its capacity was enlarged by an addition thereto. For several subsequent years the school was under the supervision of Professor H. H. Lorrimer, who was succeeded by Professor B. A. Tyler, whom the writer knew well and favorably, having met him often in connection with educational work.

In 1888 the present school building, a fine two-story brick structure of four departments, was erected, in which Prof. Tyler continued his work until 1895, when he was succeeded by the present incumbent, Prof. Chas. W. Young. According to the testimony of those who are in a position to know and are competent to judge Prof. Young has during his supervision brought the school up to a high plane of excellence, having, since he has been at the helm, graduated two classes from the school with honor to its members, which fact, of itself, tells more eloquently than mere words of the competency and ability of their instructor.

The brick building finally proving inadequate for the accommodation of the pupils, a one-story frame building was subsequently erected on the school grounds, at an aggregate cost, for the two buildings, including sites, of $13,000.00. The buildings are admirably located in the western part of the city, at the lower extremity of a sightly eminence, which gradually slopes towards the east, rendering the school easy of access to children and teachers. The number of pupils enrolled for the year beginning September, 1898 is 325, and the total indebtedness of the district is $9,250.35.

CHURCHES OF STURGIS

The first church edifice erected in Sturgis was built by the Catholic society in 1882, on an elevated plateau in the western part of the city. The site for this modest little frame structure was donated to the society by Judge Ash, then, as now, a resident of Sturgis. The society has grown since then almost beyond the capacity of the building, and a more commodious structure will, doubtless, soon have to be provided.

A little to the eastward of the church, on the same commanding eminence, is located the Catholic St. Martin's Academy, established through the unremitting labors of Rev. Father Rosen in 1888. The buildings of this excellent institution now consist of two elegant three-storied structures built of light gray sandstone, handsomely trimmed with red sandstone, mined from the quarries of the hills adjacent to the city. The stone material for these buildings was procured free of charge, it is said, from quarries belonging to Judge Ash. Aided by liberal donations of lots in different localities of the town, by citizens of Sturgis, Father Rosen selected and purchased the site and began the construction of the buildings early in the spring of 1888. In May of that year five Benedictine Sisters, of whom sister Angela, the present Mother Superior, was one, arrived in Sturgis from Yankton, having been sent by Right Rev. Martin Marty, Bishop of the Diocese, at the request of Father Rosen, to take charge of the school. In this connection, it may not be impertinent to state that these five sisters had left Switzerland in 1887, crossed the mighty deep and came to Yankton, South Dakota, where they spent an entire year in trying to master the difficulties of the English vernacular, and its pronunciation, preparatory to entering upon their life's noble work.

On reaching Sturgis no time was lost in beginning the work of building up a Catholic school. A building that stood on ground near the present residence of Max Hoehn, was secured, and a school opened with an attendance of from fifteen to twenty pupils during the first term, and, by the way, the first pupil secured by the Sisters was Miss Carrie Francis, now Mrs. H. E. Perkins, wife of the cashier of the Meade County Bank. During the last week of December, 1889, the first building of the institution though not yet fully completed was occupied by the sisters as a permanent home, and subsequently, the lower story of the second structure was finished and equipped for school purposes. In 1898 this latter building, which, in material and external construction, is an almost exact counterpart, from foundation stone to gabled roof, of the first, was built up and completed, according to the original plan of the architect.

This institution, which has acquired a wide reputation for excellence of instruction and salutary discipline, is numerously attended each year by pupils not only from all sections of the Hills, but from different parts of this and other States. Within its secluded walls numerous orphaned and half-orphaned children, find safe and comfortable homes, secure from all worldly allurements, under the tender guidance, yet firm discipline of the devoted, self-sacrificing sisters. There are usually in attendance at the institution from fifty to sixty day pupils, from ninety to 100 boarders, and twenty orphans who make it a permanent home.

METHODIST CHURCH

The Methodist Church began its religious work at a very early date in the annals of Sturgis, and appears to have been the first to organize a society though not the first to build a church edifice in the new town. Its history is but a repetition of the story of the battles of all the earlier religious organizations of the Hills with the problem of devising ways and means to build a house of worship. Away back in the fall of 1878, when Sturgis was in its swaddling clothes, a Sunday school was organized, and held first from house to house at the homes of its members alternately.

The necessity for more permanent accommodations soon becoming apparent, a movement was set on foot to raise money for the purchase of a site and the erection of a building. Through the efforts of Mr. Calvin Duke, says the church record, a fund was raised among those in sympathy with the movement, and two lots, located near the present residence of Mr. Flavin, on Sherman street, were purchased, and a small building erected thereon, which for a time was used jointly for Sunday school and monthly church services, by Elder Williams. Later, Rev. Ira Wakefield, one of the pioneer Black Hills missionaries, held alternate services at Sturgis and Crook City. One Sunday in 1880, while the school was in session, the building, unfortunately or fortunately, as one looks at it, took fire and was burned to the ground, when for a while services were held in the old public school building near the present courthouse.

In 1881 the ground now occupied by Benevolent Hall, was purchased by the society and the two lots on Sherman street were exchanged for two lots on Main street, and a parsonage commenced, for which the work and material was donated. In 1887-8, the property on Main street was sold and the present Methodist church on Cedar street was built.

The resident pastors of the church since 1881, were: Rev. Bartholomew, first resident pastor; Rev. Victor Charrion, for two years; Rev. W. D. Atwater, for three years; Rev. F. E. Lymer, for two years; Rev. T. F. J. Follenbee, Shambough, and G. C. Ulmer, each remaining one year. In 1893 Rev. Atwater returned and during his second pastorate the church was enlarged and improved. In 1895 he was succeeded by Rev. W. J. Pyle, who still watches over the spiritual welfare of the church and jealously guards his flock, to keep them in the straight and narrow way.

The Presbyterian Church entered the religious field at a much later date, and established itself under far more favorable auspices. Its first society was organized in the summer of 1886, and, during the same year, both the church and parsonage were built by Rev. J. Logan Sample, and by him donated to the society—burdened with an incumbrance of only $550.00 on the parsonage,—which obligation was assumed by the society and paid in annual payments. In the spring of 1887 the building was dedicated, Rev. W. S. Peterson, now of Lead, preaching the dedication sermon. The first pastor of the church was Rev. Eckols, who remained in charge two years, when he was successively followed by Revs. Nelson, Toby, Scroggs, and Prugh. In 1898 Rev. E. G. Wright was installed as permanent pastor. The society has a neat and commodious house of worship, fitted out with electric incandescent lights, and in its recent new coat of paint presents a very tasteful external appearance.

The St. Thomas Episcopal Society was organized in 1887, and first held services in the old Sturgis Opera House. Its present church edifice—situated on Howard street and Junction avenue, was built in 1892, and consecrated by Bishop Hare in 1893. All this was not accomplished without a good deal of hard labor and much self-sacrifice on the part of its members, but the details of the story of their struggles to build and maintain the church may, perhaps, we well remain a matter of unwritten history. Rev. North Tummon, its present rector, came to Sturgis in 1893, to assume charge of the work, and to his labors and earnest devotion, aided by the unstinted generosity of one whose hands will never again open responsive to its needs (Dr. Sanderson), is largely due the present existence of the church.

The first newspaper published in Sturgis was the Sturgis *Weekly Record*, established by Messrs. Moody & Elliott in July, 1893. The paper, which is now under the business control and editorial management of C. C. Moody, the first named member of the original firm, is a refreshingly spicy, critical and somewhat caustic sheet conducted, politically, in the interests of the "G. O. P."

The nucleus of the Sturgis Fire Department was formed by the organization of the Hook and Ladder Company on January 17th, 1887, with H. C. Alexander as Chief; First Assistant, John Behn; Second Assistant, J. A. Gaylor; President, W. E. Jones; Secretary, H. P. Hannon. The present efficient department consists of the original Hook and Ladder Company, Key City Hose Company, and Hose Company No. 1.

BANKS

By a somewhat remarkable coincidence, the first two banks of Sturgis, both unorganized enterprises, were opened for the transaction of business on the same day in the fall of 1883, one by J. J. Davenport, himself acting as cashier; the other by Stebbins, Fox & Co., with J. C. Shurtz as cashier. Two years later, in the fall of 1885, the first named of these was organized under the Territorial laws, by J. J. Davenport, as the Lawrence County Bank, with a capital stock of $25,000.00. In June, 1887, the Lawrence County Bank and the bank of Stebbins, Fox & Co. consolidated under the name of the Lawrence County Bank, which, in July, 1887, after spending thirty days in liquidating its finances, was organized into the First National Bank, by J. J. Davenport and W. R. Stebbins.

In 1896 the First National Bank went into liquidation and was incorporated under the laws of South Dakota and became the Meade County Bank, with D. A. McPherson as President; James Halley, Cashier, and Jos. Ryan, Assistant Cashier. Its present officers are: D. A. McPherson,

President; P. E. Sparks, Vice-President; H. E. Perkins, Cashier, and H. L. Conter, Assistant Cashier.

The Meade County Bank rests upon a solid foundation, and is regarded in financial circles as one of the most reliable banking institutions in the State.

On September 1st, 1889, another financial institution was opened for business by an organization known as the Western Bank and Trust Company, with Chas. C. Polk as President; Jacob W. Weeks, Vice-President, and Olaf Holweg, Cashier. The organization was incorporated under the Territorial laws with an authorized capital of $250,000, and a paid-up capital of $57,000. The original intention of the incorporators was to make a specialty of farm mortgage business, but finding the outlook along that line unpromising, it was soon dropped when the institution confined itself to an exclusive banking business until April, 1894, when it went into voluntary liquidation. In June, 1894, a receiver was appointed, who, after paying off the company's obligations, and restoring to the stockholders $28,000 in real estate and other securities, was discharged in August, 1894.

MANUFACTURES

During the three or four years subsequent to the formation of Meade County, Sturgis rapidly increased in population, wealth, and prestige, and its citizens expended large sums in the establishment of such public and private enterprises as would place it upon an enduring basis. Among the first of these was the building of the Sturgis Steam Roller Flouring Mill by George Lawrence, in the fall of 1889, at a cost of $6,000. To encourage the establishment of the industry, the citizens of Sturgis guaranteed to the builder the ground upon which the mill stands, near the western limits of the city, besides a cash bonus of $2,500. The mill, which has a capacity of fifty barrels per day, is supplied almost exclusively with wheat grown within the limits of Meade County, which also raises a surplus for shipment.

The plant is now owned and operated by George Early, who manufactures flour from native grain equal to that produced in any other portion of the West—Minneapolis not excepted.

A large plant for the manufacture of "stucco" from the extensive gypsum beds in the vicinity of Sturgis was operated for a number of years, whose excellent product found ready sale in large quantities in Eastern cities. The works were destroyed by fire a few years ago, since which time the industry has not been re-established.

WATER SYSTEM

Prior to 1893 Sturgis was lacking in one of the chief requisites to health and happiness—an abundant supply of pure, soft water. For nearly fifteen years the people had drawn their supply of that essential fluid for domestic purposes from the depths of the wells which are yet to be seen at the back doors of many of the early residences, or from the uncertain flow of Bear Butte Creek. While these wells furnished an ample supply, perhaps, their waters, though healthful, are hard and considerably impregnated with alkali, which renders them rather unpleasant to the taste, and, what is far worse, destructive to the complexion.

Fully appreciating these disadvantages, the city fathers, at their meeting of June 12th, 1892, granted to one of its enterprising citizens—Joseph J. Davenport—a franchise to supply the city with pure water from the mountains for a period of twenty years. Mr. Davenport, in accordance with the conditions of the franchise, completed the plant and turned the water into the mains on March 9th, 1893. The water supply is drawn from mountain springs located four and a half miles from the city limits, and poured into a reservoir, situated 750 feet above the level of Main street, whence it comes down through the mains with a pressure of over 300 pounds to the square inch. The water is pronounced by experts, who have analyzed its properties, to be exceptionally pure, and free from all disease-producing germs.

The system has eight and a half miles of pipe, fifty-five hydrants for fire purposes within the city limits, and also furnishes Fort Meade with water, under a ten-years' contract. It has 140 taps, which yield to the proprietor a gross income of $8,000.00 per annum.

In 1892 Benevolent Hall Association Temple, the most elaborate and costly edifice till then erected in Sturgis, was built by four of the secret societies of the city, the Masonic, Odd Fellows, Knights of Pythias, and order of United Workmen, at a cost, it is alleged, of $20,100. The building covering an area of 50x120 feet, is a two-story brick structure with iron facade, and is an ornament and credit to the business thoroughfare of the city. According to the original design, the upper story is devoted to the meetings of the above respective lodges, where the hidden mysteries of the orders are periodically practiced.

ELECTRIC LIGHT SYSTEM

The Sturgis Electric Lighting Service was established in the spring of 1897, under the terms of a twenty years franchise, granted by the Common Council of the city to the Sturgis Electric Light and Railway Company—an organization effected under the laws of the State—with Messrs. A. D.

STREET SCENE IN STURGIS, FEBRUARY 22d, 1898

Stewart, J. B. C. Baker, H. E. Perkins, and S. K. Seitz as incorporators. A fine steel-roofed power house, fitted out with the requisite electric appliances, was built by the company, at a cost of about $8,000. The plant is furnished with ample capacity for thoroughly lighting the streets, business houses, and homes of the city, and will, doubtless, in the not distant future, be equipped with additional facilities and largely increased power, for running a contemplated electric motor railway line from Fort Meade to the Elkhorn Railroad Station via Sturgis, the right of way over the military reservation having already been secured by the company from the United States government for such a line.

The consummation of such an enterprise from an economic standpoint would prove of vast advantage to the government, in the transportation of the immense amount of freight used by the post, and also to the business interests of Sturgis, besides adding to the convenience of passengers along the line.

Among the secret and other organizations of Sturgis are the orders of Free Masons, Odd Fellows, Knights of Pythias, Ancient Order of United Workmen, Modern Woodmen, G. A. R., a Women's Literary Club, a Commerical Club and Band Organization, of which latter the average citizen of Sturgis feels justly proud. The most potent factor in the business economy of Sturgis, indeed the very head and front of its commercial existence, is the "Sturgis Commerical Club." This organization is composed of its leading business men, whose aim and purpose is to promote, in every legitimate way, the material interest of the city, by inviting the investment of capital and encouraging public improvements within its limits. Its more recent efforts have been directed towards securing the permanency and enlargement of Fort Meade, upon the retention of which, the future prosperity of Sturgis, as well as the safety of the people of the surrounding country, largely depends.

The present officers of the club are H. E. Perkins, president; John Scollard, vice-president; W. C. Buderus, secretary, P. E. Sparks, treasurer. The executive committee are the president, secretary, and treasurer, of the club, M. F. Hill, Wesley A. Stuart, Geo. W. Mumford, and H. O. Anderson.

The press is now represented in Sturgis by three well conducted newspapers—the Sturgis *Record,* by C. C. Moody, *The Advertiser,* by W. S. Chase; *The Press,* by Mrs. D. T. Connor.

The Sturgis bar consists of seven lawyers and attorneys viz.: Wesley A. Stuart, Chas. C. Polk, M. McMahon, J. C. McClung, Sherman Wilcox, O. W. Jewett, and W. C. Buderus, besides several insurance attorneys, among whom are Max Hoehn, H. P. Atwater, Perkins & Conter, and perhaps others.

Owing to the extreme healthfulness of its climate Sturgis sustains, at this writing, only three disciples of Esculapius, viz., Dr. L. L. Sanderson, J. McSloy, W. G. Smith, and one dental surgeon, R. P. Smith.

The existing urban industries of Sturgis consist of an extensive sawmill, a planing mill, sash and door factory, and a large tannery and lath manufactory in the suburbs of the city. Its mercantile houses, and other business occupations of various kinds, number about seventy-five, and its present population, by a conservative estimate, numbers 1,200.

As proof of the private enterprise of the business men of Sturgis it may be stated that during the year 1898, nine stone business blocks were erected along the main business street of the city. The old frame buildings that have served their purposes for years, and outlived their usefulness, are being from time to time torn down, or moved to other sites, and in their stead massive, substantial stone structures rear their imposing fronts, forcibly reminding one that old things are rapidly receding into the misty past.

Its advantages of location, pure water, and healthful climate has predestined Sturgis to a large measure of success. Its situation at the point of convergence of all the important roadways, leading to the rich agricultural districts, which make it their market and base of supplies; its close proximity to Fort Meade, from which it draws an extensive trade; its direct railway and telegraphic connection with the great trade centers of the East, and its speaking communication by telephone with the principal towns of the Hills, insure its continued prosperity and permanency.

Sturgis, too, by the way, has had its era of disorder, crime, and speedy retribution. During the first decade of its history, it was by no means a shining

**ROUGH RIDERS LEAVING STURGIS FOR CUBA
ON MAY 23d, 1898**

example of morality and good order. According to its own confession it has frequently presented scenes of mad recklessness that outrivaled in lawlessness even the worst days of the early mining camps of the Hills. These conditions were occasioned in good part by the riotous behavior of the colored infantry men, who garrisoned Fort Meade at the time. Whisky flowed like water, and whenever they visited the town, on leave of absence, after imbibing copious draughts of the fiery fluid, they proceeded to paint Main street in all sorts of lurid colors, as if they were its sole proprietors.

Frequent collisions occurred between these black soldiers and the all-round white toughs who sometimes inflicted their unwelcome presence upon the community, resulting in black eyes, cut faces, and bruised anatomies generally. Sometimes men were held up and robbed in the public street at the muzzle of six shooters, and sometimes unoffending men were shot to death under the shelter of their own roofs, and the officers of the law had much difficulty in preserving even a semblance of good order. Sometimes the exasperated citizens took the law into their own hands, and meted out swift punishment to the wretched, trembling culprits. These carnivals of disorder usually occurred just after pay-day at the post, but the colored soldiers were not uniformly the guilty ones, which the following will serve to illustrate.

One evening in June, 1884, an inoffensive German, named Schramm, was held up in the public street, and robbed of $350.00, all he had in the world, by two soldiers and a civilian named Fiddler, if a desperado can be called a civilian.

The three highwaymen were hunted down by a special deputy and a posse of citizens, among whom were Wm. McMillan, John Scollard and others, and taken before Justice O. W. Jewett, who, after an examination, discharged the two soldiers, but held Fiddler for the crime. He was lodged in jail, from which he was taken, under cover of the third night following, by a band of masked men and suspended from the limb of a near-by tree.

On August 28th, 1885, a colored soldier wantonly fired into the drug store of Dr. H. P. Lynch, shooting and killing him instantly. The next night he also was taken from the custody of the guards, by a number of masked men, and dragged away to the western limits of the city. The next morning he was found hanging stark from the limb of a tree, that stood within a short distance of the Elkhorn Station. In the following month a squad of riotous colored soldiers while raising pandemonium, by firing their revolvers in at the doors and windows of respectable business men, shot and killed a man named Bell. Five of the rioters, after preliminary trial, were taken to Deadwood and placed in jail, from which before final trial they broke away and made good their escape.

In 1887 this deplorable state of things was reduced to a minimum, by the removal of the Twenty-fifth Colored Infantry and the substitution of four companies of the Third Infantry in their stead.

CHAPTER XLI

FORT MEADE

By order of Gen. Sheridan, issued in response to numerous appeals of the settlers of the Hills for military protection against persistent Indian depredations, a temporary United States military camp was established on Spring creek a little north of Bear Butte, in August, 1876, and named Camp Sturgis, in honor of the gallant Lieut. J. G. Sturgis, or "Jack Sturgis," as he was familiarly called by his comrades, who fought and fell with Custer on the hills overlooking the Little Big Horn. During the occupation of this camp, the present site of Fort Meade, situated just outside the eastern foot-hills of the Black Hills, and on the south side of Bear Butte creek, was selected and located as a permanent United States military post, which was established and garrisoned on the 31st of August, 1878.

It is alleged by some, that the post was first called "Camp Ruhlen" but why it was so called, and, above all, why a permanent military post should have been called a "camp" at all is not apparent. If the allegation is well founded, it must have been done without authority, as the post was soon by order of the Department named Fort Meade, in honor of Gen. George C. Meade, the brave commander of the Union forces at the deciding battle of the Civil War—Gettysburg.

The work of building the post, for which an appropriation of $100,000.00 had been made, was begun on August 28th, 1878, and completed in August, 1879. The original appropriation not proving sufficient to meet the cost of the necessary buildings an additional appropriation of $11,000, and later a special appropriation of $13,000, was made for post hospital.

On the 18th of December, 1878, the Fort Meade military reservation, comprising an area of a little more than twelve square miles, was declared, and perhaps no more desirable location for a military post could have been found throughout the length and breadth of Uncle Sam's domain. From a military standpoint, the site is admirable. On three sides the encircling hills form a spacious amphitheater which embraces an extensive plat for parade ground, smooth and level as a floor, affording ample space for all kinds of military maneuvers required by army discipline. This with the exhilarating health-giving atmosphere, in which malaria finds no foot-hold, the abundance of pure water, in which fever-breeding germs cannot exist, the plentiful supply of pine timber for fuel near at hand, and the attractiveness of its scenic environment, combine to render the location peculiarly adapted to the requirements of a military post.

According to information obtained from an officer in the Eighth Cavalry Regiment, Fort Meade has been garrisoned, since its occupation, as follows:—

The original garrison consisted of troops E and M, Seventh Cavalry, and companies F and K, First Infantry, with Major H. M. Lazelle, of First United States Infantry, in command. In June, 1879, the garrison was reinforced by the arrival of band and troops C and G, Seventh Cavalry, and on July 10th, 1879, by troops A and H, Seventh Cavalry, at which time Col. S. D. Sturgis assumed command of the post. On September, 1879, Companies D and H, First Infantry, from Fort Sully, joined, increasing the garrison to four companies of infantry and six troops of cavalry.

On May 13th, 1880, companies D, F, H, and K, left for Texas, and were replaced by Companies A, D, H, and K, Twenty-fifth Infantry (colored), with Capt. D. D. Van Valzah, Twenty-fifth Infantry, in temporary command, Col. Sturgis being absent on leave. On May 19th, 1881, Col. Sturgis resumed command, but relinquished in June, going to Washington, D. C., to take charge of the Soldiers' Home. From that time the post was commanded successively by Capt. Van Valzah, Twenty-fifth Infantry, Major Edward Ball, Seventh Cavalry, and Col. Joseph G. Tilford, Seventh Cavalry, until about 1886, when Gen. Geo. W. Forsyth was assigned to the command and remained until June, 1888.

In 1887 the four companies of the Twenty-fifth Infantry were replaced by four companies of Third Infantry. In June, 1888, the Seventh Cavalry Regiment was sent to Fort Riley, Kansas, and the Third Infantry to some other point, when the post was regarrisoned by the Eighth Cavalry Regiment, consisting of eight troops under the command of Col. Elmer Otis. In January, 1891, Col. Otis was superseded by Col. C. H. Carleton, who was retired from active service in June, 1897, when Col. John M. Bacon took command of the garrison.

Soon after the beginning of the Spanish-American war, Col. Bacon was ordered to St. Paul, Minnesota, leaving the post in charge of Major Robt. McGregor. Pending the war, the Eighth Cavalry Regiment, which had occupied the post for ten years, was broken and scattered, the last troops leaving on October 6th, 1898, for Huntsville, Alabama, whence they are to be sent to join the army of occupation in Cuba. The present garrison, October 7th,

FORT MEADE AND BEAR BUTTE IN THE BACKGROUND

1898, consists of two troops of the First United States Cavalry, fresh from the gory battle-fields of San Juan Hill and El Caney.

Fort Meade has quarters and building accommodations for a regiment of ten full troops of cavalry, and as it is regarded, from a strategic standpoint, as the most important inland military post in the whole War Department, it will, doubtless, be increased to its full capacity, and maintained for many years to come, or so long at least, as the government feels it necessary to keep a watchful eye and a restraining hand over the numerous bands of untamed, it might be said, almost untamable, Indians, partitioned off among the various reservations of the Northwest.

The present post buildings consist of twenty-five sets officers' quarters, four double sets barracks, two single sets barracks, adjutant's office, quartermaster's office, guard house, officers of the guard room, two quartermaster's store houses, one commissary, one set band quarters, post exchange, one granary, nine stables, one quartermaster's stable, new hospital of two wards, built in 1896; chapel, schoolhouse, post office, post hall, library, ordnance store house, powder magazine, one bakery, two ice houses, one saw mill, one steward house, and a beautifully located post cemetery fenced in.

The history of Fort Meade would be incomplete without a brief sketch of the brave "Comanche," for ten years an honored resident of the post. Comanche bore the gallant Capt. Keogh to the fatal battle field on the bluffs overlooking the Little Big Horn on the 25th of June, 1876, and two days and nights after the battle he was found standing in a creek, badly riddled by Indian bullets, by some of Reno's men, patiently waiting and mutely pleading for relief.

The condition of the poor creature seemed so hopeless, that the first impulse of the men was to shoot him and end his terrible suffering, but upon second thought they determined, if possible, to save his life. He was taken to Fort Lincoln, and after weeks of tender nursing and skillful treatment he recovered.

In April, 1878, Gen. Sturgis issued the following humane order: "Headquarters Seventh United States Cavalry, Fort A. Lincoln, D. T., April 10th, 1878. General Orders No. 7. (1). The horse known as 'Comanche,' being the only living representative of the bloody tragedy of the Little Big Horn, June 25th, 1876, his kind treatment and comfort shall be a matter of special pride and solicitude on the part of every member of the Seventh Cavalry to the end that his life be preserved to the utmost limit. Wounded and scarred as he is, his very existence speaks in terms more eloquent than words, of the desperate struggle against overwhelming numbers of the hopeless conflict and the heroic manner in which all went down on that fatal day. (2).

"COMANCHE"
Found standing in a creek near the Custer battle-field badly riddled by Indian bullets

The commanding officer of Company I will see that a special and comfortable stable is fitted up for him, and he will not be ridden by any person whatsoever, under any circumstances, nor will he be put to any kind of work. (3). Hereafter, upon all occasions of ceremony of mounted regimental formation, 'Comanche,' saddled, bridled, and draped in mourning, and led by a mounted trooper of Company I, will be paraded with the regiment. By command of Col. Sturgis, E. A. Garlington, First Lieutenant and Adjutant, Seventh Cavalry.''

In June, 1879, 'Comanche' was brought to Fort Meade by the Seventh Regiment, where he was kept like a prince until 1888, when he was taken to Fort Riley, Kansas, where a few years since he died, and was buried with military honors.

TILFORD

Tilford, situated in the eastern foot-hills, on a tributary of Elk creek, was laid out by an organization, known as the Pioneer Town-site Company, on January 12th, 1888, about the time of the arrival of the Fremont, Elkhorn & Missouri Valley R. R. at that point. The settlers had great hopes and expectations for the future of their town, which were destined to be shattered. It was first designated as the point of connection of the Homestake Narrow-gauge Railway from Lead, with the "Elkhorn" road, but for some reason the original plan was changed, and its railroad neighbor on the south was made the point of junction.

In 1890, when the election was held for locating the county seat of Meade County, Tilford made a creditable run for the honor, but was defeated. However, despite its defeat, it is quite a lively little hamlet. The town is

LAST HUNTING GROUND OF THE DAKOTAHS

surrounded by an excellent farming and grazing country, in which former vocation a number of the residents of Tilford are profitably engaged. In the hills adjacent thereto on the west is an abundance of good pine timber, which is being rapidly converted into lumber, which finds a ready market at its door.

PIEDMONT

Piedmont, situated on Elk creek, at the point where it debouches from the foot-hills into the open plains, about five miles south of Tilford, on the line of the Fremont & Elkhorn Railroad, was located as Piedmont in the late winter of 1887-8, upon the arrival of the road at that point. At a much earlier

HORSESHOE CURVE, ON THE FORT PIERRE RAILROAD, RUNNING BETWEEN LEAD AND PIEDMONT

date, however,—years before a railroad was projected into the Black Hills, while the Indians were yet on the rampage, the ground, upon a portion of which the town now stands, was located as a ranch, wisely known as "Spring Valley" ranch. All through the days of overland freighting, stage coaches, and "hold-ups," Spring Valley ranch was an important station along the line, from Sidney and other points to Deadwood, where entertainment was furnished for man and beast, and was also a mail distributing point for settlers, within a limited radius of the station.

The ground, which was originally located by Mark Boughton—not the Mark Boughton of early saw-mill notoriety—Geo. Adler, a Mr. Garvey, and a man whose name is forgotten, was, and is still, considered one of the most valuable ranch properties in the Black Hills. The name was suggested by the multitude of pure, cold, crystal springs which gurgle up from the depths below, causing the soil to yield its perfect crops and luscious fruitage, and keeping the meadows in a state of almost perpetual verdure. It is now recalled that one bright morning a tragedy occurred on this ranch in which the green of the meadow was crimsoned with the blood of one of its owners. In a quarrel Geo. Adler was shot to death by his copartner Garvey, it is believed in self-defense, as he was acquitted after trail by a jury of his peers.

Piedmont, because of its location at the junction with the Elkhorn of the Fort Pierre narrow-gauge railway, over which nearly all the commercial traffic of the Homestake Company is carried, is the most important station between Rapid City and Sturgis. Here are the homes of a considerable number of the company's employees, who are engaged along the line of the road, and here the company conducts a large brick store, requiring the employment of several clerks to fill the demands of an extensive trade, and a boarding house. Besides the Homestake enterprises, Piedmont sustains a store of general merchandise, one hotel, a neat church edifice, and contains a population of about 300.

Many tourists are attracted to Piedmont every year to take a trip over the wonderful Fort Pierre road to Lead which, once taken, remains a memory forever. Some of the grandest and most picturesque scenery in all the marvelous region of the Black Hills is to be found along this line, views which are well worth taking a long journey to see. The most notable attraction, however, is the Crystal Cave, on Elk creek, a few miles above Piedmont. The writer has never ventured beyond the portal of the natural cave, but visited its faint reproduction at the World's Fair in 1893, and its various chambers, gorgeous with brilliant crystalline incrustations, presented a picture which lingers in the memory still. According to the testimony of tourists and others who have explored its passages in all their ramifications, for a distance of fifteen or more miles, few of the natural attractions of the Hills are better worth visiting. A peculiar feature of the cave is a number of miniature lakes, six or eight feet deep, filled with water so transparent, that it is difficult to believe that the bottom is more than a few inches below the surface.

BLACK HAWK

Black Hawk, also on the line of the Elkhorn Railway, near the southern limits of the county, about seven miles north of Rapid City, was located and platted by Mr. C. F. and Mrs. Cornelia Ward, on December 21st, 1887. It attained but little importance until 1896, when the establishment of an extensive lumber manufactory by Baker & Price brought it into considerable prominence. The plant which has brought Black Hawk to the fore, consists of a large saw mill and planing mill, with the adjunct of an extensive wood yard, requiring the employment of a large force of men. The company also operates two or three saw mills, in the timbered region adjacent to the town, to which the manufactured lumber is brought for shipment. In connection with the industry the company has established a boarding house and a large store of general merchandise to supply the demands of its employees. In consequence of this lumber manufacturing enterprise, Black Hawk has been transformed from a secluded railway station containing a post office, a school, and a small store of general merchandise, into quite an important industrial center.

The other points of more or less importance where post offices are maintained are: Grashul, Bend, and Viewfield, on Elk creek, Smithville, on the south fork of the Cheyenne river, Doyle, Runkel, Alkali, Big Bottom, Elm Springs.

CHAPTER XLII

FALL RIVER COUNTY

Fall River County, situated in the extreme southwestern portion of the Black Hills, dates its origin back to 1883, and derives its name from one of the county's most important streams. Prior to that date the territory embraced within its boundaries constituted a part of the original county of Custer, as nearly everyone in the Black Hills doubtless already knows, but all may not know just why and how it asserted itself and became a separate organization, endowed with all the functions of individual county government.

The people of the southern portion of Custer County, like those of the eastern half of the original county of Lawrence, six years later became no longer willing to travel eighty miles over hill and dale, through bush and bracken, to attend terms of court whenever called upon to serve as witnesses or jurors; and, moreover, being essentially an agricultural and stock-raising class, they were not especially interested in mines and mining; hence, when the requisite population was acquired, they took immediate steps to bring about a separation. Reversing the old adage, they adopted the motto of "Divided we stand, united we fall."

The friends of the measure succeeded in securing the passage of a bill through the Territorial Legislature, at its session of 1883, by the provisions of which Custer County was divided on a line running due east and west near its geographical center, and the southern subdivision created into Fall River County; and henceforth the two sections traveled divergent paths. The act became a law on March 6th, 1883, and on November 17th of that year Gov. Ordway, of Dakota Territory, issued a commission to Elisha P. Chilson, Wm. P. Phillips, and Edmund Petty, to organize and construct a county government for the new county. The commissioners at their first session fixed the temporary county seat at Hot Springs, which was made the permanent capital by popular vote at the next general election.

Besides the commissioners, the other first county officers were: James A. Shepard, Sheriff; Joseph Petty, Treasurer; Geo. A. Turner, Register of Deeds and ex officio County Clerk; John Wells, Probate Judge; Dr. R. D. Jennings, County Surveyor; Gifford A. Parker, Assessor; George Trimmer, Coroner; Wm. Wells, Superintendent of Schools.

Fall River County, it appears, had no auditor until January, 1891, when J. M. Moore assumed the office, having been elected to that position at the November election of 1890.

As soon as the wheels of the county machinery were put in operation, the commissioners turned their attention to the matter of county internal improvements. Notwithstanding the fact that the young county was incumbered with its proportion of Custer County's six years' accumulation of indebtedness, inasmuch as it possessed abundant material resources, and an enterprising, progressive people, who were willing to bear the burden of additional taxation, considerable expenditures were made in the construction of such roads and bridges as would render the county seat easily accessible to all settlers within the county domain.

After the lapse of a few years, the people of the county voted to issue bonds to the amount of $25,000 for the purpose of providing funds for building a new courthouse, and, in 1890, a court building was completed, which, in point of external architecture, beauty of material, and internal finish, was the most elaborate, as well as the most costly, that had been constructed in the Black Hills. It is an imposing three-storied structure, built up from base to pediment of native white sandstone,—some call it pink, surmounted by a handsome ornamental tower, and stands in seemingly conscious dignity and pride, a little above where the hills entrench upon the border of the stream near the northern limits of the capital city.

The territory of Fall River County comprises an area of nearly 1,037,000 acres, about two-thirds of which may properly be divided into arable and grazing land, the residue consisting of rugged hills, covered for the most part with heavy pine timber. The southern portion lying along the Cheyenne river and extending south to the northern boundary line of the State of Nebraska, is peculiarly adapted to stock-raising, large herds of cattle and horses feeding all the year round on its rich grasses without other sustenance.

The principal streams draining the area are the south fork of the Big Cheyenne river, which traverses the county from its western to its northeastern boundary line, and its tributaries, Fall river and Beaver creek on the north, and Horsehead and Hat creeks on the south.

Fall river, which derives its name from the rapidity of its descent, is fed by the aggregate waters of Hotbrook and Coldbrook, its two affluents, and the surplus waters of the many never-failing springs along the narrow valley, and carries a large volume of water to the Cheyenne river at all seasons of the year without material diminution.

According to the statistics of 1897, a considerable proportion of the whole acreage of Fall River County is still open to settlement, much of which is as desirable as any land to be found in any other portion of the Hills. In the year 1897 there were 128,767 acres of land assessed at a valuation of $390,371.00; 8,726 cattle, at $89,186.00; 3,979 horses, at $53,701.00; 6,224 sheep at $6,679.00; and other stock at $1,099.00, making a total assessed valuation for the county of $541,046.00. The population of the county for the same year was 5,500 approximately.

THERMAL SPRINGS

From a scientific standpoint, a portion of Fall River County is, perhaps, the most remarkable region in the entire Black Hills, and offers a most inviting and instructive field to the student for geological and chemical research. Its most peculiar and interesting features are the groups of phenomenal springs, whose wonderful curative properties have made them already justly celebrated throughout the land. Their thermal waters, clear as crystal, issue forth from clefts in the solid rocks, but primarily, it is believed, come bubbling up from nature's heated chemical laboratory, away down somewhere toward the Celestial empire, forming numerous copious springs, in whose limpid waters the rheumatic, the dyspeptic, the neuralgic, the sciatic, the hypochondriac, and the hysterical may lave, and aided by frequent generous draughts of the tepid fluid, be made whole. It may be stated, *en passant,* that at first the beverage is not the most palatable in the world, but after several *dekaliters* each day for a week have been quaffed, one becomes accustomed to it and will want to increase the dose.

The temperature of the water of these springs, of which there are several, is said to range from ninety-six to ninety-eight degrees Fahrenheit, neither too hot nor too cold for bathing purposes, it having been already prepared in nature's dispensary to suit the temperature of the human body. The medicinal properties of these springs, all of which have been frequently analyzed by expert chemists, with nearly the same results, are as follows:—

CONSTITUENTS

Parts per gallon	Grains
Silica	2.464
Peroxide of Iron	A trace
Calcium Sulphate	16.325
Magnesium	4.320
Sodium Sulphate, Potassium Sulphate	25.620
Sodium, Chloride, and Potassa	13.790
Total	62.519

Hundreds of physicians of high repute from all parts of the country have visited these springs to examine for themselves their medicinal characteristics and have pronounced them to be unequaled by any other known mineral waters for various kinds of maladies, but more especially for all kinds of rheumatic affections. Many marvelous and well authenticated cures of that disease in its worse forms are chronicled, some of which have come under the writer's own personal observation, and if there is anything under the sun in which she has implicit and abiding faith, it is the efficacy of the thermal waters of the Black Hills' Hot Springs, for all kinds of rheumatic affections.

Their virtues were well known to the Indians, it appears, long years before they were discovered by white men. Time-worn tradition, into whose warp and woof are inter-woven many interesting pages of real history, says that more than two and a half centuries the North American tribes were striken with a fearful epidemic, which threatened to obliterate them from the face of the continent, and that many came from afar with their afflicted braves, and women, and children, to bathe in their healing waters.

Finally after the lapse of more than 200 years, they were usurped by the avaricious Cheyennes, but as to how this was done tradition is silent. The powerful Sioux, having an equal solicitous regard for the health of their squaws and papooses, disputed their title, which culminated in the waging of a fierce conflict for their possession. On the summit of a mountain, now called Battle Mountain, which stood guard over them, three miles to the eastward, the battle begun. Both sides, says tradition, fought with distinguished savage gallantry, and from behind the towering rocky battlements, poison-tipped arrows flew thick and fast from the bows of the opposing braves, resulting in a sweeping victory for the valorous Sioux, who obtained and retained possession until driven out of the Black Hills by the superior valor of the pioneers.

Moreover, there is a bit of legendary Indian lore handed down, which tells a tragic story. There was a Sioux Indian princess, reads the legend, whose wondrous beauty made her the envy of all the dusky maidens of the Sioux tribes. This royal princess, who came with her people often to lave in the wonderful waters, had plighted her troth to a stalwart young brave,— presumably beneath her in rank, whom she loved with all the fiery ardor of her race, but the unfeeling and ambitious chief, her father, had selected one in whose veins coursed the blue blood of generations of medicine men, for his beautiful daughter, and cruelly separated the young lovers, when the unhappy maiden, during one of their periodical visits to that region, threw herself headlong from a towering cliff and was dashed to fragments on the rocks below, leaving her name—Minnekahta, as a heritage to the springs. Is it not possible that the hero and heroine of the awful tragedy were romantic myths?

Many evidences are found of the occupation of this locality by Indians, but, in view of their well-known dread of the terrible electric storms which sometimes sweep over the Hills, the forked lightning splintering the giant pines from topmost branch to their roots, it is believed their visits were of short duration, and, perchance, for the most time they pitched their tepees outside the foot-hills. With her characteristic incredulity, the writer also accepts the tradition, in as far as it relates to bathing, with a good many grains of skepticism. Who ever saw, or knew, of an uncivilized Indian taking a bath? Who, indeed!

True it is that there is to be seen a shallow, moccasin-shaped tub, cut out of the solid rock, in which it is believed by many, they immersed themselves in sections when sick. Perhaps it was like this,—to quote a bit of doggerel:—

"The Indian, when sick, in hot water will lave,
The Indian, when well, devil a bit will he have."

The first white men to visit the Hot Springs' region were it is claimed: Col. Dodge, Prof. Henry Newton, and Dr. V. T. McGillicuddy, members of the Jenny Scientific Expedition in 1875. According to the notes of Prof. Newton, the three above-named gentlemen, while on a tour of exploration through the southwestern Hills, during the summer of that year, discovered a warm spring, which Dr. McGillicuddy at the time named Minnekahta.

It is not at all improbable that others also, while hunting or prospecting for minerals in their locality, may have come upon these springs at an early date, but it was left for Col. Wm. Thornby, now of Deadwood, to first locate and bring them into public notice. The history of their location, and the subsequent settlement of the region where the famous health resort now stands—based upon data obtained from Col. Thornby, is substantially as follows: In June, 1879, Prof. Jenny and Col. Thornby, left Deadwood together, on horseback, for a trip through the southern Hills, the former to complete some unfinished work, began in 1875, the latter without other object apparently than mere adventure.

COL. WM. THORNBY
Locator of the famous Minnekahta Thermal Spring and the site upon which the celebrated Black Hills resort now stands.

Their route took them through Rapid City to Rockerville—then riding on the crest of the topmost wave of prosperity—thence to Sheridan, where they met and were entertained royally by some of the old miners who had escaped from the dreaded "blue coats," and taken refuge under the mantle of the Jenny Expedition in 1875. Finding no public accommodations at Hill City—then at its ebb-tide, on reaching that point they proceeded south, and put up at a ranch then owned by L. B. Reno, a mile below. During their stay at the ranch, it was incidentally disclosed, that a ledge of very rich quartz literally covered with free gold had been discovered in the vicinity of "Chimney Rock" about eight miles south of Custer, in 1875, by W. K. Patrick, botanist of the Jenny Expedition. The next day the Professor and Col. Thornby, bent on finding, if possible, the reputed rich ledge, set out for Custer, which they made their base of operations pending the search.

Strangely enough they found no hostelry at the pioneer town and were forced to trespass upon the private hospitality of J. C. Saunders, who had been one of the guides of the scientific expedition of 1875. At that time, says Mr. Thornby, Sam'l. Booth and Sam. Shankland kept a store of general merchandise at Custer, which then contained a population of ten souls, exclusive of a few miners who were camping within the limits of the town. "How had the mighty fallen!"

Bright and early the next morning they started out in search of the "lost mine," returning at night with a large sack filled with the most promising samples of white quartz to be found in the region round about "Chimney Rock." Providing themselves with pan and mortar, they repaired to French creek, where the next day was spent in pulverizing and panning out the contents of the sack, without raising a single color. A continued and more extended research on the following day was attended with like results. Similar white quartz, glittering with gold, was brought into Custer by Alfred Gay in 1876, causing intense excitement, and what is most remarkable, he was never able to locate the mine afterwards.

During their stay in Custer, they met N. H. Ross, one of the miners of the Custer Expedition of 1874, who told them of some warm springs he had encountered while on a hunting trip through the southern Hills, when they decided to go at once and explore the region for themselves.

Of the trip, the location of the springs and the consequent settlement of that region of the Hills, Col. Thornby very entertainingly says:—

"We determined to explore that region and arose at four o'clock one morning, had lunches put up, and started. We went by the way of the Point of Rocks, where there is now a station on the Burlington road called Pringle. From this point we took an old Indian trail along the divide towards Buffalo

Gap, for six or seven miles, and passed within a short distance of the now famous Wind Cave. We then took a direct course toward Battle Mountain, and first reached what is now known as Fall river, at a point where the F. E. & M. V. depot now stands. We watered our horses, staked them out, took a bath, and ate our lunches. After hunting an hour or so at that point, we started on horseback up the stream, and when we reached the point where the Evans Hotel now stands, we found a pretty brook flowing down what is now graded as Minnekahta avenue. It was a warm day, we had been drinking the tepid water from the creek, and the sight of the bright, sparkling water of the brook was tempting. Prof. Jenny had a telescope gutta percha drinking cup with him, and, dismounting, I asked him for the cup, saying I would hand him some of the water, which looked so fresh and cool. To my surprise, I found it warmer than the water of the creek. We followed up this little stream to where the Minnekahta bath house was afterwards built, and where the famous spring boils out of the rock. At that time it was a virgin spring, and I do not think it had been disturbed by a human being, not excepting the Indians. It was covered with frog spawn, and was about six or seven feet in diameter. I cleared away the frog spawn, and the professor and I dipped our hands in it. It seemed to me at that time to be almost at the boiling temperature, and much warmer than it is now. I was very much taken with the spring, and with a hatchet I chopped off the top of a cedar tree, blazed it on both sides, and wrote on the tree: "I claim this spring." Prof. Jenny prophesied that some day the spring would be valuable. At this time the nearest habitation to the spring was Geo. Boland's ranch at Buffalo Gap, twelve miles distant.

"It was about two o'clock when we left this spring, now named the 'Minnekahta' spring, and we took a different course back, coming up what is called Hotbrook canyon, until we struck the Holman cut-off road, running from Custer to Fort Robinson, crossing near what is now Minnekahta junction, on the Burlington road. At this point I saw the first herd of elks I had ever seen. It being in the spring of the year, they had shed their antlers, and I remarked to the professor: 'There's a herd of mules.' From here we journeyed along a good road to Custer, reaching there about 7:30 in the evening.

"After remaining at Custer a day or two, and hearing so much exciting talk of the two new discoveries, known as the 'Old Bill,' and the 'Grand Junction' located six miles north of Custer, we started to investigate that camp. The 'Old Bill' locators pounded up a great many samples of their rock for the professor, and it was marvelously rich. We then visited the 'Grand Junction,' about a mile and a half from the 'Old Bill,' and were shown some fine prospects from that famous ledge. Prof. Jenny advised me to prospect in that vicinity and locate some ground. I said I would return to Deadwood with him; get my clothing and blankets, and come back to the locality, which I did soon after. From the 'Grand Junction' mine, we cut our way through the brush, down Tenderfoot gulch until we came to the Hill City road, stopping with Reno & Bond again that night. We gave them a history of the Hot Springs section, and described what a pretty place it would be to locate a ranch. Reno told me he would go down there with me when I came back. The next morning Reno accompanied us to Hill City and introduced us to George Trimmer and John Dennis, who were living in Hill City. Reno, Trimmer, and Dennis afterwards became three of the pioneer residents of Hot Springs.

"Jenny and I went from Hill City up to Newton's Fork, visiting Rochford, which was a booming camp then, and went thence to Deadwood. After spending a few days in Deadwood, I packed my outfit, moved to the 'Grand Junction' mine, and built a cabin. I was appointed on a committee with Dennis McGuire to lay out the town-site of Junction City. Shortly afterwards I took a horseback trip to George Boland's ranch, at Buffalo Gap, and tried my best to induce him to go with me to locate the Hot Springs. At that time he was the stage agent at Buffalo Gap, and distributing postmaster for all the mail that came into the Black Hills. His place was a great stopping-place for all the emigrants, and he was the busiest man I ever met.

"The night I was at his place a peculiar incident occurred. Col. John B. Fury, Post Office Inspector, with one of the high officials from Washington, was there, and he held the outgoing stage at the Gap. While he was checking up Boland in the Post Office and the distributing system, Boland was busily occupied in finding stable room for the transient stock and selling hay and feed to the emigrants, and the Washington official became very indignant because Boland did not give him greater attention. He started to reprimand Boland, when the latter became irate and gave the Washington dignitary the worst dressing down I ever heard a man get in my life. He wound up by firing the Post Office—which consisted of a beer case with twenty-four pigeon holes—out into the road, and ordered the Washington man off the reservation. It required all of Col. Fury's suavity and persuasion to pacify Boland and induce him to act as distributor until someone could be secured to take the place, at Rapid City."

The Washington official obviously did not estimate the metal of which the Black Hills pioneers are made at its true value. If he had been forewarned that Uncle Sam's mail distributor at Buffalo Gap had, with Capt. Gardner, Jack King, Dick Horsford, and others, fought several desperate battles with the redskins while en route over the dangerous trail from Fort Laramie to Custer in 1876, he might have been more discreet in his choice of words.

"The next day Boland wrote out a ranch location notice on a piece of the box that had served as the post office, and I started with it, with several nails and a hatchet, 'armed to the teeth,' to locate the Minnekahta spring. I think it was about the middle of July, 1879. In looking for the Minnekahta spring, I found the spring where the 'plunge bath' now stands, and to correct some history and stories that have been published and told about Hot Springs, I will state this was the spring that the Indians had dug out, and where they had bathed, as I found many tepee sites surrounding it, strewn with lodge poles. I was in a quandary whether to locate this spring or the Minnekahta spring, but I nailed my location notice to the Cedar tree that I had chopped down, while at the spring with Jenny, on account of the water being much warmer. Boland had instructed me to locate the ranch a half mile square, and I put up one stake next to the cement wall back of the site of the Evans Hotel as my eastern boundary. It was getting late in the afternoon, and thinking I might lose my way, I started back to Boland's ranch at Buffalo Gap. At that time there were no stakes or locations upon any of the springs, and I am positive that I was the first person to put a location on any of them.

"During the summer and fall I made several trips to the location from Custer, where I was staying,—changing the date on the notice each time, and reserving thirty days in which to make permanent improvements. Some time in August, Reno and Trimmer made a trip to the springs and located the two ranches where the old town now stands, but, before, they made any improvements, Geo. Turner and Joseph Brunschmidt built a cabin just above where the plunge bath now stands, in a cottonwood grove, and turned some cattle loose. Their cabin was the first built in that section.

"I was elected the first County Assessor of Custer County that fall, Mr. Louis Everly, who had been elected the previous fall, having refused to qualify. The next spring I went down to the springs to assess Turner and Brunschmidt, accompanying Mr. Reno and Mr. Bond. They started the second cabin upon what afterwards became the original town-site. The third cabin was built by Geo. Trimmer on ground now occupied by his fruit orchard. John Dennis built the fourth house near the Catholicon spring. During the summer of 1880, Joe Laravie and John Davidson came over from Pine Ridge Agency, bringing their families to visit Trimmer and family.

"Laravie was sick with rheumatism, and Trimmer took him to my spring to bathe, Trimmer digging out the old original bath tub.

"They built a log cabin and put up several tepees near, Laravie and Davidson being squaw men, and a picturesque scene was formed. On one of my trips, to make arrangements for building a house on my claim, I found them there, and in a joking way they told me they had jumped my spring.

"At that time the Grand Junction mine was bonded for a large sum of money, and I, having some property adjoining, that was included in the bond, and thinking that a sale would surely be made, I was feeling very generous, and told them they could have the spring if they would hold it. I thought they could make some money out of it, while I could not afford to keep some one there, and was too busy in the mining line to stay there myself.

"That summer I visited Deadwood, and wrote an article for the *Pioneer* about the springs. Dr. R. D. Jennings, read it, and questioned me considerably about the springs, and sent McKay, one of the old miners who had been with Custer, down to investigate, and give him a full report. Dr. Jennings and Dr. A. S. Stewart visited the springs in the fall of 1881, looking over the situation thoroughly. After returning to Deadwood they formed a stock company, with E. G. Dudley, L. R. Graves and Col. Fred T. Evans, and this company bought out Davidson and Laravie. In the meantime Reno had traded his ranch to Joe and Ted. Petty for a farm they owned near Buffalo Gap.

DR. R. D. JENNINGS
One of the founders of The Great American Carlsbad

They held the plunge bath spring for irrigating their farm. The new company purchased that spring also.

"Dr. Stewart, Dr. Jennings, and Judge Dudley moved their families to the springs in 1882, built themselves comfortable homes and laid out the original town-site. Judge Dudley started a saw mill, and Graves and Evans furnished the necessary means to build up and improve the town. If five men ever worked together in harmony for the upbuilding of a place, these men did."

It will be seen from the foregoing account that, contrary to the heretofore commonly accepted belief, to Col. Wm. Thornby belongs the distinction of having located, not only the first warm spring, but also, jointly with George Boland, the site upon which the main portion of the celebrated Black Hills health resort now stands. He did not perfect settlement of the ground, it is true, having, in a spasm of generosity, which he has since, no doubt, sorely regretted, relinquished his claim to Joe Laravie and John Davidson, squaw men, who subsequently sold to the Hot Springs Town-site Company for a good round sum.

The first actual settlers in the Hot Springs region were George Trimmer, George Turner, Joseph Brunschmidt, and Joseph and Edmund Pitty. Although Messrs. Reno and Bond located ranches, it does not appear that they made permanent settlement.

Col. Wm. Thornby, the locator of the wonderful thermal "Minnekahta" spring, and the site upon which the celebrated Black Hills health resort now stands, came to the Black Hills in the winter of 1876, then a young man just entered upon his twenties, and like the born "rustler" that he is, went immediately to work as an up-gulch agent for the Black Hills *Weekly Pioneer.* In June, 1879, he went to Custer, and in the fall of that year was elected as the first assessor of that county and was again elected to succeed himself. In 1884 he was elected as county judge of Custer County. In 1892 he was elected to the State Senate from Custer and Fall River Counties, by the largest majority received by any member in either branch of the Legislature. In 1887 he was appointed a Colonel on the staff of Governor Church, receiving the first Colonel's commission in the Black Hills. Mr. Thornby is now in the employ of the Government Assay Office at Deadwood, South Dakota.

Dr. R. D. Jennings, one of the founders of the great "American Carlsbad," came to the Black Hills with the Major Whitehead party from Bismarck, in June, 1876, stopping first at Crook City, then on the crest of the wave, and, as some thought, the future metropolis of the Black Hills.

After a short sorjourn at Crook City, he went to Deadwood, where he remained until 1881 when he removed to Hot Springs, where he has since resided. Dr. Jennings held the position of Deputy United States Revenue Collector for Dakota Territory from March, 1875, to June, 1878, after which time he was engaged in mining in the vicinity of Deadwood until his removal to Hot Springs, where for several years he followed the business of an architect. Many of the public buildings of the Black Hills, notably the Pennington and Custer County courthouses, the Deadwood and Custer public school buildings, as also the Minnekahta Hotel at Hot Springs, and numerous of the cottages of Deadwood, were constructed after plans prepared by his hand.

Upon his removal to Hot Springs, Dr. Jennings took up the study of medicine and graduated from a medical school at Chicago, Ill., in 1889, and in 1890 took an M. R. C. S. course in King's College, London, since which time he has been engaged in the practice of his profession at Hot Springs, South Dakota.

CHAPTER XLIII

HOT SPRINGS OR MINNEKAHTA

Located upon and between a somewhat bewildering maze of undulating hills, in the picturesque valley of Fall river, flanked by lofty ranges of mountains,—trending nearly north and south at an elevation of about 3,700 feet above the ocean's plane, may be found Hot Springs, distinguished as the Hot Springs of South Dakota, but sometimes designated the "Carlsbad of America," and perhaps its noted German prototype suffers nothing by the comparison. Indeed the Hot Springs of to-day with its numerous sanitariums and bath-houses equipped with all the best appliances for administering every kind of water treatment, including the plunge, the spray, the vapor, the salt, the Turkish, and Russian baths, its magnificent many storied and luxuriantly furnished hotels, for the entertainment of the crowds of guests who visit the resort every summer in quest of pleasure and health; its superb climate and romantic scenic environments, to say nothing of its fine public and private buildings, possibly reflects luster upon its foreign namesake.

The Hot Springs Town-site Company was organized in Deadwood, late in the fall of 1881, and in December, 1882, the town-site was laid out on ground purchased by the company of Edmund Petty, but first located as a ranch by L. B. Reno, in 1879, in the vicinity of the Catholicon spring, the original plat containing an area of 160 acres. Appropriately enough, the name applied to the new town was Hot Springs, but in this connection the thought naturally occurs that the more euphonious and attractive appellation of "Minnekahta," which, in the Sioux tongue, characterizes the thermal quality of the waters of that region, and, moreover, which speaks eloquently of sparkling rills and babbling brooks, of mossy dells and shady nooks, would be more in harmony with the romantic beauties of that delightfully sequestered spot. Perhaps, however, from a purely material and economic standpoint, it was the proper thing to give it the more practical name of plain Hot Springs. At any rate, Hot Springs it is, and it is not the purpose of the writer to question the propriety of the title bestowed.

The initial building, erected on the town-site, was a one and one-half story frame structure, built by Dr. A. S. Stewart for a stage station and hotel, for the entertainment of passengers over the line, and other guests. The building did not long stand isolated and alone, as shown in the accompanying

THE FIRST HOUSE ON THE ORIGINAL TOWN-SITE OF HOT SPRINGS, BUILT BY DR. A. S. STEWART

cut, other business enterprises of a magnitude sufficient to meet the requirements of the population, being soon established. During the following year, too, a school was opened, and the first public school building erected. This first school was taught by Miss Lottie Smith of Custer, in a small log cabin, situated at the lower extremity of the original town, with an attendance of six pupils. Subsequently, a school building was erected by the citizens of the lower town, under the auspices of the Hot Springs Library Association. This first public school building afterwards became the property of the Catholic Church.

Although the town received something of an impetus in 1883, when it became the capital of Fall River County, it was not characterized by any remarkable permanent growth during the first three years of its existence, its population being for the most part of a transient character. It did not grow up in a day like some of the early mining camps of the Hills, but developed by a sort of gradual evolution. News of the wonderful cures effected by the use of the thermal waters, in cases of rheumatism, soon spread beyond the limits of the Hills, when it became the "Mecca" of large numbers of those afflicted with that and other kindred maladies, to test their virtues. Some, who, perhaps, had experienced only occasional premonitory twinges of that peculiar disease, came provided with camping outfits, for a season of recuperation, and pitched their tents near one or another of the most reputable of the many springs, on ground once occupied by the tepees of the redmen, while others took up their quarters at a hotel or other place of entertainment; hotels and bath houses had sprung up in the vicinity of the springs as naturally as their thermal waters bubbled up from the depths below. A few helpless cripples, with drawn, distorted members, who were brought in wagons and carried to their quarters for treatment, returned to their homes in a few weeks, sound in every limb. These were only temporary guests who came and went.

With the increasing influx of invalids, and tourists on pleasure bent, the demand for sanitariums, furnished with facilities for the treatment of patients, and increased hotel accommodations for the entertainment of visitors, both sick and well, became imperative. To fulfill this demand, required the expenditure of a large amount of capital and the company prepared to meet the emergency.

In the fall of 1886 the Town-site Company reorganized and was duly incorporated under the Territorial laws, and designated the Dakota Hot Springs Company, with Dr. A. S. Stewart, Dr. R. D. Jennings, Col. Fred. T. Evans, Leonard R. Graves, and Judge E. G. Dudley as incorporators. The company was organized with a capital stock of $2,000,000, divided into 40,000 shares, of a par value of $500 each.

The 320 acres of land, purchased by the company of Laravie and Davidson, was laid out and platted for a new town-site, when the center of growth was transferred from the old town-site to the new, in the vicinity of the originally discovered "Minnekahta" spring, which is regarded as the head and front of the town's existence. From this time dates the real substantial growth of Hot Springs. Real estate became at once in active demand, and the investment of capital followed as a logical sequence. A newspaper and bank were soon established, followed later by educational and other public institutions. Elegant, many-storied structures of native sandstone, rose up in the valley, and others reared their imposing individualities on the adjacent plateaus, in the construction of which hundreds of dollars were disbursed and for the most part circulated through the town.

The first newspaper published, called the Hot Springs *Star*, was established by Dr. A. S. Stewart and W. W. Laflesh on May 28th, 1886. The first bank opened its doors for business on July 28th, 1888, with Richard C. Lake, president; Jas. Halley, vice-president, and H. S. Eaton, cashier. The institution was incorporated under the Territorial laws, and designated the "Hot Springs Bank."

The first religious society was organized by the Methodists in 1884, which society also erected the first house of public worship in 1887. There are now six religious organizations, viz.: the Methodist, Episcopalian, Presbyterian, Congregational, Baptist, and Catholic.

PUBLIC INSTITUTIONS

On an elevated plateau, known as "College Hill," overlooking the valley of Fall river on the west, half hidden by trees, stands the Black Hills College, in its sober gray sandstone attire. The college building, a solid three-storied structure, was completed in 1889 at a cost of $20,000 approximately. The institution which was established under the auspices of the Methodist church, opened its doors for the admission of students on September 11th, 1890, with an attendance of eleven students which number was increased to forty before the close of the college year. Its first president was Rev. John W. Haucher, through whose unremitting efforts the existence of the college was made possible.

Although denominational, the institution is conducted upon broad and liberal principles, its doors standing wide open for all students regardless of creed. Its course, covers a wide range of studies, in which the instruction is thorough and complete, by reason of which the institution has gained an enviable reputation both at home and abroad.

About half way up the acclivity of a hill which rises up to the westward of the business portion of the city, with groves of pine and hemlock, and tumuli of variegated gypsum on its outer environments, as I remember it, the South Dakota Soldiers' Home rears its massive pile of gray stone masonry. The Home, covering an area of 85x132 feet, wholly within its own generous domain of eighty acres of land, is a fine three-story structure with dormer roof, built of handsome gray sandstone, with double verandas in front, and stands a fitting monument in honor of the brave men who fought to preserve us a united nation. Within its solid walls and under its protecting roof, South Dakota's disabled, gray-haired veterans of the Civil War may find a safe refuge, and spend the balance of their days in peaceful comradeship, recounting stories of the terrible days when they bivouacked on the field of battle, surrounded by the bodies of the slain.

SOUTH DAKOTA SOLDIERS' HOME, HOT SPRINGS

The Home, which was secured to Hot Springs through the recommendation of the G. A. R. of the Department of Dakota, was completed in 1890, at a cost—including interior equipments and outside appurtenances—of $45,000 to Dakota Territory. The Act authorizing its construction, which became a law over the Governor's veto on the 27th of February, 1889, gives title in fee simple to eighty acres of land, within or near the limits of Hot Springs, to Dakota Territory, and by contract guarantees to the Home and its inmates all the water needed for any purpose whatsoever from the best spring in the region free of charge. It is needless to state that the title is now vested in South Dakota, and the water procured from the original Minnekahta spring.

In the valley, almost directly east from the Soldiers' Home on the opposite side of Fall river, the Evans Hotel stands out in bold relief against a background of rugged, variegated crags which rise high and still higher towards the east until they culminate in Battle Mountain, some two and a half or three miles away. The building is five stories in height, constructed of what many connoisseurs in color shades call pink sandstone, but which to my inartistic eye appears of a light brown. However, to compromise differences, we shall call it pinkish-brown. Well, it is built of pinkish-brown sandstone, mined from the Evans quarry somewhere among the neighboring hills, and is surrounded on three sides by a wide veranda, where its guests on summer evenings are wont "to trip" the light fantastic toe to the strains of the Evans House paid orchestra, and I wouldn't wonder a bit if those cured of chronic rheumatism and gout, sometimes gaily dance the "two-step" in the same spacious veranda.

In interior arrangement, finish, and furnishings, it is a model of the architect, the mechanic, and upholsterer's art, and with its mosaic-floored, fresco-walled lobby, its velvet carpeted, elegantly furnished parlors, its electroliers, anunciator, and elevator, one might easily—closing his eyes to outside environments—imagine himself in one of the palatial hotels at Newport. This magnificent structure was built by the Dakota Hot Springs Company in 1891 and 1892, at a cost of $150,000. The work of construction began on October 21st, 1891, and the big hostelry was opened for the reception of guests on August 6th, 1892.

Near the "Evans" and connected with it by an inclosed passage way is the sanitarium for the accommodation of the hotel guests, as well as the general public. It is a three-story structure of cut stone, corresponding in color and similar in style to the hotel, and furnished with the same luxuriance throughout. The lower floor is handsomely fitted up for waiting rooms, while the upper stories are separated into numerous apartments, arranged en suite for the convenience and comfort of its invalid inmates. The building is warmed with stream and lighted with electricity, is provided with capacious bath pools, and every other facility for the treatment of patients who are cared for under the special directions of a skilled physician.

Just across the stream which flows swiftly down the valley in front of the Evans, is the "Gillespie," a handsome four-story building of cut sandstone, surmounted by a dominant corner tower, and fronted by a double balcony. Although built and conducted on a somewhat less extensive and elaborate plan than its neighbor across the brook, it is fitted out with the most modern appointments, and its cuisine is reputed to be a marvel of excellence. The "Gillespie" was built in 1889 and 1890 by Fred. Gillespie, at a cost of $25,000. Its doors were opened to the public in June, 1890.

On the opposite corner north of the "Evans," stands the massive pile of stone, extending from East river to Main street, called the Minnekahta Block, which is the largest and most costly business edifice in Hot Springs. The building, a three-storied pink sandstone structure, was built by the Minnekahta Company of which Fred. T. Evans was, it is believed president, at a cost of $35,000. Conspicious among other business buildings are the Fargo-Dickover Block, and the Phillips & Boomer Block, at the lower end of the city, the former a three-storied and the latter a two-storied structure.

Let us now take a stroll around the outer limits of the city and pay a brief visit to the springs, whose magnetic waters constitute the stimulus which sustains its vitality. After crossing the bridge that spans the stream, let us proceed west to the end of Minnekahta avenue, and there in a recess of the hill which slopes down from the west, will be found the original Minnekahta Spring, in a cleft of the rock. Over the spring is erected a two-story bath house, containing sixty or more rooms, provided with handsome marble bath-tubs, and warmed by steam, where the whole category of baths are administered.

Here may be seen a moccasin-shaped tub, chiseled out of the solid rock, which is, doubtless, one of the traditional tubs, in which the Indians took their ablutions, centuries, perhaps, before they were seen by white men.

Near by, and conducted in connection with the bath-house, is a four-story sanitarium and hotel, suitably arranged and equipped for the convenience and comfort of its invalid guests, where is prepared the menu which tempts the delicate appetite of the sick.

Below the old town-site at the lower extremity of the city is the Catholican spring. Here, too, is a large sanitarium—a long three-storied building of cut sandstone and pressed brick. From a passing glimpse of the structure, obtained in 1893, it impressed me as being made up of a main central building with a right and left wing; however, it may have been added to since then. At any rate, it has a large capacity for the accommodation of guests and an extensive patronage.

Up the valley at the northern extremity of the city will be found the great Mammoth spring and the still greater ''Plunge,'' which, for the robust or those needing heroic treatment, stands without a peer. This happy conception, wrought out for the amusement of visitors, consists of an immense basin, 150x60 feet in dimensions, we are told. with gravel bottom, through which a multitude of springs bubble up, and walled on all sides with solid stone and cement masonry. Into this the Mammoth spring pours its flood of magnetic, tepid water, at the rate of 100,000 gallons every hour, the outflow leaving a depth of five feet at one end and nine at the other.

Around this immense pool is constructed a wide promenade, affording ample space for the bathers and onlookers. At convenient points in this gallery, are arranged toboggan slides, spring boards, trapeze ropes, and every other contrivance known to water sports. Over the whole is built a lofty, arched structure of iron and glass, heated by steam, lighted by electricity, and provided with a hundred well-appointed dressing-rooms, for the use of bathers and visitors. Within this unique structure an amusing and animated spectacle is presented, any day during the watering season.

Just imagine a half a hundred or more men and women, girls and boys, of nearly all ages and sizes, plump and lean, diving, ducking, sinking, swimming, floating, floundering, splashing, gasping, screaming, and laughing in

INTERIOR OF PLUNGE BATH, HOT SPRINGS

the big pond, at the same time, and you have a true mental picture of what is frequently to be seen at the "Plunge." And oh, the joy and fun of it all! This wonderful structure of stone, wood, iron, and glass, was built during the summer and fall of 1890, by the Dakota Hot Springs Company, at a cost of $20,000. About 300 yards above the "Plunge" is the Lakota spring, the fountain head of the Hot Springs' water system.

On the slope of College Hill, is another sanitarium and bath house, a private institution, affording accommodations for about twenty patients, established by Dr. A. S. Stewart. This institution is provided with facilities for all kinds of baths,—plunge, vapor, spray, Turkish, etc. An attractive feature of this establishment is a miniature "plunge" bath, twenty-five feet in diameter, in the center of the building, which may be supplied with water at any desired temperature, or any required depth. The bath rooms are furnished with handsome marble bath tubs, and floored with colored tiling of attractive design. The institution is conducted under the careful supervision of Dr. A. S. Stewart, its proprietor.

In 1890, the town was incorporated as a city under the general laws of the State, and divided into three wards, each of which is represented by two members of the city council, with J. B. Dickover as its first mayor. During the same year the city was organized into an independent school district, which was provided with a Board of Education, consisting of two members from each of the city wards.

Subsequently the board issued bonds to the amount of $20,000 to provide funds for building a new school building, and in the summer of 1893 the present fine school edifice was completed. The building which occupies a commanding site in the eastern portion of the city, is a two-storied structure of gray sandstone, divided into six departments, each of which is generously furnished with all the needed apparatus for the instruction of pupils. The school is in a flourishing condition, as is attested by the large attendance of pupils, the enrollment for the school year beginning September, 1898, being 325, making an increase of 319 pupils since the opening of the first public school in 1883.

HOT SPRINGS FIRE DEPARTMENT

The Hot Springs Fire Department was first organized on February 21st, 1891, with Henry Vanatta as its first Chief. It was first composed of three companies, viz., Hot Springs Hose Company No. 1, Minnekahta Hose Company, and Hot Springs Hook and Ladder Company. Subsequently Hose Company No. 2 was organized and incorporated into the department.

HOT SPRINGS WATER AND ELECTRIC LIGHT SYSTEMS

The Hot Springs water and electric lighting systems were built during the years 1890-91-92, by the Hot Springs Water, Light & Power Co., at an aggregate cost of $60,000. The water system is constructed upon a very ingenious plan. The water is drawn from the Lakota spring, about 300 yards above the plunge, as before stated, and carried, or rather it gravitates down to the pumping and power station, near the center of the city, where it is pumped into the mains, whence it flows into the service pipes to all parts of the city. An immense reservoir, seventy feet in diameter and eighteen feet deep, with a holding capacity of over a half million gallons, is constructed in the northwestern portion of the city, at an elevation of 200 feet above the level of the station, which receives the waste or surplus water pumped into the mains. The Evans Hotel is supplied from the same source, the water being forced into the many storied building by hydraulic pressure. The power at the station is also used for producing the arc lights, while the power and generator for the incandescent lights are located four miles below the city.

The most important industries of Hot Springs are a large stucco plant, a flouring and planing mill. The former, located south of the city, was built in 1893 by the Dakota Hot Springs Co., at a cost of $12,000. Large quantities of the product of this plant, manufactured from the immense deposits of gypsum found in that region, are annually shipped to Omaha and other Western cities, where it commands a ready market at a handsome profit.

The flouring mill, situated near the northern limits of the city, was built in 1894, by C. A. & V. G. Peterson. The plant employs the roller process, and has a capacity of sixty barrels of flour per day.

Perhaps stone quarrying may also be classed among the industries of Hot Springs. At any rate immeasurable quantities of the finest quality of building stone, of nearly every color and shade, is found among the neighboring hills, much of which has been quarried and used in the construction of the many elegant public and private buildings of the city, and some of which has been shipped to other localities. The principal quarries of the region are the "Evans," the "Elm Creek Stone Co.," the Odell Co., and the Burke quarries, all of which may, in the not distant future, prove a source of large revenue to their owners,—every facility for the shipment of the surplus product of these industries being now furnished by the "Elkhorn" and "Burlington" railways.

Branches of these great commercial arteries were extended to Hot Springs during the year 1891, the Elkhorn reaching Hot Springs in May, 1891, and the Burlington in July, 1891, the former winning the race by about two months. It was on the approach of these railroads that Hot Springs entered upon its period of commerical development. In 1892 the two companies evidenced their faith in the permanency of Hot Springs by building a handsome cut stone Union depot near the center of the city, in close proximity to the Evans Hotel.

Besides its five church organizations Hot Springs has the usual complement of secret societies, common to cities of its class, among which are the Masonic, Odd Fellows, Modern Woodmen, A. O. U. W. and Royal Neighbors. The legal and medical professions are represented by eight lawyers and five physicians—who, in the very nature of things, must needs be skilled in the treatment of all the ailments which the human flesh is heir to.

The credit of the press is maintained by two wide-awake weekly newspapers, the Hot Springs *Star* and Hot Springs *Times-Herald,* the former now published by J. A. Stanley, the latter by Edward Ames.

Besides the Evans, Gillespie, Hot Springs, and Catholican hotels before mentioned there are the Ferguson, the Fargo, and other hostelries, aggregating a baker's dozen, all of which are well patronized during the summer season when the city is thronged with visitors. It has two banking institutions, two lumber yards and over fifty other business establishments of various kinds, and contains a permanent population of 1,500 enterprising people.

However, while Hot Springs enjoys a profitable trade, it is not strictly a commercial city, that is, commerce is not its principal business. It owes its origin to its springs, and chiefly because of its springs it exists. It is essentially a health and pleasure resort, where, amid nature's lavish adornments, supplemented by wonderful creations of art, the sick and the lame may find health, and the tired and careworn rest and recreation. Every favorable, natural condition, conspires with art in making Hot Springs an ideal resort for the invalid. The wonderful curative properties of its waters, its altitude, at the golden mean, between the two extremes of temperature, its location sheltered by the encircling hills, from the fierce storms of winter, and cooled in summer by the refreshing breezes, which come down, laden with the aromatic fragrance of the pines and the hemlocks, from the canyons of the mountains, and circulates freely through the valley, combine to make it a natural sanitarium unequaled elsewhere. The fierce extremes of heat and cold, which prove so trying to the invalid, are unknown in this Black Hills elysium, the thermometer registering an average temperature of forty-two degrees above zero during the winter months, the mercury rising to ninety-two degrees Fahrenheit, during the hottest days of summer. According to the official record of the weather prophet, the average year has eighty-eight cloudy, 167 partly cloudy, and 110 days of perpetual sunshine. These favorable conditions, however, are confined to a limited area, and doubtless owe their origin to the locality and the presence of the numerous hot springs in the region.

But this is not all. Hot Springs is rich in all the scenic attractions for which the Black Hills has become noted. It has not only its bubbling springs and gurgling brooks, its lovers' glen and sylvan retreats, but also its lofty lookouts, romantic drives, and distant waterfalls, besides being the point of embarkation for the greatest natural curiosity in America. Battle Mountain, which affords a comprehensive view of hill and dale, valley and plane, for a distance of sixty miles, dominates the city on the east; Gypsum Butte, with its variegated stratification, rises upon the west, while Dennis Park rears its encroaching barrier on the south.

On its rapid descent down the valley, through the clefts of the rocky barriers that encircle the site of Hot Springs on the south and east, to the Cheyenne river, six miles away, Fall river, in its course, dashes over and around huge blocks of red sandstone, in beautiful rainbow-tinted cascades, forming what is known as the Minnekahta Falls—a vision of beauty that would delight the eye of an artist. The driveway leading to this point of attraction follows the old stage route through the narrow defiles of the mountains, where trembling, white-faced passengers furtively watched for

HOT SPRINGS

lurking road agents to stalk out and bar the narrow way in the days before the advent of railroads. At a point where the road makes a sharp curve, around a point of rocks, a tall cliff is pointed out, as the lookout from where the signal of the stage's approach was passed to the robbers in waiting below, but whether there was ever a regular "hold-up" in that particular locality is not known.

CASCADE

In a picturesque valley, surrounded by high hills, about nine miles southwest of Hot Springs, is situated the little hamlet, called Cascade, where is also a group of springs, said to possess valuable medicinal properties. Cascade, which derives its name from the beautiful waterfall that dashes down the shelving rocks a little below, caused by the overflow of these springs, once threatened to become a formidable rival of Hot Springs as a fashionable resort.

About nine years ago a syndicate of capitalists purchased a large tract of land, including the springs, platted it, and laid the foundation of a health resort, by building a large sanitarium, dancing pavilion, etc., but, it is believed, the enterprise proved a failure, and a costly experiment to its promoters. The place is a popular and pleasant resort for outing parties from Hot Springs, who go there, provided with lunch baskets, music, etc., and spend the day in dancing, bathing, and rambling about at their own sweet will.

WIND CAVE

On the southern slope of the Hills, within the limits of Custer County, about twelve miles north of Hot Springs, is the famous "Wind Cave," the greatest natural attraction in this great wonderland. This remarkable cavern with its 100 miles of labyrinthine passages and chambers, already explored, was accidentally discovered, it is said, by Edmund Petty and a party of cowboys, some seventeen years ago. They were not looking for caves, but a peculiar sound, not accounted for by the ordinary processes of nature, attracted their attention and led to the investigation which resulted in the discovery of the cave.

Through an opening at the base of a hill, long draughts of air are literally and perpetually inhaled and exhaled, producing a sound, which to those in "melancholy moods," strongly resembles the mournful soughing of the wind through the branches of a pine tree; but how long this hoary cave has chanted its solemn requiem it is impossible to know. Near the entrance, at the bottom of a dry ravine, a small hotel has been erected by the proprietor for the accommodation of visitors, who are given safe conduct through its many intricate passages and vaulted chambers, for a reasonable fee. An inclosed passageway leads from the hotel to the entrance, where the lifting of a trap door reveals a long flight of stairs, which appears to descend down, down to the underworld. I am told, however, that the flight ends at the threshold of the "Bridal Chamber," which assertion is doubtless true. I went no farther than the head of the stairs, as looking down into the darkness proved sufficient for me; besides having no ambition to crawl abjectly on hands and knees, through small apertures, leading from one chamber to another, as I was told would be necessary, I was quite content to remain near the surface, and did remain, which precludes the possibility of my giving an accurate description of the beauties and mysteries of the great cavern from personal knowledge. However, according to the descriptions given by those who have explored its recesses, it is, in many respects, the greatest natural wonder on the globe as far as known.

Hundreds of passages and vaulted chambers, more or less spacious, profusely ornamented with brilliant crystal encrustations, wrought into various honeycomb designs, which have been, probably, long centuries in process of formation, some with filaments so fragile that apparently the slightest touch, or even the faintest breath, might destroy the delicate fabric, have been explored and named from some real or fancied resemblance of the formations to familiar objects. Among these are the "Bridal Chamber" near the entrance, with an area of 150 feet, "Capital Hill," the "Bell Chamber," where a chime of sweet toned bells are rung, the tones being evoked from a series of stalactites, by human hands, the "Garden of Eden," the "Tabernacle" and the "Standing Rock" chamber, where Johnson, the mind-reader, found the hidden pin a few years ago. It is told that the wonderful beauty and brilliancy of the various translucent formations of these chambers, when illuminated by the tapes of visitors, is beyond the power of language to describe. Through the eye alone can an adequate conception of this mammoth Black Hills cave be gained.

By boarding a train of the "Burlington" road which runs from Hot Springs westward along the borders of Hot Brook, in about thirty minutes we reach Minnekahta junction. This is the point where the branch short line from Hot Springs joins the Black Hills extension of the B. & M. Railway, and where passengers and their belongings are transferred to a waiting train which carries them to the great "American Carlsbad."

EDGEMONT

At the southern gateway to the Black Hills, about fifteen miles in an air line, but several more miles by the curving lines of the Burlington Railway, southwest of Minnekahta, is situated the enterprising young city of Edgemont. Here the road divides, one division turning to the right into the Hills, which it traverses through almost impenetrable canyons and hills from their southern to their extreme northern limits, the other rounding the base of the Hills to the north and northwest towards the Big Horn Mountains. Here the company have established a division station, erected a round-house, repair shop, hotel, etc., which has made the town a place of no small importance.

The town, which was laid out and platted in 1891 by the Lincoln Land Co., is admirably located on the south bank of the Cheyenne river near the mouth of Cottonwood creek, and its broad streets and squares interspersed here and there with small groves, gives it an exceedingly attractive appearance. Its most unique and inviting feature, however, is a miniature lake situated in the center of the city, whose placid bosom is ruffled by the tiny keels of several small pleasure boats, which ply its waters through the summer, but which is utilized as a skating rink during the winter months, when the young people hold high carnival on its glassy surface.

The region surrounding Edgemont, which comprises an extensive area of fine agricultural and grazing lands, capable of supporting a dense population, is rapidly filling up with enterprising settlers, both farmers and stock men. All varieties of grain and vegetables are successfully grown along the valleys, and numerous herds of cattle, horses, and sheep may be seen grazing on the hills and plateaus adjacent to the town. To supplement the natural moisture, the lack of which has somewhat retarded the settlement of the region, a large, irrigating canal, fourteen miles in length, fed by the never failing waters of the Cheyenne river, has been constructed, through which, by lateral ditches, hundreds of acres of land have been placed under irrigation.

Edgemont, with a population of 800, has two churches, a commodious stone school building and a flourishing school. It sustains one newspaper,—a weekly publication, and what is more interesting to note, the paper is conducted by Harry Godard, who, as many of the old-timers will doubtless remember, carried the first mail over the trail from Fort Laramie to Custer during the winter of 1875-6. Several handsome business blocks grace the main street of the town, whose trade along the different lines compares favorably with any other town of its size in the Black Hills. A number of important industrial and commercial enterprises are under process of construction, among which are a grindstone manufactory, a woolen mill, and a smelter, for whose surplus products the Burlington Railway will bring a ready market to their doors. These enterprises indicate a public spirit, on the part of its business men, which is bound ultimately to bring its reward.

The other towns of Fall River County are Oelrich, once quite an important cattle shipping station on the line of the Elkhorn railroad, Smithwick, Hat Creek, Ardmore, and Evans.

CHAPTER XLIV

BUTTE COUNTY

Prior to 1880, nearly all of the territory now embraced within the limits of Butte County, and the wide scope of rich grazing lands lying contiguous thereto on the north, was practically unknown to white men. Until that time, with the exception of a few herds along the valleys of lower Belle Fourche and Redwater, and the adjacent uplands, the region was the undisputed home of the buffalo, which, "pity 'tis," owing to their wanton killing by red and white hunters alike, had become nearly extinct before the advent of white settlers. About this time, the attention of cattle owners in Colorado, Kansas, and other distant parts, was attracted to this paradise of the stock grower, and they began to drive their herds from the overcrowded ranges of the South and Southwest to the untrammeled freedom of the Northern plains, which henceforth became the stamping-ground of the dashing, festive cowboy.

Soon after, the permanent settlement of the valleys of the Redwater and Belle Fourche and their tributaries began. Among the first settlers in the valley of the Redwater and Belle Fourche were: Wm. Grimmett, Conrad Berg, Wm. Hayden, Ed. Buford, John McClure, D. F. Harrison, P. B. Stearns, J. M. Eaton, A. Giles, and Peter Brochn. The first to settle on Hay creek were: J. A. Scottney, Wm. Fieldsend, and John C. Mathias.

With the increase of population grew the demand for county government for that section of the unorganized portion of Dakota Territory, and a movement to that end culminated in the creation of Butte County, by an act of the Territorial Legislature of 1883, the county being constructed from Mandan, and a small slice from the northern border of the organized county of Lawrence.

Butte County, comprising an area of some 2,340 square miles, a goodly portion of which is traversed by a number of never-failing streams, contains some of the finest agricultural and grazing lands to be found in the Black Hills or the West. Along the valleys of the principal streams and their tributaries are thousands of acres of arable lands, whose natural productiveness has been increased by irrigation where all kinds of cereals and vegetables are raised to perfection. The water for irrigating purposes is furnished by the Redwater Land and Canal Company, through an immense irrigating canal which carries over 4,000 inches of water. This water is taken from the Redwater river, four miles above its confluence with the Belle Fourche, extending down the latter stream a distance of about forty miles.

COWBOY SCENE IN THE BLACK HILLS

There are yet within the limits of Butte County many thousands of acres of unclaimed land, open to settlement under the United States laws, much of which can be placed under similar irrigation, by taking water from the Belle Fourche by ditches, and much more of which can be made prolific by artesian irrigation. It has been satisfactorily demonstrated that the great artesian basin underlies Butte County, and that artesian irrigation can be made a practical success. It is believed by many who have made the subject a study that the day is not far distant when the so-called barren and unproductive land of that region will be made to blossom like the rose, and yield an abundance of fruitage through the medium of artesian irrigation.

On the principal streams draining the county, and their tributaries, there is an abundant growth of oak, ash, cottonwood, and other deciduous trees, and the intervening divides are intersected by numerous small valleys and gulches, where thousands of cattle and horses find shelter from the storms of winter, and feed upon their nutritious cured grasses. As a stock-raising region Butte County stands pre-eminent among the counties of the Black Hills, and in point of numbers and quality of stock raised, is easily the peer of any section of equal area in the whole Wide West. According to the assessment of 1895, there were in Butte and the unorganized counties attached to Butte for taxation purposes, 45,000 head of cattle, and 10,000 head of horses roaming over the wide range, without artificial food or shelter. At a reasonable estimate of increase, there are to-day at least 60,000 head of cattle feeding on those ranges. The raising and shipment of stock is the paramount industry of Butte County.

In 1898 Butte County had an assessed valuation of $432,557, a bonded indebtedness of $14,848.92, and outstanding warrants amounting to $23,767.48, making a total indebtedness of only $38,616.46. The commissioners appointed to organize the county government were: Henry Chamberlain, J. J. Woolston, and Christian Flucken. The other first county officers were: Harry Stevens, Sheriff; C. F. Johnson, Register of Deeds and ex officio County Clerk; John Hildebrand, Treasurer; C. H. Gores, Probate Judge; Wm. Mitchell, Coroner; G. S. Richards, Surveyor; Geo. M. Browning, Assessor; Peter Miller, Superintendent of Schools. The first meeting of the commissioners was held on July 23d, 1883, at Minnesela, which, being the first and only town of any importance in the newly created county, was naturally made the county seat.

MINNESELA

Minnesela, situated on Redwater creek, was laid out and platted by A. A. Chouteau and D. T. Harrison in 1882, on one of the prettiest sites in all that region of country. Taking advantage of the superb water power afforded by that stream, the founders of the town proceeded without delay to build and equip with all the best appliances, a large flouring mill, which, with the additional prestige gained by being made the county seat, brought the town into considerable importance. It maintained its position as the leading town of the county and *entrepot* of all the cattle ranches of the region until 1891, when the founding of Belle Fourche soon robbed it of that distinction.

BELLE FOURCHE

Belle Fourche, the capital and present metroplis of Butte County, is situated in the valley of the Belle Fourche river—from which it derived its name—about twenty-two miles as the crow flies, and twenty-nine miles by rail, nearly north of Deadwood, on the line of the Fremont, Elkhorn & Missouri Valley Railway, to which the town owes its origin.

This railroad was completed to that point, and the first shipment of cattle made, on September 16th, 1890, and during the following two months 1,300 car loads of beef cattle were transported over the line to Eastern markets. The station was opened for business on December 28th, 1890, in charge of H. H. Giles, and in the spring of 1891 Belle Fourche was platted by the Pioneer Town-site Co., and lots placed on the market for sale on the 9th of June, 1891, H. W. Brown purchasing the first lot. The town-site company set the pace for the upbuilding of the town by erecting a two-story frame building for a hotel, which was followed by a structure erected by Thos. McCumsey. From the first the town had a steady and permanent growth, as in the nature of things it should have, for, perhaps, no town in the Hills began its history under more promising conditions, in that a speedy market for the product of the region's chief industry had already been brought to its door.

During the first year, 1891, several important private enterprises were inaugurated, among the first of which was a large flouring plant known as the Belle Fourche Flouring Mill, established by B. F. Teal and F. E. Bennett, expert millers from the great flour manufacturing city of Minneapolis. The mill, which is equipped with the most approved facilities, has a capacity of 125 barrels per day of flour, manufactured exclusively from wheat grown in the neighboring valleys—which fact be speaks the excellence of the product. The water power for operating the mill is taken by ditch from Redwater creek a short distance below.

The first newspaper published in Belle Fourche, called the Belle Fourche *Weekly Bee,* was established in 1891 by W. K. Fraser and Geo. E. Hare, under the editorial management of the last named member of the firm, whose fluent pen was ever wielded in the interests of Belle Fourche and Butte County. The average citizen of the Black Hills needs no formal introduction to Geo. E. Hare, as his name has been prominently before the public for a number of years, having served the people as their representative in the South Dakota State Legislature of 1896. He will also be remembered as the captain of a troop of the Rough Riders of the Third Cavalry Regiment of South Dakota Volunteers, who marched bravely away from Fort Meade in June, 1898, to fight for Cuba Libre. Of course he never faced the Mauser bullets of the Dons, but that wasn't his fault, you know. Later, under the management of the Bee

CATTLE SHIPPING PEN AT BELLE FOURCHE

Publishing Company, the paper was largely instrumental in securing the location of the permanent county seat at Belle Fourche.

During the fall of 1895 the "Bee" fell into the proprietorship of DeKay Brothers, publishers of the Whitewood *Plaindealer* and residents of Whitewood, after which it was published for a time as a supplement of that paper. Later it came into the possession of its present publishers, Messrs. Ralston & Glassie.

In 1892 a number of enterprising citizens conceived and set on foot a project for supplying the town with water from the great artesian basin, which was believed to underlie that portion of Dakota. In furtherance of the project, a stock company was organized and some $1,500 raised for the purpose of sinking an experimental well. The experiment proved successful beyond the most sanguine expectations of the projections of the enterprise. An encouraging flow of water was soon encountered, which, upon reaching the third artesian flow at a depth of 525 feet, increased to a volume of 100,000 gallons every twenty-four hours, affording an ample supply for all purposes of pure, soft, wholesome water. This artesian well is the source of supply for the present water system of the town.

At the fall election of 1894, Belle Fourche was made the permanent county seat of Butte County by a popular vote, and during the same year a substantial two-story courthouse was built by the citizens of the new capital, without cost to the county, which gave the town a new impetus.

On September 25th, 1895, however, its progress was arrested by a disastrous conflagration, which wiped out over two-thirds of the business portion of the town. Nothing daunted by the calamity, the losers, with characteristic Western pluck, were within twenty-four hours thereafter, hard at work among the smoldering ruins, clearing away the blackened debris, preparatory to rebuilding, and in three months after the fire, buildings aggregating in value over $25,000 were erected or nearing completion in the burnt district.

Soon after the founding of the town in the spring of 1891, a school district was organized, and subsequently a commodious two-story school building, constructed of home manufactured brick, was erected, which to-day affords ample educational facilities for the children of the town. Besides the courthouse and public school building Belle Fourche has two neat church edifices, owned respectively by the Congregational and Methodist societies. It also has several secret organizations, among which are Masonic and Odd Fellows, and other lodges.

The present Butte County Bank, of which John Clay, Jr., is President, and J. F. Summers, Cashier, was established in October, 1891, since which time the institution has had a somewhat eventful history. The first building erected by the bank went up in smoke, on September 25th, 1895, when the two-storied stone structure now occupied by the institution was built upon the ashes of the old. On June 28th, 1897, a bold raid was made upon the bank by a band of six robbers, who, after securing a comparatively small amount of its assets, made good their escape. Four of them were afterwards captured.

Belle Fourche now affords patronage for two newspapers, viz.: the Belle Fourche *Bee,* whose history has been noted, and the Belle Fourche *Times.* The latter was established by Messrs. Battenberd & Martin, early in 1896, the initial number appearing on January 2d of that year, and the fact that Chester Martin conducts the editorial department of the sheet is a sufficient guaranty for its complete success. The writer of this history put Chester through a three years' course of sprouts, when he was a big, brainy lad, well up in his teens, and, well, you know the old adage: "Just as the twig is bent the tree inclines." The paper is now owned by Martin & Shocklay.

By a conservative estimate, Belle Fourche has 500 permanent inhabitants who, together with the rural population of the valleys, keep up the life of trade for at least eight months of the year. The town bears no suggestion of metropolitanism, and makes no parade or bluster, except during the shipping season. Its business houses, bank, offices, hotels, stores, and shops, for the most part occupy a comparatively small space along the main street, while the resident portion lies on the outer limits, where neat frame structures surrounded by well-kept yards bespeak the general thrift of the people. The business of Belle Fourche does not depend upon the local everyday trade but largely upon that of the many cattle outfits which periodically come from long distances to replenish their stock of supplies.

Belle Fourche, being the most accessible shipping point for the great herds of beef cattle, raised on the wide range which stretches away to the north, and into Southeastern Montana and Western Wyoming, is by far the most important shipping station in the Northwest. For the years 1896, 1897, 1898, there were shipped from that station to Eastern markets, 7,500 carloads of beef cattle, amounting in the aggregate to something over five and one-half million dollars, which, of course, proved a source of large revenue to the town. All of the cattle outfits and ranchmen, within a radius of 100 miles north and west, make Belle Fourche their supply point, creating a large volume of trade for business houses of all kinds.

CATTLE SHIPPING INDUSTRY

During the shipping season, which begins usually some time in August, and ends about the last of November, Belle Fourche presents a stirring and exciting scene, and what with the awful bellowing of the great herds as they are being rushed into the crowded cattle pens, to await their turns to be driven aboard the cars alongside, and the sudden brilliant dashes of the picturesque cowboys after the recalcitrant bovines, which now and then escape from the lines, pandemonium reigns supreme. During these cattle carnivals, the cowboy is very much in evidence everywhere, and wherever the cowboy is in force times are bound to be exceedingly lively. I must confess here to something of an admiration for cowboys despite their faults. Of course, they have been known to fire random shots as they dashed along the streets of certain towns of the Hills in the early days, and to ride their bronchos, roughshod, through the doors and up to the bars of saloons, and such playful pranks, but, after all, they are, in many respects, very manly fellows. They are perfect types of muscular development, endure hardships that would kill an ordinary mortal, are dead shots and the most expert horsemen in the world. Moreover, they love their bronchos better than anything else earthly, and regard horse-stealing as the meanest crime known to the unwritten law of the range. The average cowboy is honest, kindhearted, generous to a fault, and, in short, is not half so bad as he is painted.

BUILDING OF WYOMING & MISSOURI RIVER R. R.

An enterprise which promises much future commercial importance to Belle Fourche, is the recent building of the Wyoming and Missouri River Railroad from that point to the Hay creek coal fields, situated about eighteen miles southwest, just over the eastern boundary line of Wyoming. Ever since the discovery of coal in that region of 1876, when hostile Indians were much more plentiful in those parts than white men, the possibility of a railroad to the mines has been a dream of their owners. Facilities for putting the product of these mines on the market, the lack of which has heretofore greatly retarded their development, are now furnished. After years of waiting the road is a consummated fact.

A company of Eastern capitalists organized under the title of The Wyoming and Missouri River Railroad Co., with Geo. M. Nix as president, and in June, 1898, the work of grading was commenced along the line of the road, which was fully completed and equipped by January 1st, 1899. The successful carrying out of this project may be looked upon only as the beginning of the end, the promise of things yet to come.

The product of the mines, which made the building of this line possible, is bituminous in character, but of a dense texture and splendid quality, and will find a good demand in the Hills for fuel and gold reduction purposes, as also, now that facilities for transportation are furnished, a ready outside market for long years to come. Of course, the full extent and future productiveness of the coal measures underlying that region of the Hills, can hardly be estimated in their present stage of development, but it is believed by geologists that the deposit is practically inexhaustible.

CATTLE OUTFITS OF BLACK HILLS

Besides those mentioned the other settlements of Butte County are: Snoma, Butte, Vale, and Empire, situated on the Belle Fourche river.

The cattle outfits which ship stock from Black Hills stations, the major part of which is shipped from Belle Fourche, are as follows:—

RANGE	OWNERS	NO. OF HEAD
Little Missouri	The Franklin Live Stock Co.	25,000
" "	The Y. T. Cattle Co	8,000
" "	James M. Carey	10,000
" "	Driscoll Bros	5,000
" "	Standard Cattle Co	12,000
Moreau River	The Sheidly Cattle Co	30,000
" "	Lake Tomb and Lemmon	25,000
" "	M. J. Barclay	2,000
" "	Sam Sheffield	2,000
Bad River	C. K. Howard	10,000
" "	Peter Duhamel	10,000
" "	Scott Phillips	4,000
White River	Corbin Morris	10,000
" "	Maurice Kelliher	8,000
" "	Major W. W. Anderson	5,000
" "	J. M. Humphrey	5,000
" "	H. A. Dawson	4,000
Cheyenne River	E. Holcomb	10,000
" "	Fred Holcomb	4,000
" "	Laddingen Bros	2,000
" "	Frank Stewart	2,000
" "	F. C. Huss	2,000
Box Elder	Connor Bros.	8,000
Battle Creek	Ed. Stenger	4,000
Sand Hills	G. G. Ware	4,000
" "	Bartlett Richards	8,000
" "	T. B. Irwin	2,000
Hat Creek	Chas. Lampkin	2,000
Deer Ear	J. A. Hale	2,000

CHAPTER XLV

THE ORGANIZATION OF DAKOTA TERRITORY AND ITS SUBSEQUENT STRUGGLE FOR STATEHOOD

Out of the fairest and best portions of the vast domain acquired by the United States from France during the third year of the present century—known as the "Louisiana Purchase"—was the Dakota Territory created. The treaty for the cession of this valuable acquisition of territory, which extended from the Mississippi river on the East to the Rocky Mountains on the West, and from the British Dominion on the North to the Great Gulf on the South, was negotiated and entered into by Mr. Livingstone, then United States resident Minister at Paris, and James Monroe, who was sent thither for the purpose, and a French commission, in April, 1803. By the terms of this treaty the United States agreed to pay the French government the sum of $15,000,000, and to assume claims of American citizens against that government to the amount of $11,250,000.

By reference to any modern United States History, complete information in reference to claims as to the original ownership of this ceded territory, its cession by France to Spain, its retrocession by Spain to France, its cession by the latter to the United States, and the subsequent carving and recarving of the generous domain into Territories and States, with all the prolonged bitter struggle for the extension and restriction of slavery in connection therewith, may be obtained; hence, any further recital of facts already a matter of common history would be superfluous.

SIOUX TREATIES

When the States formed from the Northwest Territory began to fill up, the Sioux, having in 1837 ceded all their lands east of the Mississippi river to the government, were transferred to reservations on the other side of the Father of Waters, from which time all that portion of the Louisiana Purchase not included in the State of Missouri and the Territory of Arkansas was regarded and named the "Indian Country."

In 1851 a treaty was concluded by which the Sioux ceded to the United States an immense extent of territory, west of the Mississippi river, which included a narrow strip of land along the eastern border of Dakota, covering the present sites of Sioux Falls, Flandreau, and Medary,—the first piece of land relinquished by them in what is now the State of South Dakota. Owing to what the Indians regarded as "bad faith" on the part of the government in fulfilling the conditions of the treaty, years of Indian hostilities followed, during which the soil of Minnesota was freely dyed with the blood of its settlers. They were finally encountered and subdued by Gen. Harney at the battle of Little Blue Water in September, 1855, and a treaty of peace followed, which, however, secured only a temporary peace, as hostilities broke out from time to time, which were finally suppressed by Gen. Sibley in 1863.

In 1858 the final treaty, by which the Sioux relinquished to the United States all territory claimed by them in what is now South Dakota, was negotiated. In the fall of 1857 they were persuaded through the influence of J. B. S. Todd, then post trader at Fort Randall, assisted by Chas. F. Picotte, to send a delegation of chiefs to Washington to confer with the Indian Department, which, in April, 1858, culminated in the negotiation of a treaty ceding every square acre of their land, except the present Yankton reservation, to the United States.

Upon the consummation of the treaty,—even before its ratification, many, who were eagerly waiting at the threshold for the quashing of the Indian title, crossed the line and settled upon the ceded lands, and built cabins, but they were summarily driven off by the Indians and their cabins destroyed. Upon the advent in July of the agent, A. H. Redfield, of Detroit, Michigan, who was appointed to take charge of Indian affairs, buildings were erected and the Indians speedily removed to the agencies set apart for them. This done, large numbers settled upon the land, locating principally at Elk Point, Vermillion and Yankton, near the junction of the Big Sioux and Missouri rivers.

Prior to the treaty of 1858, attempts had been made to locate on this territory, but the would-be settlers were promptly driven off by the hostile Sioux. The first attempt at settlement was made in the region of the Sioux Falls, as early as 1856 by what was known as "The Western Town Company," from Dubuque, Iowa. Prominent among its members were W. W. Brookings, Dr. J. L. Phillips, and John McClellan, who, despite the inhospitable reception accorded them by the natives of the first attempt, returned a few months later of the same year, and located a half-section of land near the Falls,—perhaps the very ground upon which the metropolis of South Dakota now stands, and to them, doubtless, belongs the distinction of having located the first acre of ground in South Dakota.

Again, in May, 1857, a company styled "The Dakota Land Company" composed of W. H. Nobles, S. A. Medary, E. J. De Witt, A. G. Fuller,

Samuel F. Brown, Jas. W. Lynd, and others, hailing from St. Paul, Minnesota, made their advent in the valley of the Big Sioux river, and first located Medary, named in honor of the Governor of Minnesota, thence proceeding down the valley they located the town-site of Flandreau, named in honor of Judge Flandreau, of St. Paul. Subsequently some of the party extended their explorations down the river to the Falls where they found just two of the early pioneers, W. W. Brookings and John McClellan, who had returned and tenaciously stayed by their claims. How long this last party were suffered to remain unmolested, in the valley of the Big Sioux, is not known—supposedly not long.

The settlers on the ceded territory, finding themselves without constituted authority to exercise the political functions, proceeded at once to organize a provisional territorial government. On September 18th, 1858, the people of the Territory assembled in convention at Sioux Falls, and by resolution authorized an election to be held on the 4th day of October, for choosing members to compose a Provisional Legislature. At the first session of the Provisional Legislature, Henry Masters was chosen President of the Council, and S. J. Albright, Speaker of the House, and moreover, it is related that Henry Masters was also elected Governor of the irregularly organized Territory. During its session a memorial to Congress was formulated, praying for a regularly organized territorial government, and A. G. Fuller was selected to represent the petitioners before that body.

In 1859 similar memorials were prepared and adopted at Yankton and Vermillion, for territorial organization, to which Congress turned a deaf ear. Again, on the 15th of January, 1861, a final mass convention of the settlers assembled at Yankton and prepared an urgent memorial to Congress, which was sent to Washington bearing the signatures of nearly 600 people. At last, in February, 1861, on the eve of the great Civil War, the Organic Act creating the Territory of Dakota, was passed and approved by President Buchanan on March 2d, 1861.

The original Dakota Territory comprised not only the present States of North and South Dakota, but, besides the whole of the State of Montana, the greater portion of Wyoming and the eastern half of Idaho, embracing an area of some 350,000 square miles, constituting the largest organized Territory in the United States.

In April, 1861, Dr. Wm. Jayne, of Springfield, Illinois, was appointed the first executive of the Territory of Dakota by President Lincoln, arriving at Yankton, to enter upon the discharge of his duties, on May 27th, 1861. On the 17th of March, 1862, the first Territorial Legislature convened at Yankton, the capital city. According to a census taken at the time the population of the Territory, in the spring of 1862, numbered something less than 3,000.

Appended is a complete list of the first officers of the new Territory:—

Wm. Jayne, of Illinois, Governor; John Hutchinson, of Minnesota, Secretary; Philomen Bliss, of Ohio, Chief Justice; L. P. Williston, of Pennsylvania and J. L. Williams, of Tennessee, District Judges; W. E. Gleason, of Maryland, United States Attorney; W. P. Schaffer, United States Marshal; Geo. D. Hill, of Michigan, United States Surgeon-General; W. A. Burleigh, of Pennsylvania, United States Agent for Yankton Indians; H. A. Hoffman, of New York, Agent for the Poncas.

Members of the first Territorial Legislature were as follows:—

In the Council: John H. Shober, President; James Tufts, Secretary; W. R. Goodfellow, Engrossing and Enrolling Clerk; Rev. S. W. Ingham, Chaplain; Charles F. Picotte, Sergeant-at-Arms; E. B. Wixon, Messenger; W. W. Warford, Fireman.

House: Geo. M. Pinney, Speaker; J. R. Hanson, Chief Clerk; James M. Allen, Assistant Clerk; Daniel Gifford, Enrolling Clerk; M. B. Smith, Engrossing Clerk; M. D. Metcalf, Chaplain; James Somers, Sergeant-at-Arms; A. B. Smith, Messenger; Ole Anderson, Fireman.

Conditions during the first four years of the existence of Dakota Territory were by no means favorable to its growth and advancement. In the summer of 1862, just after the machinery of the Territorial Government was put in successful operation, the most aggressive hostilities known to the West broke out among the Sioux, which greatly retarded the settlement of the new Territory.

Notwithstanding this drawback, and the fact that the people of the North had meanwhile grappled with, and put down a mighty rebellion, and the further fact that, in 1862, the great Territory of Idaho was constructed out of Dakota, which turned the tide of emigration to the newly discovered gold mines on the eastern slope of the Rocky Mountains, and subsequently the carving out of Wyoming in 1868, the population of Dakota had expanded from 2,400 in 1862, to 14,181 in 1870.

The close of the first decade developed a general desire on the part of the people of the southern half of the Territory for division and Statehood from which time until its accomplishment in 1889, it stood waiting and periodically knocking at the door of Congress for admission, The first movement to that end was made in January, 1871, when a memorial to Congress was adopted, praying for division on the forty-sixth parallel. To make a long story short, similar memorials were adopted successively in 1872 and 1874, and again in January, 1877. From this time the Black Hills was a potent factor in the movement for division—whose people for the most part favored a tripartition of the Territory, the Black Hills to be one of the triplets.

In 1881 Congress was memorialized to divide the Territory into three States, but at no time was admission as one State desired by many.

As petitions were unavailing, a large number of the leading citizens of the Territory visited Washington, during the winter of 1881-2, and urged upon Congress the enactment of a law enabling South Dakota to form a State Constitution, but, although a bill to that effect was favorably reported in committee, it did not become a law.

The removal of the territorial capital from Yankton to Bismarck, at this time, it having held its last session at Yankton in 1883, by no means lessened the desire for Statehood on the part of South Dakota, so the people, having resolved to work out the problem without the aid or consent of Congress, called a convention to be held at Sioux Falls on September 4th, 1883, for the purpose of framing a State Constitution. The people were represented by 150 delegates who formulated a document which was submitted to the voters at the regular November election, resulting in a majority of 5,622 votes in its favor.

Again, in pursuance of an Act passed by the Territorial Legislature, providing for same, another Constitutional Convention was held at Sioux Falls on September 8th, 1885, when a new Constitution was framed, and submitted to the people at the next general election, which was this time ratified by a majority of 18,661 votes. State officers and a Legislature were also elected, Arthur C. Mellette being chosen as chief executive of the provisional State government. On the second Monday of December, 1885, the Legislature met at Huron, the temporary capital, and during its session elected G. C. Moody of Lawrence County, and A. J. Edgerton of Mitchell, United States Senators.

As no congressional action was taken in the matter, these various popular movements brought South Dakota no nearer a State government *de facto* than before. At last, however, after a prolonged and bitter struggle of eighteen years on the part of the people of the southern half of the Territory, North and South Dakota came to the parting of the ways, and, together with Montana and Washington, were admitted on an equal footing to the sisterhood of States, under the provisions of the famous "Omnibus Bill," approved February 22nd, 1889.

According to the provisions of the Enabling Act, elections were held on Tuesday after the first Monday in May, 1889, for the election of delegates for Constitutional Conventions for North and South Dakota, to be held at Bismarck, and Sioux Falls, respectively on the fourth day of July, 1889.

With certain revisions and amendments the Sioux Falls Convention adopted the constitution of the provisional State government of 1885, which was again submitted to the electors of the State and approved by a sweeping majority. The members of the Third Constitutional Convention from the Black Hills were: D. Carson and Chas. W. Thomas, Deadwood; C. L. Wood and V. T. McGillicuddy, Rapid City; John Scollard, Sturgis; W. S. O'Brien, Lead; J. W. Thompson, Whitewood; Sandford Perker, Oelrichs.

The first Legislature of the State of South Dakota met at Pierre, the temporary capital, which has since become permanent, on the fifteenth day of October, 1889, and on the seventeenth elected G. C. Moody of Deadwood; and R. F. Pettigrew of Sioux Falls, United States Senators.

On receipt of a certified copy of the Constitution, as ratified by the qualified electors of the State, Benjamin Harrison, by proclamation on the 2d day of November, 1889, declared the admission of North and South Dakota complete.

The first State officers of South Dakota were: Governor, Arthur C. Mellette; Lieutenant-Governor, James H. Fletcher; Secretary of State, A. O. Ringsrud; State Treasurer, W. F. Smith; State Auditor, Louis C. Taylor; Attorney-General, Robert Dollard; Superintendent of Public Instruction, Gilbert L. Pinkham; Commissioner of School and Public Lands, Osmer H. Parker; Public Examiner, H. E. Blanchard; Commissioner of Immigration, F. H. Hagerty; Veterinary Surgeon, Dr. D. E. Collins.

Members of the first State Legislature of South Dakota from the Black Hills were:—

Of the Senate: Frank J. Washabaugh and Chas. Parsons, Lawrence County; A. W. Bangs, Pennington; Edward S. Galvin Meade; A. S. Stewart, Fall River.

Of the House: Cyrus Cole and A. S. May, Custer County; H. A. Godard, Fall River; R. B. Hughes and Joseph Jolly, Pennington; W. S. O'Brien, Sol. Star, John Wolzmuth, W. H. Parker, Jas. Anderson, and Robert Graham, of Lawrence; M. M. Cooper and S. B. Miller, of Meade; E. B. Cummings, of Butte; Speaker of House, S. E. Young, of Minnehaha.

The first representatives to Congress were: Oscar S. Gifford, of Canton, and John H. Pickler, of Faulkton.

It was a proud day for South Dakota when, with its vast heritage of productive acres, it figuratively shouldered its equitable burden of the Territorial bonded indebtedness, including more than $70,000,000, on account of public institutions falling within its boundaries, and went out from beneath the Territorial roof to assume the dignity and responsibilities of Statehood. How well it has fulfilled its obligations and maintained its credit during its decade of history, which comprised years of great financial depression throughout the land, is attested by its present flourishing condition.

In the beginning of 1895 South Dakota was shocked at finding itself on the brink of financial ruin, wrought by the enormous defalcation of the custodian of the funds of the State,—with a depleted treasury, and a burden of floating and bonded indebtedness of $1,260,200. In January, 1897, according to the report of the State Auditor, the net indebtedness had been decreased to $983,168.31 showing a reduction for the two years of $277,031.49. In July, 1898, it had been reduced to $564,018.88, showing a decrease of $419,149.63, altogether showing an advantage to the State of $696,181.12—exclusive of trust funds from January, 1895, to July, 1898, which speaks volumes for the resources of the grand young State.

ASSESSED VALUATION OF SOUTH DAKOTA

According to the same report there are 17,779,804 acres of land assessed in South Dakota, at a total valuation, as adjusted by the State Board of Equalization, of $71,779,804, or an average of $4.05 per acre, far less than half its actual value. The assessed valuation of town lots is $14,844,959, making a total land valuation of $86,624,763. The assessed valuation of personal property is $22,315,819; railroads within the State, $9,328,053; express, telegraph, telephone, and sleeping car companies, $311,861, making a total State assessment of $118,580,496, of which $10,729,482 or nearly one-eleventh of the whole amount is assessed within the limits of the six Black Hills counties.

SOUTH DAKOTA PERMANENT SCHOOL FUND

By a wise provision of the "bill" admitting South Dakota to Statehood, sections 16 and 36, or 1,280 acres of land in each township of the State,—or their equivalent in indemnity lands—excepting the Indian, military, or other national reservations, were granted to the State for the support of its common schools. Of the nearly 50,000,000 acres of land embraced within its boundary lines, it is estimated that more than 2,000,000 of acres are school lands, which, at $10.00 per acre,—the minimum price at which it may be sold, would amount to the handsome sum of $20,000,000: and as, by the laws governing the sale of these lands, no more than one-fourth can be sold within five years, nor more than one-half of the remainder, within ten years after they become salable, their value will ultimately more than double that amount.

The fund arising from the rental and sale of these lands constitutes a permanent common school fund, the interest only of which can be expended for their support. This, together with the five per centum of the proceeds of the sale of public lands paid to the State by the general government, will accumulate into a perpetual school fund of immense proportions.

In January, 1895, the total amount in the permanent school fund was $603,250.57, all of which was invested. In July, 1898, the investment amounted to $802,822.74, and money on hand, $144,329.41, making a total of $947,152.15, while there was due the fund from deferred payments from the sale of lands, $1,302,372.89 upon which interest is accruing at the rate of six per cent per annum.

The Act also granted to the State an aggregate of a half million acres of land for the support of its educational and charitable institutions, the proceeds of the sale of which constitute a permanent fund for their maintenance.

CHAPTER XLVI

THE TREATY OF 1889 FOR THE GREAT SIOUX RESERVATION IN DAKOTA

The Act of Congress, approved March 2, 1889, dividing and setting apart a portion of the Great Sioux Reservation in Dakota, into separate reservations for the Indians entitled to receive rations and annuities at Pine Ridge, Rosebud, Standing Rock, Cheyenne river, Lower Brule, and Crow Creek Agencies, also secured the relinquishment of the Indian title to all lands outside of these separate reservations, amounting to about 9,000,000 acres, comprising some of the best lands in Dakota, which was thrown open to entry under the provisions of the Homestead law, to bona fide settlers.

By the provisions of the Act, each settler is required to pay, in addition to the fee and commission on ordinary homesteads, $1.25 per acre for all land sold within the first three years after the taking effect of this Act, and seventy-five cents per acre for all disposed of within the next two years thereafter, and fifty cents per acre for the residue, sections sixteen and thirty-two being reserved for school purposes.

For this ceded land the government deposited in the Treasury of the United States, to the credit of the Sioux Nation, $3,000,000, drawing interest at five per cent per annum, which interest is appropriated under the direction of the Secretary of the Interior, to the use of the Indians receiving rations and annuities at the agencies created by the Act. One-half of the interest accruing is expended for the promotion of education, industrial and otherwise, among the Indians, and the other half in such manner and for such purpose, as, in the judgment of the Secretary of the Interior, shall most contribute to their civilization and self-support.

It appears from the provisions of this Act that, in 1900, the government will have to purchase all the unoccupied portions of this ceded territory at fifty cents per acre, which, added to the $3,000,000 already in the Treasury, will constitute a permanent fund for the benefit of the Sioux Indians, of no small proportions.

The Act also provides for the distribution of twenty-five cows among the Indians, which are not to be sold under any circumstances; thus the number will never diminish, as when they become too old to be profitable, they are taken to the nearest Indian farmer and exchanged for young cows, the old ones being used in the regular beef issues. Although the original stock, which is branded "I. D.," the brand of the Indian Department, is not allowed to be sold, the increase becomes the personal property of the Indians and are branded with their private brand; thus many Indians, half-breeds and squaw-men, are to-day the owners of large herds of cattle, for which they find a ready market, and are really becoming rich.

Perhaps no place in the West is better adapted for stock-raising purposes than portions of the Sioux Reservation, the valleys of the streams south of the White river being green and luxuriant while many portions of the Western range are dry and withered. In these fertile valleys thousands of fat sleek cattle belonging to the squaw-men, graze, the year round, for, be it known that this favored class has all the rights of full-blooded Sioux, as far as stock and free range is concerned; but they draw no individual rations.

The Act also provides that each head of the family, or single person over eighteen years of age, who takes his or her allotment in severalty, shall be furnished with two milk cows, one pair of oxen with yoke and chain, or two horses and one set of harness, in lieu of oxen, yoke, and chain, as the Secretary of the Interior may deem advisable, also one plow, one harrow, one ax, and one pitchfork, and fifty dollars in money, to be expended under the direction of the Secretary of the Interior, in aiding such Indians to erect houses or other buildings suitable for residences or the improvement of their allotments.

In this connection, it is gratifying to be able to record that this allotment plan has worked out some desirable reforms among the Indians during the past few years, many of whom, under its beneficial operations, are making rapid strides towards self-support and resultant civilization.

NEGOTIATIONS WITH THE SIOUX

The commission, appointed in 1888 to treat with the Sioux for their great reserve in Dakota, and which met in council with the chief representatives of the Sioux Nation at Standing Rock Agency in July of that year, having proved a signal failure, a second commission was appointed in 1889 to make another attempt to secure their acceptance of the terms offered by the government in the treaty. This second commission, which was composed of ex-Governor Foster of Ohio, Major Wm. Warren, and John B. Warren of Arkansas, and Gen. Geo. Crook, visited the various agencies during the summer of 1889, for the purpose of trying to overcome the almost universal opposition met with by the commission of 1888, and by tact and skillful diplomacy, and the influence of Gen. Crook, in whose promises they had the utmost faith, finally succeeded in winning over a number of the most influential chiefs of the tribes. Subsequently a second and final council was held at Standing Rock Agency, where, in the face of a good deal of opposition and some disturbance on the part of that chronic disturber, Sitting Bull, who assumed a threatening attitude, the signatures of the requisite two-thirds of the Indians were attached to the treaty.

In the year 1890 came the "winter of their discontent." The liberal provisions of the "bill" enacted by Congress, and the verbal promises made by Gen. Crook, remained unfulfilled for many months; the scant crops sown in the spring of 1890 were utterly withered by the exceeding drouth of the following summer; the rations on some of the reserves were cut down, reducing them to a condition of starvation; sickness widely prevailed among the tribes, many dying more from lack of food than disease. All these misfortunes, it is claimed by their apologists, made them desperate. Amid this general gloom and despair among the Sioux tribe came the opportunity of the medicine-men, who heralded forth the story of the near advent of their long expected Messiah, which they hailed with great gladness.

THE MESSIAH CRAZE—THE GENERAL UPRISING—THE GHOST DANCES—THE TRAGIC DEATH OF THE GREAT MEDICINE-MAN—THE FATAL BATTLE OF WOUNDED KNEE—THE FINAL SURRENDER.

The ancestral religion of the Dakotahs, like that of all others of the North American Indians, was polytheistic. They not only worshiped numerous objects, which they deified and invested with more or less potent attributes, according to their incomprehensibility, chief among whom were their two antagonistic deities—the good and the evil spirits—and believed in and practiced the shedding of atoning blood to propitiate their incensed divinities, through the mediation of their medicine-men, whom they regard as the personification of the great Wakan—the essence of all good, but also, it is claimed by those familiar with their early legends and traditions, have long looked for the coming of a Messiah.

As far back as our knowledge of their traditions extend, there has existed among them a class of lazy, but shrewd, impostors, who, claiming supernatural powers, have, by their incantations and sorceries, imposed upon the credulity of those benighted people, the most absurd superstitions, among which was the belief that some day a "Messiah" would appear, like an avenging Nemesis at the head of an army of the red warriors who had died in battling for their possessions, and lead them against their white oppressors. From this it would appear that the coming of a Messiah had long been a part of their creed, and the "ghost dances" one of the savage rites of their religious worship.

Taking advantage of the general distress and discontent among the Dakotah tribes in 1890, the medicine-men went to work at compounding medicines, and out of the seething decoctions or mixtures, juggled the prophecy that the long-expected Messiah was due, and that their day of retribution and deliverance was at hand. To prepare for the coming event, in accordance with the messages transmitted through these impostors, the people were to dance for four consecutive days and nights, during the new of the moon, until the advent of the Messiah.

It is asserted by some that the "craze" was largely due to the teachings of a fanatical white evangelist, named Hopkins, who in the summer of 1890 went among the Pine Ridge Indians, claiming to be the true "Messiah" and strangely enough many believed in him. Later the impostor was unmasked, arrested, and banished from the agency by the soliders. Messiahs also appeared at some of the other agencies, but it is believed that with all their blind credulity, they were generally regarded by the Indians as spurious.

While the mania spread far and wide into other States, wherever there were Indian settlements, the "craze" was the most violent and pronounced among the Sioux tribes of South Dakota, and Pine Ridge, bring the largest and most important of the South Dakota agencies, became the center and hot-bed of the trouble, numerous bands from other agencies massing near that point to join the majority in their savage rites.

Although the attitude of the Indians at Pine Ridge had for some time been extremely threatening, it was not until about the middle of November that the agent wholly lost control of them. At that time large bands under the leadership of Little Wound, Six Feathers, and other chiefs, smuggled away their guns and left the reservation without leave of absence, for the vicinity of White Earth River, and on the 16th of that month began the "ghost dance," first on the Wounded Knee, a tributary of that stream, at a point about fifteen miles from the agency, and later at other points. Soon after several bands of Rosebud Indians, led by Two Strikes, Short Bull, and Big Foot arrived and began the dance on Porcupine and Medicine Root creeks, twenty-five and thirty miles distant from the agency, respectively. Almost simultaneously it began at the Cheyenne and other agencies, and at the hostile camp of Sitting Bull on the Grand River near Fort Yates.

Hideously painted and arrayed in their invulnerable "ghost dance" shirts; to the weird music of the tom-tom and other savage devices for making a great noise, the poor deluded creatures danced round and round a center pole, writhed into the most frightful contortions; pounded old mother earth until she fairly trembled beneath their savage feet; beat their plumed heads one against another in mad frenzy, until they finally sank exhausted, and almost unconscious, to the ground, when another set of braves would take their places and repeat the performance.

The dancers daily increased in numbers, and, naturally, the longer they danced the crazier and more warlike they became, and the alarm of the people at the agency, both red and white, and the settlers outside the reservation grew in proportion. All attempts of the agent and Indian police to pacify and induce them to return to the agency proved fruitless.

In the intervals of the dancing they employed their time in devastating the settlements, stealing cattle from both the settlers and the "government herd," burning buildings, and demolishing such property as could not be utilized, their depredations being principally directed against the half-breeds who refused to join the dance.

The people of the more remote settlements in Pennington, Custer, and Fall River counties in Dakota, and along the northern border of Nebraska, apprehending that the hostile bands might consolidate, and start out on the warpath, petitioned the governors of the respective States for arms for defense; organized home-guards, sent their panic-stricken women and children into the towns and larger settlements for safety, determined to make a bold stand for their homes and property.

THE ARRIVAL OF A MILITARY FORCE AT PINE RIDGE

Upon learning that the Indians had gotten beyond restraint and were leaving their reservations in large bands without leave, Gen. Miles issued orders to troops stationed at the nearest military posts to proceed at once to Pine Ridge, the most threatened point, and on or about November 20th, five companies of infantry from Omaha, and three troops of cavalry from Fort Robinson, Nebraska, arrived at the agency. The following day, or very soon after, seven troops of cavalry from Fort Meade, and seven companies of infantry from Fort McKinney, also troops from Cheyenne, Wyoming, and other points arrived at the scene of prospective war.

Gen. Brooke, chief in command of the military forces, after consulting with Agent Royer, decided to make no aggressive movement against the hostiles, who were then massed in large bands in the vicinity of White Clay creek, at least until all pacific measures were exhausted. Upon the appearance of the soldiers, the bands which, for the most part, were composed of young braves, made their escape across the White Earth river, and entrenched themselves amid the labyrinthian defiles of the Bad Lands, whither it was not

532   THE BLACK HILLS; OR,

safe for the soldiers to follow; and from where, despite the "Home-Guards" and the 400 troopers stationed at the mouth of Rapid creek, under Gen. Carr, who patroled the country bordering the Cheyenne river on the west, small bands frequently stole across that stream and raided the settlements along Rapid, Spring, and Battle creeks, in quest of the horses and other property of the settlers, who were ever ready with loaded guns for their appearance.

It early developed that the emissaries of Sitting Bull were continually passing to and fro with messages from his camp to the bands entrenched in the Bad Lands, and the malcontents outside, inciting them to continue hostilities. So, about November 27th, Col. Cody (Buffalo Bill) arrived at Standing Rock Agency, from New York, bearing a commission from Gen. Miles to visit the camp of the chief medicine-man on the Grand River, study the situation, and try to persuade him to put a stop to the ghost-dance-craze, which mission proved barren of good results.

Frequent delegations of friendly Indians, of whom there were, perhaps, between 400 and 500 left at the agency, went into their almost inaccessible retreat to induce them, if possible to send representatives into the agency to talk over their grievances with Gen. Brooke, but their efforts were unavailing. Finally, however, through the influence of Father Jule, the Catholic missionary at Pine Ridge, a number of prominent chiefs among whom were Two-Strikes, Big Turkey, Turning Bear, Big-Bad-Horse, and other influential chiefs with equally suggestive appellations, in full ghost-dance panoply, armed with Winchester rifles, and surrounded by a body-guard of several painted warriors, accompanied Father Jule into the camp of Gen. Brooke, under the protection of a flag of truce. During the conference which followed, Gen. Brooke assured them that if they would return and remain peaceable on their reservations, they would be provided with ample rations and in due time all their grievances would be redressed. The General's overtures were, however, received with ominous scowls and numerous grunts of sullen disapproval and after a few harangues from the savage orators the pow-wow closed without having received from them any promises of surrender.

All efforts to pacify the hostiles proving unavailing, the military authorities decided upon two heroic measures—first the arrest of Sitting Bull, who, it was learned, was on the eve of joining the hostiles in the Bad Lands with his followers; second the disarmament of Indians by force, and the 15th of December, 1890, saw the beginning of the end. On the night of that day, in compliance with an order from Gen. Ruger of St. Paul, dated December 12th, 1890, a detachment of soldiers consisting of troops F and H, Eighth Cavalry, under the command of Capt. Fetchet with artillery, consisting of a Hotchkiss and Gatling gun, surgeon, hospital ambulances, guide, and two trusty scouts, followed by Companies H and G, Twelfth Infantry, under Col. Drum, left Fort Yates, preceded by a force of perhaps thirty superbly mounted, splendidly accoutered Indian police in the blue uniform of United States soldiers, in command of First and Second Lieuts. Bull Head and Shave Head, from Standing Rock Agency, and marched away under the cover of darkness towards the intensely hostile village on the banks of the Grand river, to Oak creek about six miles distant therefrom, where the military made a temporary halt.

From this point, the faithful police, who were as true as steel to their sworn duty, led the band considerably in advance of the cavalry and artillery, which was to keep within supporting distance.

Noiselessly and carefully they picked their way towards the home of the great prophet, and just as the first glimmering of dawn appeared in the Orient, Lieutenant Bull Head stealthily approached the abode of the yet sleeping chieftain, lifted the latch of the unfastened door, cautiously stepped within, virtually "bearding the lion in his den," and made known his mission.

Just what immediately preceded the killing of Sitting Bull is not positively known, as there are two different, and quite antagonistic statements made in regard to the occurrences leading up to it. One is that he was seized by the police and dragged outside the door, when he sounded the alarm which brought his followers to his rescue, one of whom, Catch-The-Bear, fired at Bull Head, the captor of his chief, who then like a flash drew his revolver, and as he fell mortally wounded, sent the fatal bullet into the heart of Sitting Bull. The other is that when Bull Head entered the hut of Sitting Bull, his young son (Crow Foot) seeing through the open door that the house was surrounded by police, gave the cry of alarm, whereupon Bull Head fired at Sitting Bull, the ball entering his breast, killing him almost instantly, and that while reeling he managed to draw his revolver, which exploded as he fell, the ball entering the thigh of Bull Head, from the effects of which he later died.

In either case, the uncompromising foe of the pale-faces received his death wound—not at their hands, but at the hands of one in whose veins flowed the red blood of the Dakotahs. At the first sound of the savage slogan Sitting Bull's faithful followers gathered around their fallen chieftain, and a bloody encounter between the hostiles and police followed, in which many on both sides fell, the police, knowing that Capt. Fetchet would soon come to their support, bravely holding their ground against largely superior numbers.

At a critical juncture the dismounted cavalry, under Lieuts. Crowder, Slocum, and Steele, advanced down the hill, firing steadily as they approached, and at the same time the artillery, which had been placed in

Sitting Bull and Buffalo Bill, [Wm. Cody].

BUFFALO BILL HOLDING A CONFERENCE WITH SITTING BULL A SHORT TIME PRIOR TO HIS DEATH

position on the hills overlooking the village, opened their batteries on the hostiles, who, dismayed at the unexpected onslaught, fled precipitately towards the timber on the river.

Capt. Fetchet, fearing that when the hostiles rallied he would not be able to hold the village with the force at his command, returned to Oak creek, where he met the infantry under Col. Drum. The wounded and dead policemen, together with the body of Sitting Bull, were placed in the ambulances and conveyed to Standing Rock Agency, where Lieuts. Bull Head and Shave Head both died from the wounds received in the battle, and were, because of their fidelity, buried with military honors. What was done with the body of Sitting Bull is not known. Among the police killed in the encounter besides the lieutenants were Little Eagle, Broken Arm, Afraid-of-Soldiers, and Hawk-Man. Of the hostiles besides Sitting Bull, Crow Foot, his young son, Little Assiniboine, his adopted brother, Catch-the-Bear, Brave Thunder, and Chase-the-Wounded, were slain.

While the death of Sitting Bull was, in one sense, a great relief, removing as it did the chief obstacle in the way of a peaceful solution of the Indian trouble, it caused the most intense excitement and consternation throughout the Indian country, and a keen apprehension that many of the settlers would fall victims to the vengeance of the hostile Sioux.

THE ADVENT OF GENERAL MILES AND THE DISARMAMENT OF THE HOSTILES

The advent of Gen. Miles, the great Indian pacificator, at this crisis, was made the occasion of special rejoicing at Pine Ridge and among the people of the surrounding country, and caused a perceptible weakening and modification in the attitude of the hostiles. About December 18th Two-Strikes and the major part of his band, numbering over 800 braves, came into the agency and surrendered to Gen. Brooke. Little Wound and his band, and old Red Cloud had already returned to the ranks of the friendlies, and were making every effort to bring in the recalcitrant bands from the Bad Lands. On December 20th, Big Foot and Hump came into the agency with their bands, bringing with them 150 of Sitting Bull's warriors, who had fled after the death of their leader and joined the hostiles near Pine Ridge. The next day, however, he broke away from the agency and made for the Bad Lands, pursued by a force of cavalry under Gen. Carr. By December 25th, nearly all the bands, save those intrenched in the Bad Lands, had returned and surrendered their arms to Gen. Brooke.

The military cordon was now drawn closer and closer around the hostile entrenchment, and the only accessible pass thereto was guarded by a large force of cavalry. Much brisk fighting and skirmishing went on daily in the vicinity of Spring, Rapid, and Battle creeks, between detachments of troopers and small bands of hostiles who were trying to make their way into the Bad Lands, but of these it is needless to go into tedious detail.

On December 28th the welcome news was brought in by a scout that Big Foot was on his way to surrender, and that all the Indians in the Bad Lands had also decided to come in. Upon receiving this announcement, a part of the Seventh Cavalry in command of Capt. Whiteside hastily mounted and galloped forward to meet them, and on descending the slope of Porcupine Valley found Big Foot and his band together with Sitting Bull's warriors drawn up in battle array and heavily armed. After a short parley, the renegade chief and his entire band, and about 250 women, and children surrendered to Capt. Whiteside and were marched back to the old camp of the Seventh Cavalry on the Wounded Knee.

Reinforcements were immediately sent for, and early on the morning of the 29th of December, Col. Forsythe arrived with orders from Gen. Brooke to disarm the Indians, for which arrangements were speedily made.

He then threw his force of 500 regulars around the camp, mounted his heavy guns, and at 8 o'clock issued his order to disarm the Indians. In obedience to the command of Col. Forsythe, the Indians came forward from their tepees, leaving the squaws and children behind, when they were ordered to step forward by twenties and deliver their arms to Capt. Whiteside. They stepped forward and gave him two guns, the others being kept hidden under the folds of their blankets, or some were, perhaps, left back in their tents.

Regarding this as a lack of good faith, and suspecting treachery on the part of the desperate band, Capt. Whiteside ordered his dismounted troopers to close in about the Indians, which they did, taking a stand within twenty feet of them, in an almost complete square, when, like a flash, they drew their concealed guns from beneath their blankets, and fired a deadly volley into the closed ranks of the soldiers. Exasperated at this base treachery, the soldiers, scarcely waiting for the word of command, opened a terrific fire on the Indians, who fell before it as falls the grain before the sickle of the reaper.

After a short but terrible hand-to-hand combat, the few Indians who were left broke and fled from the unequal contest to the ravines and brakes surrounding the camp pursued by the exasperated troopers, whom it was found difficult to restrain. As soon as it became safe, the heavy guns were trained, and the batteries opened on the ambuscades of the fugitives, driving them back with shot and shell to the buttes, until there was not an Indian left in sight.

During the engagement, which lasted about an hour, there were twenty-nine soldiers killed, among whom was Capt. Geo. D. Wallace, Troop K, Seventh Cavalry; and thirty-three wounded, among whom was Lieut. E. A. Garlington, Troop A, Seventh Cavalry, who was also Adjutant of the Seventh Cavalry, at the time of the Custer battle in 1876. Lieut. Garlington, it will be remembered, rendered himself famous in connection with the expedition to the Arctic region, for the relief of Lieut. Greeley in 1883.

From the report of Gen. Miles to the Secretary of War, dated at Hermosa, South Dakota, December 30th, 1890, there were ninety dead Indian men found on and near the plain where the attempt was made to disarm Big Foot's band, which, including those killed in the ravines would, it has been estimated, swell the number to more than two hundred.

The women and children fled to the hills when the firing first began and many were unfortunately killed while on their flight and in their hiding-places, which in the confusion was, not doubt, unavoidable.

The news of the disastrous battle at Wounded Knee intensified for a time the hostility of the more warlike, and created a spirit of unrest among the Indians who had surrendered, large numbers of whom broke away from the agency and fled towards the Bad Lands. All sorts of alarming rumors, some well founded, and some baseless, were afloat, causing the greatest excitement among the friendly Indians and the settlers who flocked into the agency for safety.

From this time the history of that memorable Indian campaign may be briefly summed up. At the beginning of the new year (1891) there were near the center of hostilities, ready for active service, the First, Second, Fifth, Sixth, Seventh, Eighth, and Ninth Regiments of Cavalry, and the First, Second, Third, Seventh, Eighth, Twelfth, Seventeenth, Twenty-first, and Twenty-second Regiments of Infantry, comprising in the aggregate about 8,000 well equipped soldiers, besides Battery A of First, and Battery F of Fourth Artillery, to cope with 3,000 hostile Indians, among whom were perhaps not more than 600 warriors, who, for the most part, were safely entrenched among the inaccessible lava beds of the Bad Lands. The problem was to dislodge or induce them to come forth and surrender.

On January 5th another spirited but far less disastrous engagement took place a few miles from Wounded Knee. Upon learning that a train of wagons loaded with supplies was approaching on the Rapid City road a detachment of thirty picked troopers was sent out to meet the train and protect it from probable attack, and they were none too soon, for they had not gone more than ten miles before they discovered the train of thirteen wagons corralled, and surrounded by about fifty whooping Indians. The troopers put spurs to their horses and galloped to their relief, when the Indians retreated to a neighboring hill. The soldiers joined the teamsters, nineteen in number, and they together quickly threw up breastworks composed of boxes, sacks of grain, etc., but had hardly finished the work before the Indians returned to the attack with numbers augmented to more than a hundred warriors, leaving a large reserve force on the adjoining hills. They circled round and round, firing into the barricade at long range, doing but little damage, while an occasional redskin was seen to reel and fall from his saddle.

In the early part of the siege, a trooper named Collins made a bold dash through the circling lines of Indians, and sped swiftly away after re-enforcements followed by about twenty Indians in distant pursuit, who soon gave up the chase and returned to the attack.

After the battle had raged for three long hours, and at a critical time, when Indian bullets were flying thick and fast around the little besieged party, troops were seen coming in full charge to the rescue. The Indians broke and fled to the hills, one of the troops giving chase, which, however, was soon abandoned. Four cavalry horses were shot and killed and one soldier slightly wounded. Many Indians fell, and a large number of ponies were killed, and some captured.

On January 8, 1891, Indian affairs at the different South Dakota agencies were temporarily placed by the Secretary of the Interior, under the sole control of the military, with Gen. Miles in supreme command, when the prospect for a speedy settlement of the trouble materially brightened. Every morning reports were brought in by scouts, that the Indians were coming in to surrender, but every evening found the promise unfulfilled, and so the campaign dragged along. Finally Gen. Miles, aided by the efforts of Frank Gourard, chief of the Indian police, Buffalo Bill, and the unremitting labors of Father Jude, secured a conference with a number of the leading chiefs, which resulted in a complete surrender of all the hostile forces in the Bad Lands, the last bands reluctantly yielding up their arms to Gen. Miles on January 15th, 1891. Thus ends the story, briefly and imperfectly told, of the great Messiah Craze, and the last uprising of the Dakotahs.

INDEX

A

A.A.O.N.M.S—455
A. & A.S.R.—455
A.F. and A.M.—392
A.O.U.W.—317, 392, 431, 443, 504
A.P. Moon & Company's Mill—398
Aarons, Moses—18, 35
Abbey, Cyrus—214
Abernethy, David—412
Abrams, Lewis—465
Abt, Frank—390, 454
Abt, Jr., Frank—392
Ackey, Miss Josephine—453
Adams, G.B.—443
Adams, R.O.—201, 360
Adjudication, first case of—202
Adler, Geo.—482
"Advertiser, The," Sturgis—473
Afraid-of-Soldiers—536
Afraid-of-the-Bear—97
Agriculture & grazing—79, 355, 405, 481, 508, 510
Ainley, Hy. John—388, 456
Aken, David—18, 50
Alaskan gold fields—123
Albert Hose Company—389
Albion, Henry A.—220, 225, 298, 303
Albright, S. J.—521
Alexander, H.C.—468
Alexander mine—434
Alexander, Wesley—388
Alkali (town)—483
Alkali creek—80, 458
Allegheny City, Pennsylvania, see "Pennsylvania, Allegheny City"
Allen, Charles L.—231
Allen, Charles N.—231, 232, 233
Allen, F. M.—447
Allen, James W.—122, 449, 522
Allen, John W.—100, 122, 123, 226, 227, 340
Allinson, Wm.—456
Allison, Hon. Wm. B.—95
Alpha and Omega mines—208, 209
Alpha and Omego property—208
Alpha Lode—253
Alpha mine—208, 209
Alpha Mining Company—398
Alta Lodi mine—344, 345
Alti Lodi mine—345
Amalgamation—295, 297, 345, 370, 390, 437
"American Carlsbad"—494, 495, 508
American flag—44
American Fur Company—124
American Home Mission Society—211
American Horse, Chief—97
American Hotel—397
American House—133
American National Bank—374
Amerman, John—257
Amerman & Sutherland firm—258
Ames, Edward—410, 504
Ames, Iowa, see "Iowa, Ames"
Ammunition, Custer's Last Stand—155, 157
Anchor City—396
Ancient Order of United Workmen—389, 436, 472
Anderson, H. O.—473
Anderson, Jas.—524
Anderson, Ole—522
Anderson, Major W. W.—518
Anderson, W. M.—404
Angela, Sister Mother Superior—467
Ankeny Brothers—440

Antelope creek—88, 107, 115
"Antidote" (whiskey)—116, 117
Apex Consolidated Mining & Milling Co.—344, 441
Apron—249
Arapahoes—95, 184
Arastra—205
Arc light system—327
Architecture, Romanesque style—425
Ardmore (town)—509
Argue, John—134, 135
Argyle—307
Arizona (state)—330, 455
Arkansas Territory—519
Army, U.S.—348
Arnold, A. J.—407
Arrington, John—414
Artesian irrigation—511
Ash Extension—462
Ash, Henry—403, 404
Ash, Judge—466
Ash, U.S. Marshal—227
Ashley, W. H.—95
Ashton, George—134
Assay, certificates of—119
Assay laboratories—323
Associated Press—13
Atchinson, George—107, 269
Athletic clubs—377, 395
"Atlantic" mine—295, 296
Atwater, H. P.—473
Atwater, the Rev. W. D.—468
Aunt Sally—404
Aurora mine—398
Ayres, George Vincent—214, 449, 454, 455
Ayres & Wardman Hardware Co.—454

B

B. & M. Railway Depot—508
B. and M. Station (Railway Depot)—207, 431
Babcock, Dr. L. F.—275, 279, 356, 377, 422
Babcock, W. H.—129
Backus, Col.—211
Bacon, Col. John M.—477
Bad Lands—33, 34, 36, 111, 150, 217, 309, 531, 533, 536, 538, 539
Bad River—34, 518
Badger Mill—398
Baer & McKinnis firm—258
Baer, Ben—374
Bailey, R. A.—448
Baird, J. L.—364
Baird, W. M.—364
Baker, J.B.C.—472
Baker & Price firm—483
Baker, Van P.—428
Baker's, Justice, court—400
Bakerville—307
Balcombe, Deputy U.S. Marshal—271
"Bald Mountain News"—315, 437
Bald Mountain refractory ore deposit—372, 437
Bald Mountain region—128, 372, 373, 435, 438, 439
Balf, J. H.—269
Ball, Major Edward—477
Balthoff Ball Pulverizer—208
Baltimore and Richmond mines—440
Band Organization—472
Bangs, A. W.—524
Banks, first legitimate institution in Black Hills—361
Bank of Spearfish—418

Banking institutions—191, 202, 203, 327, 374, 417, 418, 431, 469
Baptist societies—304, 314, 392, 498
Baptiste—67
Barber, Miss Clara—465
Barclay, Charles—392
Barclay, M. J.—518
Barnes, Judge Alanson H.—358
Barrows, G. W.—315
Barry, Miss Kate—390
Barthold, Ernest—340
Bartholomew, J. S.—223, 303, 396
Bartholomew, Mrs.—465
Bartholomew, Rev.—468
Bartlett, Fred—422
Bass, F. P.—426
Bates, C.—227
Battenberd & Martin firm—515
Battle creek—80, 109, 251, 287, 292, 303, 307, 309, 337, 347, 348, 349, 353, 518, 533, 536
Battle of the Little Horn—146, 411
Battle Mountain—487, 490, 499, 505
Bear Butte—10, 11, 38, 41, 76, 77, 80, 125, 463, 476
Bear Butte Creek—124, 433, 434, 458, 462, 471, 476
Bear Butte Creek first settlers—463
Bear Creek—130
Bear Gulch nuggets—245
Bear Gulch placer diggings—432
Bear Lodge—77, 103, 185
Bear Lodge mountains—185
Bear Lodge Peak—117, 119
"Bear on slapjack"—114
Bear Paw Mountains—332
Bear Springs—235
Beatrice (town)—454
Beatrice, see "Nebraska, Beatrice"
Beauvais, G. P.—95
Beavers—128
Beaver Creek—3, 80, 92, 292, 485
Bedrock—248, 251
"Bee," Belle Fourche—515
Bee Publishing Company—514
Beef cattle, first herd in Black Hills—212
Beef issues, regular—528
Beeman, H. B.—361
Beemer, Geo.—381, 388, 454
Beer manufacture plant, first in Black Hills—205
Behm, John—469
Behrens (undertaker)—232
Belding, John—446
"Bell Chamber"—507
Bell, John—422
Bell, Leonard W.—310
Belle Fourche—512, 514, 515, 516, 517
Belle Fourche River—77, 80, 97, 172, 355, 410, 411, 414, 456, 458, 510, 511, 512, 514, 517
Belliveau's store—390
Bemis, Dr.—214
Ben Hur mine—441
Bend (town)—483
Benedict, B. B.—346, 347
Benedictine Sisters—467
Benevolent Hall—464, 468
Benevolent Hall Association Temple—471
Bengal Tiger mine—335, 336, 337
Bennett, F. E.—512
Bennett, G. G.—201
Bennett, Geo. P.—324
Bennett, Judge Granville G.—283, 284, 316, 342, 356, 358, 375, 376, 456, 457
Bennett, Mrs. J. S.—404
Benns, Henry—447
Bent & Beetkin firm—257, 258
Bent, E. C.—257
Benteen, Captain—151, 152, 154, 155, 158, 159
Benteen's battalion—151, 153, 154, 155, 158
Bentley, Thos.—448
Benton, Fort—187
Berg, Conrad—510
Berne—307
Bertchey, Geo.—336
Bethune, Frank—340
Beulah bridge—412, 413
Biennial session—323
Big-Bad-Horse—531
Big Bonanza mine—438, 440

Big Bottom (town)—483
Big Foot—530, 536, 537, 538
Big Gene—289
"Big Hit" mine—354
Big Horn—125, 126, 163, 275
Big Horn mountains—2, 6, 147, 148, 159, 186, 508
Big Horn river—9, 157, 167
Big John—178
Big Missouri mine—125
"Big Muddy"—104, 130
Big Sioux river—520, 521
Big Thunder—97
Big Turkey—531
Bigler, J. H.—407
"Billy the Kid"—331, 422
Birth, first child in Deadwood—265
Birth, first child in Rapid City—316
Birth, first white child in Black Hills—199
Bishop, E. J.—391
Bishop, H.—18, 32, 50
Bishop, J.—336, 429
"Bismarck" mine—354
Bismarck, North Dakota, see "North Dakota, Bismarck"
Bismarck wagon trail, old—414
Blackburn (outlaw)—290
Blackburn, Dunc.—331
Black Buttes—77, 125
Black Hawk (town)—483
Black Hills Canal & Water Co.—364, 389
Black Hills cession—97
Black Hills Christmas of 1874—46
Black Hills climate—80
Black Hills College—498
Black Hills, "Denver"—122
Black Hills drainage systems—80
Black Hills Expedition—88
Black Hills Expedition of 1872—6
Black Hills fever (gold)—106, 130
"Black Hills Friends"—205
Black Hills Gold Mining Company—398
Black Hills, home of Indians—3, 81
Black Hills, humorist—224
Black Hills, immigration—175
Black Hills Invasion of 1874—12, 13, 44, 146, 162, 292, 489
Black Hills literature—165
Black Hills Milling & Smelting Co.—317
Black Hills mineral deposits—81, 92
Black Hills missionary, first—379
Black Hills Pioneer and Historical Society of 1877—456
Black Hills Placer Mining Co.—350
Black Hills population—164, 184, 303
Black Hills rhymist—180
Black Hills Second Expedition of 1875—13, 104
Black Hills snowfall—80
Black Hills Superior Court—123
Black Hills survey—92
Black Hills Telegraph Line—278
Black Hills Telephone Company—456
Black Hills Telephone Exchange—364
Black Hills temperature—80
Black Hills - vegetation—77, 78
Black, J. B.—725
Black soldiers—474
Black Tail Gulch—245, 253
Black Tail mine—127, 128
Blacktail (town)—396
Blackwell, Charles—18, 30, 36, 51, 59, 236
Blair, Thomas C.—353
Blake Crusher—208
Blake, Prof. Wm.—338
Blakey, R.—140
Blanchard, H. E.—524
Blatt, Max—465
"Bleaching"—438
Bliss, Joseph—214
Bliss, Philomen—522
Blodgett, Samuel—124, 125
Bloody Knife—153
Blossom Mining Co.—345
"Blue coats"—130, 215
Blue Lead quartz mines—342
Blue Wing Lode—342
Board of Education, Deadwood—364, 365

Board of Trade flour—365
Board of Trustees, Rapid City—324
Bob Tail—253
Bobtail gulch—245, 401
Bogle, Mr.—398
Boland, George—179, 180, 231, 491, 492, 493
Boland's ranch—490, 491
Bolthoff and Ball Pulverizer—209
"Bonanza gulch"—127
Bonanza gulch, first location—128
"Bonanza" mine—297, 298
Bonham & Kelly firm—201
Bonham, F. M.—201
Bonham, Maskey & Moody firm—201
Bonham, Willis, H.—201, 373, 456
Boom camps—335
Booth, Samuel M.—216, 225, 303, 306, 446, 447, 489
Booth's Samuel, letter—217
"Boots and saddles"—151, 411
Bostwick mines—247
Bosworth's Addition—462
Bottleson, Eli—441
Bottleson group—441
Boueyer—202
Boughton, Mark—482
Boughton, Mart—212
Boughton and Berry's sawmill—211, 248
Boughton & Berry store—203, 257
Boulder Park—77, 355
Bourke, Lt. J. G.—91
Bowan, Capt. A. H.—91
Bowling Green, Kentucky, see "Kentucky, Bowling Green"
Box Elder river—11, 41, 72, 80, 103, 308, 309, 331, 458, 518
Box Elder Valley—41
Boyce, Col. D.—340
Boyd, James—315
Boyle, John—18, 50
Bozeman route—184
Bradley, General—48
Bradley, J. F.—407
Bradley, Jas.—408, 413, 414
Bradley, Kellar—408, 415
Bradley, T. K.—407
Bradley, W. W.—414, 415
Brady, T. C.—135
Bragg, Mrs. John—388
Bramble & Miner—139
Brave Thunder—536
"Break Neck" hill—268
Brelsford, J. M.—208
Brennan, John R.—104, 133, 134, 135, 136, 226, 228, 230, 231, 232, 233, 310, 312, 316, 324, 328, 331, 446
Bresnaham, C. R.—279
"Brick Store"—388
"Bridal Chamber"—507
Brigham, (Treasurer, Lawrence County)—356
British Dominion—519
Brochn, Peter—510
Brockett, J. W.—18
Brockett, Major—88
Brockett, Mrs.—88, 89
Brodie, Jas.—295
Broken Arm—536
Broman, H. H.—443
"Broncho Charley"—421
Brooke, General—531, 536
Brooke, John—389
Brookes (outlaw)—290
Brookings, W. W.—520, 521
Brough, Theodore Vos—294
Broughton, Dr.—296
Brown, Albert—136, 226, 234
Brown, Chas.—421
Brown, Col. "Stuttering"—120, 121, 217, 218, 236
Brown, Ezekiel—340
Brown, H. W.—512
Brown and Holland—274
Brown, Isaac—255, 270, 274, 275, 365
Brown, M. H.—294
Brown, Major—174
Brown, Phillip—348
Brown, Samuel F.—521
Brown, T.—7
Brown, Thos.—374

Brown & Thum's Mill—359, 398
Browning, Geo. M.—511
Browning, Wm.—234
Browning & Wringrose—256, 258
Brownsville—382, 444
Brule City—5
Brule reservation—4
Brules—95, 147, 170
Brunschmidt, Joseph—492, 494
Bryant, Frank—104, 124, 125, 126, 127, 128, 396
Bryant, John—398, 399
Bryant party—124
Buchanan, President—521
Buckbee, Arthur—462
Buckeye gulch—354
Buckhorn—77
Buckhorn Mountain—300
Buckhorn Peak—300
"Buckskin"—192, 193, 421
"Buckskin Jack"—421
Buderus, W. C.—473
Buffalo Bill, see "Cody, "Buffalo Bill" Wm."
Buffalo Gap—130, 173, 179, 216, 307, 490, 491, 493
Buffalo Gap Canyon—179, 217
Buffalo grass—79
Buford, Ed.—510
Buford, Fort—187
Building, first in Black Hills—195
Bulkhead—250, 368
Bull Head, 1st Lieutenant—534
"Bullion" mine—354
Bullock, F. E. & M. V., firm—291
Bullock Hotel—188
Bullock, Richard—291
Bullock, Seth—186, 188, 189, 191, 287, 290, 356, 362, 365, 400, 401, 440, 441, 448
Bump, J. J.—407
"Bunch grass"—79
Bunnell, W. H.—214
Burgess, P. J. M.—425
Burial of Indian victims—412
Burke, A. H.—403
Burke, H.S.—404, 407
Burke quarries—504
Burleigh, Bob—229, 231
Burleigh, W. A.—522
Burlington & Missouri Railway—304, 342, 425
Burlington & Missouri road—372, 490, 508
Burlington narrow-gauge railroad—439
"Burlington" Railway Company—372, 431, 432, 489, 504, 508, 509
Burnham, Al.—187, 188, 191, 192
Burnham, Miss—391
Burns, Chas.—286, 287
Burns, U.S. Commissioner—271
Burrows, John—214
Burton & Cook—273
Burton, Mike—185, 186, 410
Burton, W. C.—460
Burton, Wm. Vandaniker & McGavock firm—258
Busian, Miss Zella—428
Businesses—102
Business Men's Protective Association, Deadwood—454
Butcher, Jas.—407
Butler, Ben—5
Butte (town)—517
Butte County—285, 355, 510, 511, 512, 514, 515
Butte County Bank—515
Butte County, stock raising region—512
Butterfield, H. G.—298
Buxton mine—440
Bryon, G.—134, 135

C

C.A. & V.G. Peterson (firm)—504
Cabin, first in the northern Black Hills—125
Cabin, first built in Deadwood—255
Cabin, first in Rapid City—228
Cabins, first in Central City—396
Cable, Judge Wm.—403, 460
Cain, Michael—392
Calamity gulch—431

544   THE BLACK HILLS; OR,

Calamity Jane—134
Calamity Park—77, 239
Calamity Peak—301
Calcium Sulphate—486
Caldwell, J. W.—462
Caledonia—401, 402
Caledonia mills—383
Calhoun, Lieutenant—152, 161
California—245, 278, 330, 381, 393
California, gold rush—7
California Joe—101, 134, 135, 205, 234, 253
California, San Francisco—338, 381
Calihan, J. C.—443
Calumett mines—434, 441
Cameron, M.—318
Camp Crook—346, 347, 402
Camp Ruhlen—476
Camp Sturgis—400
Campbell—289
Campbell, General—227
Campbell, John—421, 422, 423
Canadian border—169
Cannon Ball river—170
Capital Hill—507
Carey, James M.—518
Carey, Thomas E.—387
Carleton, Col. C. H.—477
Carlin, A. J.—340
Carll, Jesse—328
Carney, James—226, 227, 447
Carpenter, C. W.—140
Carpenter, Prof. Franklin R.—370, 371, 435
Carpenter, Jas. E.—303, 349
Carpenter, Lieutenant—70
Carr, General—166, 533, 536
Carr, Hugh—441
Carr, W. L.—327
Carroll, H.—463
Carroll, Michael—214
Carroll, Thos. 374
Carson, D.—524
Carter, A. P.—277
Carter, Josie—388
Carter, Mrs.—388
Carty, John R.—269, 270
Cascade—506
Case Brothers—119
Case, J. I.—340
Casey, Pat—448
Cashner, John—7, 417
Castle creek—41, 93, 98, 103, 129, 130, 136, 245, 252, 254
 ,307, 343, 352, 353, 390
Castle creek gold diggings—130
Castleton—144, 254, 311, 352
Catch-The-Bear—534, 536
Catholic Church of Deadwood—360
Catholic missionaries—8, 533
Catholic societies—304, 314, 388, 392, 396, 431, 436, 466,
 496, 498
Catholicon spring—492, 495, 501
Cattle ranges—308
"Cattle-rustling"—286, 410, 420, 424
Cattle shipping—516
Caulfield, Barney G.—462
Cavalry, U.S.—25, 62, 170, 401, 410
Cavanaugh, M.—253, 380
Cedar Rapids County—337
Cement (containing gold & silver)—352, 399
Centennial—204, 273, 409
Centennial Anniversary—263
Centennial Hotel—211
Centennial Party—192, 193, 407, 421
Centennial prairie—186, 193, 273, 355, 405, 406, 407, 411
Centennial year—166
Central City—134, 295, 296, 343, 356, 368, 383, 396-399,
 401, 426
Central City, Colorado, see "Colorado, Central City"
Central, Colorado, see "Colorado, Central"
Central Gold Mining and Milling Company's Custom
 Mill—398
Central School, Deadwood—265
"Cerneau Rite"—455
Chadron, Nebraska, see "Nebraska, Chadron"
Chamberlain—138, 325
Chamberlain, Henry—511
Chambers, Major—169

"Champion," Central—396
Chandler, Mrs. G. W.—368
Chapline, Attorney A. B.—264, 269
Chapman, E. B.—325
Chapman, Martin—440, 441
Chapman, Miss L.—390
Charles Hotel—464
Charrion, the Rev. Victor—468
Chas, Sasse & Co.—177
Chase, I.—205
Chase, May—428
Chase, Mrs. Osceola—316
Chase, Osceola—316
Chase-the-Wounded—536
Chase, W. S.—470
Chaw-Skaw-Skaw-Walkapalla—124, 125
Chemical Bank, New York—322
Cheney, Dr. J. B.—448, 460
Chew, Robert—361
Cheyenne—40, 72, 75, 184, 487
Cheyenne (town), see "Wyoming, Cheyenne"
Cheyenne and Black Hills stage line—120, 139, 140,
 144, 217, 277
Cheyenne River, Big—9, 39, 40, 61, 70, 72, 75, 80, 92, 97,
 101, 109, 113, 120, 134, 139, 162, 173, 265, 290, 292, 308,
 309, 311, 355, 485, 505, 508, 509, 518, 530, 533
Cheyenne river, north fork—80, 458
Cheyenne river reservation—527
Cheyenne river, southern fork—3, 11, 80, 483
Cheyenne river stage station—122, 178, 218, 219, 237
Cheyenne river valley—309
Cheyenne road—306
Chicago, see "Illinois, Chicago"
Chicago Fire of 1871—363
Chicago, Milwaukee & St. Paul Railroad—138, 325
Chicago and Northwestern Railway—141, 192
Chicago & Northwestern Railway Company—443
Chief of the Hills—205, 253
Chilson, Elisha P.—484
"Chimney Rock"—489
Chinatown—363, 364
Chinese—378
Chinese fashions—379
Chisholm Brothers—247
Chloride—486
Chlorination—298, 317, 318, 345, 370
Chouteau, A. A.—511
"Chronicle" Custer—199, 304
Chugwater—236
Church, first in Sturgis—466
Church, Governor—133, 494
Church, Judge Wm. E.—284
Circuit Courts, Black Hills—284, 330, 342, 356, 375
City Council, Deadwood—277
City creek—364
City Hall, Deadwood—277
City Marshal, Deadwood—214, 277
Civil War—73, 476, 498, 521
Claggett, Wm.—348
"Claim-jumping"—398
Clara Nos. 1 & 2 mines—402
Clark, A. D.—441
Clark, David H.—317, 324
Clark, G. A.—214
Clark, Geo.—298
Clark, John H.—138, 429
Clark, "Red"—332
Clark & Morill firm—212, 258
Clark & Wilson bakery—404
Clay, Jr., John—515
Clayton, C. C.—202
Clean-ups—246, 249, 251
Cleghorn Springs—226, 230, 318
Clemmons Springs—429
Clerk & treasurer, Deadwood—277
Clerk of U.S. & Territorial Courts—356, 376
Clerk of U.S. Courts, first in Black Hills—265
Cleveland (town)—364, 368
Cleveland, President—284
"Climax" mine—300
Cline, Oscar—129
Clinton mine—438, 440
Clippinger, (unknown)—144, 203
Coad, Wm.—202
Coal, bituminous—516
Coats, Geo.—340

LAST HUNTING GROUND OF THE DAKOTAHS 545

Coats, Samuel H.—310
Cobalt—338
Cochrane, Deputy Sheriff—290
Cochrane, Frank—433
Cochrane, Jas.—345
Coder, Henry—127
Coder, W. H.—126
Cody, "Buffalo Bill" Wm.—165, 166, 167, 168, 533, 539
Coffee, Jules—121
Coffee & Cuny logging train—268
Coffin, first constructin in Black Hills—303
Cohen, P.—388
"Coin of the realm"—142
Cold Springs robbery of 1878—289, 307
Coldbrook creek—485
Cole, Cyrus—524
Cole, George W.—446
Cole, Jack—421
Cole, Lt. J. H.—91
College Hill—498, 502
Colletta mines—434
Collins, Charles—4, 5, 13, 14, 55, 69, 396, 464
Collins, Dr. D. E.—524
Collins, E. R.—403, 433
Collins, Trooper—539
Collins, W. H.—447
Collins and O'Leary—440
Collins & Russell Party code—26
Collins - Russell Party, donkey—22, 25, 38, 53, 60, 239, 240
Collins & Russell party (expedition)—6, 16, 20, 22, 28, 32, 88, 116, 198
Colony corporation—5
Colorado—119, 245, 295, 296, 318, 449, 510
Colorado, Central—208
Colorado, Central City—127, 396
Colorado Charlie—142
Colorado, Denver—134, 199, 202, 208, 439
Colorado, Georgetown—116, 119, 195
Colorado Iron Works of Denver, Colorado—318
Colorado Jack—407
Colorado, Kansas, see, "Kansas, Colorado"
Comanche—479, 480
Comedy in Black Hills—206
Comings, Hon. A.—95
Commercial clubs—377, 472
Commission of August, 1876 (Second)—96
Commission of Internal Revenue—265
Commission of June, 1875—95, 99
Commissioner of Indian Affairs—92, 93
Commode, Wm.—258
Common Council—172, 364
Company I of 7th Calvary—480
Comstock mine—399
Comstock's Addition—462
Concord four-horse coaches—141
Conley, Frank—227
Congdon, G. S.—326
Congdon, Joseph—436
Congregational Academy—427
Congregational Church of Deadwood—211, 212
Congregational churches, societies—304, 314, 354, 360, 388, 392, 397, 416, 431, 436, 498, 515
Congress, Fifty-first—324
Conley, Chas.—423
Connor Bros.—578
Connor, Mos. D. T.—473
Connors, M. C.—427, 429
Connors, M. F.—416
Connors, Thomas—392
Constant Mining Company—295
Constitution convention—329, 523, 524
Conter, H. L.—470
Conzette, James—433
Cook, Fayette L.—428
Cook, J. E.—185, 186
Cook, Joe—410
Cook, Prof.—429
Cooper, Attorney—222
Cooper, F. R.—185
Cooper, H. T.—443
Cooper, Harry—18, 21, 50
Cooper, M. M.—524
Cooper, O. L.—325
Cooper, Wilder—222
Cooper—297, 298

Corcoran, J. E.—394
Cordeiro, Chas.—18, 31, 32, 51
Corneille, Jas.—116, 117, 118, 195
Cornucopia mine—402
Coroner of Lawrence County, first—377
Corrigan, D.—304
Corum, F. B.—417
Cosgrove, Wm.—236
Coslett, Wm.—86
Cottonwood creek—134, 508
Council, Lincoln Territory—281
County government—283, 293, 312, 510
County Judge of Lawrence County—376
Court, Henry—425, 429
Court & Bulf's building—409
Covington—15
Cowgill, Jean—428
Craig, C. L.—407
Crandall, Mrs. C. D.—314
Crary, Chas.—295
Crawford, Capt. Jack—165, 196, 197, 200, 214, 216, 241
Crawford, E. J.—448
Crawford, J. J.—407
Crazy Horse—147, 148, 167, 169, 171, 174, 219
Crazy Horse's village—171
Creston (town)—354
Crittenden, Lieutenant—152
"Crittenden's Hill"—161
Crocker, F. C.—342
Cronen, E. P.—192
Crook City—132, 139, 172, 173, 204, 207, 208, 230, 245, 271, 273, 274, 330, 356, 381, 398, 402-404, 407, 409, 410, 416, 418, 463, 468, 494
Crook City post office—404
Crook City railway station—404
Crook, General Geo.—87, 98, 99, 100, 107, 119, 123, 125, 126, 147, 148, 157, 158, 168, 169, 170, 172, 173, 174, 196, 213, 214, 219, 230, 303, 341, 346, 402, 528, 529
Crook's column—160, 165, 170, 171, 172
Crook's, Gen., disbanding address—173, 174
Crook's order to evacuate Black Hills—99
Crook's Tower—75, 77
"Croppings"—252
Cross, Fred J.—294, 354
Crow Butte—406
Crow, Christopher—443
Crow Creek Agency—172
Crow Foot—534, 536
Crow, I. R.—315, 437
Crow Peak—77, 406
Crow reservation—275, 527
Crow scouts—150, 151, 160, 169
Crowder, Lieut.—534
Crow-king—147
Crown Hill Mining Co.—297
Cruse, Fred—341
Crystal Cave—483
Cuba—477
Cuba Libre—512
Cudney, William—126, 127
"Cues," Chinese—378
Culp, Jas.—448
Cummings, E. B.—524
Cummings, Lieut.—410, 411
Cunningham, Billy—423
"Curley"—217, 218, 238, 269
Cushman, Samuel—428
Cusick, James—386
Cusick, Patrick—443
Custer (city)—41, 44, 98, 99, 102, 111, 118, 119, 121, 122, 123, 125, 130, 131, 136, 140, 173, 178, 179, 183, 193, 195, 198, 199, 202, 203, 205, 210, 212, 213, 214, 215, 217, 218, 219, 220, 221, 222, 223, 224, 225, 235, 238, 245, 280, 286, 292, 293, 295, 296, 297, 298, 300, 301, 303, 304, 305, 306, 311, 335, 341, 346, 349, 406, 446, 454, 476, 489, 490, 491, 492, 494, 496
Custer, Boston—161
Custer, Capt. Tom—152, 161, 162
Custer, Column of 1876—1, 12, 13, 44, 146, 162, 292, 489
Custer County—285, 292, 293, 294, 295, 298, 300, 307, 308, 339, 349, 484, 485, 494, 507, 524, 531
Custer County, assessed valuation—294
Custer County Bank—304
Custer County Board of Commissioners meeting, first—292
Custer County deputy sheriff—224

Custer County, first Register of Deeds—294, 354
Custer County, location—292
Custer County, mica mines—294
Custer County mines—294
Custer Expedition of 1874—1, 12, 13, 44, 146, 162, 292, 489
Custer Expedition of 1874 wagon road—41, 42
Custer, first permanent settlers—214
Custer, first township organization board of trustees—122
Custer, first townsite survey—123
Custer, General George A.—10, 12, 91, 148, 149, 150, 151, 152, 153, 154, 155, 159, 160, 161, 162, 163, 165, 166, 168, 213, 292, 301
Custer, Gen., House—257, 360
Custer's General G. A., remains—163
Custer Gen. G. A. Report to War Department—11
"Custer minute men"—122, 216, 217, 221
Custer's battalions—151, 152
Custer's battle ground—152, 155, 159, 160, 537
"Custer's Hill"—161
Custer's Indian scouts—151
Custer's last order—155
Custer's Last Stand, see also "Indian Campaign of 1876"—152, 155, 156, 159, 160
Custer's Park—114, 134, 199, 239, 300, 301
Custer's Peak—77, 117
Custom stamp mills—380
Cuthbertson & Young firm—131, 132, 256, 258, 381
Cyanide process—345, 370, 371
Cyanide reduction works—298, 431, 439

D

D. & D. Smelting Co.—440
D. of H.—392
"Daily Evening Call," Lead—394
"Daily Journal," Rapid City—314
"Daily Pioneer," Deadwood—201
"Daily Pioneer Times," Deadwood—373
"Daily Times," Deadwood—201, 202, 357, 358, 373, 416
Dakota blizzard—136, 227
Dakota City—236, 265, 270, 354
Dakota Hot Springs Company—497, 500, 502, 503
"Dakota Land Company—521
Dakota State Fair—79
Dakota Territory organization—519
Dakotahs—1, 3, 82, 539
Dakotahs ancestral religion—529
Dakotah tribes in 1890—530
Daly, Jack—192, 454
Daly, John—387
Dan—16, 37
Darling, Prof. Ed.—390, 391
Dark Horse mine—440
Darrow, George—315
Daughters of Rebecca—317
Davenport, Iowa, see "Iowa, Davenport"
Davenport, Joseph J.—465, 469, 471
Davey, Col. J. H.—433, 434
Davidson, John—407, 492, 493, 494
Davis, Bean—421
Davis, Capt. Frank R.—304, 328
Davis, Deputy Marshall I. C.—268
Davis, E.— 341
Davis, Ed—126
Davis, L. L.—320
Davis, Marshal—269
Davis, P.—346
Davis, Scott—288, 289
Dawes, Gen. A. C.—6
Dawson, Gen. A. R. Z.—172, 173, 264, 265, 356, 446, 448
Dawson, H. A.—518
Dawson, Jack—231
Day, Col. M. H.—318, 345
Days of '76—350
DeGray, Charley—124
DeKay Brothers—443
DeLacompt—7
DeLaney, Lt.—91
DeSmet—383, 396
DeSmet, Father Peter J.—8, 13, 396
DeSmet group of mines—268
DeSmet mill—127, 398

DeWitt, E. J.—521
"Deadbroke" mill—398
Deadwood—50, 73, 77, 88, 89, 122, 124, 129, 132, 133, 134, 139, 141, 142, 144, 164, 172, 186, 187, 188, 191, 192, 199, 201-208, 211, 214, 223, 224, 230, 235, 243, 245, 246, 253, 255, 262-268, 270-275, 277, 278, 279, 280, 283, 285, 286, 287, 290, 291, 296, 303, 305, 304, 306, 317, 328, 329, 332, 335, 336, 338, 342, 343, 346, 347, 348, 350, 355-368, 370-379, 380, 396, 400-403, 406, 407, 411, 412, 413, 421, 422, 432, 433, 434, 435, 439, 446, 448, 449, 452, 454, 455, 456, 462, 465, 475, 482, 488, 491, 493, 494, 512
Deadwood Centennial celebration—263
Deadwood Central Depot—381
Deadwood Creek—366, 368
Deadwood and Delaware Pyritic Smelter—439
Deadwood and Delaware Smelting plant—370, 371, 441
Deadwood Electric Lighting System—456
Deadwood Fire Department, first company—361
Deadwood Flouring Mill Company—365
"Deadwood Gulch—120, 125, 126, 127, 128, 129, 130, 131, 210, 275, 349, 357, 362, 368, 387, 396, 398, 441
Deadwood Gulch, early claim owners—127
Deadwood Gulch, first prospecting—124, 125
Deadwood Gulch Great Stampede—102
Deadwood Gulch No. 1 below Discovery—247
Deadwood Gulch No. 2—210, 247
Deadwood Gulch Nos. 4 & 5, below Discovery—247
Deadwood Gulch No. 9, below Discovery—247
Deadwood Gulch Nos. 14 & 15 below Discovery—247
Deadwood High School building—125
"Deadwood Labor Union"—374
Deadwood Lady saves watch—288
Deadwood legal bar—375, 377
Deadwood market—136, 177, 235, 258
Deadwood medical fraternity—377
Deadwood, New—370-379
Deadwood, original site—255
Deadwood, population—164, 258
Deadwood Post Office—189, 360
Deadwood, provisional city government—189, 277
Deadwood road—230
Deadwood & Sidney Express Line—328
Deadwood Steam Flouring Mill—365
Deadwood Terra Company—382, 401
Deadwood Theatre building—211
Deadwood Treasure Coach—140, 288
"Deaf Thompson"—179, 235
Dean, Prof.—390
Death penalty, Gordon Party—32
Debris—248
Declaration of Independence—264
Decorah Lode—440
Deer Ear—518
Deetkin, Julius—257
Deffebaugh, Mr.—413
Deffenbacher, Miss Eva—360
Deitrich, C. H.—399
Delicate, Thomas W.—304
Demereau, James—298
"Democratic"—315
Democratic party—329
Dempster, James—18
Denman, J. L.—404
Dennis, John—492
Dennis Peak—491, 505
Denver, Colorado, see "Colorado, Denver"
Department of Dakota—10
Deputy Revenue Collector—265
"Devil's Tower"—77, 117, 413
Dick Dunn & Newbanks' transportation lines—139
Dickerman, Prof. A. L.—337
Dickey, David—278
Dickinson, D. K.—361
Dickover, J. B.—502
"Diggins"—125
Dirkin, William—440
Discoveries, gold—7, 13, 44, 94, 96, 214
"Discovery Claim" Deadwood Gulch—128, 129, 210
District Courts, Black Hills—284, 375
District of Dakota—265
District No. 1, Lawrence County—404
District of Wyoming—265
Ditch—250
Dividend mine—441
Dodge, Capt. S. C.—229, 230

LAST HUNTING GROUND OF THE DAKOTAHS 547

Dodge County, Nebraska, see "Nebraska, Dodge County"
Dodge, Lt. Col. R. T.—87, 90, 91, 101, 111, 115, 125, 215, 488
Dodson, Capt.—410
Dodson, Hiram—425
"Dolcode" mine—339
Dole, Leopold—297
Dollard, Robert—524
Donahue, Ed.—403
Double Standard mine—438, 440
"Down Indian Creek" (route)—180
Doyle, Miss Kate—465
Drug store, first in Deadwood—257
Druggeman—198, 223
Driscoll Bros.—390, 518
Driscoll, R. H.—394
Drum, Col.—534, 535
Drum, F. G.—386
Dudley, Judge E. G.—247, 446, 464, 493, 497
Dudley & Caldwell's Addition—462
Dudley's, Judge E. G., mill—247
Duel, first fought in Black Hills—207
Duffy, J. C.—422
Dugdale, John—229
Duhamel, Peter—518
Duke, Calvin—468
Dumont (town)—444
Dumphy, Chas.—447
Dundy, Judge—89
Dunham, Fred—460
Dunlap, Valentine—107, 108, 111, 112, 114, 115
Dunn, Aaron—208
Dunn & Newbanks transportation lines—139
Dunn, W. L.—448
Dunphy, Chas. L.—345
Durango Gold Mining Company—386
Durango Lode—386
Durham, Ed—269, 358
Durst, John—297
Dusette, David—433

E

"Eagle's Nest"—288
Early, George—470
"Early Times" whiskey—177, 464
East Deadwood—248
East Orange, New Jersey, see "New Jersey, East Orange"
Eastern Star—317
Eaton, H. S.—498
Eaton, J. M.—510
Edgar, Fred—227
Edgemont (town)—134, 508, 509, 523
Edgerly, Lieut.—401
Edgerton, Alonzo J.—375
Edwards, Pinneo Bros. & Merrick firm—201
Edwards & Pinneo firm—201, 394
Edwards, Prof. Dolph—361, 398
Edwards, Thomas—440
Edwins, Jessie—415, 416
Egan, Capt.—181, 182, 183
Egan's, Capt., post—182
Eighth Cavalry Regiment—477, 533
Eighth Judicial District State Circuit Court—284, 285
El Caney—479
El Refugio mine—433
Electric Light Company, Rapid City—226
Electricity—305
Elizabethtown—244, 247, 264, 364, 365
Elk Creek—39, 80, 124, 135, 331, 364, 458, 480, 481, 483
Elk Point—520
Elkhorn narrow-gauge railroad—439, 483, 504
Elkhorn Railroad—444, 472, 475, 482, 509
Elkhorn river—23
Elkhorn route—192
Elkhorn station—480
Elliott, John M.—417
Elliott, O. B.—336
Ellis, Fort—147
Ellis, Jud—229
Ellison shaft—386
Elsner, Mrs.—362
Elm Creek Stone Co.—504

Elm Springs (town)—483
Elsiner, Chas.—464
Ely, Capt.—105
Ely, Sheriff D. N.—294
Elysium—505
Emanuel Brothers—253, 380, 381
Emanuel, Fred—253, 280, 381
Emanuel, Moses—253, 280, 381
Emergency Hospital at Lead—392
Emigration—138
Emma mine—433, 434
Empire bakery—362
Empire State mine—438, 440
Empire (town)—517
Enabling Act—523
Engh, Alex—132
Engh, Alf.—253, 380
Englesby, Joe—128
Englewood (town)—372, 444
English—254, 394
"English Orphans, The"—57
Enos, Cyrus H.—381, 392, 452
Enos Mill—381
"Enterprise"—437
"Enterprise," Central—396
Epidemics—301
Episcopal church of Deadwood—360
Episcopal societies—314, 389, 392, 431, 498
Erin mine—396
Erquhart, John—230, 231
Estella Del Norte Company—251, 347
"Etta Mine"—337, 338
"Eureka" mine—300
Evangeline mine—343
Evans (town)—509
Evans, Fred T.—138, 329, 340, 355, 357, 493, 497, 500
Evans Hotel—490, 492, 499, 500, 503, 504
Evans House—500
Evans, Lafayette—192
Evans, Mrs. R. H.—416, 425
Evans quarry—499, 500, 504
Evans, R. H.—185, 407, 416, 425
Evans' Transportation Company—139
Evans' Transportation train—139
"Evening Bulletin," Spearfish—429
Evergreen Cemetery—232, 233
Everly, Mr. Louis—492
Evil Spirit—82
Exelbee gang—421, 422, 423
Exelbee, George—421
Express, Stage, and Union Pacific Agent—133
Express and passenger line, first regular—139

F

F.E. & M.V.R.R., see "Fremont Elkhorn and Missouri Valley Railroad"
Fairburn—307
Fairview Addition—462
Fall, Lem—327
Fall River—80, 81, 292, 490, 499, 505
Fall River County—285, 294, 484-486, 494, 496, 509, 524, 531
False Bottom Creek—80, 193, 355, 405, 410, 411, 444
Fan—16, 37
Fantail gulch—438, 440, 441
Far West, steamer—163
Fargo-Dickover Block—500
Farley, John—465
Farmers' Alliance—419
"Farmers' Club"—418
Farmingdale (town)—354
Farnum, E. B.—172, 277, 279, 407
Farnum, Ed.—447
Farrell, Andrew—447
"Father of Waters"—187, 519
Faucett & Dalahout Earnest May & S. M. Kane firm—441
Faust, Emil—104, 136, 137, 210, 214, 453
Faust, Miss Maude—454
Favorite, G. C.—429
Fay, Mrs. R. B.—277
Fayel, John J.—353
Feay, A. T.—298
"Felix Poznansky, Dry Goods, Boots & Shoes, & C."—314

Fell, L. A.—391
Fenian Convention—5
Fenianism—4
Ferguson, D. G.—327
Ferguson, Dr. S. H.—337, 338
Ferguson, Thos.—136, 226
Ferguson, Wm.—433
Feri, Esperando—433
Fertilization, lands—79
Fetchet, Capt.—533, 534, 535
Fetterman, Fort—184, 268
Feuerstein, Henry—121
Fieldsend, Wm—510
Fifth Cavalry—169
Fifth Infantry, U.S.—147, 169
Fine, E. E.—408
Finlanders—394
Finnegan, Arthur—433
Fire of 1879, great—188, 207, 361, 362, 363
Fire company, first in Lead City—389
Fire, grass—126
Fire Hunter—97
First Cavalry, U.S.—171, 479
First Infantry—477
First Judicial District of Dakota Territory—283
First Methodist Episcopal Church of Deadwood—360
First National Banks—286, 304, 306, 318, 327, 357, 361, 394
First National Bank of Custer—304
First National Bank of Deadwood—286, 357, 362, 374
First National Bank of Lead—394, 452
First National Bank of Rapid City—306, 318, 327
First National Bank of Sturgis—469
Fischel, Max—205
Fiske, Jr., Jim—5
Fitzsimmons, J.—407
Five Eyes—97
Flaherty, Ed.—340
Flaherty, John—268
Flandreau—520, 521
Flandreau, Judge—521
Flanegan, W. M.—448
Flanner, A. J.—356
Flapjacks—27
Flavin, Pat—465, 468
Fletcher, James H.—524
Fletcher, Wm.—463
Flick, Dr. D.W.—104, 105, 106, 107, 108, 110, 111, 195, 196, 198, 214, 223, 224, 303
"Float"—252
Flood, Daniel P.—460
Flood of 1878, Deadwood—365
Flood of 1883, Great—80, 122, 365, 366, 370, 464
Floodgate—250
"Floral Valley"—301
Florence mine—433, 434
"Florence Mining Company"—433
Florman, family—121
Florman, Louis—335
Florman, Mrs. Robt.—120, 121
Florman organization—121
Florman, Robert—119, 120, 121, 122, 338, 433
Flouring mill, first in Spearfish—416, 431
Flucken, Christian—511
Flume—250, 251, 247, 348, 350, 351, 364, 416
Flume, bedrock—122, 348, 351, 352, 364, 368
Flynn, J. H.—448, 449
Foglesong, Wood—208, 448
Foley, Tim—386
Follenbee, the Rev. T.F.J.—468
Folsom—307
Folsom, Henry—408, 409
Football—395
Foran, John P.—297
Forest Hill—255, 362, 378
Forsyth, General Geo. W.—477, 537
Fort Meade colored infantry—474-75
Fort Pierre—227, 231, 463
Fort Pierre & Black Hills Railway—382, 482
Fort Pierre Route—269, 482
Fort Randall Government road—25
Fort, underground—220
"Fort Wayne" mine—343
Fortune, James—416
Fortune, Wilson & Bull firm—296
Foss, Bishop—388

Foster, Governor (Ohio)—528
Foster, Lt. J.G.—91
Fountain City—364
Fourteenth Infantry, U.S.—169
Fourth Infantry, U.S.—169
Fowler, Elijah—443
Fowler, Jas. W.—317, 321
Fox, Alvin—362
Fox, M. L.—374
Fraction Lode—242
Francis, Miss Carrie—467
Franklin, Harris—365, 374
Franklin, Henry—296
Franklin Live Stock Co.—518
Franklin Mill at Golden Gate—398
Franklin, Wm B.—353, 447
Fraser, W. K.—512
Frawley, Chief—361
Frazee, Prof.—391
Frease, Milton—339
Free gold—296, 337, 386, 398, 399, 489
Free Masons—472
Free milling—295, 298, 336, 345, 353, 370, 435
Freeman, Dr. J.W.—394
Freeze, W. A.—214
Fremont, Elkhorn and Missouri Valley Railroad (F.E. & M.V.R.R.)—141, 297, 307, 325, 372, 382, 443, 465, 480, 481, 490, 512
French—394
French, Capt.—152
French creek—44, 51, 61, 65, 70, 72, 80, 87, 92, 93, 103, 110, 114, 117, 118, 119, 122, 123, 129, 134, 135, 136, 192, 195, 213, 214, 215, 217, 239, 240, 245, 253, 292, 294, 297, 300, 301, 306, 341, 489
French creek gold—306
French explorers & trappers—1
French government—519
Frenchman's Mine—253
Friend, James—295
Frost, J. R.—407
Fruit culture—79
Fuller, A. G.—521
Fuller, H. J.—447
Fuller, M. M.—309, 310
Fuller, Miss Atlanta—436
Fullerton, Geo. H.—400
Funeral, first in Rapid City—231
Furnam & Brown—256
Fury, Col. John B.—491

G

G.A.R.—392, 472, 499
Gaffey, Lorin E.—424
Gale Hill—289
Galena—433, 465
Salena Silver Camp—433
Gall, Chief—147, 163
Gallinger, John—403
Galvin, David—433
Gamble, Representative—324
Gammon's livery stable—409
Gantz, J. S.—339
Ganzio—221
Garden City—362, 437, 438
"Garden of Eden"—508
Gardner, Capt. C. V.—178, 179, 180, 181, 193, 200, 208, 209, 243, 266, 277, 279, 399, 416, 417, 446, 491
Gardner, Charlotte—327
Gardner, Judge Wm.—285
Gardner, Maude A.—428
Gardner, N. H.—230
Gardner, W. D.—214
Gardner & Brown firm—258
Gardner & Co.—205, 208, 256
Garfield Administration, President—284
Garlick Bros. Firm—258
Garlington, E. A. First Lieutenant & Adjutant—480, 537
Garretsons, Fanny—262
Garrison, A. S.—207
Garrison & Dennee firm—258
Garvey, Mr.—482
Gashwiler, Gen.—338
Gaston, J. A.—447, 448

Gaston & Shankland firm—258
"Gate City"—122, 314, 449
Gate City Hose Company, No. 1—327
Gatling guns—88, 150, 534
Gay, Alfred—86, 100, 128, 407, 489
Gay party—407
Gay, Wm.—128, 129, 396, 407, 422
Gaylor, J. A.—469
Gayville—208, 244, 245, 267, 268, 270, 278, 356, 396
Gearney, M.—407
General Custer House—257, 360
General merchandise store, 1st in Black Hills—198
General merchandise store, first in Rapid City—228
Genesee Valley Canal—450
Geology, geologists, geological reports—33, 75, 91, 92, 248
George, John S.—353
Georgetown, Colorado, see "Colorado, Georgetown"
Gerig, Tony—415
Germans—394
Getchell, I. W.—214
Gettysburg, battle of—476
Ghost Dances—529, 530, 533
"Ghost dance" shirts—530
Giant mine—127, 396
Gibbon's command—159, 160
Gibbons, General—147, 151
Gibson, B.—336
Gibson, Hugh—425
Gifford, Daniel—522
Gifford, Oscar S.—524
Gilbert, H. N.—243
Giles, A.—570
Giles, H. H.—512
Gill, John W.—269
Gillespie, Fred—500
Gillette, D. W.—449
Gillette, M. N.—258
Gillette's ranch—306
Gilman, Salisbury and Patrick, Messrs.—140
Gilt Edge mine—318
Gird, A. W.—316
Gird & Manus firm—316
Girdler & Orr's Mill—398
Glaciers—248
Gleason, W. E.—522
Glover, Geo. M.—436
Godard, H. A.—524
Godard, Harry—509
Godard, Herbert—142
Goddard, J. S.—400
Godfrey, Lieutenant—151, 153, 160
Goff, J. J.—440
Golconda—60
Gold—13, 44, 54, 55, 56, 57, 58, 59, 90, 92, 93, 103, 106, 114, 140, 209, 210, 246, 249, 250, 251, 252, 263, 294, 295, 297, 309, 323, 341, 346, 348, 351, 352, 433, 437, 454, 455, 522
Gold-bearing ledges—248, 343, 349, 353, 355, 381, 431, 432
"Gold Belt"—253
Gold Bug mine—434
Gold, coarser—251
Gold, deep gravel—93, 248, 357
Gold, discoveries—7, 13, 44, 94, 96, 214
Gold dust—129, 136, 142, 194, 203, 206, 210, 245, 246, 249, 259, 261, 262, 286, 288, 332, 350, 351, 357, 445
Gold dust, first in Black Hills—210
Gold dust postage—144
Gold dust shipment, first large from Black Hills—136, 210
Gold Fish Mining Co.—296
Gold lands—96
Gold miners—83
Gold, produced from quartz by machinery process, first in Black Hills—205
Gold-producing region—209
Gold, quartz deposits—11
Gold reduction operations, first in Black Hills—398
Gold Run—8, 286, 368, 380, 387
Gold Run Gulch—254, 380, 386, 452
Gold Run Gulch, recorder—452
Gold Scales—249
Gold & Silver Extraction, Mining & Milling Company—371
Gold testing—93

Gold, washing out—93, 249
Goldberg, J.—256, 452
Goldberg's J., store—256, 452
"Golden"—340
Golden Gate—396
Golden Reward Chlorination plant—370, 371, 439, 440, 441
Golden Sands mine—441
"Golden Slipper" mine—339
"Golden Star" mine—253, 380, 382, 383
Golden Summit mine—335, 337
Golden Terry—253
Goldman—290
Gooch, W. C.—295
Good Bull—97
Goodfellow, W. R.—522
Goodsell, M. B.—408, 415
Goose creek—148, 169
Gordon, see "Nebraska, Gordon"
Gordon, John—14, 16, 18, 29, 30, 32, 50, 55, 57, 59, 88, 89
Gordon Party (expedition)—14, 16, 28, 32, 104, 138, 139
Gordon Party code—26
Gordon stockade—48, 49, 50, 51, 53, 54, 57, 58, 59, 60, 63, 84, 86, 87, 88, 92, 100, 118, 195, 213, 239, 240
Gordon party tent fire—52
Gordon's train—105, 130
Gore, Sir George—4
Gores, C. H.—511
Gossage, Joseph B.—315, 316
Gourard, Frank—539
Government Farm—126, 134, 136
"Government herd"—531
Government intervention—25, 54, 57, 61, 70-71, 83, 84, 85, 87, 95, 98, 101, 105
Government lumbering restrictions—305
Governor, Lincoln Territory—281
Grable, Francis C.—434
Grady, Alex—421
Graham, C. H.—373
Graham, Miss Anna—388, 391
Graham, Robert—524
Graham, W. L.—418
Grambery & Co.—328
Grand Army—232
Grand Central Hotel, Deadwood—257, 279, 358
Grand Charity and Widow's and Orphans' Funds—455
Grand Council of Anointed High Priests of South Dakota—455
Grand Junction (mine)—295, 490, 491, 493
Grand Junction Company—295
Grand Master of the Grand Lodge of South Dakota—455
Grand Prize mine—401
Grand River—170, 530, 531, 534
"Grand View" mine—300
Granite Hills—300
"Granite Reef" mine—297, 298
Grant, H. S.—443
Grant, President U. S.—96
Grashul (town)—483
Graves, Leonard R.—361, 374, 448, 493, 497
Gray Eagle Lode—342
Gray, Jack—446, 449, 450
Gray, Mrs. John—448
Great Rush of 1876—7
Great Sioux Reservation in Dakota—527
Great Spirit—82
Greeley, Lieutenant—537
Green, C. J.—391
Green Mountain—440
Greenough, John—440, 441
Greenough, Mosier and Harris firm—441
Gregg, Harry M.—428
Gregory Gold Mining Co.—345
Grier, T. J.—374, 386, 394
Griffin, F. H.—340
Griffith, Andy—231
Grimmett, Wm.—510
Grimshaw, R. E.—327
Grindstone manufactory—509
Grizzly bears—111, 114
Grizzly Bear mine—335, 336
Grizzly creek—337
Grizzly Gulch—348
Grocery store, first in Deadwood—256

"Grub"—117, 239
"Grub boxes"—16, 136
"Grub stake"—249
Grubbs, Cora—428
Gulch towns—418
Gulf of Mexico—384, 519
Gun clubs—377
Gunnison mine group—441
Gurhurst, P. A.—387, 392, 394, 449, 450, 452, 453
Gypsum—79, 332, 333, 406, 432, 470
Gypsum Butte—505

H

H.F.—392
H. N. Gilbert & Son—235
H. N. Merrit & Brother—433
Hacker, Geo.—447
Hagerty, F. H.—524
Haggan, J. B.—381
Hale, Col. Hiram F.—456
Hale, J. A.—518
Hall, Miss Ada C.—465
Hall, H. S.—326
Hall, Lt. C. F.—91
Halley, James—278, 306, 307, 317, 320, 327, 348, 470, 498
Halley, John—306
Halley, Rev. C. E.—264
Haltner, John—448
Hancher, the Rev. Dr.—233
Hancock, General—6, 13
Hand, Jas.—356
Hangman's Hill—320, 331
Hanley, W. F.—304
Hann, Peter—447
Hannibal, Ross—440
Hanrahan, C. E.—356
Hanson, Andrew—439
Hanson, J. R.—310, 522
Harding, J. A.—360
Hardscrabble mine—441
Hardware store, first in Deadwood (Black Hills)—257
Hare, Bishop—360, 469
Hare, Geo. E.—412
Hare, Lieutenant—154
Harlow, W. H.—225, 288, 303, 306, 307, 429
Harlowe, W. H.—214, 305
Harmon, Capt.—463, 464
Harmony mine group—440
Harnett and Howard—6
Harney City—61, 195, 347
Harney, General—3, 4, 75, 520
Harney granite uplift—292
Harney, Henry—132, 380
Harney Hydraulic Gold Mining Co.—348
Harney Peak Consolidated Tin Company—325, 339
Harney range—77, 298, 301, 309
Harney's Peak—11, 12, 43, 61, 75, 77, 103, 109, 110, 114, 117, 127, 131, 300, 301, 308, 325, 335, 337, 338, 339
Harper, Lewis—321
Harrington, Lieut.—152
Harris, Mrs. C. B.—465
Harris, Jack—423
Harrison, Benjamin—524
Harrison, D. F.—510
Harrison, D. T.—511
Harrison, John—230
Harvey, Arthur—234, 347
Harvey, Attorney Tom—196, 197, 202, 203, 223, 303, 335
Harvey, Robt.—294
Haserodt, Capt.—303
Hat Creek Station—142, 144, 180, 181, 218, 221, 237
Hat Creek (town)—136, 166, 181, 236, 287, 485, 509, 518
Hatch, Herbert F.—434
Haucher, the Rev. John W.—498
Hauser, George—124, 125
Hawgood, Chambers & Workman firm—441
Hawgood, John—442
Hawgood & Wilcox firm—442
Hawk-Man—536
Hawley, N. H.—134, 135
Hawley, Capt. W.—91
Hay creek coal fields—412, 432, 517

Hayden, Wm.—410
Hayes, President R. B.—189, 284, 375
Hayward (town)—292, 294, 303, 348, 349, 411, 412
Hayward, Chas.—292, 293, 303, 341, 349
Hayward, Mrs. Chas.—225
Hazen, Benjamin—403
He-Takes-the Indian-Soldier—97
Hearst, Geo.—381, 382, 393
Hearst Free Library—393
Hearst, Phoebe—393
Heart river—170
Hecht, Chas.—179, 180
Heinrich, George—269
Helena, Montana, see "Montana, Helena"
Henderson, Old Bart—332, 333, 350
Henry, Brevet Brig. Gen. Guy V.—70, 72
Henry & Grant firm—417
Henzie, A. T.—258
Hepburn, James & wife—134
"Herald", Central—396
"Herald", Custer—223
Herman, John—205, 229, 456, 457
Hermosa—297, 307, 538
"Hermosa Pilot"—315
Herring, Bland—458
Herring, Henry—230
Hibbard, Capt. William H.—279, 280
Hickoc, Wild Bill—73, 74, 188, 270, 271, 379, 450
Hicks, Jas.—128
Hidden Treasure Gulch—399, 400
Hidden Treasure mine—208, 253, 399
High Bear—97
High School, first graduating class in Rapid City—322
High Wolf—97
Highland mine—380, 382, 383
Hildebrand & Harding firm—129, 258
Hildebrand, John—247, 511
Hildebrand, L. F.—176
Hill City—119, 131, 132, 193, 254, 286, 311, 325, 335, 336, 337, 339, 340, 342, 489, 491
Hill, Geo. D.—522
Hill, Henry—388, 390
Hill, M. F.—473
Hinch, Jack—267
Hinman, S. D.—95
Hodgson, Capt.—153
Hodnett, John P.—4
Hoehn, Max—460, 465, 467, 473
Hoffman, Chris—358
Hoffman, H. A.—522
Hoisting machinery—132, 336, 340, 381
Holcomb, E.—518
Holcomb, Fred—518
"Hold up your hands!"—285
"Hold-ups"—140, 286, 287, 482
Holiday, Richard—296
Holland Charles—274, 275, 365
Holman cut-off road—490
Holmes, Chas.—296
Holt County—20
Holt, R.—408
Holthausen, Gustave—368
Holweg, Olaf—470
"Holy of holies"—95
Holy Terror Gold Mining Co.—340, 353, 354
"Home Forum"—436
"Home-Guards"—533
Home Missionary Society—314
Homestake bullion—140, 141
Homestake Company—127, 132, 253, 295, 354, 361, 375, 380, 381, 382, 383, 384, 386, 388; 392, 393, 394, 398, 401, 402, 452, 482
Homestake Consolidated Company—291, 382, 383, 385
Homestake Narrow-gauge Railway—480
Homestake machinery—132
Homestake mill, old—386
Homestake Miller—132, 384
Homestake Mine No. 1—345, 381
Homestake mine, purchase price—132
Homestake mines timbering—384
Homestead, first in Black Hills—212
Homestead law—527
Homicide, justifiable—207
"Honest Dick"—134, 180
Hood, Humphrey—422, 423

Hoodoo mine—434
Hooper & Ayers firm—345
Hooper, Thos.—100, 104, 123, 183, 195, 202, 213, 214, 223, 303
Hopkins, T.—447
Hornblende—295
Hornick, John—138
Horse Creek—235
Horsehead creek—485
Horse racing—395
Horse steak—170
Horse stealing—176, 286, 331, 410, 420
Horse thieves, white—177, 331, 420, 424
Horses, U. S. Cavalry—111
Horseshoe Company—440, 441
Horseshoe mine—440
Horsford, Dick—179, 180, 491
Hose Companies Nos. 1 & 2, Spearfish—431
Hose Company No. 1, Sturgis—469
Hot Springs—207, 224, 307, 446, 484, 487, 490, 491, 494, 495-508
Hot Springs Bank—498
Hot Springs Fire Department—503
Hot Springs, first white man—488
Hot Springs Hook and Ladder Company—503
Hot Springs Hose Company No. 1—503
Hot Springs Library Association—496
Hot Springs Town-site Company—494, 495, 496
Hot Springs Water, Light & Power Co.—503
Hotbrook canyon—490, 508
Hotbrook creek—485
Hotchkiss guns—533
Hotel, first in Black Hills—198
Hotel, first in Deadwood—257
Hotel, first in Lead City—388
Hotel, first in Rapid City—228
Hotel Harney Company—133, 328
House of Representatives, Lincoln Territory—281
Howard, C. K.—518
Howard, Wm.—447
Howe, Billy—422
Hozeman, D., Browning & Wringrose firm—258
Hubbard, Judge—138
Hubbell, J. S.—400
Hubrecken, Prof.—338
Hudson Bay Company—8
Huffman, E. F.—460
Hughes, A. B.—225, 294, 303
Hughes, M. S.—343
Hughes, R. B. "Dick"—142, 200, 214, 233, 269, 315, 339, 343, 446, 594
Hull, H. F.—100
Hump—536
Humphrey, J. M.—518
Hunter, Jack—205, 253
Huntington Mill—345
Huntsville, Alabama—477
Huss, F. C.—518
Hutchinson, John—522
Hydraulic flumes—251, 348
Hydraulic Gold Mining Company—251
Hydraulic placer mines—250, 251
Hydrodynamics—251

I

I.O.O.F.—317, 392
I.O.R.M.—392
I.X.L.—257
Idaho Territory—449, 522
Iler, Walter—286, 287
Illinois, Chicago—13, 138, 169, 192, 269, 300, 340, 429, 441, 494
Illinois, Quincy—338
Illinois, Springfield—521, 522
Incandescent light—327
Incorporation, Deadwood—364
Indemnity lands—525
"Independent" Deadwood—373
"Index", Rapid City—315
Indian Agents—146
Indian Campaign of 1876 (Custer's Last Stand)—146
"Indian Country"—519
Indian creek—182
Indian Crow—7

Indian Department—146, 520, 528
Indian fighting tactics—171
Indian police—534, 539
Indian schools—324
Indian supplies—116
Indian Territory—3, 105, 106, 134
Indian territory cessions—97
Indian title—254, 266, 283, 414, 520, 527
Indian traditions—82
Ingersoll, John—416
Ingham, the Rev. S. W.—522
Ingleside (town)—364, 369, 378
Ingram, D. B. & Company—353
Inter-urban, narrow gauge short lines—372, 373
Interior Department—90, 96
International Hotel—211, 224, 328
Inyan-Kara—11, 75, 77, 118
Iowa (state)—95, 329
Iowa, Ames—192, 193, 407, 410
Iowa, Davenport,—381, 460
Iowa, Dubuque—520
Iowa, LeMars—297
Iowa, Mount Pleasant—376
Iowa, Red Oak—344
Iowa, Sioux City—6, 13, 14, 15, 18, 21, 55, 56, 59, 69, 88, 103, 104, 105, 107, 138, 139, 192, 275
Iowa State University—329
Irion, Jimmy—411
Irish—394
Irish gulch—343, 345
Irish-Americans—4, 394
Iron Creek—130
"Iron Hill"—432
Irons, Frank—374
Irwin, T. B.—518
Isadora mine group—441
Italians—394, 433

J

J. R. Mine—342
J. Vandaniker & McGavock—257
Jackson, A.—404
Jackson, E. P.—422
Jackson, General Stonewall—213
Jackson, Henry—348
Jackson, Sam.—403
Jacobs, Billy—116, 118
Jacobs purchase—198, 223
Jacoby, Jas.—340
James, (Assessor Lawrence County)—356
Jameson, G. T.—374
Janson & Bliss firm—258
Jaquette, Surgeon—91
Jayne, Dr. Wm.—521, 522
Jefferson, Thomas—407, 408
Jenny Expedition—87, 100, 122, 124, 134, 234, 488, 489
Jenny, Walter P.—90, 91, 92, 93, 135, 338, 341, 406, 488, 490
Jennings, Dr. R. D.—207, 484, 493, 494, 497
Jenny's military escort—114
Jenny's Report—91
Jenny stockage—198
Jensen & Bliss hardware store—362
Jentes' Corner—388
Jersey City, New Jersey, see "New Jersey, Jersey City"
Jesuit missionaries—13
Jewelry store, first in Deadwood—258
Jewett, Justice O. W.—465, 473, 475
Jewett, Wm. T.—336
Jewett & Dickison line—139
Jim Creek—41
Jobbing trade—132
Johnson, the mind reader—508
Johnson, Reddy & wife—231
Johnston, C. D.—207
Johnston, C. F.—511
Johnston, Edward W.—348
Johnston, Hugh—192
Johnston, John—192, 193, 407, 417, 418
Johnston, "Skew"—212
Jolly, Joseph—524
Jones, G. H.—185

Jones, G. W.—230, 231
Jones, Harry M.—428
Jones, J. C.—443
Jones, John W.—394
Jones, the Rev. H. H.—314
Jones, Smoky—253, 380, 387
Jones, Thos.—388
Jones, W. E.—208, 209, 469
Jorgans, H. M.—414
"Journal", Oakdale—20
"Journal", Rapid City—200, 314, 338
"Journal", Sioux City—6
Judd, Sylvester—297
Juderline, J.—297
Judge of First Black Hills District Court—316
Jule, the Father—533, 539
Junction City—491
Justice of the Peace, Deadwood—214, 277
Juvenile Hose Company—443

K

K. of P.—392
Kane, John—269
Kane, S. M.—441
Kane, Surgeon—91
Kansas (state)—73, 74, 270, 454, 477, 480, 510
Kansas, Kansas City—386, 439
Kearney, Fort Phil—184
Keeler, Wm—347, 350
Keets, Henry—399, 400, 429
Keets mine—399, 400
Keiffer, E. P. (Keifer) provisional justice of the peace—196, 202, 214
Kelliher, John S.—327
Kelliher, Maurice—518
Kellogg, E. F.—348
Kellogg, L. D.—381
Kelly, R. D.—201
Kemper, Kate M.—428
Kent, R.—7
Kentucky, Bowling Green—284
Kentucky, Louisville—411
Kenyon, Ralph—296
Kenyon, Robert—86, 100, 131, 247
Keogh, Capt.—152, 161, 170, 479
Key City Hose Company—469
Keya Paha river—24, 25
Keystone—348, 353, 354
Keystone Gold Mining Co.—353
Keystone State—449, 454
"Kid"—421, 422
Kiese—198
Kildonan Chlorination works—372
Kildonan plant—439, 440
Kimball, G.—336
Kimmel, Prof.—390
Kimmel, Singleton—447
Kind, Ezra—7, 8
King, Dick—135, 136
King, Dido—134
King, G. F.—440
King, Jack—179, 180, 491
King, Lt. A. D.—91
King Solomon mine—335, 337
King, Wm.—7
Kingbury, Lt. F. W.—91
King's College, London—494
Kinney, T.—192
Knight, E. D.—212
Knight of Malta in Dakota Commandery No. 1—455
Knights of Pythias—317, 365, 389, 431, 436, 471, 472
Knights Templar—455
Knowles, Freeman—373
Koppleton, Peter—447
Kubler, Joseph—199, 305
Kurtz, Keller—172, 277
Kuykendall, Judge W. L.—136, 256, 258, 264, 270, 275, 356, 407

L

Labarge, Tom—124
La Barre, L. C.—300

LeBesch, Desire—448
La Chappell, Desire—440
Lackawana mine—438, 440
Laddingen Bros.—518
Lafayette College, Easton, PA.—376
Laflesh, W. W.—498
Laham, J.—407
Lake, Harry—286, 287
Lake & Halley firm—327
Lake, Halley & Patterson firm—327
Lake, Madame Agnes—74
Lake, R. C.—317
Lake, Richard C.—327, 498
Lake Tomb and Lemmon—518
Lakota spring—502, 503
Lamb, Lyman—17, 18, 32, 43, 44, 50, 195, 232
Lame Lance—106
Lampert & Co.—317
Lampkin, Chas.—518
Lancaster Mill—398
Lance creek—290
Land Office, U. S.—212, 228, 342
Land Office, U. S., at Deadwood—212, 408
Lane, E. C.—460
Lane, Enos—443
Langrishe Comedy Company—389
Langrishe, Jack—200, 205, 206, 207, 211, 276
Langrishe, Mrs. Jack—205, 206
Langrishe Theater Building—207
Langrishe Troupe—205, 206
Laramie—48, 121, 126, 218, 237, 270
Laramie, Fort—3, 7, 10, 11, 59, 60, 61, 62, 67, 68, 69, 86, 90, 91, 92, 116, 118, 120, 125, 128, 129, 134, 136, 142, 144, 147, 163, 164, 179, 180, 181, 218, 221, 235, 236, 268, 269, 278, 280, 452, 454, 491, 509
Laramie River—9
Laravie, Joe—492, 493, 497
Lardner, party—127, 128, 130
Lardner, Wm—104, 127, 128, 129, 396
La Rue, Ella—262
La Rue, W. H.—192
"Last Chance" code—440
"Last Find"—300
Laughlin & Merrick firm—199, 223
Laughlin, W. A.—199, 200
"Laughing Sam"—331
Lavender, A. W.—356
Laverne (town)—354
Lawrence, A. G.—95
Lawrence, Col. John—356
Lawrence County—189, 191, 285, 287, 343, 355, 356, 357, 364, 403, 415, 418, 426, 436, 442, 444, 456, 458, 459, 460, 461, 464, 484, 510, 523, 524
Lawrence County Agricultural Association—418
Lawrence County Bank—469
Lawrence County, commissioner—134
Lawrence County farmers—418
Lawrence County, first sheriff—189
Lawrence County Republican Central Committee—454
Lawrence County sheriff—191
Lawrence, George—470
Lawson, Lt. James—91
Lawyer, first in Deadwood—258
Lawyers, first to practice in Black Hills—202
Lazelle, Major H. M.—462, 477
Le De Moss, Wm.—258
Lead (city)—105, 115, 125, 191, 192, 210, 295, 343, 345, 372, 373, 380, 381, 382, 383, 386, 387, 388, 392, 394, 395, 401, 402, 426, 432, 436, 449, 452, 453, 480, 482, 524
Lead City Hose Company No. 1—389
Lead City Hose Company No. 2—389
Lead City Opera House—389
Lead City water system—389
Lead School Building—390
Lead Town-site Company—452
Ledges, gold-bearing—248, 343, 349, 353, 355, 381, 431, 432
Ledwich Brothers' Mill—398
Lee & Brown's log cabin—255, 256, 258
Lee, Craven—255
Lee Street bridge, Deadwood—367
Leedy, Cassius M.—321
Leedy springs—231, 321
Legislative Assembly, Lincoln Territory—281
Legislature of 1883—324

LAST HUNTING GROUND OF THE DAKOTAHS 553

Legislature of 1885—322, 428
Legislature of 1887—322
Le Gro, Capt. E.—231, 232, 233
Le Gro, Vena—312, 316
Le Mars, Iowa, see "Iowa, Le Mars"
Lent, W. S.—346
Leopold mine—441
Leroys, Kittie—262
Lessell, the Rev. E. J. K.—360
Levings, Homer—404
Lewis Hall—312
Lewis, J. H.—339
Lewis, Wm.—312, 339
Liberal League— 365
Liberty Lode—440
Library Association, Rapid City—316
Library Hall—232, 316, 317, 318
Liebman, M.—418
"Lightning" mine—295, 297
Limerick—5
Limestone—432
Limestone ranges—80
Limestone Springs—230, 321
Lincoln, Fort Abraham—10, 147, 148, 162, 163, 164, 170, 187, 479
Lincoln Land Co.—508
Lincoln Territory location—281, 282
Lindley, W. P.—418
Little Assiniboine—536
Little, B. A.—192
Little Big Horn—148, 149, 152, 154, 164, 168, 170, 210, 219, 476, 479
Little Big Horn tragedy—146, 411
Little Blue Water, battle of—520
Little Bonanza mine—441, 452
Little Eagle—536
Little Horn river—148, 150, 152, 153, 160, 167, 230
Little Missouri river—149, 411, 418
Little Muddy—149
Little Rapid creek—41, 127, 128, 129, 343, 390
Little Spearfish creek—128, 130
Little Wound—97, 530, 536
L. S. Parkhurst & Co.—205
Livermore, S. S.—230
Livery barn, first in Deadwood—257
Livery Stable, first in Black Hills—212
Livingstone, Mr.—519
"Lizzie" mine—297
Lo family—115
Lobdell, A. C.—269
Lockouts—39
Locomotive, steam, first in Black Hills—324
Log cabin in Black Hills 1875, first—104
Logan, B. B.—18
"Logan" outfit—49
Lone Horse—97
Lonegan, Father John—360
Long Branch Hall—212
Long, Chas.—18, 50
Long Pine—23
Long-haired Chief (Custer)—151
Lookout (town)—345, 353, 354
Lookout mine—345
Lookout Mountain—7, 8, 274, 406, 409, 420
Lorrimer, H. H.—466
Lost Bonanza mine—298
"Lost Mining District"—128
Lot-jumpers—267
Loudon, A. H.—396
Louisiana Purchase—519
Louisville, Kentucky, see "Kentucky, Louisville"
Louthan, Dr. J. M.—417, 421, 423, 429
Loveland, Edwin—309, 340
Low grade mining statistics—345, 370, 383
Lowe, Richard—124, 125
Lower Brule reservation—527
Lower Central—398
Lowie, Dr.—388
"Lucky Boy" mine—354
Ludlow, William—10
Lumber shipping station, largest—305
Lundt, Henry—441
Lundt and Toney firm—440
Lutheran societies, churches—314, 392
Lymer, the Rev. F. E.—468

Lynch, Dr. H. P.—270, 475
Lynd, Jas. W.—521

Mc

McAleer, Jack—247, 296
McCain, L. P.—436
McCall, Jack—270
McCarthy, Bill—421
McCarty, Jerry—267
McCarty, P. B.—328
McClellan, John—520, 521
McClung, J. C.—473
McClure, John—510
McConachie, J. T.—425
McCoy, Pearly—388
McCullough, Hugh—335
McCumsey, Thos.—512
McDon, Luke—448
McDonald, Angus—18, 50
McDonald, B. W.—338
McDonald, Dan, "Black"—18
McDonald, Dan "Red"—18, 60, 61, 62
McDonald, J. C.—336
McDonald, L. W.—337
McGee, Judge Levi—285
McGillicuddy, Dr. V. T.—91, 92, 488, 524
McGovern, heirs—441
McGovern, Hugh—441, 447
McGovern, Thos.—441
McGregor, Major Robert—239, 477
McGuire, Dennis—491
McGuire, Phil—447
McHenry, J.—407
McIntosh, Lieutenant—152
McIntyre, J. D.—387
McKay, Ed—128, 129, 396
McKay, Hugh—231
McKinney, Dr. A. W.—258, 264
McKinney, Fort—531
McKinnis, Chas.—356
McKirihan, Joe—343
McLaren, R.—447
McLaren, Thos.—18, 51, 59
McLaughlin & Cassel's Custom Mill—398
McLaughlin, Ford—297
McLaughlin, Frank—297, 457
McLaughlin, Judge D.—364
McMahon, Frank—327
McMahon, Hugh—311
McMahon, Mike—404, 473
McMaken mine—298
McMasters, Angus—286
McMillan Extension—462
McMillan, J. C.—465
McMillan, Wm.—462, 464, 475
McMillan's Southwestern and Southern Addition—462
McMurtie, Wm.—339
McNamara, John J.—317
McPherson, D. A.—361, 374, 469, 470
McPherson, James—187, 188, 191, 361
McShearer, James—297
McSloy, J.—473
McVey, E.—447

M

M.W.A.—392
M. H. Day & Son Co.—318
Mackin, the Rev. Father—388
Madden, Thos.—234
Madding, Jas. H.—414
Madison, Pap—231
Madison, Rufus—229, 339
Maggie claim—441
Magnesium—486
Maguire, Judge H. N.—264, 367
Mail carrier, U. S., first—415
Mail sacks—142
Mail service for Black Hills (private & U. S.)—140, 141, 144, 179

"Mail" Spearfish—429
Mallory, T. H.—99, 130
Mammoth spring—501
Mandan County—510
Manitou—163
Manning, John—186, 187, 191, 287, 356, 361, 456
Manning, Mrs. John—448
Manning, W. F.—316
"Mansion, the" mine—343
Manufacturing—205, 317, 365, 470
Manuel brothers, see "Emanuel"
Marble—432
Mark Twain mine—441
Marriage contract—415
Marriage, first in Lead—453
Marriage, first in Rapid City—316
Marsh, R. R.—257
Marshal, U. S.—421
Marshall, C. W.—227
Marsten, Wm—136, 226, 227, 340
Marthin & Shocklay firm—515
Martin, Samuel H.—458
Martin, W. P.—136, 226, 227
Marty, the Right Rev. Martin—465
Maryland and Virginia mines—440
Masonic funeral services, first in Black Hills—207, 275, 365
Masonic Hall—317, 388, 415
Masons—365, 388, 431, 455, 471, 504, 515
Masters, Henry—521
Matheieson & Goldberg firm—258
Mathews, Tom—415
Mathias, John C.—510
Matkin & Co.—258
Matteson, Chas D.—329
Mattox, Geo.—403
Maurer, John—426
Mauvaises Terres—33, 113
Maxwell, Joe—400
May, A. S.—524
May & Appel fast freight line—208
May, Col.—270
May, D. B.—290
May, Ernest—388, 392, 394, 440, 441, 442, 454
"Mayflower" mine—295, 297
Mayo—307
Mayor of Cheyenne—279
Mayor, Deadwood—173, 277, 364
Mayor, first of Greater Deadwood—277, 364
Mead, Joel—295
Meade County—285, 355, 458-461, 462, 470, 480, 524
Meade County Bank—467, 469, 470
Meade County Land and Improvement Company—460
Meade, Fort—459, 462, 464, 471, 472, 473, 476-480, 512, 531
Meade, Gen. George C.—476
Meade, John—366
Mealy & Smith grocery store—388
Meat shop, first in Deadwood—257
Medary—520, 521
Medary, S. A.—521
"Medicine man"—146
Medicine Root Creek—530
Medill, Alexander—338
Mellette, Arthur C.—523, 524
"Melodeon"—262
Memorial to Congress—264, 266
Merchants, merchandise in Black Hills—131
Merchants' National Bank—362
Merrick, A. W.—199, 200, 201, 279, 304, 305, 374
Merrick & Adams firm—201
Merritt, H. N.—433
Merritt (town)—354
Merritt Nos. 1 & 2—433
Messiah Craze—529, 530, 539
Metcalf, M. D.—522
Metallic Streak—431
Metallurgical laboratory—322, 323
Methodist Episcopal services, first in Rapid City—314
Methodist societies—304, 354, 360, 368, 388, 392, 397, 416, 431, 436, 443, 465, 467, 468, 498, 515
Metz, Mr.—121, 237
Metz, Mrs.—121, 219, 237
Metz Party massacre—120, 179, 217, 218

Mica—294, 298, 300, 337, 338
Mica, large sheets—300
Mica lubrication factory—304
Mica mines, Custer County—298
Mica mine, first workable—298
Mica trust—300
Michigan (state)—187
Michigan, Detroit—520
Michigan Southern Railway Co.—340
Miles City—421, 422
Miles, General—174, 531, 536, 538, 539
Military expedition, first in Black Hills—213, 292
Military opposition to immigration, see also "Government Intervention"—25, 54, 57, 61, 70-71, 84, 85, 101, 108, 113, 114, 125, 129, 130, 131, 134
Military reservation—236
Mill, J. R.—339
Mill, P. O.—407
Miller, George—185
Miller, H. A.—429
Miller & Mather firm—258
Miller & McPherson banking house—191, 258
Miller, J. K. P.—187, 188, 191, 373
Miller, John—335
Miller, Judge Joseph—258, 264, 270, 356
Miller, Mel—327
Miller, Peter—511
Miller, R. H.—192
Miller, S. B.—524
Millett, R. D.—426
Mills, Capt.—88, 170, 171, 172
Mills, G. H.—214
Mills & Hollis law firm—269
Mills, the Rev. B. F.—397
Mills, Stephen H.—304, 328
"Milton's Paradise Lost"—57
Milwaukee parties—348, 353
Mine, first to be tested chemically and found to be refractory—438
Mineconjons—95
"Mineral belt"—309
"Mineral Hill"—352
Mineral Ridge—298
Mineral Water—487
Mineralogy—323
Miner's claims—96
Miners' gold pan—246
Miners' Hotel—388
Miners' inches—124
Miners' jury—196, 198
Miners' & Mechanic's Bank—203
Miners' meeting, first in Black Hills—118, 134, 195
Miners' pecularities—254
Miners' petition—99
Miners' property guardians—100, 104
Miners' Union—365, 392, 436
Miners' Union Hall, first in Lead City—388, 389
Miners' Union Opera House—393
Mining Camps—102, 132, 164, 203, 205, 228, 244
Mining district, first organization in northern Black Hills—127
Mining machinery—445
Mining notice—333
Mining regions—119
"Mining Review"—373, 374
Mining, systematic—94
Minnehaha County—524
Minnekahta—488, 508
Minnekahta Falls—505
Minnekahta Hose Company—503
Minnekahta Hotel—494
Minnekahta junction—490, 508
Minnekahta legend—487, 488
Minnekahta spring—490, 492, 494, 495, 497, 499, 501
Minnesela (town)—446, 511
Minnesota mine—343
Minnesota (state)—140, 424, 428, 520
Minnesota, St. Paul—138, 253, 477, 521, 533
Minstrel troupe, first in Black Hills—212
Missing persons—84
Missionary of Black Hills, martyred—203
Mississippi river—1, 23, 519
Missouri, Kansas City—6
Missouri river—1, 4, 6, 10, 15, 55, 68, 72, 97, 124, 125, 138, 164, 174, 176, 187, 229, 380, 519, 520
Missouri River Agencies—174, 235

Missouri River Indian Reservations—422
Missouri (state)—95, 454
Missouri, St. Louis—95, 295
Mitchell, D. L.—447
Mitchell & Thompson firm—443
Mitchell, W. H.—315, 316
Mitchell, Wm—512
"Mitchell's bar"—348
Mix, Capt.—48, 66, 67
Moccasin-shaped tub—501
Modern Woodmen—431, 472, 504
Mohr, F. H.—320
Moliter, Albert—441
Monahan, Thos.—86
Money, first coined in Black Hills—203
Monroe County—450
Monroe, James—519
Monroe mine—402
Montana—119, 184, 186, 189, 245, 248, 275, 341, 449, 516, 521, 523
"Montana" bar—341
Montana City—264, 364
Montana Company—135, 407
Montana hay-makers—410
Montana, Helena—184, 187, 188
Montana Herd—186, 204, 410
Montana Herd, Indian raid—273
Montana Lake—412
Montana Mine—345
Montana miners—129, 176, 184, 349
Montana, Stonewall—422
Monteverdes—262
Montezuma hill—343
Moody, C. C.—462, 469
Moody & Elliott firm—469
Moody, Jim—231
Moody, Judge Gideon C.—284, 375, 523, 524
Moon, S. M.—269
Moon, Thos.—124, 125
Moore, Homer E.—456
Moore, J. M.—485
Moore, Judge Joseph A.—285
Moore, Judge Joseph B.—373
Moore, Thomas—403
Moore, Thos.—207
Moreau River—170, 418
Morgan, David—389
"Moriah Cemetery"—271, 379
Morris & Co.—329
Morris, Corbin—518
Morris, Jacob—329
Morris, Wm.—234
Morrison, Jas.—343
Morristown, New Jersey, see "New Jersey, Morristown"
"Mortar and pestle" era—252
Moulton (town)—354
Moulton, C. H.—447
Moulton, Frank P.—234, 310
Moulton, J. M.—192
Mount Pleasant, Iowa, see "Iowa, Mount Pleasant"
Mountain fever—454
Moylan, Capt.—152
"Mud March"—170, 172
Mumford, Geo. W.—473
Munson, Capt.—91
Murder, first authenticated case of in Black Hills—202, 267
Murder, first in northern Black Hills—198
Murphy, Ed—126, 247, 448
Murphy, J. F.—198, 223
Murphy, T. G.—407
Muse, Col.—440
Muskle, Dan—127
Musical clubs—377
Musicals, monthly—393
Myers, Dr. C. W.—200, 266, 279
Myers, Wm.—463
"Mysterious Jimmies"—262
Mystic (town)—354

N

N.W. & M.V. Railroad—23
Nadowessioux—1
Nahant (town)—444
Naja Temple—455
Narcouter, Lephiere—124
Narrow gauge railroad—325, 372, 373, 382, 384, 439
Nasby (town)—444
National banks—374, 394
National Cemetery—163
Nebraska (state)—2, 18, 23, 25, 88, 106, 107, 173, 454, 485
Nebraska, Beatrice—95, 455
Nebraska, Dodge County—142
Nebraska, Gordon—88, 138
Nebraska, Norfolk—21
Nebraska, Omaha—89, 172, 291, 297, 360, 392, 434, 439, 450, 504, 531
Nebraska, Sidney—115, 139, 142, 144, 216, 220, 225, 288, 346, 381, 482
"Needles"—110
Negotiations with Sioux—75, 519, 520
Neill, Robert—465
Neill, Mrs. Robt—465
Nelson, the Rev.—468
Nemo (town)—444
"Nevada" gulch—125, 436, 437, 438, 439, 440, 441
Newbanks, Noah—231, 446
New Eldorado—84, 100, 116, 179, 209, 339
New Holland—340
New Jersey, East Orange—434
New Jersey, Jersey City—434
New Jersey, Morristown—284
New Mexico—119, 330, 455
New Mexico & Dakota Mica Mining Company—300
"New York" mine—296, 300
"New York, Mining Journal"—338
New York, Northport—328
New York, West Point—163
Newspaper, daily—199, 201, 202, 223, 357, 393, 396
Newspaper, first daily in Black Hills—199, 201, 373, 416, 429
Newspaper, first in Custer—223
Newspaper, first in Rapid City—315
Newspaper, first in Hot Springs—498
Newspaper, second daily in Dakota Territory—202
Newspaper reporter, first—200, 304, 315
Newspapers, weekly—396, 404, 417, 437, 443, 469, 504, 509, 572
Newton, Prof. Henry—92, 488
Newton's Fork—335, 339, 491
Nichols, Elliott—460
Nicholson, Oscar—228, 231, 232
Nickel—338
"Nickel Plate" mine—338
Nickson, N.—192
"Nigger Hill"—245, 432
"Nigger Hill" tin district—432
Nimrod—28, 228
Ninth U. S. Infantry—91, 169
Niobrara, Old Fort—23, 173
Niobrara River—24, 55, 88, 105, 138
Nix, Geo. M.—517
"No good Indians but dead Indians"—106
Nobles, W. H.—521
Noland, W. A.—192
Norcross, the Rev. L. P.—211, 212
Norfolk, Nebraska, see "Nebraska, Norfolk"
North American tribes—487, 529
North Dakota, Bismarck—176, 186, 187, 229, 234, 413, 427, 523
"North Pole" mine—295
North Star Mine—297
Northern Gold Belt—354, 370, 450
Northern Pacific Railroad—140
Northern plains—510
Northington, Ben—229
Northport, New York, see "New York, Northport"
Northwest Territory—519
Northwestern Express, Stage and Transportation Company—140
Northwestern Iowa Conference—360, 397
Northwestern Stage & Transportation Line—328
Northwestern Transportation Company—6
Northwestern Water and Gas Supply Company of Minneapolis—320
Norton, Frank—126
Norton, Lt. C.—91
Norton, John—341

Norway Pine—216
Norwegians—394
Nowlin, John W.—285, 329, 330
"Nugget, The"—241, 244
Nuggets, gold—103, 205, 249, 333, 341, 350, 351
"Nutshell Bills"—262
Nuttall & Maw's saloon—270
Nuttall, Wm.—226, 227
Nutt's store—409
Nye Block—255
Nye & Co.—258

O

O.E.S.—392
O.S.C.—392
Oak Creek—534, 535
Oak Grove Springs—443
Oakes, Edward—328
O'Brien, W. S.—524
Occidental Hotel—292
O'Connor, Bishop—360
Odd Fellows—275, 365, 388, 431, 437, 471, 472, 504, 515
Odell Co.—504
O'Donnell, Daniel J.—392
Oelrich (town)—509, 524
Offenbacher & Haight firm—298
Ogalallas—95
Ogden, Joseph—373
Ogden, Judge David B.—396, 397
O'Grady, Pat—389
O'Harra, Jack—422
Old Abe—253, 295, 382
Old Abe mine—127, 380
Old Bill (mine)—295, 296, 490
"Old Charley" mine—295, 296
"Old Mike" mine—300
Old Woman's Creek—3
Olds, W. N.—296, 297
Oleson, Andrew—374
Olson, A.—192
Omaha, see "Nebraska, Omaha"
Omega mine—208, 209
"Omnibus Bill"—524
O'Neal, Thomas—208, 253
O'Neill—192
O'Neill, Peter—447
O'Neill's Colony—18, 22, 23
Onge, Osman—422
Opera House, Central—397
Opera House, Lead City's first—389
Order of Free Masons—455
Ordway, Gov. N. J.—427
Organ—212
Organic Act—521
Oro Fino mine—434, 435
Orr, Joseph L.—439, 441
Osborne, Flora—416
Oskosh—216
Ostram, Charlie—286
Ostram, Mattie—286
Otis—307
Otis, Col. Elmer—477
Otto, Mr.—192
Outlaws—290
Overman, Dr.—192, 264
Overman, Frank—429
Overpeck, A. L.—327
Ox freight trains—132

P

Pacific Coast—413, 445
"Packing the feet"—45
Pactola—117, 118, 196, 234, 251, 346, 347, 377
Palaezoic rock formation—437
Paleontology—323
Palmer, Geo.—134, 135
Palmer Gulch Mining District—135
Palmer, H. E.—460
Palmer's gulch—134, 135, 136, 226, 339
Pan, panning, gold—94, 113
"Pancake Bills"—262

Parker, E. B.—269
Parker, Gifford A.—484
Parker, Osmer H.—524
Parker, Sandford—524
Parker, W. H.—524
Parshall, A. J.—132, 214
Parsons, Chas.—524
Paslin, H. F.—400
Passenger traffic to Black Hills—138, 140
Paste—414
Patrick, W. K.—489
Patterson, Alex—441
Patterson, J. W.—230
Patton, John D.—428, 459
Patton's First and Second Additions—462
Peace Commissioners—75
Pearson, J. B.—127, 128, 380
Pearson, John B.—124, 125, 126, 396
Pearson Mill—398
Peierman, James—124
Peirce, E. T. "Doc"—183, 224, 303, 332
Pendleton, Thos. E.—230
Pennell, the Rev. Geo. C.—360
Pennington County—284, 294, 295, 308, 309, 311, 312, 335, 337, 339, 342, 344, 352, 353, 355, 376, 377, 380, 490, 524, 531
Pennington County Bank of Rapid City—328
Pennington County Board of Commissioners first meeting—311
Pennington County Commissioners—254, 354
Pennington County depository—328
Pehnington County fire department—311
Pennington Counts, Judge of Probate—330
Pennington County organization—309
Pennington County Sheriff—224, 229, 234
Pennington County, Superintendent of Public Instruction—312
Pennington County's first courthouse—311
Pennington, Governor John L.—133, 189, 266, 309, 311, 354
Pennsylvania, Philadelphia—336
"Penobscot" mine—295, 296
Pensinger, Martin—136, 226, 231
Perkin's & Conter firm—473
Perkins, H. E.—470, 472, 473
Perkins, Mrs. H. E.—467
Peroxide of Iron—486
Perry (town)—444
Persimmons Bill's gang—177, 178, 218
Peters, E. C.—310, 311
Peters, S. S.—407
Peterson, the Rev. W. S.—468
Peterson and Woodward firm—296
Pettigrew, Charles W.—413
Pettigrew, Eugene T.—428
Pettirgrew, Miss—185, 416
"Pettigrew" party—413
Pettigrew, R. F.—375, 524
Pettigrew, Senator—324
Petty, Edmund—484, 493, 495, 507
Petty, Joseph—484, 493
Phifer, the Rev. W. D.—388
Philadelphia, Pennsylvania, see "Pennsylvania, Philadelphia"
Philbrook, H. C.—172, 277
Philips, Wendell—5
Phillips & Biddle firm—258
Phillips & Boomer Block—500
Phillips, Chas.—348
Phillips, Dr. J. L.—520
Phillips, Scott—518
Phillips, Wm. P.—484
Physician, first in Deadwood—258
Pickett, the Rev. J. W.—314
Pickler, John H.—524
Picotte, Chas. F.—520, 522
Piedmont—41, 382, 481, 482, 483
Pierce, Governor—428
Pierre—138, 139, 141, 227, 228, 230, 321, 328, 329, 375, 524
Pierre, Fort—227, 231, 463
Pilcher, Joseph—296, 304
"Pilot", Hermosa—315
Pincus, Pauline—390
Pine Ridge Agency—225, 492, 527, 531, 536
Pine Ridge Indians—530

Pinkerton, Prof. C. M.—390
Pinkham, Gilbert L.—524
Pinneo, Mr.—394
Pinney, Geo. M.—522
Pinney & Lorton—208
Pinney, Milton E.—208
"Pioneer," Black Hills—164, 199, 200, 201, 279, 305
"Pioneer" Deadwood—201, 202, 373
Pioneer Hook and Ladder Company—361
Pioneer Times Publishing Company—201, 480
"Pioneer Times," The—202, 373, 493
Pioneer towns—102
Pioneer Town-site Company—443, 512
Pipe—250
Pitty, Edmund—494
Pitty, Joseph—494
Placer claims—118, 346, 352
Placer deposits, gold—94, 124, 128, 186, 210, 245, 248, 251, 253, 339, 349, 351, 357, 380, 402
Placer gold—103, 119, 229, 347, 348, 352, 353
Placer gold, first discovery in northern Black Hills—124
Placer mining in Deadwood gulch—127, 245
Placer mining operations—122, 245, 246, 248, 252, 335, 348, 349, 350, 368, 387
"Plaindealer," Whitewood—443, 514
Planing mill—431, 483, 503
Planing mills (Steam)—305
Platt, Senator Thos. C.—399
Platte Department—147, 172
Platte River—2, 68, 91, 116, 118, 126, 134, 179, 236
Plaudney, Wm.—407
Pleasant Valley—122, 134
Plowman, Judge A. J.—285
Pluma—372, 439, 440
Pluma Mill—286
"Plunge"—501, 502
Plutas mine—441
Poem to Custer's Last Stand—165
"Poet-scout"—165, 196, 197
Point of Rocks—179, 489
"Poker Flats"—254
Poland, Harry—297
Pole Creek—236
Polk, C. C.—460, 465, 470, 473
Pollock, Major—98, 101, 196
Pollock's Capt. troopers—130, 136, 195
Pony express mail service—144, 223
Pony Express Service—145, 463
Population proportion of foreign residents—394
Porcupine Creek—530
Porcupine Valley—537
Porter, Dr.—159
Porter, Lieut.—152
Porter, Wade—86, 87, 99, 112, 113, 114, 129, 130
Portland Consolidated Mining Company—439, 441
Portland Mine—438, 439
Posses—267, 270
Post, Jas. W.—327
Postal facilities in Black Hills—141, 354
Postal service, regular in Rapid City—312
Postal service, U. S.—283, 303
Postmaster, Custer's private—223
Postmaster, Deadwood—141, 189
Potassa—486
Potassium Sulphate—486
Potato gulch—221
Potter, A. C.—394, 417
Potter, John T.—465
Potter & Powers firm—295
Powder river—147, 149, 150, 169, 185
Powers, Albert—428
Powers, James—18
Powers, W. F.—427
Poznansky, Felix, Poznanska (sic)—314, 318, 320
"Prairie craft"—95
Pratt, Nettie M.—428
Pre-emption law, first settler to use in Black Hills—212
Presbyterian societies, churches—314, 389, 392, 443, 468, 498
"Press, The"—304, 473
Price (outlaw)—290
Price, Cassius—327
Pringle—307
Pringle station—489

Private mail service—142, 144
"Progressive Hall"—358
Prosecuting Attorney, first in Pennington county—376
Prospect Park—301
Provisional courts—202
Provisional government for Black Hills—214, 330
Provisional Legislature—375, 521
Pruden, J. B.—421, 422
Prugh, the Rev.—468
Pryor, Sallie R.—428
Pryor, Thos.—390
Public school system, first in Dakota Territory—397
Public schools, Rapid City—312
Pugh, Bob—225
Pyle, the Rev. W. J.—468
Pyritic smelting plant—370, 371

Q

Quakers—168
Quartz-bearing gold—120, 253, 295, 297, 335, 336, 349, 357, 380, 489
Quartz claim in Black Hills, first—135
Quartz, first ton transported out of Black Hills—119, 195
Quartz mill, first in Black Hills—208, 253, 278
Quartz mills—208, 209, 353
Quartz mine, first discovered in "gold belt"—253
Quartz mining—119, 127, 252, 253, 283, 296, 309, 335, 338, 343, 345, 347, 348, 389, 396
Quartz properties—252
Queen Bee—340
Queen Bee gold mine—340
Queen City—185, 193, 424, 429, 432
Queen City of Black Hills—406, 424, 425
Queen of the Hills mine—402
Quick Bear—97
Quicksilver—249
Quincy, Illinois, see "Illinois, Quincy"
Quiner, Thomas—18

R

R.A.M.—392
R.N.—392
R.S.—392
Racine Mining & Milling Company—381
Racine, Wisconsin, see "Wisconsin, Racine"
"Ragged Top"—431, 437, 438
Ragged Top Mining district—431, 432
Raids on Custer—216, 217
Railroad, first in Deadwood—372
Railroad, first to reach Rapid City—324
Rain-in-the-Face—162
Rainwater, E.—447
Ralston & Glassie firm—514
Ralston, Robert—134
Ramsdell Addition—407
Ramsdell, Joseph—186, 407, 416, 426, 427
Randall, Fort—24, 72, 520
Ransdell, Joseph—212
Rapid City—79, 120, 136, 203, 222, 223, 224, 226, 227, 228, 229, 230, 231, 232, 233, 234, 285, 291, 308, 311, 312, 313, 314, 315, 318, 321, 322, 323, 324, 325, 327, 328, 329, 330, 331, 332, 333, 338, 340, 342, 344, 346, 348, 377, 446, 454, 482, 483, 489, 491, 524, 538
Rapid City, first Board of Trustees—133
Rapid City, business—120
Rapid City, Chlorination plant—317, 440
Rapid City Electric and Gas Light Company—326
Rapid City, Fire Department—327
Rapid City founders—133, 312
Rapid City Hook and Ladder, No. 1—327
Rapid City, first hostelry—133
Rapid City Incorporated—324
Rapid City & Keystone Stage Line—352
Rapid City Lodge A.F. and A.M.—317
Rapid City, first postmaster—133, 312
Rapid City Street Railway—325
Rapid City, township organization—122
Rapid City Water Co.—318

558 THE BLACK HILLS; OR,

Rapid Creek—43, 80, 81, 92, 103, 226, 231, 233, 234, 245, 251, 252, 308, 309, 324, 346, 347, 352, 533, 536
Rapid Creek Mining District—346
Rapid Creek Mining & Manufacturing Company—347
Rapid Creek Valley—136, 323, 449
Rapid River Milling Co.—317
Rapid River Valley ranches—234
Raw Hide Butte—3, 134, 181
Raymond, A. A.—421, 422
Raymond (Scout)—87
Read, G. W.—185
Rebecca Mine—438, 440
Receiver of Public Moneys of U. S. Land Office, Rapid City—454
"Record," Terry—437
Red Beds—406
Red Canyon—61, 120, 121, 134, 177, 178, 216, 217, 218, 237, 280
Red Canyon Creek—80
Red Cloud Agency—67, 69, 86, 87, 92, 95, 97, 116, 132, 179
Red Cloud, Chief—70, 71, 97, 235, 536
Red Dog—97
Redfern (town)—354
Redfield, A. H.—520
"Red Head Mike"—290
Red Leaf—97
Red Oak, Iowa, see, "Iowa, Red Oak"
Reduction plants—370, 382, 387, 392, 398, 431, 517
Redwater creek—80, 81, 185, 274, 355, 406, 410, 413, 414, 510, 511, 512
Redwater Land and Canal Company—511
Ree scouts—150, 153
Reed, Geo.—408, 416
Reed, Jacob—353
Refractory ore—295, 370, 371, 372, 436, 437, 442, 452
Religious organization, first in Deadwood—360
Religious organization, first in Rapid City—314
Religious service, first in Black Hills—203
Religious services, first in Central—396
Religious society, first in Black Hills—211
Remington rifle—142
Reno & Bond—491, 494
Reno, Fort, old—147
Reno, L. B.—495
Reno, Major—150, 152, 153, 154, 155, 156, 167, 479
Reno scouting party—150, 151
Reno's casualties—154
Reno's retreat—154, 155, 162
Reppert, A. P.—343
Republican Fork, Smoky Hill River—2
Republican Publishing Co.—315
"Republican," Rapid City—314, 315
"Republican" West Point—20
Rescue Hose Company No. 1—443
Reservation, permanent—97
Resorts, health & pleasure—505
"Rest"—204, 274
Restaurant, first regular in Deadwood—257
Restaurant, first in Deadwood—257
"Retreiver" mine—440
Revenue Collector, Deputy U. S. for Dakota Territory—494
Revenue Department—265
Rewman, Paul—449, 455, 456
Reynolds, Prof. Arthur—443
Reynolds, Capt. Expedition—4
Reynolds, Charlie—11, 162
Reynolds, General—148
Reynolds, Joseph—104, 116, 117, 118, 119, 196, 203, 214, 220, 225
Rhinehart Judge—105, 115
Rhode Island (state)—95
Richards, Bartlett—518
Richards, G. S.—511
Richmond Mining Company—433, 434
Richmond, Wm.—439
Riffles—248, 249, 250, 251
Riley, Fort, Kansas—477, 480
Riley, Lieut.—152
Riley's cabin, P. C.—409, 414, 415
Ringsrud, A. O.—524
"Road agents"—140, 506
"Roaring Camp"—254
"Roasting"—438
Robbins, C. W.—298, 318

Robert Chew & Co.—366
Roberts, Jas.—199, 223
Robinson, Camp see "Robinson, Fort"
Robinson, Fort—69, 70, 88, 89, 174, 490, 531
Robinson, Hawgood & Hoskins Company—345
Robinson, J. N.—265
Robinson, Mrs.—236
Robinson, Mrs. J. N.—236
Robinson, Revillo F.—265
Robinson & Ripley firm—408
Robinson & Ross firm—258
Rochford—254, 311, 342, 343, 344, 345, 387, 491
Rochford, John—344
Rochford, M. D.—343
Rochford, Nyswanger & Co.—343
"Rocker"—55, 103, 249, 250, 350
Rockerville—250, 251, 333, 349, 350, 351, 352, 353, 489
Rockerville flume—250
Rockerville Gold Mining Co.—351
Rockfellow, H. G.—142
Rockford, J. J.—327
Rocky Mountains—1, 332, 419, 522
Rocky Mountain District—314, 452
Rodebank Addition—462
Rodebank, J. W.—462
Rodebank, Mrs. Nellie—465
Rodebank's Second Addition—462
Rogers, G. W.—192
Rogers, Jas.—415, 429
Rogers, Miss—390
Roman Catholics—360
Roman Nose, Chief—170
Rooney, Felix—271
Rosebud Reservation—527
Rosebud River—148, 150, 151, 160, 168, 169
Rosen, the Rev. Father—466, 467
Rosenbaum, G. W.—185
Rosenbaum, Wm—339
Ross' Bar—127
Ross, H. N.—12, 103, 296, 489
Ross, Hiram—185
Rossiter, Jas.—448
Rothrock, G. W.—214
Rough Riders—512
"Round Table," Thursday—377
Rowland, M. V.—209
Roy, Rob—239
Royal Arch Mason—455
Royal, Neighbors—504
Royal, Agent—531
Ruby, Basin—372, 437, 438
Ruger, Gen.—533
Runkel (town)—483
Russell, Capt. G—91
Russell, J. H.—425
Russell, Capt. Thomas H.—5, 6, 13, 14, 18, 28, 29, 50, 111, 195, 348, 446, 448
Ryan Fraction mine—441,
Ryan, J. C.—407, 415, 418
Ryan, J. W.—322
Ryan, Jas.—185, 356, 408, 415, 446, 470

S

S. of St. G.—392
Sabin, W. W.—465
Saddlery & Harness Shop, first in Deadwood—258
Sadler, Edwin—230
St. Ange—444
St. Elmo mine—335, 336
St. Louis, see "Missouri, St. Louis"
St. Martin's Academy—466
St. Thomas Episcopal Society—469
Salisbury, O. J.—361, 374
"Salmon" mine—295, 296
Salvation Army—389
Sample, the Rev. J. Logan—468
Sampson, A.—296
Samuel Soyster, Knowles & Marshmand firm—258
San Francisco, California, see "California, San Francisco"
San Juan Hill—479
Sand Creek—80, 125, 130, 413
Sand Hills—518

LAST HUNTING GROUND OF THE DAKOTAHS 559

Sanderson, Dr.—469
Sanderson, Dr. L. L.—473
Sands, Nicholas—447
Sandstone, native—497
Sandstone obelisk—271
Sans Arcs—95
Santee Agency—95
Santees—95
Sasse, Alvina—199
Sasse, Chas.—177, 178, 199
Sasse, Mrs. Chas.—178, 199
Saunders, J. C.—303, 489
Saw Mill, first in Black Hills—198, 223
Sawmill, portable steam—351
Sawmills, (Steam)—247, 305, 347, 363, 415, 431, 458, 480, 483
"Sawyer's Trail"—111, 112
Schaffer, W. P.—522
Schell, Lule—460
Schenck, Henry—297, 337
Schlawig, Mrs.—88
Schleuning, Sr., Ernest (Schlewning)—222
Schleunning, Ernest—214, 303
Schlittenger, Mr.—439
Schmitz, Henry—394
Schnasse & Grambery Co.—328
Schnasse, G.—317
Schneider, Geo. F.—328
Schnell's Addition—462
School building, first public in Custer—304
School district, first in Black Hills—404
School district meeting, first in Lead City—390
School District No. 66, Lawrence County—443
School District No. 76, Lawrence County—436
School, first in Custer—303
School, first in Deadwood—258
School, first in Hot Springs—496
School, first in Lead City—388
School, first in Rapid City—312
School, first in Spearfish—185, 416, 425
School Fund permanent—525
School of Mines—322, 323, 325, 330
School of Mines of the Territory of Dakota—133
School, public building, first in Deadwood—361
School, public system Lawrence County—356
School, second in Custer—303
School system, first public in Dakota Territory—397
School lands, Lincoln Territory—282
Schrader, Chas.—441
Schugardt, G.—269
Schultz, James—440
Schurtz, J. C.—469
Scollard, John—257, 464, 473, 475, 524
Scoop, D.—422
Scotch—394
Scotland, Scotsmen—50
Scott, C. A.—294, 303
Scott, Carrie—303
Scott, Charles—212
Scott, Dan—6
Scott, Fort, Kansas, see "Kansas, Fort Scott"
Scott, Gen.—225
Scott, J.—448, 463
Scott, Samuel—226, 227, 228, 230, 231, 233, 318, 358
Scottney, J. A.—510
Scroggs, the Rev.—468
Searle, John K.—392
Searles, J. R.—390
Second Cavalry—91
Second U. S. Cavalry—169
Secret Orders—317, 365, 392
Secret Orders and Benevolent Associations—365
Secretary of the Interior—95, 96, 106, 282, 462, 527, 528, 539
Seip, Chas.—347
Seitz, S. K.—472
Seventh Cavalry—149, 150, 158, 163, 170, 537
Seventh Cavalry, U. S.—477, 479, 480
Seventh Day Adventists—392
Seventh Judicial District of State Circuit Court—284, 285, 330
Seymour and Utter Pony Express Mail Service—142
Shambough, the Rev.—468
Shankland, S. R.—294, 303
Shankland, Sam'l—100, 104, 107, 112, 113, 114, 115, 131, 214, 215, 303, 446, 489

Shannon, Jas.—207
Shannon, Thomas—403, 404
Sharp, J. J.—327
Sharp's rifles—130, 196, 221, 463
Shave Head, 1st Lieutenant—534, 536
Sheep ranches—410
Sheffield, Sam—518
Sheidly Cattle Co.—518
Shelby D. Reed & Co.—315
Sheldon Edwards Mill—398
Sheldon, Governor—133
Sheldon's Ranch—423
Shenn, V. P.—104
Shepard, James A.—484
Sheridan—251, 311, 336, 337, 340, 341, 342, 350, 351
Sheridan, General Phil—13, 146, 168, 340, 476
Sheridan House—464
Sheriff of Lawrence County—287
Sherman, Wm.—441
Sherman House—347
Sherman, Jas. C.—346, 347
Shingles—49
Shive, John—256
Shober, John H.—522
Short Bull—530
Shoudy, J.—257
Shoun, V. P.—130, 131
Shule, C. W.—269
Sibley, General—520
Sidney and Black Hills stage coach—286, 288
Sidney coach—287
"Sidney Cut-off"—115
Sidney, Nebraska, see "Nebraska, Sidney"
Siever, Noah—358
Silica—435, 439, 486
Siliceous gold ores—432
Silliman, D. G.—350
Silver—338, 352, 353, 433
Silver Brothers dry goods store—388
Silver City—352, 353, 354
Silver Creek—343
Silver mill—323
Silver-lead carbonate camp—432
Silver mining operations—433
Silver reduction industry—433
Simmon, A. J.—348
Simmons, Major A. J.—338, 343, 353
Simonton, O. H.—269
Sioux—1, 6, 10, 13
Sioux City and Black Hills Transportation Co.—89, 138, 139
Sioux, domain, reserve, territory—20, 57, 60, 90, 116, 445
Sioux Falls—329, 520, 523, 524
Sioux hostilities, last in Spearfish area—413
Sioux Nation—1, 20, 21, 23, 40, 42, 58, 69, 75, 83, 84, 85, 95, 98, 101, 146, 147, 148, 151, 155, 157, 174, 175, 178, 179, 181, 182, 183, 184, 187, 215, 229, 232, 235, 244, 266, 312, 402, 406, 411, 449, 487, 495, 519, 520, 522, 527, 529, 530
Sioux reservation—16, 90, 96, 325, 528
Sioux treaties—75, 519, 520
Sioux Treaty of 1876—283
Sister's Hospital—390
Sitting Bull—146, 147, 148, 165, 167, 169, 175, 230, 529, 530, 533, 534, 536
Sitting Bull, killing of—534
Sitting Bull mine—433, 434
Sitting Bull (town)—352
Six Feathers—530
Sixth Judicial District of South Dakota—424
Skeating, George—421
Skidmore, I. V.—396
Skinner, John H.—347
Skinner, John Henry—415, 416
Slate (rock wall)—295
Slate Creek—41, 125, 340
Slater, E. F.—407
Slaughter, Johnny—286
Salvonians—394
Slim Buttes—170, 171
Slocum, Lieutenant—534
Slow Bull—97
Sluice Boxes—124, 247, 249, 250, 251
Sluice, wide—250

Sluicing, sluices—92, 93, 124, 130, 246, 247, 248, 249, 250, 251, 350
Smead, W. E.—394
Smelters—318, 345, 434, 509
Smiley Lundt mine group—440
Smith, A. B.—522
Smith, A. G.—286, 287
Smith, A. H.—327
Smith, A. J.—441
Smith, B. P.—286
Smith, Custer Justice of the Peace—202
Smith, D. Tom—236
Smith, Dr. W. G.—460
Smith, E. C.—400
Smith, Eugene—129
Smith, F. B.—214
Smith, Frank—126, 223
Smith, Frank B.—294, 303
Smith, Geo. G.—345
Smith, H. C.—254
Smith, Henry Weston—379
Smith, Hon. E. P.—93
Smith, J. E.—407, 408
Smith, L.—346
Smith, Lieut.—152
Smith, M. B.—522
Smith, Miss Lottie—496
Smith, Mrs. Viola—425
Smith party—407
Smith, R. P.—473
Smith, S. R.—388
Smith, the Rev. H. W.—203, 204, 269, 274, 404
Smith, W. F.—524
Smith, W. G.—465, 473
Smith, W. H.—256
Smith's canyon—344
Smithville (town)—483
Smithwick (town)—509
Snake Creek—88
Snake River—105
Snelling, Fort—6
Snively, D. K.—214, 303
Snively, D. T.—131
Snoma (town)—517
Snowfall in spring of 1878—366
Snowstorm of March 6, 1878, great—132
Snowstorm mine—438, 440, 442
Snyder, Julia B.—390
Social clubs—377, 472
Society of Black Hills Pioneers—446, 449, 450, 454, 455, 456
Society of Black Hills Pioneers, death list—447
Society of Black Hills Pioneers, membership—446
Sodium—486
Sodium sulphate—486
Soldiers Home—477, 498, 499
Somers, H. H.—327
Somers, James—522
Sonter, W. F. L.—465
Soule, Charles S.—6, 13
South Bend—396
South Dakota—323, 324, 328, 329, 330, 375, 380, 392, 394, 415, 521, 523
South Dakota assessed valuation—525
South Dakota Soldiers' Home—477, 498, 499
South Deadwood—211, 248, 266, 267, 360, 361, 364
South Deadwood platting—266
Spades, C. C.—407
Spanish American War—477
Sparks, Joseph—403, 404
Sparks, P. E.—470, 473
Spaulding, Capt.—91
Spaulding, John—409
Spearfish—7, 81, 193, 212, 273, 274, 288, 303, 305, 372, 373, 406-419, 420, 421-427, 429-432
Spearfish Buttes—125
Spearfish Canyon—372
Spearfish Creek—80, 185, 355, 406, 407, 416
Spearfish Cyanide Co.—431
Spearfish Electric Light—429
Spearfish Fire Department—429
Spearfish Hotel—415
Spearfish Milling Company—415, 416
Spearfish Normal School—427
Spearfish Post Office, first—414

Spearfish Valley—117, 125, 185, 193, 241, 406, 407, 408, 418
Spears, Albert—307
Spencer, Chas.—341
Spencer, Chas. N.—327
Spilman, E. G.—348
Spokane—297
"Spokane" mine—307
Spooner, C. L.—294
Spotted Tail—101
SpottedTail Agency—92, 130
Spread Eagle mine—345
Spring Creek—41, 43, 80, 103, 119, 122, 124, 125, 135, 136, 233, 245, 251, 252, 274, 292, 308, 309, 335, 336, 340, 342, 349, 350, 351, 364, 376, 449, 533, 536
Spring Creek Military Comp U. S.—476
Spring gulch—208, 253
Spring Valley—229, 230, 405, 446
"Spring Valley" ranch—482
Springfield rifles—306
Spruce gulch—124, 125, 372
Square Creek—441
"Squatter's" rights—436
Squaw Creek—109, 436, 438, 439, 452
Stafford, Dan J.—224
Stage Robberies—286, 287, 482
Stage robbery, first attempt—286
Stamp batteries—209
Stamp Mill, first in Black Hills—208, 209
Stamp mills—208, 209, 295, 296, 297, 323, 335, 336, 337, 340, 342, 343, 344, 345, 346, 352, 353, 354, 370, 380, 381, 382, 383, 396, 398, 401, 433, 434, 435, 437, 438
Stampedes, mining—303, 332
"Stand-by"—343
"Stand Off Bar"—122, 135, 341, 449
Standard Cattle Co.—518
"Standing Rock" Chamber—508
Standing Rock Indians—176
Standing Rock Reservation—527, 528, 529, 533, 534, 536
Stannus, John—447
Stapleton, Con—277
Star & Bullock's hardware store—188, 257, 258
"Star", Hot Springs—498, 504
Star of Empire—186
Star, Sol.—186, 187, 189, 207, 277, 360, 365, 524
State Banks—394
State Board of Equalization—525
State Constitution—523
State Normal School—322, 425, 426, 431
State of Black Hills—282
State Railroad Commissioner—133
State University—322
Stearns, B. F.—465
Stearns, Fred E.—324
Stearns, P. B.—510
Stebbins, Fox & Co.—417, 418, 469
Stebbins, Post & Mund—362
Stebbins, W. R.—358, 362, 469
Stebbins, Wood & Post (banks)—202, 286, 357, 358, 359, 361, 374
Steele, Lieut.—534
Steele, Mrs. Wm.—312
Steele, Wm. F.—231, 316, 331, 447
Stein, Dr. H.—457
Stenger, Ed—518
Sterling, A. P.—339
Sterner, Jacob—434
Stevens, Harry—511
Stewart, A. D.—472
Stewart, A. S.—524
Stewart, A. F.—5
Stewart, Dr. A. S.—493, 495, 497, 498, 502
Stewart, Frank—518
Stock raising industry—305
Stockade, Custer, see "Gordon Stockade"
Stockade in 1875, see "Gordon Stockade"
Stockade, see "Gordon Stockade"
Stockton, Col.—347
Stokes, Billy—236
Stokes, Geo. W.—134, 135, 200
Stone, Col. L. R.—353
Stone, L. W.—425
Stone table—8
Stonewall—213, 214
Stonewall, Montana, see "Montana, Stonewall"

LAST HUNTING GROUND OF THE DAKOTAHS 561

Stool, first—186
Stotts, George—417
Stout Brothers—422
Strader lode—242
Strawberry gulch—434
Street & Thompson's mill—248
Street and Thompson's transportation trains—180
Strikes—392
Strobe, John—440
Stuart Lode—441
Stuart, Wesley A.—466, 473
Stucco plant—470, 503
Sturgis (city)—41, 208, 209, 257, 442, 446, 460, 462-474, 482, 524
Sturgis, Col. S. D.—477
"Sturgis Commercial Club"—472
Sturgis Electric Light and Railway Company—471
Sturgis Electric Lighting Service—471
Sturgis Fire Department—469
Sturgis, first store—463
Sturgis, General—462, 479, 480
Sturgis legal bar—473
Sturgis, Lieut. J. G. "Sturgis, Jack"—152, 476
Sturgis Opera House, Old—469
Sturgis Steam Roller Flouring Mill—470
Sturgis Water System—471
Sullivan, John L.—386
Sully, Fort—477
Sulphur—401
Summary justice—420
Summers, J. F.—417, 418, 428, 429, 515
Summers, Joseph—295
Sundance Mountain—77
Sundance, Wyoming, see "Wyoming, Sundance"
Sunday gulch—301, 336
Sunny Side mine—339
Superintendent of Schools of Pennington County, first—133
Superior Court for Black Hills—214
Superior flour—317
Supreme Court Territory of Dakota—434
Supreme Court, United States—434, 460
Survey, government, first in Black Hills—212
Surveyor General for South Dakota, U. S.—200, 282
Suter, W. F. L.—460
Sutherland, J. J.—257
Swartout—202
Swede Bar—347
Swedes—394
Sweeney, Thos.—311, 327, 329, 332, 333, 334
Sweetman, V. P.—373
Sweetwater Rivers—9
Swift, John A.—277, 447
Swift, Joseph—373
Swift, W. H.—373
"Switzerland of America"—301
Sylvan Lake—301

T

"Tabernacle" chamber—508
Talbot, J.—422
Tallent, Annie D.—15, 18, 30, 31, 39, 42, 43, 44, 46, 48, 49, 53, 54, 58, 64, 65, 73, 83, 177, 221, 235, 237, 239, 240, 241, 243, 250, 254, 493
Tallent cabin—50
Tallent, D. G.—18, 136, 235, 407
Tallent, Robt. E.—18
Tallent's Annie, trunk—62, 86
"Tanglefoot" Creek—109
Tanglefoot Gulch—109
Tanner, Dr.—332
Taxes in Black Hills, federal—265
Taylor, Jack—327
Taylor, Louis C.—524
"Tea" mine—339
Teal, B. F.—512
"Telegraph", Lead City—388
Telegraph lines—278
Telegraph road (old Custer to Deadwood)—347
Telluride test—297
Temple, W. O.—373
Tenderfoot gulch—491
Terra mill—401

Terraville—401, 402, 446, 449, 450
Territorial bonded indebtedness—524
Territorial legislature—283, 308, 330, 364, 375, 376, 426, 458, 465, 484, 510, 522, 523
Terry, Brig. Gen. A. H.—95, 147, 149, 151, 157, 160, 168, 169
Terry Hose Company No. 1—437
Terry (town)—435, 436
Terry's column command—159, 165
Terry's Peak—75, 77, 125, 436, 440
Tetrault, P. S.—447
Tevis, Lloyd—381
Texas Jack—230
Texas, Oakes—114
Theatre building, pioneer—206
Theatre, first legitimate in Black Hills—205
Theatrical performance, first—206
Theatrical performance, first in Lead City—389
Thermal Springs—486
Thiens, John—448
Third Cavalry Regiment of South Dakota Volunteers—512
Third Cavalry, U. S.—91, 147, 169, 170
Third Infantry, U. S.—475
Thoen, Lewis—7
Thomas, C. F.—407
Thomas, Chas. W.—524
Thomas, Henry—18, 40, 60
Thomas, Judge Chas M.—284, 285
Thomas, Judge A. D.—375
Thompson, Alex—100
Thompson, C.—79
Thompson, Col. Daniel—122
Thompson, J. S.—390
Thompson, J. W.—524
Thompson, M. D.—292, 293
Thompson, Miss W. A.—428
Thompson's Custom Mill—398
Thorburn, Robt.—317
Thornby, Col. Wm.—488, 489, 493, 494
Thornby, W. J.—361
Three Bears—97
Thulen, Frank—235, 446
Thullen, Frank C.—275
Tigerville—337, 340
Tilford, Col. Joseph G.—477
Tilford, (town)—460, 480, 481
Timber Culture Entry No. 1—212
Timber homestead, first in Black Hills—212
Timber line—308
Timbering the mines—382, 384
"Times", Belle Fourche—515
"Times", Deadwood—201, 373
"Times", Oskosh (sic)—216
"Times", Sioux City, Iowa—4, 6, 13, 14, 55
"Times Herald", Hot Springs—504
Timmish—107, 112
Tin—294, 300, 337, 338
Tin-bearing rock—338
Tin Belt—339
Tin discovery, first—337
Tin discovery public announcement, first—338
Tin districts, Harney Peak—325
Tin stream—339
Title 23 of the Revised Statutes of United States—281
Titles to property, valid—197
Toby, the Rev.—468
Todd, Green—275
Todd, J. B. S.—520
"Tom Austin" mine—354
Toney, Lewis—441
Tongue River—148, 150, 169
Tonn, M. G.—408
"Topsy"—435
Torbet, C. L.—400
Tornado mine—437, 438, 439, 440, 452
Town, first in Black Hills—195
Town, first to establish a public school system in Dakota Territory—397
Town lot, first sold in Black Hills—198
Towner, F. A.—295, 304
Town-site Company—99, 213, 407, 408, 413
Town-site Company original stockholders—407
Town-site, first in Black Hills—61, 195
Trainor, Bill—267, 268
Trask, A. D.—100, 104, 117, 118, 195

Travis, West—287
Treaty of 1851—2
Treaty of 1868—1, 2, 3, 97, 98
Treaty of 1889—527
Treaty ratification—97
Treaty rights—96, 107
Treaty violations—68, 146
Treber, John—374
Tremble, H. B.—443
Trespassers, Indian Reserve—95
"Tribune", Crook City—404
Tribunal—214
Trimmer, George—484, 491, 492, 494
Trojan Enterprise mine group—441
Trout creek—113
Trout, Lt. J. F.—91
Trout, Lt. M. F.—91
Troy (town)—356
Tufts, James—522
Tuley, James—374
Tummon, the Rev. North—469
Turner & Wilson's saloon—267
Turner, Geo.—492, 494
Turner, Geo. A.—484
Turning Bear—531
Tuttle, Capt. P. H.—91, 92
Tuttle, Cephas—399, 400, 423, 424
Twelfth Infantry—534
Twenty-fifth Colored Infantry—475, 477
Twenty-third Infantry—90, 91
Two Bit Gulch—318, 372
Two Lance—97
Two Strikes—530, 531, 536
Tyler, Prof. B. A.—466

U

Uhlig, Otto—186, 407
Uhlig's Addition—186, 407
Ulmer, the Rev. G. C.—468
Uncapapas—95, 147
"Uncle Nute"—50, 60, 100
"Union," Black Hills—314, 315, 316
Union depot—504
"Union Hill" mine—297, 298, 434
Union Mill company—398
Union Hill Mining Co.—434
Union Pacific Railway—275, 452
Union Aid Society—314
United States Commissioner—99, 130, 146
Upham, Major—172
Upper Rapid—234
U. S. Government Assay Building—373
Utter, Charlie (Colorado Charlie)—142

V

Vale (town)—517
Valentine, L. W.—403, 404, 418
"Valentine Scrip"—462
"Valley Gazette", Spearfish—417
Vanatta, Henry—503
Van Cise & Wilson firm—377
Van Cise, Edwin—296, 371, 376
Van Fleet, Wm.—343
Van Horn—110, 111
Van Luvin, Dan—204
Van Valzak, Capt. D. D.—477
Vanocker & Merrick firm—201
Vanocker, Frank—201
"Variety Theatre"—262
Veasel Bear—97
Vermillion—406, 520, 521
Viewfield (town)—483
Volin's freight wagons—230, 231
Voorhees, Superintendent—140, 277, 288
Vosburg, R. H.—309, 310
Vroman, H. M.—403, 404

W

W. of W.—392
W.R.C.—392
W.U. Tele. Co.—192
Wade, Wm.—403
Wager, W. A.—317
Wagner, C. H.—257, 258
Wagnus family—404
Waite, Cephas—440
Wakan—529
Wakefield, the Rev. Ira—314, 468
Wakeman, W. D.—403, 404
Walk, M. V.—414
Walker, Capt.—88
Wall, (outlaw)—290
Wallace, Capt. Geo. D.—537
Wallace, Lieut.—152
Walton, J. A.—185
Walton's Isaac—109
War Department—146, 479
"War pipe"—147
Ward, Mr. C. F.—483
Ward, Mrs. Cornelia—483
Ward. E. G.—214, 292, 293
Ware, G. G.—518
Warford, W. W.—522
Ward's cabin, John—409
Warner, Porter—201, 202, 357, 358, 373, 416, 456, 457
Warren, E. H.—429
Warren Expedition—3
Warren, J. H.—429
Warren, John B.—528
Warren, Lt. Governor K.—3
Warren, Major Wm.—528
Warren, Newton—18, 50, 60
Washabaugh, F. J.—310
Washabaugh, Frank J.—376, 426, 428, 456, 457, 524
Washing out gold—350
Washington D. C.—266, 281, 387, 394, 477, 520, 521, 523
"Washington School House"—392
Water—33, 305, 382, 429, 471
Water, leasing—248
Water power—317, 325
Water systems for fire control—363, 364, 389
Watts, Mr.—346
Waugh, Billy—181
Weatherby, Frank—297
Webb, G. W.—291
Webb, Prescott—291
'weber, Antoine—387
Webster, Chas.—107, 108, 109, 110
Webster, Daniel W.—304
Webster, T. J.—396
"Weekly Bee", Belle Fourche—512
"Weekly Democrat", Black Hills—315
"Weekly Pioneer", Black Hills—199, 269, 315, 357, 494
"Weekly Record", Sturgis—469, 473
"Weekly Register" Dakota—417
Weeks, Jacob W.—470
Welch—220, 221
Welch, Frank—429
Welch House—363, 366
Welch, Mrs.—221
Welcome mine—317, 440
Wels, John—484
Wells, Wm.—484
Wenkie, John—465
Wentworth Hotel—258
Wessels, Capt. W. H.—91
West Point, New York, see "New York, West Point"
Western Bank and Trust Company—410
"Western Town Company"—520
Western Union Telegraph Co.—280
Westford—307
"Whacker"—44
Whealen, Mike—311
Wheeler Brothers—210, 247
Wheeler, Prof.—390
Wheelock, R. P.—338, 339
Wheelock, Richard P.—348
Whipsawing—247
Whiskey—116, 117
Whitbeck, L. F.—446
White, Judge J. W. C.—214, 294

White Bow—97
White Clay Creek—531
White Earth Creek—107
White Earth River—107, 111, 530, 531
White man, confined, legend—83
White River—31, 33, 92, 95, 518, 528
White Rocks—255, 379
"White Spar" mine—300
White Tail Creek—128, 390
White Tail Gulch—125, 437, 440
Whitehead, Chas.—216
Whitehead, Judge—279
Whitehead, Major—494
Whiteside, Capt.—537
Whitewood—164, 207, 208, 214, 245, 271, 291, 372, 442, 443, 446, 514, 524
Whitewood Creek—80, 124, 125, 126, 128, 129, 255, 266, 275, 355, 360, 366, 368, 379, 402, 403
Whitewood Fire Department—443
Whitewood Flouring Mill—443
Whitewood gulch—245, 246, 247, 349, 357, 362, 405
Whitewood, Major James—403
Whitewood A.O.U.W. society—443
Whitewood Water System—443
Whitman, Lt. R. G.—91
"Whitney" outfit—50
Whitney, R. R.—18, 50
Whitney, Richard G.—428
Whitson, B.—356
Wiek, John—448
Wier, Capt.—151, 154
Wier's troops—154, 155
Wigginton, Wm.—403, 404
Wilbur, the Rev. Dr.—233
Wilcox, M. A.—436
Wilcox, Major J. C.—462, 463
Wilcox, A.—295
Wilcox, Sherman—473
Willard, Capt. A. M.—422
Willard, Deacon—340
Willard, Deputy Captain—290, 291
Willard, Fred A.—421, 422, 423
Williams, Andrew J.—340, 341
Williams, Dan—229
Williams, Elder—468
Williams, Geo.—396
Williams, Gus—135
Williams, J. J.—18, 35, 60, 61, 62, 129, 198, 255, 256
Williams, J. L.—522
Williams, Rev. Jas.—314, 360, 397
"Willie Wassel" mine—438, 439, 440
Willis, Judge—348
Williston, L. P.—522
Willow Creek—110
Wilson, Deputy Sheriff—412
Wilson, John R.—377
Wilson, W. A.—441
Wilson, Wm.—441
Wiltsie, M.—318
Winchell, Prof.—12
Winchester rifles—17, 30, 237, 533
Wind Cave—307, 490, 507
Wind River—9
"Window Light" mine—300
Winona Normal School, Minnesota—428
Wisconsin—50
Wisconsin, Broadhead—296
Wisdom, C. P.—291
Witcher Company—104
Witcher, Eaf.—18, 30, 51, 55, 59, 88, 105, 139
Witcher Transportation Company, H. N.—104
Wixson, E. B.—522
Wolf, Ed—403
Wolf Mountain Stampede—275, 276
Wolf mountains—151, 275, 276
Wolsey, Jas.—209
Wolsey, Jones & Rowland—253
Wolzmuth & Goewey's Mill—398
Wolzmuth, David—447
Wolzmuth, John—355, 428, 452, 524

Woman to enter Hills in 1875, first—404
Woman (white) in Black Hills, first—63, 134
Women, Black Hills pioneers—120
Women literary clubs—377, 472
Wood, A. F.—407
Wood, B.—336
Wood, B. C.—448
Wood, C. L.—524
Wood, Chauncey L.—329, 330, 332
Wood, G. W.—7
Wood, Gus. M.—414
Wood, S. N.—361, 374
Wood, W. H.—100, 433
Woods Hotel—207
Woods, J. M.—139, 203, 258, 328
Woods, Paul S.—328
"Woodmen of the World"—437
Woodville—382
Woodward, M.—214
Woolen mill—509
Woolsey, Jones, and Rowland—208
Woolston, J. J.—511
Woonsocket—303
World's Fair of 1893—483
Worth, Howard—231, 325
Worth, John—361
Wounded Knee—107, 530, 537, 538
Wounded Knee, Fatal Battle of—529
Wrestling—395
Wright—107
Wright, D.—214
Wright, Harry—225
Wright, John—296
Wright, the Rev. E. G.—468
Wyman, Frank—227
Wyoming—309, 325, 355, 410, 420, 449, 450, 516, 517, 521
Wyoming and Missouri River Railroad—517
Wyoming, Carbon—450
Wyoming, Cheyenne—69, 72, 74, 90, 91, 99, 116, 119, 120, 127, 130, 131, 132, 134, 136, 139, 177, 179, 195, 208, 210, 212, 217, 222, 235, 236, 268, 271, 278, 280, 347, 399, 450, 452, 454, 455, 456, 531
Wyoming, Sundance—123, 446
Wyoming, unceded Indian Territory—2, 97

Y

Yankee traditional (language)—254
Yankton—55, 89, 130, 138, 139, 187, 227, 266, 269, 271, 292, 329, 346, 375, 376, 467, 520, 521, 523
Yankton Indians agent, U. S.—522
Yankton penitentiary—358
Yankton reservation—520
Yanktons—95
Yates, Capt.—152
Yates, Fort—530, 534
Yellow creek mines—126
Yellowstone Expedition of 1876—146, 149, 168, 173
Yellowstone river—4, 9, 10, 147, 150, 169, 175, 184, 281
Yellowstone river, upper—147
Yerkes, Abram—214, 255, 303
Youmans, Miss Bertha—428
Young, H. B.—104, 131, 132, 380, 381, 407
Young, Prof. Chas. W.—466
Young, S. E.—524
Young & Chapline firm—269
Young-Man-Afraid-of-His-Horses—97
Y. T. Cattle Co.—518

Z

Zink, W. A.—425
Zoellner Bros. & Co.—418